THE LIFE AND TIMES
OF
CAVOUR

IN TWO VOLUMES

VOLUME II

Cavour's Last Portrait

THE LIFE AND TIMES

OF

CAVOUR

BY

WILLIAM ROSCOE THAYER

WITH ILLUSTRATIONS AND MAPS

VOLUME II

" I am the son of Liberty ; to her I owe all that I am "
CAVOUR to MADAME DE CIRCOURT
December 29, 1860

BOSTON AND NEW YORK
HOUGHTON MIFFLIN COMPANY
The Riverside Press Cambridge

CONTENTS

ILLUSTRATIONS

THE LIFE AND TIMES
OF
CAVOUR

THE LIFE AND TIMES OF
CAVOUR

CHAPTER XXII

BEGINNING OF THE WAR WITH AUSTRIA

FEW human enterprises wear such a double face as modern war. In earlier times news of battle traveled so slowly that weeks might elapse before the result of a campaign was known. The electric telegraph has made not only entire countries but the civilized world consentaneous. The War of 1859 was the first in which the contestants realized the double necessity of winning battles and of editing bulletins which would be read the next day in the great European capitals. The French chroniclers easily excelled the others. They had the tradition of the Great Napoleon's flamboyant despatches; they had a language as direct as a rifle bullet, as clear as crystal, as resonant as a trumpet, and they needed to supply France with a daily banquet of glory in return for the treasure she was reluctantly spending on a war she did not desire. Napoleon III constantly remembered that the Austrians were in front of him and French public opinion behind. So the historian must distinguish what actually happened from the official reports of what happened, and from the popular state of mind which these superinduced. Read in the light of the French bulletins the War of 1859 was a glorious military pageant, in which the Allies had only to meet the enemy in order to rout him; a competition in which every army corps envied its fellows sent ahead of it into battle, a tournament of fame where marshals' batons might be won in a morning, where promotions were awarded to many and medals to all. Among this host military genius was so common that a Frederick or a Napoleon I would have found many peers. Glory beamed everywhere, and the Austrians were obliging enough to offer so manful a resistance

2

that the French by overcoming them proved themselves heroes. Such the iridescent legend: let us now look at the facts.[1]

France was unprepared. Although the Emperor knew from the beginning of January that war was possible, he gave no general order until April to put his army into condition. Up to the last moment he wished to be able to declare that he did not intend to break the peace; he still doubted whether Cavour would succeed in forcing a provocation from Austria; and he was temperamentally disinclined, after the fashion of idealogues, to translate his grandiose plans into irrevocable acts. During the winter months, therefore, he worked furtively, hoping to attract little attention, and embarking in few arrangements which, if the project should fall through, might rise up to embarrass him. Most important was his withdrawing the seasoned troops from Algeria. When, however, early in April, Austria mobilized her reserves and sent a second army into Italy, Napoleon massed every available regiment on the Piedmontese frontier, with orders to cross Savoy at the first signal, and he concentrated other forces at Toulon and Marseilles, to go by sea to Genoa.

On April 26, when Cavour rejected Buol's ultimatum, the effective of the French army destined for Italy counted on paper 132,200 infantry, 9000 cavalry, 10,000 artillery and miscellaneous and 300 cannon:[2] but several weeks elapsed before these 151,200 men, equipped and organized, faced the Austrians. The Emperor decided to lead the army himself, with Marshal Vaillant

---

[1] The principal sources for the War of 1859 are the official French, Piedmontese and Austrian reports. Then follow many unofficial works, among which the following may be cited: W. Rüstow: *Der Italienische Krieg*, 1859. Bazancourt; Moltke: Zurich, 1859; F. Lecomte: *Relation Historique et Critique de la Campagne d'Italie en 1859*. Paris, 1860 (2d edit.). The most important subsequent works are *Précis;* A. Duquet; C. Mariani; La Gorce; Della Rocca; Hohenlohe-Ingelfingen; Pagani; Massari,' lives of *Vittorio Emanuele II*, and of *A. La Marmora*,' Carrano, Guerzoni, La Varenne, and his own *Memorie* for Garibaldi's operations. In general, I have found Moltke, Duquet, Rüstow, and the *Précis* the clearest guides. Mariani is most elaborate for Piedmontese operations; La Gorce, always consistently anti-Italian, lays himself out to paint a literary panorama; the official reports — Randon's, Moltke's, and the Austrian — slight the Piedmontese, and especially the Garibaldian campaign. The formal historians, Zini, Reuchlin, and Tivaroni, should also be consulted, and for special points, the Italian, French and English contemporary newspapers, and the biographies of the principal generals — Cialdini, Fanti, MacMahon, Vaillant, Lebrun, Fleury, Canrobert, Benedek.   [2] Moltke, 16.

as his chief of staff. General Regnaud de Saint-Jean d'Angély, a
veteran of the Moscow campaign, commanded the Imperial
Guard: Marshal Baraguey d'Hilliers, another relic of the Napoleonic Wars, had the First Army Corps: General MacMahon,
who had distinguished himself in the Crimea and in Africa,
led the Second Corps; Marshal Canrobert, the savior of the
French army at Sebastopol, the Third; and General Niel, chief
of engineers at Sebastopol, the Fourth. To Prince Napoleon
was assigned the Fifth Corps, which, instead of accompany-
ing the main army, was to move southward to Tuscany.

Piedmont, thanks to Cavour and La Marmora, had mobilized
most of her army. It numbered on paper 64,000 men,[3] of whom
9400 were cavalry, and 120 pieces of artillery. In addition, Garibaldi had three regiments enrolled in his Hunters of the Alps,
and the National Guard, composed chiefly of volunteers, mustered 26,000 men, whose duty it was to defend the capital and
fortified towns. Their military value was small. Victor Emanuel
assumed command of all the forces, with La Marmora as special
adviser, Della Rocca chief of staff, and the five divisions of infantry commanded respectively by Castelborgo, Fanti, Durando,
Cialdini, and Cucchiari. Sambuy led the division of cavalry.[4]

The Austrian forces were estimated at 200,000 men of all
arms: but of these 65,000 served in garrisons, along the eastern
frontiers, and in the Duchies and Legations.[5] The original army
of occupation was reinforced by a second Army of Italy under
General Wimpffen, but this did not come into play for several
weeks. While General Gyulai, who held the chief command, was
hated even by his soldiers for his cruelty, his chief of staff, Colonel Kuhn, inspired the greatest confidence; his bravery was un-
questioned, and his book knowledge of warfare, although he was
only 40 years old, was regarded as unequalled.[6] Prince Edward
Liechtenstein (II), Prince Edward Schwarzenberg (III), Count
Stadion (V), General Zobel (VII), General Benedek (VIII)

[3] But this number fell short of the nominal war-strength, 84,000 men. *Précis*
gives the total as only 55,648 (p. 258), but Cavour estimated on May 6 that Piedmont had 70,000 men in the field. *Lettere*, III, 72. Hohenlohe-Ingelfingen, I, 126,
says that on May 20, Piedmont had an army of 60,000 men, including 3120
Garibaldians.   [4] Moltke, 13. *Précis*, 258-59.   [5] Moltke estimates the Austrian
effective at 115,000 ; *Précis* at 118,000.   [6] Hohenlohe-Ingelfingen, I, 209, confirms the generally favorable opinion of Kuhn.

commanded the infantry corps of the Second Army, and Count Schaffgottsche led the cavalry corps. All these officers except the last were field marshals: Liechtenstein, Schwarzenberg and Stadion bore illustrious names, and were soon to prove that military genius can neither be inherited nor passed on with patents of nobility. The Austrian army, in spite of being well equipped, lacked experience of actual fighting. Those of its officers who had made the campaigns of 1848 and 1849 had acquired a dangerous self-conceit from having defeated — too easily — the inferior army of Charles Albert and the brave but undisciplined forces of the Revolution. But men who had seen no service at all filled many of the posts, and arrogance was their prevailing characteristic. They had looked down so long on the subject populations of Italy and the unwilling Slavs and Magyars, that they had forgotten that any men existed tall enough to look them squarely in the eyes. Peculation was practised so outrageously that before the campaign was well under way the troops frequently suffered for want of supplies and sometimes went into battle starving: and the dishonest and incompetent commissariat was matched by the department of logistics. Austria now paid the penalty for her refusal to provide the Italian provinces with adequate railway communication. The only trunk line in the kingdom connected Milan with Verona and Venice; but between Venice and Trieste there was a gap of seventy miles which had to be covered on foot by every soldier, with a loss of at least five days. The single-track railway from Vienna to Trieste became so clogged that one regiment marched the entire distance from Vienna to the front. In April, however, Europe accepted the Austrians at their own valuation as mighty men of Mars.

Piedmont, on the contrary, had access by a well-planned network of railways to every important part of her Subalpine provinces. From Turin to the River Ticino, the eastern boundary, through Vercelli and Novara, was 70 miles; to Genoa, 103 miles, with Alessandria lying almost exactly half way. One line ran north from Novara to Arona on Lake Maggiore; another, connecting Vercelli with Alessandria, passed through Casale; a fourth joined Cuneo with the capital; a fifth, stretching westward to the Mount Cenis Tunnel, had been completed as far as Susa. Even at the slow rate at which trains then ran, it was possible between morning and night to travel from one end of the country to the other. The highroads, too, like those in Lombardy and Venetia, were broad and well-kept. Everything favored, therefore, the rapid distribution of the Piedmontese troops, their concentration in haste on a given point in case of emergency, and their prompt receipt of forage and provisions.

Since the obvious move for the Austrians was to invade Piedmont, and having either destroyed or driven back the Piedmontese army, to take Turin before the French came up, the French and Piedmontese strategists had been debating, since January, how best to prepare the little country to hold out for a week or ten days. They decided first to fortify Alessandria and Casale to the utmost, and to mass at these places the bulk of the army, — precautions which might be expected at least to check the Austrians coming from Pavia; and then to establish a second line of defense along the Dora Baltea, an Alpine river which flows into the Po twenty miles east of the capital. Except in times of freshet, however, the Dora, being fordable, rendered only an uncertain protection. The Stura, a similar stream, on the eastern outskirts of Turin, might serve as the last ditch for Victor Emanuel's troops to die in if the enemy captured the outposts.

But on April 28, when Marshal Canrobert inspected these positions, he pronounced them useless, and ordered the troops guarding them to join the main Piedmontese army, which could most efficiently harass the Austrians on their flank and rear if they should venture to assail the capital.[7] From Turin due east as far as Valenza stretches a ridge of hills, high enough and rugged enough to serve as a natural bulwark; at their feet the Po curves in a flattened crescent, and the plain broadens northward till it meets the last spurs of the Alps. A score of streams and many canals irrigate the level country, in some parts of which extensive rice fields are often under water. To an army not in control of the highroads, the Piedmontese plain offered a succession of minor difficulties, which, however, could easily be surmounted by a properly equipped pontoon corps. Provisions were plenty.

On April 25, Count Gyulai had under his command in the triangle bounded by lines connecting Milan, Pavia and Piacenza

[7] *Précis*, 55–56.

about 100,000 men. To enter Piedmont he needed only to cross the bridge over the Ticino at Pavia: then a march of less than forty miles would bring him to either Alessandria or Casale. Late in the evening of the 26th Kellersperg arrived with Cavour's reply. It had been understood that, if this were negative or evasive, the Austrian invasion would begin at once. Throughout the 27th, however, Gyulai did not stir. April 28 came and went, and still the Austrians seemed asleep. At last, on the 29th, the vanguard and three army corps crossed the Ticino at Gravellone and two other corps at Bereguardo. Having spent the next day in strategic developments, the army marched on May 1 at a snail's pace towards the Agogna. May 2 its headquarters were at Lomello and its van had reached the Po and the Sesia. In six days, Gyulai had advanced only twenty miles. He had thrown away his magnificent opportunity. A competent general would have hurled the Austrian army on the Piedmontese as early as April 27, when the result could hardly have been doubtful. What held back Gyulai's initiative during that precious week? Austrian apologists hint that — by his Emperor's orders — he waited in the expectation that England would succeed in mediating, even after Cavour rejected the ultimatum: it seems likely, however, that incurable incompetence paralyzed his will. Being one of those parade generals whom the rude pell-mell of actual warfare disconcerted, he would not fight unless all the conditions suited him exactly.[8] He felt that the propitious moment had passed two or three weeks before — that it was too late to crush the Piedmontese before the French arrived — that after the Allies were united, he should need large reinforcements: but he boldly promised his Emperor to protect Lombardy by manœuvring and to profit by any blunders the enemy might make.[9] These are hardly the sentiments of a born fighter. The news that the French forerunners were disembarking at Genoa or descending the Alps, caused Gyulai to proceed with greater caution, instead of to atone by swiftness, if he could, for the time already lost.

In contrast with the Austrian procrastination was the energy

[8] Hohenlohe-Ingelfingen, I, 208–09, gives a sketch of Gyulai. Ollivier, 131, makes a rosy pen-portrait of him, for which I find no justification elsewhere.

[9] *Précis*, 57; Gyulai to Francis Joseph, April 25.

at Turin. On April 23, Parliament having conferred dictatorial powers upon the King, Cavour set in motion all the wheels, military, administrative and diplomatic, of war. The last battalions were sent to the front at Casale and Alessandria. The bakers prepared great stores of bread; the railway carriages were collected at Genoa and Susa; and already plans were laid for calling out the reserves and summoning the new levy of conscripts. The great enthusiasm which prevailed was the long, groundswell enthusiasm of a people that knew the danger it ran, and not the gusty excesses of 1848. Cavour waited with almost equal impatience to hear that the Austrians had begun operations on the East, and that the French had entered Piedmont on the West.

In France, especially at Paris, public opinion had suddenly whirled round. "We are a droll nation!" Mérimée confided to Panizzi on April 29. "A fortnight ago I wrote you that there was only one man in France who desired war, and I believe I told the truth. Today, consider the opposite as true. The Gallic instinct is aroused. Now there is an enthusiasm which has its magnificent side, and also its dreadful side. The people accepts the war with joy: it is full of confidence and of spirit. As for the soldiers, they depart as to a ball. Day before yesterday they chalked on their wagons: 'Pleasure trains for Italy and Vienna.' When they pass through the streets on their way to the railway stations, the populace cover them with flowers, bring them wine, embrace them, adjure them to kill as many Austrians as they can. The regiment of Zouaves of the Guard had its orders to start a week ago. They shouted, 'This is war; no more police hall for us!' and the regiment disappeared for two days. They had to say goodby to all the cooks of their acquaintance. At the moment of departure, not a man was missing: every one of them had a sprig of lilacs in the muzzle of his gun. In this French gaiety there is a considerable element of success. Our fellows are convinced they are going to win, and in war that counts for much. They regard themselves as knights errant going to fight for their lady. I hold the Austrians for very brave soldiers; but every one of ours imagines he is going to become at least a colonel, and a Croat has no such ideas."[10]

The Emperor issued orders on April 23 for the Army of the

[10] Mérimée, I, 29-30.

Alps to enter Savoy immediately. Thenceforward, there was incessant bustle, especially in the despatch of trains.[11] To expedite transportation, the Third (Canrobert) and Fourth (Neil) Corps crossed the mountains, whilst the First (Baraguey d'Hilliers) and the Second (MacMahon) shipped by sea to Genoa. The Cavalry of the Imperial Guard skirted the Mediterranean on the recently opened Corniche Road. The crossing of the Alpine passes at that season was both difficult and dangerous: for snow and ice still covered the upper slopes, and rains soaked the roads, converted rills into torrents, and unleashed avalanches and landslips. From St. Jean de Maurienne, the eastern terminus of the Savoy railway, to Susa, by way of Mount Cenis, was 62 miles (101 kilometres). A second route, from Briançon over Mont Genèvre, required at least two days [12] for the heavily laden foot soldiers [13] to cover. The transport wagons stuck in the mud and soon fell behind. Suffering much from the inclement weather and lack of shelter, the troops marched with little discipline, and yet on April 29, the first columns of both Canrobert's and Niel's corps came swinging into Susa. As to all their predecessors in that interminable caravan of soldiers who, since Hannibal led his swarthy Carthaginians over the Alps, had entered Italy to succor or despoil, to these regiments also, bedraggled, weary and wet, the first glimpses of the far-off plains brought a strange joy. It seemed to them that they stood indeed on the threshold of the Promised Land. For Italy was still, even to those who had only a glimmer of enlightenment, the home of beauty, the abode of romance, where, by some touch of magic, day-dreams must come true; to soldiers of France it was the garden where laurels grew exuberantly.

Leaving their troops to rest at Susa, Canrobert and Niel hurried on to Turin, where the King welcomed them fervently. The mere sight of "red pantaloons" relieved him, because it was the visible proof that Imperial France was involved in Piedmont's

---

[11] Prince Hohenlohe-Ingelfingen states that 17 trains a day were sent southward. Eleven years later, in spite of improved methods, the Germans were able to send only 18 trains a day over the same line. *Précis*, 48.   [12] Lecomte, I, 30.
[13] Moltke, 23, says: "Le soldat était extraordinairement chargé. Il portait dans son sac la veste, une paire de souliers, un caleçon, trois chemises, les guêtres, des brosses et 80 cartouches, les sacs de campement, une couverture, des piquets, la marmite, le bidon, des outils, et cinq jours de vivres."

fate. Canrobert insisted on abandoning the line of the Dora Baltea and the King reluctantly consented. Beginning on April 30, the French troops traveled from Susa as fast as the single-track railroad permitted, to Alessandria, where the Allies had the base of their operations. Simultaneously, the First and Second Corps, which began to land at Genoa on the 26th,[14] were sent forward to Alessandria. Disembarkation was a perpetual festival. The inner harbor of Genoa, like the arena of an amphitheatre, was small enough for the scores of thousands of spectators ranged along the quays, and on the balconies, roofs and slopes of the city, to witness all that went on. They cheered each boatload at the landing, but especially the swarthy Turcos, native Arab warriors from Algeria, who were expected to work havoc among the mere white troops of Austria: they cheered the Zouaves, whose Oriental uniforms and reputation for fighting made them conspicuous: they cheered the generals, many of whom were known in Italy since the days of the Crimea — none more popular than MacMahon, victor in many a desperate encounter with Bedouins and Khabyles, hero of the storming of the Malakoff. The medieval usage still prevailed in Mediterranean ports of loading and unloading vessels by lighters, instead of providing docks or wharves for them to lie up at; and this occasioned so great a delay that it took as long to embark and disembark a corps as to send it by rail and on foot over Alpine passes. But whether by land or by sea, almost every day after the 28th of April from 8000 to 10,000 French troops entered Piedmont.

Victor Emanuel quitted Turin for the front on April 30, having appointed his cousin, Prince Eugene of Savoy Carignan, lieutenant general during his absence.[15] Cavour took La Marmora's place as Minister of War and Marine.[16] His labor increased enormously, but he despatched it with ease because his heart was light. The details of transportation, of furnishing rations, of procuring equipment for fresh levies, of establishing quick communications, of making contracts, fell to his charge. In addition, he had to conduct international relations, to inspire enthusiasm in the press, to prevent disorders, to conduct secret negotiations

---

[14] Baraguey's first troops landed on the 26th, and his corps was all ashore on the 29th. On May 6, by occupying Gavi, he came into touch with the Piedmontese at Novi. Moltke, 24.   [15] April 26.   [16] May 3.

with the Liberals outside of Piedmont, to watch the Mazzinians, and to keep a firm hand on the operations of the National Society. His most pressing anxiety was for the safety of Turin, which seemed to lie at the mercy of the Austrians. Their delay in advancing, coupled with their irregular tactics, led to the belief that they might attempt a rapid descent on the capital. On May 6 Cavour wrote to La Marmora that, while the little garrison would do its best, it would be shameful if the Allies should fail to attack the Austrians in the rear and on the flank. He evidently supposed that Canrobert would not stir until his troops were in thorough condition: in which case, said the Minister of War, our Piedmontese army ought to act on its own initiative; and "it is strong enough to get us out of our scrape by ourselves." [17] For the political and moral effect it would produce, Cavour desired that the Piedmontese should meet the enemy first and unaided. He suggested movements, but left the professional strategists to decide. If worst came to worst, he would transfer the government to Genoa, but he would grieve to his dying day, if the King, with 70,000 men under his orders, did nothing to save the capital. "The Turinese," he added, "would never forgive him." [18]

During more than a fortnight the good people of Turin had to endure this suspense, which they bore with perfect self-control. The Austrians, after crossing the Ticino and spreading themselves over the Lomellina during the first week in May, seemed to stagnate. Torrential rains made the streams unfordable, raised the level of the Po fifteen feet in a short time, carried away a bridge of boats, and discouraged marching. By the rules of war, Gyulai's objective should have been the Piedmontese army. Every hour that he delayed, by bringing the French to the front, lessened his advantage in numbers. Military critics agree that, if he had attacked in force by May 1, he might have driven the enemy back from Alessandria and Casale. A secondary operation should have been pressed to the southward, with a view to capture the railway at Novi, and so to check the advance of the French coming up from Genoa. But dunces and geniuses are a law unto themselves. Concluding to let the Piedmontese army alone and to march on Turin, Gyulai, with a sudden access of

[17] *Lettere*, III, 71; C. to La Marmora, May 6; see also p. 70.   [18] *Ibid*, 72.

energy,[19] moved his forces northward, occupied Novara, took Vercelli, and followed the main route towards the capital. On May 8, his vanguard had already reached the Dora Baltea, with orders for one detachment to seize Ivrea.

That evening, when Turin fully expected to be attacked, Cavour counted up his resources and estimated them at from 7000 to 8000 men, of whom only 2000, Sambuy's cavalry, with 20 field-pieces, were regulars. Still, he betrayed no alarm. He asked for a division to be despatched from Alessandria. "I am not a tactician," he wrote La Marmora; "but I have enough sense and firmness to carry out whatever orders you might send me." [20] To the astonishment of the Piedmontese, the Austrian troops began to fall back at noon on May 9 — Turin was saved.[21] What caused this sudden change of plan? When Gyulai learned that his patrols had reached the Dora Baltea and looked in vain for Piedmontese pickets on the other bank, he suspected a trap. Spies reported that some 40,000 French had left Turin for Alessandria; a telegram from Vienna warned him that two corps had already landed at Genoa, and that the French Emperor was starting for Italy. From these various data he inferred that if he advanced to attack the capital, he would find it amply defended, and that the Allies, rushing out of Casale, would batter him, flank and rear. A tyro in strategy knows that he ought not to allow himself to be caught between two armies: Field-Marshal Gyulai, therefore, ordered a retreat, marked by "inexcusable precipitation and disorder," and proceeded to station his troops in cantonments in the Lomellina.[22] Then he wrote for Emperor Francis Joseph an account of his operation, making it plain that he regarded his having kept his army safe from battle during fifteen days as a proof of supreme generalship. But troops, like money, are useless when hoarded. The over-cautious commanders have lost more battles than the over-daring.[23]

[19] Moltke, 32. In two days he advanced 8 leagues and more.

[20] *Lettere*, III, 75; C. to La Marmora, May 8.

[21] Moltke, 33. The Austrians felt so sure of taking Turin that their officers had their letters addressed there; and the letters kept coming for several weeks.

[22] Moltke, 33. *Précis*, 66-67.

[23] Some years later, when it was proposed to erect at Turin a monument to commemorate the Campaign of 1859, Victor Emanuel said: "It ought to be dedicated not to me but to Gyulai, who spared us till the French came." Della Rocca, I, 411.

On the very day when Gyulai was congratulating himself that he was likely to accomplish his retreat without accident, Napoleon III quitted Paris for the front. He had been detained by the need of arranging for a regency, under the Empress, during his absence, and of organizing the Army of the Rhine, to guard Eastern France against a possible attack by the German Confederation. The smaller German States, completely in Austria's control, were pledged to go to Austria's assistance if the Allied Armies menaced the frontiers of the Confederation at any point. This was equivalent to declaring that, if the French and Piedmontese, having succeeded in driving the Austrians over the Northern or Eastern border of the Lombardo-Venetian Kingdom, should attempt to pursue them, the German Confederation would invade France. Prussia too, although she reserved more liberty of action, had still to be a party to this agreement. To show that he wished to keep on good terms with the Germans and had no thought of attacking them, Napoleon quartered his Army of the Rhine, over which he placed Marshal Pélissier, as far as possible from the frontier. The Army itself, for some time to come, flourished chiefly on paper. Unpreparedness marked every act of the War Department, which, having forwarded the troops into Italy, left them so ill-provided for that, more than once, they would have starved, if Cavour had not been able to succor them out of the abundance of rations which he had stored up. After nearly three weeks' warning, the heavy military trains started on their slow journey to the front. Such dilatoriness would have caused no comment earlier in the century: but now the railroad and the steamboat had revolutionized transportation; and after all, the French Army had had several months in which to make ready.

Napoleon steamed into Genoa on May 12. Cleopatra in her burnished galley could not have been more welcome to Antony than he to the Italians. He came, as he told them, "to free Italy from the Alps to the Adriatic." Even the cynical were astonished into admiration by his Quixotic venture. The masses saw him through the radiant nimbus of idealization which their hopes threw around him. Here at last was the Veltro, prophesied by Dante six centuries ago! The Emperor of the French, the arbiter of Europe, smitten with sympathy for the downtrodden, was

NAPOLEON III

In 1859

come in person, to succor and redeem a people. So grateful were they at that moment that they would joyfully have given him almost anything that he might have asked. They trusted his sincerity and his chivalry. Throughout his long career, chequered as it was by tragedy and ridicule, garish with false glory, turgid with counterfeit greatness, mottled with crime and guile, and finally engulfed in disaster, there were no other moments of unalloyed satisfaction, like those in which he entered Genoa. From the deck of *La Reine Hortense*, the Imperial yacht, he saw the buildings of the city, like the benches of an amphitheatre, rise tier on tier, crowned by battlemented walls and massive forts, where the tricolor of France and the tricolor of Piedmont flew side by side. Every window was decked for festival: the palaces of the rich with precious tapestries, — heirlooms which may have seen the pageants of doges in the old ducal times, — the dwellings of the poor with bunting and flags. The harbor and inner port were covered with boats, large and small, on which crowded myriads of gaily-appareled holiday-makers. The ships were dressed with flags; sailors manned the yards; and amid a salutation of cannon, the Imperial yacht came to anchor. The Prince of Carignan, Cavour, and other officials formally greeted the Emperor, who was then conveyed on the King's barge to the landing at the Royal Palace. Standing in the stern of the launch, he faced the city, with its gorgeous decorations and multitudes of spectators. Flowers strewed the water so thick that it seemed not water but an oriental garden, through which the boat cut its way merrily, and left only a little wake which the flowers quickly closed over. It was roses, roses all the way, as befitted that May afternoon and the May-time of hope in every Italian heart. Then, if ever, Napoleon might believe himself to be a benefactor of mankind.

Having set foot on Italian soil, he issued to his army the following manifesto: "Soldiers! I have just put myself at your head to lead you to the combat. We are going to second the struggle of a people reclaiming its independence and to rescue it from foreign oppression. This is a holy cause, which has the sympathy of the civilized world. I do not need to stimulate your ardor: every day's march will remind you of a victory. On the Sacred Way of Ancient Rome the inscriptions crowded each other on the marble to recall to the people their great deeds; so also to-day, in passing Mondovì, Marengo, Lodi, Castiglione, Arcola, Rivoli, you will march along another Sacred Way, amid these glorious memories. Maintain that severe discipline which is the honor of the army. Here, do not forget it, there are no enemies save those who fight against you. In battle, keep compact, and do not quit your ranks to rush on ahead. Beware of too great impetuosity, it is the only thing I dread. The new arms of precision are dangerous only from afar. They will not prevent the bayonet to be, as it was formerly, the terrible arm of the French infantry. Soldiers! let us all do our duty, and place our trust in God. The mother country expects much from you. Already from one end of France to the other resound words of happy augury: 'The new Army of Italy will be worthy of her elder sister!'"[24]

In English, the manifesto loses some of its effect: for French rhetoric, like French millinery, goes out of fashion. The Anglo-Saxon mind has not a turn for epigrammatic polish, and therefore suspects it, especially at an emotional crisis. But to Frenchmen of 1859, especially to the army in Italy, the Emperor's words were like a bugle call. With rare ingenuity he covered every important point, and so briefly that the whole could be read in a moment. In the phrase where he warned his soldiers that the only thing he feared was their eagerness to get at the enemy, he displayed an audacity almost sublime. But he knew his audience: time, place and people applauded him. And so after landing, he passed from ovation to ovation. On May 14 he proceeded to Alessandria, where he took command of the Allied armies. Napoleon the Third's qualifications for generalissimo were twofold: he knew the art of war as taught in the books;[25] and he was the supposed nephew of the world's master in warfare. The military glories of the First Napoleon would not let the younger sleep. He yearned not only to equal but, so far as changed conditions allowed, to reproduce and outdo them. Gladly would he have fought a battle at Marengo, which lies two miles to the east of Alessandria, in order to show that he would not fall into the blunder which nearly wrecked his uncle.

Though we smile at closet strategists, yet they may be helpful

[24] Text in Bazancourt, i, 75–76.
[25] Ollivier, 128–29, rates Napoleon III's military capacity high.

as critics, and when Napoleon III reached his headquarters, he perceived that the lines of the Allies were stretched too far and too thin.[26] Having ordered their concentration, he bethought him of a new plan of campaign. Instead of driving the Austrians out of Southeastern Piedmont, back through Pavia to Piacenza, their base, he proposed by a rapid march, to transfer his armies as secretly as he could to the North, and pounce upon Milan before Gyulai could overtake him. This project rested partly on the well-known rule that it is desirable to carry the war into the enemy's country, partly on the belief that it might require several weeks to dislodge the Austrians from their chosen fortified region along the Po, and partly on the need of furnishing, as soon as possible, a spectacular victory for the French public to gloat over. Every day saw his Army of Italy in better condition to take the offensive. The trains were coming up, the regiments welcomed their tardy quotas, discipline improved, the lines of organization were perfected.

Before this movement was begun, however, the first battle of the campaign took place. Field-Marshal Count Gyulai either had direct reproof from Vienna for his Fabian tactics or himself felt that he ought to make a show of boldness. In three weeks to have marched and counter-marched, retreated, kept carefully out of the enemy's gun-range, and dug endless trenches, might be the height of prudence, but it earned no glory. Gyulai determined, therefore, on a reconnaissance in order to get some information about the Allies' main positions; for he lacked scouts, whereas the French and Piedmontese learned of his doings from the peasants who sold supplies to his troops.[27] In some places the country people themselves were rebellious and received muskets from the French.[28]

Gyulai had his headquarters at Mortara, but a large part of his army was stationed in the neighborhood of Pavia and south of the Po along the highroad to Piacenza. He ordered Stadion's corps, advancing in three columns, to make a reconnaissance towards Voghera on May 20. Stadion's divisions, setting out from Stradella on the morning of that day, marched gaily till noon. As you journey from Stradella to Voghera, you have on your left

[26] On May 15, the Allies' front stretched over 43 miles.
[27] Moltke, 37.   [28] *Ibid.* 38.

the last spurs of the Apennines, and on your right the level valley of the Po, through which the river winds leisurely. The country is fertile: along the slopes vineyards rise in terraces; over the plain long, rambling farm-buildings, each walled round as if it were a fort, break through the foliage in summer and give a human touch to the bareness of the landscape in winter. The central column of the Austrians passed unmolested through Casteggio, a cross-roads village, where they expected to find the French, and on to Montebello, two miles to the southeast, which also they occupied without resistance: but a mile and a half farther on, beyond Genestrello, they came upon the French, whose outposts were distributed along the Fossagazzo stream. Hearing the firing, General Forey, in command of the first division of Baraguey's corps, hastened to the front, and decided, although he realized that the Austrians were in large force, to engage battle. "Under the detestable pretext that his troops were facing the enemy for the first time, he gave the order to advance."[29] For two hours the Austrians contested his passage hotly, and if their commander, Urban, had been equal to the occasion, they might more than once have crushed the overdaring Forey. But Urban fought too much by the manual, — and, having failed to bring into action two other columns which were only an hour's march north of him, he fell back to Montebello. The crest of that town rises one hundred feet above the plain, and the hill which it crowns is laid out in terraced vineyards, step on step, like a giant's staircase. Forey's battalions, undeterred by the natural strength of the place, scaled from terrace to terrace to a point above the town, and then poured into the streets, where the Austrians fought them valiantly. The French won their way from house to house, and finally took the church and the cemetery, a walled rectangle, which served the enemy as a last refuge. Then Marshal Stadion, who directed in person the later phase of the battle, ordered a retreat, and his anxiety to be thorough led him to continue the retreat as far as Stradella. Like his Commander-in-Chief, Marshal Stadion relished everything about war except the fighting. The French and Piedmontese — Son-

---

[29] Duquet, 16–17. "Let his division perish, if necessary!" adds this excellent French military historian, "but do not let him lose the chance of winning, singlehanded, the first success."

naz's cavalry had done good service — did not hold Montebello, because General Baraguey judged that the Allied force there was too small to withstand the attack which he supposed the Austrians would make the next day. So, having lighted their bivouac fires as a subterfuge, the Allies retired towards Voghera. The battle of Montebello cost the Austrians nearly 1300 men and the Allies 730. The Austrians brought 27,000 into action and the Allies only about 8000 — a number which, considering the nearness of two army corps, does little credit to the strategy of their commanders.[30] The battle gave the Allies great prestige: Europe soon knew that four and even five Austrian soldiers were no match for one Frenchman. The confidence of the Allies increased accordingly, and that of their enemy fell. The total result obtained by Gyulai from this costly reconnaissance was this — that on the 20th of May a division of the French army happened to be on the road from Alessandria to Piacenza, not far from Voghera: this he might have learned, says Moltke with laconic sarcasm, "by other means."[31] But Gyulai was misled as well as beaten at Montebello: for he jumped at the conclusion that the French intended to move against his right wing.

The time had come, indeed, for the Allies to take the offensive. The French army had been raised to its war footing; its guns and trains had arrived; it had tasted victory and hungered for more. Three plans lay before the Emperor. He might, as the Austrians expected, march against Piacenza; but the road between the mountains and the Po was narrow, and the Austrians, swooping from the north upon his left flank, could cut his column in two. He might concentrate the Allied armies and give battle to the Austrians on their front: but the terrain was very difficult, cut up by irrigation, and partly under water in the rice bottoms; and even if successful in battle, the Allies could hardly hope to destroy the Austrian army, which had a fair line of retreat open to it. The third plan seemed the most audacious, and perhaps for that reason the Emperor preferred it. The Allies were to make a flank movement to the north, as far as Novara, then turn east, cross the Ticino, brush back the fringe of the Austrian right wing, and

[30] I quote Duquet's figures (p. 14) which seem more reliable than those printed by the earlier writers. General L. Nava's monograph *Combattimento di Montebello* (Modena, 1909) gives the most detailed account of the battle. He states the losses: Austrians, 1010; Allies, 705.   [31] Moltke, 50.

2

reach Milan before Gyulai could defend it. Grave objections were patent. By stripping Alessandria and Casale, the Allies would leave the line to Genoa an easy prey, endanger their main communication with Turin, and expose themselves to a flank attack during their march. In case of defeat they might be driven into neutral Switzerland.[32] Nevertheless, this plan prevailed. The political advantage to be won by capturing Milan could not be overestimated; and probably Napoleon counted on Gyulai's slowness and incompetence. While keeping up a show of menacing the Austrians in the southeast, therefore, the Allies moved the bulk of their forces northward as fast as possible.[33]

Before the great armies came into collision, however, Garibaldi and his Hunters of the Alps blazed like a meteor before the eyes of Europe. For three weeks he had chafed in camp on the Po. On May 8 the King gave him a roving commission, bidding him to harass the Austrian right, then believed to be stationed along the southern shores of Lake Maggiore, and authorizing him to enroll as many new volunteers as he saw fit. Only on the 18th could Garibaldi begin his march, glad to shake free from the formal routine of a large army, in which his command was merely a cog in the wheel, and to embark once more on that life of the guerilla in which no European has ever approached him. Compared with the carthorse movements of the regular regiments, his battalions of Hunters were like leopards, lithe, swift, alert, indefatigable; as ready for mountain paths or pathless forests as for the highroad; yet disciplined after their fashion; and above all, responsive, every man of them, to the eye or beck of their commander. Garibaldi complained, indeed, that the Piedmontese War Department had picked out all the able-bodied volunteers and sent on to him only the hunchbacked and the halt; but in this he exaggerated, for his Hunters of the Alps of 1859 proved themselves the peers of his Roman Legion of 1849.

On the 21st he crossed the Sesia at Romagnano, marched to Borgomanero, where he left his men, and pushed on himself in disguise to the lake. Having reconnoitred there, and arranged secretly for boats to cross the river, he returned to Borgomanero.

[32] *Ibid*, 54.   [33] Napoleon decided on May 26 to carry out this plan. " I cannot contradict you," says Hohenlohe-Ingelfingen, "if you call it incomprehensible that the headquarters of the Austrian army had no idea of the enemy's intention of turning the Austrian right at Vercelli." I, 170.

The next afternoon he led his little division forward, having lightened them of their knapsacks, for which he substituted a bag sewed into each cloak, and of every other impediment. They reached Arona at nightfall, rested a little, dropped down to Casteletto, where Viganotti had boats waiting for them, and before the dawn of the 23d they were safely in Sesto Calende, the first of the liberators to tread Lombard soil. The exploit was hazardous, beyond the approved etiquette of war. Garibaldi, with nominally 3000 men, had abandoned his base of supplies, lost touch with the extreme left of the Piedmontese army, and thrust himself into the enemy's country, which was occupied, presumably, by at least an army corps. But danger merely whetted Garibaldi's spirit: as for provisions, his men would get them on the way. That same night of May 23 he entered Varese, almost unopposed.

When Gyulai heard that this swarm of revolutionists, as he persisted in regarding them, had flown into Lombard territory, he feared that their motive might be as much political as military: for it required only the stimulus of a fascinating leader like Garibaldi to rouse the native population of Northern Lombardy. Gyulai accordingly ordered Urban to take a sufficient force, hurry to the scene, and destroy the Garibaldians. Urban was one of the hyenas whom the Austrian government kept to do its butcher's work — brutes whose highest model was Marshal Haynau, the flogger and torturer of naked women at Brescia. In 1849 Urban served his apprenticeship in Hungary, with such sinister efficiency that he was held in special favor by his chiefs. He affected to treat the present conflict not as war, duly declared between the combatants, and therefore subject to the rules in force among civilized nations, but as an insurrection. His action towards the peasantry caused Cavour to issue a protest, denouncing him as a "ferocious and cowardly assassin" — a stigma well-earned: for when he discovered a little powder and some bird-shot in a bottle in a dwelling at Casteggio, he caused the entire family to be stood up in a lane and shot. Eight dropt dead, Cignoli, the head of the family, was left mortally wounded, still alive on the heap.[34] So when Urban reached Como and

---

[34] Bersezio, VII, 195. For other examples of Urban's brutality see Mariani, III, 478, and La Varenne, chap. 22.

gathered four battalions of infantry, two squadrons of horse, and a battery, no one was astonished to hear him swear his great oaths that he would "catch and hang Garibaldi and all his brigands."[35] He also gave warning that he would hand over to fire, sword and sack any town or village which rebelled against the Imperial authority or in any way aided the enemy.

At four o'clock on the morning of May 26, Urban attempted to surprise the Garibaldians entrenched on the outskirts of Varese; but after holding their own, they advanced, and finally drove the Austrians back almost to Como. The following day Garibaldi had the effrontery to go in search of Urban, and to assault his outposts at San Fermo. After an obstinate fight, in which the brave De Cristoforis was killed, he took that position, the key to the town of Como, and before dark Urban was in full retreat on Monza.[36] On the 30th Garibaldi made a dash at Laveno, on Lake Maggiore, hoping that by pouncing unawares on the garrison there, he might get control of navigation on the lake; but at the critical moment his accomplices failed him and his own men lost their bearings in the dark. Garibaldi retreated to the neighborhood of Varese almost as stealthily as he had come. On June 1 he found that Urban had returned there with 12,000 men and 18 guns. The brutal Croat not only levied on the town a tribute of 3,000,000 lire, but of provisions, wine, leather, tobacco and cigars; he seized hostages, whom he kept in momentary terror of death; and finally, when the inhabitants could raise only 300,000 lire, he bombarded the place and let loose his wolfish soldiery to pillage it.[37] He did not, however, go out to take vengeance on Garibaldi, whose forces his own now outnumbered five to one, but contented himself with damaging Varese, defenseless, and occupied for the most part by women, children and old men. Having news of Urban's strength, and recognizing the risk of fighting a battle on terms so unequal, Garibaldi decided to retreat to Como, and he had begun his march thither, during the evening of June 1, when Urban himself received instructions to rejoin the main army at once. Leaving behind a rear guard two thousand strong to watch Varese and Como, he set out for the Ticino,

---

[35] Bersezio, VII, 205; Mariani, III, 470, n. 1.   [36] Urban believed that Garibaldi had 15,000 men, with cavalry and cannon. See his despatch after San Fermo: Varenne: *Chasseurs*, 568.   [37] Varese's population was only 8000.

where a crisis was impending. This sudden departure removed Garibaldi's anxiety. The formal military historians, who naturally pay as little attention as possible to his guerilla operations, imply that his dance was almost up when Urban withdrew: this opinion, however, has no warrant from the relative ability displayed by the Garibaldians and Austrians during the preceding nine days, and it ignores Garibaldi's cat-like agility in gliding out of difficulties. Had he been forced to take to the mountains, he might have eluded his pursuers for weeks.

Perplexed at Urban's unexpected retreat, Garibaldi stood on the alert till the afternoon of June 5, when news of the battle at Magenta reached him. He understood its import in a flash, and, without waiting to communicate with the Allied armies, he started eastward at full speed. Skirting the Lombard plain, he passed through Bergamo and Brescia and reached Lake Garda. Everywhere his coming roused the countryside. Left to his own motion, he would probably have pushed forward into the Trentino, in the hope of cutting that Austrian line of approach to Italy: but on June 20 he received at Salò orders from the King to retrace his steps and guard the Valtellina. Evidently, Napoleon III did not wish the Garibaldians to take part in operations which he himself commanded. The suspicion of his own sympathy with revolution must be quenched. Garibaldi, reluctant, and divining the true reason for his being condemned to inactivity, obeyed with soldierlike promptness.[38]

Tidings of his exploit circulated far and wide, and helped to popularize the Italian cause in quarters where France was distrusted and the war frowned upon. [39] The world felt instinctively that whatever Garibaldi fought for must be noble. His success against superior numbers roused general admiration. But most important was the symbolic value of his presence in the campaign: this meant that all Italy, irrespective of political party or of geographical divisions, had a stake in the war. And by keeping Urban busy during the last week of May, Garibaldi contributed to the successful carrying out of the Allies' colossal strategic venture. But as no bulletins reached him from either

[38] See Trevelyan, I, chap. v, for a vivid account of Garibaldi's campaign.
[39] Even the London *Times*, which had been staunchly pro-Austrian, was moved to admiration by the news from Varese.

headquarters he could only conjecture on the 2d of June why Urban had marched southward without striking a blow.[40]

On May 27 the Emperor, having lost a week by inactivity after the battle of Montebello, began to move. On the 29th he issued this order: "The 30th of May the Army of the King will establish itself beyond Palestro." His purpose was to enable the Third Corps (Canrobert's) to pass the Sesia unmolested. Palestro is but a small village, raised a few metres above the plain, and accessible only by the roads which converge upon it as a centre: for the country here is cut up by ditches and dikes. A little before noon on the 30th Cialdini's division attacked the place, which Weigl's brigade, much inferior in numbers, occupied. Owing to the narrow approach, however, the Austrians had the advantage of position and held the Piedmontese at bay for some time. Then the Queen's Brigade made a gallant charge, gained a foothold, and sent the enemy flying. In vain did Weigl himself come up with more men, Cialdini could not be dislodged. At Vinzaglio, Austrian Fleischhacker, with only three companies, bravely resisted Durando's division for an hour and a half, and then barely escaped with the remnant of his men.[41] By nightfall, the Piedmontese were established in the position the Emperor had marked out for them. But the King knew that if the Austrians returned on the morrow with more troops, he might be driven back, and he sent for reinforcements. During the night the Third Regiment of Zouaves joined him, bringing his effective up to about 14,000 men.[42] The news of this fight perplexed Gyulai, who could not understand how it happened that the Piedmontese should be pushing forward in the Northeast, if, as he assumed, the Allies were preparing for a grand advance on Piacenza in the Southeast. He saw, however, that his first need was to recapture Palestro, and he accordingly gave orders for two divisions (Jellacic and Lilia) to attack that place on the morning of the 31st. At ten o'clock the Austrian columns, advancing from the southeast, opened fire. They were checked and gradually driven back. The Austrian left, gliding along the Sesia, seemed to be more fortunate; for while they rolled up the Piedmontese outposts, they dropped

[40] Guerzoni: *Garibaldi*, I, 435–65. Garibaldi, *Memorie*, 2d period, chap. xi. Moltke, 56–57. La Varenne: *Chasseurs*, chaps. 16–23. Mariani, III, 464–86.

[41] *Précis*, 106, gives the Austrian loss 560, the Piedmontese, 316.

[42] Moltke, 61. Fleury: *Souvenirs*, II, 18–20.

shells on the bridge over which Canrobert's corps was crossing the river. If Palestro were lost, the advance of the Allies would be endangered. There was a moment of terrible suspense. Then, like unleashed bloodhounds, the Zouaves dashed forward and waded through a canal, with water rising above their waists, sprang at the Austrian battery, captured it, sabred the gunners, and swept the infantry, astonished, beaten and exhausted, down the road it had come by. The Piedmontese sharpshooters and the 16th of the Line reinforced the Zouaves, who gave the Austrians no respite till they reached the Bridda, where many of the fugitives were huddled together and killed in trying to cross the bridge, and hundreds more leapt or were hurled into the river and were drowned. Victor Emanuel himself, oblivious of discretion, rode in the great charge. A third Austrian column, directed against the Piedmontese left behind at Confienza, could make no headway against Fanti's superior numbers, and withdrew. General Zobel, who commanded the Austrians that day, ignorant alike of the destruction of his left wing and of the retreat of his right, made a final attempt to storm Palestro with his centre: but when he encountered fresh French battalions joining Cialdini's division in front of him, he understood that he was too late, and retreated to Robbio. The Austrians lost 1605 men, of whom 774 were missing.[43]

The Allies exulted over the victory — and well they might; for a defeat would have disgraced them. The number of their troops actually engaged — about 20,000 — equaled that of the Austrians; but they had 50,000 or 60,000 more men within two hours' march, and, although it was only four o'clock when the Austrians gave up the fight, the French did not pursue them. While two divisions properly handled were securing Palestro, the rest of the Allied Armies might have advanced to Novara, thereby hastening their passage of the Ticino. To waste a day on a march which must be rapid if it were to succeed, to assign 80,000 men to an operation and employ only a quarter of them, and to fail to convert the enemy's retreat into a rout, certainly did not indicate high generalship. On their side, the Austrians could congratulate themselves that by their valor they had interrupted the Allies' advance and had penetrated their strategic secret.

[43] Moltke, 67.

Marshal Gyulai, however, still clung to his belief that the fighting at Palestro was only a reconnaissance on the part of the French, until he heard, early in the morning of June 1, the details of the second battle. Almost at the same time his troops evacuated Novara, and brought word that they had seen not only the French and Piedmontese in large numbers, but also the bearskins of the Imperial Guard, an indication that the Emperor himself must be near. This news threw the Austrian commander into a flutter of doubts. He had so long taken it for granted that the Allies meant to plough their way through his army to Piacenza that he could not quickly adjust his mind to new possibilities. Having allowed the enemy to accomplish unhindered a flank movement along an arc sixty-five miles in length, he was staggered by the sudden need of action. Thirty-six hours elapsed before he could come to a decision.[44] He did not even send out patrols to seek definite information of the position and strength of the Allies, but kept brigades and divisions marching hither and yon in response to his weather-cock resolutions. How longingly he thought of Mortara, entrenched among her swamps and ditches, so comfortable — and so safe! Why had not the enemy attacked him there, where he could have certainly overwhelmed them? A fighting general, like Grant or Lee, would, of course, have cut the Allies' line in two as soon as he had discovered its length: but the Field Marshal Count, though a military man, was no fighter. He saw only the awful dangers which beset him. Early on June 2 he gave orders to retreat into Lombardy, and forthwith his troops quitted hastily the country which they had occupied to so little purpose for thirty days. To justify this humiliating move Gyulai telegraphed Emperor Francis Joseph, who had reached Verona on May 30, that he "regarded it as his first duty to maintain the strength of the army for further operations." [45] He was already looking forward to the happy day when he should have led it back beyond the Mincio into the security of the Quadrilateral. His immediate object, however, was to occupy the East bank of the Ticino, in order to prevent the Allies from invading Lombardy and threatening Milan.

[44] "I must invite your attention to the pernicious consequences of the frequent counter-orders, when issued by so high an authority as the commander of an army. *Ordre! Contre-ordre! Désordre!* once said an authority, I forget who." Hohenlohe-Ingelfingen, I, 189.   [45] *Précis*, 123.

CHAPTER XXIII

MAGENTA AND SOLFERINO

GYULAI'S inexplicable indecision puzzled Napoleon III, who, having drawn his military knowledge out of the books, expected his opponent to follow the rules. Napoleon himself, also neglecting to maintain an efficient scouting service, assumed that the Austrians would attempt to join battle with him before he could gain a foothold in Lombardy. Having this in view he concentrated his army at Novara, and then instructed General Camou, with his division of light infantry of the Guard, to seize the bridge over the Ticino at Turbigo. Camou made the passage unopposed, and bivouacked in the little town. MacMahon and Espinasse, finding the still more important crossing at San Martino undefended, seized the bridge-head, and set their engineers to work to strengthen the viaduct the Austrians had weakened but failed to blow up. Thus on that night of June 2, two French commands were picketed on Lombard soil. The next day, early, MacMahon reached Turbigo, and rode on to Robecchetto, a village a mile and a third beyond, where, on climbing into the belfry, he saw a battalion of Austrians within gunshot of him, tramping along the wooded road. He had barely time to mount his horse, gallop back to Turbigo and send his men against them. They proved to be a column under General Cordon sent to block the passage at Turbigo: but they were too late; and after a two hours' hot encounter with La Motte-rouge's division and the Algerian sharpshooters, they retired. Being thus in possession of two entrances into Lombardy, Napoleon determined to move his entire left wing across the river on the following day. He was in the position of a novice who, through good luck which he ought not to have banked upon, had made a stroke that would have glorified any professional. Nothing seemed impossible now to the planner of the amazing flank movement. For a while, Europe attributed to his genius success that should be credited to Gyulai's incompetence.

Coming east from Novara, you pass at six miles the little town of Trecate; thence in two miles you reach the village of San Martino, crowning the bluff which forms the western boundary of the Ticino water-way. The river itself, except in times of flood, flows a mile still farther eastward and in 1859 it was crossed by a viaduct which carried both the railway and the high-road. The highroad runs thence in a straight line to Magenta, five miles off; the railway to the south bends a little and then touches the town on its northern outskirts. Half way between the river and Magenta both roads cross the Naviglio Grande, a canal thirty feet wide and averaging six feet deep, with a lively current which irrigates the country to the south. The steep inner sides of the Canal are twenty-five or thirty feet high, and either wooded or, where the erosion is greatest, are paved with stone; the top, rising six or eight feet above the level of the ground, is banked at so gradual a slope that you often do not perceive the Canal until you stand on its brink. The Ticino itself meanders among many islands, which spread out or dwindle according to the height of the water, and are covered with a thick growth of riverain bushes and trees. Between the Ticino and the Canal stretches a tangle of vegetation, amid which, wherever practicable, patches of barley and rice are under cultivation. Eastward from the Canal begins that Lombard Plain whose fertility remains, after two thousand years, unex-hausted. No square foot of its soil lies idle. Every shrub, vine or tree contributes its share to the annual profit. The mulber-ries feed the silkworms and serve with the elms as supports for the endless festoons of grapevines. The acacias give a refreshing shade, their vivid green pleases the eye, and their graceful pendu-lous twigs, responsive to every breath of wind, suggest coolness even amid the heat of summer noons. The land is cut up into large farms, each with its massive group of buildings, and each subdivided into plots two or three acres in area, where maize and other grain and vegetables are grown according to the season. In June, the maize is already taller than the tallest man; and as each precinct is bounded by hedges or by the vine-draped mul-berries and elms, the views, except along the highway, are shut in. A tangle of narrow lanes, in which the stranger quickly loses his way, connects farm with farm, hamlet with hamlet. Small

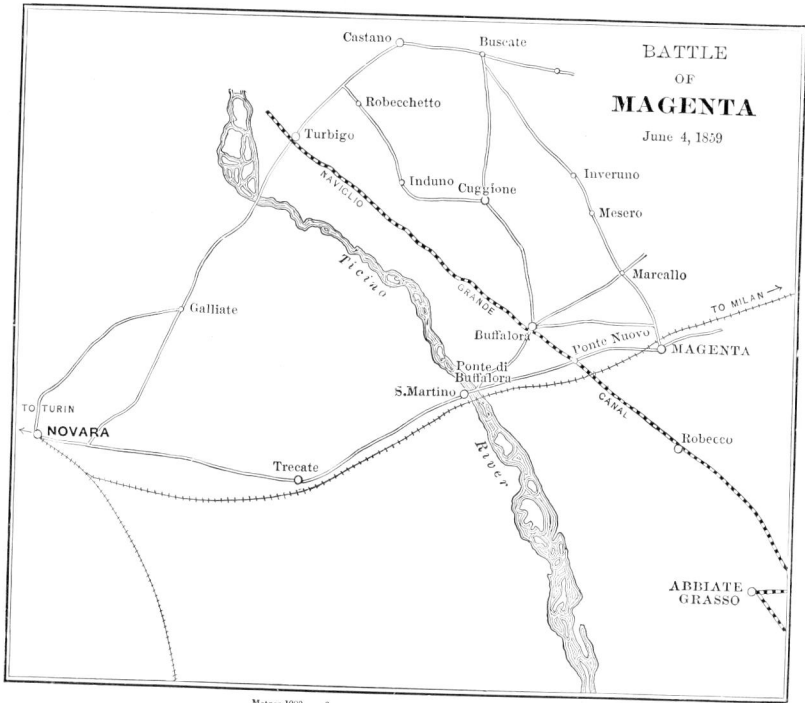

BATTLE
OF
MAGENTA
June 4, 1859

Castano
Buscate
Robecchetto
Turbigo
NAVIGLIO
Induno
Cuggione
Inveruno
Mesero
Ticino
GRANDE
Marcallo
Galliate
Buffalora
TO MILAN
Ponte Nuovo
Ponte di
Buffalora
MAGENTA
S.Martino
TO TURIN
NOVARA
River
CANAL
Robecco
Trecate
ABBIATE
GRASSO

Metres 1000   0
0   1   2   3   4 Kilometres

ditches for irrigation spread their meshes in all directions. This land of plenty, smiling, luxuriant and trim, so noble a witness to the virtues of Man at Peace, presented nothing but obstacles to Man at War.[1]

Napoleon III, still expecting the Austrians to attack him on the Piedmontese side of the Ticino, planned on June 4 to have his left wing occupy Magenta, to leave his right wing at Novara, and to échelon his centre between Trecate and the river. His Second Corps being firmly placed to the north at Turbigo, on the Lombard side of the Canal, some nine miles, as the crow flies, from Magenta, he ordered MacMahon to march in two columns on that town, where, by the middle of the afternoon, they would be joined by the main army following the highroad. The Emperor laid his plan on the belief that there would be no general engagement that day, because he supposed that, at most, he might be engaged with a few divisions of the enemy to the east of the Ticino. Half of the Piedmontese army, bivouacking at Galliate, was to cross the river at Turbigo, and act as reserves to MacMahon.

The Austrian commander, equally ignorant of the intentions of the French, did not prepare for a great battle. He had hardly completed the transfer of his army into Lombardy. His men were tired with long marches. On June 3 his Second Corps had actually had no rations.[2] In spite of the skirmish at Robecchetto on the 3d, he counted on having time enough to bar the march of the French to Milan, and by blowing up three or four bridges to delay their passage over the Ticino and the Naviglio. A new army corps, under Count Clam Gallas, which had reached Milan on the 1st, had been immediately sent forward to Magenta. To reinforce this, Gyulai ordered up from the south three corps, Zobel's, Prince Schwarzenberg's, and Prince Liechtenstein's. Gyulai's total strength was 113,000 men; but so clumsy were the arrangements on both sides that the Austrians brought only 58,000 and the French only 54,000 men into action during a battle which lasted twelve hours.

Gyulai expected that the bridge-head at San Martino would

---

[1] Descriptions of the campaigning ground are given by all the military historians. I have drawn also on notes made by myself when visiting the battlefield of Magenta.   [2] Hohenlohe-Ingelfingen, I, 196.

be hotly defended by his men, who, when obliged to fall back, would destroy the viaduct. If, however, the French should still succeed in crossing, the Austrians could hem them in on the long and impassable strip between the river and the Canal. Finally, if the French should drive the Austrians before them, the latter had merely to demolish the bridges on the Canal itself. But his expectations were dashed: for, on June 2, the Austrians abandoned San Martino without even contesting it, and they failed to destroy the viaduct.

At eight o'clock on the morning of June 4 Mellinet's division of the Guard left Trecate, reached San Martino unopposed, and having strengthened the shattered arches with beams, crossed safely. Other regiments followed on pontoons, and by half past ten they were pushing forward towards Magenta. The Emperor arrived about noon, and took up his headquarters on the highroad a third of a mile east of the river. Looking down the road he saw a thousand yards ahead of him at the Canal the buildings of Ponte Nuovo di Magenta piercing the foliage. To his left, not more than a mile distant, on both sides of the Canal, was Buffalora, his nearest point of contact with MacMahon's Second Corps. To his right, three miles away in a straight line, lay Robecco, a largeish village, where the Austrian commander had his quarters. The day was sunny and hot; a south breeze blowing. The clear passage over the river put the Emperor in good spirits, but on learning that his grenadiers had encountered a desultory fire from Austrian sharpshooters in the brush, he began to have misgivings and he therefore decided to hold his men in until the time came for a general advance. At half past twelve, according to agreement, MacMahon ought to be at Buffalora; then the Imperial command would sweep forward to join him in capturing Magenta. Impatient, and growing every moment more anxious, Napoleon waited for MacMahon's signal. The flat country, enveloped in luxuriant foliage, made the battle as indistinct as a sea-fight in a fog: but this obstacle troubled both contestants equally.

Gyulai, however, had a great advantage in being on the east of the Naviglio, where he commanded the bridges, and in having comparatively free communications. He had pushed his men northward three miles above the highroad and up to noon he supposed that he held victory in his hands. About that hour, his outposts were in contact with MacMahon's vanguard. Starting from Turbigo at nine o'clock, MacMahon moved his corps in two columns toward Magenta. He himself led La Motterouge's division, which took the western route, through Cuggiono to Buffalora. Camou's division followed in an hour. Espinasse meanwhile, passing to the east, after making a long circuit through Buscate, Inveruno, Mesero, and Marcallo, was to attack Magenta from the north. The distance for MacMahon might be twelve miles, for Espinasse fifteen. The roads were narrow, and they ran through a country which, as has been described, rendered marching across the fields always difficult and often impossible.

It was one o'clock when MacMahon approached Buffalora, only to find it occupied by the Austrians. He opened fire from a battery, expecting to dislodge them quickly; but they proved to be present in such large numbers that he thought it wiser to draw back and wait for Camou's regiments to overtake him. Hearing the cannonade, the Emperor asssumed that MacMahon was executing the plan agreed upon, would easily capture Buffalora and be at Magenta in an hour; so he gave the impatient Imperial Guard the word to advance, and it sprang forward eagerly. One regiment rushed towards Buffalora, to support MacMahon; another stormed the redoubt that commanded the railroad bridge over the Canal; the third, holding the middle course, hurried along the highroad to Ponte Nuovo di Magenta, where the Austrians were prepared to defend the bridge stoutly. Having seized the redoubt Wimpffen's grenadiers within twenty minutes drove Ban Jellacic to the other side of the Canal. In the centre, the grenadiers cleared the west bank, but when they attempted to cross the bridge, they were mowed down by a hail of bullets from the heavy granite buildings opposite, which served as forts for the Austrians. To realize the peril of these combats at the bridges, one must remember that the distance between the windows of the houses on the east and of those on the west was not more than forty yards, and that the moment a soldier came into the open, he had nothing to protect him while he was crossing. Nevertheless, Mellinet captured Buffalora and in half an hour, his four thousand soldiers of the Imperial

Guard had possession of the eastern bank of the Canal as far south as Ponte Vecchio di Magenta. But their task was only beginning. General Reischach, having disentangled a fresh brigade from the mass of teams that cumbered the highroad, marched on Ponte Nuovo, while Prince Schwarzenberg, from Robecco, hurried a brigade through the lanes on the West side of the Naviglio, to smash the flank of the French at Ponte Vecchio and at the railroad bridge. Then Baltin's division, reinforced, recaptured Buffalora.

On hearing MacMahon's welcome cannonade, the Emperor rode forward from San Martino to a point almost halfway between the river and the Naviglio, whence he might direct more rapidly the victorious advance on Magenta. Very soon, however, MacMahon's guns ceased to thunder; then even the rattle of musketry died out in the direction of Buffalora. The Emperor's first inference was that the Second Corps must have captured the place; but as the silence continued, anxiety gained upon him, and after anxiety, alarm. One hour, two hours, three hours passed — yet no sound, no news, from MacMahon. Only his utter rout could account for such neglect. Napoleon had not been long in his new position before he began to be beset by requests for reinforcements from his troops at the bridges, who were being hard pressed by the fresh regiments massed against them. He despatched orderlies and aides in all directions with the single command "Hurry!" To Mellinet and Cler, to Cassaignoles and Wimpffen, frantically appealing for more men, he could only reply, — "Help soon!" "Hold fast!" "Block the passage!" Some of the official chroniclers say that throughout this terrible suspense, he maintained an unruffled manner and uttered words of cheer only; although he perpetually lighted cigarettes, puffed a few whiffs at each and then threw it away: if that be true, he never dissembled better.[3] For the imminent danger was apparent. Unless relief came speedily, he himself would be compelled to retreat, with the remnant of the Imperial Guard, across the Ticino,[4] and he had no assurance that the Austrians had not already pushed north to Turbigo and cut off the Second Corps's line of escape. Other historians, however, unhampered by obli-

[3] Fleury: *Souvenirs*, ii, 42–45; describes Napoleon's coolness. Moltke, 91.
[4] Hohenlohe-Ingelfingen, i, 252.

gations of eulogy, tell a very different story. They describe Napoleon as being in a state of utter collapse, unable to speak, much less to command, paralyzed by the thought that though the fate of his Empire hung on his decisions he was powerless to decide. When the bullets began to whistle round him his staff turned his chestnut horse, Buckingham, to the west, and they led the Emperor towards Piedmont. He rode speechlessly, mechanically. From a walk, the group broke into a gallop, as if in flight, and they had ridden across the river before General Frossard prevailed on the Emperor to stop. Half an hour later when their nerves were quieter, they recrossed the bridge, and Napoleon dismounted behind a brickyard to await his doom.[5]

To add bitterness to his foreboding, he realized that within a radius of ten miles from where he was standing, Canrobert and Niel had 41,000 men inactive near Novara, Baraguey d'Hilliers had 40,000 more at Lumelongo, and Victor Emanuel was chafing inactive with 22,000 at Galliate. As soon as he understood the situation, he sent urgent commands; but owing to his fixed idea that the Austrians intended to attack in force on the right side of the river, he kept Canrobert's corps, the nearest to him, drawn up in battle order, and summoned his reinforcements from Niel's corps, which lay farthest to the west. Niel's men found their way blocked by Canrobert's and, it was after half past three before Picard's brigade came on the scene. A great shout of exultation went up from the regiments of the Guard[6] — Mellinet's division had fought on for six hours — at the sight of their comrades. They drove the enemy back to Ponte Vecchio, seized the buildings on the right bank, and were about to cross, when the Austrians blew up the bridge. Then heavy reinforcements gave new life to the Austrians, who in turn drove the French foot by foot from Ponte Vecchio to Ponte Nuovo, which they held desperately, as a drowning man clutches a plank that is slipping away from him. The French understood that if they failed there, they would lose the Naviglio, be unable to re-form on this side of the river; and before they could retire over the viaduct, the Austrians, multiplying in numbers every moment, might put them to utter rout and cut off their escape.

[5] *Revue Historique*, Mars-Avril, 1904, 84; G. Bapst: "Napoleon III à Magenta." [6] On that day the Imperial Guard numbered 13,223 men.

It is a quarter to five, and here at last is another wave of succor. Vinoy's division, the head of Niel's column, is signaled at
San Martino, and a little later it has come up and is supporting
Picard's fagged battalions and the long-suffering grenadiers.
Close in their dust follows Charrière with the 85th and 86th of
the Line. The Emperor may now breathe more freely, although
as yet he can see only the possibility of holding his own till nightfall. For he is still ignorant of MacMahon's fate.

Where was the Second Corps? After MacMahon early in the
afternoon found Buffalora occupied in force, he retired a mile or
two to the north, to Bernate and the neighboring farms, in order
to give time for Espinasse with the left wing to approach within
striking distance of Magenta. But Espinasse, fearing an attack,
had marched in order of battle, which greatly decreased his speed,
and when the Austrians discovered that a wide gap yawned
between his column and MacMahon's they drove Baltin's and
Koudelka's brigades in to separate them permanently. Thereupon, MacMahon, with a few aides, dashed across country
in search of Espinasse. More than once he came within pistol-
shot of the Austrian lines, risking death or capture; but luck
served him, and, having bidden Espinasse to hurry, he rode back
unscathed. Such rashness, of course, had no justification. By
five o'clock, however, MacMahon had disposed his corps for a
general advance. La Motterouge's division moved south on
Buffalora, Camou filled the dangerous void in the centre, and
Espinasse pushed forward as fast as he could on the left, followed
by Fanti's divisions of Piedmontese.[7] The belfry of Magenta,
one of the few landmarks visible above the trees, was their common rendezvous. For more than an hour the Austrians held out
doggedly. They contested each farm; they rallied at a brick-
kiln; they converted the village of Marcallo into a fortress: but
MacMahon's men were fresher, and Gyulai's reserves were too

---

[7] The French afterwards complained that the Piedmontese were slow. But
the Emperor's original orders did not call for Piedmontese participation in the
battle. He prevented them from crossing the river until his own troops had
passed, and he called on Fanti so late that he barely succeeded in reaching
Magenta at the end of the day. The Piedmontese claim that Fanti's coming up
decided the battle: the French claim that he did not arrive until the fighting was
over. Compare the official military authorities, and Carandini, 213–36; Della
Rocca, 1, 445; Castelli: *Ricordi*, 298.

far away to succor the exhausted brigades of Baltin, Lebzeltern, Gablenz and Szabo, which retired badly disorganized to Magenta.

This place, although flat, offered a good means of defense. On approaching it by the highroad from Piedmont, you still see the walled cemetery and the massive church which served the Austrians as a redoubt. The buildings at the entrance to the town were of masonry, well-adapted to sharpshooters. Cannon commanded the main exits to San Martino and to Buffalora. The railroad station on the northern edge of the town, was proof against musketry, and behind the low embankment on which the track was laid riflemen stretched prone found a shelter. Within and behind Magenta, Gyulai counted 33 battalions, some, indeed mere remnants, and the best much battered, decimated and terribly fatigued. Yet they had the advantage in numbers and in acting on the defensive; and they still kept a residue of courage. At half past six the French began their double attack from the west and from the north; at half past seven, they were still fighting stubbornly. They took the cemetery; they forced the sharpshooters back into the town; they silenced the guns; they fought hand to hand in the streets; they stormed the loopholed houses. Leading his men against a tower-like edifice from which 300 Tyrolese carabineers were working havoc among the French in the open, Espinasse was shot dead: but his Zouaves captured the place. By eight o'clock, when the long summer day was sinking into dusk, the French, aided by Fanti's division of Piedmontese,[8] occupied Magenta, and the Austrians, beaten and almost panic-stricken, took refuge at Cubetta and in the villages to the South.

While MacMahon was thus engaged, the Imperial Guard, now still further strengthened, engaged in a final furious struggle for possession of the Naviglio. First, they won Ponte Nuovo di Magenta; then, the railroad bridge, and finally they held Ponte Vecchio, which had been taken and re-taken seven times in as many hours. As the twilight deepened, the Austrians withdrew in fair order, unpursued, to Robecco.

On that day the French lost 4535 men, of whom 655 were prisoners or missing,[9] and the Austrians 10,226 men, including

[8] Carandini, 233–36, makes Fanti's coöperation the pivotal element in Mac-Mahon's success. See also his notes to pp. 237–40, including MacMahon's letter of March 14, 1861.

[9] Moltke, p. 97, gives the totals: French, 4444, Austrians, 9713.

2

4500 prisoners or missing. The latter part of the day the Emperor spent in scolding for their delay the generals who were hurrying to his support. He shuddered as the long file of the terribly wounded passed him. Only when MacMahon sent word that he had driven the Austrians out of Magenta, did the Emperor's spirits revive. Not yet sure of his victory,[10] having placed a brigade at Magenta, and another at the Naviglio, he retired with the rest of his troops to San Martino, to prepare for renewing the struggle on the morrow, when he estimated that he could put 100,000 men, nearly all fresh, into the field. Gyulai also expected to bring up at least 100,000 troops, more than half of whom had not fought on the 4th, and to deliver a great battle: but at three in the morning Clam Gallas informed him that his corps was too demoralized to fight again so soon. The Austrian commander-in-chief gave orders, therefore, for a general retreat to the Adda. Lombardy was lost.

The battle of Magenta, which, for the brilliance of its immediate results, rivaled some of the spectacular victories of Napoleon I, furnishes abundant material to critics who love to perform autopsies on by-gone strategy. For the French, it was a battle without a commander-in-chief. Both commanders erred in plunging unawares into a vast engagement;[11] both erred in bringing less than half their troops into action. The failure of Gyulai's officers to blow up the bridge upset his plans, but even so he had the advantage of free communications with all his forces, of position and of numbers. During several critical hours, when a different commander would have won the day, his 25,000 men along the Naviglio were held in check, and more than once dislodged, by the 8000 grenadiers of the Imperial Guard. Napoleon, after being misled by MacMahon's cannonade into ordering an advance, could do nothing but wait. For MacMahon himself, who was glorified as the hero of the battle, praise and blame mix freely. No excuse has been offered for his failure to notify to the Emperor his withdrawal from Buffalora. As the bridge was in-

---

[10] His despatches were so ambiguous that the Empress rewrote them before printing in the *Moniteur*. *Revue Historique*, l. c., 275–76.   [11] "Napoleon III in 1859 committed as many blunders as he did in 1870. But the Austrians had no Moltke to direct them ; their army corps were commanded by men who knew less of generalship than a Prussian major, and their armament was inferior." G. F. R. Henderson: *The Science of War*. London: Longmans, 1906, p. 14.

tact at Bernate, an orderly could have ridden in twenty minutes to headquarters. That neglect nearly ruined the French centre, and might have resulted in complete disaster. The rest of his work MacMahon did well: like Sheridan, he shone in undertakings requiring dash and spirit. But the real hero of the battle was the French soldier. In discipline and endurance, as well as in valor, he excelled the Austrian; although the latter, with competent officers, would have made a better showing. Many of the Austrian regiments were composed of new recruits. No proper attention was paid to the soldiers' welfare. They were sent on over-long marches; they were ill-fed, or not fed at all. Clam Gallas's corps, just conveyed from Bohemia by rail, suffered so much from hunger and fatigue that some of the privates committed suicide "and many swooned." Gyulai and his lieutenants had not learned the first wisdom of war, — armies win few battles on an empty stomach.[12]

After holding himself on the alert during June 5, until he learned that the Austrians were in full retreat, and the Allies had really triumphed, Napoleon moved his headquarters to Magenta. In the flush of victory, he bestowed upon MacMahon a marshal's baton and the title of Duke of Magenta, — excessive rewards for the general who almost wrecked the French plan of battle. The victory had already been won by the Imperial Guard before MacMahon dislodged the shattered fragments of the Austrian army that rallied at Magenta.[13] Napoleon therefore created Baraguey d'Hilliers a marshal in recognition of the superb valor of the Guard. But the horrors of the slaughter impressed him. Magenta was filled with thousands of wounded, and many of the dead were still unburied. Passing a stretcher bearing a general's body he had the cloth removed. There lay the intrepid commander of MacMahon's second division. "Poor Espinasse!" said the Emperor, after looking intently; and again, "Poor Espinasse!" Did the idealogue realize for a moment not merely the brutishness of war, but the stupidity of it as a means of establishing ideals among civilized men?

---

[12] Moltke, 96. Hohenlohe-Ingelfingen, I, 196. *Revue Historique*, l. c. For eyewitnesses' reports see Eber's accounts in the London *Times*, and Arrivabene's in the *News* (reprinted in his book). Bapst's account in the *Revue Historique* shows up Napoleon's incapacity. *La Revue Militaire Suisse*, Aug. 29, 1859, prints an apology apparently by Gyulai himself for his generalship at Magenta. Reprinted in Lecomte, I, 232–34. [13] Moltke, 102.

The Allies took no steps to pursue the Austrians. For forty-eight hours, indeed, they hardly measured the extent of their victory, and for several days Europe believed that the Austrians had won.[14] Only on the 7th did they continue their march to Milan, where, on the 8th, the two monarchs made a triumphal entry.[15] Ignorant as usual of the enemy's movements, and suspecting from the silence that they were hatching mischief, Napoleon ordered Baraguey d'Hilliers, supported on his right by Niel's corps and on his left by MacMahon's, to attack Melegnano on the 8th. Baraguey started at five in the morning, and it was five in the afternoon of a sultry day before he had covered the eighteen miles, and come within attacking distance of the town. There General Benedek, whose Eighth Corps was serving as rear-guard for the Austrians' retreat, had left a single brigade under General Roden. At six o'clock Baraguey opened fire: but the Austrians were well-placed and brave; Benedek sent Boer's brigade to assist them; and they could be dislodged only after the French had carried their position at the point of the bayonet. A terrific thunderstorm and the fall of night rendered pursuit impossible. During the entire conflict, Niel's and MacMahon's troops stood idly by, about three miles distant on the west and on the east respectively. In this brief fight at Melegnano, Baraguey lost some 950 men, and the Austrians about 1480.[16] The operation was a sheer waste: for the Austrians intended to evacuate the town the next morning, and the French put their success to no use. Instead of pressing on to harass Benedek's rear, they turned back to Milan, and joined the movement of the Allied armies towards Venetia.

The Allies' plan of campaign was opportunist. They went in search of the enemy, and hoped to rout him in a decisive battle: but they seemed to be in no hurry to conclude. From Milan to Desenzano, on Lake Garda, skirting the southern spurs of the

---

[14] On June 6, having heard nothing from the Piedmontese headquarters, Cavour telegraphed the Emperor for details. *Revue Historique*, l. c., 285.

[15] Napoleon, says Fleury, "had veritably the air of a prophet; the women waved their handkerchiefs, the men cheered, shouting, 'Long live the Liberator of Italy!' Flowers were showered, bouquets hit us, the people came to touch his hands, to embrace his knees: it was a delirium." *Souvenirs*, II, 46.

[16] *Précis*, 121. But the French loss in killed and wounded was 887 and the Austrian only 360; but the Austrians had 1124 missing.

Alps, is only seventy miles: yet the Piedmontese and French advanced so leisurely that not until June 23 were they within sight of the lake. The Italian summer heat affected the French, many of whom succumbed to malaria and fever. The railway, which should have given swift transportation, had been disabled by the Austrians, who carried off all the rolling-stock. Supplies had to be hauled; the procession of teams blocked the road for the marching regiments; and every day's advance added to the difficulty.[17] Perhaps also, Napoleon III hesitated to risk another engagement which, even if successful, must force dangerous political problems upon him. Although the Austrians appeared to be more forthright, whoever frequented their headquarters perceived that irresolution and incompetence reigned there. Emperor Francis Joseph, a man of mediocre ability in government, the plaything of one adviser or sycophant after another, and wholly without knowledge or experience as a warrior, took command of the two armies into which his forces in Italy were divided. Dismissing Gyulai, he chose for his chief-of-staff old Baron Hess, a veteran of the Napoleonic wars [18] and an understudy of Radetzky. Marshal Wimpffen commanded the First Army, which consisted of the Third, Ninth, and Eleventh Corps, with adequate reserves; and Count Schlick, a cavalry general who had found favor at court, commanded the Second Army (First, Fifth, Seventh, Eighth Corps, four battalions of the Sixth Corps, and a division of reserves). Every province of the Empire north of the Alps was stripped of its garrisons and conscripts to make good the losses from battle and disease: yet in spite of these additions, the regiments fell below the peace standard of strength. By the middle of June there were 50,000 sick soldiers within the Austrian lines; three weeks later there were 80,000!

Day by day Francis Joseph's hosts slipped back toward the Quadrilateral, evading an encounter as the Russians had retreated before the great Napoleon in 1812. The Allies followed them slothfully, whilst Europe looked on surprised: for the popular belief was that the Austrian armies far outnumbered their adversaries, and that they were a match for the French on even terms.

[17] The lack of food and forage was paralyzing. The French suffered worse than the Piedmontese, but the latter more than once nearly dropped from hunger and exhaustion. See, for instance, Della Rocca, I, 456–57.

[18] Hess first distinguished himself at Wagram in 1809.

But they let go the line of the River Chiese, which offered a splendid opportunity for a defensive battle, and on June 22 they had crossed the Mincio, thereby abandoning Lombardy. The following day Francis Joseph changed his mind, recrossed the Mincio and distributed his forces in front of the river, from Pozzolengo on the north to Guidizzolo and Medole on the south. The Emperor having been persuaded by Marshal Hess to take the offensive and go and meet the enemy, a general advance of ten miles was planned for the 24th. The Allies enjoyed the 23d as a day of rest, except that their scouts reconnoitred as usual, and so ineffectively that they failed to note the return of the Austrians. A balloonist, who looked down on the country, reported only three Austrian horsemen in sight. Napoleon gave orders that on the 24th the Allied Armies should move eastward, in nearly parallel columns, a distance of some ten miles.

The battlefield of Solferino may be enclosed by lines which run almost due south from Desenzano to Medole, thence east to Volta, thence north to Lake Garda. This oblong strip, which measures about 12 miles from north to south, and six miles in width, has a most diversified character. From the lake shore the land begins to rise, gradually and in regular slope for a while, and then in a succession of hills. The first of these, San Martino, may be three hundred feet above the lake. Beyond this, southward, crops up a succession of ridges and rounded crests, until, six miles away, you reach the hill of Solferino which, with a height of 700 feet, dominates the entire cluster of miniature mountains. On its very top perches a massive tower, The Spy of Italy, whence one of the most beautiful panoramas in Europe stretches before you. On its western side, the hill drops very steeply; along the ridge there is a walled cemetery. The village of Solferino itself nestles in the hollow to the south. Outposts of this central crest, and separated from it and from each other by narrow valleys, are the hill of Madonna della Scoperta, the Mount of Cypresses, and Monte Fenile. A short two miles away to the southeast Cavriana, another unimportant village, which destiny chose to make a pivotal point in this battle, straggles at the foot of another cluster of hills. Beyond Cavriana, lies Volta, where the ridge melts gently into the plain. The glacier-made chain of hills, which culminates at Solferino, extends on the northwest to Castiglione and Lonato. Many of them are bare, or clothed only with brush along their slopes. The general impression one gets, especially among the lower or detached hillocks, is of their symmetrical, breastlike form.[19] The valleys, though cultivated, are less fertile than the plains to the south: in many places, the gravel and stones of the moraine coming to the surface give the farmer but scant encouragement; yet he persists in terracing the slopes for his vines, and in planting his mulberry trees wherever there is soil enough to cover their roots.

On its southern side, this chain slopes into the vast Lombard plain, level, luxuriant, populous, stretching on the southeast to Mantua — Virgil's Mantua, and the Mantua of the Martyrs of Belfiore — and on the south to the Po. Here are Medole and Guidizzolo, two villages situated at about three miles from each other and from Solferino. A flat open field, a square mile in area, and known as the Campo di Medole, marks out this section as particularly fitted for cavalry fighting. Besides the villages, massive farmsteads, like those which served as points of defense in the battle of Magenta, dot the plain. Many roads and lanes intersect the level country and wind through the folds in the hills, and there are four main highroads, running east and west and north and south. A single stream, the Redone, flowing lazily eastward through the valleys between Pozzolengo and Solferino meets the Mincio near Monzambano. Such the varied country which Nature had made beautiful, and Man the Tiller had converted into smiling gardens and orchards and vineyards, and which Man the Killer was to use as shambles on Friday, the 24th of June, 1859.[20]

On the 23d, Emperor Napoleon issued the following orders, his general purpose being to bring the Allies within a short march of the Mincio: the left wing, composed of the Piedmontese under Victor Emanuel, and bivouacking at Lonato, Desenzano and Rivoltella, must converge on Pozzolengo; Marshal Baraguey d'Hilliers was to lead the First Corps from Esenta to Solferino; MacMahon, with the Second Corps, should advance from Castiglione to Cavriana, while Marshal Canrobert, with the Third Corps, made a detour from Mezzane, through Castel Goffredo to

---

[19] Hence the French, *Mamelon.*   [20] The region is described in most of the authorities referred to. I add details from notes made by me on the spot.

Medole; General Niel, with the Fourth Corps, should take the shorter route from Carpenedolo to Medole; the Imperial Guard, replacing MacMahon's corps at Castiglione, was to be ready to support any imperiled division. The Allies brought into action about 138,000 men, distributed as follows: Left Wing, Piedmontese, 44,700; Centre, Baraguey (24,334) and MacMahon (17,503), 41,837; Right Wing, Canrobert (12,317) and Niel (22,012), 34,329; Imperial Guard, 17,281. The artillery numbered 366 pieces, and the cavalry, already reckoned in the above total, had 108 squadrons. Opposed to these 138,000 men were about 129,000 Austrians, with 429 cannon and 80 squadrons of horse. Their First Army consisted of three corps — Schwarzenberg's (18,775), Schaffgottsche's (19,208) and Weigl's (13,046) — and Zedwitz's division of cavalry (2970). The Second Army had four corps — Clam Gallas's (15,670), Zobel's (16,208), Stadion's (20,076) and Benedek's (20,720) — and Mensdorff's cavalry (2600). Although the Allies had a small advantage in the number of troops they brought into action, and were superior in cavalry, the Austrians were much superior in position and in artillery, and, except on their left, they fought on the defensive.

When those 270,000 men bivouacked on the night of June 23–24, with the outposts of the hostile armies less than five miles apart, nobody suspected that within a few hours the hosts of France and of Piedmont and the polyglot myriads of Austria would be engaged in the vastest battle fought in Western Europe since Leipzig.

On account of the great heat, Napoleon ordered his corps to make an early start, and he expected that during the morning they would occupy the positions he assigned to them. By two o'clock, therefore, they were astir; by half-past two, having swallowed a hasty breakfast, the first columns set off, and as soon as possible thereafter the others followed. Baraguey and MacMahon in the centre and Niel and Canrobert on the right had to take care not to block each other's progress. So the five army corps marched through the growing dawn, saw the sun rise over the Eastern hills, and felt the slight cool of the summer night pass away before the heat of day. Niel's van had approached to within a mile and a half of Medole, when his scouts ran upon Austrian outposts, and the battle began with a desperate cavalry engagement on the highroad. The French won; the Austrians rode back in disorder; and before nine o'clock the French had captured Medole itself. On this occasion, Zedwitz and his cavalry, before coming to close quarters, were so smitten with fear, that they gave rein to their horses and rode ten miles to Goito, where they spent the day vainly trying to recover their nerve.[21] Hour after hour Niel, who threw Luzy's division into the village of Rebecco, over two miles southeast of Medole, held at bay three Austrian corps, — Schaffgottsche's, Schwarzenberg's and Weigl's, — which beat against him, and strove to open a passage between his left and MacMahon's right. MacMahon's corps, marching in single column, came upon the enemy at five o'clock near Casa Morino. The marshal quickly reconnoitred in person, and having assured himself that the Austrians were massed in great force in his front, he decided to deploy his corps, stand his ground, and await reinforcements. He took Monte Medolano, one of the breast-shaped hills on the edge of the Campo di Medole. Niel on his right and Baraguey on his left looked in vain for assistance from him; and he doubtless believed that in maintaining his position he was doing his share. Canrobert, with the Third Corps, had the longest road to travel, but he reached and took Castel Goffredo at about seven o'clock; his next duty was to protect the army from a flank attack from the south, and to keep in touch with Niel on his left. Baraguey's corps, having the Solferino Tower as its objective, fell in with the Austrians two miles or more to the west of Solferino, and found itself involved in the task of carrying one after another of the outlying hills.

The Piedmontese left wing meanwhile were gallantly endeavoring to obey instructions, by moving across the plateau of San Martino on Pozzolengo; but the Piedmontese were so far from the French centre as to be practically isolated, and, to weaken them still further, they marched in two columns, neither of which had its proper strength. Inevitably, therefore, when Mollard's division, which followed the easternmost road, encountered part of Benedek's corps, near San Martino, it was obliged to fall back, and shortly afterwards Mollard's colleague, Cucchiari, instead of waiting until they could make a united attack, hurled his division at Benedek's superior force, proved that his men were

[21] *Précis*, 217. Duquet, 142. Moltke, 157.

fighters, and then had to retire. A similar disaster befell Durando, at Madonna della Scoperta, where he led his division, the Piedmontese right wing, against a part of Stadion's corps, which was well protected by artillery.

Before eight o'clock on that sultry morning battle raged at half a dozen places along an irregular front starting from Castel Goffredo on the south to beyond San Martino, a distance of twelve or thirteen miles. Most of the Allies' soldiers had been on their feet since three o'clock; whereas the Austrians were either just finishing their breakfasts or had only recently begun to move. There was, on either side, no general direction; each corps commander handled his local problem as best he could. Napoleon was still lingering at Montechiaro, ten miles from the front, when aides brought him word that a great struggle was in progress. He drove to Castiglione, climbed the look-out tower there, and recognized at once from the puffs of smoke rising above the creases in the hills and over the Plain of Medole, the extent of the encounter. Then he went in search of MacMahon, whom he found awaiting Niel's support, before pushing forward to Cavriana. If Napoleon had had any doubt that the encounters might be mere skirmishes between his troops and the Austrian outposts, he was speedily undeceived. Quitting MacMahon, he hastened to learn why Baraguey delayed at the centre. He soon ran across that marshal, who had been checked by the cannonade the Austrians poured down from the Solferino heights. Divining that Solferino was the key to the battle, he redoubled his efforts to win it. After hauling the guns up slopes which their horses could not climb, the French planted batteries on adjoining crests. The Emperor stationed himself on Monte Fenile, in range of the enemy's shots: for the Mount of Cypresses was only 500 yards to the north and the Rocca of Solferino only twice as far on the northeast. By eleven o'clock, therefore, the commander-in-chief of the Allies was where he should have been, directing the pivotal operations of the battle.

Francis Joseph, on the other hand, breakfasted comfortably at Valeggio and only at nine o'clock moved his headquarters to Volta, where he was so poorly served by aides that he had no idea of the extent of the engagement. He supposed the firing at Robecco to be merely a skirmish; the heavy air and the breeze deadened the noise to the northwest, and intervening hills cut off the view. At eleven, the young Emperor and his staff rode forward to Cavriana, whence he could at last follow at short range the shifting fortunes. Convinced that he had the whole body of the Allies on his hands, he ordered his Second Army, under Count Schlick, to defend Solferino as long as possible, and his First Army to advance toward Castiglione with a view to disengage the enemy from his centre.

About noon, therefore, the second phase of the battle opened. Instead of fighting more or less independently, each host now moved on a concerted plan. The supreme object of the French was to drive their main force up the heights of Solferino, and beat back or destroy the Austrian centre; while the Austrians, massing four army corps on their left, designed to sweep from the southeast upon the French right, shatter it, overwhelm it, and cleave the French army in twain. The struggle round Solferino was among hills and in ravines; the combat to the southeast was in the open.

To capture the central height of Solferino seemed an impossible feat. Almost inaccessible on one side, it was defended on the other by strong batteries and by as many men as could be stowed on its comparatively small area. As early as eleven o'clock Napoleon had called for his reserves of the Imperial Guard to assist Baraguey's corps which had the task in hand. The French carried the surrounding hill-tops, one by one, and quickly planted them with cannon, which about one o'clock began to pour a converging fire on the Austrian defenders. Bils's brigade, worn by many hours' fighting, had to retire under that rain of shells; Puchner, too, found Monte Carnale and Monte Mezzano untenable: but Festetics could not be shaken from Solferino, and three fresh brigades hurried to support him. The French artillery continued its fire. When finally the Emperor gave the word of assault, Forey urged one of his brigades against the Hill of Cypresses; Bazaine stormed the cemetery; Picard and Manèque, of the Imperial Guard, led Camou's division to support the attack. Festetics's men, astonished to see the French blue-coats rush up the slopes, as if impervious to the volleys of bullets with which they greeted them, stood up for only a few minutes: then they were swept off the top of the hill, as the wind blows dry leaves off the roof of a house, and at last only one Austrian regiment held the cemetery, with its walls loopholed. But the French soon captured this, though after much slaughter, and the last Austrian defenders of the centre went rolling or tumbling down the steep hillsides, while their pursuers occupied the town of Solferino. It was then about two o'clock.

And yet, the plight of the Austrian centre was not hopeless. Two miles to the east of Solferino, at Cavriana, where the Austrian Emperor had his headquarters, the hills offered a fine opportunity for defense. Francis Joseph bade Marshal Zobel to hold Cavriana at all costs. But now MacMahon, who had played a waiting game since early in the forenoon, judged it safe for him to move: and he accordingly sent the main part of his corps forward to San Cassiano, a little village commanding the approach to Cavriana. Joined there by Mellinet's grenadiers of the Guard, he carried the place, and forced Zobel to rally on Monte Fontana, a hill less than a thousand yards from Francis Joseph's headquarters.

While the French grand attack on the Austrian centre was prospering in this fashion, Marshal Wimpffen was straining every sinew to deliver the Austrian grand counter-attack on the French right. As waves follow each other shoreward, so battalion after battalion and brigade after brigade came at his summons, and broke against Niel's defense. Niel had posted the front of his First Corps, which had fought almost without respite since six o'clock that morning, in the hamlets of Robecco and Baite and in some of the massive farms. Each of these points was taken and lost, and taken and lost again by the Austrians, who outnumbered the French on several occasions by more than two to one. But Niel, always a hardy fighter, was furious now at being left in the lurch, as he thought, by Canrobert, who, in response to urgent appeals for support, replied that he dared not weaken his defense as he expected an attack from the southeast. The fate of Niel's corps, perhaps the result of the war itself, hung on the tattle of a single, nameless, irresponsible peasant, who early in the day reported that a great force of Austrians had quitted Mantua for the field of battle. Afternoon had come, and brought no signs of them: yet Canrobert held doggedly on the alert. By this time Niel knew that, even though he himself were obliged to

fall back, a mighty park of artillery, and most of the French cavalry, assembled on the Campo di Medole, would check the Austrians' progress. But Niel did not fall back: and Marshal Wimpffen, unable to dislodge him, at two o'clock sent this despatch to
the Austrian Emperor: "I have tried twice to take the offensive,
and have employed my last reserves; I can hold out no longer, and
I find myself forced to beat a retreat, under the protection of the
Eleventh Corps. . . . I regret not to be able to announce to
your Majesty a better result."

The Emperor received this note at Cavriana about three
o'clock. Almost simultaneously came word that San Cassiano
had been abandoned. The French projectiles began to fall round
the house where Francis Joseph had his headquarters. After a
conference with Schlick and Hess, he decided, at half-past three,
to order a general retreat. An hour later, Wimpffen was still
fighting at Guidizzolo, and the French had just stormed Monte
Fontana, the last bulwark of Cavriana, when a terrific summer
tempest burst over the combatants. First, clouds of dust swept
down the trampled roads and parched fields; then rain fell in
torrents, and with the rain hail. The soldiers on both sides, who
had faced volleys of shot and shell all day long, ran to cover,
seeking the protection of tree and bush, of house and hedge.
The myriads who were perishing for water, could at least moisten
their lips. An hour later, when the tornado had past, the Austrians might be seen making off towards the Mincio. But the
French were too exhausted to pursue. They had been going for
fourteen hours, marching or fighting, and few of them had eaten
anything since their hasty breakfast at two o'clock that morning. If Canrobert's corps, however, which was comparatively
fresh, had been sent after the fagged and panicky Austrians, it
might have caught them at the passage of the river and turned
their defeat into a rout.

For the French at Medole on the south and at Solferino in the
centre the battles of the 24th of June ended victoriously; but
the contest on the north at San Martino still seemed an Austrian
victory, when Benedek received his orders to retire. He burst
into tears and exclaimed, "What damned jackass is our commander-in-chief!" As the Piedmontese were about to charge
again, he could not in honor withdraw. He, therefore, used his

own discretion, weathered the tempest, and repelled the enemy, who made a fifth assault at about six o'clock. Nothing could exceed the pluck and endurance of the Piedmontese throughout that day except the obvious errors of their commanders. From a plateau well adapted for defense they had to dislodge a corps of 21,000 men, among the best in the Austrian army, commanded by Louis Benedek, the only Austrian general of real military capacity during that campaign. They numbered, indeed, some 45,000 men; but these were never employed simultaneously, nor was ever a considerable portion of them massed for a concerted operation. Instead of that, they were sent up, a few battalions or regiments at a time, now by this road, now by that, against the enemy, who had throughout the immense advantage in position and always a great superiority in numbers to the detachments sent against him. The Piedmontese troops vied with their officers in their eagerness to crush the white-coats: but though they won a position over and over again by the impetuosity of their charge, they could not hold it. The King, longing to plunge into the thick of battle, — he envied the wearer of the White Plume of Navarre, he envied the glorious exploits of Ney and Murat, — could scarcely contain his impatience: and as fast as a brigade was available, he hurled it against Benedek's entrenchments. All day long the King rushed over the field, now at a gallop, now at a trot, pursued by his staff, as in a hare-and-hounds race, to whatever point there was fighting. His generals did not know where to find the commander-in-chief. His aides were puzzled; their horses blown. There was no mainspring of action. Only after half past three in the afternoon did General Solaroli persuade him to station himself on the height of Castel Venzago, whence he could see everything, and direct his forces intelligently.[22] Having news that the French had captured Solferino and were conquering in the Plain of Medole, he resolved that the day should not close until Piedmont's army had won its share of laurels. "Boys," he said, in Piedmontese slang, urging the troops on, "we must take San Martino; if we don't, the Aus-

[22] Castelli: *Ricordi*, 304–09. Della Rocca, I, 462–66. La Marmora, who should have been the chief in command, spent most of the day as a "simple spectator," until he was permitted to direct the final assault. The action of the Piedmontese in supporting the French left is described in detail by General A. Pettitti Bagliani di Roreto: *Madonna della Scoperta*. Turin, 1909.

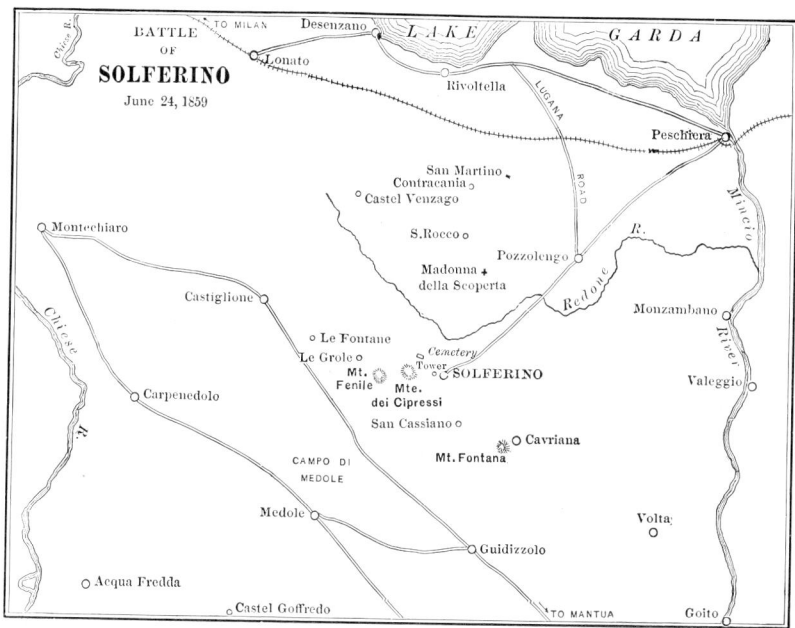

BATTLE
OF
SOLFERINO
June 24, 1859

TO MILAN
Desenzano
Lonato
LAKE GARDA
Rivoltella
LUGANA ROAD
Peschiera
Chiese R.
San Martino
Contracania
Castel Venzago
Montechiaro
S.Rocco
Pozzolengo
Mincio
Madonna
della Scoperta
Redone R.
Castiglione
Monzambano
Le Fontane
Cemetery
Le Grole
Tower
SOLFERINO
Mincio River
Mt.
Fenile
Mte.
dei Cipressi
Valeggio
Carpenedolo
San Cassiano
Chiese R.
Cavriana
Mt. Fontana
CAMPO DI
MEDOLE
Medole
Volta
Guidizzolo
Acqua Fredda
Castel Goffredo
TO MANTUA
Goito

0   1000   3000   5000 Metres

trians will make us move out."[23] This time the Piedmontese gained a foothold on the plateau, but were slowly driven back down the slope. Then Benedek, with tears in his eyes, and face to the foe, like a reluctant lion, slowly prepared to withdraw. His first divisions were already winding their way deliberately to Pozzolengo, and dusk was gathering, when the indomitable Piedmontese returned in reinforced vigor and gradually took possession of the plateau. The Austrian rear-guard checked their onslaught sufficiently for Benedek's main force to get safely to Pozzolengo. Night had fallen before the firing ceased. The Austrians left behind them four cannon, proof positive, the Piedmontese urge, that Benedek was driven away too hurriedly to take them with him; but the Austrians rejoin that the cannon were not worth taking because they had been disabled. As further proof that they did not retreat under compulsion, the Austrians show that they reached Pozzolengo unmolested; had theirs been a rout or a flight, the enemy would surely have pursued them. To this the Piedmontese reply that darkness made pursuit impossible. Benedek regarded himself so much the master of the day's combats that he intended to attack the Piedmontese the next morning, but was forced by Imperial orders to retire with the Eighth Corps beyond the Mincio.

The final phase of the battle of San Martino is one of those military puzzles, which seem likely never to be solved. The Italians claim that they captured the heights and drove Benedek away; the Austrians claim that Benedek did not retire until he chose, and that then he went at his own gait. Unfortunately for posterity, which desires to form an impartial judgment, the evidence comes wholly from the Piedmontese and the Austrians — that is, from prejudiced witnesses who contradict each other. It cannot be questioned, however, that Benedek's day-long defense of San Martino saved the Austrian centre at Solferino from being defeated early in the day, and protected its retreat in the afternoon. On the other hand the Piedmontese soldiers by their pluck, endurance and discipline proved themselves equal to the best fighters in Europe. Under adequate leadership, they would not have been wasted by a series of partial charges, foredoomed to

[23] Massari: *Vitt. Em.* 271. Martinmas was moving day in Northern Italy. Hence the King's joke.

failure; but would have been massed as soon as possible, instead of at twilight, for a grand concerted advance.[24] Their greatest service was in keeping Benedek's corps so harassed all day long that it could not support the Austrian centre at Solferino. That service was indispensable.

That night they bivouacked on the heights of San Martino. The King and Della Rocca, utterly exhausted, threw themselves on the earth floor of a peasant's hut.[25] Napoleon III slept at Cavriana in the house which Emperor Francis Joseph had occupied during the afternoon. He telegraphed Empress Eugénie: "Great battle — great victory." The next day, he visited parts of the field, and heard reports from his generals. The losses surpassed the most anxious forebodings. Seventeen thousand of the Allies were killed, wounded or missing.[26]

These figures seem to indicate that the Allies fought more fiercely than the Austrians. Stadion's corps, which held Solfer-

[24] After examining all available evidence, I am forced to these conclusions. The Piedmontese side is zealously stated by Della Rocca, who, however, did not take part in the final assault, and by Carandini, 260–64, whose statements are confused. C. Rovighi: *Storia della Terza Divisione* (Turin, 1860) gives a contemporary's report. General Luigi Nava, in *Rivista Militare Italiana*, April–August, 1907, furnishes a detailed report of the movements of the Piedmontese army throughout the day. Pagani, 216–23; also, *Corriere della Sera*, June 24, 1909; Revel: *Il 1859*; Luzio: *Studi e Bozzetti*, II, 229–312; A. Sandonà: *Rivista d'Italia*, July, 1909; 120–53. For the Austrian side see Benedek; Friedjung: *Kampf*; Ramming: *Zur Polemik über die Schlacht von Solferino;* and self-defenses of other Austrian generals. H. C. Wylly: *Magenta and Solferino* (London, 1907) gives a colorless statement.

[25] The King refused a straw mattress, saying that he wished to be like all the rest. "If V. E.," writes Solaroli, "had a quarter as much ability as he has courage, he would be the foremost general in the world; but he has neither memory nor eye, and he will not concentrate his attention; but he is very decisive when he has understood the situation." Castelli: *Ricordi*, 309.

[26] I give the figures of *Précis*, pp. 238, 239, 264, 265, 268, which seem the most likely to be near the truth.

ALLIED ARMY

	Strength.	Killed.	Wounded.	Missing.
Imperial Guard	(17281)	181	704	63
First Corps (Baraguey d'Hilliers)	(24334)	610	3162	659
Second Corps (MacMahon)	(17503)	234	987	275
Third Corps (Canrobert)	(12317)	37	257	19
Fourth Corps (Niel)	(22012)	560	3420	502
		1622	8530	1518
Piedmontese	(44690)	691	3572	1258
	138137	2313	12102	2776
		Total	17191	

ino and suffered the hardest hammering, lost sixteen per cent, in killed and wounded, while Niel's corps, defending the plain against the onslaught of four successive Austrian corps, lost nearly nineteen per cent. Benedek alone, of the Austrians, came through the ordeal with great credit. The divisions of Zedwitz and Mensdorff [27] reduced their losses to a minimum by running away. The Austrians had the advantage in position, in the freshness of their men and in the numbers they brought on the field: [28] but they could neither defend the extraordinarily strong hills in the centre, nor crush a far inferior force in the open. 24,000 Frenchmen stormed the heights of Solferino in spite of 35,000 Austrians; whereas less than 40,000 Frenchmen in the open round Medole repelled and finally drove back Marshal Wimpffen's horde of 65,000. The French troops were better drilled and more seasoned, while among the Austrians there were many recent conscripts, who spoke seven or eight languages and were strangers to each other. The French had the better cannon, the Austrians the better musket; but the French infantry excelled so greatly as marksmen that they offset the inferiority in their weapons. The French inherited from their fathers the use of the bayonet: whenever they could charge with cold steel they were formidable, if not irresistible. Several of their division and brigade commanders displayed not merely bravery but ability to act on the spur of the moment. The Austrians, on the contrary, felt in every nerve the handicap of being commanded by an Imperial amateur. Francis Joseph and his military advisers

AUSTRIAN ARMY

First Army.	Strength.	Killed.	Wounded.	Missing.
Third Corps (Schwarzenberg)	(18775)	331	1978	898
Ninth Corps (Schaffgottsche)	(19208)	315	1903	2131
Eleventh Corps (Weigl)	(13046)	378	1403	780
Division (Zedwitz)	(2970)	7	3	29
Second Army.				
First Corps (Clam Gallas)	(15670)	282	1116	1426
Fifth Corps (Stadion)	(20076)	468	2249	1725
Seventh Corps (Zobel)	(16208)	132	800	946
Eighth Corps (Benedek)	(20720)	336	1648	631
Division (Mensdorff)	(2600)	43	67	72
	129273	2292	11167	8638
		Total	22097	

[27] Sandonà, *op. cit.*, 138, says that it was Laningin's brigade and not Zedwitz's entire division that ran away.   [28] The Allies exceeded in the grand total, but the Austrians always had the larger number of men in action.

2

were infected by the same stale hauteur which had ruined Buol and his political circle: they believed that any Austrian plan, simply because it was Austrian, must prevail. The young Emperor, watching the battle from the slopes of Cavriana, would not credit the signs of defeat. His generals proved almost as green as he in the details of battle, and Nugent and Ramming were accused of pursuing an independent plan of action. Occasion after occasion slipped by when, had a few battalions, lying idle, been massed at a critical point, the result might have been different. It was aptly said that General Soldier won whatever honor came to Austria on that day: raw, misled, or led half-heartedly, he showed how deeprooted the instinct of plain courage lies in the average human animal. Benedek alone of all Francis Joseph's corps commanders enhanced his reputation: and he had the good fortune to be placed where he suffered little interference from headquarters. The Piedmontese proved by their losses that for mere fighting they were equal to the best soldiers on the field.

Solferino was the first modern battle fought over so vast an area, and amid conditions so diverse, that it strained to the utmost the channels of communication and rendered a central direction very difficult. Like Magenta, Solferino was a surprise battle; and although the French troops displayed remarkable endurance in holding out until their reinforcements came up, the fact could not be disguised that a masterful commander would neither allow himself to flounder into an engagement unexpectedly nor dispose his columns so clumsily that it required several hours for one detachment to support another. Victory under these conditions filled the French generals with that unwarranted belief in their military genius which made them in 1870 an easy prey for German forethought, discipline and caution.

On June 25 Napoleon III created Niel a marshal of France. As he visited several parts of the battle-field he was horror-stricken. Nearly five thousand dead were awaiting such hasty burial as the soldiers of the day before, and sextons now, could give them. Most agonizing were the shrieks and groans of the wounded, of whom ten or twelve thousand had not yet been removed, for to transport such a host called for more vehicles than could be procured. The number of surgeons fell so far short that days elapsed before all the sufferers could be attended to. Medicines and bandages gave out. And all the while the broiling sun sapped the vigor of the strong and intensified the tortures of the stricken. By degrees the army of wounded was conveyed to Brescia, and thence to Milan, where they joined their brothers from Magenta and Melegnano.[29] But the non-combatants, to whom the sixty square miles of battlefield had been home, the farmers and peasants, the dwellers in the hamlets, the artisans and small tradesmen and landed proprietors in the villages, who had escaped with their lives from the carnage, found deserted fields, trampled crops, roads and water-ways torn up, buildings demolished, cattle and food gone, their hopes blighted, and themselves plunged in a single day from peaceful thrift into calamity: and that not by earthquake, not by flood, not by volcano, but by the remorseless passions of their brother men.

[29] During the month of June, the Milanese hospitals cared for 15,908 wounded, French, Piedmontese and Austrian, alike: during July, for 12,302; during August, for 7455; and during September, for 2108. Mariani, III, 654, n. 1. Brescia, a town of only 40,000 inhabitants, cared for 19,665 sick and about 10,000 wounded between June 15 and Aug. 31. Reuchlin, pt. III, 342. Rovighi, 161-75, describes the medical equipment of the Piedmontese.

The reader should be warned that in this description of Solferino, and in that of Magenta, the times stated, as well as the numbers engaged, are the subjects of heated dispute. No two authorities agree. I have given the figures which seem to conflict the least with probability.

CHAPTER XXIV

THE STAMPEDE TO UNITY, APRIL–JULY, 1859

WHILST these military affairs were absorbing the attention of Europe during May and June, a campaign
equally important and exciting, but less spectacular, was going
forward in the fields of politics and of diplomacy. Lacking imagination, mankind in the mass can be roused only by the crude
heroism and horrors of war, or by the devastation of nature and
disease. But as civilization advances, men become aware of the
significance of the cosmic drama in which every human being
has a part, and they perceive that the battles fought out in the
conscience and the will often transcend the physical shock of
armies and of fleets. Thought antecedes action. The explosion
of brute force at Gettysburg or Solferino would be as vain as the
churning of a storm-swept sea, unless a Thinker were at hand to
lead on to new issues, to the attainment of new ideals. The
Brute in Man is constantly dragging him down to settle his
quarrels with life after the common brute fashion: the Spirit in
Man struggles with unwearied devotion to lift his activities to
the plane of Reason and of Conscience. The five thousand
corpses hurriedly shoveled into their shallow graves on the day
after Solferino were indeed mere clay; but an Idea survived
them, and it was for the Statesmen and not for the Soldiers to
profit by it.

On April 26, when Cavour handed his ultimatum to Baron
Kellersperg, he knew that the coming war, though indispensable to national liberation, would not of itself suffice. It might
require only a short time to strike off Italy's shackles: but what
would she be when free? To prepare for freedom was Cavour's
incessant care: to prevent European diplomacy from interfering
with the war before the task of liberation was completed, his
immediate concern. The twofold task gave him no repose. At
Plombières he promised Napoleon that he would force Austria
to declare war, that Austria should be isolated, and that the war

should have no revolutionary taint to alarm the reactionary governments of Europe. These three things he had brought to pass, with such adroitness that although Europe hated the very thought of war, yet on April 26 she withheld her sympathy from Austria. Nevertheless, the Western Powers refrained from encouraging Piedmont, because they regarded the enterprise as Napoleonist rather than Italian. With justifiable cynicism, they scouted the pretense that the French Emperor had embarked on an unselfish mission: they could not picture to themselves Louis Napoleon as a knight-errant protecting beautiful damsels in distress. The French reputation for conquest rose up to shake their confidence.

At the moment of rupture the English Ministers were agitated by the rumor that Napoleon had concluded a secret alliance with Russia; but when the Emperor and Walewski formally denied this, they had to appear satisfied.[1] The further gossip that Piedmont would cede Savoy to France as soon as Lombardy should be won, was also contradicted. Austria's ultimatum deeply chagrined Queen Victoria and Prince Albert because as she wrote, it "entirely changed the feeling here, which was all that we could desire, into the most *vehement* sympathy for *Sardinia*, though we hope now again to be able to *throw* the blame of the war on France."[2] A fortnight later she laments that the Austrians did not destroy the Piedmontese before the French came up in force. "It is indeed distracting, and most difficult to understand them or do anything for them."[3] In spite of the Queen's distraction and of Albert's vexation, however, the British Government adopted a policy of strict neutrality and exerted itself to localize the war.[4]

In this, it was ably seconded by Russia. The Czar hated Austria, and although he was supposed to have hinted that he would forcibly prevent the Germanic Confederation from giving military aid to the Austrians, he contented himself during the month

[1] *Lettere*, III, clviii.
[2] *Q. V. L.*, III, 328; Victoria to Leopold, April 26, 1859. On May 3 she writes her uncle: "God knows we *are* in a sad mess. The rashness of the Austrians is indeed a *great* misfortune, for it has placed them in the wrong. Still there is *one* universal feeling of *anger* at the conduct of France, and of *great suspicion*. The Treaty with Russia is *denied* but I am perfectly certain there are engagements." *Ibid*, 331.   [3] *Ibid*, 332; Victoria to Leopold, May 9, 1859.
[4] *Correspondence;* Malmesbury's Circular of May 2, 1859.

of May with warning the German States that their Confederation existed for mutual defense alone, and that any offensive act on their part might precipitate a general war.[5] The smaller States, however, had already pledged themselves to Austria, so that neither Malmesbury's circular nor Gortchakoff's moved them. Too many Germans were still alive who had known in youth the horrors of a French invasion not to make it easy to rally the Germanic Confederation to the standard of the monarch who was now at war with the French. Still, Prussia, next to Austria the most powerful of the confederates, hesitated, not because she cared for France but because she did not wish to contribute to Austria's aggrandizement. When Archduke Albert went on a special mission to Berlin to secure a promise of support, the Prince Regent replied that Prussia would remain neutral unless German interests should be menaced.[6] Ten days later, the Prussian Premier, Schleinitz, sent a sedative message to the smaller German States, to remind them that, by the Treaty of Vienna, Austria herself [7] had no right to call for the support of the Germanic Confederation in a war over her Italian provinces.[8]

While the contest went on because the Great Powers, for fear of starting a continental struggle, did not dare to interfere, Cavour labored with might and main to extend its scope in Italy. Austria must not only be driven out of Lombardy and Venetia by the Allied Armies, but her influence must be uprooted in every capital South of the Po. Let Italy once be independent, and the political questions — unity and constitutionalism — would be quickly solved. Independence was the one object to which Italians of all political principles should rally: but Cavour, who planned far beyond the day's march, had no intention that, as the National movement broadened, it should slip out of the control of the leader who had for ten years been preparing it. The first proof of his forethought came from an unexpected quarter — Florence.

Although Tuscany had been leading the most inglorious existence of any of the Italian States since the restoration, she could not escape from the prestige of her patriotic past. The very city

[5] *Correspondence:* Gortchakoff's Circular of May 15/27, 1859.
[6] *Stor. Doc.,* VIII, 64–65. See also Sybel, II, 365–67.
[7] Treaty of Vienna, § 46.
[8] *Lettere,* III, clvi–clvii; Schleinitz's Circular of April 22, 1859.

of Florence was a temple to liberty and independence. Whoever walked her streets met Dante and Savonarola and Machia-
velli, Buonarotti and Galileo; men still alive had seen Alfieri,
the haughtiest of Democrats, hastening along the Lungarno:
Giusti, whose satire pierced every despot's steel shirt, was but
lately dead: Niccolini, venerable and leonine, lived on. It was
no secret that the best Tuscans sympathized with Piedmont: but
they were men unfitted for conspiracy or violent revolution, men
whom the failure of 1849 had caused to sit down quietly and
wait for some outside power to assist them. They had to tolerate
their Grand Duke, but they loathed him, as members of a club
would loathe one of their number whom they caught cheating
at cards, but could not expel. Their enforced toleration was not
wholesome for the patricians and professional men whom the
patriotic Tuscans looked up to as their natural chiefs.

After the Austrian garrisons left, Cavour took more direct
means for infusing national, or at least anti-Austrian ideas
through the Grand Duchy. Early in 1857 he sent Carlo Boncompagni as minister to Florence, instructing him to allay the suspicion that Piedmont was selfishly ambitious, and to persuade
the Grand Duke's advisers that a frankly national policy such as
Victor Emanuel had adopted was the only safe one.[9] With the
best intentions in the world, Boncompagni was neither aggressive nor insinuating enough for this special task. Nature
moulded him for the bench and not for diplomacy. At the beginning of 1859, when the great crisis drew near, Boncompagni had
qualms: though he desired the end his government had in view,
he hesitated before the means. Cavour saw the danger of drift-
ing, and summoned him to Turin. "I confess to you candidly,"
he wrote, "that I am a little less scrupulous than you, and that I
have a conscience (in political matters) a little more elastic than
yours. Still, I recognize that while I am free to put my soul in
jeopardy to serve the country, I ought not likewise to drag with
me on the road to perdition the souls of my friends." [10] A short
sojourn in Turin so strengthened Boncompagni's nerve that he
returned to his post willing, if not eager, to keep pace with
Cavour's audacity. Happily, the Tuscans themselves forced the

[9] For Boncompagni's instructions, dated Jan. 13, 1857, see *Stor. Doc.*, VIII,
77–80.   [10] *Lettere*, III, 23; C. to Boncompagni, Feb. 8, 1859.

issue, earning by their own right, and not by Piedmontese instigation, their participation in Italy's redemption.

The National Party in Tuscany was composed of Radicals or Democrats, mostly artisans and tradesmen, who had been Mazzinians until La Farina drew them into the National Society. Giuseppe Dolfi, their most popular leader in Florence, was a baker: a man of colossal frame, handsome features, sterling character and level head, — the incarnation of the legendary Rienzi. Pietro Cironi, who had a better education and equal tact, ably seconded him. The indispensable link between the populace and the dominant classes was Marquis Ferdinando Bartolommei, a noble who possessed the art of fraternizing with plebeians without turning demagogue. He joined them, because he believed that through them alone the National ideal could be attained. His palace in Via Lambertesca became the centre of preparations which, though they aimed at revolution, wore a cloak of legality. He carried out to the letter Cavour's instructions: 'Agitate, but so as to leave the future unpledged. Do not talk of a constitution, but of independence, of nationality. We wish the Tuscan troops to unite with the Piedmontese to fight for the common cause; therefore, avoid friction with your soldiers.' [11] Cavour advised that they should prod the Government with petitions, and even try a public demonstration, if this were likely to succeed.[12] Bartolommei and Dolfi and Cironi and their colleagues did their work well. They won over the troops. They promoted the exodus of Tuscan volunteers to Piedmont. The marquis himself furnished fifty cavalry horses and contributed generously to the fund for the patriotic enterprise. So many volunteers set out, that it was thought wise to check the movement in order to keep energetic men for use at home in case of need. By April, the National Party was ready for action.

The Conservatives, on the other hand, shrank from any step which might lead to violence. They dreaded anarchy much more than Leopold's despotism. They organized a society, which put forth mildly Liberal publications. They hoped, at the most, to persuade the Grand Duke not to ally himself with Austria in the coming struggle. They were all men of unimpeachable character

---

[11] Gioli, 238; La Farina, II, 137. Gioli gives Feb. 2, 1859 as the date of the letter; La Farina, Feb. 12.   [12] Gioli, 239; C. to Bartolommei, Feb. 19, 1859.

whose devotion to Tuscany could not be questioned. Don Neri Corsini, a three-ply patrician, Marquis Cosimo Ridolfi, Baron Bettino Ricasoli, Count Cambray Digny, and venerated Gino Capponi formed the aristocratic core of this group, and with them worked lawyers, like Corsi, Cempini and Galeotti, and several professors, among whom Giorgini enjoyed the highest esteem. Boncompagni, the Piedmontese Minister, had stronger social and personal ties with them than with the National Party, but he made it his duty to propitiate everybody.

The Grand Duke, meanwhile, surrounded by the antiquated Baldasseroni, the detested Landucci and a crowd of sycophant courtiers, saw the storm gathering, but would not heed it. There would be something sublime in the stubbornness with which the obsolescent princelings of the Old Régime clung to their ruinous ways, were it not evident that this stubbornness proceeded from moral and intellectual decadence, which produced incapacity to make new adjustments with life. Their tenacity was not fortitude, but merely the quality of the leech and the barnacle. On March 14, Boncompagni proposed to Leopold's ministers an alliance with Piedmont. War he assured them was inevitable. If Tuscany joined the National movement, the Grand Duke would so secure his popularity, that he need fear no attack on his throne. Baldasseroni replied that the Grand Duke would remain neutral.[13] This was equivalent to siding with Austria; for it deprived the National Cause of the coöperation of an important Italian State. But the barnacle Leopold, who could conceive of no existence detached from Austria, had a blind faith that Austria must, in any event, win, and he suspected that patriotism was another name for perdition. He attached no weight to the alternative possibilities that if the National Cause should triumph without him he could hope for no favors from it, and that the thousands of patriotic Tuscan enthusiasts, forbidden to spend their zeal in the war, would seek an outlet for it at home. Still, neutrality was Leopold's last word.

In April, however, his ministers began to feel a little anxious. Leopold consulted Don Neri Corsini, the patrician figurehead, as to the desirability of restoring the constitution. Corsini, after conferring with Boncompagni, replied that it would do no harm,

[13] *Stor. Doc.*, VIII, 82–83.

but that the real safeguard was an alliance with Piedmont.[14] Walewski was urging the same action on Nerli, the Tuscan minister
at Paris. But Leopold and Baldasseroni dozed. Recognizing the
importance of forcing the Grand Duke's Government to give an
official answer, and so to range itself either with or against the
National Cause, Cavour bade Boncompagni, as soon as war was
certain, to make a formal offer of alliance. This he did on April
24, Easter Day. Lenzoni, the Tuscan Foreign Minister, thought
it sufficient to say that the matter would be examined, but that
his Government had already decided on its course.[15] He too was
incredulous at the suggestion of an internal revolution. When
Austria sent secretly to ask whether the Grand Duke would like
to have some Austrian regiments despatched to keep order,
Leopold felt so sure of his position that he replied no.[16] Little
did he understand the temper of his people. On that Easter forenoon the crowds which he saw thronging Via de' Calzaioli and
Piazza della Signoria, as he returned from hearing mass in the
Cathedral, were primed for revolt, and were restrained only by
the wise leaders of the Democrats.

As the crisis approached, the divergence between the Democrats and Conservatives grew more evident. Both parties
desired concord, but neither would give way. The Conservatives
were plagued by the spectre of anarchy; the Democrats by the
dread of letting slip the propitious moment for making Tuscany
Italian. At length, on Easter night the two parties had a lively
meeting at Ricasoli's palace. When Professor Giorgini, for the
Conservatives, proposed to recommend to the Grand Duke to join
the National movement, and to send his son with the Tuscan
contingent to Piedmont, the Democrats jumped up, said that
they had misjudged the purpose of the conference, begged to be
excused, and turned to go out. The astonished Conservatives
asked for an explanation. Marquis Bartolommei replied that
they had no intention of merely pushing the Government in one
direction rather than in another, but of overthrowing the dynasty
and making a clean slate of all the States of Italy. The Conservatives protested that this was "crazy," "impossible." Bartolommei replied that it was not only easy, but almost already

[14] *Stor. Doc.*, VIII, 82–83. Boncompagni's letter is dated, April 17, 1859.
[15] *Ibid*, 87–88.   [16] Baldasseroni, 539.

accomplished — for at a signal the city and province would hoist the tricolor banner and expel the Grand Duke. "Ricasoli," Giorgini adds, "fell from the clouds." So did his friends.[17]

During the next two days the Conservatives strove to persuade the Grand Duke, by showing him the danger of the situation, to make concessions. But Leopold stolidly clung to neutrality and Baldasseroni accused the Conservatives of having caused the trouble. On April 26 an abnormal calm brooded over Florence. All day long Marchioness Bartolommei, with her little daughters and servants, worked in the tower of her palace on two large red-white-and-green banners and several basketfuls of tricolor cockades.[18] The Democratic leaders met at Dolfi's house.[19] Bartolommei himself staid at home, arranging the last details. The Conservatives took counsel with each other at Ricasoli's and tried vainly to impart it at the Pitti Palace. Late in the afternoon Ricasoli, despairing of influencing the Government, started for Turin. About sunset, when Ferrari da Grado, the unpopular Austrian commander of the Tuscan army, was returning to his quarters, a mocking crowd accompanied him. That was the first warning of the storm. At eight o'clock that evening, the Democrats, meeting at Dolfi's, with Celestino Bianchi there to represent the Conservatives, voted to make a pacific demonstration on the following morning and to set up a People's Junta. News had come from Turin that war had been declared, and that the first French contingents were landing at Genoa.

Grand Duke Leopold did not sleep late on April 27, 1859. Very early a lackey brought him a letter from Cosimo Ridolfi, who urged him, in most respectful language, and by a circumlocution worthy of a Persian court poet, to abdicate in order to save the dynasty. Leopold waited. Then Baldasseroni arrived, with an alarming note from Galeotti. Next entered two officers, Danzini and Cappellini, to report that the troops of the garrison could not be counted upon. Leopold sent in haste for Don Neri Corsini, who reached the Palace at nine o'clock and was told by Baldasseroni that he was to form a ministry: for the Grand Duke had decided to join the Franco-Piedmontese alliance, and, after the war was over, to grant a constitution. The Grand Duchess and

---

[17] Gioli, 247–91, from Giorgini's own account. Rubieri, 57–60.
[18] Torre dei Lamberti in Via Lambertesca.   [19] In Borgo San Lorenzo.

her second son, Carlo, had taken refuge betimes in the Belvedere Fortress, which connected with the Pitti Palace. There they had ample evidence that the troops were disaffected. Grand Duchess Marie Antoinette, the sister of the King of Naples, was the most imperious of women: but, though the officers at the fortress treated her respectfully, her flashing eyes and scornful commands did not move them. They broke the seals of secret instructions, which hinted that even the bombardment of Florence was to be resorted to in case of rebellion, but, beyond informing the Grand Duchess and her son how much ammunition and what guns were ready, the officers did nothing. Every messenger who came, whether to the Belvedere or to the Pitti Palace, brought tidings that the town was up. The great tricolor banner had been raised on the tower of Bartolommei's palace, and at that signal, tricolor cockades and flags blossomed in all parts of Florence. A great multitude, gathered in Piazza Barbano, was shouting "War! Independence! Victor Emanuel!" And now, throngs were converging on the fortress.

While Leopold summoned the Diplomatic Corps to an audience, the self-sacrificing Corsini hastened to Boncompagni's, where he found several of the Conservatives, and Rubieri and Malenchini, the only members of the People's Junta who had consented to serve. Corsini probably expected that his announcement of Leopold's yielding would delight everybody and put an end to the danger. But the company at Boncompagni's would be satisfied with nothing short of Leopold's abdication, which, the mild Corsini believed, Boncompagni could effect with little trouble.[20] When some one suggested to Bartolommei that the crowd should shout, "Long live Ferdinand IV," in front of the Pitti Palace, as a hint which would surely be followed, that aristocratic Democrat, whose motto was "Thorough," laughed in the face of his noble friend. Corsini returned to the Grand Duke with this ultimatum: Leopold must abdicate; his ministers and officers must resign; Tuscany must ally herself with Piedmont and send as many troops as possible under General Ulloa to the front; her political reorganization would be determined at the general reorganization of Italy.

"With death in his heart"[21] Corsini reported the terms to

[20] Galeotti: *Storia di Quattr' Ore.*   [21] Tivaroni, II, 91.

Baldasseroni and then to Leopold. At last the Grand Duke realized that his hour had struck. If he had hoped to gain time, or
to repeat the duplicities of 1848–49, he now saw his mistake. He
conferred with his cabinet, with the Diplomatic Corps, and with
the Austrian Minister. He protested that, although his treaties
bound him to an alliance with Austria, he had consented to remain neutral. But this did not appease his subjects, who insisted
on his joining Piedmont in the war: this too he had agreed to,
since his troops had been corrupted; still unsatisfied, the enemies
of order demanded his abdication. But rather than abdicate —
which would be an offense against his personal dignity and an
injury to the monarchical principle — he would retire to Austria
and await the triumph of justice.[22] Leopold's sudden fit of dignity, in the opinion of many critics, saved Tuscany from an angry
revolution and simplified the way to Italian unity.[23]

Having announced his refusal and besought the Diplomatic
Corps to protect him from personal danger, Leopold quitted the
Pitti Palace for the Belvedere, where a tricolor flag[24] was flying
in spite of the fury of the Grand Duchess, who declared that 'she
would not have it,' and of Prince Carlo's protest that it was
'indecent.' At six o'clock in the afternoon, the grand-ducal
family, their loyal courtiers and some of the foreign diplomats,
drove in their traveling carriages out of the side portal of the
Pitti, through Porta Romana, and skirted the city walls to Porta
San Gallo, and so onward into the country, till they disappeared
from sight on the Pellegrino Hill.[25] The crowds, which had refrained all day from approaching the Pitti Palace, saw them depart without hiss or jeer, or even talk. Sittoli, a popular patriot,
sat on the box beside Leopold's coachman, to serve as protector:
but he was not needed, for nobody showed any desire to molest
the fugitives; rather, by a remarkable silence, did the voluble
people of Florence express their utter contempt. As his berline
rumbled away, the Grand Duke gave sarcastically the familiar

[22] As man, says Baldasseroni, 541, he felt the wrong done him by demanding
that he should resign a crown which his conscience told him he had always worn
honorably; as sovereign, he regarded the revolt as consummated; as father, he
could not sacrifice his young son to an unscrupulous faction.
[23] See, for instance, Tivaroni's comments, II, 91–92.
[24] To make the flag, a green curtain from the soldiers' infirmary was sewed to
the red and white Tuscan banner. Gioli, 359.
[25] *Monitore Toscano*, April 28, 1859.

farewell greeting — "Till we meet again!" at which one of the crowd, with characteristic Florentine irony, replied, "In Paradise!" Thus ingloriously, despised, undefended even by those who had enjoyed its favors, the House of Lorraine slunk like a dismissed lackey out of Florence into the night and into Oblivion. It was 122 years since Grand Duke Francis, the first of the line, had succeeded to Gaston, the last of the bastard Medici. Leopold's apologists insisted that his mild rule deserved the gratitude and not the aversion of his people. They pointed out that under him there had been no terrible persecutions, no floggings, no bestial imprisonments. But the Tuscans knew that beneath the cloak of mildness, Leopold was bent on slaying their souls: and they preferred to be more than mere bodies, however well-fed and comfortably housed.

Since Florence was left without a government, Boncompagni suggested to the Municipality that they should nominate a provisional triumvirate. As soon as they could be convened — the timid, or discreet among them were 'prevented' from attending the meeting — they chose Ubaldino Perruzzi, Vincenzo Malenchini and Major Alessandro Danzini. At six o'clock, said Salvagnoli, the revolution had done its work, and went to dinner. "We have made at Florence a revolution of rosewater," wrote a sympathizing Englishwoman.[26] "A revolution in which not a drop of blood was spilt, or, to the astonishment of the French minister, a pane of glass broken."

The Grand Duke had been got rid of with unexpected ease: now came the ticklish work of reorganization. Turning at once to Victor Emanuel, the Provisional Government offered him the dictatorship of Tuscany. The King, Cavour and Napoleon III thought that it would be impolitic to accept this, but they agreed that Victor Emanuel ought to assume the military command of the Grand Duchy in order to secure unity in the conduct of the campaign. The King accordingly appointed Boncompagni his commissioner extraordinary for the war of independence;[27] the

[26] Theodosia Trollope: *Social Aspects of the Italian Revolution* (London, 1861), p. 1. For the Tuscan Revolution see also Jarro: *Vita di U. Peruzzi* (Florence, 1897). Gotti: *Ricordi.* The anniversary pamphlet, XXVII Aprile MDCCCLIX (Florence, 1909), contains a large number of interesting documents, portraits, etc. Also, V. Soldani: *La Pasqua di Liberazione* (Florence, Soc. Edit. L'Etruria, 1909.)   [27] *Lettere*, III, 62-63 ; C. to Provisional Government, April 30, 1859. *Stor. Doc.*, VIII, 92.

Tuscan troops swore allegiance; a step seemed to be taken towards annexation to Piedmont.

Every day the pivotal importance of Tuscany increased. The provinces north of the Po would presumably soon be able to join Piedmont; the Duchies and Legations were already seething with the same purpose: but Tuscany lay south of the Apennines, and her decision could not fail to exert a determining influence on the fate of Central Italy. Up to Leopold's flight, Cavour took it for granted that the House of Lorraine must not be disturbed at Florence, at least until the consummation of the Kingdom of Italy came within reach, and he therefore studiously avoided every appearance of exciting Leopold's alarm. But now by a stroke of good fortune Tuscany was free — a fair prize for the most daring. Recognizing the imprudence of direct interference, Cavour worked unofficially, through his acquaintance with Tuscans of various cliques, to hasten the union of Tuscany and Piedmont. He suspected, and with reason, that Napoleon hoped to create a Kingdom of Central Italy, obedient to French protection, if not actually ruled by a Bonaparte. Almost equally to be feared was the Tuscan instinct for autonomy. The people who had for seven centuries been known as Tuscans, did not wish to lose their identity by becoming Italians: to their thinking that would be as if a saucerful of cream were to be mixed and lost in a great jar of milk. While a considerable fraction of the upper classes felt this reluctance, every class, on the other hand, had some politicians who might uphold autonomy, because it gave them a better field for their selfish ambitions to work in. But the majority of the Democrats set union with Piedmont above either Tuscan independence or the establishing of a democratic government.

Within a week Boncompagni saw that it would be better to create a ministry, and after much persuasion the following consented to serve: Bettino Ricasoli (Interior); Cosimo Ridolfi (Instruction and Foreign Affairs); Raffaele Busacca (Finance); Enrico Poggi (Justice); Vincenzo Malenchini (War); and Vincenzo Salvagnoli (Worship). Bartolommei was gonfaloniere, or mayor of Florence; and Tommaso Corsi, the lawyer who had defended Guerrazzi in his trial for high treason nine years before, was prefect. It soon appeared that among them they had one

strong man — Ricasoli. As a patriotic duty he accepted office
for two months, but resolved, punctually "on the 60th day," [28]
to return to the Cincinnatus life which he loved. To make Italy
great by securing her independence, and to unite with Piedmont
were his aims: but he would do nothing precipitately. "Order
and War" was his motto. Fearful lest order should be disturbed,
he urged Cavour to send a small Piedmontese force into Tuscany;
but Cavour replied that every Piedmontese soldier was needed at
the front. The Tuscans shuddered at the suggestion of a military
levy. "Three centuries of corrupting governments," Cavour
wrote, "have not disposed them to the sacrifices which war
exacts. They detest the Austrians, without having a decided
taste for employing the means which must be employed in order
to drive them out." [29] Ricasoli, however, judged that his people
must be humored: he, being on the spot and responsible, knew
how many compromises must be made with Tuscan temperament
and prejudices. His colleagues held such divergent views that
the task of securing among them even a semblance of unity in
essentials was not slight. Don Neri Corsini went to Piedmont to
take counsel of the King. Salvagnoli hurried to Alessandria as
soon as the French Emperor reached there, and endeavored, by
drawing an alarming picture of the condition of Tuscany, to
probe his intentions.[30] The Emperor received him cordially and
announced that the Fifth French Army Corps, under Prince
Napoleon, had been ordered to Tuscany. At this, Salvagnoli
betrayed surprise and perhaps anxiety. The Emperor protested
that the expedition was "purely military," without any civil
purpose, but must strengthen the cause of order: and he insisted
that the status of Tuscany should not be prematurely settled.[31]
Salvagnoli's alarm was not easily quieted. Prince Corsini, who
also had an interview with the Emperor, surmised that a French
Kingdom of Central Italy was projected.

At the first hint of this, Cavour took train for Alessandria.
Less than a week before, at Genoa, the Emperor had embraced
him cordially, saying: "You ought to be satisfied. Your plans
are being realized." [32] Now Napoleon withdrew into his habitual

[28] Ricasoli, iii, 16.   [29] *Lettere*, vi, 402; C. to Prince Napoleon, June 8, 1859.
[30] Poggi: *Memorie*, i, 69.   [31] Ricasoli, iii, 30, 33, 41; Salvagnoli to Ricasoli,
May 18 and 20.   [32] *Lettere*, iii, clxix–clxx.

reserve. When he admitted that he had authorized the French expedition to Tuscany, Cavour candidly told him that it would justify the suspicions of Europe that the French were fighting for aggrandizement and that it might easily lead to a general war.[33] Napoleon denied that he intended to put any French prince on any throne in Central Italy, and he consented that Prince Napoleon should be technically under Victor Emanuel's military orders.[34] Here began the little rift which was to widen into a chasm between Cavour and Napoleon. Until we shall know the Emperor's secret desires, we can only conjecture whether he was sincere or not in protesting his disinterestedness. Appearances ran strongly against him. If his sole purpose had been to uphold the Party of Order in Tuscany, he needed only to despatch two or three regiments under a brigadier-general; whereas Prince Napoleon's arrival with an army corps could not fail to be interpreted as a political move. Even the plea that the presence of the French right wing south of the Apennines would distract and divide the Austrians along the Po, seems specious when we remember that, on May 25 or 26, the Emperor changed his plan of campaign and proceeded to carry on the war without reference to Prince Napoleon. On the other hand, the Emperor had good reason to distrust the turn events had taken in Italy. Before he rejoined his army in the middle of May, the Duchies, Legations and Tuscany were already so restless, that there could be little doubt that, left to themselves, they would unite with Piedmont. He had agreed to free Lombardy and Venetia, and to set up the Kingdom of Upper Italy with ten million inhabitants. With these other provinces added, this Kingdom numbering fifteen millions would stretch almost to within sight of Rome, and create a political situation which he had not reckoned on. His jealous neighbors would insist on being consulted: his own subjects, always restless and until recently opposed to the war, would require him to explain why he lavished French blood, treasure and prestige on so Quixotic an enterprise. Possibly, there flitted through his mind a suspicion that he was being duped by his Italian accomplices; certainly, he must have begun to suspect that the Italian movement might get beyond his control. He had

---

[33] *Stor. Doc.*, VIII, 497–99; C. to Villamarina, May 21, 1859.
[34] *Lettere*, III, clxxii.

2

stipulated that he should not be involved in the Revolution; yet here was the Revolution, triumphant in Central Italy, threatening to dislocate his plans: here was the Revolution, personified by Garibaldi and the Hunters of the Alps, actually fighting under Victor Emanuel's banner. Doctrinaire that he was, Napoleon III thought that he could prescribe the limits within which war could be made and the consequences that should flow from it.

Not so Cavour, who knew that war is the mother of surprises. Taking it for granted that many new combinations, not provided for in the compact of Plombières, would spring up, he watched in order to turn each of them to the advantage of the Italian cause. The revolt of the provinces offered unexpectedly a great opportunity which he did not hesitate to grasp. It was a fair contest between him and Napoleon. In their joint undertaking, the campaign against Austria, Cavour was faultlessly loyal; in the concerns outside of their agreement, he sought, and had every right to seek, the benefit of Italy. With this in view, he opposed Plon-Plon's military expedition. Finding the Emperor immovable, he redoubled his efforts to neutralize the effect of the French occupation of Tuscany. He sent his nephew-in-law, Carlo Alfieri, and his most trusted secretary, Costantino Nigra, to Florence, to sound the Tuscan leaders; but their mission seems to have borne no fruit. Prince Napoleon, who reached Leghorn on May 23, was cordially received wherever he went. He disavowed political intentions, laughed at the suggested dynastic ambition, and formed so poor an opinion of the ability of the Provisional Government that, in order to prevent its collapse, he unofficially favored immediate fusion with Piedmont. Ricasoli, who had now a zealous supporter in Salvagnoli, even went so far as to sign an address to Victor Emanuel and to propose to summon the Tuscan Consulta to ratify an act of annexation: but the opposition of Ridolfi, Poggi and other Moderates and Autonomists warned him that it would be prudent to wait. From Turin Cavour frankly told him that the time had passed. Too tactful to attempt to force his own policy through after the Emperor had said emphatically that the status of Tuscany must not be fixed until the war was over,[35] Cavour had to content himself with promoting close, but unofficial, relations with Tuscany. He

[35] *Stor. Doc.*, VIII, 100; C. to Boncompagni, June 15, 1859.

spurred on Boncompagni, whom he found too easy-going, to take
the initiative to which, as royal commissioner, he had a right. Instead of leading, however, Boncompagni seemed often to Cavour
too willing to be led; and indeed he was no match for Ricasoli,
who henceforth dominated the counsels of Tuscany. At news
of the victory of Magenta, Prince Napoleon departed northward
with his corps, in the hope of joining the Allied Armies in time to
strike a decisive blow. General Ulloa, exile, revolutionist, and
recently commander of the Hunters of the Apennines, took charge
of the Tuscan military preparations, while General Mezzacapo
organized a troop of volunteers from the Papal States. The Provisional Government preserved order which, indeed, nobody
threatened. So at last Tuscany was contributing, after her fashion,
to the national uprising.

In the Duchies the patriotic plan unfolded more swiftly,
because the political situation was simpler. The despots there
were undisguisedly Austrian, dependent upon Austria for support; but as the populations, unlike the Tuscans, had no strong
feeling for Autonomy nor fondness for their ruling houses, they
looked forward to union with Piedmont as the natural outcome of
any change. The National Society had honeycombed both provinces. La Farina sent word to his agents that war was to be
declared: and on the night of April 27–28 Massa and Carrara duly
rose,[36] drove out their Modenese garrisons and governors, and
proclaimed themselves subjects of Victor Emanuel. The immediate appearance of Piedmontese carabineers to aid them, gave the
Duke a valid reason for protesting: but protests availed nothing,
and Francis V busied himself during the month of May in marching his toy army to and fro in the Duchy itself and in collecting,
by forced taxes, as large a sum as possible. On June 11, when the
Austrians had retreated from the north bank of the Po, he
thought it safer to take refuge in Mantua, carrying with him
what treasure and rare objects he could, as if he were a victorious
enemy laden with spoils. The Regency which he left behind him
succumbed in forty-eight hours to a bloodless revolution, the
achievement of the patriots, who voted for fusion with Piedmont. On June 19 Luigi Carlo Farini was appointed governor in

[36] Cantù asserts that Cavour telegraphed the Carrarese the single word,
"Rebel!" Tivaroni, III, 101.

the name of the King. His first acts were to abolish torture and to suppress the Jesuits — twin accompaniments of despotism — and to reorganize the fiscal and legal departments. Posterity must ever be grateful to him for publishing without change or comment a large number of documents from the Modenese secret archives — documents that reveal with damning frankness the practices of the last rulers of the House of Este. When Francis V protested against Piedmont's usurpation, Cavour replied by a circular note that, in view of the known alliance of Modena and Parma with Austria, Victor Emanuel was justified in putting no trust in their pretended neutrality, and that he therefore regarded himself as at war with the Duke. Sure of his personal safety, Francis awaited at Mantua the outcome of the campaign.

Duchess Louisa, the Regent of Parma, took flight for Mantua on May 1, when some of her officers asked permission to enlist with the Allies. A provisional junta worked for fusion with Piedmont, but the soldiers, with whom the Duchess was popular, demanded her restoration. Back she came on May 4, and out went the patriots in hot haste. She announced that Parma should remain neutral. During the next month she lived unmolested in her capital, but everyone realized that her tenure depended on the ascendency of the Austrians. After Magenta, when they blew up the vast fortifications of Piacenza and withdrew their troops to the Mincio, Duchess Louisa hoped, by granting a popular town government to Parma, to save her throne: on the next day however, she decided to flee again (June 9). Her garrison consigned their banner and cannon to the Austrians and disbanded. The patriotic party organized, declared Piacenza and Parma restored to the dynasty of Savoy, to which they belonged, by the vote of March 17, 1848, and on June 16 welcomed Count Diodato Pallieri, whom Victor Emanuel appointed governor.

Tuscany, Massa, Carrara, Modena, Piacenza, Parma — had all joined the National Cause, and all of them except Tuscany had formally united with Piedmont, before the battle of Solferino was fought. Equally enthusiastic were the subjects of the Pope, who, if they had had a free hand, would have been the first to cast in their lot with the new Kingdom of Italy. But up to June 11 Bologna and the Romagna were occupied by Austrian troops. That night the Liberals, impatient at the long wait, organized in Bologna; the next morning they marched from the Pepoli Palace to the Town Hall, and told Cardinal Milesi, the Papal Legate, that while the war lasted the people demanded a dictatorship under Victor Emanuel. Not being obtuse, the Cardinal wasted no time in expostulation, but promptly departed for Rome. A provisional government, headed by Pepoli, was acclaimed: the Bolognese spent a day of exquisite patriotic satisfaction parading up and down the streets, proudly displaying their tricolor cockades, cheering and congratulating each other, "but all with a calm and grave sobriety." The Junta telegraphed Victor Emanuel to beseech him to assume the dictatorship, but Cavour replied that for obvious reasons it would be imprudent for the King to accept their invitation at present. The Junta continued in office, therefore, and became the centre of an uprising which included three quarters of the Pope's Kingdom. Ravenna, Forlì, Ancona, Sinigaglia, Perugia, Fano, rose simultaneously. By June 13 the tricolor of liberty and independence waved from every town hall.[37] The delirium of patriotism caused Romagnoles and Umbrians, Marches men and Legations men to fraternize, and to enjoy for a day the dream, which they knew was only a dream, that they were their own masters. Strive, cheer, legislate as they might, their fate depended on other wills than theirs. Even while they battled valiantly, some god without consulting them, had decided to give the battle to their adversaries.

For the Pope's subjects were entangled in that coil of the Pope's Temporal Power which had for centuries strangled Italy's struggle for unity and independence. In the early spring, when war between Austria and France seemed imminent, Cardinal Antonelli tried to lure native recruits to the Papal army by the promise of fivefold pay: Europe believed and Pius the Ninth's government always acted on the assumption that Pius's rule could be maintained only by force of arms. Since recruits did not flock to the Papal barracks, however, Antonelli besought Emperor Francis Joseph not to withdraw his Austrian garrisons from Bologna, Ferrara and Ancona, and he persuaded Emperor Napoleon not to leave Rome unprotected by the French troops. Nothing could better illustrate the incongruity of a Pope-King

[37] Pesaro was a noticeable exception.

than that he had to rely for his existence upon the protection of two Powers which were then at war with each other.

Napoleon felt more grievously than ever the burden of his obligations to the Clericals. During the winter they had thwarted his plans at every step, and they so intimidated him that, on quitting Paris he publicly proclaimed: "We are not going to Italy to foment disorder, nor to disturb the power of the Holy Father, whom we restored to his throne, but to shield him from that foreign pressure which weighs on all the Peninsula." [38] The Pope announced that he should remain strictly neutral, as his unique office required. Antonelli gave out that the French government had promised to observe neutrality and not to permit any outbreak in the Papal States : [39] another instance of the Cardinal's characteristic unconcern for the truth; for the French actually promised to prevent outbreaks only in that part of the Papal States which they themselves were occupying, and to respect neutrality only in case the Austrians should not increase their garrisons. If Antonelli was privately urging Austria to send more troops into the Legations to hold down the "populations seduced by Piedmontese wiles," his purpose in garbling the French promise could not be misconstrued. [40] On the other hand, since France was intriguing to force a collision between the Pope and Austria, Antonelli could plead that he was simply holding his own in the game of diamond-cut-diamond.

From of old, Cavour understood that the Roman Question lay at the bottom of the Italian Question. The solution he proposed for it was the abolition of the Pope's Temporal Power: but many things must be gained before it would be politic even to suggest a discussion of this most delicate matter. He wished to guard against every act that might justify the Pope in charging Piedmont with hostile intentions; yet at the same time, he hoped that the Papal States would rise, as if spontaneously, in behalf of the National War. Antonelli was no doubt right in hinting that Piedmont was stimulating the spontaneity. Cavour pledged his government to respect Papal neutrality until the campaign advanced into Venetia. [41] Before that happened, the evacuation of the Aus-

[38] Napoleon's proclamation, Paris, May 3, 1859; text in Zini, ii, ii, 143–44.

[39] Zini, ii, ii, 182-83, for Antonelli's despatch of May 3 (or May 7, according to *Stor. Doc.*, viii, 103).   [40] *Stor. Doc.*, viii, 103.

[41] *Stor. Doc.*, viii, 105; Della Minerva to Antonelli, May 20, 1859.

trian garrisons, the popular revolution and the request that Victor Emanuel should accept a dictatorship, thrust upon Cavour the very entanglement he had hoped to escape. The dictatorship had to be declined, not only to save Piedmont from an open breach with the Vatican, but also because it was disapproved by Napoleon, who wished neither to irritate the Pope nor to encourage the extension of Piedmontese influence south of the Po. Events rushed on so rapidly, however, that the King and Cavour decided that, as a war measure, it was necessary to send Massimo d'Azeglio as commissioner extraordinary to Bologna.[42] To this Napoleon consented, to head off anarchy and to organize the volunteers of the Papal provinces for service in the Allied Armies. D'Azeglio accepted the work, for which his undiminished popularity commended him, choosing as his assistants Marquis Pepoli for finances, Professor Montanari for internal affairs, and General Pinelli, a Piedmontese officer, to direct the military preparations.

The Pope and his advisers watched this dissolution of the Papal States with undisguised alarm: his Papal anathemas had no longer any effect upon the rebellious patriots: for the avenging spirits whom Pius frantically called from the vasty deep did not obey him. Cardinal Antonelli, always the most practical of the Romish hierophants, leaving to His Holiness the employment of spiritual means, put his trust in the Papal troops, which numbered more than ten thousand. The Cardinal ordered a detachment of these, some 2300 men, that lay at Spoleto, to march on Perugia, and suppress the insurrection there. The strength of the troops was made up of a regiment of Swiss mercenaries, commanded by Colonel Anton Schmid, and their zeal was whetted, according to credible report, by the hint that they would be allowed to plunder the town.[43] To mercenaries, the lure of plunder is like raw beef to bloodhounds. Schmid was exhorted to use great vigor, as an example for terrorizing the other provinces, and he was authorized to behead the rebels whom he found in the houses in order to save the government the expense of trying them, and to levy food and money on the provinces themselves.[44] At three

[42] His instructions bade him to rally all the live forces of the Romagna, to give them a wise administration, and to refute the assertion that the Italians are unable to govern themselves. *Stor. Doc.*, viii, 106–07.   [43] Degli Azzi, 56 ff.
[44] *Narrazione Storica dei Fatti Accaduti in Perugia dal 14 al 20 Giugno, 1859.*

o'clock in the afternoon of June 20, Schmid led his force up the ridge which slopes from Perugia southward. His cannon battered the suburb and church of St. Peter. The Perugian insurgents, of whom not more than 600 seem to have been armed, and their arms were antiquated muskets, could not long withstand the assault. They retired within St. Peter's Gate, only to be driven back into the town. Then the Swiss availed themselves royally of the Papal license to sack and pillage. They broke into and despoiled houses, set fires, shot down innocent women and children, and but for being suddenly diverted from their purpose they would have massacred an American family which happened to be staying in one of the hotels. They robbed even the churches, and ravished two of the inmates of a girls' orphan asylum. The Perugians resisted as long as they could, at first in the streets, at last from windows and roofs. When they had to capitulate, their representative who went with a white flag in search of Schmid was shot down in cold blood. The barbarous orgy continued far into the night. "The devastation wrought by the soldiers has been great," Schmid telegraphed with bandit pride to the Papal Legate, Giordani — "about 70 dead, including some women killed in their homes."[45]

Not content with this bloody reprisal, the mercenary chief levied a tribute of 320,000 lire on the inhabitants, compelled them to illuminate their houses as for a jubilee, and exacted victuals and pay for his troops. He reported to Rome that he had vanquished 5000 rebels,[46] which was at least five times as many as took part against him. Pope, cardinals and prelates, forgetting for an instant their professed vocation of peace, rejoiced exceedingly.[47] Antonelli promoted Schmid to a generalship, and Pius caused a medal to be struck and distributed, with his blessing, to the devoted soldiers of Mother Church, who committed these atrocities. The only soldiers who failed to receive their reward

[45] Mariani, iii, 686.   [46] Between 700 and 800 seems the probable number, although 1000 is also estimated. Only 600, however, had firearms.

[47] A detailed account of the massacre is given by H. N. Gay in *Uno Screzio Diplomatico*, reprinted from *Archivio Storico del Risorgimento Umbro*, iii, nos. 2–4, iv, no. 2. The vigor with which the American Minister, Stockton, demanded an indemnity and brought Antonelli to terms is vividly described. Mr. Gay's monograph is inserted in G. Degli Azzi's *L'Insurrezione e le Stragi di Perugia del Giugno, 1859* (Perugia: Bartelli, 1909, 2d edit.). This work, a monument of research, is likely to remain the authority on this episode.

were those who, having plundered churches, made off to Tuscany with their booty.[48] Cardinal Gioacchino Pecci, Archbishop of Perugia, conducted the funeral services for the few Papalini who were killed. War is war, a recognized letting loose of the beast in Man: but Europe was shocked that the Pope, who was forever harping on his extreme regard for religion, should license his soldiery to ravish, rob, and slay. It was bad enough that he had to hold himself on his throne by the aid of foreign troops; it was worse that he handed over one of his own towns to such ferocity as foreign conquerors used to wreak on enemies of an alien race. That free Switzerland hired out her young men to support the worst government in Italy did not escape censure.[49] Small wonder that the assertion gained credence that William Tell was merely a myth, when his degenerate compatriots of the nineteenth century took so willingly to the vocation of mercenaries. In the eighteenth century, the word Hessian earned an evil significance from which it could never be purged: in the nineteenth Swiss became its synonym.

The subjugation of Perugia quelled the insurrection in the other Umbrian towns and in several places along the Adriatic. The reoccupation of Ancona, where the Liberals, from being unprepared and unorganized, failed to seize the fortress when the Austrians marched out,[50] checked for a moment the wave of patriotism. All parties awaited anxiously the result of the great campaign north of the Po. The news of the "massacre of Perugia," which the Italians painted in more than its original horror,[51] was soon overshadowed by the reports of the battle of Solferino.

[48] Coppi; quoted by Reuchlin, III, 388.

[49] The 10,000 Swiss who worked in hotels and at trades in Italy were in danger of being boycotted for the sins of their compatriots. Reuchlin, III, 388.

[50] Balan, the Papal historian, argues from their inaction that the Anconitans heartily endorsed the Pope's government. II, 131.

[51] The official Papal historian devotes one sentence to the Perugian fight, with characteristic suppression of facts, as follows: "Perugia, where a handful of impudent conspirators aided by persons from outside and led by Tuscan officials, had rebelled against its legitimate sovereign, returned to its obedience, the felons having been subdued by a band of Swiss, commanded by Colonel Schmid, who in four hours of combat forced the entrance with slight loss, although he had to fight in the streets and against some of the houses where the rebels had barricaded themselves." Balan II, 13. Balan hardly deigns to mention the "very ferocious and rabid accusations against the Pontifical troops," and the "unheard-of calumnies" against them of "pillage, of frightful slaughter, of the barbarity of the *Papal satellites*." After all, he says, the dead numbered only 27: then he adds that anyhow the Italian generals, Cialdini, Fanti and others, were guilty of much worse.

Napoleon himself gave a great stimulus to the Italian patriots through the proclamation he issued after the victory of Magenta. He told them boldly that their enemies were his, that he knew his times so well that he aspired for moral influence and not for mere sterile conquests, in order that he might free one of the most beautiful parts of Europe. "Your welcome," he said, "shows that you have understood me. I do not come among you with a preconceived system to dispossess sovereigns or to impose my will; my army will busy itself with only two things — to fight your enemies and to maintain internal order; it will oppose no obstacles to the free manifestation of your legitimate desires. Providence sometimes favors people and individuals, giving them occasion to become great all at once, but only on this condition, that they know how to profit by it. Your desire for independence, so vaguely expressed, so often dashed, will be realized if you shall show yourselves worthy. *Organize yourselves militarily;* fly to the banner of King *Victor Emanuel*, who has so nobly shown you the way of honor. Remember that without discipline there is no army; and, burning with the holy fire of patriotism, be today all soldiers, to be tomorrow the free citizens of a great country." [52]

To the Italians this exhortation had no oracular ambiguity; but it both urged to action and seemed to guarantee protection. June 8, the day when it was published, saw the entry of the Emperor and the King into Milan,[53] amid such outbursts of gratitude as only the realization of redemption could inspire. "We came back by way of the Corso," writes Fleury to his wife that afternoon, "where an immense crowd awaited us. (Napoleon) had really the air of a prophet. Women waved their handkerchiefs; men applauded, crying, 'Long live the Liberator of Italy!' Flowers were showered, the bouquets even fell upon us; the people came to touch his hands, to embrace his knees: it was a delirium!"[54] That moment proved to be the crest of Napoleon's career. Had he died then, he would have been immortalized as the most unselfish despot in history.[55]

[52] Ialian text in Zini II, ii, 18–59.   [53] Della Rocca, I, 452.
[54] Fleury, II, 46.   [55] P. O. Vigliani was appointed Governor of Lombardy. C. telegraphed him on June 13: "We are no longer in 1848; we admit no discussion. Pay no attention to the sensations of those around you. The least act of weakness would wreck the government." *Lettere*, III, 96.

These risings during April, May and June confirmed Cavour's repeated assertions that at the first opportunity the Central Italians would shake off their yoke, and showed also that the desire for unity had taken hold of all classes, and was no longer, as Mazzini claimed, the monopoly of his disciples. By the way in which each town turned instinctively, in the first moment of liberation, to Victor Emanuel, the ten years' policy of Piedmont was crowned. But while the Central Italians, by popular enthusiasm and by revolutions which, except at Perugia, were bloodless, proved themselves eager for independence, they fell far short in volunteering for the war. Cavour had hoped that for every French soldier who came over the Alps there would be a Piedmontese regular or an Italian volunteer. "Woe unto us," he said, "if we owe our emancipation to the French." He welcomed volunteers from all parts of the Peninsula, and, as we have seen, they flocked to Turin in great numbers: but they seemed to vanish before the war began. No one has explained what became of the 40,000 or more men who were enrolled up to the middle of April. The best of them, according to Garibaldi's complaint, went into the Piedmontese army; his Hunters of the Alps numbered less than 3500, and Mezzacapo's Hunters of the Apennines fewer still. If the effective of the Piedmontese army reached 60,000 as was estimated, that is only 12,000 more than its peace footing in 1858.

From his arrival at the seat of war, Napoleon hinted that the coöperation of the Italians in men and arms did not correspond with what he had been led to expect; and he inclined to interpret the smallness of the contingents in the Central States as an indication of indifference or of cowardice. The Bolognese, he said, waited till the Austrians had evacuated their city, before making a sign.[56] Plon-Plon, with customary outspokenness, expressed his contempt for the Tuscans, who after six weeks of freedom had only five or six thousand men sufficiently equipped and drilled to accompany him northward. A people that earnestly desired independence ought to muster at least two per cent of its inhabitants to fight; but Tuscany, according to him, would contribute only one seventh of this minimum. Was it worth while, he asked sarcastically, to shout "Hurrah for war!" and to

[56] *Lettere*, III, clxxxi.

change the form of government.[57] So far as in him lay, Cavour strove to impress upon the Central Italians their military duty. Although her own effective troops fell below two per cent, Piedmont was doing her share, having expended a great sum on fortifications and munitions, and on equipping non-Piedmontese volunteers; not to speak of the losses she incurred by voluntarily flooding her territory and by Austrian depredations. Napoleon overlooked three facts, or refused to give them due weight: his prohibition against any league with the Revolution diminished the number of recruits, and those who were accepted, including Garibaldi's Hunters, would never have been enrolled if Cavour had stood strictly by the letter of the Emperor's instructions; next, the people of the Duchies, Legations and Tuscany had been held by their despots in so unmartial a state that very few of them had ever handled a gun; thirdly, when suddenly freed, they lacked arms, uniforms, discipline, and leaders — those essentials of war which can never be improvised. While, therefore, the smallness of the Central Italian contingents surprised the Emperor, and evidently annoyed him, he was not justified in inferring that those provinces deliberately planned to live in pleasant sloth while he fought their battles for them.

During May and June, however, these things did not come to the surface. What astonished Europe was the spontaneous rush for liberty of the Italians — that, and the orderliness with which they carried through their revolutions. Among the Italians themselves there was patriotic enthusiasm which fell little short of exaltation. Contrasted with the delirium of 1848, it seemed almost sober; certainly, it was more sophisticated, because men knew that a nation cannot be built on iridescent dreams alone. They understood, also, that even after the Austrians and Bourbons were expelled, many complications must be cleared up before Italy could face the world in the glory of her freedom, independence and unity. But to their morning hopes, all seemed attainable.

In the South there was no such ferment. To leave no stone unturned, Cavour endeavored to bring the King of the Two Sicilies into the National cause: for he did not yet dream that Italy could be united under Victor Emanuel in a brief campaign. The most

[57] *Lettere*, III, cxix; Prince Napoleon to Boncompagni, June 9, 1859. In 1858, Tuscany's population was 1,793,965; two per cent of this would give more than 35,000 soldiers.

that he hoped from the promised war was the expulsion of the Austrians, the expansion of Piedmont, a union in Central Italy, and the continuance of the Bourbon Kingdom in the South. Most politic was it, therefore, in him to arrange, if he could, for concord among the Italian rulers who might soon be reigning side by side without foreign interference. But Ferdinand II was being consumed by a swift and loathsome disease, and his ministers dared not act. When the war began, however, Bomba, propped up in bed, wrote down instructions that neutrality should be strictly preserved.[58] Surrounded by holy pictures, charms, and amulets, and attended by the constant services of priests, in spite of the administration, more than once, of the viaticum, in spite even of the Pope's special benediction sent by telegraph, Bomba spent his last weeks miserably. These agents were as powerless as the incantations of an Indian medicine man to exorcise his fears. He died at Caserta, May 22, 1859. There have been worse rulers and many much wickeder men, but so long as the name of Bomba is remembered it will call up the most abhorred European monarch of the 19th century. Nature intended him for a lazzarone; fate indulged a wild whim in making him a king. He died young; but long before his death he had established a record still unapproached for lying, cruelty and vulgar deceit.[59]

Cavour seized the occasion to send Count Gabaleone di Salmour to Naples on a special mission. Being no intriguer, Salmour frankly said that he would not undertake any underhand propaganda in behalf of Piedmont:[60] he would simply go, deliver his message, look over the field and report. This he did. Cavour instructed him to persuade the new King, Francis II, that his only safety lay in adhering to the Italian cause.[61] When the victory of Magenta seemed to foreshadow the success of the Allies, Salmour was told to suggest that by joining them Francis II might annex Umbria and the Marches. The King rejected this proposal indignantly, and Salmour returned to Turin.[62] All the

[58] Text, dated April 28, 1859, in *Stor. Doc.*, VIII, 16.

[59] For Ferdinand's last days see De Cesare; *La Fine di un Regno* (edit. 1895), chap. xv; De' Sivo, I, 472–75. N. Bernardini: *Ferdinando II a Lecce*. Lecce (1895) says three causes were given for Ferdinand's death — Milano's poisoned weapon; poison administered in his food on his journey; and venereal disease, caught "da una meretrice." But pyæmia, he declares, was the real disease. 176–77.   [60] Crispolti.   [61] C.'s instructions, dated at Turin, May 27, 1859, in *Stor. Doc.*, VIII, 121–26.   [62] De Cesare: *Fine*, II, 330.

while Napoleon III was secretly working to keep Naples neutral, and Muratist agents, with or without his cognizance, were striving to resuscitate the following of Lucien, the aspirant.[63]

Prince Metternich died on May 6, just early enough to escape the disgust of being ferried across the Styx in the same boatload with Bomba, whom he abominated. His passing had no political significance; it simply marked the close of an epoch. In his 86 years he had seen more than Methuselah in his ten centuries. A new force, Democracy, whose coming had been prophesied for ages by poets, dreamers and lovers of their fellowmen, had begun to transform society, and although no one could foresee whither it would lead, everyone saw that Privilege must go down before it. Metternich's glory was to gauge more accurately than any one else the longevity of Privilege. When Napoleon the First's ambition drove all the monarchs of Europe into coalition against him, Metternich made them understand that the preservation of the order in which their general interests flourished must take precedence over their mutual jealousies. The Treaties of 1815 registered the solidarity of the Privileged Classes. Metternich believed that in the long run it is safe to count on selfishness. He knew not only that the semi-feudal conditions, through which fifteen generations had expressed themselves, would, though decayed, outlast his time, but that the fact of Privilege would survive, by whatever name it might be called, and that Privilege would appropriate as fast and as far as it could the tools of Democracy. His policy of make-shift he maintained, with a spurious Jovian poise, from 1815 to 1848.

The best thing he owed to fortune was that his lot was cast in Austria: in Prussia or in France he could not have prospered. He cherished no illusions. He was skeptical, but this did not prevent him from keeping up the bluff that the political and religious doctrines which had held society together when the foremost men and women believed them could be regalvanized indefinitely to serve as checks for the ignorant masses. He had the master workman's contempt for Papal and Bourbon bunglers, but since Pope and Bourbons were a part of the system, instead of abolishing them he had to take care that their bungling did as little harm as possible. "If he had been present," said Prudhon,

<hr>

[63] De Cesare, *Fine*, II, 328. *Stor. Doc.*, VIII, 126.

"when God began to bring order out of chaos, Metternich would have prayed fervently, 'O God, preserve chaos!'" Like all who interpret life in terms of selfishness, he was cynical. He had a pin for every Utopian bubble. His intellect served his ends perfectly. His wit was less vitriolic than Talleyrand's, but it permeated action in a way that Talleyrand's did not. Metternich had principles, and he managed to be the dominant political figure in Europe for 35 years; Talleyrand had no principles and could not dominate France for even 35 weeks. Had Metternich been less consistent, less thorough, or less rigorous, Italian patriotism would have taken a different course. Shortly before he died he is reported to have said, gloomily: "There is only one statesman in Europe today. That is M. de Cavour, — and he is against us."

CHAPTER XXV

VILLAFRANCA

DURING the night of June 24–25 the Austrians retired beyond the Mincio. The Allies, exhausted by that terrible day's fighting, did not pursue them. A few days later they too crossed the river to carry the war into Venetia. Napoleon established his quarters at Valeggio. The Piedmontese prepared to besiege Peschiera, while the French turned to Verona on the east and to Mantua on the south. The arrival of Prince Napoleon with the Fifth Corps and the Tuscan division under Ulloa added 35,000 men to Napoleon's effective. A week passed in comparative inactivity — little enough time for reorganizing armies which had just lost a thousand officers and 20,000 men, and for starting them on their next task. As soon as the Italians realized that the Allies had won a great victory at Solferino their hopes rose almost to the pitch of delirium. When the Allies entered Venetia everyone took it for granted that the Venetians — the patient, brave Venetians — were as good as free. The Cabinets of Europe, and the press too, discussed with amazement the reports of the battle, which surpassed Waterloo in magnitude and might prove to be another turning point in history. Such consternation reigned in Austria that Emperor Francis Joseph hurried to Vienna. At Turin, on the contrary, amid profound satisfaction, the bustle of preparation was redoubled. Cavour was placing orders for new guns and uniforms, was raising new regiments, and sending to the front supplies and men. "In eight days," he wrote La Marmora on July 6, "you will have 600 new officers. Will that be enough for you?" [1]

That very afternoon, at half-past six o'clock, Emperor Napoleon at Valeggio gave to General Fleury a letter to deliver at once, and with secrecy, to Emperor Francis Joseph, who had returned to Verona. Fleury drove post-haste in one of the Imperial closed carriages, accompanied by an officer bearing a flag

[1] *Lettere*, III, 106; C. to La Marmora.

of truce. Being admitted within the Austrian lines, a troop of Uhlans escorted him to Francis Joseph's quarters, where Marshal Hess received him courteously. The Emperor had gone to bed, but on learning of the arrival of a special messenger on an urgent errand, he rose, hastily (we may assume) wrapped himself in his Imperial dressing-gown, and had General Fleury admitted. Francis Joseph expressed great surprise at Napoleon's letter, and said that before answering he should need time to think it over. Fleury replied that he awaited his Majesty's pleasure, but that as the French fleet already occupied the island of Lossini,[2] and was ordered to attack Venice the following day, he hoped there would be no long delay. The young Emperor promised to give a reply early the next morning. This he did, and in handing Fleury an autograph letter for his master, he told him that he agreed to the armistice. By eight o'clock Fleury was returning post-haste to Napoleon.[3] Before noon, the Allied forces, which had been speciously drawn up as if for attack along the hills facing the Austrians, received notice that the two Emperors had agreed to a truce. Later, Victor Emanuel was formally advised that as the terms of the armistice were to be signed at Villafranca early on the following day, his chief of staff, Della Rocca, must be present. Incredulity faintly describes the emotion which surged through the Piedmontese army at this word. Everybody had a foreboding of impending disaster. Each asked his neighbor what had happened, what was going to happen: all were equally mystified. Twenty-four hours later, when the telegraph had spread the news through Europe, the political world was overcome by wonder. What did it mean that the French Emperor, after a brilliant campaign of only six weeks, crowned by two colossal victories, should pause midway in his triumph? A little later, when the despatches announced that Napoleon himself — the victor, not the vanquished — had sued for a truce, the general wonder grew.

What puzzled contemporaries has become reasonably clear to posterity. Napoleon's sudden halt was not due to his love of causing sensations, but to a combination of influences among

[2] The slowness of the French fleet deserves notice. Had Venice been attacked several weeks earlier, as was quite possible, the Austrian military operations in Venetia would have been upset.

[3] See Fleury, II, 111–22, for details of his mission.

2

which he himself might have been unable to say which was paramount. At Valeggio he seemed to be the arbiter of Europe: in reality, Europe held him as firmly in her web as a spider holds a glossy, much-buzzing fly. The fates which enmeshed the Emperor were political and military. His own France, Italy and the rest of Europe, far from being fixed quantities, had varied, each according to its nature, as the war progressed. The French public relished the glory their army won for them, but the soberer minority had begun to count the cost. Glory, like rubies or yachts or Lucullus feasts, may demand more than its devotees can afford or care to spend. Up to July 1, the Italian War had drained France of 750 million francs, and the end was not in sight. What equivalent could she hope for, even if she finally routed Austria? The Bismarckian plan of exacting from a beaten adversary a stupendous indemnity had not come into vogue; and Austria, in any case, was too nearly bankrupt to make rich picking. So the French capitalists favored peace. Joined with them were the Clericals, who dreaded, with reason, the slightest jar that might disturb the Pope's senile despotism. The Imperialists also, the horde of self-seekers whose rank or wealth depended upon Napoleon the Third's stability, grumbled at his continuing to risk his fortunes and theirs in a visionary enterprise.

Italy, as we have just seen, presented a new problem after the 27th of April. Napoleon had unwittingly abetted the Revolution. The Roman Question, annexations, a Kingdom of Italy beyond his calculations and entirely against his wishes, loomed up to menace him, like the genie whom the unwary Arab uncorked. Let him protest as he might, the Italians were bent on making the most of his assistance in order to secure their long dreamed-of independence. Well aware that Cavour, ordinarily affable, tactful, seductive, could be, at need, overwhelming, terrible, Napoleon began to feel towards him the aversion which a wilful and obstinate but variable man instinctively feels towards one whose will is stronger, and whose principles are out of reach of whims. In their first interview over Tuscany,[4] the two perceived that their policies could not coincide. Cavour deferred then, because it was politic: but Napoleon knew that deference was not the masterful statesman's favorite rôle, and he believed,

[4] See above, II, 40.

with good reason, that the agitations south of the Po had Cavour's sanction, if not his active direction. To get out of Italy before the entire Peninsula required his remodeling hand, seemed therefore more and more desirable to the disenchanted Don Quixote. For when he looked beyond the French frontier, he saw neither ally nor well-wisher. Even Russia, his loyal supporter during the winter months, grew cool as the campaign restored liberty to the Italian patriots. The Czar, apparently, dreaded lest the Revolution, spreading to Naples, should sweep away the Bourbons, whom he had, for special reasons, protected; and perhaps also, his Romanoff loathing for constitutionalism took umbrage at the likelihood of the extension of a Liberal government through Central Italy. Although no documents have been published, it seems most probable that Russia wished to prevent a general war into which she would necessarily be drawn, without prospect of benefit for herself.

If Napoleon might expect no aid from Russia, he had much to fear from Germany, which since the early spring was seething with Gallophobia. The smaller States gave themselves over completely to Austria. Prussia, phlegmatic, at first, and hesitant, gradually came to the conclusion that she must show her strength in order to enhance her reputation in the Germanic Confederation. Anti-French feeling increased and served as an excuse for her intention, which she did not disguise after the Austrians were driven from Lombardy, of mobilizing her army.[5] At Berlin, Napoleon got no reassurances. Everything foreboded that the political phase would, at a moment's notice, turn military. National hatred has a long memory: the Prussians of 1859 had not forgotten, they would never forgive, the humiliations heaped upon them after Jena in 1806.

In England, too, there was taking place a great change which, in proportion as it benefited the Italian cause, checked the Emperor's designs. During the month of May, Lord Derby's Ministry lost popularity day by day. The middle classes, in whom still flourished the Anglo-Saxon love of liberty, sympathized with the Italians. The Tory Cabinet and party, taking their cue from Windsor Castle, were pledged officially to neutrality, but ardently desired the Austrians to win. We have read how both

---

[5] For an authoritative account of Prussia's conduct see Sybel, II, 361–90.

Victoria and Albert deplored Gyulai's failure to destroy the Piedmontese army before the French troops arrived. On May 29, Lord Malmesbury wrote in his diary: "The Queen and Prince feel very strongly the defeat of the Austrians, [at Montebello] and are anxious to take their part, but I told her Majesty that was quite impossible; this country would not go to war even in support of Italian independence, and there would not be ten men in the House of Commons who would do so on behalf of Austria."[6] Victoria and her husband, however, were too discreet to allow their personal preferences to clash with her constitutional obligations, and the public little suspected the Queen's eagerness to aid the Austrian Emperor, whose despotism had become a stench in the nostrils of civilization. Neither was it commonly known how tirelessly Lord Derby's Ministry, and especially Lord Malmesbury, had labored — not unlike an "old aunt," but with unflagging zeal — to preserve peace.

On April 19 the Queen prorogued Parliament, the Government having been defeated in the vote on the Reform Bill.[7] In the election which followed, the Whigs had a valid majority,[8] and in a full house on June 11 they carried by 13 votes an amendment to the address from the Throne.[9] Lord Derby resigned, taking into retirement the reputation of a mediocre statesman with good intentions — a politician of the stop-gap order, who is usually found at the helm in moments of transition, and is invariably swamped. Lord Palmerston and Lord John Russell, the recognized leaders of the Whigs, had made up their differences and agreed to serve in the same Cabinet. But the Queen, who loved flattery always, and expected obsequiousness in prime ministers even, had reason to recollect that neither Pam nor Lord John had been to her taste: she therefore sent for Lord Granville, who was young enough to be the son of either,[10] and whose personal deportment was more attractive to her and the Prince.[11] We need not suppose, however, that in choosing a man who could not unite the Liberals Victoria and Albert hoped to hasten the downfall of the next administration and the return of the Tories.

[6] Malmesbury, 488.   [7] 330 ayes; 291 nays.   [8] Liberals 353, Conservatives 302, as classified by the London *Times* of May 21, 1859.   [9] 323 to 310.

[10] Palmerston was born in 1784, Russell in 1792, Granville in 1815.

[11] The Queen's professed reason for summoning the young man first, was because she did not wish to show a preference between the two veteran chiefs.

Granville, however, failed to form a ministry, and the Queen, with ill-concealed reluctance, summoned Palmerston.[12] On June 18 the new British Ministry, which surpassed every other in the 19th century for the ability of its individual members, kissed hands. Palmerston was Premier; Gladstone, Chancellor of the Exchequer; Lord John Russell, Foreign Secretary; Sidney Herbert, War Secretary; and Granville, President of the Council.[13] To this Cabinet, or at least to Palmerston and Lord John, Italy was to owe hardly less than to Napoleon III and the armies of France.

Those two British champions of liberty, as liberty was conceived in the third quarter of the 19th century, had been such outspoken advocates of Italian rights and so friendly to the French Emperor, that both the Italians and the French joyfully hailed their triumph. Lord Malmesbury, with the natural acerbity of a very virtuous man who believes that he has been beaten by the very wicked, records that the French Ambassador spent money lavishly to secure the Liberals' victory. "That one gentleman received £480, the cost of his late election, is," he says, "well-known." [14] He further relates that on the morning of the parliamentary division, Marquis E. d'Azeglio "and some other foreigners were waiting in the lobby outside, and when Lord Palmerston appeared redoubled their vociferations. Azeglio is said to have thrown his hat in the air, and himself in the arms of Jaucourt, the French attaché, which probably no Ambassador, or even Italian, ever did before in so public a place." [15] "Or even *Italian* " — the noble lord's slur, written down in the moment of defeat, is excusable: like most of his class, he regarded the Italians as a noisy, degenerate people who had succeeded in disturbing the peace of Europe. But Tories, French Imperialists and Italian patriots were alike deceived in supposing that the new Ministry would actively support the Allies in the campaign.

[12] Palmerston's letter of June 11, 1859, offering to serve under Granville but reminding the Queen of the proper etiquette in the formation of a Ministry, could not have pleased her and the Prince. Text in Ashley, II, 363–64.

[13] "The Cabinet," writes Malmesbury to Cowley on June 18, "is remarkable for its *personnel* of talent, and for having *three* Dukes in it" (Somerset, Argyll and Newcastle). Malmesbury, 494. "The Administration was looked upon as the strongest that was ever formed so far as the individual talents of its members were concerned." Ashley, II, 364.

[14] Malmesbury, 491; June 12, 1859.   [15] *Ibid*, 490; June 11, 1859.

True to the instinct which, from the year 1815 restrained Britain from risking a man or a shilling where British interests were not directly involved, Palmerston had no intention of reversing Derby's policy of neutrality. The difference was that, though England would remain officially neutral, her ministers, and especially Lord John at the Foreign Office, had the advancement of Italy and not that of Austria, at heart. The French Emperor suspected, even before he sounded the Liberal leaders, that they would support him only so long as he promoted the liberation of Italy. His brilliant military successes were beginning to alarm the British public against him. Men of all parties asked themselves, "Is it possible that he is disinterested? Will he, with a generosity unparalleled in history, bestow on Italy her independence and demand no recompense? Having crushed Austria, will he spare Germany? If he covets Belgium, who shall prevent him? Glory won in North Italy kindled in his uncle the desire to conquer Europe: will the nephew be more moderate?" This dread was nowhere more prevalent than at Court, where the Queen and Prince had been early inoculated with it by their Uncle Leopold. For a long time past, the King of the Belgians, obeying the instinct of self-preservation, had systematically cast suspicions on the Emperor of the French as plotting to swallow up Belgium. By lineage and marriage Leopold had access to the hereditary enemies of Bonapartism,[16] each of whom cherished his special reason for harkening to him.[17]

Reduced to lowest terms, the political problem left Napoleon without a militant ally except Piedmont. The opposition and distrust which isolated him, increased with each victory: if he fulfilled his promise and drove the Austrians out of Venetia, how could he persuade the alarmed chancelleries of Europe that he was less formidable than before he began the war?

From the military standpoint the outlook was even more un-

[16] Thus Victoria and Albert were his niece and nephew. Through his second wife, Princess Louise of Orleans, he was son-in-law of Louis Philippe, and in touch with the powerful Orleanist faction. His daughter, Princess Charlotte, was married to the Austrian Archduke Maximilian, viceroy of Lombardy-Venetia. His family ramifications in Germany were almost equally important.

[17] Rothan states that Victoria was receiving secret despatches from Leopold instigating her against France. De Moustier confirms this, and declares that Bismarck at St. Petersburg had wind of Leopold's purposes. *Revue des Deux Mondes*, Feb. 15, 1899; pp. 760–71.

favorable. The first of July saw him on the left bank of the Mincio with an army of less than 100,000 available troops, terribly battered by its struggle at Solferino. Of this force, 25,000 men were in hospital, many stricken with typhus, although this fact was kept as secret as possible, and those in active service, worn by battle, marches, insufficient rations and the scorching Lombard sun, were not eager to continue the campaign. They had won enough glory: what other recompense was there to fight for? The fierce jealousies which invariably accompany the exercise of war shed their bane through the army. At officers' mess, in barracks, at campfires, rank and file discussed each episode of the recent battles and spattered each other with recriminations. The feud between Niel and Canrobert spread to their respective corps, and became so bitter that the Emperor himself was forced to command silence.[18] MacMahon had his critics and his eulogists. Generals of division or of brigade nursed their mutual grievances. Promotions were inevitably attributed to favoritism. When such family quarrels prevailed in the French army, no wonder that the feeling between the French and Piedmontese lacked cordiality. In public, of course, they treated each other with suspiciously effusive courtesy, but among themselves they spoke out. The French did not disguise their contempt for Italian unsoldierliness. They complained that Fanti had dawdled at Magenta, and that, but for Benedek's voluntary retreat, the Piedmontese would have been crushed at San Martino. They ignored the incontestable instances of Piedmontese valor, the Emperor's clumsy orders which blocked Fanti's march, the support given by Victor Emanuel to the French left centre at Solferino, the obvious intent of the Emperor to reserve for his own men the best chances for glory, and the way in which the Piedmontese commissariat had supplied deficiencies in the French.

A veteran commander-in-chief would have taken it for granted that bickerings and recriminations should go on as a part of the daily life of a large army: but to Napoleon, the civilian who had been fascinated through books by the glamour of war and only at fifty-one had experienced its disenchanting realities, these things seemed grave. Far more important, however, was the direct military problem: How long would it take to drive the Austrians

[18] La Gorce, III, 98.

from the Quadrilateral? The four fortresses, Peschiera, Mantua, Verona and Legnago, must be reduced in turn. Their investment called for siege trains, great stores of ammunition, and, above all, for more troops. It was computed that at least 300,000 men would be required: that meant that France must furnish 100,000 new troops and that Piedmont must raise her army to 100,000. But already Napoleon had difficulty in drawing even another regiment from home. Marshal Randon, at Paris, growing more alarmed every day at the prospect of a war on the Rhine, was unwilling to strip his home defense for the benefit of the army on the Po, and he sent brusque replies to Marshal Vaillant's requisitions from the Imperial headquarters. Napoleon did not believe that Piedmont could double her effective force, even if she recruited every available volunteer in the insurgent provinces. Unquestionably, also, the awful carnage of Solferino had horrified him.[19] His nerve had been shaken by the sight of the 15,000 dead and wounded on the field. He saw flies and carrion birds swarming for their feast. He heard, appalled, the shrieks, groans and curses of thousands of frantic human beings. For a time at least, glory seemed unreal before the intense reality of agony. Grim campaigners, like Grant or Moltke, look on such scenes unmoved, having learned that war cannot be otherwise: but Napoleon III, accustomed to the luxury of Paris, where he was carefully screened from contact with suffering, could not regard this piece of hell as a matter of course. He felt also the great heat and the stifling dust and the fatigue of camp life to such an extent that on July 6 he telegraphed the Empress that he was physically worn out:[20] yet there might be eight or ten weeks before the heat abated. The arrival at headquarters of Prince Napoleon exerted a further influence, because the Prince had a habit in private of treating Napoleon as his cousin and not as his Emperor. He now brought pessimistic reports from Tuscany and the Legations, where the lack of military spirit disgusted him, and he probably told Napoleon that it was madness to flatter

[19] Francis Joseph was equally horrified: "General Benedek . . . related afterwards that, in the council of war on the following morning, he had urged an immediate renewal of the battle, arguing that the French had had quite as severe losses, and had fewer fresh troops in reserve than the Austrians; but the Emperor cried out, with tears in his eyes, 'Rather let us lose a province than go through such horrible things again.'" Sybel, II, 377.   [20] *Lettre*, III, cci.

himself any longer on being a great general. By lucky blunders the French won at Magenta and at Solferino, but luck could not be depended upon forever. What if the Imperial Guard had given way at Ponte di Magenta, before Picard's reinforcements came up? What if Niel had been overwhelmed at Medole, or the Piedmontese shattered at San Martino? What if the French centre had failed at Solferino? To stake any longer the fortunes of a dynasty on the possible tardiness or flinching of a brigade would be suicidal. These thoughts, which formed the burden of every letter from Paris, Prince Napoleon cast at the Emperor without ceremony.[21] They led him to put into deed the decision which his heart had already prepared.

The deciding stroke came from Prussia. At Berlin the Prince Regent, who aspired to military laurels and had never forgotten the cruel indignity his mother received from the first Napoleon, would have welcomed war against France. But his prime minister, Schleinitz, urged a waiting policy, and in this Bernstorff, the Prussian Ambassador at London, and Bismarck at St. Petersburg, supported him, until the time for mediation should come. William, however, formally offered Francis Joseph to guarantee to him his Italian provinces, if Prussia, in return, should be allowed full sway in Germany.[22] The Austrian Emperor held off. Then William sent Baron Werther to Vienna with a similar message, adding that Prussia foresaw that her interest would soon require her to seek to mediate.[23] Francis Joseph, still hopeful of a great victory, replied that he reserved his liberty of action.[24] Finally, on June 24, Schleinitz addressed to Bernstorff and Bismarck a note in which he urged them to secure the coöperation of England and Russia to bring about a peace which should reconcile the rights of the Austrian Emperor and the hopes of the Italians. Schleinitz particularly referred to Napoleon's frequently expressed disavowal of ambitious intentions as a good augury for the Powers in their effort to mediate. By a coincidence which did not escape notice, Prussia called on the Diet to mobilize four additional army corps to be united with the Prussian army of

[21] Fleury, II, 93–99. Fleury and other officers were secretly urging Walewski to "strike the big blow" for peace before Napoleon changed his mind again. *Ibid*, 99.   [22] *Stor. Doc.*, VIII, 137.

[23] *Ibid* for Schleinitz's note of June 14, 1859.

[24] *Ibid*, 138, for Rechberg's despatch of June 22, 1859. Cf. Sybel, II, 377.

observation.[25] These two moves indicated that Prussia felt that
if she delayed taking the lead, her prestige in the Germanic Confederation would suffer. If Austria should suddenly win the
campaign by a brilliant victory, Austria's influence in Germany
would be irresistible: if France and Piedmont won, the other members of the Confederation might complain that Prussia had not
sufficiently upheld their common cause: whereas if Prussia, supported by England and Russia, could carry through her scheme
of mediation, she would both assert her commanding position in
Germany and put both Austria and France under obligations to
her.[26] To this despatch Lord John Russell replied, that Austria
ought to abandon all her Italian possessions, in order that Piedmont might expand into a kingdom large enough to keep Italy
independent of both Austrian and French interference.[27]

During the first three weeks of June, rumors of Prussia's purpose circulated freely in Paris: and the mobilization of her forces
was immediately construed as a threat to France. On the eve of
Solferino, Napoleon and Victor Emanuel rode out together, apparently to inspect positions. When they were beyond the hearing of everyone except Della Rocca, the King's chief of staff,
Napoleon read a letter from Eugénie. He spoke slowly, doling
his words out one by one. The Empress painted the situation in
all its gravity, and insisted that the war must stop then and
there. From the Emperor's tone, the King and Della Rocca inferred that he was taking this way of announcing his own decision. The King, having listened in silence, made no reply. "He
understood, as I did," says Della Rocca, "that everything was
over."[28]

The next day Solferino was fought. Immediately thereafter,
the Emperor, without a hint to Victor Emanuel, secretly set
out in search of a mediator.[29] He applied first in London, where
Persigny, by his orders, asked Palmerston to propose to Austria
an armistice on the following terms: Italy to be entirely in control of the Italians; Venetia and Modena under an Austrian
archduke, but independent; Lombardy and Parma annexed to

---

[25] Sybel, II, 378.   [26] The German troops mobilized along the Rhine would
have numbered nearly 400,000 by July 16. Sybel, II, 378.

[27] *Stor. Doc.*, VIII, 136–37: Russell despatch of June 26, 1859.

[28] Della Rocca, II, 459–61.   [29] On June 25 Fleury writes to his wife that Europe
' will not let us give ' Lombardy and Venetia to Piedmont. *Souvenirs*, I, 77.

Piedmont; the Grand Duke restored in Tuscany; the Legations, separated from the Papal States, to be governed by a lieutenant of Victor Emanuel under the high suzerainty of the Pope; the Italian States to be united in a Confederation presided over by the Pope.[30] These were the proposals of La Gueronnière's pamphlet. The Emperor counted on the personal friendship of both Palmerston and Russell, but he soon discovered that those statesmen declined to mix personal with State affairs. The Premier's reply foreshadowed England's new policy, which, in adopting the program, " Italy for the Italians," did not include the furtherance of Napoleon's ambition. Palmerston told Persigny that the British Ministry could not accept the proposed terms and press them as if they had originated at the Foreign Office; at most, he would transmit them to the Austrian Ambassador without comment. "If the French Emperor is tired of his war," he wrote Lord John, "and finds the job tougher than he expected, let him make what proposals he pleases, and to whomsoever he pleases; but let them be made as from himself formally and officially, and let him not ask us to father his suggestions, and make ourselves answerable for them." [31] The veteran statesman, whose eyes at seventy-five had no superiors in England for seeing through the wimples of diplomacy, penetrated to the marrow of Napoleon's scheme. "It would obviously fall short of the wishes and expectations of Italy; and if we made it, we should be accused of having interposed and stopped the allied armies in their career of victory, and of having betrayed and disappointed the Italians at the moment when their prospects were brightest." [32]

To create a new state out of Venetia and Modena, and set an Austrian archduke over it would, he pointed out, give an inlet to the same Austrian influences which had been the curse of Tuscany, and, through Modena, it would admit Austria into Central Italy. "The freedom of Piedmont would excite the aspirations of the Venetians. Discontent and disturbance would arise. Austria would intervene: she could not see an archduke in trouble and not come and help him." Fresh wars would inevitably follow on fresh grievances. "If the scheme is the Emperor's own, it is suggested by jealousy of Sardinia and tenderness for the

---

[30] Text in *Lettere*, III, cxcviii.
[31] Ashley, II, 367; Palmerston to Russell, July 6, 1859. [32] *Ibid*, 366.

Pope; but we feel neither of these mental affections, and are not bound to adopt them. The scheme, moreover, throws wholly out of question the wishes of the Italians themselves, and we are asked to propose to the belligerents a parceling out of the nations of Italy, as if we had any authority to dispose of them." [33] To Persigny Palmerston remarked: "What the Emperor proposes does not mean Italy *restored* to herself, but Italy *sold* to Austria." [34]

A few hours later, a telegram from Persigny announcing Palmerston's declination was in Napoleon's hands at Valeggio.[35] Having set his heart on peace, or rather, on an escape from his present difficulties, Napoleon quickly resolved to cut short further suspense by appealing directly to Francis Joseph. Like many men who seem unable to make up their minds, he brooked no delay when once he had made his up. Just as he had declared war because Cavour's superior will drove him to it, so now he sought for peace because he felt himself coerced by events which he could not control. He loved also to startle the world by doing the unexpected thing, and in this case the unexpected seemed to his harassed imagination the most natural way out. So at half past six o'clock that same Wednesday afternoon he summoned Fleury, and sent him with the secret message to Francis Joseph.[36] It was characteristic of Napoleon's nature that, instead of suspending the military operations planned for July 7 until a reply should come to his request, he kept sixty or seventy thousand men in battle array throughout that morning, marching and countermarching in expectation of an attack, which he knew the Austrians had no intention of delivering. This was his way of mystifying his own army and of impressing upon Francis Joseph that, although willing to talk of an armistice, he was thoroughly prepared to go on with the war. But as Francis Joseph gave Fleury his reply before knowing of the French demonstration, he could not have been influenced by it.

In printing the news of the suspension of arms the *Moniteur*

[33] Ashley, II, 366–67. Ollivier, 225.

[34] The play on *rendue* and *vendue* cannot be literally repeated in English.

[35] Martin, IV, 458.   [36] " Have a care, Sire," said Marshal Vaillant, as Napoleon gave his instructions to Fleury; " the armistice means peace." " Marshal," replied the Emperor brusquely, " that is no affair of yours." " But, Sire, you have promised the Italians to free them from the Alps to the Adriatic." " I repeat, that is none of your business." Massari: *Vitt. Em.*, 283–84.

added that it was still impossible to foresee the end of the war:[37] for Napoleon now played the rôle of a victor, who would out of his benevolence, if it suited him, grant peace to the vanquished. At five o'clock on the morning of the 8th the representatives of the three monarchs met at Villafranca, and signed an armistice to expire on August 16. When the *Moniteur* published the terms, it forgot to mention that Della Rocca as well as Vaillant and Hess signed them.[38] The omission, which seemed a mere oversight, was premeditated. During the past few days, Napoleon had held Victor Emanuel off at arms' length, seeing him as little as possible, retiring into his sepulchre of taciturnity, revealing nothing either of Persigny's negotiations in London or of his own intentions.[39] The King, who had an open nature coupled with much astuteness, mulled over the news on the 7th; on the 8th, unable longer to remain in suspense, he went to Valeggio, determined to compel Napoleon to "unbutton" his thoughts. Napoleon did not unbutton, but he knew how to seem expansive towards his ally. He protested that the armistice, being purely military, would in nowise affect their agreements; that he should be glad if Austria, by submitting to his conditions, would allow him to restore peace to Europe; but that his terms were "*so hard, so very hard*" (he repeated these words several times) that he had no expectation that Austria would accept them; the Allies, therefore, must prepare to renew hostilities with a larger host than before. The French must number 200,000 and the Italians 100,000, besides Garibaldi's 12,000 volunteers.[40] Napoleon understood his man, and evidently dropped hints and half-disclosures which Victor Emanuel instinctively filled out to suit his hopes.

Yet the King drove back to Monzambano far from satisfied. He knew of course that Napoleon was keeping something in reserve, and he was enough of an intriguer himself to assume that this something must be most advantageous to the Allies. The belief in Louis Napoleon's extraordinary craft was then almost universal, so that each act of his was regarded merely as a blind to hide some deep-laid plot. When the news spread of Fleury's

---

[37] *Moniteur*, July 8, 1859.   [38] *Moniteur*, July 9, 1859.

[39] As proof of the ignorance in which the Piedmontese were kept, La Marmora on July 8 wrote Cavour that the armistice was being concluded at that moment. "I am utterly unable," he adds, "to find out how and by whom it was proposed." *Lettere*, III, 107.   [40] *Lettere*, III, 411.

night errand to Verona, it was rumored that Francis Joseph had that morning ordered a general attack on the Allied Armies but that his troops refused to fight; whereupon Napoleon, getting wind of Francis Joseph's plight, fired at him the proposal of a truce.[41] In like manner, when the armistice was arranged, it was interpreted as a trick by which Napoleon, the old fox! saved himself the trouble of besieging Verona during the worst month of the summer, and secured an interval for augmenting his forces.[42] The King, as junior partner of a wizard, felt reasonably sure that, although there might be some secrets kept from him, their mutual interests would not suffer. Assembling his chief officers, he described his interview with Napoleon, spoke encouragingly, and ended by bidding the division commanders to take special care to drill the new levies and the chief of ordnance to create new batteries at once.[43] For another thirty-six hours the King and his generals clung to the hope that the truce would help their cause.

On the 9th Napoleon announced the armistice. In an order of the day he told his troops that he was going immediately to Paris, leaving Vaillant in command, but that he would return at the first signal and lead them to fresh glory. That day and the next autograph letters passed between the two Emperors, and when their commissioners had tried in vain to agree upon the preliminaries, Napoleon III requested a personal interview with Francis Joseph. In like manner Napoleon I at Tilsit concluded by word of mouth a treaty with Czar Alexander. What better example for the mimetic nephew to follow? He did not, however, let the result depend wholly on his eloquence, but telegraphed Persigny to urge the British Government to give its moral support to the French demands. Persigny saw Palmerston and Lord John, who were inclined to consent, because the terms which Persigny outlined seemed to them as favorable to the Italians as could be hoped for, unless the French should renew the war and drive the Austrians beyond the Isonzo. But Queen Victoria and Prince Albert, echoing the opinions of King Leopold, who had come to London to work on Austria's behalf, could not approve. The Queen condemned the terms as too vague. England, she pointed

---

[41] *Lettere*, III, 412.
[42] So clear an observer as Dina wrote thus to Chiala, July 10. *Ib.*, 412, n. 3.
[43] *Lettere*, III, 410–12; from Solaroli's diary.

out, had pledged herself to neutrality; by supporting the demands of one of the belligerents she would break this pledge. Victoria added, in one of those clear phrases in which we recognize Albert's inspiration: "She [the Queen] sees no distinction between moral and general support; the moral support of England *is* her support and she ought to be prepared to follow it up." [44] The Ministry upheld the Queen, and Persigny was obliged to telegraph his master that France must get on without British backing. While solicitude for peace was a sufficient reason for Victoria's decision, there is no doubt that her dread of Napoleon III's aggrandizement, which had become almost a mania at Windsor, and her pro-Austrian sympathies, made it easy for her to insist on a neutrality which benefited Austria. Uncle Leopold, whose influence over his niece and nephew was never greater than at this epoch, naturally hoped to rescue for Austria the Lombardo-Venetian Kingdom, over which his daughter's husband, Archduke Maximilian, reigned as Viceroy.

At nine o'clock on the morning of July 11, the two Emperors met at Villafranca, a village which lies about halfway between Valeggio and Verona. The sovereigns and their staffs wore undress uniforms, their escorts were in full dress. Like a flight of gorgeous birds, the hundred picked men of the Guards, the gaily appareled Guides, swept after Napoleon, along the dusty highroad. As Francis Joseph had not yet reached the Guadini Morelli house, the modest dwelling chosen for the conference, Napoleon rode forward a couple of furlongs, and met him more than halfway, accompanied by his troop of Uhlans and Court gendarmes. The escorts stopped; the Emperors cantered up to each other and greeted with friendliest gestures. A few minutes later, they were seated alone in the upper chamber of the Morelli house, while their followers fraternized in the street below, and two guards, one French, one Austrian, stood as sentries outside the door.

Francis Joseph was not twenty-nine years old.[45] His slender person made him seem tall. His features and complexion were commonplace Teutonic, hair and whiskers blond, eyes blue. Although he had escaped that blight of imbecility by which various sons of the House of Hapsburg were expiating the sins of their

[44] *Q. V. L.*, iii, 353; Queen to Russell, July 10, 1859.   [45] Born Aug. 18, 1830.

fathers, his force, whether of intellect or of character, hardly rose above mediocrity. Hoisted into the throne when his crazy uncle had to be removed from it to a madhouse, his strength lay in the fact that he served as buffer for a dozen antagonistic racial and political elements. Other nations have been strong in proportion to their unity; the Austrian Empire lived on its discords. During the early years of his reign, Francis Joseph was dominated by his mother, an imperious, bigoted woman, completely at the beck of the priests. For not even a mess of pottage he had sold his sovereign birth-right in agreeing to the Concordat of 1855. Reaction was his religion, because he had been taught no other. Cardinal Rauscher, not content with making the Pope supreme in Austria, urged the young Emperor to begin the "Holy War" against Piedmont and Liberals in Italy.[46] He believed absolutely that the Almighty made the world in order that the sovereigns of Hapsburg might enjoy by divine right a large portion of it. So a bird that stays its flight on a sea-girt crag, might imagine that the crag was created solely to be its momentary perch. Fond of court splendors, given to the ordinary licentiousness of his rank and time, little addicted to the serious work of government, he was so hemmed in by flatterers that he had no means of testing his own ability. By the simple device of making him suppose that the policy which they suggested originated with himself, prelates, ministers and marshals ran the Clerical, political and military affairs of the Empire for their respective advantage. Yet, so deep-rooted is mankind's trust in the innate goodness of youth, that the public clung to the belief that he could not be cognizant of the mistakes and iniquities of his administration. Amiable in disposition, with less of the Hapsburg hauteur than usual, he would, under ordinary circumstances, have made an excellent royal figure-head; but Fate had sent him on the stage, cast for a leading part in a high tragedy. And now, in the modest best room of Casa Morelli, he was pitted against the reputed arbiter of Europe, the man who by his own efforts had crowned himself Emperor, the politician whose astuteness was regarded as both boundless and successful, the commander who, in five weeks, had driven the armies of Austria from the heart of Piedmont to the Quadrilateral.

[46] Sybel, ii, 370.

Neither Emperor left a report of that interview, but much leaked out, and much has been inferred. At the outset, Napoleon played the chords of magnanimity. He had not come to dictate terms to a conquered foe, but to discuss with a brother monarch how to make a peace that should satisfy both. Like himself, Francis Joseph had been horrified by the carnage at Solferino, and would gladly find an honorable way to prevent more bloodshed. Napoleon seems to have given full value to the probability that the other Great Powers, dreading a general war, would intervene. If they did, it was clear that he and Francis Joseph would do better to settle by themselves, than to have Prussia, England and Russia thrust on them terms they would be forced to accept. On the other hand, if Prussia, for instance, acted as mediator in behalf of Austria, she would unquestionably demand some recompense. Very possibly the elder Emperor, who was all blandness and apparent candor, went further and hinted that by patching up their quarrel, they might divide the mastery of Central and Western Europe between them. The triumph of Prussia would be as damaging to Austria as to France. If Francis Joseph persisted, therefore, and the Germanic Confederation declared war, Austria would suffer. For if in that war France should conquer on the Rhine and on the Po, France would impose whatever conditions she desired on both enemies; if, on the contrary, the Germanic Confederation, led by Prussia, should win, Prussia might be counted upon to humiliate Austria. Whether actually uttered or not, these arguments lay in the foreground of the minds of the two Emperors.

At this point we can imagine that Francis Joseph asked very pertinently, "What does your Majesty propose?" and then Napoleon unfolded the conditions which, he promised Victor Emanuel, should be "*so hard, so very hard*" that Austria would reject them. His apologists imply that he intended to demand the liberation of Lombardy and Venetia, but that the sight of the young Emperor, whose good intentions had been dashed by misfortune, touched his compassion and closed his lips. More probably, Francis Joseph reminded him that, as the Allies had not conquered Venetia, it was idle to suppose that he would surrender it. Napoleon took the hint, and agreed that the Venetians should remain under the Austrian sceptre. Francis Joseph, on his side,

2

would cede Lombardy to Napoleon, who might make it over to Piedmont. The Grand Duke of Tuscany and the Duke of Modena should return to their states, but "without recourse to force." Italy should be united in a confederation under the honorary presidency of the Pope. Both Emperors would request the Holy Father to introduce reforms into his government. Amnesty should be everywhere extended to the revolutionists; and a European congress would ratify the new arrangement. Napoleon seems to have returned more than once to the fate of Venetia, but Francis Joseph naturally repeated that he would not give up territory which he had good reason to believe the Allies could not wrest from him. In England, it was charged afterwards that Napoleon tried to strengthen his case by asserting that he had the moral support of the British Ministry; [47] but if he did resort to this falsehood, which seems unlikely, he gained nothing by it. The young Hapsburg Emperor simply shook his head. During this conference, which lasted an hour, the sovereigns vied with each other in urbanity. Having set a time when he would receive Prince Napoleon to consider a formal draft of the preliminaries, Francis Joseph accompanied the French Emperor a short distance on the way to Valeggio. Then they parted amid most gracious salutations.

With a monstrous load lifted from him, Napoleon III returned to his headquarters. He had secured peace, his supreme desire at that crisis: what mattered the details? He flattered himself that he and not the Austrian had triumphed in the parley. So a year before, at Plombières, he supposed that Cavour was merely a tool in his hands. Beginning with himself, Louis Napoleon had a fatal incapacity for measuring men. He imagined that no one could resist his persuasiveness. During his Imperial career, he had three historic interviews,[48] yet only at the last, when he faced the pitiless Bismarck in the upper room of the peasant's cottage at Donchèry, did he realize that he was beaten.

On his return to Valeggio on that torrid Monday morning in July, Napoleon found Victor Emanuel waiting to hear the proposed terms of peace. The Emperor stated them as favorably as

---

[47] Malmesbury, 500–01.   [48] With Cavour, at Plombières, July 21, 1858; with Francis Joseph at Villafranca, July 11, 1859; with Bismarck, at Donchèry, Sept. 2, 1870, the morning after the disaster of Sedan.

possible, perhaps even too favorably.[49] According to some reports, the King denounced the arrangement as inconclusive and disloyal; according to others, while not concealing his regrets, he assured the Emperor that he was grateful for the benefits received. Early in the afternoon, he rode back heavy-hearted to Monzambano. Napoleon summoned Prince Napoleon, gave him a minute of the treaty, added oral instructions, and sent him to finish the business with Francis Joseph. Since Plon-Plon was no respecter of persons, he might be counted on not to grow tender at the sight of the unfortunate young monarch. But, on the other hand, Plon-Plon was thoroughly disgusted with the war — cynics said that he cooled when he found there was no desire to make a king in Central Italy — and he had been scaring his Imperial cousin with prophecies of disaster.

At half past four the Prince was closeted with Francis Joseph at Verona. They took up the clauses in order. The Emperor had only a tepid interest in the proposed Italian Confederation, but consented to it. He saw no reason for calling the Pope "honorary," instead of actual, president, but yielded. When, however, they reached Paragraph Three, which stated that the French Emperor should transfer Lombardy, in accordance with the vote of its inhabitants, to Piedmont, Francis Joseph asked what that meant. The Prince replied that it was simply the acknowledgment that modern sovereigns derive their authority from the consent of the governed: this was the token by which Napoleon III reigned in France, by which he was waging this war, by which Victor Emanuel ruled. The King of Piedmont did not claim to have conquered Lombardy: he had helped to emancipate the Lombards, and it was for them to show, by popular vote, what they desired. Francis Joseph pertinently pointed out that these were purely the doctrines of the Revolution. Plon-Plon proceeded to argue, but the Emperor cut him short, saying with unintentional humor, "My dear Prince, we are not here to take a course in international law." He would agree to hand Lombardy over to Napoleon, but without mention of popular vote, or of Piedmont. Rather than acknowledge publicly that he would concede anything to Piedmont direct, Francis Joseph would continue the war. A significant avowal!

[49] Castelli: *Ricordi*, 317. The adjutant who rode back with the King at 2.30 P. M. records that the King said the Austrians would cede as far as the Piave.

The next difficulty arose over Peschiera and Mantua. Both fortresses being in Lombard territory, the Prince insisted that they should be given up; but again the Emperor would not yield. They were fortresses, he said, which his army was now actually occupying: they had not been conquered; they should not be sacrificed. Plon-Plon, fully aware that Napoleon III had no intention of pressing this demand, simulated disappointment — and passed on. Paragraph Five declared that the two Emperors should do their utmost, short of resorting to arms, to restore the rulers of Tuscany and Modena, who should offer an amnesty and grant a constitution. Here Francis Joseph balked. "I may make personal sacrifices and give up what belongs to me," he said; "but I cannot abandon kinsmen and allies who have remained loyal to me." The reply rings with chivalry: but the negotiators were concerned with hard facts, not with chivalry or with fine phrases. In the end, they agreed that Leopold and Francis V should return to their states and grant an amnesty; but Francis Joseph would never, never listen to the suggestion of requiring them to promise a constitution. He remarked naïvely that France seemed to him to have not much more of a constitution than Austria had. He consented, however, to the annexation of Parma to Piedmont — for the Duchess was only a Bourbon, not a Hapsburg, and, after all, Parma and Piacenza did not belong to him. So it was easy to be lavish with rights that were not his.

The clock now marked quarter past six. The Emperor rose, professed to be inclined to conclude the treaty, but added that first he must think it over and take counsel. Prince Napoleon dreaded the interference of the military and court cabal. "I am commanded to be at Valeggio at ten o'clock," he told Francis Joseph; "that means that I must leave here not later than a quarter past eight. My sovereign will be most grieved to receive a negative reply. The war in that case would be resumed and the revolution would flood all Italy and perhaps Hungary."

The Prince retired to a room, where dinner had been prepared for him. With characteristic brass, he called out of the window, to his postilions in the courtyard, 'to have his carriage ready at 8.15 sharp.' During the interval, he is said to have heard sounds of a heated discussion — Imperial sobs, even! — between Francis

Joseph and his advisers. At half past seven the Emperor entered the Prince's room and handed him a paper in which the terms of peace were set down precisely as he had stated them earlier. Prince Napoleon read them with apparent chagrin. "I am a poor diplomat," said he. They took up again, briefly, the irreconcilable points, but soon saw that it was hopeless to argue further. The Emperor's only concession was that the Pope should be "honorary" president of the confederation. When he had inserted that word, the Prince begged him to sign the paper. "But will you sign it?" Francis Joseph asked. The Prince replied that he had no authority, but he pledged his word of honor that the document should be restored to Francis Joseph the following morning, with or without Napoleon's signature. The Emperor then signed, remarking as he did so that it was hard to cede his most beautiful province.[50]

Francis Joseph's reasons for consenting to the peace were obvious. He saved his position in the Germanic Confederation; he saved his treasury, already drained very low, from bankruptcy; he ran no further risk of defeats in the field; and he gained a recognized right to dominate in Italy: all at the sacrifice of a single province. "The gist of the thing is," wrote Moltke to his brother, "that Austria had rather give up Lombardy, than see Prussia at the head of Germany." [51]

Punctually at ten o'clock the Prince brought the paper to Napoleon, who read it and in his joy embraced his cousin. Victor Emanuel also read it, but without joy. "Poor Italy!" he is reported to have exclaimed. As the realization of the calamity swept over him he broke forth into protests. He told the Emperor that these were not the terms he had been led to expect; he explained that the outraged Italians might rush to any extreme; he even talked of prosecuting the war alone. "Do so and welcome," replied Napoleon; "but instead of one enemy you might possibly have two." Before taking leave, however, the King grew calm. His Guardian Angel, who inspired him to say the

---

[50] The official account of this interview is in Prince Napoleon's " Les Préliminaires de la Paix, July 11, 1859. Journal de ma Mission à Vérone auprès de l'Empereur d'Autriche." *Revue des Deux Mondes,* Aug. 1, 1909. Bianchi evidently had access to this document for his narrative in *Stor. Doc.,* VIII.

[51] H. von Moltke: *Briefe an seine Mutter und an seiner Brüder* (Berlin, 1891), 163; letter to Adolf, July, 1859.

right word in the great crises of his career, whispered to him now not to forget his obligations for the favors already received. "Whatever may be your Majesty's decision," he said, "I shall keep the liveliest gratitude for what you have done for the independence of my country; and I beg you to believe that in all circumstances you can count on my fidelity."[52] With a copy of the document in his pocket, the King rode back to his quarters at Monzambano to face Cavour.

For forty hours the Piedmontese Prime Minister, like an avenging Fury, had been ranging to and fro between Monzambano and Valeggio. Never was statesman more amazed than he at the treachery of an ally. During the seven weeks of the war he had worked night and day at Turin to send forward troops, arms and supplies; he had furnished transportation, and, in more than one emergency, rations to the French. He knew, of course, that Napoleon frowned on the risings in Central Italy, but he knew also that Napoleon, by contradiction, grumbled because the Italians had not flocked in multitudes to the Allied Armies. Cavour also had been watching the shifting currents of European politics. He saw the Prussian menace on the horizon, but he did not believe that the Prussians would fight. He noted the apparent coolness of the Czar, who disapproved of any revolutionary stir, but he knew that Russia would not forcibly intervene. He rejoiced at the triumph of Palmerston and Russell. Immediately after Magenta, La Marmora seems to have had doubts of the Emperor, which he communicated to Cavour,[53] who did not, however, regard them as alarming. It does not appear that, after Solferino, he made a calm estimate of the time and men the conquest of the Quadrilateral would require. His guiding thought was that Napoleon III was under oath to accomplish a certain task, and that, if he chose, he could accomplish it, let Europe snarl as it might.

While the King was in the field, Cavour had much to complain of. Della Rocca, chief of staff, not only refused to give the War Minister information, but often left his despatches unacknowledged. It was the old antagonism between the professional soldier and the civilian. Della Rocca was a man of many engaging

[52] There is doubt as to when the King said this.
[53] Massari: La Marmora, 235–37.

qualities — handsome, a good comrade, brave, a high-bred aristocrat through and through. He would preserve military etiquette though the heavens fell; at all times, or anywhere, he was the general to lead a parade, or lend dignity to a reception, or take his master's greetings to a passing prince. But he could neither plan nor fight a battle — as the sad blunders at San Martino proved. Whilst he and Cavour had been friendly enough in private, Della Rocca was too uncertain a Liberal to win Cavour's confidence. The King, however, had a strong liking for him. Victor Emanuel was a genuine constitutional monarch, but he never lost, on that account, his preference for great nobles and for soldiers, the traditional props of a throne. Brusque to a fault himself, he looked instinctively for courtly manners in his entourage. Della Rocca's knightly grace pleased him: no doubt, it contrasted only too favourably with Cavour's businesslike despatch. And then Della Rocca was by profession what the King aspired above all things to be — a soldier. Della Rocca could discuss tactics, arms, the commissariat: Della Rocca knew what was considered good form in every General Staff Office in Europe.

Cavour endured the official slights as a patriotic duty. He protested, however, when Della Rocca carried his punctilio so far that he refused to furnish lists of the killed and wounded after each battle, so that the suspense of the multitudes who thronged the Ministry of War for news might be relieved. Not merely the good people of Turin, but the Prime Minister and the Regent had often to wait till the Paris newspapers came, in order to know what the Piedmontese troops were doing. The second day after Magenta, Cavour had actually to telegraph to Napoleon to learn whether the battle had been won or lost. In all his public career, Cavour never submitted to such indignity.[54] Della Rocca will go down in history as the personage who for two months snubbed the greatest statesman of his time, a feat he could not have accomplished without the King's cognizance.[55]

[54] *Lettere*, III, 68, 69, 71, 73, 74, 75, 78, 81, 90, 91–92, 94, 99, 102.

[55] For the other side, see Della Rocca, I, 412–14. Della Rocca also succeeded in chilling the King towards La Marmora. "I talked little or not at all with La Marmora," he says; "I let him go about our quarters at his pleasure, dictating laws or advice more or less heeded, playing the professor now here now there, even with the French, whom he went to teach how to use their rifled cannon. . . . Little by little La Marmora tired of coming to our headquarters, and went to lay

Victor Emanuel had very naturally never forgiven Cavour for the Rosina affair. He was too high-spirited not to find the pressure of so masterful a minister irksome at times; for no monarch likes to appear to be governed by one of his advisers; and Cavour, we surmise, did not always coquette sufficiently with his sovereign's pride. Since the meeting at Plombières, he had inevitably played the part of Jupiter in Piedmont. He it was who had persuaded Napoleon into the alliance, he who had forced the war, he who, besides doing the work of four ministers, was directing the supplies for the army in the field and conducting the negotiations with patriotic insurgents throughout Northern and Central Italy. His enemies accused him of inordinate ambition. In truth, however, he possessed a Titan's capacity for exertion, and since he had prepared every detail, it was logical that he should direct the work to its consummation.

In camp, Victor Emanuel felt relief at being out of range of his taskmaster's eye. The generals of his staff paid proper deference to him, and encouraged him in thinking himself cut out for a great commander. They made merry over the officiousness of the little minister, toiling night and day to keep them fed and equipped. If Cavour suggested a military plan, they treated it as an impertinence — what could a civilian know about war? But if it be not the duty of a war minister to express an opinion on the war for which he is responsible, whose duty is it? On the day after Magenta, when the King was breakfasting with the Emperor, Napoleon said, laughing, that he had received a letter from Cavour begging him not to leave Turin unprotected. "That fellow," said Napoleon, still laughing, and looking at the King, "is always alarmed about Turin. I replied to him that I had ordered the last division I had in Alessandria to come here at once." On this there was a general burst of hilarity. Victor Emanuel said later to his officers, "It serves Cavour right for meddling where he has no business." [56]

The King, properly solicitous that Napoleon III should have no cause to complain of his treatment in Italy, left nothing undone to show respect, even when this involved a slur at Cavour.

down the law elsewhere, where it was not always so easy as with us." *Ibid*, I, 414. The point to be noted is that the chief of staff plumes himself on side-tracking the Piedmontese general who was supposed to know the most about warfare.

[56] Castelli: *Ricordi*, 298; from *Diario inedito*, June 5, 1859.

Perhaps he listened without protest to the Emperor's charge that Cavour's intrigues in the Romagna had fatally complicated the situation. The King was too outspoken and independent by nature, to perceive that his extreme politeness might be interpreted as obsequiousness; accordingly, he was hardly aware that Cavour's efforts during May and June aimed at preventing the ruler of tiny Piedmont from becoming merely the vassal of the mighty Emperor of France. The European cabinets acted almost as if Victor Emanuel were a negligible quantity. When they negotiated, it was with Paris and not with Turin; and they believed that, at the day of settlement, Napoleon would order and the King would obey. They assumed that the Kingdom of Upper Italy, won by French arms, would be in fact, whatever it might pretend to be, merely an appanage of the French Empire. This was what Cavour strove to prevent; this was what his connivance in the patriotic revolutions did prevent. His insistence that the Italians should be their own masters, no matter how deep their cause for gratitude to their French helpers, sprang from the soundest wisdom. Napoleon began to draw away from Cavour as soon as he discovered that there was no possibility, whilst Cavour blocked the way, of turning the results of the war to the direct extension of Imperial influence in Italy. Neither the King at the time nor Italians subsequently recognized the immense service which Cavour rendered in preventing the Imperial ally from becoming their permanent overlord. He knew the risk in the partnership of lamb and lion.[57]

Had Victor Emanuel been in a friendly mood, he might have kept Cavour near him and possibly have checked the peace project; but he was so irritated, that he did not even confide to the minister what Napoleon had read on the eve of Solferino.[58] He had his laugh, instead, over the French and Piedmontese jests at Cavour's officiousness. Cavour would gladly have resigned the Ministry of War, if an efficient successor could have been found.

[57] As long before as Nov. 28, 1858, he wrote Boncompagni: " I too lament the necessity we are in of getting Russia's support. I should prefer the support of England. . . . Deserted by England, how can we help seeking Russia's support? Ought we to trust in Napoleon alone? It would be a grave error. We seek at St. Petersburg the counterpoise that London denies us." *Risorg. Ital.*, April, 1909; II, 308.

[58] La Marmora states, however, that they were about to telegraph to Cavour at 6 A. M. on June 24, when the great battle began. Massari: *La Marmora*, 236.

He applied to Dabormida, but Dabormida refused, although La
Marmora added to his own entreaties the reason, "Cavour has
too many portfolios." [59] La Marmora himself wandered about
headquarters like an unbidden guest, bearing the vague commission of Minister in the Field. By rights, being the most experienced soldier in Piedmont, he ought to have led the army: in
fact, however, he might speak if the King asked his opinion, but
he had no real responsibility, and his proud and punctilious
spirit chafed at being outranked by Della Rocca, who, until the
campaign opened, had been his subordinate.

Despite these incidents, which have their counterparts in every
war, Cavour never expected that Napoleon would dare to fall
short of his promise. He was irritated rather than alarmed by
the apparent lethargy which followed the victory of Solferino.
He himself was redoubling his efforts, and during the first week
in July he conferred with Kossuth, who had just met the Emperor and Prince Napoleon (July 3). The Emperor virtually told
Kossuth to go ahead and fire the revolution in Hungary, so as to
draw part of the Austrian forces out of Italy. It was on July 5
that Cavour, who at last began to suspect that European diplomacy might impose a "half-peace," urged Kossuth to organize without delay a Magyar troop of volunteers, to fight in the
King's army. "That will compromise us," he said, "and I desire
that we be compromised; for then there will be no half-peace." [60]
The very next afternoon, Napoleon sent Fleury to Verona to
request the armistice. News of this mission reached Cavour,
by way of Paris, on the 8th,[61] the day on which La Marmora
sent his laconic despatch.[62] The following morning brought
a telegram from Prince Napoleon announcing the signing of
the armistice. Cavour summoned his confidential secretary,
Nigra, told him the message, and asked, "What do you think
of it?" "This means peace," Nigra replied. "Do you really
believe that?" said Cavour, searchingly. "Yes." "Then we
will start for the camp," Cavour said. There might yet be
time.

At half-past six that evening, he, Nigra and Alessandro Bixio
took train; at daybreak the next morning they got out at

[59] *Lettere*, III, 94, n. 1; La Marmora to Dabormida, June 10, 1859.
[60] *Lettere*, III, clxxxvi–cxci.   [61] *Lettere*, III, 107.   [62] *Lettere*, VI, 412, n. 1.

Desenzano. While they were waiting there for a carriage, they learned from the bystanders' talk that the two Emperors were to meet that very day and arrange for peace. Cavour's impatience grew insupportable. At last a wretched vehicle was found, and in it he drove over the weary road to Monzambano, through the valleys and across the uplands where the Piedmontese had fought their battle less than three weeks before. "Are you the great Cavour?" the rustic coachman inquired. "Hurry up! hurry up!" was the only answer. When Cavour landed in the square of Monzambano, it seemed as if "a tempest were roaring within him"; he had no jovial smile, not even a word of greeting for Arrivabene and the officers who chanced to be there. He asked where the King was. "At his quarters, in Villa Melchiorri outside the town." To Villa Melchiorri accordingly Cavour and Nigra hastened.

The interview between the Minister and the King lasted two hours. Only shreds of their talk, like the mutterings of a thunderstorm, have been reported. It was one of those moments when titles, rank, and all the social accidents whereby men ordinarily hide their common origin drop away. King and Minister faced each other as man to man. Cavour was nearly overwhelmed by the realization that peace would blast irretrievably the hopes of the Italians. It might mean also the end of Piedmont's leadership, if Piedmont, by acquiescing, became a party to the treachery. What could the King or his Government reply to their people when they asked whether this were a fair return for the heavy taxes they had borne for many years, for the losses by invasion, for the thousands of sons killed and wounded in the war? To his own dashed hopes, and the stigma of bad faith which he knew would be branded on him, he felt the added sting of wasted opportunities. The statesman in him rebelled at the thought of throwing away, on the eve of accomplishment, the labors of a lifetime. And how could the King pacify his subjects when the day came to surrender Nice and Savoy? It was Cavour who had persuaded Victor Emanuel to make that bargain — Cavour who was now dishonored in the eyes of his master, as he must soon be before the world. He would not believe that it was too late to stop Napoleon. Victor Emanuel, to whom the odious probability of peace was already three days old, rehearsed the reasons which the Emperor had given. Cavour tore them to pieces, one by one: as his rage mounted, they seemed less and less worth considering. He besought the King to prosecute the war alone — to prove to the Italians that he was honorable — to win, possibly, the great stake they were fighting for — to fall, if it must be, with reputation unsullied. The King offered obvious objections. Cavour grew insolent. "Calm yourself; remember that I am the King." "I am the real King," Cavour shouted, beside himself; "the Italians recognize me first of all!" "What do you say? *You the King? You are a rogue!*" replied Victor Emanuel, and turned his back on him.[63] As soon as Cavour, still raging, left the room, Victor Emanuel summoned Della Rocca and said: "Do you know what Cavour wants? He wants me to continue the war alone; I am as furious as he over this peace, but I don't lose my compass, I don't lose my reason."[64]

As a last resort, Cavour sought an audience of the Emperor, but Napoleon would not see him. Napoleon too evidently feared to meet the terrible little man who had hypnotized him at Plombières and had forced him in March to stand true to his promise. "A talk under actual conditions can be of no use," he said. "The Count wishes to heap reproaches on me; I have plenty to make to him, but it will do no good, for everything is now settled. I will see him willingly at Milan, on condition that he does not speak to me about the past."[65] Napoleon was, indeed, bent on making Cavour the scapegoat for his own action: for he told Dr. Conneau and others how badly Cavour had behaved,[66] and he complained to the King that Cavour's meddling in the Romagna was a reason and an excuse for stopping the war.[67] It was by Napoleon's express order that the King failed to summon Cavour to headquarters. An honorable ally would have consulted his partner before taking a step which might be fatal to

---

[63] I quote this stock anecdote from Canini's *Bricciole di Storia;* but nobody has verified it.   [64] *Lettere,* vi, 413. Della Rocca says that the King told him that, at a certain point, feeling that he should lose his self-control, he turned his back on Cavour and left the room. Della Rocca, i, 472.

[65] *Stor. Doc.,* viii, 159. Della Rocca, i, 478, repeats the camp rumor that the Emperor did receive Cavour at Valeggio; and he quotes, in evidence, Robilant's diary; but Robilant was at Monzambano and merely recorded current gossip.

[66] *Lettere,* vi, 414.   [67] *Lettere,* vi, 417. The King said to Solaroli on July 12: "Napoleon says he has reason for grievances against Cavour, but ought he to sacrifice a nation for a man?"

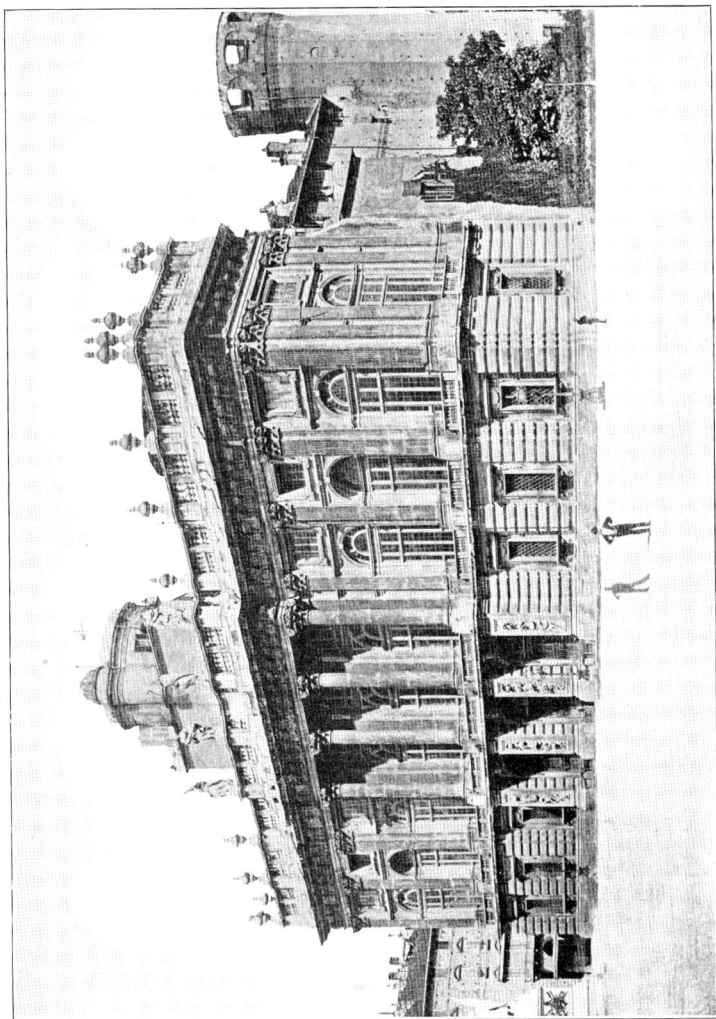

PALAZZO MADAMA, TURIN

The building beyond is part of the Ministry of State

both; and that partner, being a constitutional monarch, would have sent for his prime minister: [68] but Napoleon III, treating Victor Emanuel like a vassal, kept at a distance the one man whom he feared. Had Cavour been cheaply vain, he might have gloried in this proof of his own importance: but it only increased his exasperation; and it is not impossible that he hurled this also at the King in their distressing interview.

Shut out from the Emperor, Cavour attacked Prince Napoleon and stated to him over and over again why the peace would be shameful. Plon-Plon returned volley for volley, now insisting on the danger to France in continuing the war, and now vilifying the Italians. The arguments and sarcasms of his angry visitor goaded Plon-Plon, always noted for his unbridled tongue, to unusual license. He would admit nothing favorable to the Italians, until at last Cavour said to him ironically, "Ah, Monsignor, when one wants to drown a dog, one says that it is mad."[69] "But after all do you wish us to sacrifice France and our own dynasty for you?" asked Plon-Plon angrily. "Promises are promises and must be kept," Cavour replied, as inflexible as Cato. He threatened to head a revolution rather than leave the work half done.[70]

How Cavour passed the rest of July 10, and how he spent the next day, is not recorded in detail. We have glimpses of him, darting to and fro like a Fury, sleepless, preternaturally excited, now stifling his emotions, now arguing or urging with all the vigor of his intellect, now denouncing with the combined vehemence of his wrath, chagrin and regret. To La Marmora, his closest friend in the army, he hinted that, if other means failed, they ought to resort to revolution. La Marmora, who had not lost his compass, replied that England would support them even if France should desert them: and he did not hesitate to tell Cavour that he was crazy in advising the King not to accept Lombardy.[71] Any hope Cavour may have had that Francis Joseph and Napoleon would clash over the terms of peace, was soon quenched. Late in the evening of Thursday, July 11, he went again to Villa Melchiorri. Towards midnight the King, escorted by Nigra and

---

[68] La Gorce regards it as proper that Napoleon should play this trick on the King and Cavour: but would he be equally pleased if England had treated France in this way in the Crimea?   [69] *Lettere*, VI, 414.

[70] Della Rocca, I, 473.   [71] Massari; *La Marmora*, 239.

General Solaroli, returned from Valeggio. "We are ruined," said the King to Solaroli, on their way back. "They gave us more in 1848, when we were alone, than today! They intend to give us only the line of the Mincio — without Mantua and Peschiera, and without the Duchy of Modena! Napoleon has allowed himself to be softened by the young Emperor; he yields everything, because he says his interests no longer permit him to make war!" [72]

As soon as the King reached his private study, he sent for Cavour and Nigra. The heat, even at midnight, was intense. Victor Emanuel took off his coat, lighted a cigar, and sat with bare elbows propped on the table. His face, always ruddy, was flaming. Cavour stood at his left, Nigra leaned against the wall in front. By the King's command, Nigra handed Cavour a copy of the preliminaries. At a glance, Cavour saw the general tenor of the paper, which he threw down on the table. Then he burst forth into an impassioned protest and appeal: "Sire!" he said, "to what end keep the Subalpine throne, to what serves even the annexation of Lombardy, if all Italy continues under the political and military supremacy of Austria? How can you leave Naples and Sicily to the Bourbons, with Emilia, Tuscany, Romagna oscillating between the formation of ephemeral republics and the return of their old rulers? Rather than bow the head to the new terms, let your Majesty listen to the voice of his heart. Try the contest once again with only your own forces, and if fortune is again unfavorable, retire sooner to Sardinia, or wander through Italy and Europe. Let the Italians understand that your dynasty has henceforth no other future, no other hopes than the future and hopes of Italy!" [73] This he said, and much more — much that the King approved in his soul, but that, addressed to him by a subject, he found insolent. The King's instinct, however, was a safer guide than the Minister's rage. Better the half-loaf than no bread: better the infamous treaty, which freed Lombardy, than war single-handed, which might wipe out even Piedmont. Unable to shake the King's resolution, Cavour announced that he resigned, and turned to go. "Take him off to sleep," said

[72] Castelli: *Ricordi*, 317.   [73] I. Artom: *Vittorio Emanuele e la politica estera*. (Bologna, 1882.) Artom has evidently crystallized in literary form what must have been a much longer, impulsive exhortation.

the King to La Marmora, who was waiting in the villa; "he needs rest." [74]

Throughout these distressing scenes Victor Emanuel held himself in with unexpected forbearance. Grant that he had allowed unwarranted slights to be put upon Cavour during the campaign, still he could with truth say that it was Cavour who led him into the war which had plunged them so abruptly into this pit of shame. And after all, a king is not king to be rebuked point-blank by any of his servants. They had another interview at seven o'clock the next morning, but neither had changed his mind, and another storm threatened. "Cavour behaved very badly with me," Victor Emanuel said to Solaroli; "he was almost insolent. But I pity him, because for some time past his head has been whirling. . . . I have been wrong in following his advice too much. But I shall find other friends." [75]

Still Cavour's words — fiery, insolent, unreasonable, though they seemed, as he poured them out — sank into the King's soul; and that forenoon (July 12) La Marmora was despatched to Valeggio to inform Napoleon of the King's great repugnance to signing the preliminaries. "After a very long interview," says La Marmora, "it was agreed with the Emperor that the King should sign only for that which concerned him. This phrase, 'for what concerns me,' is what saved us," says La Marmora, "and allowed us to do all that was done afterwards." [76]

On La Marmora's return from Valeggio, Cavour exchanged a few words with him, and then, accompanied by the faithful Nigra, he drove back to Desenzano, and took the evening express for Turin. The strain of those four terrific days and nights told at last on his wonderful endurance and he fell asleep. As the train drew into the station at Milan, a crowd had gathered to cheer him for his desperate efforts in behalf of Italian independence: but when they saw him sleeping in his carriage, they made no sound. Before daybreak on the 13th, "beaten down in morale, but trusting still in the destiny of Italy," he reached Turin: "in three days aged by many years." [77]

[74] *Corriere della Sera*, July 10, 1908; L. Minguzzi. Della Rocca, I.

[75] Castelli: *Ricordi*, 318–19. *Lettere*, VI, 416–17.

[76] Massari: *La Marmora*, 238. *Lettere*, III, ccxx.

[77] Artom, cited by Chiala: *Lettere* III, ccxxi. See also Arrivabene, I, chap. 13, for notes made on the spot during this crisis.

At their headquarters, the monarchs' business was soon de-spatched. Victor Emanuel signed the preliminaries, adding the saving clause, "for what concerns me." Napoleon, light of heart, spent the 13th at Desenzano, where he fished from the balcony of his hotel.[78] He was rowed over to beautiful Sermione, where the local doctor, Forgioli, told him that "Napoleon I also visited the Scaliger Castle after the Peace of Campoformio." [79] Systemat-ically imitative of his uncle, the nephew here unwittingly blun-dered into imitation. But the parallel between Campoformio and Villafranca was too close to be overlooked by the Italians. As soon as the terms of the compact were published, they could think of but one explanation — betrayal. What was at first a fearful suspicion quickly became a conviction; and, even in later years, when the facts were known, this conviction prevented them from weighing calmly the reasons which compelled Napoleon to stop the war before freeing Italy from the Alps to the Adriatic. In Milan, on his homeward journey, he received an apparently genuine welcome, for the Milanese, at least, had every reason to regard him as their liberator. But when he came to Turin he met an arctic chill. In the shop-windows his portrait had been dis-placed by Orsini's. A troop of French cavalry reinforced the Pied-montese regiments that guarded him. The multitudes in the streets cheered the King with a will, but their voices sank when they gave perfunctory hurrahs for the Emperor.[80] As a new Minis-try had not yet been formed, Cavour and his colleagues awaited their majesties at the station, but he merely bowed, a correctly official bow, to the Emperor, and he did not attend the court ban-quet. Later in the evening, Napoleon sent for him and they had a brief conversation, at which a stranger might have found it hard to distinguish the "victor of Villafranca" from the "vanquished." Napoleon justified the peace on military grounds exclusively. He harped on the immense number of troops — 300,000 or more — required to take Verona. Cavour listened incredulously but refrained from arguing; he only allowed himself to remark on the unhappy fate of the countries abandoned to their former rulers. The Emperor assured him that he would plead their cause in the European Congress; meanwhile, he hinted, the peoples had sim-

[78] The Hôtel de la Poste.   [79] *Lettere*, III, ccxxi.   [80] Even Della Rocca, I, 477, admits that the reception to Napoleon was " very cold."

ply to keep the tyrants from returning.[81] Instead of devoting another day, as he had planned, to receiving showers of gratitude from the Piedmontese, Napoleon was enough of a weather expert to know that the wind did not lie in the right quarter for gratitude, and so he cut short his stay. "You shall pay me the cost of the war," he said to the King, as if pricked with remorse, "and we will think no more of Nice and Savoy." The King accompanied him to Susa, and when he saw the Imperial berline well-started on the Mt. Cenis road, he heaved a deep sigh of relief and exclaimed, "Thank God, he's gone!" This was Saturday, July 16, exactly nine weeks since the Emperor sailed into the flower-strewn harbor of Genoa, to be acclaimed the noblest of benefactors.[82]

The news of Villafranca fell like a thunderbolt at Turin, and when, a few hours later, Cavour's resignation followed, the Piedmontese stood aghast. Cavour took no pains to hide his feelings. We can still hear the savage irony with which he spoke to Count Pasolini of Napoleon: "He would have given up Milan — Turin. *He was tired! the weather was hot!*"[83] More memorable was the interview with Kossuth, at which Pietri, the Emperor's confidant, was present, and remarked that the Emperor would regret greatly that he had resigned. This roused Cavour, who, knowing that his words would reach Napoleon, burst forth: "What would you have? In politics one often compromises on questions as to time and mode of action, sometimes even on principles; but there is one point on which the man of heart never compromises. That is, honor. Your Emperor has dishonoured me." Kossuth, having declared that the French were getting much for little, ridiculed Napoleon's pet plan of the Italian Confederation. "I picture to myself the King of Piedmont in this grotesque company," said he, "in which the Pope presides, with Austria on his right and the four Austrian satellites round him. Victor Emanuel is mediatized, if he accepts this position." "Perfectly right!" Cavour broke in; "but I say to you — and I say it before Monsieur (and speaking before Monsieur is as if I were talking to his Emperor) — this peace will never be made! This treaty will never be executed! If necessary, I will take Solaro della Margherita by one

[81] *Lettere*, III, 110–11; C. to La Marmora, July 16, 1859.
[82] Castelli: *Ricordi*, 323.   [83] Pasolini, 237.

2

hand, and Mazzini by the other. I will turn conspirator! [Striking his breast.] I will become a revolutionist! But this treaty shall not be carried out. No, a thousand times no! Never, never! . . . The Emperor of the French departs. Let him go. But you and I, M. Kossuth, remain. We two will do what the Emperor of the French did not dare to accomplish. By God! *we* will not stop half way!"[84]

This was not merely unreasoning anger venting itself: it was the conviction of Cavour's inmost soul that the gates of hell itself should not prevail against Italy's redemption. Compared with that supreme end, the distinctions between Black and Red faded away. Not only in wine but in agony may a man's true nature be revealed.

It required until July 19 to form a ministry. The King summoned Francesco Arese, a high-minded, patriotic Lombard, who had the advantage of being the intimate friend of Napoleon III; but he lacked the stuff of which even stop-gap premiers are made. Finally, Alfonso La Marmora took the presidency, with Rattazzi, the King's favorite, Minister of the Interior, and Dabormida, a safe, routine man, in charge of foreign affairs. In the few days intervening, Cavour foreshadowed the policy which he believed would save Central Italy. His last instructions as *minister* to the Royal Commissioners at Modena, Bologna, Parma and Florence were to retire; as *simple citizen*, he bade them stay. When Farini telegraphed from Modena for orders, saying that he would compromise neither the government "nor the future," Cavour replied: "The minister is dead. The friend grasps your hand and applauds the decision you have taken."[85] To Pallieri he telegraphed: "Parma must remain annexed to Piedmont. Have the oath administered, and act with the greatest energy."[86] He told Massimo d'Azeglio at Bologna to pursue his own way, regardless of the treaty, regardless of threats and lures. He urged the Tuscans to organize at once a Liberal government, resolved to resist pressure of every kind, and looking to a union

---

[84] Kossuth: *Souvenirs*. Chiala; *Politica Segreta*, Turin, 1895, 61–62.

[85] *Lettere*, III, 112; Farini to C., July 16; C. to Farini, July 17. On July 15 Farini telegraphed: "Be warned that if the Duke, relying on agreements of which I am ignorant, makes any attempt, I shall treat him as an enemy of the King and country. I shall allow myself to be driven out by nobody, though it were to cost me my life." *Ibid*, 109.   [86] *Lettere*, III, 108; C. to Pallieri, July 13.

with Piedmont.[87] He sent Frapolli, a Republican leader, to aid Farini at Modena; and when Malmussi, president of the Modenese Assembly, called and asked him for arms, Cavour exclaimed, "Bravo! I am no longer Minister of War, but we will try an experiment. Take this card to the Arsenal, and if they let you have arms, pack them up and be off." [88]

As soon as the new Cabinet was installed, Cavour retired to Leri, to give his successor a free field and to refresh himself, body and mind, after his Herculean labors. It was just a year since he glided unnoticed into Plombières. "Two months ago," writes Massimo d'Azeglio on July 24, "if any one had proposed the following problem: To go to Italy with 200,000 men; to spend half a milliard francs; to gain four battles; to restore to the Italians one of their most beautiful Provinces, — and to come away cursed by them, the problem would have been declared insoluble. Well, it was not; the fact has proved it." [89] Cavour was among those who cursed most bitterly. To the Italians, all that Napoleon had done was as nothing compared with what he had promised to do, with what, they insisted on believing, they might easily have had, if he had been true. He had deceived them in their hope: no material compensation can offset that. They were like a wrecked crew, starving on a raft, to whom a ship came with food and offered to tow them to land: but a gale sprang up and the ship, to save itself, had to cut loose; and as the shipwrecked crew saw it depart, they forgot to be grateful for the food. We must recall the exaltation of hope in which the Italians had been soaring until Villafranca, in order to understand their fury.

Nothing can be clearer now than that Napoleon was justified by the interests of France and of his dynasty in stopping the war. "To serve Italian independence," he told the great dignitaries of France on his return to St. Cloud, "I made war, against the wish of Europe; as soon as the fate of my country seemed to be imperilled, I made peace." [90] Even if the European situation was not actually so threatening as he imagined it — and as to this opinions differ — he was bound to act on the evidence that he had. Why, then, was he followed out of Italy by a tempest

[87] *Lettere*, III, ccxxiii.   [88] *Stor. Doc.*, VIII, 161.
[89] D'Azeglio: *Politique*, 108; D'Azeglio to Rendu, July 24, 1859.
[90] *Moniteur*, July 20, 1859. Also Zini, II, ii, 283–84.

of imprecations instead of blessings? why was the incredible service which Massimo d'Azeglio describes forgotten? why was the
charge of treachery hurled at him? Because he had not been
frank. When he discovered that the revolutions in Central Italy
traversed his plan, he should have warned Victor Emanuel and
Cavour that this new condition would warrant him in breaking
his compact. Later, when the military task seemed gigantic and
he thought a war with Germany imminent, he ought to have
spoken out honestly. Instead of that, like a sneak he went about
to make peace without taking his ally into his confidence, and
having failed in one intrigue after another, he secretly appealed
to the Austrian Emperor and concluded terms with him. Having
kept Victor Emanuel in the dark up to the last moment, he forbade him to summon his prime minister for consultation. Then
he exploded the terms of peace, as Orsini had thrown his bomb,
and resented that the Italians were stunned and wounded. If
this disingenuous, not to say underhand, conduct were permis-
sible between allies, — partners in an enterprise involving the fortunes of two nations, — then all faith in the everyday dealings
of man with man would perish from the earth.

We need not charge Napoleon with premeditated deceit, much
less with deliberate treachery. His conduct proceeded fatally
from his nature and environment. He was an incarnation of contradictions. The conflicts and insincerities, which lay side by side
quite harmlessly in his mind, appeared in their true characters,
irreconcilable or mutually destructive, as soon as they became
concrete through action. Except when he struggled for the Imperial crown, he was never thorough. His lack of tenacity was
coupled with timidity or at least with hesitancy. In politics as in
war, a theorist, he was too meticulous over the thousand opposing opinions which flitted across the European horizon. The doctrinaire in him made him anxious to present a plausible front to
each of those opinions. The great man rests on some bedrock of
principle; Napoleon had no bedrock principles; he had only the
uncertain footing of the rider at the circus whose horses face
different ways. In Victor Emanuel, in Cavour, in Garibaldi, in
all the Italians who wrought for Italy in 1859, he had to do with
men inspired by patriotism: what he supposed was a force which
could be turned on or off like water at a faucet, was to them a

principle dearer than life, stronger than death. He had, indeed, broken down the dam behind which for forty years the rising flood of national desire had been pent up. The rush of waters startled him; he foresaw that they might sweep out of his control.

Although Villafranca fell like a calamity on the Italians, the common sense of the King and the wrath of Cavour prevented it from being more than a temporary check. The King remained as the unspotted standard-bearer of the Italian cause. Repudiating the treaty, Cavour embodied in his outburst the anger of all his countrymen, enormously increased his popularity, and saved himself for further service. Napoleon III, in dishonorably concluding the peace without consulting Victor Emanuel and Cavour, unwittingly shielded them from the odium of his action, to achieve in due season the very end which he hoped to avert. But Italians should not forget that it was indeed he who broke down that dam which had rendered stagnant the flood of Italian patriotism. Napoleon III was indeed that Veltro whose coming Dante predicted five centuries and a half before.[91]

[91] Among the multitudes of reasons given to account for Napoleon's suing for peace, besides those already referred to, see Massari: *La Marmora*, 237, and *Vittorio Emanuele*, 282–83; Ollivier, 219–23; Pagani, chap. 8. In Panzani: *Il 1859*, Milan (Treves, 1909), is a readable narrative of these events.

CHAPTER XXVI

RICASOLI

ON July 19, the day when the new Ministry was sworn in at Turin and Cavour retired to Leri, Napoleon III, with his talent for manifestoes, addressed at the Tuileries the chief functionaries of France. Nothing could be more politic than the openness with which, after detailing the splendid victories won for France, he admitted that, though the war might have been continued, the risk would have been too great for the possible gain. Napoleon posed as the benefactor who had freed Lombardy and had, by his moderation, saved Europe from a general war. He took it for granted that the world would recognize his prior right to direct the Italians in their reorganization. Had he not deserved it? Had he not revealed to them at Villafranca the way of their salvation? France had earned laurels by the war: many of her officers had been promoted; and Paris was to have a perpetual reminder of the campaign in a Bridge of Solferino and a Boulevard of Magenta. The Emperor, who had skirted disaster at Valeggio, now seemed more secure than ever in his rôle of arbiter. His prosperity worried Victoria and Albert and caused tingles of anxiety to shoot through all the layers of the British public. Prussia was the most discredited in reputation of the Great Powers;[1] for she had attempted to mediate, but the belligerents had settled their quarrel without her. She could claim that it was their fear of her which spurred them to make peace; but mere claims for the recovery of unacknowledged glory are sterile. The Prussians and the Germans learned that mobilizing army corps and maintaining them inactive for many weeks is expensive. Russia had spent nothing and profited nothing.

Paradoxical though it seemed, Austria was the principal gainer

[1] " Bach" in *Giornale d'Italia*, July 15, 1908, tersely sums up Prussia's situation: " The Prussian policy displeased everyone: France, whose victories she had put a stop to; Austria, who blamed her for defeats; South Germany, who accused her of separating herself; German patriots, who chided her hesitation and incertitude."

by the peace terms, which gave her, legally, that dominant position in Italy which she had held illegally since 1815. Although she would now sit in the diet of the Confederation by virtue of owning Venetia, counting only 2,500,000 inhabitants, she would exercise the authority which belonged to her as an empire of 40 millions. The rulers of the Duchies would be her henchmen. The Pope and the King of Naples, in so far as their existence depended upon preserving reaction, would look to her for support. Against such odds, what could Piedmont do, especially when by joining this confederation she must formally sanction it? To set up the Pope, whose misrule was the recognized shame of Europe, as the president of this motley league, was a diabolical joke. In compensation for the loss of her independent action in Italy, Piedmont was to receive Lombardy; but Lombardy, without Peschiera and Mantua, lay at the mercy of Austrian armies in those fortresses. This was the scheme of salvation which Napoleon III offered for the outraged Italians. It bore his stamp in being a tangle of contradictions: it gave with the right hand and took back with the left. Most certainly, as Cavour declared, that treaty would never be carried out. Did Napoleon intend that it should be carried out? Did he slily weave his tissue of paradoxes so that it could never be used? Was this a makeshift for escaping from a pressing embarrassment? Or was it his way of letting the Italians infer that, though he could not openly support their national movement, he would not interfere with it? Events proved that Napoleon was neither so sly nor so far-seeing as men supposed when they first scrutinized the Villafranca compact.

That Napoleon clung to the chimera of a confederation was due to the doctrinaire in him. He seems to have been fascinated by the idea when Gioberti presented it in grandiose outlines fifteen years before; he returned to it at Plombières; he expounded it brilliantly in La Gueronnière's pamphlet. In insisting upon it now, he affected to be blind to the fact that Austria's inclusion, which he did not originally contemplate, completely changed the condition: for the position of Austria in the Confederation was, as Massimo d'Azeglio said, that of a wolf in the sheepfold. Napoleon's conduct after the battle of Magenta cannot be explained if we suppose that the welfare of Italy was his first concern. All his acts had in view the interests of his Imperial dynasty, of

France or of the Pope. The first two he assumed to be identical, although he could not persuade a growing minority of Frenchmen that they were; the last was the incubus he had rashly shouldered in 1849 and which he could neither throw over now nor placate.[2] As he desired to make no move in Italy which, by exasperating the Pope, would mass the Clericals against himself in France, so he clung to a confederation as a protection against the perils he dreaded in Italian unification. When Marquis Pepoli urged him to allow the insurgent states to unite with Piedmont, the Emperor replied: "If annexation should cross the Apennines, unity would be accomplished, and I will not have unity, I will have independence only. Unity would stir up for me dangers in France itself, on account of the Roman Question; and France would not be pleased to see rise beside her a great nation that might diminish her preponderance."[3]

The success of the Confederation depended on the Pope's accepting the honorary presidency. Napoleon therefore wrote, in his best vein, a letter to Pius, announcing the terms of peace, and expressing the hope of a dutiful son of the Church, that His Holiness would acquiesce. "Brute force," he said, "no longer suffices to solve questions and smooth over difficulties." As a man who knew the needs of his epoch, he besought the Pope to approve of a separate administration for the Legations and for the Marches. Scotland and Ireland, he said, had laws of their own without losing their membership in the British Empire. The glory of Catholicism required that the Pope should preside over the destinies of Italy, just as the Doge of Venice once seemed able by a gesture to raise or calm the billows of the Adriatic. The Emperor gave warning that he should withdraw his troops as soon as Italian affairs were regulated.[4] "It is all very fine to talk about the Doge controlling the billows of the Adriatic," Pius replied, with an apostolic twinkle of the eye; "but I will have none of this confederation or of this lay government . . . The French occupation

[2] Napoleon wrote Victor Emanuel, Oct. 20, 1859: "In assigning to the Holy Father the presidency of the Confederation, we satisfy the religious sentiment of Catholic Europe, we augment the moral influence of the Pope throughout Italy, and that permits him to make concessions conformable to the legitimate desires of the peoples." Zini, ii, ii, 530.

[3] The interview took place at Turin, July 15. *Lettere*, iii, ccxxxviii.

[4] Ollivier, 290; Napoleon III, to Pius IX, July 14, 1859.

is an honor for you rather than a debt for me; if you did not protect me, others gladly would: and, besides, I am organizing an army of my own, so that I shall need no outside help." As to reforms, "*Non possumus.*—We cannot." Reforms and a lay government led straight to damnable heresies. At the utmost, he would render the administrative departments more efficient, if that were necessary, but not until the rebellious provinces humbly submitted to him. If the Emperor is sincere, he concluded, let him publicly utter a single word to check the revolution in my kingdom.[5] Knowing clearly what he wanted, and having decided that any change must threaten his Temporal Power, the Pope had the advantage over Napoleon, who hoped so to juggle events as to make them seem equally favorable to himself, to the Pope and to the Italians. You may use logic to prove that white is black, if you stick to that conclusion: but when you go on to prove black yellow, and then yellow blue, your logic becomes suspiciously pliable. Pio Nono's sharp refusal to be lured into the Confederation, his attitude of no compromise towards reform, and his threat against meddling with the Temporal Power, left the Italians under no delusion as to Papal policy.

In the Homeric poems, the gods watched from Olympus the struggles of the Greeks and Trojans in which, at their pleasure, and without warning, they interfered. A similar situation prevailed in Central Italy during the remainder of the summer and early autumn of 1859: Romagnoles and Modenese, Parmesans and Tuscans, toiled and planned while the Great Powers strove to agree among themselves as to what fate they should send to the pygmies on whom they looked down. The two dramas went on simultaneously, often interlocked but never harmonious: for the Olympians were strangely unable to control the mere mortals whom they regarded as their puppets. Within a fortnight of Villafranca, the European Cabinets realized with alarm that the Italian Question, which they had smothered, side-tracked or dodged since the oldest minister among them was a stripling, was lifting its head against their express commands.

The first shock of Villafranca had not passed away before the Italians of the insurgent States saw that the vague preliminaries left an opening for their own efforts. The old rulers were to be

[5] Ollivier, 291-93.

restored — by whom? By nobody with drawn swords. That excluded Austria singly, or France singly, and implied that the restoration must be achieved, if at all, by European mandate. This, in turn, could be given only after a general congress. But the main thing, as every Italian politician realized, was to secure the present. Every day that the return of the despots could be staved off lessened, or at least seemed to lessen, the likelihood of their returning at all.

The local problem in each of the four States differed from that of its neighbors. Parma and Modena desired immediate fusion with Piedmont, but Modena was menaced by possible attack from the Duke, who waited just across the border, while Parma ran no such risk. The Papal complication, however, had added to the burden of the Romagna. In Tuscany, on the other hand, provincial ties were strongest. When the Rattazzi Ministry took office, therefore, the possible readjustments included the restoration of the old rulers and an Italian Confederation, as outlined in the Villafranca scheme; the creation of a Kingdom of Central Italy; or the annexation of the four States to Piedmont. And in every place three antagonistic causes were competing for mastery — the Reactionist, the Liberal Monarchist, and the Republican.

On July 9, in sending to the Piedmontese commissioners in Milan, Florence, Bologna, Modena and Parma official notice of the armistice, Cavour bade each of them "augment the army with energy and with solicitude." [6] His messages after his resignation struck the keynote of the policy he believed would save the day. At Modena, the post most exposed, Farini was fortunately in control: for he proved himself a man who grew with the emergency. "If the Duke, relying on arguments which I know nothing of, makes any attempt, I treat him as enemy of the King and of the country," he telegraphed. "I will not resign my authority except by the King's order. I will allow no one to drive me out, though it costs me my life." On receiving his official recall, Farini resigned, but was immediately elected dictator by the Modenese,[7] and thenceforth he directed their affairs with remarkable tact and decision. When Pallieri and Massimo

---

[6] *Lettere*, III, 108; July 15.
[7] Proclamations of July 27 and 28 in Zini, II, ii, 305–08.

d'Azeglio, on the other hand, obeyed instructions and returned
to Turin, the people of Parma chose Farini for their dictator,[8]
and the Romagnoles elected Leonetto Cipriani, a man of determination, as their governor general.[9]

Setting one of the noblest examples of moral support recorded
in modern times, England came now to the rescue of Italy: not
entirely, nor suddenly, but validly. The motto of Lord John
Russell and of Palmerston was "Italy for the Italians." Those
statesmen were too genuinely British to dream for a moment
that England could send army or fleet to support a people in
whose concerns British interests were not involved: but they
showed how the moral support of England might be as powerful
as the military support which France had embodied in eight
score thousand soldiers. Palmerston and Lord John had the
great mass of English opinion with them, but they encountered
dangerous opposition in the Queen and Prince Albert. Out of
respect for Victoria in her old age the conflict which took place
during the summer of 1859 between her, inspired by her husband,
and her chief ministers, has been generally passed over by later
English historians with as little comment as possible: but enough
documents have now come to light to enable us to follow the
main course of a struggle on which the future of Italy very truly
depended, and in which Prince Albert's systematic endeavor to
extend the power of the Crown at the expense of the Constitution was frustrated. The Prince Consort did not, of course,
meditate a constitutional overturn, but he knew that the British
system was so elastic that the sovereign might, by tact and determination, gradually exert more influence; and he was himself
too ingrained a German to believe that the ruler of even the
most constitutional of countries should be merely a figurehead.

The Queen, who felt bitterly the defeat of Austria, regarded
Napoleon as a danger to the peace of the world. "He will now
probably cajole Austria as he has done to Russia," she wrote
Lord John on July 12, "and turn her spirit of revenge on Prussia
and Germany — the Emperor's probable next victim. Should
he thus have rendered himself master of the entire Continent,
the time may come for us either to obey or to fight him with terrible odds against us. This has been the Queen's view from the

[8] Zini, ii, ii, 309–10; Aug. 18.   [9] Zini, ii, ii, 302–04; July 28.

beginning of this complication, and events have hitherto wonderfully supported them." [10]   In replying, Lord John remarked that "Napoleon is left, no doubt, in a position of great power. That position has been made for him by allowing him to be the only champion of the people of Italy." [11]   On that same day Palmerston wrote a private letter to Persigny, the French Ambassador in London, in which he trenchantly criticized the peace preliminaries, and declared that "England could never join in so bad an arrangement." "On the contrary," he said, "we might think it our duty to protest emphatically and in the face of Europe against such an enslaving of the peoples of Italy. Austria ought, instead, to be strictly excluded from all meddling, political or military, beyond her frontiers. And if that is not done, nothing is done, and all will need to be begun again in a very short time. . . . Be well assured that if Austria is not carefully excluded from all interference, of every sort, in the affairs of Italy, French blood will have been shed in vain, and the Emperor's glory will be of only short duration." [12]

The Queen and Prince Albert quickly got wind of this letter, which Persigny communicated to the Emperor, the Emperor to Walewski, and Walewski to Cowley. Victoria wrote Palmerston, indulging in justifiable sarcasm at his expense, since it was he, and not herself, who had been deceived into putting trust in the Emperor. She said that she could never share the Prime Minister's "sanguine hopes that the '*coup d'état*' and 'the empire' could be made subservient to the establishment of independent nationalities, and the diffusion of liberty and constitutional government on the Continent." [13]   She laid down the astonishing proposition that as England had not protested against the war she could hardly protest against the peace; [14] absolute neutrality must be England's position until the peace was signed. Her Majesty further advised the Prime Minister not to let it appear that the persecution of Austria was his personal aim.

"Neutrality" had an alluring sound: but in this case the Queen and her husband used it for the unneutral purpose of benefiting Austria. They not only deplored Austria's humiliation, but they

[10] *Q. V. L.*, III, 354.   [11] *Ibid,* 355; July 13.
[12] Ashley, II, 368; Palmerston to Persigny, July 13, 1859.
[13] Martin, IV, 463; Queen to Palmerston, July 18, 1859.   [14] *Ibid.*

feared lest Austria should turn for friendship from them to France. The Austrian Emperor had good reason to curse England's bungling attempts to prevent the war — attempts which simply allowed time for the French to cross the Alps. Victoria herself blamed Prussia both for acting too late, and for restraining the minor German States from aiding Austria early in the campaign.[15] To win back Austria, therefore, the Queen deemed essential. She was most exercised, however, over Palmerston's and Lord John's enthusiasm for Italy, which, she believed, would plunge them, without consulting herself or the Cabinet, into embarrassing engagements. She wished to discipline Palmerston for holding private communications with Persigny or with any other foreign representative: as if every premier in Europe were not having every day unofficial relations with members of the diplomatic corps. Palmerston's reply was characteristic: "If your Majesty's meaning is that Viscount Palmerston is to be debarred from communicating with Foreign Ministers except for the purpose of informing them officially of formal decisions of the British Government, Viscount Palmerston would beg humbly and respectfully to represent to your Majesty that such a curtailment of the proper and constitutional functions of the office which he holds would render it impossible for him to serve your Majesty consistently with his own honour or with advantage to the public interest."[16] Palmerston further denied that he had attempted to persuade Napoleon to break the promise made at Villafranca. The Queen, or Prince Albert behind her, evaded Palmerston's reference to the constitutional rights of a British Prime Minister, only to repeat that Palmerston's letter had not been shown to her. What would the British public, then and always so jealous of foreign meddling, have thought if it had known that the Queen and Prince were constantly sending to the King of the Belgians and to Baron Stockmar secret reports of British political action and unfavorable personal criticism of British ministers?

The Royal couple were hardly more successful in arguing for neutrality. To lay down the law that, between the moment when

[15] *Q. V. L.*, III, 359; Queen to Russell, July 18. Yet in the spring Albert had urged Prussia to play a waiting game; Martin, IV, 382–86, 396–98.

[16] *Q. V. L.*, III, 371; Palmerston to Queen, Sept. 9. On Sept. 5, the Queen wrote also to Russell that his distinction between his official and his private opinion given to a foreign minister was a most dangerous and untenable theory.

two nations declare war and the moment when they sign a peace, no other nation ought to tender suggestions to either of them, was an extraordinary slip on Prince Albert's part. It might at least have seemed sincere, if both the Prince and the Queen had not been working with all their might, until the fall of the Derby Ministry, in behalf of Austria. Up to July 14 even, when the Queen wrote Lord John Russell that she trusted that "we" should ask for "justice and consideration" for "the poor Duchess of Parma,"[17] her Majesty was quite willing to employ England's influence *before* the treaty was signed. But when Palmerston and Russell expressed their opinion that the terms of peace could not bring peace, when they kept repeating that, in the interest of Europe, justice must be done to the Italians, the Queen and Prince Albert accused those statesmen of unwarranted interference. Victoria protested, "above all," "against the principle of England volunteering at this moment the intrusion of a scheme of her own for the redistribution of the territories and Governments of Northern Italy."[18] To this Lord John replied that he never proposed to reverse the principle of non-intervention. "If intervention were to mean giving friendly advice," he wrote, "or even offering mediation, your Majesty's Government from January to May would have pursued a course of intervention, for they were all that time advising Austria, France, Sardinia, and Germany. If by friendly and judicious advice we can prevent a bloody and causeless war in Italy we are bound to give such advice. If we refrain from doing so, we may ultimately be obliged to have recourse to intervention; that is to say, we may have to interfere against the ruthless tyranny of Austria, or the unchained ambition of France. It is with a view to prevent the necessity of intervention that Lord John Russell advises friendly representations."[19]

Lord John's reference to the Tory interference was not relished

[17] *Q. V. L.*, III, 355; Queen to Russell, July 14, 1859.

[18] *Ibid*, 361; Aug. 23, 1859.

[19] *Ibid*, 361; Russell to Queen, Aug. 23, 1859. That same day Palmerston wrote the Queen: "The whole course of the Derby Government, in regard to the matters on which the war turned, was one uninterrupted series of interventions by advice, by opinions, and by censure now addressed to one party and now to another. Whatever may be thought of the judgment which was shown by them, or of the bias by which they were guided, the principle on which they acted was undoubtedly right and proper." *Ibid*, 362–63.

by the Queen, who replied that she was "placed in a position of much difficulty, giving her deep pain." As fast as she objected to one draft sent to her from the Foreign Office, she complained, another came with exactly the same purport.[20] Palmerston went to Osborne, but Victoria refused to talk with him on this burning subject, and referred him to her mentor, Prince Albert.[21] A Cabinet meeting was held, which both sides deemed satisfactory. Lord Granville was secretly furnishing Prince Albert with the views of his chief,[22] and the Queen continued to feel "much pain" at Lord John's action.[23] She accused Palmerston of committing her and the Cabinet without advising with either,[24] and by implication she insisted that until peace was signed, the Cabinet had no right to consider any proposition that might come from France. She also insinuated that Lord John was deceitfully hiding his opinions from his colleagues.[25] A rupture was near. At this point it was that Palmerston wrote in his candid fashion that, if her Majesty meant that the British Prime Minister was to be permitted merely to inform foreign governments of the decisions of the British Government, he could not be a party to such a curtailment of the constitutional functions of his office, and should resign.[26] The Queen and her husband, knowing that in any attempt of the Crown to encroach upon the Constitution, the British Nation would be against them, avoided an open breach. The Queen argued that the Prime Minister had misstated her question, and reminded him how his private remarks to Persigny in early July had been used to "our" disadvantage by Napoleon. Had Palmerston been aware that, as late as May 29, the Queen and Albert wished openly to take sides with Francis Joseph after Austria's first defeats[27] the high-spirited old premier might have spoken in language unadorned with the customary obsequious phrases with which British ministers addressed their sovereign. Consistency is a jewel! The Royal Couple were throughout consistent in their support of Austria.

This side conflict among the Olympians has to be borne in mind while we follow the Italians themselves in working out their

[20] *Q. V. L.* iii, 362.   [21] *Ibid*, 365. On Aug. 26, Albert notes in his diary: "We had, alas, discussions during the day with Lord Palmerston."   [22] *Ibid*, 364-67; Aug. 29, 1859.   [23] *Ibid*, 367; Sept. 5.   [24] *Ibid*, 367, 368, 369. [25] *Ibid*, 369-70; Russell to Queen, Sept. 7.   [26] *Ibid*, 371; Palmerston to Queen, Sept. 9.   [27] Malmesbury, 488; quoted above.

own salvation. The determination of Palmerston and Lord John Russell, in spite of the hostility of Victoria and Albert, swung the great influence of liberty-loving Englishmen to the support of Tuscans and Sicilians struggling to be free. Disinterested in a high sense was the purpose of the English Liberal chiefs, and for that reason they observed with increasing distrust the manœuvres of Napoleon III. On his return to Paris, the Emperor discovered that by his Villafranca makeshift he had escaped from the heat of Lombardy, but not from the Italian Question. The contradictions in his scheme could not be reconciled. Outwardly, he seemed the Arbiter of Italy; in reality, he shrank from uttering a command which the Italians might dare to disobey. The problem of the Pope's Temporal Power spread like a cancer over his plans. The Clericals at home were threatening him with disaster for permitting the Italians to throw down, even temporarily, the Pope's authority in the Romagna, and, just as they had tried to terrorize Victor Emanuel when his wife, mother and brother died, so now they assured the Empress that the Pope's God would punish Napoleon's disregard for the Pope by smiting the little Prince Imperial. Eugénie was a bigot of the Spanish type; the fanatic in her did not need this cruel excitation of the mother's alarm in order to make of her a tireless Papal champion. Except during those periods when she and her husband were estranged, thenceforth until 1870 she dinned into his ears the opinions which her Jesuit advisers had stealthily caused to glide into hers. In the summer of 1859, Eugénie unquestionably expressed the sentiments of the French upper and middle classes when she cursed the dangers which the war had raised. She wrote to Arese: "I wish as *hard as I can* to become Italian. . . . Aren't you afraid that we shall prove to Europe that the trade of Redeemer is a fool's trade?"[28] The ingratitude of the Italians who kept howling "traitor" at the peacemaker of Villafranca might well excuse his resentment: and yet Napoleon let them infer, privately, that they might still count him their friend. Too perplexed to act resolutely, he waited, in the hope that events would of themselves relieve him of the distraction of choosing. Although the French and Austrian envoys had met at Zurich, the treaty was unsigned, a delay which left everything open. The Emperor

[28] Arese, 185; Eugénie to Arese, Aug. 26, 1859.

bethought him of a European congress as the best device for
settling the affairs of Italy: but when he sounded England, the
British Foreign Secretary "replied by objecting to certain provisions of the peace, and supposed intentions of the Powers." [29]
Delegates from every part of Italy besieged the Tuileries, unless
they were headed off on the Quai d'Orsay by Walewski, who kept
urging his master to carry out the Villafranca terms without
further procrastination. Walewski and Eugénie now found an
ally in Plon-Plon, who had not yet recovered from his disgust at
the unmartial and ungrateful Central Italians.

But Napoleon was chiefly troubled by England. The hostility
of the Queen and Court, though unpleasant, was less formidable
than the adverse criticism which reached him indirectly from
Palmerston and Russell. "The people of the Duchies," wrote
Palmerston to Cowley, "have as good a right to change their
rulers as the people of England, France, Belgium, and Sweden;
and the annexation of the Duchies to Piedmont would be an un-
mixed good for Italy, and for France, and for Europe. I hope
Walewski will not sway the mind of the Emperor to make the
enslaving of Italy the end of a drama, which opened with the
declaration, 'Italy free from the Alps to the Adriatic,' and 'l'Italie
rendue à elle-même.' If the Italians are left to themselves all will
go well." [30] Lord John's attitude was not less resolute, nor his
language less candid. "I could not answer . . . in a despatch,"
he wrote privately to Cowley, "for I should use terms of abhorrence and indignation too strong for eyes and ears diplomatic.
The disposal of the Tuscans and Modenese as if they were so
many firkins of butter is somewhat too profligate." [31] It was
because Napoleon knew that the clear-sighted English statesmen
saw the facts as they really were and not as he wished them to
be, that their criticism worried him: for next to propitiating the
French, he aimed at standing well with the English.

Austria waited. Whilst her armies bivouacked in Venetia,
ready at a moment's notice to cross the Po and put down the
revolution, she thought it more discreet to hold back until the
peace was signed than to dash in and cause a general war. More-

[29] Ashley, II, 370; Russell to Palmerston, Sept. 11, 1859.
[30] Ashley, II, 371; Palmerston to Cowley, Aug. 22, 1859.
[31] Walpole: *Russell*, II, 313, n. 1; Russell to Cowley, Sept. 9, 1859.
2

over, the stipulation that the despots should not be restored by force gave Austria pause.

In Piedmont the summer passed amid manifold anxieties. Rattazzi was a vigorous prosecuting attorney, and in many respects he made an able Minister of the Interior in a country where that official interfered in the details of local government more than is salutary under healthy decentralization; but he was no statesman. He could imitate Cavour up to the point where a new combination required a new special handling: then, like the mimic who goes through the motions of a magician, he could produce no magic results.[32] The Ministry had two objects — to keep the goodwill of Napoleon III, and to support, as far as it dared, the aspirations of the revolted provinces. Count Arese, the most intimate of Napoleon's Italian friends, hastened to Saint Cloud on a private mission.[33] He and the son of Queen Hortense had been youths together in Rome. They had shared the retreat of Arenenberg. They had lived together in their young men's visions, during those dark days of the Restoration when conspiracy seemed the only hope of Liberals. Together they had traveled; and after Louis Napoleon's fatuous invasion of Strasburg and banishment to America, Arese crossed the Atlantic and stood on the wharf at New York to greet his astonished friend. It was Damon and Pythias between them. When the ridiculed Bonaparte became Emperor, their old intimacy was strengthened. The finest of Louis Napoleon's traits was his loyalty to his friends, among whom Francesco Arese stood out as the most disinterested. Unlike the crew of brigands and adventurers who exploited the Emperor for their personal gain, he sought nothing for himself. He gave no surer proof of his friendship than in speaking as frankly to the autocrat as in times gone by he had spoken to the comrade.[34] Now, however, Napoleon listened unmoved to his plea for Italy, and replied that he intended to execute to the letter the terms agreed on at Villafranca. He would not hear of uniting Tuscany to Piedmont; he wished the complication in the Romagna to cease before it led to an open quarrel with the Vatican; though he despised the Dukes, he saw

[32] Aspromonte in 1862 and Mentana in 1867 are monuments to Rattazzi's tragic lack of originality in statesmanship.

[33] He reached Saint Cloud Aug. 3; Arese, 198.   [34] Arese, 15–53. This book, one of the best of Italian biographies, should be read entire.

nothing better than for them to return; and in the Duchess of
Parma, either from personal or political motives, he felt a strong
interest. Nevertheless, he did not hint of interfering by force to
put any of them back on the throne.[35]

To Chevalier Desambrois, the Piedmontese plenipotentiary at
Zurich, who had an interview with him on almost the same day
as Arese, the Emperor uttered similar opinions.[36] The prospect
of non-intervention was a sheet-anchor of hope for the Italians
during the next few weeks. "Don't be precipitate," Castelli
wrote Minghetti: "there is no danger of attack, from any quarter."[37] To the delegations from the liberated provinces, Napoleon was non-committal, letting them feel that his personal sympathy for Italy would not blind him to the paramount interests
of France. He neither disguised his abhorrence of the Revolutionists, who, he believed, were foremost in accusing him of betrayal, nor concealed his intention of preventing Austria from supplanting him in the protectorate of Italy. Massimo d'Azeglio
thought, and appearances justified him, that the Emperor wished
to help the Italians, but not beyond the point where they
should be as dependent on him as a vassal on his lord. Imperial
agents visited Emilia and Tuscany with instructions to see what
could be done to restore the old rulers: but they reported that the
impetus towards restoration would never come from within.

While Napoleon still hesitated, trusting fortune to bring the
happy solution which he could not compel, and while Piedmont
desired far more than she dared, the Central Italians went their
own way, just as if there were no Olympians above them. The
conduct of the Romagna, being involved in the coils of the Temporal Power, had the widest international significance: but the
decision of Tuscany exerted the chief influence on the national
destiny. Had the Tuscans taken back the Lorrainese or had they
consented to form the largest element in a separate kingdom, the
redemption of Italy would have been long postponed. That they,
the least aggressive of the Italians, kept a straight course to the
goal was due chiefly to Bettino Ricasoli. His patriotism was of
that simple, intense, unyielding type which we moderns, remem-

---

[35] Arese, 198. La Gorce, III, 144–45.
[36] *Stor. Doc.*, VIII, 191; Desambrois's despatch is dated July 29, 1859.
[37] Castelli: *Carteggio*, I, 204; Castelli to Minghetti, Aug. 11, 1859.

bering Plutarch and forgetting our many modern instances, choose to call antique. At the news of Villafranca, Ricasoli made his will, and, in his own rough expression, "spat upon his life." Rather than yield to any pressure whatsoever, though it were even armed intervention, he would have died. Nay, more: "There was no excess," he wrote long afterward, "which I would not have committed in 1859 and '60, if I had been put to the desperation of losing the Unity of Italy, in which I saw the sole harbor of safety for the future of Italy: I would have killed my daughter, who was my great affection on earth, if she had been an obstacle to achieving the great end towards which so many Italians were straining."[38] Ricasoli preached unity; Ricasoli planned unity; Ricasoli would not be content until, by joining Tuscany to her free and independent neighbors at the North, he had made her a living example of unity. Hitherto, Mazzini had enjoyed a monopoly as champion of Unitarianism. No doubt patriots all over the Peninsula had cherished unity as the final ideal, but in proportion as they were responsible, they had seen the need of waiting. Cavour, for instance, dared to dream at twenty-two that he was to be prime minister of United Italy; but as prime minister of Piedmont he had never been so foolish as to make an open avowal which must have done his cause great harm. Ricasoli, on the other hand, could preach this gospel with impunity, for nobody would impute to him or to Tuscany motives of aggrandizement. Ricasoli would not merge Tuscany in Piedmont; he would say to Piedmont and to the other provinces that they should put off their local names and prejudices and put on the large-natured Italianism.

On August 7 was held the election to the Tuscan Assembly; on the 11th the 172 deputies[39] met in the Hall of the Five Hundred in the Palazzo Vecchio. To Florentines, ever-mindful of their glorious past, it seemed that day as if three centuries and a half had been bridged: for when the clerk read the roll, name after name rang out of the descendants of the men who had made Florence great, and from the walls the faded vestiges of the frescoes designed by Leonardo and Michael Angelo looked down. On the

[38] Gotti, 216–17. [39] List of deputies in Zini II, ii, 358–63. According to Tivaroni's analysis, III, 128, there were 44 patricians, 7 grand-ducal chamberlains, 4 high magistrates, 4 ecclesiastics; the rest were mainly of the upper bourgeoisie; few democrats — a sign that there had been no violence.

dais, among the officers of the Assembly, one figure predominated — that of a man of middle age, strong and bony, with a gaunt, thin face, a scant reddish beard and dark red hair, aquiline nose and piercing black eyes which, from being a little crossed, lent at first almost a sinister expression to the face. But when he spoke, his tone of earnestness and his utter sincerity seemed to illumine his granite features. This man was Bettino Ricasoli, the last of the great barons of Italy. In plain words, he told the story of the past four months during which Tuscany had been governed tranquilly without other force than that which rested on public opinion. He bade the deputies not to be disheartened by the smallness of their state, "because" he said, "there are moments in which even small states may achieve great things. Let us remember that in this hall, mute for three centuries to the voice of liberty, whilst we deal with Tuscan affairs, our thought ought to aim at Italy. The City without the Nation would be today a contradiction. Without clamors and without vainglory, let us say what as Italians we wish to be; and Tuscany will set a great example, and we shall rejoice that we were born in this part of Italy; nor, however events may turn out, will we despair of our beloved country."[40] Ricasoli was no orator, if ability to intoxicate be the test of oratory; his words were a tonic, which his fellow Tuscans had most need of. On August 16, after a motion by Marquis Ginori declaring the House of Lorraine deposed, and after a thrilling speech by Ferdinando Andreucci, 168 deputies marched up to the urn, their hands on their hearts, and cast their secret votes. When the teller counted, there were 168 ayes. With similar unanimity four days later the Assembly voted that "Tuscany should form part of a strong Italian Kingdom under the constitutional sceptre of King Victor Emanuel."[41]

At this juncture Ricasoli was beset from two opposite sides. The patriots of the Duchies and Legations urged Tuscany to enter a confederation of Central Italy, organize a common government and recruit a common army, for mutual protection against outside interference. Ricasoli agreed that the four States should act together, as far as possible, with their purpose

[40] Ricasoli, III, 216–17.
[41] Montanelli, advocate of a Bonapartist kingdom, and Mazzoni, did not vote. For Giorgini's report see Zini, II, ii, 380–88. For Mansi's resolution of Aug. 16, and the form in which it was adopted, *Ibid*, 388.

set towards a union with Piedmont as the indispensable step towards national unification: but he saw the danger of tying the fate of Tuscany and of the Duchies to that of the Legations, entangled in the Papal Question, and he suspected that a central confederation, closely knit together, would be an easier prey, if the French Emperor, for instance, should push his scheme of a Central Italian Kingdom. He hurried forward, therefore, his preparations for fusion with Piedmont.

From another quarter came the menace of an attempt by the Party of Action. Mazzini had stolen back to Italy and was in hiding at Florence. Having predicted before the war that Napoleon would betray Italy and sacrifice Venetia, he could exult that his prophecy was fulfilled.[42] In the confusion, he hoped to regain his leadership of the Revolution, even though he failed to establish his Utopian Republic. There could be no better proof of Ricasoli's self-reliance than the fact that he knew of Mazzini's concealment, consented to it, and himself had intercourse with the Great Conspirator, whom he warned that, if he tried to embroil Tuscany he should depart at short notice; and when that happened, Ricasoli had the courage to apply his warning as if Mazzini were a common incendiary. But during three months Mazzini hid undisturbed in the house of Dolfi, the baker patriot.[43] "To the Centre, to the Centre looking towards the South," was his war cry.[44] He planned to start an insurrection in Umbria, to liberate Perugia, and sweep on to the Abruzzi. Simultaneously, Sicily would rise; probably Naples also.[45] Genoa, Lombardy, the Duchies and Romagna stood on tiptoe for the signal. He professed that so long as the Monarchy fought for Unity he would fight under its banner; but he insisted that as soon as Unity was achieved, the united Nation should decide whether it would be Monarchical or Republican.[46] No one could doubt that he would then work with might and main for a Republic. If we win, he wrote Roselli, "we can speak as Power to Power." The Provisional

[42] Mazzini, x, 331. No one has taken the trouble to count the hundreds of Mazzini's Cassandra warnings which did *not* come true.   [43] Mazzini, x, lxxix. Only Cironi, Gianelli and a few others knew of his presence.   [44] *Ibid*, lxxxii.

[45] He assigned Pilo, Crispi and La Masa to Sicily; Liberati and a few recently released prisoners to Naples; Mario, Campanella, M. Quadrio, Pianciani, Montecchi and others to the Centre. *Ibid*, lxxxiii.

[46] *Ibid*, cxxix. See also his program in his letter "To Genoese Friends" (64–66), and most of his articles in vol. x.

BETTINO RICASOLI

Governments, he insinuated, had not backbone enough to resist the first drastic threat: they would simply issue a protest, and then submit to the Restoration, in order to save their cities from useless bloodshed. White-livered Piedmont, having allowed them to offer annexation, would refuse it, from fear of France; but would cite as a precedent afterwards that "those populations in 1859 gave themselves to us."[47] In a letter postmarked "Pistoja, 26 August, 1859," Mazzini assured Ricasoli, that for a year past he had not talked of a republic, and that, while protesting against the immoral alliance with French Imperial despotism,[48] he and his friends had accepted the Monarchy, provided that it meant honestly to work for unity. "I am, was, and shall be before everything, Unitarian."[49] His professed acceptance of the Monarchy could hardly be called zealous.

Ricasoli drew up a remarkable set of maxims to guide the Tuscan officials, and on this document Mazzini jotted down a not less remarkable series of comments. Ricasoli insisted that above all things order must be preserved, so that the Great Powers could have no excuse for interfering. Mazzini rejoined that the Italians ought no longer to wait servilely on the Great Powers, but to act for themselves as they saw fit. Tuscany, he declared, should display not only internal orderliness but external energy, and lead in extending freedom through the States of the Church and the Two Sicilies. He painted the chances of success in rainbow colors. But, by a strange lapse from his doctrinaire consistency, he said that, to avoid collisions, Rome should not for the present be included in the enterprise. This unwitting acknowledgment that there might be facts which even the Coryphæus of Republican visions ought to respect, passed almost unnoticed, however, amid his description of the auspicious situation. Austria, he asserted, was politically, militarily and financially unable to interfere; if she should move, Piedmont and Lombardy would be more than a match for her. Prussia and Germany held Louis Napoleon in check. Russia was

---

[47] Ricasoli, III, 225, n. 2; Mazzini to Roselli, Aug. 15, 1859.

[48] *Ibid*, 232; Mazzini to Ricasoli, Aug. 22, 1859; also printed in Mazzini, x, xciii. He used to say, that to expose Italy to the intervention and malefic influence of L. Napoleon was a crime similar to that of a man who should infect a young life with a mortal disease. *Ibid*, x, xviii, n. 2.

[49] Mazzini, x, xc; Mazzini to Ricasoli, Aug. 22, 1859.

not worth talking about. Twenty million Italians in a state of latent revolution were a power — they needed only some flaming beacon, like the liberation of Perugia, to rise up in their might. Hard-headed Ricasoli, however, persisted in declaring that any violation of the Pope's territory would enrage Catholic Europe; that the duty of Tuscany was to refrain from a war of expansion, however patriotic its aims ; and that Mazzinians and Reactionists were equally dangerous.[50] Although Mazzini staid on in Florence till November,[51] Ricasoli did not bend. He was not sorry, apparently, to have the Apostle infuse virile precepts, especially the doctrine of unity, into the doubting masses; but, on getting evidence that Mazzini was instigating a raid into Umbria, he sent him off with short shrift.[52] The arrogance with which Mazzini took credit for the new situation, which had, in fact, been brought about first by the Franco-Piedmontese alliance and next by the National Society and by thousands of former Mazzinians who had abandoned him, was as humorous as his pretense of still being the recognized leader of the twenty millions of latent revolutionists. Prophets have short memories; indeed, to practice their calling successfully they require no memory at all.

With sure instinct, Ricasoli wished to hasten the welding of Tuscany to Piedmont: that accomplished, whatever the Great Powers proposed must apply to both partners; that accomplished, Modena and Parma, if not the Legations also, would join the Union. Ricasoli had overcome the reluctance of the Tuscan autonomists and, as the vote of August 20 showed, the deputies were practically unanimous for annexation. But France frowned upon it. At Paris, Count Walewski stoutly obstructed every desire of the Italians. He told Peruzzi, the Tuscan suppliant, that though the war lasted five years France would never consent to the union. When Peruzzi suggested that, if the legitimate aspirations of the sober classes were thwarted, Mazzini would triumph, Walewski replied: "We fear Mazzini when he sends out his murderers from London; in Italy he does not frighten us."[53] A month later, at the end of August, Walewski talked even more

---

[50] Ricasoli, III, 257–64; dated Sept. 1, 1859.

[51] Mazzini, x, lxxxix; Piero Cironi and Andrea Gianelli acted as his chief agents.   [52] Saffi implies that Mazzini went of his own accord. Mazzini, x, cvii.

[53] *Stor. Doc.*, VIII, 200; Peruzzi to Ricasoli, Aug. 2, 1859.

brutally to Peruzzi, declaring that there was no government but only a faction in Florence, and giving warning that if Piedmont continued to meddle in Central Italy, France and Austria would sign the Peace of Zurich without her, and would put it in operation.[54]

Unterrified by Walewski's hostility, Ricasoli and the Tuscans made a formal offer of their State to Piedmont. On September 3, Victor Emanuel received their deputation.[55] He gave them, however, only a guarded reply, in which, instead of accepting Tuscany, he promised to champion her cause at Zurich and with Napoleon III.[56] After the formal meeting, the King talked in his habitually outspoken fashion to the delegates, and let them understand, though they did not need such proof, how heartily he regretted that he could not annex Tuscany forthwith.[57] The official speech in nowise expressed what either the Government or the people felt. From the moment the deputation left Florence until it returned, it was overwhelmed with affectionate demonstrations. The sedate Piedmontese greeted the Tuscans as brothers, as Italians. There was a continuous rivalry of racial and patriotic outbursts. At Genoa not less than at Turin, banquets and receptions, with glowing speeches, went on indoors, while outside there were illuminations, arches, showers of bouquets and cheering from the joy-stimulated multitudes. It was impossible to show more enthusiasm, wrote Constance d'Azeglio, "without going into convulsions." [58] The envoys, overcome with emotion, could not speak when they appeared on the balcony of their hotel.[59] The two peoples had united, let Diplomacy say what it would. At Florence, the discerning read between the lines of the King's speech. The arms of Savoy were raised on the Pitti Palace and on the Palazzo Vecchio, and the Government tacitly acted as if it had the Royal authority behind it. Talk of a regent, until the King could prudently assume control, began to be heard.

[54] *Stor. Doc.*, VIII, 201; Peruzzi's despatches of Sept. 3. Peruzzi's letters are printed in Zini, II, ii, 321–44.

[55] The deputation consisted of Count Ugolino della Gherardesca, Count Scipione Borghese, Dr. Rinaldo Ruschi, Professor G. B. Giorgini, and the banker, Adama.

[56] Tuscan address and King's reply in Zini, II, ii, 474–75.

[57] Giorgini describes audience in letter of Sept. 3, to Ricasoli; Ricasoli, III, 269.   [58] C. d'Azeglio, 617.   [59] Hôtel d'Europe, Piazza di Castello, Turin.

Napoleon III, however, would not take a resolute stand.
Officially, he professed his loyalty to the Villafranca agreement;
and whilst he allowed Walewski to thunder away against the
Italians, he privately assured them that he was their steadfast
friend. When the approaching visit of the Tuscan delegation
threw the Cabinet at Turin into a tremor, Count Arese hurried
to St. Sauveur to draw from the Emperor a hint as to how the
Ministers should act. He advised the greatest circumspection:
hence Victor Emanuel's Delphic reply to the Tuscans. Yet Napoleon declared to Arese: "I hope that after all the peace of Villafranca will have freed Italy: this is the dearest of my wishes." [60]
At the same moment, he was urging Victor Emanuel to consent
to the restoration of the Grand Duke, which Austria made the
condition antecedent to granting "very generous terms" to the
Venetians. To the alternative, "either the Grand Duke at Florence, or Austria armed to the teeth on the Po," the King replied,
truly enough, that the restoration did not depend on him, and
that Austria, though armed to the teeth, could do nothing, because Napoleon III would not permit intervention. [61] While Napoleon was still assuring the Austrians that he intended to carry
out the peace preliminaries with almost absolute precision, he was
writing the British Government that he would forcibly stop the
return of the despots. He had supposed, he said, that they would
publish a Liberal program and would be welcomed back with
open arms, but he had deceived himself. From London Persigny
blew a counterblast to Walewski, asserting that he alone knew
and represented the Emperor's real intentions; and that the
strategic move for Central Italians was to force his hand. Persigny went even further and urged that Victor Emanuel should
accept provisionally the offer of annexation, a policy which
England would support, France could not disavow or Austria
prevent. [62] At Florence, at Modena, at Bologna the leaders were
ready to put this policy of audacity to the proof, but at Turin
the ministers took counsel of their prudence. The Emperor
printed in the *Moniteur* of September 9 an adroit statement of his
official position, showing how reasonably he had acted through-

---

[60] Arese, 199; Napoleon to Arese, Sept. 5, 1859.
[61] *Stor. Doc.*, VIII, 217; Napoleon to V. E., Sept. 3 and 4, 1859.
[62] *Stor. Doc.*, VIII, 570–71; E. d'Azeglio, from London, Aug. 22, 25, 27, 1859.

out, both in making peace at Villafranca and in accepting conditions which, if loyally executed, would heal at last the chronic ills of Italy. Only restore the despots, and Utopia would follow: reject them, and a policy of hatred and defiance would revive. He warned the Italians not to expect too much from a European congress: for a congress would grant only what was just — the Emperor's sense of humor failed him here! — and it would not be just to ask Austria to make important concessions without fair compensation. If the Congress failed, war would be the only other method possible: but, he concluded sententiously, "there is only one Power that would make war for an idea: that is France; and France has accomplished her task." [63]

The Central Italians did not allow themselves to be disconcerted by this warning. They assumed that the Emperor was keeping up appearances; at any rate, they would so solidify their new régime that, if either he or Francis Joseph should decide later to interfere, there would be a compact state to resist him. Their military league furnished an army of 25,000 men,[64] who could be massed at any point, and were commanded by General Fanti,[65] the most popular of the regular officers in the recent war. On September 15 the deputations from Modena and Parma were received by Victor Emanuel with the non-committal welcome he had given the Tuscans. On their heels came the Emilians.[66] The Italians had spoken out their wishes boldly. Europe, except that part of it that was struggling to restore the Restoration, admired the orderliness and the shrewdness, the foresight and the courage with which those peoples till recently oppressed by Austrian, Papal and Bourbon despotism governed themselves. Patriots in the Peninsula chafed at Piedmont's reserve. "Madame Potiphar had to do with one Joseph, but Central Italy has six of them," remarked Massimo d'Azeglio, when the votes of annexation perplexed the Cabinet at Turin

[63] *Moniteur*, Sept. 9, 1859; reprinted in Zini, II, ii, 501–02; Italian version in Artom, II, 329–34. Napoleon believed at this time that he could persuade Austria to give Venetia a quasi-independent position in the Italian Confederation, like that of Luxemburg in the Germanic Confederation.

[64] See conventions of Tuscany, Modena, Romagna and Parma, dated Aug. 10 and Sept. 3, 1859; Tuscany furnished 10,000 troops, Modena, 4000, Romagna, 7000, Parma, 4000. Zini, II, ii, 310–14; Carandini, 276.   [65] Rattazzi accepted Fanti's resignation from the Piedmontese Army on Aug. 23. Zini, *l. c.*, 314–15.

[66] For addresses and King's replies see Zini, II, ii, 497–501.

with its six members.[67] Nevertheless, though delay was hard to
bear, haste might have brought ruin. The very capacity to
endure the long suspense, which the Italians displayed, had its
effect on the Great Powers, whose envoys at Zurich could still
come to no agreement. The conference dragged on, without conclusion, but not without angry interludes, after one of which the
Austrian and French gentlemen were barely restrained from a
duel. More than two months had elapsed since the Emperors
met at Villafranca, yet nothing was settled, unless it were that
the peace which they had planned could never, as Cavour had
predicted, be executed. In September, Italians were already
hinting that they might profit more by the elastic and abortive
peace than they could have done by prolonging the war. The
principle of non-intervention, unacknowledged in July, was now
practically accepted. Having allowed things to drift, Napoleon
discovered to his anxiety, that the current had set away from
his purposes. Thanks to Ricasoli and to Farini, this current had
thus far flowed safely along the channel they had banked in; but
the waters were rising and threatened to overflow the dykes.

At Turin throughout the summer everybody was conscious of
a void, for the public, like Massimo, put little confidence in Rattazzi and his colleagues. The drama went on, but without its
hero. A great statesman in eclipse is too often either a danger to
his country or a destroyer of his own fame. The world will not
soon forget the sorry spectacle of the dethroned Bismarck, —
the Titan who had lifted the German Empire out of the earth
and borne it for twenty years aloft on his shoulders, — spending
his last years in cursing the mere man who overthrew him. Very
different the dignity of his great forerunner, Stein; very different
the fruitful retirement of Jefferson and John Quincy Adams, and
the noble disdain of Turgot. Happy Mirabeau, happy Pitt,
whom premature death spared the supreme test which too often
shows patriotism to be subordinate to self-love.

Though Cavour resigned in a tempest on July 12, it was not to
evade the consequences of the peace, but to serve Italy best. He
had had too long a discipline to be moved by unpopularity now.
If his continuing in power would have helped the country,

[67] D'Azeglio: *Lettere*, 299.

he would have sacrificed himself; but, as he wrote Emanuel
d'Azeglio, his duty was to retire. "The peace preliminaries," he
said, "have established only a few general points; there remains
a crowd of questions to be decided, either directly with Austria,
or by means of a European congress. Now, before a diplomatic
tribunal, the Italian cause would lose by being pleaded by me.
I am the aversion [*bête noire*] of diplomacy. You had a chance to
convince yourself of this during your last stay in Paris. Walewski detests me for a thousand reasons, and above all because of
the sarcasm and jokes we made with Clarendon during the treaty
of Paris. Cowley has nervous fidgets when he sees me. I think I
should give the Austrian plenipotentiaries a nightmare. In short,
I am the man least likely to obtain concessions from the diplomats. These gentlemen would refuse to me, the man, that which
they might perhaps grant to the country, provided it were represented by some sympathetic personage." [68] "My retirement,"
he explained to Villamarina in Paris, "ought to render your task
less difficult. . . . Make a scapegoat of me in order to regain
the friendship of the French government. That is indispensable
to us, so that the sacrifice of Villafranca may not be consummated at Zurich." [69] Neither pique nor rancor found lodgment
in his spirit. Although no longer in the game himself, he watched
the play with the zest of an expert. We have seen how he gave
the Emilians and Tuscans their cue. Not less vigorously did he
aid in the formation of the new ministry, suggesting men not because they were identified with his policy but because they seemed
the best fitted, in that crisis, to restore harmony. Then, to give
them a clear field, he quitted Turin.

He went first to Leri where he realized, on being free, how
much the burdens and disappointments of the past year had
worn upon him. The Circourts urged him to visit them, and he
would have accepted gladly if Bougival, their country-place,
had been in an out-of-the-way corner of France instead of at the
gates of the capital. If he stopped there, without entering Paris,
he would have the air of sulking. "There is nothing in the world
so ridiculous," he said, "as a fallen minister who sulks, especially
if he is so ill-advised as to sulk in the city above all others in the

[68] Cavour: *Politique*, 351; C. to E. d'Azeglio, July 16, 1859.
[69] *Lettere*, III, 114; C. to Villamarina, July 21, 1859.

world the most mocking and indifferent to misfortune. I was
going into Switzerland — that hospital for the political wounded;
but, as the announcement of the Congress of Zurich might give a
suspicious tinge to my innocent project, I shall confine myself to
Savoy and establish myself at the foot of Mont Blanc, there to
forget, amidst the wonders of nature, the miseries of the affairs
guided by men. . . . Having suffered a startling defeat, it would
for a long time be impossible for me to return to the arena as
general-in-chief; but I am fully decided to fight as a simple soldier under new leaders, who will be, I hope, more fortunate than
I. . . . My cruelest enemy, the *Times*, said the other day:
'*Poor Cavour! he was honest and zealous!*' I ask for no other
testimony or panegyric." [70]

He wrote with perfect sincerity, but with more cheerfulness
than he felt: for having resolved to show the world only courage
and a cheerful face, he guarded against every hint of moping.
Only at Pressinge, with his devoted De La Rives, did he make no
effort to hide his inmost thoughts. "He was not at all crushed,
but in revolt, or absent-minded, preoccupied, sombre, turning
over in his mind the projects destroyed, the combinations of the
battle lost." His appearance revealed the fever of his thoughts.[71]
In a few weeks the change of scene, rest, Swiss air, the robust
sympathy and intellectual stimulus of his Genevan friends, and,
above all, his wonderful temperament, made him in fact what
he had willed to be.[72] From his intimates at home, especially
from Castelli,[73] he heard what was passing there. He would not
thrust his advice on the Ministers, but he let them know that if
they wished to consult him, he would listen gladly; for he
regarded it as a sacred duty to coöperate with all his strength to
render less arduous the undertaking of those who worked in a
spirit of genuine patriotism.[74] "Greet Rattazzi," he wrote
Castelli, "assure him of my concurrence in everything and for
everything. . . . You know that in politics I practise largely
the penultimate precept of the Lord's Prayer. Rattazzi, in accepting the ministry after the peace, displayed courage and patriotism; therefore, he has a right to the support of good and

[70] Circourt, 91–92.   [71] La Rive, 301–02.   [72] *Lettere*, vi, 428; to
Corio.   [73] *Lettere*, vi, 427; C. to Castelli, July 22, 1859.   [74] *Lettere*, iii,
122; C. to Oytana, Aug. 10, 1859.

Liberal citizens; he shall have mine, frank, loyal, energetic. As minister, he shall have me among his followers. As man, I reserve my full liberty of action." [75] Questions came from many quarters. The Central Italians turned instinctively to Cavour, rather than to the Piedmontese Ministers, for counsel. He told the Tuscans to resist to the end the restoration of the Lorrainese, — "better Austria herself than her despised proconsul"; to pass a vote for union with Piedmont; and accept ultimately a plan for creating at Florence a government resting on a broad and liberal base, without any bonds with Austria.[76] "It is well," he wrote Farini, "that the Duchies, Tuscany and the Romagna should mutually help each other; I could wish, however, that you established a perfect solidarity among these states, whose destinies, *at least for the present*, cannot be identical." [77]

Most charming is the sketch which William de La Rive draws of Cavour's weeks of repose in Switzerland. We see that simplicity without which greatness in any field seems an alloy: we see also that straightforwardness which was characteristic of Cavour when he was among his trusted friends. One hot day in early August, he landed at Hermance, on Lake Geneva, and walked with brisk step to De La Rive's cottage. Not finding his friend, he procured a rude farm-cart, on which he jolted up the steep slope to Pressinge, cross-questioning the farmer-driver all the way as to crops, soil, rents, profits, as if agriculture and not the peace of Europe were his absorbing interest. Finding nobody at Pressinge, Cavour walked on to Auguste de La Rive's house, his coat on his arm, his eyes taking in every object far and near. Unannounced, he strode into the drawing-room, embraced the surprised and delighted Professor, threw himself into an easy chair, and asked for a glass of iced water — all as natural as life, but not at all as it used to be the fashion to describe the daily life of great men. To those friends he poured out the story of the catastrophe of Villafranca, but he did not linger long over that. His nature "came back at a gallop" — a sanguine, indomitable nature, which could never be content with futile brooding over the past, but must look forward, measure the new conditions and conjure out of them the results which the past had

---

[75] *Lettere*, III, 119–20; C. to Castelli, Aug. 7, 1859.   [76] *Ibid*, 121; C. to Massari, Aug. 9, 1859.   [77] *Lettere*, VI, 430; C. to Farini, Aug. 10, 1859.

frustrated. All was yarn that came to his loom. Within a week his irritation, not less than his sterile reveries and vain regrets, had passed. "I will not say that Cavour got on his feet again," remarks his loving biographer, "because he had never been beaten down"; but he had recovered his calm judgment which no rancor could long mislead, and with this his penetration and lucidity returned. "We must not look back, but forward!" he told his friends. "We have followed one road — it is blocked — very well, we will follow another. We shall take twenty years to do what might perhaps have been accomplished in a few months. . . . England has thus far done nothing for Italy — it is her turn now. I will busy myself with Naples. They will accuse me of being a revolutionist, but above all we must go ahead, and we will go ahead! They will force me to spend the rest of my life conspiring!" [78] As in his capacity for quickly recovering his normal poise and buoyancy he showed the sanity of his nature, so in his power to face new combinations with a new policy he showed himself master of that Opportunism which has been the secret of the few consummate statesmen in history.

Cavour returned to Turin on the last day of August, having received at Aix and other places [79] significant ovations which assured him of his undiminished popularity. It was of vital importance to Italy that she should not, owing to Villafranca, lose faith in her pilot. At home, where he could not doubt that his influence was greater than ever, he now expressed his opinions, being unofficial, without reserve. To Leri came Cabinet officers, leaders of all political parties, foreign ministers, — Verdi, friends, disciples, — and Cavour banteringly declared himself well satisfied with the very quiet life he led among his cows. Holding annexation to be a question which must wait, he approved of the King's reserve towards it, until the treaty was signed: then, and not before, Piedmont's liberty of action would be untrammeled. But he watched with growing concern the inability of the Cabinet even to seem to act resolutely. Already Napoleon III was beginning to realize that unless the Central Italians were crushed by a force which necessarily must be either French or Austrian, they would surely join Piedmont. Armed intervention Cavour could not countenance: but what could he reply to France when she

[78] La Rive, 301–03.   [79] *Lettere*, III, 125, 126.

PRESSINGE NEAR GENEVA

Country Place of the De La Rives

should ask him why he had allowed a kingdom of Italy, twelve millions strong, to spring up without compensation to her. The French journals, inspired and uninspired, were talking of the cession of Savoy and Nice. Cavour would have closed boldly with the Emperor and submitted to the loss of two provinces with their 800,000 inhabitants, provided the Emperor consented to the addition of seven millions to the subjects of Victor Emanuel. But Rattazzi was too subservient to French opinions, and his colleagues were too fearful of rousing a storm among the Italians, to do more than tread water. When Cavour found that even at Leri he could neither speak nor move without embarrassing the Cabinet, he thought of traveling abroad; but the proprieties shut him out from France and England; he had not the courage to face the cold and heavy climate of the German cities, and seasickness precluded a transatlantic voyage.[80] He ended by staying at Leri, whither the seekers of advice continued to flock.

In spite of the most honorable intentions on both sides — for the Ministers, though lacking boldness, unquestionably were patriotic, and Cavour, though he differed frankly, engaged in no intrigue to overthrow them — the Cabinet had an unenviable position. The Athenians tired of hearing Aristides called the just; Rattazzi, La Marmora and Dabormida could not enjoy being reminded at all hours of the master statesman whose place they were trying to fill. Foreign critics regarded it as a foregone conclusion that Cavour would soon be at the helm again. The Piedmontese, however, or at least those familiar with affairs on the inside, suspected that the King's antipathy would postpone his recall; they speculated whether he might not be President of the Chamber, or Regent of Central Italy. Cavour himself bided his time, as he had done in 1852. He dismissed the suggestion of the Regency as impracticable. He saw that until events compelled the King to summon him, it would be folly to force his way back to power.

The crisis dragged on.[81] The course of destiny seemed to wait for Napoleon's command, and he hesitated. But the French Ultramontanes, getting their signal from Rome, kindled the

[80] *Lettere*, III, 129; C. to Mme. de Circourt, Sept. 1859.

[81] "The negotiations at Zurich are at a complete standstill," wrote Cowley to J. Russell, on Sept. 16, and intimated that the conference would never conclude. *Correspondence*, 1860, LXVIII, 116.

2

wrath of the French Clericals in the hope of thereby scaring the
Emperor. Monsignor Dupanloup, Bishop of Orleans, and Monsignor Pie, Bishop of Poitiers, denounced as a sacrilege the spoliation of the Papal States. Many other prelates joined in the attack, which, they knew, was heartily approved by Empress
Eugénie and by Walewski. Returning from Biarritz, Napoleon
listened at Bordeaux to a homily from Cardinal Donnet, who
besought him "to put an end to the anxieties of the Catholic
world." After praising the Cardinal's moderation and expressing
the wish that a day of new glory would dawn for the Church, —
a day when everyone should perceive that the Pope's Temporal
Power need not conflict with the liberty and independence of
Italy, — the Emperor announced that the French army would
soon evacuate the States of the Church. "Will it leave behind it
anarchy, terror, or peace?" he asked.[82] Returning to Paris, he
received a swarm of Italian envoys, to whom, amid many oracular remarks, he made clear one thing, — his determination to
enforce the principle of non-intervention.[83] When Dabormida,
the Piedmontese Foreign Secretary, proposed Cavour as Regent
for Central Italy, Napoleon replied that "he would frighten
Europe." "That might have its use," Dabormida had the wit to
answer. The Emperor, however, evidently disliked the idea of
a regency, which would be a tacit acknowledgment that the Central Italians were their own masters, and, if the regent were an
Italian, would quench the last gleam of hope for Plon-Plon, or for
any other Napoleonid, to reign at Florence. The Emperor spoke
unreservedly in favor of annexing Savoy to France, if a plebiscite indicated, as he believed it would, that the Savoyards desired
to be reunited to the nation to which they belonged by their
language, race and geographical position. Dabormida remarked
that if the principle of nationality ruled in Savoy, it ought also
to rule in Emilia and Tuscany.[84] The Piedmontese Minister got
the impression that the Emperor was wholly bound to Austria —
an impression which Napoleon explained away in a letter to
Victor Emanuel. Although he wrote, apparently, with only the
welfare of Italy at heart, yet by a characteristic face-about he
made that welfare hinge on the immediate and loyal acceptance

[82] *Moniteur*, Oct. 11, 1859.
[83] *Stor. Doc.*, VIII, 597–616; Peruzzi to Ricasoli, Oct. 16, 17, 20, 1859.
[84] *Lettere*, III, ccxlvi–ix.

of the Villafranca proposals.[85] Again it seemed as if he wished to put himself on record as being for and against each of the suggested policies, so that he could claim as his own whichever finally prevailed. In truth, however, he was trying to keep up the semblance of being master of a situation which had run far beyond his control. Only by actually leaguing himself with Austria and beating the Italians back into a state of servitude, could he expect to put into operation the program that he published so light-heartedly on July 12. The state of Italy, the certainty that such a compact between France and Austria could not be lasting, the dread of precipitating a general war, the attitude of England, warned him that it was better to tack to and fro than to dash headlong on the reefs.

England's moral support more than once saved the Italian patriots during these crucial months. Let the Queen and Prince Albert, and their Tory courtiers, work as openly as they dared in behalf of Austria and the Treaties of 1815, yet they did not represent typical English public opinion which, since the days of Chatham and of Burke, had upheld the cause of liberty. In the autumn of 1859 the great majority of Englishmen sympathized with the Italians, and found in Palmerston and Lord John Russell spokesmen willing to go to any length short of war in behalf of Italy. In their instructions to British diplomats abroad, in private talk with foreign ambassadors in London, and, so far as they might prudently do so, in their official despatches, Lord John and Palmerston preached the policy, "Italy for the Italians." They advised Victor Emanuel to promise the Tuscans that he would defend them against the danger of internal disorder. They encouraged Tuscans and Emilians alike to express their wishes by popular vote: had not these peoples, they asked, as good a right to change their rulers as the people of England, France, Belgium and Sweden? Napoleon III would have preferred that the plebiscites which made him despot should be forgotten; and perhaps Queen Victoria did not like to be reminded that the King of the Belgians, her own "Uncle Leopold," had no better warrant for his crown than that which the Central Italians now relied upon for their own redemption. The logic of the English statesmen carried with it sarcasm and reproof. But,

[85] *Lettere,* iii, ccxlix–li.

although charges of inconsistency could not dash the French Emperor, he was troubled, deeply troubled, to perceive that he had lost the goodwill of the British Government, without gaining that of any other Great Power as an offset, and that England, without striking a blow or even inditing a manifesto, was supplanting France in the hearts and hopes of the Italians.

The crisis dragged on. Despairing of reaching a durable agreement through the peace conference of Zurich, Napoleon revived the project of a European Congress, in which new sanctions should be formally adopted for a new international combination. It was indispensable that England should accept the invitation to the Congress and yet neither the English Premier nor the Foreign Secretary saw in it more than an attempt on the part of the Emperor to wriggle out of his untenable position. "I can see no reason sufficient to induce us to go," Lord John wrote to his chief, on October 21. "We cannot object to the transfer of Lombardy, but the clause about the Duchies and the article about the Pope[86] are especially objectionable. I cannot but think that by going into a congress we should give some sanction to the Austrian doctrine of the divine right of Kings. The notion of a confederation we have always scouted as a way of leading Sardinia back to the house of bondage. I should therefore be inclined to say in answer to Walewski's despatch that our objections on the score of Venetia being part of the Italian Confederation are by no means removed — that the Pope's assurance that he will grant reforms when his authority is restored is of no value in our eyes, as we do not see how the authority of the Pope is to be re-established without the employment of foreign force — that to such employment of foreign force, either to re-establish the authority of the Pope or to restore the Archdukes in Tuscany and Modena, we have insuperable objections. The rights reserved to the Archdukes and to the Duchess of Parma by the Treaty of Zurich appear to us in the same light as the rights of the Count de Chambord and Prince Wasa — rights to respect and observance, but not to obedience and subjection on the part of France and Sweden. That if the independence of Italy mentioned in the Treaty of Zurich is not to be illusory, the rights of the Italian people ought to be respected and observed. Yet if

[86] See draft of Treaty of Zurich.

the Congress should decide to use force, what would be the position of Great Britain? She would only have to protest and withdraw. France would be in a similar position, but France has bound herself by engagements to which Great Britain is not a party."[87]

The Queen and Prince Consort also objected to the Congress, because they suspected that Napoleon schemed thereby to make England the persecutor of Austria.[88] Nevertheless, as England and France happened to be entangled in several other questions, — the upheaval in China, the Suez Canal, the situation in Morocco, — Palmerston and Lord John decided that it was expedient not to break with France at that juncture; and accordingly, on their proposal the Cabinet voted to accept the invitation to the Congress, but with several reservations, and the sovereign approved.[89]

The Emperor's satisfaction at securing England's consent was shattered by the Central Italians themselves. Their League preserved order without difficulty, but every week showed them the increasing perils of a provisional government. They knew that since the Treaty of Zurich merely confirmed the stipulations of Villafranca, they must, as a last resort, create such a situation that the ousted princes could not possibly be restored. Ricasoli stood like a rock for annexation to Victor Emanuel's Kingdom, as the only way to ensure the unification of Italy. Once joined, he kept preaching, they would survive or perish together. The King's declination to receive their offer was merely a temporary check. With their innate talent for political adroitness, they proposed to choose Prince Eugenio di Carignano as Regent, until such time as Victor Emanuel should find it prudent to welcome them under his sceptre. The lynching at Parma of Colonel Anviti, an odious tool of the ducal régime, gave an impetus to this movement. Although this was the only act of violence recorded during

---

[87] Ashley, II, 372–73; J. Russell to Palmerston, Oct. 21, 1859. Palmerston indorsed this note: "I entirely agree with John Russell, and had already come to the same conclusion."

[88] Martin, IV, 504–05; Queen to J. Russell, Oct. 28, 1859.

[89] Ashley, II, 373. Martin, IV, 506. Walpole: *Russell*, II, 315. Walpole: *History*, I, 268. See also *Correspondence*, 1860, LXVIII; Walewski to Persigny, Oct. 22 (147–50); Russell to Cowley, Oct. 31, stating England's terms (150); Cowley to Russell, Nov. 3, reporting interview with Walewski (164); Russell to Cowley in reply, Nov. 5 (165).

many months of crisis, it caused a deep impression: the Reactionaries pointed to it as a proof that anarchy reigned; the Liberals cited it as a reason for hastening the consolidation of the Kingdom. The larger reason, however, was the prospective convening of a European congress. Unless the Central Italians managed to dispose of themselves before that met, they would be parceled out at the pleasure of the Great Powers. By the middle of October the plan of a regency was revived; by the end of the month the Assemblies of the League had been summoned. Ubaldino Peruzzi, the special Tuscan agent in Paris, found Napoleon opposed to a regent, but friendly, in general terms, to the Italians. Dabormida, the Piedmontese Foreign Secretary, divined that the Emperor would kiss the hand of anyone who would free him from his pledge to Austria.[90] The Italians were quick to note the change in the wind. Prince Corsini telegraphed on November 3 that London was more important than Paris; and that Palmerston advised waiting until peace had been signed between Piedmont and Austria before setting up a regent. Four days later he reported that Lord John agreed, but that, above all, they must maintain order, for England and Victor Emanuel could not defend the Revolution. "Garibaldi must keep quiet," he added; "look out for Mazzini."[91]

The Emperor's disapproval of a regency was attributed to his desire to reserve the crown of Central Italy for Prince Napoleon. So long as the States of the League lacked a final organization, the Prince had a chance; but if Carignano were chosen, the Centre would be the prize of Piedmont. Plon-Plon himself recognized that the time for his own candidacy had passed; but he urged that some one — any one — Carignano, Cavour, D'Azeglio — be nominated at once, but that Victor Emanuel must be careful not to send troops south of the Po, because, by sending them, he would give Austria a pretext for armed intervention. "You will suffer a second Novara," he said, sarcastically, "and you will be

[90] Ricasoli, III, 396–402; Peruzzi to Ricasoli, Paris, Oct. 16, 1859.

[91] *Stor. Doc.*, VIII, 622; Corsini to Ricasoli, Oct. 30, Nov. 3 and 7, 1859. On Oct. 27, Corsini telegraphed from London to Ridolfi at Florence: " England is mistress of the situation at Turin. She is in favor of the Congress, but wishes one thing more — Carignano as Regent. Elect him at once. . . . Let Victor Emanuel act with independence and save Italy. Let us take advantage of the occasion; if not, we disgust England. *Cavour must now be minister. Act like lightning.*" *Lettere,* III, cclxiii.

well-advanced when you have caused the Emperor's ruin and the arrival of the Prussians in Paris."[92] Cavour also advised the League to consolidate, and to elect a regent without delay; above all, he insisted, "do not allow yourselves to be separated —that would be your perdition." [93] On October 30, Fabrizi, the Tuscan agent at Turin, after a long interview with the King, whom he described as "resolute and willing," telegraphed Ricasoli to nominate Carignano.[94]

On November 7 the Tuscan deputies met in the Hall of the Five Hundred. Having told them in his straightforward fashion what the Government had done since August, Ricasoli described the present situation, and gave the reasons for calling in Prince Carignano as regent to "govern in the name of His Majesty the King Elect."[95] On the 9th the Prince was elected, with only one dissenting vote.[96] Bologna and Modena followed suit, but with the difference that instead of defining Carignano as regent in the name of Victor Emanuel, they made him regent with full powers by virtue of their own vote.[97] This difference, apparently trifling, might provide diplomats in search of a quibble with the thing they desired. It would have been well if there had been no delay between the passage of the vote and the arrival in Turin of a delegation from the Assemblies: for during the interval, Victor Emanuel sounded Napoleon III and received his veto of Carignano's regency, which would, he asserted, prevent the meeting of the Congress, and thereby throw upon Victor Emanuel the responsibility for losing Italy.[98] Alarmed and perplexed, the Ministry held a special session[99] to which they invited Cavour, Massimo d'Azeglio and Boncompagni. Cavour suggested that Prince Carignano should formally receive the delegations, and tell them that, as the Congress was about to meet, it would be imprudent for him to assume office immediately, but that he would appoint Boncompagni to oversee the affairs of Central Italy. By this subterfuge, Piedmont would virtually accept the States of the Centre, without rousing Napoleon's anger, and would avoid wounding the feelings of the Tuscans and Emilians by a refusal.[100] The King laid this plan, to which Rattazzi and

[92] Ricasoli, III, 437; Peruzzi to Ricasoli, Oct. 20, 1859.   [93] *Ibid*, 469; Minghetti to Ricasoli, Oct. 28, 1859.   [94] *Ibid*, 475.   [95] *Ibid*, 501–09.   [96] Poggi, I, 394.   [97] *Ibid*, 391, 395.   [98] *Stor. Doc.*, VIII, 230; Napoleon to V. E., Nov. 9, 1859; this date seems incorrect.   [99] On Nov. 11.   [100] *Lettere*, III, cclxv. Ricasoli, IV, 10; Peruzzi to Ricasoli, Nov. 12, 1859.

Dabormida objected, before the Emperor, who declared it to be deplorable because, as he justly said, it prejudiced the situation and rendered a Congress futile.[101] The King replied that he could not withhold his friendly services from the people who had recently drawn closer to him.[102] Cavour returned to Leri full of scorn for Dabormida's timidity and hesitation.[103]

It happened that Peruzzi, the Tuscan envoy, on his way home from Paris, was at Turin, and that Minghetti, the spokesman of the Romagna, persuaded him of the wisdom of Cavour's plan. Taking the matter in their own hands, they offered the regency to Prince Carignano, who delegated his authority to Boncompagni (November 13). On receiving this news, which reached him late owing to a muddled cipher, Ricasoli felt that the salvation of Italy hung by a thread. "Either Carignano or Nobody," he telegraphed; "but by all means Carignano; and if it truly is impossible for him to come, let him accept and not come; and if even this is not possible, let the King speak up as an Italian to the peoples of Central Italy, and to Europe at the same time."[104] The Piedmontese Cabinet despatched Castelli to beseech Ricasoli not to send the committee that was to inform Prince Carignano of his election; but Ricasoli, who had promptly disavowed Peruzzi's action as unauthorized, insisted that the committee should go to Turin. Its mission could not be other than an empty function, for the King and Ministers were bent on regarding Boncompagni's appointment as an accomplished fact. The Iron Baron was not reassured by a despatch from Boncompagni who proposed to come to Florence as regent, to appoint Fanti as Minister of War, and Ricasoli and Farini as governors "with full liberty of action " in their respective provinces.[105] This scheme indicated that the Regent did not intend to be more than a figurehead. Ricasoli insisted, therefore, that Boncompagni must come, if he came at all, as the official representative of the Prince, and not as if he had in himself any symbolical virtue. Ricasoli insisted further that during the period of transition Tuscany and Emilia should be autonomous. But again Dabormida, fearing to offend the Emperor, hesitated; and now Austria an-

---

[101] *Stor. Doc.*, VIII, 231; Napoleon said Boncompagni ought at least to be called dictator and not regent.   [102] *Ibid*, 232; V. E. to Napoleon, Nov. 12, 1859.
[103] *Lettere*, III, 149.   [104] Ricasoli, IV, 21; Ricasoli to G. Fabrizi, Nov. 14, 1859.
[105] *Ibid*, 20; Boncompagni to Ricasoli, Nov. 14, 1859.

nounced that not only would she not enter the Congress until this complication was unsnarled, but that she should regard the crossing of the first Piedmontese soldiers into Central Italy as a cause for war.[106] Farini, who had the most urgent reason for grasping almost any rope thrown to him by Piedmont, begged Ricasoli not to break with the government at Turin.[107] But Ricasoli had two vital issues to defend, and compromise was not easy for him. He would neither allow the fate of Tuscany to be merged with that of Emilia, nor would he consent to any temporary arrangement which might imperil the complete union of Tuscany and the Kingdom of Italy. A European Congress, rather than face open warfare over the Roman Question, might restore the Papal provinces to the Pope; it was imperative, therefore, that Tuscany's claims should not be confounded with those of the Legations. When the deadlock had lasted a fortnight, Ricasoli went to Turin, where he was courteously welcomed by the King and Prince, and where, after a little further discussion, a compact embodying his principles was drawn up.[108] With the title of governor-general, Boncompagni was to guard the common interests of the League, and to promote its union with Piedmont; but Emilia and Tuscany retained each its independent government and conducted through its own agents diplomatic relations with foreign countries.[109] On December 21 Boncompagni arrived at Florence, was formally received by the Ministers and installed in the 'modest and remote' Palazzo della Crocetta. They continued to govern from the Palazzo Vecchio without troubling him.[110]

Ricasoli's firmness during those anxious weeks must be counted among the great factors in the unification of Italy. By preventing the creation of a single central state, by insisting that the Tuscans should speak for themselves, and by denying that any concession short of unity could be final, he converted portentous risks into victory.[111] In the crisis when Piedmont and Victor

[106] *Stor. Doc.*, VIII, 234; Dabormida to Ricasoli, Nov. 21, 1859.   [107] Ricasoli, IV, 38–39; five despatches of Nov. 17, 1859.   [108] *Stor. Doc.*, VIII, 234–37.

[109] On Nov. 20, Napoleon telegraphed V. E. that he regarded Boncompagni's nomination as unavoidable, but that he must not be the delegate of Carignano as Regent. Ricasoli, IV, 52. This despatch reached Ricasoli on Nov. 21. Minghetti wrote, Nov. 24, that the Emilians would have preferred the title of " Regent." Castelli: *Carteggio*, I, 250.   [110] Text of conventions in Ricasoli, IV, 79–80. Also, *Monitore Toscano*, 1859, No. 304.   [111] Rubieri, 298–99.

Emanuel, looking to France for advice and permission, seemed to abdicate the leadership of the Italian cause, Ricasoli showed Europe that one Italian State dared to be unreservedly Italian. In demanding "Carignano or Nobody" as Regent, he blocked the road for Prince Napoleon, or for any other Napoleonid. In vetoing a Kingdom of the Centre, he set up the Kingdom of the Whole as the only alternative. He faced with equal steadfastness the rage of Walewski, the threats of Mazzinians, the reproof of the Piedmontese[112] and the entreaties of his friends. Critics at home charged him with acting unconstitutionally; political enemies, accusing him of ambition, attributed to that his delay in coming to a settlement.[113] His colleagues — estimable gentlemen, but without a grain of the iron which was Ricasoli's very nature — said afterwards that he got credit which belonged equally to them,[114] and yet they asserted that more than once he dictatorially gave an important order without consulting them.[115] Dictator he was, in fact, whatever his legal title; a far-seeing, benevolent dictator, worthy to rank with Daniele Manin in 1848–49. That some of his acts were technically arbitrary cannot be denied: in revolutions, when the old laws no longer bind and the new code has not yet been sanctioned, many necessary acts must be illegal if not lawless. Happy the State which in its hour of extreme peril finds a leader as indomitable, as courageous, as unselfish, and as wise as Ricasoli.

[112] Even Castelli, the peace-maker, had no patience for the " mulishness " of the Tuscan policy. *Carteggio*, i, 246. " You know my opinion of that eunuch of a — ," he wrote Minghetti on Dec. 13.   [113] Rubieri, 290, 293.
[114] Poggi, i, 428.   [115] *Ibid*, 271, 310, 338, 352, 377.

CHAPTER XXVII

CAVOUR'S RECALL

IN the midst of this struggle, another danger sprang up. The Party of Action, withheld by no diplomatic engagements, sought to realize the dreams which Mazzini and others painted for it. The prospect, indeed, was good, because the Pope's subjects in the unredeemed provinces, were stimulated by the example of free Emilia and free Tuscany. The presence of Papal troops on the frontier was a constant provocation. But, above all, Garibaldi, aching to strike down the most detested of the despotic governments in the Peninsula, had an army at his call, and only a short march to the border. After disbanding the Hunters of the Alps, he had come southward at the end of August, had been proposed by Fanti to command the Tuscan contingent, and to be second to Fanti himself as commander of the entire army of the League. During September, Garibaldi drilled his men at Bologna. He was probably let into the secret that the National Society, with Farini's collusion or at least with his knowledge, was preparing a rising in Umbria and the Marches. La Farina busily directed the Society from Turin. Mazzini, from Dolfi's back room at Florence as his headquarters, laid the trains for explosions which he himself expected to profit by and to control. Fanti conferred with Farini, and they agreed that the surly temper of the Papal troops warranted sending the Army of the League to the frontier. Feeling sure that in any encounter the League's regiments must win, they hoped, of course, that the Papalists would attack, but they would not grieve if, through some accidental collision, their own men started the fight.

With this in view, Fanti ordered Generals Mezzacapo and Roselli to concentrate their forces on the borders of La Cattolica, and Garibaldi to move his men forward to Rimini. He further instructed Garibaldi not merely to defend the frontier but also, in case any province or single town should revolt, to send arms and troops to it, and to protect it from such a massacre as Perugia

had recently suffered.[1] To give Garibaldi this command was like
giving a boy a bunch of matches and telling him to go and play in
a powder-magazine. For more than a week these instructions seem
not to have leaked out. Then the rumor went about that Garibaldi and Fanti did not agree;[2] next, that he was as submissive
as a lamb to Fanti, and would not lift a finger unless the Papalists
attacked him;[3] finally, that he was the most dangerous person in
Italy, as he had just accepted the presidency of the Society of the
Nation Armed, a fact which might of itself furnish a pretext to
France or to Austria to interfere. The hero, as every one knew,
believed in a dictatorship with himself as dictator. What if he
should decide that the day for the Man on Horseback had come?[4]
On October 28, Ricasoli, consulting at Pratolino with Farini and
Cipriani on the Regency, and on the military situation, declared
emphatically that Garibaldi's projected invasion of the Marches
must be prevented. He requested Farini to compel Fanti to return to the purely defensive preparations for which he had originally been engaged, and to recall the instructions issued to Garibaldi. On the 30th, Fanti received telegrams from Ricasoli and
Cipriani, ordering him to avoid even the risk of a collision with
the Papalists. Fanti talked the matter over with Farini; they
came to the conclusion that some anti-patriotic influence was at
work; and Fanti telegraphed back, "I do not accept orders, except from the three governments acting together." If he had not
been in too great haste to think, he would have perceived that in
obeying one government and ignoring two he cast consistency
to the winds.[5]

The ticklish situation threw the friends of Italy everywhere
into alarm. They foresaw a general war if Garibaldi broke loose
in the Papal States. The fear of his rashness delayed the diplomatic settlement of the Italian problem, and supplied reactionaries with the proof which they greedily snatched up that the
National movement was really an enterprise of the Reds. At

[1] Carandini, 287; instructions dated Oct. 19, 1859.
[2] Ricasoli, III, 421; C. Bianchi to Ricasoli, Oct. 18, 1859.
[3] Ibid, 451; Salvagnoli to Ricasoli, Oct. 21, 1859.
[4] Ibid, 454; Salvagnoli to Ricasoli, Oct. 22, 1859. Fabrizi, on the other hand,
wrote from Turin on Oct. 24 that they need not fear any disloyal act on the part
of Garibaldi himself, "but that his very name is an incitement, and here lies the
danger." Ibid, 461.   [5] Ricasoli, III, 273-74; Ricasoli to Garibaldi, Oct. 29,
1860. Poggi, I, 349. Guerzoni, I, 494.

Turin, the greatest anxiety prevailed, until the King, with one of his happy audacities, wrote Fanti a note hinting that he and Garibaldi would be wise to resign their commands, because there was a plan on foot to dismiss them.[6] Coming to Turin from Leri the next morning, Cavour heard of this letter, but not accurately; and realizing that there would be a revulsion of feeling against Piedmont, if the Central Italians had reason to suspect that the King, who had no official control over either Fanti or Garibaldi, was interfering in the military affairs of the League, Cavour urged La Marmora to intercept by telegraph the "insensate" message.[7]

Fanti received the countermand promptly, and promptly decided to resign, but he found nobody ready to accept his resignation. October 31 Cipriani, either disgusted or dazed by the course of events, retired from the virtual dictatorship of the Romagna, which immediately fused with the Duchies, under the dictatorship of Farini. Henceforth, Central Italy comprised Emilia, north of the Apennines, and Tuscany south.

Within a few hours of writing the letter to Fanti, the King had a private meeting with Garibaldi. The interview lasted four hours, and although nothing authentic has been reported of it, we know that it strengthened Garibaldi's enthusiasm for Victor Emanuel. He thought that the King was as bluff and naïf as himself; he admired the soldier in him, and the outspoken patriotism; he believed that the delay in unifying Italy was due to Victor Emanuel's timid or wicked ministers, and not to any taint of royal prudence. The truth is that Victor Emanuel had a lifelong passion for intrigue. He would unquestionably have preferred to cut each Gordian knot with a blow of his own sword; but he was not less canny than bluff, not less discreet — except in private conversation — than chivalrous. Throughout his reign he continually held secret negotiations with persons whom his ministers dared not approach. Whatever was said in their talk of October 29, Garibaldi returned to Rimini only to hurry on the preparations for the rising in La Cattolica and for its invasion at the first

[6] Telegrams in Carandini, 288–90. *Lettere*, III, cclvii; V. E. to Fanti, Oct. 29, 1859. [7] *Lettere*, III, cclvii, and 145; C. to La Marmora, Oct. 30, 1859. "The King has sent to Fanti the order to resign. If this happens, I hold that everything is lost, and that the responsibility for the disaster will fall on the King and his ministers."

signal.[8] To his officers, who asked him as to the probability of crossing the Rubicon, he replied: "I think that we shall be attacked ourselves; but *perhaps we shall not lack an occasion for marching ahead all the same.*"[9] Historians have inferred with good reason that Victor Emanuel left in Garibaldi the conviction that, while the Piedmontese Government could not officially meddle in the military or political affairs of the League, much less abet an attack on Papal territory, it would rejoice over every foot of soil redeemed for Italy. Perhaps he did not say frankly, "Go ahead with my blessing; but if trouble comes, I will deny you like Peter," as Cavour had said to La Farina; nevertheless, there can be little doubt that he intimated as much.[10] And Garibaldi, prone to interpret the King's words according to his own wishes, needed only a hint: for to him it was monstrous that an army of free Italians should not as a matter of course march to liberate their Italian brothers. Having no misgiving of the outcome, it was all the harder for him to be leashed in. Surrounded by enthusiasts who chafed at the delay, Garibaldi grew more and more restive, and being by nature very suspicious, he readily assumed that Fanti and Farini and everyone else who suggested moderation were either disloyal or cowardly. The crisis called for the Strong Man, the Dictator, who, unrestrained by pettifogging diplomacy, would pour all the resources of the League into the War of Liberation.

Fearing an explosion, Farini summoned Garibaldi to Modena, where, in company with Fanti, and with General Solaroli from Turin, they held a long conference. If it began in storm it ended in calm, for Garibaldi professed to recognize the need of keeping the peace, and went away promising to do so. On quitting the Palace, however, he was beset by his Red friends, who insinuated that Farini was making a fool of him, and that it would be base to abandon the patriots of the Marches, to whom he had already pledged his word.[11] At Imola,[12] Garibaldi received a spurious message, announcing that the revolution had already broken

---

[8] Garibaldi himself states, *Memorie*, 293, that it was agreed that he should act for the good of the common cause, according as he judged it opportune — the King, however, not giving his consent for the invasion of Papal territory.

[9] Guerzoni, I, 495–96. This must have been on Nov. 4 or 5. Guerzoni, who records it, was one of the officers.   [10] Guerzoni, I, 497.

[11] Guerzoni, I, 499–500; Carandini, 294.   [12] Carandini says Bologna, 295.

out. He telegraphed the news to Farini, adding that he was going to the patriots' assistance. The somewhat simple hero was indeed the dupe, although not of the men whom he suspected. He hurried forward, with what troops he found at Bologna, to begin operations. Farini and Fanti, having telegraphed to the frontier for news and learned that there was no revolution, sent messengers to order the officers of every regiment to return to their quarters under pain of arrest. How Fanti could have carried out his threat in case of refusal, which would have meant that the army took its orders from Garibaldi and not from him, does not appear. Garibaldi, however, who talked vociferously of a dictatorship, never thought of seizing it when it came within his reach: either a subconscious, soldierly respect for Victor Emanuel as his chief, or an intuition that he might throw Italy into civil war, restrained him. Fanti's messenger overtook the troops, some of whom were just about to cross the frontier,[13] and on November 13 they wearily retraced their steps over the roads down which they had dashed on the double-quick the day before. Alarm reached Turin long before it was known what Garibaldi would do. "The King must act directly, and without hesitation," Cavour wrote La Marmora; "a delay of twenty-four hours might be fatal."[14] The King lost no time in sending a despatch to invite Garibaldi to come at once to Turin. The Knight Errant obeyed.

There is a legend that on his journey north he stopped at Bologna and had with Farini and Fanti a stormy scene, in which he demanded of them to deliver to him the civil and military dictatorship. Farini replied: "You may pitch me out of the balcony into the square, but you cannot make me yield to a military sedition."[15] Garibaldi knew a firm man when he saw one, and quitted Bologna without attempting to lay violent hands on Farini. At Turin on the 16th he had another long talk with Victor Emanuel, who cast the usual spell over him.[16] After describing the ruinous result which the invasion of Papal territory at that crisis might lead to, the King artfully hinted — referring to Naples — that there might soon be a field where a great blow could be struck for Italy. Garibaldi went away "without rancor

---

[13] Guerzoni, I, 501, n. 1.   [14] *Lettere*, III, 149. Guerzoni says, I, 503, that on the same day, Nov. 12, Cavour wrote Rattazzi: "Sole means of smothering the nascent discord, invite Garibaldi to lay down his command."   [15] Guerzoni, I, 501, who discredits the story.   [16] *Lettere*, III, cclxi; Guerzoni, I, 503, says Nov. 17.

and even satisfied,"[17] resigned his command, and retired to Caprera, looking forward to the happy moment when the King should summon him for further service.[18] At parting, he addressed to the Italians a manifesto in which he told them that, finding his liberty of action shackled by deceitful arts, he had resigned. "The wretched vulpine policy," he said, "which for a moment disturbs the majestic progress of our affairs, should persuade itself more than ever that we must rally round the valiant and loyal soldier of Independence, [who is] incapable of receding from his great-hearted and sublime purpose, and more than ever [we ought] to prepare gold and iron to welcome whosoever may attempt to plunge us back into the ancient disasters."[19] In two other public addresses, he urged everyone to contribute to the Million Muskets Fund, which he had recently organized, and he bade his "companions in arms in Central Italy" not to disband, but to be ready to secure, "perhaps tomorrow," by force, that which Europe was vainly trying to concede to them by justice.[20]

Garibaldi's departure relieved the suspense along the Papal frontier. A few of his most zealous followers resigned with him, a few angry protests were made, but there was no mutiny. Ricasoli expelled Mazzini from Tuscany with as little deference or fear as if he had been an unbefriended spy.[21] The Party of Order had showed that it dared to deal firmly with the two demi-gods who held themselves above the law. Mazzini indeed was compelled to go, because, in spite of his boast, he had only a small backing: but Garibaldi was immensely popular, not merely among all cliques of the Party of Action, but with the Liberals also. Mazzini's policy is summed up in this sentence of his in a letter which Farini intercepted: "Our only hope now is to excite the ambition of Garibaldi; he must be made commander-in-chief, and, if necessary, even dictator of Central Italy." [22] Knowing that Garibaldi, except when on the battlefield, was controlled by the person last with him, Mazzini planned to be the real wielder of whatever power the hero might acquire. This letter, written in September, Farini read to Garibaldi, who opened his eyes in

---

[17] *Lettere*, III, cclxi, n. 3.   [18] Ciàmpoli, 117; Garibaldi to V. E., Nov. 23, 1859.   [19] Full text in Ciàmpoli, 116. Guerzoni, I, 504, and *Lettere*, III, cclxii, give incomplete version; dated, Genoa, Nov. 19.   [20] Ciàmpoli, 117, 118; both dated, Genoa, Nov. 23.   [21] Gotti, 224.   [22] La Farina, II, 210–11. "The work must now be done in Garibaldi's name, a popular name."

astonishment: nevertheless, the warning did not prevent him, during the six weeks' complications which we have just reviewed, from allowing himself to be approached, and at times to be dominated by Mazzini's agents. That he listened at the critical moment to Victor Emanuel seemed a glorious accident.

The fortunes of Central Italy during that autumn resemble the eddies on a slowly-moving stream. Fix your attention on any eddy, and you forget both its neighbors and the general movement of the stream. The wonder was that the Central Italians, with so many motives for separate action, could work collectively towards a common end. Farini in the Legations had special reasons for urging annexation to Piedmont upon almost any terms. Ricasoli at Florence had equally good cause for not casting in the lot of Tuscany with that of the Legations, involved as they were in the Papal coil. Piedmont, longing to annex, was compelled to heed Napoleon's warning: "If one Piedmontese soldier crosses the frontier, 50,000 French will occupy Parma, Modena and Bologna." [23] Whatever the King and his Cabinet did, therefore, must be done by indirection. Thus Fanti, as a Piedmontese general, could not command the Army of the League; but having resigned his commission, he satisfied the proprieties, — which are often the hypocrisies, — and gave a Piedmontese turn to the League's military policy. Still more contradictory was Garibaldi's position, fluctuating between the confidence of Victor Emanuel on one side, and the instigations of Mazzini on the other. Republican by conviction, he had accepted the royal leadership, but always with the reservation that, if he thought the King hesitated or went too slow, he would join any other party that promised quick action. With the temperament of a prima-donna — wayward, wilful, superficially vain; living through his emotions at the expense of his intellect, ready to share his last crust with a beggar or his cloak with a shivering soldier, but equally ready to do great injustice by denouncing patriots who did not agree with him; simple with the lowly, but haughtier than Lucifer with the mighty, in order to show them that their rank had no awe for him — Garibaldi was a most embarrassing ally. While his immense popular prestige made it suicidal not to propitiate him, his habit of regarding himself as

[23] La Farina, II, 234.

2

a personage above the law, kept the heads of the League in perpetual anxiety. He had the patriotism to accept the post of second in command, but not to refrain from complaining that he deserved to be first — nay, to be dictator. No other modern hero, not even Nelson, has recorded such a mass of childish grievances as Garibaldi.[24] He was always whining that his unique qualifications were not appreciated, always suspecting that jealous rivals were intriguing against him. Bereft of political sense, he denounced statesmen and diplomats, with their slowness and their devious ways, and their system of authorized insincerity. For him — the belated Paladin — it was enough to arm one's self with good intentions and a sword. And yet, more than once at a critical moment, he displayed the noblest self-abnegation as naturally as a saint; and in spite of his frequent piques, his suspicions, his hurt feelings, his rages at having his opinions slighted, he possessed almost unparalleled charm — charm which caused myriads of Italians to flock after him on the most desperate errands; charm which enthralled women, young and old; charm which roused the stolid populace of London to boundless enthusiasm, and captivated the fastidious Tennyson.[25]

The mythical demi-gods of antiquity appeared unheralded at the crisis of a battle, smote down their worshipers' enemies, and then considerately vanished. To the great inconvenience of his friends, Garibaldi staid on. So Farini who, on October 31, protested to Ricasoli that nothing must be done to irritate the hero, was moving heaven and earth, ten days later, to keep the hero from ruining the cause: and although Farini ostensibly enjoyed the closest relations with Victor Emanuel's government, he found himself hampered at every step by the fact that the King was secretly conniving with Garibaldi.[26] Farini himself did not escape the accusation of working for a Bonapartist candidate in

[24] For his state of mind in these months read *Memorie*, 286–99.

[25] After Garibaldi's visit to Farringford, in April, 1864, Tennyson wrote the Duke of Argyll: " What a noble human being! I expected to see a hero and was not disappointed. One can not exactly say of him what Chaucer says of the ideal Knight, ' as meke he was of port as is a made '; he is more majestic than meek, and his manners have a certain divine simplicity in them, such as I have never witnessed in a native of these islands, among men at least, and they are gentler than those of most young maidens whom I know." *Alfred, Lord Tennyson. By his Son.* New York, 1905. II, 3.

[26] L. Rava in *Nuova Antologia*, Sept. 1, 1903; 140, 141, 142. Farini epitomizes the affair in his letter to Cavour of Nov. 22; 144–47.

Central Italy: but no evidence exists that either he, or Cipriani, similarly suspected, wavered in their preference for annexation to Piedmont. Cavour's splendid praise of Farini leaves no doubt as to him: for Cavour never planned to get rid of Austrian or Papal despotism merely to replace it by French,[27] and he would not have thanked any Italian who undertook to do so. Farini himself believed in conspiring with the Party of Action just as long as he could control the situation. He saw Crispi, Mazzini's emissary, and, if Crispi is to be credited, he not only encouraged his plan of an insurrection in Sicily, but gave money and promised still more.[28] On the other hand, Mazzini made no pretense of not plotting: he burrowed underground because he was not allowed to work in the open. Ricasoli alone would neither compromise nor intrigue.

Out of this interval of make-believe, cross-purposes and suspense, there came, however, the salvation of Italy. The Treaty of Zurich, signed on November 11,[29] simply registered the views of the Emperors at Villafranca four months earlier. Their plans, except the cession of Lombardy to Piedmont, had not been carried out: the Pope had scoffed at the Federation, and the Central Italians had maintained their independence since the spring; nothing save armed intervention could compel them to submit to their old rulers. Who should interfere? Austria longed to but dared not, for Napoleon had proclaimed non-intervention. Only Europe, speaking through a Congress, could set up a new authority. The treaty of 1856 was supposed to amend and supersede the treaties of 1815, but events had torn it to pieces, as easily as an acrobat plunges through his paper-covered hoops at the circus. Napoleon was from the first most eager to have a Congress assemble, to throw upon Europe, instead of upon himself, the responsibility for settling the Roman Question. It might also, incidentally, sanction French aspirations in Central Italy. But he had difficulty in persuading the Great Powers to favor his project. Russia expected nothing from it for herself, and she could not sanction the declaration of the principle of nationality, or the ratification of the doctrine that states might rebel and

---

[27] *Lettere*, III, 161; C. to Farini, Dec. 25, 1859.   [28] Crispi: *Mille*, 80–82.

[29] "I bring you a peace, but not peace," said Bourqueney, one of the French envoys, on his return to Paris. La Gorce, III, 163.

choose their own sovereigns. Prussia knew that if the discussion of the rights of small states extended beyond the Italian, embarrassing questions might be asked concerning members of the Germanic Confederation. England — that is Russell and Palmerston — insisted on reserving full liberty of action, and made non-restoration in Central Italy a condition precedent to entering the Congress. On November 17 the invitations were announced, the object of the Congress being to receive communication of the Treaty of Zurich, and "to take into consideration the pacification of Central Italy." [30] Paris was to be the place of meeting. Then followed weeks of diplomatic manœuvring, in which each cabinet tried to get assurance that its particular views should prevail. On December 1, Rechberg, Buol's successor as chief minister in Austria, insisted that the Legations must be restored to the Pope; by December 8, he had so far relaxed as to acquiesce generally in the English policy, provided Lord John Russell would join in putting an end to the revolutionary intrigues of Piedmont [31] — a humorous proviso, which evidently minimized the value of his acquiescence. Prussia was inclined not to offer any programme. [32] The Pope gave warning that his envoy must take precedence of all others, and walk first after the president of the Congress. To this Russell replied flatly, no. "Great Britain," he said, "cannot acknowledge the spiritual supremacy of the Pope, nor any pretension arising therefrom." [33] The sole reason for admitting a Papal representative was the fact that Pius was a petty temporal prince; yet the Pope presumed, with the arrogance which since the Renaissance had become a fixed policy at Rome, to enjoy the dignity which attached to him as the spiritual head of the Roman Catholic Church. Austria and the expelled despots sowed rumors of terrorism and Piedmontese "agency" in the Duchies and the Romagna, and of Piedmontese plots in Venetia and the Tyrol. [34] The Tuscan army was described as yearning to call back the Grand Duke. Iridescent pictures of the perfect happiness enjoyed under the Old Régime were circulated. Austria labored to exclude Piedmont from the Congress: but Napoleon and Russell stood firm. In spite of

[30] *Correspondence*, 1860, lxviii, 201, 219. The formal invitations issued from Paris and Vienna on Nov. 21.   [31] *Ibid*, 252; Loftus to Russell, Vienna, Dec. 8.
[32] *Ibid*, 200; Lowther to Russell, Berlin, Nov. 19.
[33] *Ibid*, 230; Russell to Cowley, Dec. 6.   [34] *Stor. Doc.*, viii, 246–51.

bickerings and hesitation, by December 12 every invited State had accepted.

The upholders of the doctrines of the Restoration noted with dismay the steady growth of Lord John Russell's influence, through which England was supplanting France as the promoter of Italian liberty and independence. Many Frenchmen also resented this, but they had only themselves and Napoleon's policy of fast-and-loose to blame for it. From his entry into the Foreign Office Lord John never hid the fact that his motto was "Italy for the Italians"; every link of his policy, every despatch that he wrote had that in view. And strange to say, although the Queen and Albert opposed him, he made Europe understand that that was England's purpose, and that England's purpose was not to be disregarded now, as it had been when Malmesbury and the Queen attempted to prevent the war. From his vantage-ground of London, Lord John could speak out boldly, whereas Napoleon, even if he had been by nature straightforward, was hindered at Paris by many internal and international considerations. Still, whatever he affirmed or denied, the Emperor drew nearer month by month to the Russell-Palmerston policy, whether because at heart he approved it, or because he believed that it offered the safest escape for him out of his perilous predicament. How closely he agreed with the English statesmen was revealed in startling fashion on December 22, when an inspired pamphlet, "The Pope and the Congress," [35] appeared.

It required little acumen to perceive that this tract came from the same hand that wrote "Napoleon III and Italy." Official gossip hinted that "an august personage" had dictated it, while La Gueronnière held the pen. Judge its substance as we will, we can hardly deny that, as a specimen of special pleading, it is a little masterpiece. In apparent frankness and urbanity; in artfully assuming the conclusions that ought to be proved; in ignoring, quite as artfully, difficulties that could not be solved; in making the unsubstantial seem plausible and the plausible seem indisputable; in the use of innuendo; in the appeal to the highest interests of mankind; in the apparent absence of self-seeking, whether personal, national or sectarian — this pamphlet is a model. It was as if the Angel of the Lord had come in a dream

[35] *Le Pape et le Congrès.* Paris: Dentu, 1859.

to the pious Autocrat of the Tuileries, and bidden him to teach Pius, the Pope, deafened and misled by the sophistries of designing prelates, the simple way to restore peace to the world.

The pamphleteer, who professes to be a "sincere Catholic," begins with the assertion that both Catholic doctrine and political reason require that the Pope shall have Temporal Power: because, if he were not an independent sovereign, "he would be French, Austrian, Spanish or Italian, and the title of his nationality would deprive him of the character of his universal pontificate."[36] The interests of all the Powers, Protestant and Greek, as well as Catholic, demand therefore that the Pope shall be independent.[37] But the double nature of the Pope-King creates insuperable contradictions. How can he whose mission it is to pardon be at the same time he whose duty it is to punish?[38] What form of government can reconcile these antagonisms? Not by monarchy, not by a republic, not by despotism, not through liberty can the end be reached, but by paternalism.[39] A paternal ruler needs neither a large kingdom nor many subjects; indeed, if he is to be like a father to his people, they must be few. "The smaller the territory, the greater the sovereign. A large domain, ordered for the Pope's requirements, would either stagnate, or require foreign garrisons to protect it." "Grievous extremity!" exclaims the Sincere Catholic, in one of his telling epigrams; "because any power which does not live by its national forces and by public opinion, is not an institution: it is only an expedient. The Church, far from finding therein a condition of independence, would find only a cause of discredit and of impotence."[40]

Having declared that the minimum of domain is the ideal, the Sincere Catholic proceeds to show that the City of Rome, or at the utmost the Patrimony of St. Peter, will suffice. The only politics possible to that restricted sphere will be those of municipal government. The Pope will not need an army: since his function is not to draw the sword but to cultivate the olive, the troops of the Italian Confederation will serve to protect him. In a larger sense, he will be guarded by the Catholic Powers, which will contribute gladly a generous offering to maintain him in fitting splendor. So "there will be in Europe a people which will have at

[36] *Le Pape et le Congrès*, 7.　　[37] *Ibid*, 8.　　[38] *Ibid*, 9.　　[39] *Ibid*, 10.
[40] *Ibid*, 12.

its head less a king than a father and whose rights will be guaranteed rather by the heart of the sovereign than by the authority of laws and of institutions. This people will require no national representation, no army, no press, no magistracy. Its entire public life will be concentrated in its municipal organization. Outside of this narrow circle, it will have no other resource than contemplation, the arts, the cult of great memories, and prayer. It will be forever disinherited from that noble part of activity which, in all countries, is the stimulus of patriotism and the legitimate exercise of the mind's faculties or of superiorities of character. Under the government of the Sovereign Pontiff, no one can aspire to the glory of the soldier, or to that of the orator or the statesman. That will be a government of repose and meditation, a sort of oasis where the passions and interests of politics will not intrude, and which will have only the mild and calm perspectives of the spiritual world." [41] The Sincere Catholic who, in this passage, comes dangerously near to irony, admits that the eight or ten score thousand human beings may find it hard to be thus shut out from their normal rights, but he bids them to remember that this sacrifice will benefit scores of millions of Catholics, and that they must seek consolation in the benefits of a paternal administration, in the absence of taxes, in the thought that their country is the centre of the Catholic faith, and in the pomp of the Papal Court, of which they will form a part. [42]

Such the ideal: can it be achieved? Ought the Pope to consent to see his kingdom reduced to a minimum? Events have already helped towards a reply. For the best part of a year the Romagna has been independent. The Pope cannot bring it back under his sceptre; shall some outside Power force it back? In the name of religion, No! in the interest of the Pope himself, No! The Romagna did not add an iota to his true strength; on the contrary, it meant paralysis to his authority. The Holy Father has no need of material space in order to be loved and revered. His possession of Bologna, Ancona, Ravenna, adds nothing to the puissance of the Holy See. "The Pope, enthroned in Rome and seated in the Vatican, is what strikes the world. One descries with difficulty the sovereign of the Roman States." [43] Suppose, however, that it were decided to subjugate the Romagna and restore Papal

[41] *Le Pape et le Congrès,* 17, 18, 19.   [42] *Ibid,* 19.   [43] *Ibid,* 21, 23, 25.

authority, who could accomplish this? Not France: France, as a devout Catholic country, would never consent to deal this blow to the moral power of Catholicism; France, a free nation, could not coerce other peoples to suffer a government which their will rejected.[44] What fell at Bologna was not so much the Papal authority as the influence of Austria. Will the Papalists look to her for succor? France would never allow Austria thus to undo the results of the recent war: to permit Austria to set up her dominion in the Peninsula, would be tantamount to acknowledging that Magenta and Solferino were fought in vain, and that the principles which had guided France were false. France must not allow the rights of Italy to be infringed; neither must she grant to Austria the right of armed intervention which she herself disclaimed.[45] France would never surrender her glorious rôle of defender of the great principles of justice, reparation and nationality and leave Protestant England to reap the harvest sown by the initiative of the Emperor and by the triumph of French arms.[46] With France and Austria excluded, it was idle to talk of Naples as the Pope's champion.

The only body competent to impose its authority on Italy is a European congress: for it is from such a body that international law emanates. The majority of the Powers at the Congress of Vienna in 1815 were schismatic; yet the Pope recognized its competence in restoring to him his Italian States. In like manner, the Congress of 1860 will have authority. At Vienna, the ancient Papal title to Avignon was canceled; at Paris, it may be decided that other parts of the Papal territory are, like all secular domains, subject to changes. But in fact, Papal territory is neither indivisible nor unchangeable.[47] "The spiritual authority of the Pope is alone immovable, as are the truths it represents and the dogmas it teaches."[48] The Sincere Catholic concludes, therefore, that the convening of the Congress will bring speedy relief, if his remedy be adopted. He reiterates his declaration that the Temporal Power must be preserved. He deprecates again the anomalous position of the Pope-King whose Kingship has brought odium on his Popeship. He does not hesitate to assert that Napoleon III perceived that "it was necessary to save the

---

[44] *Le Pape et le Congrès*, 28, 29.   [45] *Ibid*, 32, 33.   [46] *Ibid*, 31.
[47] *Ibid*, 36, 39.   [48] *Ibid*, 40.

Papacy by freeing Italy. God has blessed his design," he adds, "and given him victory. But his glory would be sterile if, in restoring to a people the titles to their nationality, it failed to guarantee security and independence." Napoleon I, by the Concordat, reconciled the new society and faith; Napoleon III prays that he may have the honour of reconciling the Pope with his people and his age.[49]

The pamphlet created an uproar which went resounding through Europe. Clericals of all shades shot off pamphlets in reply. Some exposed the inconsistencies of the Sincere Catholic; some assailed his statement of facts; many accused him of guile, many of falsehood; all cried out in horror at the suggested sacrilege. The tone, the arguments, the methods of the defenders of the Pope's Temporal Power resemble, as one twin resembles another, the tone, the methods and the arguments of many estimable defenders of American Slavery at that epoch. The Papalists, however, had their customary advantage of being able to denounce as an attack on the Catholic religion that which solely concerned the Papal political institution: were it not for this juggle there would never have been a Roman Question. These pamphlets of rebuttal are stronger in passion than in logic. They are weak in historical supports. Even Montalembert taunted the Romagnoles with inconsistency for revolting from the bland rule of Pius IX, after they had submitted uncomplainingly in the Middle Age to the House of Este and to many other tyrants.[50] Without exception, the Papal defenders accepted as axiomatic the necessity that the Pope should be a temporal monarch. None of them considered how it happened that, if worldly pomp were indispensable to the furtherance of religion, Jesus had neglected to make himself King of the Jews.[51] None of them referred to the fact that Pope Paul III in 1545 invested his bastard, Pier Luigi Farnese, with Parma, thereby alienating a part of the Papal domain. This precedent, which does not stand alone, did not trouble the Papalists: while they ignored modern instances which told against them, they would cite Isaiah to serve their purpose.

---

[49] *Le Pape et la Congrès*, 42, 46.   [50] Montalembert: *Pie IX et la France en 1849 et en 1859*. Paris: *Douniol*, 1860, p. 23. This pamphlet appeared just before the Emperor's.   [51] "Here we are in 1860," L. Veuillot writes the Bishop of Lille; "the year which is to see officially proclaimed the deposition of Christ as a terrestrial King." L. Veuillot: *Correspondance*, VII, 365.

In this they were wise, for the appeal to history, as the candid
admitted, had fatal gaps, and the authors of Isaiah lived before
the Papacy was dreamed of. The question of morals was also
ignored although many of the most loyal Catholics, beginning
with Dante, had condemned the unholy wedding of spiritual and
temporal, and to justify them there stood the Papacy of the
Renaissance, immutably fixed in history as the culmination of
worldliness and corruption. The preferences of the inhabitants
of the Papal States were as little regarded as were the preferences
of the negroes by the pillars of the American Slaveocracy. That
the Pope's subjects desired to be free men, according to the best
standard of the time, was imputed to their wickedness. The
Revolution — which included Victor Emanuel not less than
Mazzini — had poisoned them. Under the mask of political
reform, the Devil was submerging the world in irreligion. Viewed
thus, the attack on the Temporal Power was only an incident
in a universal calamity. The loss of that power, the Bishop of
Arras declared, "would be the most terrible of tempests." Why?
Because without it the unimpeded transmission of the Pontiff's
word to the faithful might be impossible; the Pontiff himself
might be gagged by the monarch in whose kingdom he was enslaved; for want of his words Catholicism would languish.[52]
Montalembert and Villemain, as became men who were literary
first and theological next, laid less stress on doctrinal than on
picturesque considerations.[53] Villemain concluded that the
Papacy would never have its Charles I or its Louis XVI; Montalembert asked triumphantly who would wish to be the Pilate
of the Papacy.

The argument most commonly used by the Papalists was: The
Pope is the Vicar of Christ: therefore, he must be a very good
man; therefore, the charge that the Papal government is abominable can have no foundation. One defender, who concedes that
"the temporal sovereignty of the Pope is not doctrinally an
absolute necessity for his spiritual sovereignty," insists nevertheless that it has been Providentially established,[54] and he denies
that the Church has been a bar to progress. "Either Catholi-

[52] [Parisis.] *L'Evêque d'Arras à l'auteur de la brochure Le Pape et le Congrès.*
Paris: Lecoffre, 1859, pp. 10, 12, 15.   [53] Montalembert, *op. cit., passim.*
M. Villemain: *La France, l'Empire et la Papauté.* Paris: *Douniol,* 1860.
[54] A. Nettement: *Appel au Bon Sens.* Paris: Lecoffre, 1859, p. 11.

cism is true," he argues bluntly, "and then if it does not advance, this is because it is the immortal goal towards which everything advances, and in advancing the world will not leave it behind; or if, in advancing, the world leaves it behind, Catholicism is false."[55] Monsignor Dupanloup, Bishop of Orleans, in the pamphlet which gave the Clericals the greatest comfort, has also his rejoinder to the accusation that the Church is condemned by its dogmas to immobility. "There is," he says, "the glorious immobility of the sun, fixed at the centre of the world, which animates all, gives light to all, and round which are accomplished the most splendid movements, round which the world advances without the light remaining ever behind."[56]

The cry of joy which went up from the Liberals everywhere convinced the Clericals that the Sincere Catholic's proposals emanated from the Devil: otherwise, how account for the mutual satisfaction of Protestant England, Radical France and Revolutionary Piedmont? The official organ at Rome declared the pamphlet to be homage rendered to the Revolution; and the Pope, "prostrating himself before the Most High," stigmatized it as a "signal monument of hypocrisies and an ignoble tissue of contradictions." Whilst the inspired press in France hinted that the Pope, being long in the hands of the Jesuits, could not speak his own mind, the Imperial censor discreetly permitted the defenders of the Papacy to print without hindrance.[57] Although some of these rejoinders were written by the ablest Catholics in France — the fervid Dupanloup, the magisterial Montalembert, the gravely academic Villemain, the pugnacious Veuillot — they fell short collectively of the Emperor's pamphlet; and with good reason, because while that was clear, adroit and urbane, they followed no regular line of rebuttal, but fired off volleys now at one point and now at another,[58] and exploded in outbursts of passion which seriously blurred their dialectics.[59] The genuinely pious

[55] Nettement, 18–19.   [56] [Dupanloup.] *L'Evêque d'Orleans: Lettre à un Catholique.* Paris: *Douniol*, 1860, p. 14. See also his Second Letter.
[57] An attempt by the *Univers* to instigate a monster address to the Pope, was, however, forbidden, on the ground that, under the pretense of religion the *Univers* was organizing a political agitation. *Moniteur*, Dec. 28, 1859. The *Univers* was suppressed Jan. 30, 1860.   [58] True even of Dupanloup, whose two letters seem to me to be the ablest.   [59] Compare L. Veuillot's comments in the *Univers*; reprinted in his *Mélanges*, 2d series, VI, 201–34. For his more systematic argument, see his "Le Pouvoir Temporel des Papes," *ibid*, 163–99.

among them seem to be almost too overwhelmed at the proposed outrage, to speak intelligibly.

The deepest fact is, however, that this storm of controversy registered the incompatibility of the Temporal Papacy with modern life. That ideal of Pope-King, which sprang as naturally as Feudalism out of medieval conditions, was outworn. The attempt to unite God and Mammon, the spiritual and the worldly, had failed. The world had learned by terrible experience that the confounding of religion and politics pollutes both. As head of his Church, what the Pope said was the law: but when he declared that the Temporal Power was necessary to the exercise of his religious functions, laymen more expert than he in secular affairs doubted him and then denied. Having assumed that as a pontiff he dwelt on a plane exempt from all human jurisdiction, he wished to carry this exemption over to his position as a secular prince. But he held his temporal States by exactly the same rights as his neighbors. Like them he was bound by the treaties which ruled Western civilization, — by compacts which were subject to change from age to age, to correspond with the changed conditions of governments and nations. In 1859, as they matched neither facts nor ideals in Italy, a new compact had to be framed. The Pope, however, insisted that he should continue to rule according to a different, earlier, and now discredited compact. It was as if the descendants of the aboriginal Indians of Manhattan — if any survived — should demand to live in New York today by the tribal law of their ancestors.

Had it not been for the Papal monarch's dual nature, his title to temporal sovereignty would have received no more consideration than that of the petty despots of Modena and Tuscany. The Imperial pamphlet was a warning, couched in the form of a suggestion, that the Papacy, in the last stage of senile gangrene, must either conform to the standard of the European body politic or die. The Pope and the Curia chose dissolution; indeed, they could not help choosing it, because their training and tradition, not less than their interests, drove them to that choice. The Papacy sprang up and flourished in the Middle Age: it was an anachronism in the era of advancing democracy, a contradiction in a world that had come to see the necessity of separating Church and State. It was as idle to claim that the head of the

Roman Catholic religion must be a temporal ruler as that the
Archbishop of Canterbury ought to be King of England or that
the senior bishop of the American Methodists must be President
of the United States. But emotion is the stuff of which religion
is chiefly woven; and many good persons, including some of the
hierarchy, blindly believed that to divorce the temporal from the
spiritual in the Pope's functions would destroy the Catholic
religion: and cynics like Antonelli, and the Jesuits, who had
Pius IX under complete control, encouraged the misconception.
Ten years were to elapse before the final snuffing out of the
Papal Power. In the interval the Vatican issued protests, curses,
bulls of excommunication; it denied that it was too moribund or
too medieval to adapt itself to modern conditions, and then it
launched the Syllabus of 1864, in which it condemned principles
that are the very foundation of modern life.

The death of an institution should touch the imagination, if
not the heart. Much of the world's chivalry has been gladly
spent on lost causes.

> " Men are we and must grieve when even the shade
>   Of that which once was great is passed away."

The Papacy, as conceived by Hildebrand, was one of the amplest
visions vouchsafed to man. Under Innocent III, it was an awe-
inspiring experiment. By Dante's time, it had already begun to
encroach upon its spiritual mate, the Church. Thenceforward,
through the Renaissance, it outvied in worldliness the most
worldly secular princedoms, and its sovereigns — the Della
Rovere, the Borgia, the Medici, the Caraffa, the Farnese —
either made new records for personal depravity, or revived the
social ideals of Paganism in its decadence. Exhausted, with the
exhaustion that overtakes at last the most insatiate worldling, the
Papacy, stripped of its Hildebrandine universality, reduced to be
only a petty state in Italy, herself only the name for a collection
of petty states, might soon have succumbed, had not new blood
from outside poured into its veins. The Jesuits saw their opportunity, and during its last three centuries, with occasional intervals when other factions drove them out, they shaped the policy
of the Papal institution.

But whatever faction dominated, in one respect, in priestcraft, the training of a thousand years did not fail the Italians in the Vatican. They contrived to keep their monopoly of the hierarchical machine. Although foreign Catholics outnumbered them by seven or eight to one, the Italians took care to fix an effective majority in the College of Cardinals; so the eighth part controlled the whole, and it not only always elected an Italian pope, but also filled with Italians nine-tenths of the offices at Rome in which ecclesiastical ambition might enjoy wealth or power. In adroitness, no other example of political management can be compared with this. At a time when France was supplying a large share of the Pope's funds and most of the ablest polemics for his defense, France was allotted only seven cardinals, while Italy had forty-eight![60] And yet the French, and the world in general, looked down on the Italians as incapable of learning even the rudiments of the art of politics!

When the first breath of the new era came from France, it was evident that the Papacy could not live unless it adjusted itself to the new climate. Its guides, however, scoffed at adjustment or compromise: and as its feebleness increased, they tried to transfuse into it some of the supernatural equipment of the Church. Short of declaring the inviolability of the Papacy as a dogma, they stopped at no shift for saving the Temporal by identifying it with the Spiritual. But the end came — ingloriously. There is nothing noble or dramatic in death by inanition. In the forenoon of September 20, 1870, while the Italians were entering Rome, Pius IX was unconcernedly amusing himself in the Vatican by composing a charade.[61] From Hildebrand to him the descent was hardly less amazing than from Julius Cæsar to Romulus Augustulus.

The pamphlet of the Sincere Catholic promoted the Italian Cause in a way he did not intend. Austria required France to promise not to allow the anti-Papal suggestions in it to be

---

[60] The "Almanach de Gotha" for 1859 gives the nationality of the 66 cardinals as follows: Italian, 48; French, 7; Austrian, 5; Spanish, 2; Belgian, German, English and Portuguese, 1 each. In December 1910, with 18 vacancies in the college, the proportion of Italians was still overwhelming, viz.: Italian, 32; Austrian, 6; Spanish, 4; French, 3; German, 2; Irish, 2; American, Belgian, and Portuguese, 1 each.

[61] De Cesare: *Fine*, II, 456. The word chosen by Pius was *Tremare:*

Il tre non oltrepassa il mio *primiero*,
È *l'altro* molto vasto e molto infido
Che spesso spesso fa provar *l'intero*.

broached in the approaching Congress: France declined to bind herself. Then Austria, having heard secretly that Pius would not send a delegate, refused to take part in a Congress in which the Pope had no representative. On January 3, 1860, Walewski formally announced that the Congress, which was to have assembled on January 19, would not meet at all.[62] This left the Italians, whose doom was to be assigned to them by the mandate of Europe, to shift for themselves. They had reached another turning-point in their zig-zag climb to independence.

The most important event, however, was Cavour's return to office. Since September, the Piedmontese public had regarded his recall as merely a question of time; since November, Liberals in all parts of Italy wondered why there was so long a delay. Although Cavour himself could have forced a crisis, he would not complicate the situation, for he had pledged his support to the Ministers so long as they seemed to him to safeguard Italy's interests. When they asked his advice, he gave it. But he grew more and more disgusted with what he dubbed ministerial incompetence. Instead of taking the initiative, Rattazzi and La Marmora waited for instructions from Paris. Apparently Cavour thought it possible, since Napoleon III upheld non-intervention, to hasten the union with the Central States. He feared also, and with good reason, that Rattazzi would revert to his old cronies of the Left. Rattazzi, in fact, was no sooner in office than Brofferio, Valerio, Depretis, Capriolo and their friends flocked to support him; and his personal attraction was so great for Victor Emanuel that, at his suggestion, the King welcomed Brofferio and Guerrazzi freely. The anti-Cavourians, long held in check, naturally made the most of their opportunity. The Rattazzians announced that their chief would devote his attention to internal affairs, which had been shockingly neglected by Cavour, yet they pretended to excuse Cavour's neglect on the plea that for eight years he had been too busy with Piedmont's foreign policy to give proper attention to home needs. They said that he had the fatal defect of being an autocrat. Everything must be done by him. As he would trust no able men to divide with him the burden of government, his satellites were mere mediocrities or nonentities.

[62] *Correspondence*, 1860, 274; Cowley to Russell, Jan. 1, 1860; Walewski to Jaucourt, Jan. 3, 1860, p. 275.

Inevitably, when his great personality was removed, there was disclosed only a void. And now, even his foreign policy had been wrecked, with the result that Piedmont had nothing but disappointment and a huge debt to show for his Icarian schemes.[63]

Rattazzi sent Brofferio and Depretis into Central Italy to report on the situation there. Stigmatizing the people as timid and slothful, and their governors as either lukewarm, illiberal or treacherous, Brofferio recommended that they should be turned out of power, and that the King, leaguing himself with Garibaldi, should call on Italy to rise and fight as one man. Such a course, the Subalpine Cleon admitted, would require audacity, but he assured Rattazzi that on Garibaldi's promise "*a million men and a million guns*" would respond. "And then, forward!" said he, with that grandiose sweep of the hand with which political prestidigitators conjure away facts. What Rattazzi would have preferred, we do not know; but he had sufficient discretion to wait awhile: for the Treaty of Zurich, signed on November 11 and ratified on the 17th, provided for the European Congress, and he saw that it would be discreet to give that precedence. Much debate arose over the question who should represent Piedmont. Public opinion from the first designated Cavour; the dominant class in the Central States called for Cavour; foreigners identified the Italian cause with Cavour, and thought that without him Italy would not be represented at all. Nevertheless, objections loomed up on three sides. Although Rattazzi and his colleagues desired him to accept,[64] the King had neither forgotten the passionate outburst at Villa Melchiorri, nor forgiven the Rosina affair. He also wished to consult the Emperor's preference. To send to the Congress an envoy odious to Napoleon would be the height of folly. The King therefore secretly despatched an agent to Paris and got direct assurance that Cavour would be acceptable. Presumably Napoleon had now abandoned hope of creating a kingdom in Central Italy for Plon-Plon; he was disturbed by the way England had cut in and appropriated his sponsorship of the Italian cause; he was charging his anti-Papal bolt; he

---

[63] *Diritto*, Aug. 1, 1859; Valerio's organ.　　[64] Castelli writes Minghetti on Nov. 22, 1859: "Rattazzi agrees, and has had a long talk with C., who accepts." *Carteggio*, I, 247. Again, on Nov. 26: "Cavour was informed by despatches from England and from Gortchakoff that those two governments desire him and request him of our [government] for the Congress." P. 254.

must very soon be able to appease Frenchmen with some tangible compensation for his Quixotic war. To harp upon Cavour's wrath after Villafranca would do no good; better welcome him to the Congress and secure his aid against Ultramontanes and Reds. As usual, however, what the Emperor agreed upon in secret had no effect on Walewski, who appeared before the world as the authoritative spokesman of French foreign policy. Having consistently opposed every suggestion favorable to Piedmont or to Italy, he could not be expected, after his experience in 1856, with all that had happened since, to desire to sit with Cavour in another congress. Empress Eugénie, who was always hostile to Cavour, opposed him now, and with her intrigued the Ultramontane clergy and many of the influential women who played an important though officially unrecognized part in politics at the Tuileries.[65]

To these obvious enemies, were added accomplices of the Piedmontese Radicals, who sought to swell the opposition to Cavour at Turin by printing denigrations of him at Paris. Charles de La Varenne, a journalist at once facile and plausible, eulogized Rattazzi's superiority as organizer and administrator, and his tactful pliancy in effacing himself before the King's wishes. He pictured Cavour, on the contrary, as merely an agitator, with a passion for spectacular policies and with a talent for putting himself where the dazzling light was focused on him alone; one who brooked no rivals, employed no men of ability, and was responsible, by his shocking conduct towards the Emperor, for the brusque stopping of the war.[66] Other writers echoed La Varenne's opinions. At Turin, Brofferio founded a political club, "The Free Assemblies," and edited, as its organ, the *Stendardo*, which proved its fierce patriotism by abusing and ridiculing the hated statesman. Brofferio hoped to seal an alliance between the Left and Left Centre which, with Rattazzi at its head, should supplant the old Cavourian majority. Rattazzi's sympathies were naturally Radical, and his personal influence on the King was counted on to win the royal consent to Radical measures very thinly disguised.[67] The *Stendardo*, however, overreached itself so far that a group of twenty-five deputies who

[65] *Lettere*, III, ccxcvii, n. 1. [66] *Lettere*, III, cclxxxvi, 59.
[67] How the Radicals succeeded was shown at Aspromonte and Mentana.

2

had deliberated whether to join the Free Assemblies or not, voted to have nothing to do with that society (December 21). Although Rattazzi was in constant communication with Brofferio, yet he insisted during these very weeks that Cavour must represent Piedmont at the Congress. The Emperor acquiesced, the Cabinet favored, the public demanded; it remained only to persuade Victor Emanuel. This task fell to Dabormida, the Foreign Minister, who "urged the King so hard" that he could no longer refuse.[68] On December 22, Nigra went to Leri with a command for Cavour to meet the King on the following day.[69] Their interview was satisfactory, and on December 24 the official gazette announced Cavour's nomination.[70]

With growing indignation he had waited in the country for the Ministers' decision. He did not make sufficient allowance for their embarrassment. It was bad enough in his eyes that they should be as servile "as valets" to the French Emperor;[71] it was worse that they should truckle to the Radicals. The thought of Brofferio frequenting the King's Palace and acting as mentor to Rattazzi angered him; the suggestion that Valerio and other anti-Cavourians should be sent to oust Farini and Ricasoli disgusted him: for he believed that the salvation of Italy depended upon the maintenance in power of the great Liberal Party which included the largest possible number of supporters. A policy directed by the Republicans would be as narrow and exclusive as one controlled by the Clericals. He was kept informed of the base intrigues and wretched plots against himself, and although he held Dabormida and La Marmora innocent, his affection for the latter began to ebb. As to facing the hostile Imperial clique at Paris, he had no qualms: he never brooded over the past, and he had now ceased to regret Villafranca.[72] "Bless the peace," he

---

[68] Dabormida to Desambrois, Dec. 22, 1859; the interview took place the preceding evening. *Lettere*, III, ccxcix.   [69] *Lettere*, VI, 514: Dabormida to C., Dec. 22.   [70] "The King received him very graciously," Castelli writes Farini, on Dec. 23, "and the interview was satisfactory on one side and the other; and I know it, from one side and the other." *Lettere*, VI, 515.

[71] "What credit," he writes Castelli on Dec. 10, "can a government give me that does not dare to nominate its representative without first having obtained the express permission of a foreign prince?" *Lettere*, VI, 500. "These ministers are ignoble valets." C. to Castelli, Dec. 17; *Ibid*, 510.

[72] After reading Napoleon's reply to the Archbishop of Bordeaux on Oct. 11, C. said: "I forgive the Emperor the peace of Villafranca; he has just rendered a service greater than the battle of Solferino." C. to W. de La Rive, Jan. 7, 1860; *Lettere*, III, 167.

CAVOUR'S HOUSE AT LERI

wrote Prince Napoleon; because by it, but contrary to the intentions of the two Emperors, the Italians had gone further towards independence than they might if the war had been fought out,[73] and they had escaped from obligations to Napoleon that might have reduced them to tutelage. Cavour could meet the Emperor, therefore, unprejudiced by their rupture in July; and he stood in no awe of either Walewski or the Austrian envoys. He accepted the nomination, however, without deceiving himself as to the difficulties before him. He felt that the long wrangle over his nomination deprived him of the semblance of a unanimous backing. In 1856, he went to Paris as Prime Minister, to carry out his own projects; in 1860, he must go with instructions from a Cabinet he despised. "In spite of all, I have accepted," he wrote Farini; "because by refusing I must of necessity proclaim an antagonism fatal to Italy; but in accepting, I believe I have made the greatest sacrifice that a public man can make for his country, not merely by consenting to bear in silence cruel insults, but also by accepting a mandate from a government which inspires in me neither esteem nor trust."[74]

The Radicals, led by Brofferio, made a final effort to prevent Cavour from going to the Congress. They needed a popular figurehead, and they found one in Garibaldi[75] who, feeling sore over his forced abandonment of the invasion of the Pope's domain, was easily coaxed into resigning the honorary presidency of the National Society. He cherished his rainbow vision that if a Million Muskets were provided, a Million Italians would leap from the soil and shoulder them. The Radicals, pretending to share his delusion,[76] made him president of the Free Assemblies, which they rechristened the Nation Armed. Brofferio, Sineo, Beolchi, Asproni, and other Garibaldians and Republicans were among its directors. They evidently deluded him into believing that if this society showed its vigor, the European Congress would let the Italians settle their own destiny: "the affair would be done in a fortnight," he confidently predicted.[77] On December 31 he issued an address "to Italian Liberals," bidding them to rally round Victor Emanuel, to embrace each other fraternally,

---

[73] *Lettere*, VI, 539–40; C. to Prince Napoleon, Jan. 25, 1860.
[74] *Lettere*, III, 162; C. to Farini, Dec. 25, 1859.   [75] *Lettere*, III, ccclii.
[76] Jessie Mario admits the existence of the Brofferian plot. *Bertani*, I, 422 *ff*.
[77] Ciàmpoli, 121; Garibaldi to Türr, Dec. 18, 1859.

and to understand that their only enemy was the foreign oppressor.[78] Since the Nation Armed existed to destroy the National
Society, to bury Cavour, to oust Farini and Ricasoli, and to
side-track if not to shatter the Liberal Party, Garibaldi's appeal
for union resembles the proverbial invitation of the lion to the
lamb, but as he had absolutely no sense of humor, he failed to
see the inconsistency. All he asked for was to be allowed to fight,
and to fight without delay. The announcement that, under the
protection of the King's government, he had formed a society
whose object was to attack the "oppressor," called out so many
protests and received so little support[79] that on January 4 he
published a second proclamation in which, after denouncing the
minions of corruption and insolence and the modern Jesuits who
took fright at the idea of the Italian Nation in Arms, he declared
the society dissolved.[80] Pressure had evidently reached him from
above, from a source which, happily, his instinct warned him it
would be imprudent to disregard. Then he devoted himself with
all the greater zeal to collecting funds for the Million Muskets,
an object countenanced by the Ministry.

The plot to crush Cavour failed. Garibaldi attributed to him
and not to the Brofferians, this check on his impatient patriotism.
Throughout the intrigue Rattazzi protested to be no party to it:
but his denial does not agree with Brofferio's report of meetings,
at which, we may suspect, they discussed some topic other than
the weather or folk-poetry.[81] The dissolution of the Nation
Armed had just cleared the way for Cavour's mission to Paris,[82]
when the Congress itself was indefinitely postponed. The Imperial Pamphlet had killed it.

That this was indeed Napoleon's secret motive in issuing "The
Pope and the Congress" seems now indisputable. On coming to
terms at Villafranca, he and Francis Joseph supposed that the
Italians would acquiesce in their arrangement, which a European
Congress would simply need to legalize. But the Italians had
gone their own gait, the Roman Question, with its hydra heads,
was alarming France, and it required no unusual foresight to mark

---

[78] Ciàmpoli, 121; dated Dec. 31, 1859.

[79] La Farina, II, 272, states that in four days no members joined it at Turin.

[80] Ciàmpoli, 125.   [81] "Rattazzi exclaimed this morning, 'who will free
me from such friends!'" Castelli: *Carteggio*, I, 280; Dec. 29, 1859.   [82] He
had engaged rooms at Hotel Bristol. Desambrois was to be his colleague.

the Roman Question as the rock on which the Congress would split. Napoleon wished to avoid that peril and the likelihood that Francis Joseph would accuse him of disloyalty if he failed to uphold their mutual agreement. Having determined, therefore, that there should be no Congress, at the time when he acted as if its assembling were fixed, he shot off his pamphlet. This shifted the blame of a refusal on Austria and on the Pope, and gave him a delusive sense of being freed from a nightmare. He had now two leading projects: At home, he wished to appease the public, and especially the army, discontented over the unfruitfulness of the Italian war, and, further, to propitiate the masses, who complained of heavy taxation, and were disaffected by Clerical propaganda. Abroad, he regarded the recovery of England's friendship as his chief need. Weeks before the pamphlet appeared, French politicians and officers were discussing the annexation of Savoy. Simultaneously, Palmerston was urging that the Emperor should consent to the union of the Central Italian States with Piedmont. To this Persigny replied that the French would take umbrage at the creation of a kingdom of eleven millions of Italians on their southeastern frontier; he hinted, however, that the cession of Savoy might calm them. Palmerston objected that this would make Napoleon's great enterprise for liberating Italy appear as a ruse for filching from the House of Savoy the little province where that family originated, and that the lofty and generous policy of the Emperor would be denatured, and a very mean interest would be substituted for a noble principle. Unabashed, Persigny told Palmerston that England, by proposing to astonished Europe the cession of Savoy, would heal the wounds of 1815, and prove the sincerity of that friendship which the ancient rivals now professed. Palmerston said nothing: but Persigny, "who had the happy gift of believing that when he had spoken his hearer was convinced," assured the Emperor that he could see by Palmerston's manner that his reason was captivated by the grandeur of the rôle he might play.[83]

Napoleon embodied his scheme for propitiating the French masses in a commercial treaty with England. The distinguished French economist, Chevalier, on visiting London had a hearty

[83] Ollivier, 343–45; quoting Palmerston's notes to Persigny on Dec. 2 and 4, and Persigny's despatch of Dec. 16.

welcome from Cabinet Ministers, financiers and City magnates.
Cobden, who spent the autumn in France, made important con-
verts, if not to the entire doctrine of free trade at least to reci-
procity or to a low tariff between France and England. When
he quoted the motto on Peel's statue, Napoleon exclaimed that
that was the fame he chiefly yearned for. Cobden supplied him
with arguments against protection, and assured him that, if his
friendship for England were genuine, he could prove it in no
more practical way than in adopting this policy of peace. Napoleon was persuaded. Then Palmerston and Russell, who had
been too busy over a trifling quarrel in Morocco to pay much attention to Cobden when he first broached his project, saw its
importance, and appointed him a special envoy to draft and
sign the treaty. In less than a month he accomplished his task
(January 18).[84] By this measure, Napoleon expected to capture the goodwill of England and to win the devotion of the
French masses, to whom it cheapened the necessaries of life and
promised better wages.

Meanwhile Cavour was waiting at Turin for definitive news of
the Congress. He did not dissemble his scorn for the intrigues of
the Radicals. He told his old friend, La Marmora, only too
plainly, that the honest members of the Cabinet had been duped
by tricksters — candor at which the brusque soldier naturally
took offense; "he kept silent, and went off angry and aggrieved."[85]
Recriminations among the partisans of both factions were inevitable: bitter words, uttered in private by the leaders, went the
rounds. With Garibaldi's departure (January 5) the Radicals
seemed to have played their last trump. The Ministry, after intriguing with them for many weeks past, must now face the crisis
alone.[86] The country repudiated it; Italy prayed for its dissolution: but it had neither the pluck nor the grace to die. On January 4, the Emperor dismissed Walewski: proof positive, as Palmerston's *Morning Post* announced, that Napoleon had decided to
act in concert with England on the Italian Question.[87]

[84] Morley: *Cobden*, II, chap. 11, for detailed account of Cobden's negotiations.
[85] *Lettere*, VI, 527; C. to Cugia, Jan. 3, 1860. Castelli: *Carteggio*, I, 279. *Lettere*,
III, cccxxxiv; La Marmora writes to Pettiti on Jan. 14, 1860: "I am utterly disgusted, especially with Cavour, who, being in Turin, declared not only that he
did not care to see me, but did not even send once to inquire for me."
[86] La Farina, II, 273.   [87] *Moniteur*, Jan. 8, 1860, translates *Post's* leader.

As Walewski fades away into oblivion, we bid farewell to a mediocre man who consented for five years to live in a false position. Possibly the timid business man's policy he advocated for France might have served her better than the Emperor's rashness; but he never had the character to stand by it. He knew that the Emperor's schemes were at odds with his own; that he might talk and negotiate with all the swagger fitting to a Foreign Secretary, but that, when the time came to act, the Imperial will would prevail, without even consulting him. In consequence, many persons construed his conduct as deceitful, whereas it was simply weak. A man of principles would have resigned on the first occasion when he caught his sovereign making a dupe or a decoy of him: [88] but Walewski, like all his colleagues, found the post of minister too lucrative and too pleasantly adorned with seeming power and with pomp, to dream of resigning.[89] He would gladly have been transferred to the Ministry of Finance, but the Emperor needed in that office an able and unscrupulous money-getter, to provide funds for his own and Empress Eugénie's boundless extravagance. Exit Walewski, with his anti-Italian, anti-Liberal sympathies, and his determination that Tuscany should be restored to the Lorrainese or given to a French aspirant; enter Thouvenel, a diplomat of ampler capacity, who believed in the Emperor's favorite doctrines — the English alliance, non-intervention, and the spirit of nationality.[90]

Walewski's downfall caused joy at Turin, where it was accepted as the confirmation of the policy outlined by Napoleon in the famous pamphlet. As it rendered the convening of the Congress still more improbable, Cavour doubtless chuckled over it: but his own position became every day more ambiguous. If there were no congress, his appointment to it would be void: in that case, why should he linger in Turin? The Cabinet persisted in making believe it was alive, thus blocking his return to office; the King persisted in holding him at bay. Yet Prince Napoleon,

[88] Rouher said to Cobden on Dec. 9: "There is but one man in the government, — the Emperor, and but one will, that of the Emperor." Morley: *Cobden*, II, 254. M. Émile Ollivier assures me, however, that Walewski was not cognizant of the Emperor's conflicting intrigues. [89] Walewski's resignation and Thouvenel's appointment were gazetted in the *Moniteur* of Jan. 4, 1860.

[90] The best, if not the only, eulogy of Walewski in our time is in La Gorce, III, 182. Indeed, La Gorce's history of the relations between France and Italy from 1855 to 1860 is a pæan dedicated to Walewski.

speaking in part for the Emperor, urged that Cavour be sent to Paris to drive matters ahead and to conclude.[91] Congress or no Congress, Lord John Russell wrote to Hudson, "I hope Cavour will come to Paris and London." "As oaks grow from acorns," Hudson remarked, "so even did this curt invitation produce its fruit in the downfall of the Cabinet."[92] The Ministers were willing, if not glad, to have Cavour set out on this special mission, and relieve them by his absence of the feeling that he was dogging their hesitating steps in the very streets of Turin. They could rely upon his winning the utmost concession for Italy. Cavour, however, declined to start unless they gave him a guarantee that they would convene the Piedmontese parliament on the earliest possible date (March 20). They demurred.[93] The King, they reported, felt offended at the notion of Cavour's requiring a guarantee. Cavour rejected the appointment forthwith. This threw the Rattazzians into consternation, while the Cavourians, although regarding his act as justifiable, feared that it would lead to an open feud which might be fatal to the great cause. The devoted Farini wrote from Modena to Castelli: Cavour "has so lofty a post that he cannot and should not honor with his scorn certain of his enemies."[94] Friends of harmony sought a way of reconciliation:[95] but the matter dragged, and Cavour, disgusted, determined to go back to Leri and devote himself 'to milking his cows.' On the afternoon of January 6, whilst he was calling at Hudson's to say good-bye, Solaroli came to submit to Hudson some documents from the Ministers. The conversation turned on Cavour's demands. To avoid misunderstanding, Solaroli asked Cavour to jot them down: but he was irritated and weary, and did not suppose that it would be of any use. Then Hudson took a scrap of paper and offered to write, if Cavour would dictate. In two minutes the ultimatum in black and white was in Solaroli's hands; if Parliament shall meet in March, Cavour will accept the mission.[96] Solaroli hastened with this reply to the

---

[91] Prince Napoleon in an interview with Desambrois, Jan. 2, 1860: *Lettere,* III, cccxx.   [92] Walpole: *Russell,* II, 317.

[93] The ministerial statement is given in Dabormida's letter to Desambrois, Jan. 18, 1860; *Lettere,* III, cccxxxvi ff.

[94] Castelli: *Carteggio,* I, 283; Farini to Castelli, Jan. 8, 1860.

[95] Walpole: *Russell,* II, 317. *Lettere,* III, cccxxxvi.

[96] *Lettere,* III, 182–83, for C.'s detailed account in letter to Desambrois of Jan. 23. The *Perseveranza* printed the brief note. *Ibid,* 183, n. 1.

Ministers, who would not assent to it. One of them recognized Hudson's handwriting: whereupon La Marmora, the Premier, declared that as this was clearly an attempt on the part of a foreign ambassador to interfere in the internal affairs of the State, the Cabinet must resign.[97] Shortly afterward they handed their portfolios to the King, who, though ill and surprised, rose to the occasion. As usual, his judgment worked best in a crisis. Recognizing that the Cabinet could not keep up longer even a show of viability, he accepted their resignations, and sent for Cavour. The Count's carriage was at his own door, to take him to the station; but he drove instead to the Palace, where, a quarter of an hour later, he found the King in bed.[98] The interview was an ordeal for both, but especially for Victor Emanuel, who stipulated that Cavour should never again, either directly or indirectly, meddle in his relations with Rosina. As to public policies, they came to an agreement, although Cavour was much startled when the King told him that Napoleon had recently demanded the cession of Nice besides Savoy.[99] A statesman less courageous or less patriotic would have declined a responsibility which might make him odious: but Cavour evaded no duty; perhaps he hoped, in this case, to prevent the worst; he certainly knew that if he could not, no one else could. That evening he left the Palace with instructions to form a Cabinet.[100] This he did without difficulty. On January 21, the new Ministry, in which he was Premier, Minister of Foreign Affairs, Minister of Marine, and provisional Minister of the Interior, took office. Only two of his colleagues — Mamiani (Public Instruction), and Fanti (War) — were conspicuous: the others — Vegezzi (Finance), Jacini (Public Works), Cassinis (Grace and Justice) and Corsi (Agriculture) — were routine men, who might be replaced whenever political exigencies required.

Look back on the half-year of his eclipse. See how, instead of

[97] Hudson wrote: "I was not a little astonished to learn that I was accused of having exercised an undue pressure upon the Rattazzi Cabinet (if I had the power it would have been by the application of hemp to its windpipe, and not by sending a scrap of paper), which had forced its chief to tender his resignation to the King. . . . I cannot say that I was particularly affected by the intelligence but I deemed it advisable to enter a protest against the truth of the assertion." Walpole: *Russell*, II, 371, n. 1.

[98] Massari: *Vitt. Em.*, 313–14; also, Massari: *La Marmora*, 260; more extended version in Tavallini: *Lanza*, I, 217. [99] *Lettere*, IV, 12. [100] *Lettere*, III, cccxxxv.

being disgraced or even discredited by the peace of Villafranca,
he grew steadily in reputation. His enemies disparaged his
statesmanship, because he had been checked by Napoleon; they
accused him of cowardice, because he resigned the premiership
in the hour of danger; they imputed to him selfishness, vanity,
a dog-in-the-manger spirit, unfairness, disloyalty. Still his influence grew. The very Ministers, who believed that they could
prove themselves abler than he, were forced to consult him. The
King, who had reasons enough for resenting the conduct of the
man, realized that Piedmont could not do without the genius of
the statesman. That Cavour was impatient,[101] that he chafed
at the Cabinet's timidity, that he underestimated its handicap
as well as the value of its actual achievement, cannot be doubted.
Nor can we deny that he, too, had just cause for resenting the
ignoble tricks employed to prevent him from attending the Congress. In view of the clash of interests and of the passionate
natures of the men, we marvel not that there was some friction,
but that there was any restraint.

The self-control of the Central Italians deserved the highest
praise. Since May they had governed themselves without disorder. When diplomacy said to them, "Restoration," they replied, "Annexation and Italian Independence." By their firmness, they blocked alike Napoleon and Francis Joseph and they
forced Diplomacy into a new channel. Thanks to Ricasoli's
immovability, they were saved from any transient arrangement,
which might have diverted them from the final consummation —
unity. The policy of some of the Party of Action to take the lead
by using Garibaldi, first, in a mad raid on the Papal States, and,
next, in an attempt to capture the government of Piedmont,
must be censured as fratricidal, if we judge it by common sense;[102]

[101] " You know," writes Dabormida to Desambrois a few days after the change
of ministers, "that I have always recognized the right of Count Cavour to be
called to finish the work which he began with so much talent and energy, and
with excess of courage. I was impatient to cede my place to him; however, he
has shown himself still more impatient than I; I thought that it would not be useless for him to visit Paris and London before coming back to the helm of affairs.
I regret that he has worked so hard to force an open door! But he has the right
to have the ambition!" Lettere, III, cccxxxvii.

[102] Bertani repudiated and deplored the plot to make Garibaldi a catspaw.
Medici stigmatized the " discredited men " by whom Garibaldi allowed himself
to be played. Even Jessie Mario, implacable towards Cavour, characterizes the
Brofferian attempts as " miserable affairs." Mario: Bertani, I, 421–27.

but if we remember that the Republicans and Radicals regarded the Liberal Monarchists as either too slow or too cowardly, or as wholly mistaken, and if we consider further that they had as much at stake in Italy and professed as disinterested a patriotism as their rivals, though we may censure their judgment we need not doubt their sincerity. Their attempts demonstrated the practical inefficiency of the Party when it came to action, and the willingness of Garibaldi to obey Victor Emanuel rather than to risk a revolution. But the fact which was soon destined to exert a baneful influence on the course of Italian unification, was that Garibaldi came out of these months feeling personally aggrieved, and that, as his grievance grew and rankled, the men who coaxed him away from the National Society poisoned his heart against Cavour. In doing that they injured Italy far beyond the power of Pope or Bourbon to harm her. On the other hand their frustrated agitation in the Centre proved that Ricasoli could no more be shaken by Mazzinians than by Reactionaries. That the King, in recalling Cavour, sacrificed his private aversion for the sake of his country's welfare, was another significant outcome of this momentous half-year. Add to all this that the Papacy already felt the death chill at its extremities, that Italy could now look to England for help if France deserted her, and that Napoleon was ready to support the Italians as a means of propitiating England and of retaining his ascendency in the Peninsula, and we see how Fate had changed the political elements since Cavour quitted his office on July 19, 1859.

CHAPTER XXVIII

ANNEXATION AND CESSION

THOUGH Cavour found the task complicated which Rattazzi handed over to him, yet he could not complain that it was harder than that which he had left for Rattazzi after Villafranca. It was, however, different, and demanded the application of his supple genius to new problems. Since her cession to Piedmont, Lombardy had been governed by royal mandate: Cavour insisted that all parts of the Kingdom should enjoy the same constitutional safeguards, and he therefore called a general election. Still more momentous was the case of the Central Italians, who could not safely be left longer dangling between possible anarchy and the fear of restoration. Napoleon had thus far forbidden annexation; Cavour now prepared to bring it about. "Two men," said Guizot, "divide at this moment the attention of Europe: Emperor Napoleon and M. de Cavour. The match has begun; I bet on M. de Cavour."[1] The wager showed that Cavour's prestige had not been lessened by his apparent defeat at Villafranca: but perhaps Guizot did not know that Cavour's success would now depend upon whether his courage were equal to a great sacrifice. A few days before the La Marmora Cabinet resigned, Baron Talleyrand, the new French Ambassador, reached Turin with instructions to sound the government as to the cession of Savoy and of Nice. Cavour would prevent the sacrifice if he could: if he could not, he would get the largest possible compensation for it.

The very day when he took office, he laid down the cardinal principles on which his policy should turn: at home, "we shall be Liberal conservatives; abroad, out and out Italians [*Italianissimi*], up to the extreme limits of possibility."[2] He gave his Cabinet an Italian rather than a Piedmontese complexion: Jacini was a Lombard; Fanti commanded the Army of the League; Mamiani had been a Papal subject. He planned to have Minghetti and

---

[1] Mazade, 314.   [2] *Lettere*, III, 176; C. to M. d'Azeglio, Jan. 20, 1860.

Farini[3] for colleagues as soon as the unions were completed: he destined Massimo d'Azeglio — ever popular, though ever querulous — for the Governorship at Milan, and young Costantino Nigra — alert, discreet, and successful — for the embassy at Paris.[4] In a few days, he reopened his old channels of communication and influence. Dissolving the Chamber of Deputies on January 21, he fixed the date of the elections for early March. He sent Arese "to propitiate the Emperor by his friendly presence" and to serve him "as goad, as cushion or as lightning-rod."[5] Living up to his avowal that "in politics he practised the next to the last precept of the Lord's prayer," he took every means to let it be understood at the Tuileries that he nursed no rancor. To Prince Napoleon, with whom he had already come again to a friendly footing, he wrote the following letter, at once true and most politic: "Since my last interview with your Highness what great events! How many germs contained in the treaty of Villafranca have developed in a marvelous fashion! The political campaign which followed the peace of Villafranca has been as glorious for the Emperor, and more advantageous for Italy, than the military campaign which preceded it.[6] The Emperor's conduct towards Rome, the reply to the Archbishop of Bordeaux, his immortal pamphlet, the letter to the Pope, are in my eyes titles to the gratitude of the Italians greater than the victories of Magenta and Solferino. How often in reading in my solitude these historic documents, have I exclaimed 'Blessed be the peace of Villafranca!' Without that, the Roman Question, the most important of all, not only for Italy, but for France and Europe, could not have received a complete solution, sanctioned without reserve by public opinion. In striking a mortal blow, not at religion, but at the Ultramontane principles which denature it, the Emperor has rendered modern society the greatest service it is possible to render it. He has thereby earned the right to be classed among the greatest benefactors of mankind."[7] No doubt, this letter passed without delay from the Palais Royal to the Tuileries.

[3] "Will you share with me the responsibility of the government? With you I shall *dare*, with you, we will make Italy: alone I cannot." Frapolli: *L. C. Farini,* 33.   [4] *Ibid,* and 186. Villamarina had recently been transferred by Rattazzi from Paris to Naples.   [5] *Lettere,* IV, Arese, 214.   [6] I keep the syntax of the original.   [7] *Lettere,* III, 186–87; C. to Prince Napoleon, Jan. 25, 1860.

Not less energetically did Cavour prepare the field at home. To his right-hand man, La Farina, he gave these instructions: 'Demand resolutely, even *sharply*, a solution. Keep repeating that, at whatever cost, even running the risk of committing an irregularity, the electoral colleges must be convoked without further delays. Agitate for an armament, pointing out that to wish to rely on diplomacy alone is a fearful thing, since diplomacy cannot recognize a situation based on the destruction of so-called legitimate thrones, except as accomplished facts. The tone should not be hostile, but yet a *little bit menacing*.[8] Not of course that I need pressure to go ahead, but it will be useful to be able to say that I am pressed.'[9]

La Farina was to shape public opinion indirectly, in unofficial but not less effective ways. Cavour sent to Piedmont's representatives abroad a circular letter setting forth the situation and outlining the attitude they must maintain. He told them that the Congress, which the King's government had eagerly desired, was shelved. The hearty agreement between England and France on the Italian question; the prorogation of the Congress; the Emperor's pamphlet; the Emperor's letter to the Pope — here, he said, were four facts the least of which would suffice to precipitate a solution. A restoration was now as impossible at Bologna and at Parma as at Florence and at Modena; the one way out was to legalize the annexation, already established, of Emilia and Tuscany to Piedmont. Finally, as the Italians had waited so long patiently but vainly for Europe to put their affairs in order, on the basis of non-intervention and of respect for popular wishes, they had earned the right to go forward and provide a government for themselves.[10]

Events hurried on. The commercial treaty between France and England was signed on January 24. The next day, at the opening of Parliament, Queen Victoria spoke at least politely of the Italians. Quick upon this followed proposals which Lord John Russell first made privately to the French Government, and then, when they had been cordially received at Paris, communicated to Cavour. He proposed that France and Austria should agree not to interfere forcibly in the internal affairs of the Penin-

---

[8] "*Un tantino minaccioso.*"   [9] La Farina, II, 289; Feb. 24, 1860. *Lettere*, IV, xlii, n. 2.   [10] Circular note of Jan. 27, 1860; *Lettere*, IV, v–viii.

From a photograph of 1860

LORD JOHN RUSSELL

sula, unless they were unanimously requested to do so by the five Great Powers; that Napoleon should arrange with the Pope to withdraw the French troops from Rome, and at the same time should recall his army from Northern Italy;[11] that the internal government of Venetia should not be discussed; that Victor Emanuel should promise not to send Piedmontese troops into Central Italy, before the several States had solemnly expressed their desires through assemblies newly elected.[12] England was at last to do something for the Italians: not however, without opposition from the Queen and Prince Albert. Victoria refused to nominate Hudson as second British plenipotentiary to the Congress, because she said he was too friendly to the Italians, and she rebuked Palmerston for urging Napoleon to consent to the annexation of even the Duchies to Piedmont.[13] On January 17 she wrote to Uncle Leopold: "Affairs are in a sad and complicated state, and though we modify matters as much as we *can*, we can't entirely keep our Ministers (*the two*)[14] from doing *something*. You will hear no doubt of the last proposal soon. . . . We could not prevent this *proposal*, which I doubt being accepted — as the rest of the Cabinet thought it could *not* be opposed, and entailed *no* material *support*."[15] The Queen and Prince, more than distrustful of Palmerston and Russell, — who declined to be as putty in their hands, — and thoroughly suspicious of Napoleon III, — even when he came bearing gifts, — stood loyally by Austria to the end. To Lord John's suggestion that England should join France in the settlement of the Italian Question, the Queen replied that France and Austria, the parties interested, might very well agree not to meddle in Italy, but that that was no reason why England and France should make a compact; and she thought it "worth remembering" that Austria at that moment had no troops in any part of Italy except her own (Venetia), whereas France still occupied Rome and a portion of Lombardy. "French interference," she adds triumphantly, "is therefore the only one existing."[16] The Prince Consort criticized with equal speciosity the Commercial Treaty, one of his reasons being that

[11] Since the end of the war, he had kept more than 50,000 soldiers in the north, chiefly at Piacenza.   [12] Italian text in C. to Ricasoli, Feb. 1, 1860; Ricasoli, IV, 233–34.   [13] *Q. V. L.*, III, 375; Queen to Russell, Dec. 6, 1859.
[14] Palmerston and Russell.   [15] *Q. V. L.*, III, 384.
[16] Martin, V, 9; Queen to Russell, Jan. 9, 1860.

it "will give the Emperor our coals and iron, which he will want if he should come into collision with us."[17] In spite of Royal opposition, however, the Treaty was signed, and Lord John's Four Proposals, having been accepted in their general drift by Napoleon, were communicated to the European governments. Austria inevitably resented them; if Napoleon wished to provide a permanent peace in Italy, and to remove the ancient cause of rivalry between France and Austria, said Rechberg, he needed only to carry out the compact of Villafranca.[18] But having broken with the Pope and with Reaction, having taken up the English alliance, and being absolved, by the failure of Europe to meet in a congress, from his obligations to Francis Joseph, which were conditioned on their approval by the congress, Napoleon politely informed the Austrian Foreign Minister that France could no longer be bound by the Villafranca terms.[19]

Cavour realized that England's powerful support, though indispensable for carrying out the annexations, was not a substitute for that of the French Emperor. He needed both Lord John Russell and Napoleon, using Lord John as lever for overcoming the Imperial reluctance. Napoleon, coveting the English alliance and jealous of being supplanted by England in Italy, had a still more pressing object at home: the time had come for him to appease the French people by some compensation adequate to their craving. In short, he must secure Savoy and Nice. Thus cession to France and annexation to Piedmont were the warp and woof of diplomatic negotiations during February and March. But at the mere mention of cession, England took alarm, and at the rumor Piedmont shook with indignation. Cavour could not defy Napoleon, for that would lead to the immediate withdrawal of French troops from Lombardy and to the cutting off of French support: those gone, what could prevent Austria from restoring the dukelings of the Centre, or from reconquering Lombardy? If Napoleon insisted, therefore, that the Piedmontese must surrender Savoy to pay him for his campaign of 1859, how could they refuse him? English sympathy, precious though it was, would furnish them with not one soldier in their plight.

This solution had much to commend it to the Emperor, as an

---

[17] Martin, v, 13; Albert to Stockmar, Jan. 15, 1860.
[18] *Stor. Doc.*, viii, 255; Rechberg Note, Feb. 17, 1860.   [19] *Ibid*, 256.

escape from increasing difficulties. It would quash his dispute with the Papacy, relieve him of responsibility for Italy's reconstruction, enrich France with a province which geography intended to be hers, and serve besides as an intimation to the French that their sovereign had foresworn Quixotic enterprises. His pride and theirs might feel a momentary twinge at seeing Austrian influence become paramount again in the Peninsula; but they could console themselves by reflecting that they withdrew of their own accord, and by enjoying solid gains in exchange for slippery possibilities. Whether Napoleon, if driven to bay, would have taken this course we can never know; but in judging Cavour's action during the next two months we must remember that this alternative had always to be reckoned with by him as a danger which might lead to irremediable calamity. Count Rechberg, the Austrian Premier, could with perfect truthfulness assure the British Ambassador at Vienna that Francis Joseph had no intention of interfering in Italian affairs: [20] but he did not say what Austria would do if the French abandoned Italy. In the dubious task of annexation and of cession which confronted Cavour he must not let his right hand know what his left hand was doing. Since only he and Napoleon were in the secret of both transactions, neither England nor Italy must suspect that cession had been agreed upon until annexation was accomplished. Such a business could not be straightforward.[21] It involved evasions and mental reservations, guile and downright double-dealing which no historian with moral sense would attempt to defend or to justify. But then, no historian can justify human nature; his duty is to describe it as truly as he may. The public which watched the progress of the campaign for annexation did not understand — or at most, it only dimly surmised — how far this campaign was affected by the hidden struggle over cession.

In consenting to Lord John Russell's Four Points, Napoleon stipulated that Emilia and Tuscany should not be annexed to Piedmont unless those States expressed their desire by an affirmative vote given by assemblies to be elected in the most suitable

[20] Martin, v, 9, n. 5; Loftus to J. Russell, Vienna, Jan. 24, 1860. That the Austrian army was exhausted and Austria's treasury on the verge of bankruptcy, would not have prevented her from attempting to reconquer Lombardy and Central Italy, if the French had gone. War is frequently the last resource of despots threatened by political or financial collapse.   [21] *Cf*. Arese, 215.

2

way. On reflection, he preferred a plebiscite, — the method by which he had legitimized his own crown, and by which he might most plausibly acquire Nice and Savoy. "This most happy news," Cavour wrote, "not without profound emotion," to Ricasoli, "proves that annexation may now be regarded as achieved." [22] Difficulties, however, sprang up at once, because Ricasoli declared that as Tuscany, through its duly authorized Assembly, had voted in the preceding August to unite with Piedmont, a plebiscite was unnecessary and that recourse to it would cast doubt on the legality of the Tuscan Assembly and of the government itself. Lord John Russell supported him in this contention: but Napoleon, who now regarded the plebiscite as essential to his purposes in Savoy and Nice, insisted that Tuscany must submit to it. Then Ricasoli, adamant as usual where principles or the dignity of his State were concerned, refused to compromise. "We will not budge by a hair's-breadth," he wrote, on February 1, to Massimo d'Azeglio. [23] He hoped to force the King's hand. [24] Cavour requested him to go to Turin to confer, but he declined. [25] Tuscany regarded herself as being already under Victor Emanuel, and would elect deputies to the Italian Parliament on the dates and according to the rules prescribed by royal decree. [26] "Why, in God's name," he asked Cavour by letter, "demand another vote on the question of annexation? At most, the Tuscan Assembly might meet to reaffirm its original votes, sanction the election for deputies, and dissolve." [27] Either this, or nothing, was his ultimatum. His friends reasoned with him. Giorgini used the argument that enemies would construe his refusal to hold a plebiscite as proof that he feared the result. [28] At Napoleon's desire, Pepoli, the Romagnole agent at Paris, accepted for Emilia the recourse to universal suffrage, and thereby traversed Cavour's statement that there should not be universal suffrage. [29] Unable to talk face to face with the Tuscan Dictator, Cavour wrote him a frank letter, in which he said that, while Tuscany and Piedmont considered annexation an accomplished fact, they had still to persuade the Great Powers to sanction it, and that, in order to get this sanction, it would be criminal not

[22] *Lettere*, III, 194, C. to Ricasoli, Feb. 1, 1860.   [23] Ricasoli, IV, 229.
[24] *Ibid*, 228.   [25] *Ibid*, 242; telegrams of Feb. 3, 1860.   [26] *Ibid*.
[27] *Ibid*, 245; Feb. 4, 1860.   [28] *Ibid*, 249; Giorgini from Turin to Ricasoli, Feb. 5, 1860.   [29] *Ibid*, 259; Ricasoli to G. Fabrizi, Feb. 8, 1860.

to acquiesce in such unessential formalities as Europe required. If Tuscany still relucted, let her throw the responsibility on Piedmont: but above all, let her not imperil, or perhaps shatter, the prospect of national unity, by holding out for a mere matter of punctilio.[30] To drive home his plea, Cavour sent Massari, a resourceful and persuasive advocate, to Florence. The Iron Baron yielded. "I cannot deny my faith in the King I have chosen," he said. "My reign is ended; I should have preferred that the great principle should triumph in a great way, but I sacrifice my personal conviction to the common good." [31] This was on February 10. The sight of the Cross of Savoy on the Palazzo Vecchio moved Massari deeply. The fact that he, a Neapolitan by birth, acting now as agent for the Prime Minister of Piedmont, had the assent of Ricasoli, the virtual dictator of Tuscany, testified that their cause was indeed national.

With Emilia already as good as annexed, and with Tuscany acquiescent, Cavour could at last count on his Italian allies, but when he looked to Paris to complete the work of readjustment, he saw a sudden change. The Emperor was caught in an undertow of reaction. So long as his chief desire had been to escape the Congress, he had promised much; now that a month had elapsed, however, and the dread of the Congress no longer troubled him, he repented of his complaisance. As usual, he was astonished to find that the consequences of his acts wore a very different face from that which he had expected. Outwardly, he still appeared to be the arbiter of Europe, but he knew, and he feared that the chancellors of Europe suspected, that he was in no position to dictate.[32] England had superseded him in the respect and affection of the Italians: Austria covertly charged him with being too weak to compel the wards for whom he went to war to obey his

---

[30] Ricasoli, IV, 261–69; C. to Ricasoli, Feb. 8, 1860.

[31] Ibid, 279; Massari to Cavour, Florence, Feb. 10, 1860.

[32] Nevertheless, monarchs and chancellors had not yet outgrown their exaggerated estimate of Napoleon's power. Thus on Jan. 23, 1860, Duke Ernest II, Prince Albert's brother, wrote to their Uncle Leopold: "We have an antique tyrant before us, educated by life itself, and full of a host of cosmopolitical views of the 19th century, *who has a power at his command, such as probably no ruler in Europe has ever had in so absolute a form, indeed, not even his uncle.*" Ernest II: *Memoirs,* IV, 3. The italics are mine. The opinions expressed measure the political acumen at that time of Albert, Ernest and Leopold, whose views in regard to the Emperor were interchangeable.

orders; Prussia and Russia had no sympathy with political Quix-
otry of any kind; the Pope, having denounced the spoliation of
the Romagna, which, he implied, Napoleon had abetted, was in-
flaming still further the French Clericals; finally, the Italians
themselves did not scruple to say openly that they had no
stronger desire to be under French domination than under Austrian. Napoleon understood only too well that he could not go
back; yet he did not enjoy going forward. To soothe Austria he
must make it appear that he had not betrayed the Villafranca
compact; to pacify the Clericals, he must also shift, if he could,
the odium of the overturn in the Romagna. Less intelligible was
his sudden objection to the annexation of Tuscany to Piedmont.
Did he merely wish to procrastinate? did he still nurse the hope
that a Napoleonid might reign at Florence? or was he shrewd
enough to foresee that, if Tuscany were not then annexed, he
might postpone the thorny business of demanding the cession of
Nice to France? Again we are left uncertain; but we infer that
all these considerations weighed with him and that, according as
one or another came uppermost, his policy veered.

During February, the key to the situation was at Rome, as the
despatches which passed between Thouvenel and Gramont [33]
amply prove. Thouvenel, a foreign minister of different calibre
from Walewski, labored honestly to effectuate the Emperor's
plans, instead of countermining them by intrigues of his own.
In addition to truly statesmanlike qualities, he was honest and
urbane. A seasoned diplomat, he set himself to devise techni-
cal quibbles to enable Napoleon to adopt a new line of action
without incurring the charge of traitor. Gramont was by nature
too overbearing to be a good negotiator, but he had no illusions
as to Pius IX or the Curia. In his second despatch, Thouvenel
told Gramont that he had unearthed some very interesting documents telling how, in 1814 and 1815, Austria and Naples had not
blushed to enrich themselves with Papal spoils — the same
Austria and Naples that were now screaming to have the inviolability of the Legations accepted as a dogma.[34] Gramont found
Antonelli suspiciously conciliatory. The wily Cardinal declared
that not France but Austria was responsible for the loss of the

[33] Formerly French Ambassador at Turin: transferred to Rome, Aug. 16, 1857.
[34] Thouvenel, I, 6; Thouvenel to Gramont, Jan. 29, 1860.

Romagna: that the Pope could not expect Napoleon to interfere and restore it by force; that all they asked was that he should not legalize the spoliation. "We regret keenly," Antonelli continued, "all the incidents of these last days," — the Pope's allocution, the unauthorized publication of the Emperor's letter, — "and even the last encyclical." "The Pope ardently desires," he added, "to return to his old frank relations with the Emperor." [35] This interview took place on February 3. Five days later, when Gramont saw the Pope himself, Pius said bluntly: "The situation has cleared; I know that I have nothing further to expect from the Emperor; he will let them take the Legations and the Romagna from me, and I cannot prevent it. . . . He has the force and he is master." The Pope then intimated that he should make an "enormous" distinction between Napoleon and Victor Emanuel. His last hope was to persuade the Emperor not to countenance the wicked scheme of the Piedmontese, against whom he intended to launch a bull of major excommunication.[36]

Finding Pius immovable, Napoleon cast about for another scheme which, although it might be rejected at Rome, would serve to exonerate himself. On February 15 Arese wrote Cavour that Thouvenel was going to send a "rose-water ultimatum" to the effect that France would consent only to the annexation of Parma, Modena and the Legations to Piedmont, but with the proviso that the Legations should be held in the Pope's name by a vicar and should pay tribute to the Holy See. Tuscany must be a separate kingdom under a Savoy prince. If this offer were declined, France would withdraw her troops from Italy and leave Piedmont at her own risk and peril to seek something better.[37] Cavour was in Milan, and received Arese's letter a day late. He wrote at once to General Fanti to hurry forward military preparations with the greatest secrecy.[38] He bade Arese to persuade the Emperor that by opposing the annexation of Tuscany, he would incur the indelible hatred of the Italians, whereas, if he

[35] Thouvenel, I, 22; Gramont to Thouvenel, Feb. 4, 1860.
[36] Ibid, I, 32–33; Gramont to Thouvenel, Feb. 11, 1860.
[37] Arese, 222; Arese to Cavour, Paris, Feb. 15, 1860. Lettere, III, 210; C. to Fanti, Milan, Feb. 18, 1860. Thouvenel, I, 41–42; Thouvenel to Gramont, Feb. 19, 1860. As an alternative, Napoleon suggested giving Parma, Modena, and Tuscany to Piedmont, and making the Duke of Parma vicar of the Legations; but he preferred plan I. Thouvenel, I, 42.   [38] Lettere, III, 210–11.

consented, they would forget Villafranca, and hold him in greater
popularity than ever. Joined with the French, the Italians would
form a compact whole of 50,000,000 souls — a power which might
defy any European coalition. If Napoleon had any doubts as to
the wishes of the Tuscans, Cavour proposed that they be asked
whether they preferred to remain independent, or to become
members of the Kingdom of Italy. The King and he would do
their utmost to second Napoleon's views, but they could not,
even at the risk of being abandoned by the French, deny the
principle of popular suffrage on which the new Italian throne
rested. Single-handed, they would face the Austrians, rather
than coerce the Tuscans.[39]

With the Pope protesting that he would have none of their
vicariate, and with Cavour declaring that Piedmont would never
abet the violation of Tuscany, Napoleon III and Thouvenel were
mightily perplexed. Gramont kept sending irritating despatches
from Rome, where the Austrian Ambassador (Baron Bach) and
Count Buol, who happened to be recreating himself among the
antiquities of the Eternal City, had the ear of Pius and his advisers.[40] In Paris, Monsignor Sacconi, the Papal Nuncio, poured
out so turgid a stream of denunciations that Gramont advised
Thouvenel to hand him his passports.[41] Through all these weeks
England never stopped recommending immediate annexation.
At length Napoleon judged that he had made a sufficient pretense of defending the Pope's interests to protect himself from
the wrath of the French Papalists. Gramont suggested that he
should formally urge the people of the Legations to return to
their allegiance to the Pope;[42] advice which, of course, they
would not heed. Then Gramont urged the Pope that the Vicariate alone would both rescue for him the nominal sovereignty
of the Legations, and save the rest of his territory and Naples.[43]
Pius, however, determined to remain passive;[44] there was nothing, absolutely nothing, Gramont wrote, to hope for from him.

[39] *Lettere*, III, 211–14; C. to Arese, Feb. 19, 1860.   [40] Thouvenel, I, 46.
[41] *Ibid*, 39. Sacconi asserted that while he was instructed by Antonelli to
be as violent as possible at Paris, the Cardinal himself at Rome pretended to be
conciliatory. Sacconi is "more and more detestable," Thouvenel writes on Feb.
26. *Ibid*, 47.   [42] *Ibid*, I, 45; Gramont to Thouvenel, Rome, Feb. 25, 1860.
[43] *Ibid*, I, 47; Thouvenel to Gramont, Paris, Feb. 26, 1860.
[44] *Ibid*, I, 50; Gramont to Thouvenel, Rome, March 3, 1860.

"One cannot be more Popish than the Pope," Gramont added. "We are justified in the eyes of Europe. Now let the Emperor wash his hands of the Legations." Pius's control over his temper slackened so notably under these trials, that when the Portuguese Minister ventured to speak in behalf of conciliation, the Pope burst out: "In truth, to have advice from this little fellow, representing that little country, is like being kicked by a donkey." And he denounced the "infernal policy which changes every minute." "All that is deplorable," Gramont comments; "all the worse because there is no remedy for the evil. It is in the Pope that stubbornness and blindness dwell, and from him that the resistance springs. That is whither feebleness and incapacity on the throne lead! The saintly virtues do not suffice for reigning."[45]

The delay in coming to a decision exasperated Ricasoli. True to his duty of shielding Tuscany from seeming to act by compulsion, he chafed at Victor Emanuel's failure to give the word to proceed to an election. From Fabrizi at Paris he first learned of the veering in the Emperor's policy,[46] and he must have laughed to hear that Napoleon pretended to have changed his mind because he thought that the Tuscans did not wish to be annexed to the new Kingdom of Italy. Montanelli, indeed, and other doctrinaries, spread that falsehood, the friends of the deposed Lorrainese echoed it, and later French historians have cited it as a valid reason for the Imperial backsliding:[47] but facts were overwhelmingly against it. If circumstantial evidence can be trusted, the true explanation is that early in February Napoleon and Thouvenel vaguely foresaw that, if Tuscany joined the new Kingdom, the Italian yearnings of the Neapolitans would be stimulated, a revolution might break out and overthrow the detested Bourbon dynasty, and then Naples and Sicily would unite under Victor Emanuel and hasten to complete the unification of Italy. But Napoleon intended that the Italian Kingdom should not exceed ten million inhabitants, and he was still dreaming that a French sovereign might replace the Bourbon at Naples. So long as he could keep Victor Emanuel from crossing the Apennines, there-

[45] Thouvenel, I, 55.   [46] Ricasoli, IV, 296–98; G. Fabrizi to Ricasoli, Paris, Feb. 16, 1860.   [47] Cf. Rambaud et Lavisse. Ollivier, 389. Montanelli said to Ollivier: "How could we submit to barbarians? Just fancy, Boncompagni says *lingeria* instead of *biancheria!*"

fore, he might check the furor for unification in the South. Tuscany, if independent, even though nominally ruled by a prince of Savoy, would serve as a neutral zone.[48]

News of the Emperor's latest plan merely whetted Cavour's resolve. On February 20 he telegraphed to Ricasoli from Milan, where he was still in attendance on the King: "The moment to make an energetic decision approaches, but is not yet come; count on my devotion, and, in case of need, on my audacity also."[49] This did not satisfy Ricasoli, who fretted for immediate action. Two days later he learned that Cavour had telegraphed to London: "Sooner than abandon Tuscany, sooner than accept a new conference on the affairs of Italy, we ask to be left alone to struggle with Austria,"[50] — and that Palmerston had approved. Still, the Iron Baron could not persuade himself that the King and Cavour were moving as fast as they might, and he sometimes suspected that they were dallying with him. In fact, however, Cavour was waiting to strike at the first signal that he could certainly rely upon England. In the interval, he had to hold up against the strongest pressure from Paris. At half past two in the morning of February 22, as he and the King were returning from a court ball, M. de Talleyrand overtook them in the courtyard of the Royal Palace and requested an audience of the Count. Cavour consented, and in five minutes the French Minister was reading to him a most urgent despatch in which Thouvenel announced that the Emperor intended to withdraw his troops at once and to resume negotiations for the immediate cession of Nice and Savoy. Nothing disconcerted, although somewhat surprised, Cavour remarked that the news ought to give great satisfaction in Vienna. If the English had occupied Genoa under similar conditions, he said, they would hardly abandon Italy so hurriedly. What concerned him most was the second part of the despatch. "Does your Emperor really set such store by Savoy and that unfortunate town of Nice?" he asked. Talleyrand replied that the Emperor regarded the affair as already settled.[51]

It was amid such threats that Cavour worked during the last fortnight in February. Having the English Liberals behind

[48] Ricasoli, IV, 304; G. Fabrizi to Ricasoli, Paris, Feb. 16, 1860. Arese, 223-24.   [49] *Lettere*, III, 215. Ricasoli, IV, 313.   [50] *Lettere*, IV, xxxviii; C. to E. d'Azeglio, Feb. 20, 1860. Ricasoli, IV, 316.   [51] Ideville, 79-81.

him, and the patriotic Italians with him, he seems to have divined that Napoleon would content himself with thundering. The Austrian army in Venetia was a very real menace, but, as he wrote Arese, "I think it is better to run the risk of being crushed by Austria, than to lose all prestige, and to be unable to govern further except by the aid of bayonets."[52] Palmerston, questioned by E. d'Azeglio, replied: "We do not take the initiative to give you advice, but our opinion is that you ought to uphold the Four Points." Through oversight this message was telegraphed without cipher to Turin,[53] and being read on the way in Paris it caused irritation, which appeared presently in the tone of Thouvenel's long-expected ultimatum. The French Foreign Minister repeated the Emperor's proposals that Piedmont should annex the Duchies, hold the Romagna as a vicariate of the Pope, and restore Tuscany as an autonomous grand-duchy. Thouvenel expatiated on the unwisdom of absorbing Tuscany, because the Tuscans, tenacious of their past glories, would not willingly merge their identity in that of Italy. He pointed out also three dangers — from Austria, from internal revolution, from the Pope's displeasure. If Piedmont accepted the Emperor's plan, she might count on his support in any emergency; otherwise, she must suffer whatever consequences might follow on her action, for the Emperor would be guided solely by the interests of France.[54]

A copy of this despatch reached Lord John Russell on February 27. The next day, when Talleyrand presented it to Cavour, the latter had already heard from Hudson that Lord John regarded the French terms as entirely subversive of Italian independence. Cavour telegraphed Arese to tell Thouvenel that the Piedmontese government, "*so far as it was concerned,*" did not reject the Imperial propositions; but that it would transmit them to the governments of Central Italy and would loyally accept the result of a plebiscite.[55] On the 29th, Arese announced that Thouvenel agreed to a vote in any form, but not to the annexation of Tuscany.[56] The next morning at six o'clock Ricasoli received from Cavour this telegram, brief but sufficient: "Proceed to the election." A duplicate was sent to Farini at

[52] *Lettere*, III, 223; C. to Arese, Feb. 28, 1860.   [53] *Ibid.*
[54] Text in Ricasoli, IV, 364–70.   [55] *Lettere*, III, 223.   [56] Arese, 248.

Bologna. To Arese Cavour telegraphed: "Whatever the French proposition may be, we can accept nothing which has not been subordinated to the vote of Tuscany. *We are going to call the four classes under arms.* This measure is purely defensive."[57]

Ricasoli and Farini issued their proclamations without delay. When Count Mesbourg, the French diplomatic agent, officially warned Ricasoli that the Emperor disapproved of Tuscany's move and would not stand by the verdict at the polls, he was politely but clearly informed that the Tuscans, after waiting ten months, were determined to act for themselves. Out of respect for France, however, they were even going to resort to a plebiscite. If the Emperor should think of coercion, Ricasoli bade him reflect that the Italians had not labored simply to exchange Austrian for French oppression. Count Mesbourg went away without further illusions.[58] Napoleon discreetly refrained from open interference. The elections took place on March 11 and 12, the question being put in this form, which was criticized as disingenuous: "Do you prefer union with the constitutional monarchy of Piedmont, or a separate kingdom?" In Emilia 426,006 voted for union, and only 756 for separation;[59] in Tuscany, where the desire for autonomy was supposed to predominate, 366,571 voted for union, and 14,925 for separation.[60] Victories so sweeping might suggest intimidation at the polls, or fraud in the counting. In fact, however, 75 per cent of the registered voters in Tuscany and more than 80 per cent in Emilia cast their ballots, and there is no evidence that the returns did not accord with the wishes of an overwhelming majority.

Late in the afternoon of March 15, crowds began to pour into the Piazza della Signoria at Florence to hear the result. Darkness fell, night came, yet they waited patiently, their numbers having been swollen by anxious country-folk. At length, just at midnight, the small central window of the Syndic's Room in the Palazzo Vecchio opened, allegorical pieces outlined in gas-jets were lighted, and Ricasoli and his colleagues,[61] with torches, came out on the balcony. Enrico Poggi, Minister of Justice, was

---

[57] Arese, 247–48.   [58] Ricasoli, IV, 391–92; Massari to C., Florence, March 4, 1860.   [59] Zini, I, ii, 546. In Emilia, 526,258 were registered; 750 defective ballots were rejected.   [60] Total registration, 534,000; total vote, 386,445; defective ballots, 4,949. Ricasoli, IV, 425. Tivaroni, II, 162.   [61] Except Salvagnoli, who was ill.

on the point of announcing the plebiscite, when the premature setting off of a rocket gave the signal for the great bell of the Palace to toll and for the cannoneers at the Fortress to fire their salute of one hundred and one guns. The crowds in the Piazza and in the tributary streets and alleys set up frantic cheers, and it was some time before the numbers which Poggi shouted at the top of his thin voice were heard. Then the multitude, wild with joy at the unexpected unanimity of the vote, cheered and cheered again. Later, Ricasoli, who loved to link the past with the present, sent out heralds, dressed in medieval garb, and drawn on the ancient civic chariot, accompanied by torch-bearers and bannermen, to proclaim the news. All night long they went up and down the narrow streets, through the squares, along the quays, trumpeting the wonderful tidings — that Florence, who had played many parts in her ten centuries of mercurial existence, was at last, on those Ides of March, 1860, a member of the Kingdom of Italy.[62] "Little-Tuscany is done for, and can never come back to life,"[63] Massari wrote prophetically to Cavour ten days before the election. Little-Tuscany, with her provincialism, with her musty vainglory over the past and her sterile hypercriticism of the present, was indeed no more. Ricasoli had welded her fortunes to those of a young nation, thereby saving her from falling back into sterile autonomy, a prey for any reactionary despot.

As long as Italy honors her great sons, Ricasoli shall be revered. Without him, the unification of the Kingdom would have been long delayed. To be single-minded in a high cause, is much; to have courage, is much; to have character above suspicion and proof against every temptation, is more: having all these, to succeed, is to be a benefactor of the race. Ricasoli resisted alike Cavour and Mazzini, Napoleon III and Farini, Garibaldi and the various Tuscan partisans of separatism or of a Central Kingdom. He was the most conspicuously victorious modern champion of the policy of no compromise. "When you are following a line as narrow as the blade of a knife," he said, "you must go straight ahead, without looking to the right or left, and without stopping at advice."[64] Yet this man, whom kings and diplomats

[62] Poggi, II, 239–47. Rubieri, 316–19. [63] Ricasoli, IV, 388; Massari to C., Florence, March 3, 1860. [64] Quoted by La Gorce, III, 199.

could not bend, whom acquaintances found austere and intimates reserved, was beloved by the common people. They called him familiarly "Bettino"; so children caress a mastiff, and fear no harm.

Emilia and Tuscany celebrated the plebiscite with great rejoicing. On March 18 Farini formally presented the vote of his province to Victor Emanuel, who, from his throne, accepted it with gracious words. On the 20th the Tuscan Assembly met and sanctioned the plebiscite. At a motion to thank the Government for standing loyally by the principle of unity, Montanelli — whose separatism seems often to have been inspired by jealousy of Ricasoli — arraigned the Iron Baron as a tyrant guilty of one illegal act after another. Neither the Assembly nor the Government deigned to reply,[65] and only three deputies — Manzini, Caldini and Mordini — supported the egotistical professor. Then the Assembly voted to dissolve forever — and independent Tuscany ceased to be. Two days later, Ricasoli, in a few noble words, announced to Victor Emanuel the decision of the Tuscans to form part of United Italy. The decree of annexation was officially published, and the opening of the new parliament, which should consolidate the Kingdom, was set for April 2. Cavour strengthened the Cabinet by giving to Farini the portfolio of the Interior. The King created Prince Eugenio of Savoy Lieutenant of Tuscany, and Ricasoli, who declined the offer of the presidency of the Chamber, he made Governor General.[66]

In the very hour when his countrymen were throbbing with joy at the annexation of Central Italy, Cavour's soul was racked by the necessity of an immense sacrifice. Throughout his negotiations with France over Emilia and Tuscany the cession of Nice and Savoy loomed in the background, for Napoleon III assumed that the transfer was as good as made. Cavour, regarding it as inevitable, instead of wasting time over vain repinings, set about accomplishing the odious task in such a way that it should cause as little harm as possible. With the foresight of a statesman who had generations, if not centuries in view, he knew that the annexed provinces were immeasurably more important to the unifi-

---

[65] Rubieri, 326, construes this silence as a confession that Montanelli was right.   [66] Zini, ii, ii, 600–06, for royal proclamations. Ricasoli, iv, 475–76, for Ricasoli's address and King's reply.

CAVOUR IN 1860

cation of Italy than the retention of the Transalpine possessions could ever be; he knew also that sentiment, as well as politicians in search of an issue against him, would judge the act not by the permanent good it promised but by its transient painfulness. His first care was to secure Tuscany and Emilia by plebiscite, after the six weeks' conflict, which we have just followed, with the shifting and devious Emperor. Enemies insinuated that Cavour was in collusion with the Emperor, in the hope that, by appearing to force annexation through in spite of French threats he might lessen the odium that awaited him for ceding Nice and Savoy; but this charge has absolutely no basis. His apparent change of front was due to the indecision of Napoleon, who, up to the last, hoping to keep Tuscany separate and thereby postpone taking Nice, delayed publishing his plan, which would have aroused the hostility of the Great Powers. Cavour acquiesced in this silence in order to complete the business of annexation before that of cession had to be dealt with. Once announced, such a storm arose that Napoleon would have been glad if he could disavow any designs on Nice.

Next to the bitterness of giving up a single foot of the heritage of the House of Savoy, the duty of maintaining a false face towards his English supporters wrung Cavour's heart. To confide in them, however, meant to lose Emilia and Tuscany; because Napoleon would not have consented to their annexation unless he were to be compensated elsewhere; and if the English government had known in January what every one knew in March, it might have conjured up a coalition against which Napoleon would not have dared to move. Most solicitous to recover the goodwill of England, Napoleon could not be expected to make a clean breast of a project which the English were sure to brand as piratical. Unless, therefore, Cavour were prepared to sacrifice the results of the War of 1859, to blast the hopes of Italian unity and to lose the favor of both France and England, he must dissemble. And he did dissemble: for he was a practical statesman, at a time when the code of honor no more required statesmen to spoil their chances by showing their hand prematurely than it does to-day; or than it requires a general to-day to send the enemy word of his intentions, or a lawyer to ruin his client's cause by voluntarily exposing his crime. Like legal procedure, like the duel, like warfare, diplomacy and statecraft were and are governed by a standard of their own which does not correspond to an ideal standard of right and wrong.

French designs on Savoy had been talked of for at least a year. The fitness of uniting Savoy to France had been remarked upon from time to time for over two centuries. Geography predestined the union, which mere arbitrary political interests prevented. So long as European States were passed to and fro with dowries and family jewels as marriage portions, a rational amalgamation according to racial, geographical and economic interests was ignored. In 1860, however, when Savoy was tested by these criteria, it appeared at once that by race and language, by location and by commercial interest she was French. By tradition, she belonged to the family which, from humble beginnings in the Viennois, went eastward, climbed the Alps, saw the richness of the Italian plain and made that their home. But the spirit of nationality, which was now superseding the old idea that peoples were the chattels of their rulers, plainly designated Savoy for France.

In the summer of 1859, when Lord Cowley questioned Walewski as to the Emperor's intention to annex Savoy, Walewski made light of it, as of a contingency which the Peace of Villafranca had set aside. Still the rumor persisted; the French newspapers not only repeated it, but claimed the cession as a natural offset to the expansion of Piedmont. On January 14, 1860, Prince de Joinville told Prince Albert that Napoleon had given out in the Army that he had obtained Savoy.[67] This could only mean that the Emperor had Victor Emanuel's personal promise, because the Emperor himself, before quitting Turin on the previous 15th of July, had assured both the King and Cavour that there should be no more question of Savoy. But Joinville's hint set the British Foreign Office in motion. Without delay,[68] Cowley interviewed Napoleon, and urged him against taking a false step; to which Napoleon replied that, as the Savoyards desired the change, their wishes ought to be respected like those "of any other population." [69] Lord John admitted that Cowley's report was "rather alarming." Queen Victoria had now good reason for being sarcastic at the expense of her "Ministers, *the two*," whom she

[67] Martin, v, 10, n. 6.   [68] Jan. 18, 1860.   [69] Martin, v, 11–12.

reminded that she had always warned them that it was most dangerous to bind England to common action with the French Emperor.[70] To King Leopold she wrote: "I think Parliament has had a wholesome effect upon certain people; and that they are *altogether frightened*. There has been a strong despatch written relative to Savoy. . . . The feeling of *all* parties and this *whole* country is — to *let Italy settle its own affairs* — and *England to keep quite out of it*." [71] Prince Albert, "tired to death with work, worry and vexation," regaled Baron Stockmar with a diatribe against "Louis Napoleon" who, he said, was trying to make Europe believe that his iniquities were committed for the sake of the English alliance.[72] When Parliament met on January 24, Disraeli questioned the Government as to the disquieting rumors.[73] Palmerston was able to reply, quite truthfully, that England was under no engagement whatever with any Foreign Power concerning the affairs of Italy.[74] On January 30 Disraeli returned to the charge, asking for downright information in regard to the cession of Nice and Savoy. Lord John requested a day or two before answering.[75] Disraeli, whom few have excelled in the rôle of parliamentary picador, thrust again into the subject on February 2, and drew from Lord John a report of the July conversation between Cowley and Walewski.[76]

Meanwhile the Ministers were doing their utmost, at Paris and at Turin, to discover the Emperor's plans. At length Cowley drew from Thouvenel the admission that, since Piedmont was likely to become a kingdom with a population of fifteen millions, the Emperor, in order to protect France, must insist on annexing Savoy. This annexation, he said, had nothing menacing in it, and ought to be considered neither as an act of conquest nor as an augmenting of the strength of France.[77] In forwarding Cowley's letter Lord Russell wrote to the Queen: "The same reasons which are given for the frontier of the Alps apply more strongly to the frontiers of the Rhine, inasmuch as the German armies will at all times be much more formidable than the Piedmontese, Lombards and Tuscans." [78] The Queen gave vent to a natural

[70] *Q. V. L.*, iii, 384–85; Queen to Russell, Jan. 21, 1860.
[71] *Q. V. L.*, iii, 386; Queen to Leopold, Jan. 31, 1860.   [72] Martin, v, 13–14.
[73] iii, Hansard, 88, *sqq.*   [74] *Ib.*, 108, *sqq.*   [75] *Ib.*, 262.   [76] *Ib.*, 445–46.
[77] Martin, v, 26; Cowley to Russell, Feb. 5, 1860.
[78] *Ibid*, v, 27; Russell to Queen, Feb. 5, 1860.

outburst of irritation, coupled with the self-gratulation of a Cassandra whose unheeded warnings have come true. She replied to Lord John: "We have been made regular dupes (which the Queen apprehended all along). The return to an English alliance, universal peace, respect for treaties, commercial fraternity, etc., etc., were the blinds to cover before Europe a policy of spoliation. We were asked to make proposals about Italy, to 'lay the basis for a mutual agreement with France' upon that question, and to enable the Emperor 'to release himself from his engagements to Austria.' In an evil hour the proposal is made, and is now pleaded as the reason for France seizing upon Savoy. 'The Emperor was ready to carry out the Treaty of Zurich, but having agreed, to please England, in a scheme leading to the further aggrandizement of Sardinia, must be compensated by Savoy!' . . . Sardinia is being aggrandized solely at the expense of Austria and the House of Lorraine, and France is to be compensated!" [79] This letter, in which Prince Albert's dictating mind protrudes at every sentence, shows how unwilling they were to recognize in the Italian movement the patriotic attempt of a downtrodden people to win possession of their own souls and bodies, and how completely they had turned away from Napoleon since the time when he consulted the Queen about midwives and wet-nurses and she admired him as a family man to be unreservedly trusted. Now it was only too true, they were the dupes of their modest, velvet-mannered Imperial Brother!

On January 31, Lord John Russell, who saw that all Germany would rally to Austria and discredit England's championship of the Italians, wrote Hudson that the question of Nice was pressing. If Napoleon had exacted it in his bargain at Plombières, he had no right to claim it, because he had not fulfilled the promise of freeing Venetia. "I hope Cavour is under no engagement," he wrote, anxiously. "If the King sell his inheritance of Savoy to obtain Tuscany, he will be disgraced in the eyes of Europe, and we shall not hesitate to affix to his conduct the fitting epithets." [80] Hudson went straight to Cavour with Russell's private letter. After listening to it Cavour replied: "'I declare to you that at this moment no engagement exists between us and France for the

---

[79] Martin, v, 27-28; Queen to Russell, Feb. 5, 1860.
[80] Walpole: *Russell*, ii, 319; Russell to Hudson, Jan. 31, 1860.

cession of Savoy. If the Savoyards, by a great numerical majority, petition Parliament for separation, the question will be treated parliamentarily. But I tell you frankly that the best way to meet this question is openly and frankly, and in no other way will I ever consent to meet it. I agree with Lord John,' said he, 'that the King would be disgraced were he to cede [*céder*], swap [*troquer*], or sell Savoy." [81] This declaration was literally and technically true. Piedmont's agreement made the year before to cede Savoy to France had been contingent on the liberation of Italy from the Alps to the Adriatic; that having failed, the engagement, by the Emperor's own admission, lapsed. Cavour henceforth made a plebiscite the cornerstone of his policy: for if Piedmont annexed Emilia and Tuscany after that test, she could not consistently refuse to let the Savoyards go to France, if they should express that preference by popular vote. On the other hand, Napoleon III, who owed his throne to a plebiscite, and plumed himself on being the apostle of the rights of nationality, could not complain if the Savoyards showed by universal suffrage that they wished to remain with Piedmont. Cavour spoke, therefore, the literal truth to Hudson; but he did not speak the whole truth; and, if intent to deceive be the essence of a lie, he cannot escape that censure.

Whether Hudson was deceived, or not, is another matter. England certainly assumed that Napoleon was a trickster, a view which, held by the Queen and Prince Albert, spread from them to the aristocracy, and on to the middle classes, with such rapidity that the Government gravely doubted its ability to carry through Parliament the Commercial Treaty with France.[82] Cavour saw that the supreme object for Piedmont was to hasten the annexation of the Central Italians; and this he accomplished in the manner we have detailed. When Napoleon found that he could no longer postpone this conclusion, which displeased him, he came out boldly with his determination to have an equivalent for the expansion of the Kingdom of Italy. Cavour sent his telegram to Ricasoli and Farini on February 29. On March 1 the Emperor, in addressing the French legislative bodies, stated that

---

[81] Walpole: *Russell*, II, 319. *Correspondence*, 1860, vol. 67, pt. i, p. 35; Hudson to Russell, Feb. 10, 1860.   [82] Malmesbury, 512, writes on Feb. 8: " It was evident that the great majority if not the whole House, was against France."

2

Victor Emanuel was pursuing a policy in regard to Tuscany and the Holy See, which the Emperor disapproved — a policy which seemed to be dictated by the desire to absorb all the States of Italy and to threaten new conflagrations. "Confronted by this transformation of Northern Italy, which gives to a powerful State all the passes of the Alps, it was my duty," said the Emperor, "for the safety of our frontiers, to reclaim the French slopes of the mountains. This revendication of a somewhat extended territory has nothing in it to alarm Europe, or to give the lie to the policy of disinterestedness which I have more than once proclaimed; for France does not intend to carry through an aggrandizement, no matter how slight, either by a military occupation, or by a superinduced insurrection, or by underhand intrigues, but by frankly stating the question to the Great Powers."[83]

That same afternoon Cowley asked Thouvenel what the Emperor meant by the "French slopes" of the mountains. Nothing less than Savoy and the County of Nice,[84] the French Premier replied. The report of the Imperial speech passed like a torch from capital to capital, kindling indignation. Schleinitz told the French Ambassador at Berlin that Prussia viewed the proposed absorption with the greatest distrust: she had incurred great unpopularity by restraining the Germans from joining in the recent war, but she might not be silent now. The question was European, not to be decided arbitrarily by any Power. Foreign diplomats worried Thouvenel to explain what the Emperor meant by the ominous word "revendication." Today you revendicate Nice, Lord John Russell remarked; Europe will dread lest tomorrow you revendicate the Rhine and Belgium; the slight advantage France will get now will be more than outweighed by the distrust of all the European Powers.[85] The Emperor himself, irritated by the gales of abuse which swept across the Channel to the Tuileries, lost his temper at a public audience and spoke sharply to Cowley, who, by an admirable display of dignity, compelled the Emperor to apologize.[86] Russia alone gave Napoleon a hearty support. True to his Absolutist principles, Prince Gort-

---

[83] *Moniteur*, March 2, 1860.   [84] *Correspondence*, 1860, vol. 67, pt. vi, p. 33.
[85] Russell to Cowley, March 22, 1860.
[86] Martin, v, 39–43. *Correspondence*, 1860, vol. 67, *l. c.*

chakoff told the Duke of Montebello that it was nobody's business to prevent Victor Emanuel from giving away as much or little of his possessions as he chose; the King owned them, and he could therefore dispose of them like any other property. Europe's sole concern was whether the transfer would disturb the international equilibrium. Evidently, it would not; for France would not endanger Swiss neutrality. France must not, however, base the transaction on a plebiscite; if Piedmont wished to consult the people, that was purely an internal affair. The actual cession should be a personal arrangement between the two sovereigns.[87]

While Napoleon felt keenly the outspoken hostility of England, and the less demonstrative opposition of Prussia and Austria, he did not allow himself to be shaken. Perhaps he discounted their barking because he believed that they would not bite. More probably, he was in one of his periodic states in which he was ready to risk everything in order to attain the object that came uppermost. Since Cavour had cut short diplomatic dawdling and was going ahead with annexation, he himself must realize his scheme of revendication, or the French nation would be upon him. Accordingly, he instructed his ambassador at Turin to arrange with the King's Government for the cession of Savoy and Nice. As a preliminary, Cavour urged that they destroy the secret treaty of December 18, 1858, the existence of which had often been denied, and conclude another suitable to the present situation. This was done: the copies of the old instrument were burned; the new ones were signed on March 12. Still this failed to satisfy Thouvenel. A recent comer in the spider's web of international intrigue at Paris, he believed, not unnaturally, that no man could be trusted. He suspected that Cavour and the King might foment popular demonstrations in Nice and Savoy against France; for already protesting deputations had appealed to Victor Emanuel, to the Emperor and to the British Government. He had assured foreign cabinets, as their anger increased, that France would of course consult Europe before taking any irrevocable step: but Europe soon learned that instead of being consulted, she was to be merely informed of the Emperor's decisions. Thouvenel judged, therefore, that his safety lay in haste.

[87] Ollivier 399–401; letters of March 17 and 20.

The ink of the secret treaty was scarcely dry, before he peremptorily demanded the execution of another treaty which could be published immediately, and serve to counteract the announcement of the annexations, now imminent, of Emilia and Tuscany. Cavour would have preferred to wait until the Italian Parliament met on April 2, in order to allow it to formulate the terms of cession: but knowing that to suggest delay would arouse suspicions at Paris, and being from the first bent on loyally carrying out the bond, he acquiesced.[88] The Emperor ordered Benedetti, chief of the political bureau of the Ministry of Foreign Affairs, to take the first train to Turin and not to return until he could bring the treaty, signed, in his pocket. "No delay, no concessions," summed up his instructions. Benedetti, though a second-class man, was a first-class bureaucrat, through whom Fate, on this occasion and on another still more calamitous,[89] wrought ill to France.

Reaching Turin on the morning of March 22, he had interviews with the King and Cavour. The King seems to have hesitated for a moment, but Benedetti assured him that the Emperor regarded the treaty as indispensable and that he would not be put off. Cavour, with no thought of not fulfilling his part of the compact, still strove, as he honestly might strive, to make the sacrifice as small as possible. While Benedetti was closeted with Cavour, a deputation of Nizzards was beseeching Victor Emanuel not to desert them. Cavour himself used every argument to save Nice: it was Italian; therefore, if the principle of nationality were respected, it should remain Italian; its cession had not been originally demanded; therefore, if the Emperor insisted on it now, he would justify those who accused him of land greed. Its people had already so plainly indicated their desire to remain under Victor Emanuel's crown that an honest plebiscite would show an anti-French majority. To these and other arguments Benedetti bluntly replied: "The Emperor wishes absolutely Nice and Savoy, even though he should have all Europe against him." [90] When Cavour pleaded that Nice be neutralized, Benedetti replied with a downright no. As a last hope, Cavour suggested that they delay long enough to resubmit the matter to the

[88] Thouvenel evidently accompanied his demand by a threat.
[89] Interviews with Prussian King at Ems, July, 1870.　[90] *Lettere*, IV, lxv.

Emperor and get his answer. Again Benedetti cut short the negotiation with his no. He made no pretense of hiding the fact that the Emperor could and would dictate. "Cavour resisted some of the demands of Benedetti, and so stoutly," Hudson wrote Lord John Russell, "that upon his telling Benedetti, who threatened the withdrawal of the French troops, 'that the sooner they were gone, the better,' the Frenchman drew a letter from his pocket, which contained the private instructions of the Emperor, and said, 'My orders are to withdraw the troops, but not to France. They will occupy Bologna and Florence.' And then, but not till then, Cavour knocked under." [91]

Now came Cavour's turn to be immovable. He insisted, first, that the treaty should be void unless it were ratified by Parliament, and, secondly, that neither Savoy nor Nice should be ceded unless the plebiscite were favorable to France. Benedetti, who saw no reason for bothering over the sanction of Parliament, wished to strike out that clause, but Cavour would not yield, and Benedetti could not consistently hold out against the test by popular vote. In winning these two essentials, [92] Cavour kept his conscience clear. No one could justly accuse him of abandoning Nice and Savoy without making every effort to save them; nor of truckling to France; nor of disregarding the constitution in order to escape from a desperate plight. How grave his action was he understood fully. "You know that a treaty carrying a modification of territory is only valid when it has received the sanction of Parliament," he wrote an intimate friend, the day before he signed the earlier treaty. "Also, in countersigning a secret treaty which calls for the cession of two provinces, I commit an act highly unconstitutional, which might have the most serious consequences for me. If the Chamber of Deputies were composed of a majority of Carottis and Dabormidas, I should run the risk of being accused of high treason and of being condemned, if not to lose my head like Strafford, certainly to several years' imprisonment in a fortress like Polignac and Peyronnet. In spite of this conviction, I have not hesitated to advise the King to put his signature to the treaty, for which I assume the entire responsibility.

[91] Martin, v, 33, n. 5. Hudson's letter is dated May 1, 1860.

[92] In winning these, Cavour fulfilled the promise made to a friend in a letter dated March 12: "Have no fear: I am conciliatory as to the *form*; as to the *substance*, I am firm as a rock." *Lettere*, IV, lviii, n. 1.

But in so doing I do not mean to tear up the Statute and to dispense with Parliament. . . . The King and I have no doubts; for he stakes his crown, and I, if not my head, my reputation, which is a great deal dearer to me. . . . I shall lose in this affair all my popularity in Piedmont; but a great number of Piedmontese deputies, while blaming me, and while biding their time before making me pay dearly for what they will consider a kind of treason, will not dare to provoke a crisis which would gravely compromise not merely the Government but the King himself." [93]

So, with full understanding of the risk he ran, Cavour signed the Treaty on March 24. [94] In his private office, at the Foreign Ministry, he, Benedetti and Talleyrand, and Farini, recently confirmed as Minister of the Interior, were gathered. Count d'Ideville, serving the French Ambassador as secretary, read aloud the copy of the secret memorandum and the minutes of the Treaty, which were to be given to the Piedmontese Government, while Artom, Cavour's private secretary, followed the duplicate. Cavour walked up and down, silent, preoccupied, his head bowed, his hands in his pockets, until D'Ideville finished reading. Then he took a pen and signed both documents with a firm hand. His face lighted up at once, his habitual smile returned, and he passed the pen to Talleyrand. "Now we are accomplices!" he said sardonically, as soon as he saw the Frenchman's name written. [95] The devoted Farini insisted on signing also, so that he might share whatever odium or penalty this act drew down upon Cavour.

The next morning Napoleon triumphantly announced in the *Moniteur* the outline of the Treaty, but with characteristic guile he omitted the reference to a plebiscite, thus leaving the public to suppose that he had dictated his terms and that Piedmont had servilely accepted them. [96] That same day the new Kingdom of Italy held its parliamentary elections. The citizens of Savoy and Nice voted for their deputies, just as if the cession had not al-

---

[93] *Lettere*, III, 226–27; C. to an Intimate Friend, March 11, 1860.

[94] All of the Ministers except Fanti were agreed that the cession of Nice was necessary. Carandini, 317–18.   [95] Ideville, 116–17, also his Appendix A. Benedetti: *Ma Mission en Prusse* (1871), introduction, gives Benedetti's letters to the London *Times* in December, 1870.

[96] *Moniteur*, March 25, 1860, which said: "This reunion shall be effected without any constraint on the will of the peoples." The Treaty was signed" with the reservation of the sanction of the Chambers."

ready been agreed to, and when the French Government protested, Cavour replied that until the legislature had ratified the treaty, no distinction could be recognized among the King's subjects. By a great majority, the Ministry was endorsed. Eight colleges, representing all the great cities of the New Kingdom, — Turin, Milan, Florence, Genoa and Bologna, — chose Cavour.[97] The Clericals were almost wiped out; and the Radicals were much shorn of their strength. On Monday, April 2, the King opened Parliament. The oval hall in Palazzo Madama was far too small for even the official throng that overcrowded into it. These men who up to a few months before were Tuscans or Lombards, Modenese or Romagnoles, sat at last side by side as Italians. All eyes turned instinctively to the narrow Ministerial table below the Throne, where Cavour, smiling and light-hearted as a boy, showed neither traces of the ordeal he had just gone through nor foreboding of trials to come. Farini, slender, nervous, typically Italian, foreigners would say, made a sharp contrast with Fanti, massive and military in form and bearing. Mamiani, though scarcely three score years old, seemed patriarchal, a man of books, strangely strayed out of a library of parchment folios into the hurly-burly of this political arena: but when he spoke, all listened. The other Ministers had only a local reputation. Not so the venerable Cesare Alfieri, President of the Senate, whose presence reminded men that it was he who had urged Charles Albert to grant the reforms of 1847, whence issued the glory of Piedmont; not so Lanza, President of the Chamber, whose achievement as Minister of Finance had raised him among the notables. As the eye ranged along the deputies' benches, it recognized the veterans of the Subalpine Parliament: Rattazzi with the air of a lawyer sure of his case; Brofferio, always ready to hurl comments at the member who had the floor; Valerio, somewhat less belligerent than formerly, but still by preference a fighter. From a newer group emerged Depretis, already well on his way to become one of the sleekest politicians that Europe produced during the next quarter of a century; Biancheri and Mancini; Minghetti, with high-bred features and incisive speech, and Berti, philosopher rather than publicist. Imbriani, once Min-

[97] I Turin, II Genoa, I Bologna, II Florence, I Milan; also Intra, Brescia, and Vercelli. He preferred his old constituency, the I Turin.

ister at Naples, then victim of Bomba, exile and professor at
Pisa, hardly smothering the volcanic fire in his heart, was one of
the newly elected; along with whom came many of the patriotic
leaders of Lombardy, Emilia and Tuscany. Guerrazzi, who enjoyed his brief hour of apotheosis in 1849, had outlived his vigor
and his reputation, but had supporters enough to seat him in this
Italian Parliament. Every one looked hard at Medici, the hero of
the Vascello, Garibaldi's lieutenant, with a ballast of common
sense which Garibaldi himself lacked. Mordini and Sirtori, ex-
conspirators, came out of exile. Tuscany sent Giorgini, Ubaldino Peruzzi and Filippo Gualterio — the last known for his
stirring history of the revolutions of 1848–49. Among the Ministerialists towered Emilio Visconti-Venosta, whose tawny hair
and whiskers framed a face of indomitable firmness. La Farina,
on whose faithful labors the meeting of that Parliament depended
far more than most of those present imagined, stood out promi-
nently among the Cavourians. Near him was Sommeiller, the
engineer of the Mont Cenis Tunnel. At another bench sat Alear-
di, the poet whose verse had for years carried the cry of anguish
of oppressed Lombardo-Venetians throughout Italy and beyond
the Alps. Pasini, another Venetian, represented Cremona. But
most eagerly were all eyes turned to discover Garibaldi, not
present on that day, and Ricasoli, who required no pedestal in
order to be recognized as a man of iron purpose.

Among the recently created senators, Manzoni kindled the
greatest enthusiasm — Manzoni who, in the darkest days of the
Restoration, when the world sneered at the Italians as a played-
out race, redeemed the fame of the Italic genius by a masterpiece,
and who now, at seventy-five, venerable and revered, witnessed
the first festival of Italy's progress towards unity. Other senators for whom everybody looked were blind Gino Capponi,
for forty years the adviser of Tuscan Liberals: Pallavicino, tiny
of stature, but with the strut of a man of importance (which he
was); Massimo d'Azeglio, whose face was known in all parts
of Italy; Pasolini, friend of the early, unrecanted Pius IX,
model of the enlightened aristocrat; Cosimo Ridolfi, who enjoyed a vogue in Tuscany which, when put to the touch, he never
seemed able to justify: and Castelli, the most loyal of friends
and the most skilful smoother of political or personal quarrels.

The galleries — small at best — were packed: but one noted in the section reserved for foreign diplomats several significant absences. Russia, Prussia, Spain, Belgium, and Naples forbade their ministers to attend: to some of those monarchs the new Kingdom was an upstart, not to be hastily welcomed into their circle; to all, it was an experiment. But the Italians, who assembled that day to celebrate the birth of their nation, were too full of joy to be cast down by any slight. Through innumerable hardships, in spite of losses, failures and mistakes, against incredible odds, their fathers and they had endured ; and now they gave thanks. It was just forty years since the revolution in Naples, by which Italian patriotism uttered its first warning to reactionary despotism. So for forty years the Israelites wandered in the desert, ere being permitted to enter the Promised Land.

Victor Emanuel read a stirring address, which Farini had drafted and Cavour revised. The King himself, as was his wont, added a trenchant phrase.[98] He alluded to the magnanimous ally with whose aid Lombardy had been freed, to the prowess of the soldiers, and to the persevering concord of the peoples which, under God, had brought their union to pass. When he spoke of sacrificing Nice and Savoy as the thing which cost his heart most dear, his voice trembled with emotion. He promised to uphold every right, and every liberty. Three days before, the Pope had launched a bull of major excommunication[99] against the principal authors of the annexation of the Romagna to Piedmont. When therefore Victor Emanuel declared with solemn emphasis that though he, like his ancestors, was firm in his devotion to the Catholic Religion and to its Head, nevertheless, if the ecclesiastical authority adopted spiritual arms for temporal interests, he should find strength to maintain undiminished civil liberty and his own authority, — for which he owed an accounting to God alone and to his own people, — at these words, senators and deputies jumped to their feet, clapped their hands and cheered so wildly that it was many minutes before he could finish the sentence.[100] The conscience of Italy repudiated the attempt of the

[98] C. d'Azeglio, 633.   [99] Text of the bull *Cum Catholica Ecclesia*, dated March 26, 1860, in Chantrel, 627–33. Its publication was forbidden in France. Translations in *Correspondence*, 1860, vol. 67, pt. 3, pp. 122–33.

[100] Official report. Also *Correspondence*, 1860, vol. 67, pt. 3, p. 115; Hudson to Russell, April 2. "It is the King who insisted on saying that he drew his author-

moribund Papacy to repeat its worn-out juggle of spiritual and temporal.

Much would we give to know the thoughts that coursed through Cavour's brain as he watched that transport of emotion. For the first time, and the last,[101] the parliament chamber in Palazzo Madama was serving as a Valhalla for Italy's *living* heroes, who, putting aside the Past and the Future, took their full measure of exultation in the Present. For Cavour himself, though they little suspected it, the bitter mingled with the sweet. He knew that the very unity they were celebrating would be disputed, perhaps imperiled, when the Chambers next met. By accepting the inevitable, he had made France the accomplice of the new Kingdom, and while it was with France rather than with Italy that the incensed European Powers would reckon, the enemies whom he must face were sitting on the benches before him, cheering the King that afternoon. When the truce ended, they would turn on the Prime Minister and demand satisfaction.

To the immense injury of United Italy, it happened that Nice was the birthplace of Garibaldi. Had he been born at Savona or at any other town along the western Riviera, the later history of Italian unification would not record a blighting dissension, which after fifty years, still rankles, and the fame of Garibaldi would not be sullied by an outburst of egotism which went far to offset his splendid services to Italy. At the earliest whisper of the possible cession of Nice, Garibaldi gave free rein to his megalomania. Nice was his birthplace; therefore it was a place apart from all others — almost a holy place; and no one except him should determine its fate. On January 17, 1860, he wrote Colonel Türr to ask Victor Emanuel whether Nice was to be ceded to France, and to telegraph the reply, "Yes or No."[102] Türr found the King sick in bed, but not too sick to appreciate the humor of the situation. On reading the note he exclaimed: "By telegraph! Yes or no! The cheek of the fellow! Reply 'Yes'; but tell the General not Nice alone, but also Savoy! And that if I can reconcile myself to giving up the land of my forefathers, of all my race, he

ity from God alone and from his people, and he said it with energy. At the passage about Rome, your Father rose instinctively to applaud, which caused all the others to rise." C. d'Azeglio, 633; to her son, April 4, 1860.

[101] Thenceforth, the Senate met here and the Deputies in Palazzo Carignano.

[102] Ciàmpoli, 126; Garibaldi was at Fino. Mario: *Bertani*, I, 429, n. 1.

ought to be able to reconcile himself to losing his home, where only he was born. . . . It is a cruel destiny that *I* and *he* should have to make for Italy the greatest sacrifice that could be asked." [103] If Garibaldi, in his dealings with the King, arrogated to himself the tone of a monarch addressing a monarch, it must be borne in mind that the King, whether from personal fondness for the soldier or from motives of policy, did not resent it.

Garibaldi had no intention, however, of being a submissive martyr. Nice was Italian; his career had been devoted to Italy; if Nice became French, he would be a foreigner in his native town. The very thought of this compulsory metamorphosis enraged him. He hated the French, because they tolerated and even glorified Napoleon III; to see Nice fall a prey to such a villain, more than doubled the sting of his resentment. Always scornful of Diplomacy, as a system by which rascals accomplish and attempt to legitimize projects against the welfare of the people, he asked for no stronger proof of the rightness of his view than this proposal to immolate his birthplace. He believed that, if they would tell the Great Powers to mind their own business, the Italians would not be further troubled by foreign interference. With equal inability to understand actual conditions, Marie Antoinette naïvely suggested that, if the poor were really starving for want of bread, they ought to eat cake. Garibaldi not only persuaded himself that the cession was unnecessary, but that the Ministers who seriously proposed it must be traitors. As usual he absolved the King, whom he assumed to be the dupe of his unpatriotic advisers.

On April 6, before the Chamber, by electing its officers, was legally ready for business, Garibaldi appeared and demanded to be allowed to interpellate the Minister of the Interior on a matter "very vital to *me* and to the country" — to wit, the cession of Nice. Cavour instantly protested that constitutional procedure must be respected — an impertinent consideration in the eyes of Garibaldi, who always regarded himself as a privileged personage to whom the law and the constitution did not apply. Nevertheless, the House, by an overwhelming vote, supported Cavour. On the 12th, the Chamber of Deputies having been organized with Lanza as its president, Garibaldi denounced the impending

[103] *Lettere,* IV, xiv–xv.

cession, declaring it to be historically and constitutionally indefensible, scoring the undue pressure exerted on the Nizzards, and asking that the vote should be postponed until the treaty had been ratified.[104] Cavour replied briefly, that, at the proper time, the Ministers would give the Chambers a full account of the transaction, but that for the moment he could say only that "the cession of Nice and Savoy was a condition essential to the prosecution of that political road which had led them [us] in so short a time to Milan, to Florence, to Bologna!" It might have been possible he added, to refuse to cede; but that refusal would have endangered the Central Italian provinces, if not the future of the country.[105] When Mancini, hoping to soothe matters, moved that three deputies from Nice and three from Savoy should oversee the elections in their respective districts, Cavour said irrevocably, no. "If we were to follow this advice," he explained with fervor, "I should believe that we were betraying the nation itself. It is a small matter that ministers compromise themselves, either at home or abroad; a small matter that ministers draw down on their heads powerful enmities; but it would be an immense and irremediable harm if this anger, these enmities were to be drawn down on the representatives of the nation. The ministers of a constitutional country must be able to sacrifice themselves for the public good, and never so long as we are ministers will we retreat behind the vote of Parliament to cover our responsibility. We assume entire responsibility for the Treaty, and if there is odium attached to it, we do not shrink from having it fall on us. We are as eager as any one for popularity, and on many occasions my colleagues and I have indeed tasted that beverage which sometimes inebriates; but, so far as our duty requires it, we know how to renounce this popularity. In signing this Treaty, we had a firm conviction that immense unpopularity would descend upon us: but we faced it, because we were persuaded that by so doing we acted for the interest of Italy."[106]

---

[104] Guerzoni: *Garibaldi*, II, 9, n. 1, frankly admits that Garibaldi's speech was inspired, if not actually written, by persons who were using him. This agrees with La Farina's view: "The petition for Nice is a party weapon, and nothing more; the cession of Nice is a grievous necessity. Nice might not be ceded; but in this case the making of Italy must be abandoned: who does not see this is either blind or dishonest." La Farina to C. Tamagni, April 10, 1860; *Epist.*, II, 312.

[105] *Discorsi*, XI, 54.   [106] *Discorsi*, XI, 59–60.

The debate on the Treaty was postponed until the end of May. In the mean time, the British Foreign Office unavailingly poured persuasion, sarcasm, warning into the Palace of the Quay d'Orsay. The French blandly regarded annexation, which they now called "restitution," as a matter of course. Prussia, though approving England's protests, remained passive. Austria contented herself with refusing to recognize the annexation of Central Italy, intimating that she reserved the right to act whenever she should think it necessary. Russia repeated that any monarch might perfectly well give away part of his territory to another, so long as the transfer did not disturb the European equilibrium.[107] The British public fell into a fever over a war with France — a possibility which the statesmen of both nations seriously discussed.[108] Lord John said boldly in the House of Commons "that such an act as the annexation of Savoy will lead a nation as warlike as the French to call upon its Government from time to time to commit other acts of aggression."[109] Listening to this speech from the Ambassadors' Gallery, Persigny could hardly contain his rage. "What language!" he shouted; "must I hear such things against my master?"[110] Palmerston told Flahaut, who was starting for Paris, to repeat the speech to the Emperor. "But that means war!" said Flahaut. "Very well!" replied Palmerston, "if it means war, war be it. . . . We are prepared."[111] Persigny became so abusive that his recall was rumored.[112] Paris Jingoes talked war, and figured out that it would be easy in a few hours to throw an invincible army across the Channel and conquer perfidious Albion. In political circles, the annexation of Belgium and of the Rhine Provinces to France began to be discussed as inevitable.[113] Rebuffed in their attempt to prevent France from swallowing Savoy and Nice, Palmerston and Lord John Russell insisted that the Treaty of 1815 must be respected: that pact declared that Chablais and Faucigny, two districts in Upper Savoy, should revert to Switzerland. Cavour could honestly profess that

[107] Vitzthum, II, 54. [108] See, for instance, Palmerston's memorandum of his talk with Flahaut on March 27. Ashley, II, 392–93, and Martin, v, 72–74.
[109] III Hansard, March 26, 1860; also Walpole: *Russell*, II, 320. Greville III, 532–33. [110] Walpole: *Russell*, II, 321. Malmesbury, 518. But Palmerston does not quote this remark in his Memorandum. [111] Vitzthum, II, 77–78.
[112] Malmesbury, 520. Greville, III, 536. [113] Senior: *Conversations*, II, 295, 296, 312–13, 323, 339, 349. Greville, II, 538.

the Italian Cabinet wished to see justice done to Switzerland. Reams of despatches on this subject passed to and fro.[114] Napoleon occasionally hinted at a congress. Gossips had it that Palmerston and Lord John were really working in secret against each other. Queen Victoria and Albert smarted more and more at the realization that they had been "regular dupes" of the French charlatan. She wrote Russell "that she would consider it the *deepest* degradation to [England] if she were compelled to appear at the Emperor's Congress, summoned to Paris, in order to register and put her seal to the acts of spoliation of the Emperor."[115] The Queen clung to her opinion that Cavour was a political trickster in collusion with Napoleon the Wicked. Albert was already worrying over the probability that in a year Victor Emanuel would be strong enough to wrest Venetia from Austria.[116] The Emperor himself, while taking no steps to prevent his people from relieving their wrath by bellicose speeches, did not intend to be stampeded into a war with England. He understood that Lord John's utterances meant "thus far and no farther" to Imperial ambition. He had gauged the anger of the Great Powers exactly, when he counted on their not going to war over Nice and Savoy, and to make his acquisition of these provinces seem moderate, he countenanced talk of much larger expansion. He even told Richard Metternich, the Austrian Ambassador, that he should be satisfied with those provinces and the Rhine frontier.[117]

When Nice held its plebiscite on April 15, out of 25,933 voters, 25,743 voted for and only 160 against annexation to France.[118] In Savoy, where the result was a foregone conclusion, 130,533 voted yes and 235 no.[119] The efforts of the French agents were so thorough as to be suspicious. Although in February and March, 12,500 citizens of Upper Savoy petitioned to be united to Switzerland, with which, by language, geography and economic interests, they naturally belonged,[120] in April, only about 100 persons in those communes voted against union with France. They had

---

[114] The important documents are in *Correspondence*, 1860, vol. 67.

[115] *Q. V. L.*, III, 397; Queen to Russell, April 26 (?), 1860.

[116] Vitzthum, II, 60; April 30, 1860.   [117] *Ibid;* but Vitzthum had this at second hand.   [118] *Moniteur*, April 27. Non-voting, 4743; defective ballots, 30.

[119] *Moniteur*, April 29. Total registration, 135,449; defective ballots, 71; non-voting, 4610.   [120] W. de La Rive cannot forgive Cavour for letting France take Upper Savoy; 308–09.

simply not been offered the Swiss alternative. In Savoy proper, the majority unquestionably preferred France to Piedmont. The clergy were Ultramontane; the nobles, still steeped in the memories of the Old Régime, thought their chances better under an Imperial despotism than in a constitutional monarchy of doubtful stability; the army likewise looked for higher pay and quicker promotions, and the court functionaries and even the school-teachers knew that the French stipend was more generous than the Piedmontese.[121] Ever since the princes of the House of Savoy followed their manifest destiny eastward, the Savoyards saw that crossing the Alps [122] did not benefit them. Recently, they had been attached to the person of the sovereign, rather than to his kingdom; and now they felt no serious wrench at parting. Nice, on the contrary, was more Italian in sympathy, despite a large mixture of French or Provençal blood; yet, if her people could have foreseen that under the French she would become in a few years one of the most prosperous pleasure resorts in the world, it is possible that they would have made less outcry against cession. Except for Garibaldi, the transaction would have left no bitterness: but he, and, much more, those who used him as their stalking-horse, fomented an agitation among the Nizzards; and, being beaten in the elections, they brought their rancor into the Italian Parliament, and long kept it alive there, as if it were a holy flame. That the vote of Nice as announced by the French government was dishonest, does not prove that the majority wished to stay under Victor Emanuel's sceptre. The ultimate question, however, went deeper than whether the vote were honest or not: it was simply this: If Napoleon III insists on taking Nice, who can prevent him? The plebiscite, employed fairly, was then the best means of ascertaining the crude wishes of a people; controlled by a despot or a demagogue, it was a convenient device for throwing a veil of legality over an act of brute force. From the plebiscite, which registered the desire, the overwhelming desire, of Nice

[121] Under Piedmont, the poorest parish priests received only 500 or 600 francs a year; under France, they might expect 1000, 1200 or even 1500 francs. Primary school-teachers in the mountains got from 200 to 300 francs; the French minimum was 600 francs. The many laborers who migrated every season from Savoy and Nice to France, required a passport; in becoming French, they would be saved this expense and bother. *Discorsi*, XI, 127–28.

[122] All Savoyards over 45 and under 68 had been *born* French; for Savoy was a part of France from 1792 to 1814.

and Savoy, there was no appeal. Foreign statesmen might think what they chose; unless they were prepared to go to war against France, the cession could not be prevented. The English prolonged their negotiations to save Upper Savoy for Switzerland, but without avail.[123] They criticized Cavour for not aiding them, but this he could not honorably do, being bound by his compact to cede all Savoy to France. Even had his honor not restrained him, he would not have been such a fool as to anger Napoleon by keeping back part of the compensation promised him. The English stigmatized Cavour's conduct as Machiavellian.[124]

On May 26 Cavour defended the Treaty before the Chamber of Deputies. Eight members, among whom were Guerrazzi and Rattazzi, had inveighed against it from every side.[125] According to them it was unpatriotic, unnecessary, unjustified, treasonable. They were listened to with intense interest, even by those members who did not intend to vote with them. Although some of their eloquence was inspired by political motives, especially by the desire to punish or destroy Cavour, — the stumbling-block to so many ambitions, — yet genuine grief at parting from the oldest province of the dynasty predominated. Cavour himself did not hide his emotion. When the little man rose to speak, his followers must have wondered what arguments he could find to stem the flood of objections which had been launched against him, but in the very first sentence, he captured the sympathy of the House. If the previous orators, he said, felt so much sorrow and bitterness, what must he feel — he, on whom the responsibility lay? Guerrazzi [126] had cited the case of Lord Clarendon, impeached

[123] Ollivier, 414, intimates that Napoleon at one time favored transferring the two districts to Switzerland.

[124] For the Savoy Question " Documents et Souvenirs rélatifs à l'Annexion de la Savoie en 1860 " (Geneva: Imprimerie de *La Tribune de Génève*, 1908) is indispensable. Also, "L'Affaire de Savoie, en 1860 et l'Intervention Anglais," by Prof. Ed. Rossier (Paris, 1906, reprint from *Revue Historique*, xc), is excellent.

[125] The ablest argument of the opponents appears in a memorandum sent by Mazzini (*Scritti*, xi, xix-xxiii) to Bertani. Its only defect is that it leaves fact out of sight and builds up its conclusions on visions.

[126] Guerrazzi's ten reasons for voting no will serve as an example of the argumentation of the Opposition. (1) My duty is to increase Italy: therefore, I cannot vote to curtail it. (2) If Nice is ceded, Italy will remain in perpetual servitude. (3) I cannot believe that generous France desires to subject us to such Caudine Forks. (4) Ministers have shown neither a necessity for the sacrifice, nor that they have tried to prevent it. (5) The Principle of Nationality may apply to Savoy, but never to Nice. (6) Neither present nor future advantage has been

and exiled for ceding Dunkirk to France; but, he added, if Clarendon had freed several million English and united several counties to his sovereign's crown, there would be some parallel between his acts and Cavour's.

Thereupon the Prime Minister unfolded the history of Piedmont since 1848, showing how the two chief aims of Victor Emanuel's reign — to develop the principles of liberty at home, and to promote within the bounds of the possible the principle of nationality abroad — had been carried out. The cession which they all deplored was the inevitable price Italy had to pay for her redemption. If Piedmont had followed a policy of cowardice or of isolation, they would not, he reminded them, be assembled that day as members of the first Italian Parliament. To escape from impotent isolation, Piedmont had required an alliance, which she had found in France. Thanks to that alliance, they had seen Lombardy freed and the principle of non-intervention enforced which permitted the independence of Emilia and Tuscany. He dismissed with brief notice those visionaries who insisted that Italy ought to pay no heed to Europe, but settle her own affairs and rely upon her volunteers. Taking up the military objections, he pointed out that, since the Alps were the natural bulwark of Piedmont, the possession of Savoy, which had no defensible frontier against France, was a great disadvantage. As to Nice, it was not to be supposed that, if the French wished to invade Piedmont on the south they would waste time to lay siege to that town, when in twenty-four hours they could transport an army by sea to the Ligurian coast. Cavour took pains to emphasize the French proclivities of both Nice and Savoy.[127] He

shown. (7) This vote tramples legality under foot. (8) This cession may serve as a precedent for some other foreign power to seize part of Italy in order to offset French preponderance. (9) I do not vote for it, because while Garibaldi risks his life to win for us our mother-country with his sword, to deprive him of his country would be a crime. (10) A favorable vote in the urn means a nail in Italy's coffin. " To bury the dead, sextons are called, not the free Italians of the first Italian Parliament."

[127] Later, in his speech before the Senate, on June 9, he showed how the Princes of Savoy, from the time when they first turned towards Italy, never scrupled to relinquish their Transalpine possessions. Charles Emanuel I made a treaty with Henry IV by which Lombardy was to be joined to Piedmont and Savoy to France. Victor Amedeus II, in 1700, wished to exchange both Savoy and Nice to get Lombardy and Parma; and he actually ceded Barcellonetta by the Treaty of Utrecht. *Discorsi*, xi, 150–51.

2

refrained from reminding his hearers how persistently Savoy, steeped in Ultramontanism, had opposed every effort since 1847 to liberalize Piedmont and to rescue oppressed Italy. He was too magnanimous to quote the threats of Savoyard deputies only the year before, that Savoy would secede if the King's Government undertook a war of Liberation.[128] He made short work of one speaker who based the Italianism of the Nizzards on their having voluntarily given themselves in 1388 to Amedeus VI, the Red Count, who was a Provençal not an Italian prince. As to the fairness of the recent vote, while admitting French pressure, he believed that the result truly registered the will of the majority: how otherwise explain that the Nizzard soldiers, free to choose, and voting wherever their regiments happened to be in Italy, were almost unanimous for France? He concluded by asserting that this act of cession, instead of ignoring, confirmed the principle of nationality. When Rattazzi slily suggested that it might serve as an excuse for giving away other parts of Italy, Cavour replied with fervor: "God knows how much we commiserate the fate of Venetia, God knows our grief when we were forced to abandon the hope of breaking her chains. And yet, gentlemen, I take you to witness, and consequently I take Europe to witness, that if, in order to acquire Venetia, we had to cede a hand's-breadth of Italian soil in Liguria or in Sardinia, I would reject the proposal without hesitation." [129]

Three days later, replying to Rattazzi's criticism that France had not guaranteed the union of Emilia and Tuscany, Cavour said that his government had avoided even discussing such a guarantee, which would be equivalent to placing Italy under the protection of the Emperor. After a brief explanation to Valerio and Biancheri, he ended his defense. Among the seven or eight speeches of his which are not only foundation documents of the Risorgimento but also specimens of the highest parliamentary oratory in the nineteenth century, this apology for the cession of Nice and Savoy is the most subtle. In many respects it required the greatest effort, just as the cession itself cost him the keenest

[128] Treitschke called Savoy, "the Italian Ireland"; but this is inexact: because Ireland had long-standing valid grievances against England, whereas Savoy was a favored part of Victor Emanuel's Kingdom. Savoy resembled Ireland in that its masses were most bigoted and superstitious Ultramontanes.

[129] *Discorsi*, XI, 130.

suffering. Having made a virtue of necessity, he had to persuade a hostile Parliament that the necessity existed. Following his habit, he spoke the truth as fearlessly in enumerating the objections as in stating the reasons why the Treaty must be ratified. Fully realizing the responsibility that weighed upon him, he was yet buoyant in his manner, as of one performing a duty with alacrity. He passed from grave to gay, interspersing his business-like statement of facts with characteristic touches of irony, or with appeals to conscience and to ideals. Never had he greater need than now of that gift of "seduction" in which, as La Marmora confessed, he was unrivaled, and never did he employ it more successfully in the Chamber of Deputies. When the roll was called, 229 supported him; 33 voted no; and 23 abstained.[130] The most critical act of his career was sealed; for the Senate, after further discussion, in which similar arguments went back and forth, confirmed the decision of the Chamber.

In judging the cession of Savoy and Nice, if we would be fair to all parties we must put ourselves into the conditions of March and April, 1860. Today, no one can seriously maintain that the Kingdom of Italy would be strengthened by possessing these States. In 1860, however, Italian tradition and sentiment clung to both of them; and Cavour would have saved both, or either, had it been possible. But he bowed to necessity. The critics who attacked him could offer absolutely nothing, except their fine phrases, as a substitute. Without the Emperor's acquiescence, the Centre could not have been annexed: against the Emperor's will, Savoy and Nice could not have been retained. The Austrian army, though in bad condition, would have marched into the Legations and Tuscany at a day's notice, and there is no likelihood that it could have been prevented from recovering Lombardy. Except Napoleon, the young Kingdom had no active

---

[130] On the secret ballot, with 282 members present instead of 285, the result was: Ayes, 233; noes, 36; non-voting, 23. On the open vote among the *noes* were: Anelli, Asproni, Bertani, Bertea, Berti-Pichat, Biancheri, Bottero, Castellani-Fantoni, L. Castelli, Cavalleri, Depretis, Dossena, Ferracini, Ferrari, Franchini, Guerrazzi, Maccabruni, Macchi, Massei, Mellana, Murardet, Mordini, Mosca, Pareto, Polti, Regnoli, V. Ricci, G. A. Sanna, G. Sanna, Sineo, Tomati, Valerio, Zanardelli. *Non-voting* : Amelio, D. Berti, Bonatti, Cabella, Capriolo, Casareto, Cavallini, Carlo, Coppini, Cornero, Cotta-Ramusino, Cossetti, De Amicis, Gentili, Giovanola, Mathis, Melegari, G. B. Michelini, Montezemolo, Monticelli, Rattazzi, Rubieri, Sperino, Tecchio. Artom-Blanc, II, 473-74.

friend in Europe. Prussia, Germany and Russia frowned at a State born of revolution and baptized by universal suffrage. Queen Victoria and a large section of official England, regarding the Italians merely as cunning brigands, wished to maintain towards them a rigid neutrality, which should favor Austria by every means short of open alliance. Palmerston, Russell and Gladstone, the loyal supporters of the Italian cause, never dreamed of helping the Italians by an army, and had grown lukewarm towards them, and especially towards Cavour, for making the secret bargain with Napoleon. It was the hope of frustrating the Emperor's grasping ambition, rather than of saving Nice and Savoy to Victor Emanuel, that induced the English statesmen to try to rouse the other Great Powers to interfere. Cavour measured the political field exactly, therefore, saw that he had no alternative, and accepted the inevitable not begrudgingly, nor with whimpers and repining, but with the air of one who recognized that the inevitable itself might conceal benefits. Just as in 1849 some members of Parliament refused to vote for the treaty of peace in the hope of winning a cheap popularity by their spurious patriotism, so now there were deputies and senators who prided themselves on being too patriotic to consent to cede a foot of Italy. Such buncombe deceives nobody. When amputation is necessary, how stands the surgeon who, in order not to risk his reputation, refuses to perform it?

The real loser by the cession was neither Cavour nor Italy, but Napoleon III. France gained; her Imperial ruler lost. The Nemesis which had been tracking him ever since, in 1849, he destroyed the Roman Republic in order to curry favor with the Papacy, now turned his acquisition of Nice and Savoy to his disadvantage. In getting Savoy, he added to the multitude, already menacingly large, of his Ultramontane subjects; in taking Nice, he embittered the Party of Action, who idolized Garibaldi. But this was of slight concern compared with the forfeiture of not only the goodwill but the confidence and respect of England. That goodwill for which, next to keeping himself on his throne, he had striven most indefatigably, now vanished in a day, and it never came back. Palmerston, his earliest supporter among the British, acted henceforth on the belief that he was a liar and a knave. Queen Victoria and Albert, grown suspicious that the

Third Napoleon intended to imitate the First and clutch at universal empire, saw, in this seizure, their suspicions confirmed. Europe accepted it as a certainty that he would next "revendicate" the "natural frontiers" of France by taking Belgium and the left bank of the Rhine. The Italians, who branded him a traitor at Villafranca, and had then slowly come to feel more kindly towards him, when he tacitly allowed the Central States to join the new Kingdom, plunged into resentment which has lasted until this day. They accused him of extorting full payment for half his service: an unjust accusation, because Emilia and Tuscany were much more than equivalent to Venetia. But outraged patriotism deals in emotions and not in figures; and Napoleon, caught in his web of contradictions, laid himself open to misconstructions. Instead of the unselfish Liberator, who had sailed into the flower-strewn harbor of Genoa less than a year before, he was loathed as a political Shylock — and, indeed, the comparison maligned the usurious Jew, for he at least had performed his part of the contract. But Napoleon could do nothing straightforward. He had neither tact as to method, nor sense of fitness as to time. In exacting Nice and Savoy, he set a precedent which the Germans followed remorselessly eleven years later, when they wrenched Alsace and Lorraine from France.

CHAPTER XXIX

GARIBALDI AND THE THOUSAND

EVEN before the Italian Parliament voted to accept the treaty, Italy and Europe were watching breathlessly the course of an adventure without its counterpart in the modern world. Garibaldi, who could ill accommodate himself to the restraints of constitutional government, who scorned diplomacy, despised the suggestion that Italians should pay heed to the Great Powers, loathed Napoleon III, and cherished henceforth unqualified hatred of Cavour as the betrayer of Nice, Garibaldi now became the hero of an exploit which took on from the beginning a legendary glory. His Italian Expedition recalled the mythic prowess of the Argonauts whom Jason steered to Colchis; it reproduced the triumph, which Dion, the ancient liberator, won in Sicily over Dionysius, the ancient tyrant; it matched in improbability the epic feats of Joan of Arc. Unlike Joan, Garibaldi lacked the faith that moves mountains: but he had invincible courage. In time of peace he was easily led, a prey to the last comer; on horseback, however, with face towards the enemy, he acted on his own motion, decisively and swiftly. Had it been left to him, the Thousand would not have sailed on May 5, 1860; but he was in the hands of abler planners, who knew neither caution nor scruple.

Naples and Sicily under Bomba's reign had been, as we have seen, the objective of conspirators. The fate of Agesilao Milano and of Count Bentivegna, and the ill-starred attempt of Pisacane, were symptoms that the patriotic ferment was working. After the Congress of Paris the Party of Action redoubled their efforts for fear of being forestalled by the Muratists. During the War of 1859 they kept quiet; then they roused themselves, and under the guidance of Mazzini and Crispi, they hoped to set off an explosion in Sicily in October. That missed fire. "To the Centre! to the Centre! aiming towards the South!" was next Mazzini's war-cry, until Ricasoli prevented his operations in

Tuscany, and the King dissuaded Garibaldi from invading the Papal States. All parties realized that the Two Sicilies were the most hopeful field for endeavor. The Government of young King Francis, or "Bombino" (Little Bomba) as his subjects nicknamed him, seemed tottering. Enthusiasts believed that a mere shove would push it over. As when the discovery of gold is announced in some remote place, fortune-seekers rush thither from every quarter, so the prospectors of Cavour and Mazzini, and of Napoleon III also, gathered secretly at Naples and in Sicily. The Party of Action, which included many who, though not devout Mazzinians, were eager to serve under his guidance, focussed their attention on Sicily.

Many reasons caused them to prefer the Island to the Mainland for their enterprise. First of all, there was the long-standing feud between the Sicilians and the Neapolitans: the former had been yoked to the latter by a dynastic bond which they hated. In 1848, Sicily, having won independence at a single stroke, maintained it after Naples had succumbed. The memory of Ferdinand's bombardment, which gave him the evil name he bears in history, rankled. The régime of martial law, under which the Islanders had been persecuted like a conquered people for a decade, kept them exasperated. The somewhat slacker rule since Bombino's accession they rightly attributed to feebleness and not to a desire on his part for reform. They thought the army rotten and suspected that much of it, whether rank or file, was disaffected. The alliance of France with Piedmont, the war with Austria, the victories of Magenta and Solferino, the emergence of the Kingdom of Upper Italy like an unbidden genie after the fumes of Villafranca, revived their hopes. There was in the Sicilian a love of independence which three thousand years of oppression had not succeeded in stifling. Could the anthropologists today reduce him to his elements, we should see the most astonishing among racial composites. For in his veins runs the blood of prehistoric Elymians, Sicels and Sicans; of Greeks, Doric and Ionic; of Phœnicians and of their offspring the Carthaginians; of Italiots and Romans; of Byzantines and Saracens; of Normans, Germans, French and Spanish. The issues of civilization, so long as civilization was restricted to the Mediterranean countries, circulated through his little island as all the sands slip through the waist of an hour-glass. Sicily was the stepping-stone for armies passing between Italy and Africa, the half-way post for fleets bound from Tyre to the Pillars of Hercules and beyond. Geography doomed Sicily never to be a nation: she was too central to be let alone, too small to defend her independence. But in spite of sequent conquests, her people never lost their love of liberty. Though they seemed quiescent for centuries, yet like imperial Etna now and again they would burst forth irresistibly: as the French learned to their sorrow at the Massacre of the Vespers in 1282, and the Bourbons at the uprising of 1848. Temperament, tradition and his daily life amid brutalizing conditions, seemed to mark the Sicilian as a predestined revolutionist.

The strategic importance of liberating Sicily before Naples was obvious. Once freed, the Island could hold out for a long time against any forces Bombino could send to reconquer it, and in the interval, Northern Italy, if not Europe, might intervene. The Sicilian shores could be reached from all sides. Malta, where Fabrizi had long been storing a lot of old muskets, and where a flock of agitators had grown gray watching for a signal, was only sixty miles from Cape Passero. For the Party of Action itself the liberation of Sicily might have tremendous consequences. The recent annexations, by which the Kingdom of Upper Italy had come into being, was the achievement of the Monarchists, allied with the Garibaldians and all those ex-republicans whom the National Society had drawn to Victor Emanuel's banner. To every observer of insight it was plain that Ricasoli had done more by taciturn inflexibility in ten months, than Mazzini by his unceasing propaganda and miscalculated risings in ten years. The great Exile, and his dwindling body of disciples, knew that, unless they could point to some province in Italy as redeemed by them, they would be forever discredited. They must act soon, or the Monarchists would forestall them. If Mazzini could free and hold Sicily, he might establish his republic there, and possibly go on to republicanize Naples and the Papal States. On the other hand, if Victor Emanuel were the liberator, the Monarchy would inevitably absorb all Italy. Thus party ambition as well as patriotism spurred the Mazzinians forward.

If they had had to depend on Mazzini himself, they would have failed as surely as they had always failed under his active

direction since the fizzle at Annemasse in 1834. But Francesco
Crispi, and not Mazzini, was the real preparer of the Sicilian
Expedition. Crispi, himself a Sicilian, born in 1819, had lived for
ten years in exile. In figure he was above middle height, spare
rather than stout, of undistinguished features even in the days of
his power, but of a manner which bespoke supreme self-confidence. He had an innate passion for domination, and capacity almost equal to his passion. In youth he accepted Mazzini's gospel
without reserve; but as he matured, he developed in the highest
degree that habit of seeing things as they are and of dealing with
them point-blank, which stamps the born men of action. He believed every means lawful to a patriot. Italy was his religion: like
the Crusaders, he lived as if he took it for granted that his zeal absolved him from the cardinal virtues which are the true witnesses
of religion. He was more than a theoretical approver of regicide:
indeed, it is still debated whether he was not the thrower of the
third bomb in Orsini's attempt on Napoleon III's life.[1] Men followed him, obeyed him, trusted him — but did not love him.
Except in open danger, when his nerve deserted him, he was a
perfect agent for a conspiracy. Give him a disguise, and he would
filter as naturally through a crowd of Bourbon or French police,
as a breeze through a thicket. Cool, alert, resourceful, he was,
and above all, clear-headed. Set Mazzini in Genoa, and his
fanatic vision would magnify a thousand adherents into a hundred thousand; Crispi would count just a thousand, or five more
or less, as the case might be. Mazzini's supreme value lay in his
power as a moral awakener: but his disciples had long needed not
so much to be persuaded of their duty to patriotism, as to be led
to some sane and fruitful achievement. Toward this Crispi possessed the rare qualification of seeing things as they were.

In August, 1859, Crispi, bearing an English passport made out
to "Manuel Pareda" from Argentine, and wearing English side-
whiskers and two pairs of blue goggles,[2] went from London to
Sicily, conferred with the revolutionary chiefs, taught them how
to construct Orsini bombs,[3] saw the number and location of the
Bourbon troops, planned minutely the proposed rising, and quitted the Island with the belief that the Revolution would come
at the appointed time. Late in September, however, Mazzini

[1] See *ante*, vol. I, p. 496, n. 6.   [2] Crispi, 229.   [3] *Ibid*, 235.

became anxious at the delay, and sent Crispi on a second mission. This time his passport read: "Tobias Glivaie (British Subject, a native of Malta)." Reaching Messina on October 11, he learned that the rising set for the 4th had been put off till the 9th, and then, after an insignificant skirmish, it had been abandoned.[4] Quick to realize that the local leaders had lost heart, he reasoned that the impetus and guidance of a revolution in Sicily must come from outside the Island. What troubled him most was to find that Moderates were supplanting Mazzinians on the committees. As Mazzini and Crispi used the epithet "Moderate" it sounded worse than "traitor." They applied it to the supporters of Victor Emanuel, to members of the National Society, to everyone, indeed, who doubted the possibility of redeeming Venetia, the Papal States and the Two Sicilies by a conspirators' insurrection. The effect of the War in the North and of the provisional independence of the Central States, had caused so many good Sicilian patriots, hitherto devoted followers of Mazzini, to perceive that their best hope lay in coöperating with the King's Government, that Crispi wrote Mazzini that unless their influence could be counteracted by the arrival in the Island of "a large number of exiles friendly to us," everything would be delayed and "our work may easily be lost."[5] In December, Crispi conferred with Farini, who was disposed to favor the Sicilian enterprise. "If it is a question of money," he said, "I will contribute as much as a million francs." [6] But Farini declared that he could not give aid openly without the sanction of the King's Government. Crispi, therefore, went to Turin and held several interviews with Rattazzi. Although we have no direct evidence, we are justified in suspecting that Crispi abetted, if he did not oversee, the plot to detach Garibaldi from the King's influence, by making him head of the Free Committees and of the Nation Armed — a plot which aimed also at the political destruction of Cavour. On July 14, 1859, Crispi wrote in his diary: "The papers bring news of Cavour's resignation, which indicates that the terms of the peace cannot be honorable or useful for Italy." [7] Sufficient proof that Crispi, in spite of his Mazzinianism, regarded Cavour at that time as representing the honor

[4] Crispi, 254.   [5] Ibid, 272; Crispi to Mazzini, Malta, Oct. 29, 1859.
[6] Ibid, 302.   [7] Ibid, 229.

and welfare of Italy; but by December, the Mazzinians, whose attack on the Papal States had been prevented, realizing that their principal obstruction might come from the Moderates, had entered upon a campaign of vilification against the Moderates, and especially against Cavour.

Crispi's report of the unpromising conditions of the Sicilian conspirators did not discourage Mazzini: but even the Great Exile, who had so far lost his grip on reality as to preach that the Italians need fear neither France nor Austria, even he understood that his little band of disciples could not unaided liberate Sicily. This band included Crispi, a man of clear sight and tireless energy, but neither widely popular, nor magnetic; Nicola Fabrizi, whose forty years of conspiring had left him a zealot, intense and narrow, but necessarily incapable of leading a large movement: Maurizio Quadrio, another patriarch, a doctrinaire whose proper weapon was the pen and not the sword; Rosalino Pilo, an enthusiast, fitted to serve as lieutenant, but without the first requisites of generalship; and Alberto Mario, who could write caustic indictments, who impressed both friends and enemies by his Draconic austerity, but who, like Pilo, could lay no claim to military authority. Men bred up as conspirators, experience has proved it a thousand times, are ill-qualified to organize and command a wide-reaching campaign. They can throw a bomb, or stab a despot, or start a riot: but they cannot conduct a war. They can no more take a broad view of the political situation than a cat, with eyes riveted to a rat-hole, can see what is going on in the house. Mazzini knew that he must ally his little party with the Garibaldians, whose chief enjoyed that prestige as a warrior and that magic popularity which would draw multitudes to support their common cause.

From January to May, 1860, the Party of Action concentrated their efforts on winning over Garibaldi. He was not a Mazzinian; and although he had resigned from the National Society, he still looked up to Victor Emanuel as his leader: but his loyalty did not extend to the Monarchists as a body. His ideal was the Republic: but his dearest wish was to fight for Italy's independence, no matter when, or where, or under whose banner. Garibaldi was, however, as Mazzini petulantly declared, "weak beyond expression"; and by subscribing yourself his friend, or pat-

ting his shoulder, you could do anything with him.[8] By these
easy tactics, "Brofferio and Company," Mazzini's allies in Piedmont, captured Garibaldi, and exploited him for their own ends
in the often mentioned attempt to destroy Cavour in December,
1859. He quitted Turin with the realization that he had been
played upon, only to be trapped into an unseemly marriage,
which he repudiated on the day of the ceremony. He was a
creature of such fascination, however, that neither foibles nor
mistakes could permanently lessen his popularity.

Garibaldi's intimates, Bertani, Medici, Bixio, were too rational
to favor any expedition unless its success could be counted upon.
They knew that Crispi's report on the impotence of the Sicilians
to rise without outside instigation, was sound. While they kept
up friendly and even confidential relations with the Mazzinians,
they placed more faith in the King's ability to complete the work
of liberation: hoping, very naturally, that they could influence
the King. "The difficult task now, and quite the most useful
for our cause," Bertani wrote Panizzi in January, "is to bring
Garibaldi and Cavour together. Garibaldi has absolutely in
hand the people of Italy and the King. Cavour could contribute
the intelligence and the guidance that are lacking, along the very
difficult paths, to both. Cavour with the King and Garibaldi can
emancipate himself in great part from Napoleon." [9]

Bertani also suggested using Napoleon as far as Italian inter-
ests might benefit thereby, and he urged Panizzi to persuade the
British Ministers of the desirability of effecting a league between
Cavour and Garibaldi. "If we do not succeed in associating
Garibaldi with the men and affairs of high political significance,"
Bertani added wisely, "he will never be more than a guerilla . . .
and we shall have lost all the usefulness that can be derived . . .
from the popular prestige which that man enjoys."[10] The shrewd
Bertani even suggested that Garibaldi be invited to England, to
be feasted by the Liberal magnates, so that he might return
better disposed towards the Royal direction, and lead the Sicilian
revolution.[11] Partly on this mission of reconciliation and partly
in behalf of the Garibaldian Volunteers, whose neglect by the
Government was one of Garibaldi's standing grievances, Medici

[8] Trevelyan, I, 121; letter of Mazzini; Nov. 1859.
[9] Panizzi, 411.　　[10] *Ibid*, 412.　　[11] *Ibid*, 413.

went to Turin, saw Cavour several times, admired his "mind at the level of circumstances," and his energetic and sensible and thoroughly Italian purposes, and accepted a commission as lieutenant-colonel in the Piedmontese army.[12] Bixio also had a cordial welcome from Cavour, whose views he pronounced satisfactory.[13] That great section of the Party of Action which we may now call Garibaldian, composed of ardent patriots who accepted his watchword — "Italy and Victor Emanuel!" — and asked only that Garibaldi should lead them, were inclined, during the months of January and February, to wait for a signal from Turin.

Cavour's attitude towards the projected Sicilian Expedition has been the most criticized by his enemies of all his political acts. Not even the cession of Nice supplied them with so unfailing a secretion of venom. And yet, although all the documents have not been published, and much oral testimony is lost forever, we can almost unerringly trace his course, surmise the reason for each decision and for each change of front, and if we do this dispassionately we cannot escape the conclusion that he was guided throughout by the keenest foresight and by the highest patriotism. The fundamental mistake made by Mazzini, and by later critics who have echoed his vituperation, is that they identified their own program with Italy itself. When, therefore, Cavour differed from them, he was indisputably, according to their argument, a traitor to Italy.

During his early career, Cavour's guiding principle for the redemption of Italy was, as we have so frequently seen, the expulsion of foreign influence. Until Austria could be driven out, he condemned as futile sporadic assassinations and explosions. To drive Austria out, Italy required an ally. This Mazzini denied. For thirty years he preached that the Italians could do the work unaided. Yet in 1858 the Austrians seemed to be as firmly rooted as ever in Italian soil. On July 21, 1858, Cavour secured an ally; on July 21, 1859, Austrian control over the Peninsula had been loosed forever, except in Venetia. As to the one thing indispensable — the foreign alliance — which was right, Mazzini or Cavour? Which was really making Italy — Mazzini, with his record of abortive attempts, or Cavour, with Lombardy and

---

[12] Panizzi, 419; Medici to Panizzi, Genoa, Feb. 25, 1860.
[13] Mario: *Bertani*, II, 2; Jan. 26, 1860.

the Legations, the Duchies and Tuscany, redeemed in a few months at a single trial?

At the Congress of Paris, Cavour pleaded for the emancipation of the Peninsula. He could not openly propose the extinction of the Bourbon dynasty in the Two Sicilies; but privately he would have preferred Murat to Bomba at Naples, because Murat's presence would shut out Austrian influence from half of Italy. A doctrinaire like Mazzini argued from this that Cavour had not a drop of Italianism in him, that his patriotism was a sham, that he simply wished to substitute a French despot for a Bourbon despot, and Bonapartist influence for Hapsburg. The next year, after the Sapri failure, although Cavour supported the claims of the owners of the *Cagliari* and broke off diplomatic relations with Bomba, this did not deter the Mazzinians from denouncing him as Bomba's counterpart in persecution. At Plombières it was assumed that the French and Piedmontese allies should make no overt attack on Naples: but both Napoleon and Cavour understood that Bomba's throne might topple over at the least jar. It would have been suicidal, however, for Cavour to suggest then that, in case of revolution, the Kingdom of Naples should be united to Piedmont. Having secured the French alliance, Cavour, true to his fundamental principle of ridding the Peninsula of the foreigner, preferred the Bourbon to a French prince at Naples: the Bourbons would go to the wall very soon unless they reformed, whereas a Murat or a Bonaparte would have Imperial backing. With this intent, Cavour, in April, 1859, urged Bomba's government to join the National movement: but Bomba declared that he should remain neutral, which was equivalent to his siding with Austria. A similar invitation to the new King, Francis II, met with a similar rebuff. "There is nothing to hope for here for the Italian cause," wrote Salmour on June 22, 1859. To Mazzinians, taking their short views of the future, these negotiations seemed sacrilege, explainable only on the theory that Cavour's assertion of patriotism was pure deceit. They would not have believed in his sincerity even if they had heard him assure his friends after Villafranca that he would turn revolutionist, devote himself to Naples, and, at any cost, drive the national movement ahead.[14] When,

[14] *Ante*, p. 114.

however, Emilia and Tuscany gravitated irresistibly to Piedmont, to form the Kingdom of Upper Italy, Cavour realized that his next duty was to control, if he could not retard, the revolution in the South. Being a statesman, fully convinced that well-knit states do not spring, like Athena, full-grown from the brain of Zeus, Cavour wished to hinder a premature union. He would first train the new states in constitutional government, make them feel their common interests, teach them to be Italians, instead of Tuscans and Lombards, let Europe acknowledge them as a self-sufficient, well-fused and united nation, and then welcome the brethren of the South.

But, without any preparation, to join eleven or twelve millions of the most backward Italians to those of the Centre and the North — to yoke Neapolitans, Sicilians, Romans, each with their special problems, their inveterate provincial characteristics, their feuds, their backwardness in education and morals, their degeneracy due to the organized corrupting influence of Popes and Bourbons, — to yoke these to the Piedmontese, already seasoned in parliamentary experience, and to Lombards, Emilians and Tuscans, who had long had contacts with civilization, was an immense imprudence. There comes a point where the Leaven is too small for the Lump. That Cavour did not favor the sudden liberation of the South was, therefore, a proof of his patriotism not less than of his wisdom. Like an honest builder, he knew the danger of laying on the upper stones before the foundations were solid.

The course of events, however, paid no more heed to the dictates of reason, than a freshet pays to the dykes it has overflowed. All sections of the Party of Action clamored to strike off the shackles from the South Italians, who were described as unanimous for the Revolution, and resolved to rise to a man at the first call. It was a race to rescue them. Although Cavour preferred that the actual state of things should last several years longer, he recognized that the inundation was near, and adapted his policy to make the very cataclysm he would have averted serve the larger cause of Italy.[15] He had to avoid, on the one hand, a triumph of the Revolution, which should transmute the Two Sicilies into a republic; and, on the other, he had to

[15] *Lettere*, III, 236; C. to Villamarina, March 30, 1860.

beware of traversing the popular movement to such a degree as to render the Royal Government odious. Whatever happened, he must show a perfectly correct front to international diplomacy, which eyed him with well-founded distrust, because he was achieving, against the wishes of official Europe, the creation of the Kingdom of United Italy. The various means he now employed were intended to control, if he could not head off, the Revolution. He instructed Villamarina, recently transferred from the Paris to the Naples embassy, to do his utmost to discourage the patriots from revolting, and to urge Francis II that his one chance of salvation lay in adopting sincerely the National cause. Victor Emanuel wrote the young King that Italy might be divided into a Northern and a Southern Kingdom, mutually friendly and both upholding the great idea of the time — national independence. "If you repudiate my advice," said Victor bluntly, "the day may come in which I shall be placed in the terrible alternative of putting in jeopardy the most vital interests of my dynasty or of being the chief instrument of its ruin. . . . If you allow some months to pass without heeding my friendly suggestions, Your Majesty may, perhaps, experience the bitterness of those terrible words — 'too late' — as happened to a member of your family in 1830, at Paris."[16]

Being a true Bourbon, Francis would not learn from experience; and indeed, he could not be blamed for suspecting any offer from Piedmont, the source, as he had been taught to believe, of all the ills that had harried the despots of Italy since 1849. In the autumn he had secretly arranged with Austria and the Pope to send his army into the Marches and, when a favorable moment came, to attack the Romagna. The Austrian Ambassador did not cease to urge Pius to proclaim a crusade of loyal Catholics against the modern reprobates who were despoiling his kingdom.[17] Though he would not officially do this, yet he and Antonelli gladly embraced a project which would, if successful, restore the lost provinces to the Holy See, bring back the petty

[16] *Lettere*, iv, cxxi; V. E. to Francis II, April 15, 1860.

[17] "The Austrian Ambassador labors ardently to drive the Holy Father to extreme measures. An Appeal to Catholicism, a Catholic League, can alone, he says, save the pontificate and society." Very confidential despatch of De Martino, Neapolitan Minister at Rome, to Neapolitan Minister of Foreign Affairs, Jan. 6, 1860. Bianchi : *Cavour*, 89.

despots to Tuscany, Parma and Modena, re-establish Austria's primacy and raise what they hoped would be an impregnable bulwark against further Piedmontese aggression.[18] This plot failed. A few months later, the French Emperor, worried over his inability to force either Pius or Victor Emanuel to accept his views in regard to the Romagna, told both that he should withdraw his troops from Rome, and leave them to make the best of it. He went so far as to propose that a Neapolitan army should protect the Papal government, and occupy the Northern frontiers. Cavour checkmated this scheme by announcing that, unless Ancona were garrisoned by the Piedmontese, as a safeguard, he should construe the entrance of the first Neapolitans as a cause of war.[19] He pointed out to Talleyrand that, if Francis II were so foolish as to order his troops into Umbria and the Marches, he would create a revolution in Naples and Sicily.[20] The Pope himself settled the matter by organizing under the Belgian fanatic, Mérode, a Papal Army, composed of Catholic volunteers from various countries, especially from Austria and France, and by appointing Lamoricière, a French general, to command it. The garrison of Ancona, nominally composed of Papal volunteers, really consisted of some 6,000 seasoned Austrian troops, whose underhand enrolment the Pope winked at. Before the end of March, therefore, the Papal-Austrian-Neapolitan coalition loomed up as a very real menace to Victor Emanuel's Kingdom. It had, on paper at least, some 200,000 men, and if the French troops evacuated Rome and Lombardy, it would require no urging to attack the Piedmontese. Could they repel such a force?

On learning, some time afterward, of Cavour's attempt to draw the Bourbons into the Italian movement, the Mazzinians gloated over it, as another proof that he was a reactionary, bent on blasting the unification of Italy. They accused him also of duplicity, on the assumption that he tried to entice the young King into a snare. If we understand, however, that Cavour wished to stave off a revolution in the Two Sicilies until Victor Emanuel's new Kingdom should have time to weld itself into one

---

[18] Bianchi: *Cavour*, 88–89.
[19] *Lettere*, IV, 234; C. to Villamarina, March 30, 1860.   [20] See also for this episode, Thouvenel, I, 60 *ff.*, 80 *ff.*, 88, 93. Bianchi: *Cavour*, 85–90.

2

strong nation, we shall see that he might with perfect sincerity urge Francis to constitutionalize his government and to work for Italian Independence. Had Francis followed this suggestion, the improvement in his Kingdom might have quieted discontent, if only for an interval: but there could be no doubt that, in the long run, the Bourbons would fail, and that their subjects would unite with their brethren of the North. In order to fight fire with fire, Cavour encouraged La Farina to spur on the National Society, which, since the preceding autumn, had extended its activity through the Centre and South. As before, La Farina's purpose was to attract to Victor Emanuel as large a number as possible of the Revolutionists. To those still groaning under the Bourbon régime he passed the word to wait, lest by a premature rising they should bring ruin on the cause.[21] The abuse which the Mazzinians showered upon him is the best measure of his efficiency.[22] But he was equally alert in preparing to send an expedition to Sicily, in case it were necessary to outstrip a Mazzinian venture; and he held himself ready to start at a moment's notice.

While the La Farinians kept logically to their Fabian policy, the Mazzinians labored night and day to force a crisis. Mazzini himself fired his partisans at Genoa with his appeals from a distance. Crispi, who had the advantage of being on the spot, conferred with everybody, spread the Master Conspirator's vehement instructions and gave to them a gloss of practicability which Mazzini never could give. For Crispi was no dreamer, no idealist; he nursed no delusions as to the situation in Sicily: but he believed that, though the odds were ten to one against them, it was advisable to make the attempt without delay. Every week they put off, the hated Moderates would be sapping the revolutionary propensity of the Sicilians. Towards the end of January, Bertani adopted this view. With these two in accord, the two ablest heads and most indefatigable workers of the Party of Action joined in directing its campaign. They were, indeed, the Preparers of the Expedition, and in Nino Bixio they had an efficient coadjutor. They all realized that Garibaldi must lead. For a long time the Sicilians had looked to the hero of the defense of

[21] De Cesare : *Fine*, II, 159–60; Benza's trip to Palermo in February, 1860.
[22] E. g., see Mario's *Bertani*, passim.

Rome as their predestined savior. In September, 1859, they invited him to take command of their impending insurrection. Being still hopeful of invading Umbria, he replied that they must, first of all, unite themselves indissolubly to his program — "Italy and Victor Emanuel!" If there were any possibility of succeeding, he bade them rise; if not, he would have them cleave to each other and gain strength. He would willingly go to Sicily, but he must first have a closer acquaintance with them and their prospects. They replied: "A handful of men with ensigns, several hundred guns, a few cannon and a flag consecrated by your breath, will suffice to shatter the grievous stagnation in which the affairs of Italy now stand, and to redeem Sicily from the apparent apathy in which she believes herself accursed. Come, Sir, and this country will sound anew its Vespers!" [23] Aged people in adversity have long memories: it was nearly six hundred years since the Sicilians slew their French oppressors: ever since then the thought of those Vespers had lain in Sicilian hearts as an incentive.

In spite of his whims and his surface naïveté, Garibaldi was too canny to be a pliable conspirator.[24] He distrusted Mazzini, as the spinner of impracticable and often mad plots; at Rome, where the two had come into collision, Garibaldi resented Mazzini's dictatorialness. Achievement for achievement, why should the elder Joseph dictate to the younger, especially when the younger had no illusion as to his own importance? And now Garibaldi left unanswered for three months an appealing letter from Mazzini. He asked for nothing better than to unsheathe his sword for Italy, but he required evidence that success was at least probable. Mazzini had no reputation to lose by an abortive plot, but Garibaldi was too shrewd to stake his prestige without due warrant. Bertani, friend of both, sent an agent, Nicola Mignogna, to Caprera, where Garibaldi was revolving black thoughts over the pitfalls of marriage, the proposed betrayal of Nice, and the tedious delay in attacking the Pope, the Austrian or the Bourbon. He promised to give Bertani 3000 lire and the muskets stored in Genoa.[25] Mazzini, despite Garibaldi's silence, had already written to reassure him: "There is only one aim:

[23] Mario: *Bertani*, II, 6; Garibaldi's letter is dated Sept. 29, 1859.
[24] Guerzoni: *Garibaldi*, II, 24, says truly: "Garibaldi was never an initiator, nor a conspirator."
[25] Mario: *Bertani*, II, 10; Garibaldi to Bertani, Feb. 15, 1860.

Italy free, Rome the centre, the French ousted. I understand
the times, I respect the wishes of the country, I will not work
against the King, I will not conspire for the Republic; I give
only the watchword *Unity!* I urge to annexation and to bring
about a rising in Sicily or elsewhere, only stipulating immediate
acceptance." [26] Mazzini asked whether, in case the Sicilian venture succeeded, Garibaldi would support a movement in the
Centre. In his fervid imagination he already saw the Pope stript
of his temporal power, and the Austrians of Venetia. Garibaldi
left no doubt of his goodwill towards every attempt to destroy
the enemies of Italy, but he warily avoided pledging himself to
lead a wild-goose chase.

Growing frantic at Garibaldi's caution, Mazzini besought
Bertani, Medici and Bixio to win the General over to them at any
cost. He sowed his letters thick with the seeds of discord, which
sprang up promptly and have borne many crops. While Garibaldi made "Italy and Victor Emanuel" his battle-cry, Mazzini declared that Victor Emanuel and Cavour were, morally,
cowards, and lackeys to the commands of "L. Napoleon." He
pretended to have secret information, much of which, however,
must have originated in his own brain. The impending cessions
confirmed his reiterated warnings against the deceit of the Piedmontese policy. He knew Garibaldi's loathing of "L. Napoleon,"
and sprinkled pepper on that rankling sore by making Garibaldi
appear a mere puppet in the Emperor's hands. He tried to rouse
Garibaldi's self-love, by hinting that he was losing his energy.
Mazzini himself had everything ready — "a multitude of elements *organized* in the Centre," the army of patriots drilled and
eager and only awaiting a general to lead them to victory! Without a quiver of humor he wrote, that last November "we were
within *forty-eight hours* of a rising." The one thing which Mazzini hoped for even beyond Garibaldi's personal coöperation, was
the gift of the money and muskets which Garibaldi controlled.
He begged for 10,000 or 12,000 lire, not to start an outbreak in
Sicily, but to pay the way of his agents, "some important individuals," who were going there. If Garibaldi refused to perform
his task of initiator, there were other men in Italy to take his
place: "Why not you, Medici?" asked Mazzini.[27]

[26] Mario: *Bertani*, ii, 9.   [27] Mazzini: *Scritti*, xi; letters to Bixio, Feb.
19; to Bixio, Medici, and Bertani, Feb. 20; to Garibaldi, March 17.

The Great Conspirator suffered torments to think that only the stubbornness of the very man who ought to be first in the field prevented the Party of Action from scoring at last a speedy and conclusive victory. While he goaded on his friends at Genoa, he also spared no effort to arouse the Sicilians. "Brothers!" he wrote them, in a manifesto dated March 2, "it is necessary that I should tell you from time to time the true state of affairs. . . . I confess that in the Sicilians of today, I no longer recognize the men of the defiance of 1848." This he attributes not to loss of patriotism but to their having been deluded by false prophets — to wit, La Farina. "First of all, I repeat to you that which we have been printing these two years past — *There is no longer question of Republic or Monarchy; the question is National Unity — to be or not to be.* . . . If Italy wishes to be a Monarchy under the House of Savoy, let it be, and welcome. If, when all is done, it wishes to acclaim the King and Cavour liberators or what not, so be it. What we all will is that Italy shall be made; and if she is to be made, she must be made by her own inspiration and conscience, not by giving free swing, as to methods, to Cavour and to the King, while we remain inert and wait. Wait for what? In good faith, can you believe that Cavour, the King and L. Napoleon will come to give you liberty? Suppose they desire to do this, how could they do it? . . . Cavour has only a single aim — to add Venetia to the Monarchy, as was agreed at Plombières. L. Napoleon has only a single aim: to secure Savoy and maintain French supremacy in Italy. . . . Fixed in his single purpose, Cavour does not desire new complications. L. Napoleon fears them. Neither from one nor the other, therefore, can you expect salvation." Mazzini goes on to tell them how the patriots, but for a menacing note from L. Napoleon, would have redeemed the Centre and South last November. With sublime disregard of fact, he implies that the liberation of Emilia and Tuscany was his work. Why, indeed, should not a visionary claim dominion over an imaginary past, as well as over a dream-born future? He next assures the Sicilians that, if they only will rise, the Piedmontese army will be forced to invade Umbria and Naples. A "vast" movement to that end exists in the army itself. "Farini approves of it. Garibaldi is bound to aid. . . . For heaven's sake, dare! You will be followed. But dare in the name of

National Unity; it is the indispensable condition. Dare: summon to power a little nucleus of energetic men; let their first acts speak of Italy, of the Nation; let them call on the Italians of the Centre and of the North. You will have them." [28]

Meanwhile the Preparers — Crispi and Bertani, Medici and Bixio — were working from Genoa as their headquarters to make everything ready, in the belief that, sooner or later, the expedition would sail. They and their associates had constant communication with La Farina and the National Society leaders, who were in touch with Cavour. Probably even thus early the King also had private knowledge of their plans. It was no secret to anyone who chose to inquire, that a plot against the Bourbon King was hatching. Up to February 20 Garibaldi himself assumed that Cavour was with them, and he dreaded lest Cavour should dominate their enterprise, for he wrote to Bertani on that day: "Leave as little as possible to Cavour's disposition." [29] To Finzi and Besana, directors of the Million Muskets Fund, he wrote at the same time: "I advise using the greatest deference to Cavour's desires. But, since near him there are men likely to oppose us, we must have patience and courage, and sagacity to let ourselves be entangled as little as possible." [30] From this it appears that Garibaldi did not yet feel downright hatred for Cavour, but distrusted his followers, among whom we may suspect he had La Farina especially in mind. The Million Muskets Fund, of which Garibaldi was president, already amounted to a large sum: the cash and 15,000 weapons were controlled by a board in Milan, but Giuseppe Finzi was the responsible director. Subscriptions flowed in generously from all quarters: the King gave 10,000 lire, Mazzini gave 250. On his return to office, Cavour, far from thwarting this very suggestive project, encouraged it: only, he took steps to guard against its involving Piedmont in international inquiries. He assigned certain government buildings as depots for the guns and ammunition, intimating that they would help to equip the National Guard, which, a little earlier, it had been proposed that Garibaldi should organize, but the scheme was temporarily shelved. Cavour went even further, and

---

[28] Mazzini: *Scritti*, xi, xlviii-li.	[29] Trevelyan, i, 333; Garibaldi to Bertani, Feb. 20. Jessie Mario gives the note misdated, "Feb. 15," and carefully omits the postscript with this sentence. *Bertani*, ii, 10.	[30] Ciàmpoli, 128.

AGOSTINO BERTANI

FRANCESCO CRISPI

GIACOMO MEDICI

NINO BIXIO

PREPARERS OF THE SICILIAN EXPEDITION

allowed the guns, which were bought in Germany, to be admitted free of duty. He stipulated, however, that they should not be distributed without notification to the Government:[31] a necessary precaution, in view of Garibaldi's propensity for agreeing with the latest comer. What guarantee had the Government, for instance, that Mazzini might not wheedle the arms into his own possession and use them in an insane attempt to capture Genoa, such as he had made less than three years before? The Directors of the Fund heartily concurred in Cavour's requirements, and so did Garibaldi himself. "He intends to act, on his part," Finzi wrote on February 17, "in perfect agreement with the views of the National Government." [32]

Towards the end of February, Rosalino Pilo, Mazzini's most unqualified disciple, made it his express business to persuade Garibaldi. Pilo was one of those whole-souled natures born to be eager and fruitful martyrs. He wrote the General that "something concrete" was already prepared in Sicily; that Bertani and his friends needed only money to launch operations from Genoa; that Mazzini stipulated nothing about a republic; that Garibaldi himself should command "militarily" the insurgent South, and thus have the best guarantee that his program would be carried out.[33] Three weeks elapsed before Garibaldi replied. In the interval, the rumored cession of Nice and Savoy became a certainty. Garibaldi promised Pilo arms and money, but thought the time unfavorable for any rising. "Today," he said, "the cause of the country is in the hands of political intriguers, who wish to settle everything by diplomatic negotiations. . . ." The time to act will be "when the Italian people understand the inutility of these doctrinaires." Garibaldi pledged himself to support any attempt, no matter how perilous, provided it were opportune; and he bade Pilo to remember that their battle-cry was "Italy and Victor Emanuel." [34] Undiscouraged, Pilo determined to go himself to Sicily, and carry from group to group the fiery message, "Begin, and Garibaldi will come!" Leaving behind him a letter to inflame Garibaldi, by suggesting that an immediate revolution in the South might block the diplomats in

[31] The first agreement was made with Rattazzi, shortly before his resignation.
[32] Luzio: "Garibaldi, Cavour e Crispi," *Giornale d'Italia*, May 5, 1907.
[33] Mario: *Bertani*, 10–11; Pilo to Garibaldi, Feb. 24.
[34] Ciàmpoli, 130; Garibaldi to Pilo, Caprera, March 15.

the North and save Nice,[35] he and a companion named Corrao, hired a small fishing-boat, sailed from Genoa on March 25, and after a precarious voyage, landed undiscovered near Messina on April 9.[36]

Meanwhile, the Patriotic Committees in Sicily, shamed out of their inertia by Mazzinian and La Farinian messages alike, prepared to act. Their membership included many aristocrats, and even more of the lower classes, to whom it fell to take the lead. They planned to assemble in the Convent of La Gancia, where a small supply of poor firearms and bombs had been collected, and, on the morning of April 4, to rush out and seize Palermo before the 20,000 troops garrisoned in the city could oppose them. At the first success, they expected bands of peasants to dash to their aid from the countryside, and the soldiers to desert and join the Revolution. The news would spread through the Island, kindling a local rebellion in each important place; the victorious patriots would seize the men-of-war in the harbors; the garrisons would surrender; Sicily would be free before the Bourbons could recover from their amazement. "Never had an insurrectional movement," a devoted Mazzinian declared, "been better and more precisely organized and prearranged." [37]

Alas for rainbow dreams of conspirators! Throughout the night of April 3-4, brave Francesco Riso, master plumber and leader of the plebeian conspirators, waited with his little band of comrades in the convent. At dawn, they heard the tramp of troops outside and knew that their plot was discovered. "It is too late to retreat!" said Riso to his men. Seizing their arms, they went out to face the enemy. They were soon driven back, and for a time there was a hand-to-hand struggle in the Gancia courtyard itself. They rang the tocsin frantically, but no help came. The Bourbon soldiers overpowered them, killed several, arrested the others, looted the convent, bound the friars and took them off as prisoners. Before Palermo had breakfasted, the glorious and perfectly organized Mazzinian attempt was crushed under foot. The rural bands (squadre) kept safely away from the city, only appearing from time to time on the neighboring mountains, where they exchanged shots with the Bourbon soldiery and

[35] Mario: *Bertani*, II, 12-13.   [36] Mazzini: *Scritti*, XI, lv-lxi, for account of the voyage by Motto, the pilot.   [37] Mazzini: *Scritti*, XI, lvii, note.

then disappeared. These Parthian skirmishes continued until April 18, when a band led by Piediscalzi, the Albanian, was caught at Carini and badly worsted. In Palermo itself Marshal Salzano set up a reign of terror. He crowded the prisons with political suspects, and caused thirteen of the rebels taken in the Convent to be shot (April 14), while, by an infamous trick, Maniscalco, the Chief of Police, persuaded Francesco Riso, who had been mortally wounded, to reveal the names of some of the nobles who had failed to stand in the breach on April 4.[38]

When Pilo landed at Le Grotte on the evening of April 9, he heard of the lamentable collapse of the revolution in Palermo — a collapse which soon put an end to the sympathetic risings in other cities.[39] Instead of being nonplussed, however, the zealous Pilo wrote at once to Bertani: "The Revolution in Sicily is prospering well." [40] Having perpetrated this pious fraud,[41] he started to cross the Island, whispering to every one whom he could trust, "Courage! Garibaldi is coming!" After a journey of almost incredible dangers, he stole on April 20 into Piana dei Greci, where Piediscalzi was just about to disband his troop and to emigrate. Pilo told him the joyful news. Word flew round in a mysterious way to the other bands, some of which had already broken up, to rise again to receive Garibaldi; and they rose. Patriotic leaders in Palermo spread the glad tidings. Even the prisoners in the Vicaria fortress taunted their keepers with the cry, "*Piddu* is coming!" [42] Before the end of April, Pilo in his mountain refuge had reassembled a goodly number of *Picciotti*,[43] galvanized the patriots throughout Northwestern Sicily with new hope, and painted Garibaldi in such marvelous terms that he seemed to the superstitious and imaginative natives at least a demi-god or an archangel who was descending to free them. So Pilo, the Precursor, assured them; and so they began to believe: but would he come?

In Piedmont, meanwhile, preparations went forward without pause, and with so little attempt at concealment, that the uninitiated could not help suspecting what was up. Crispi and Ber-

---

[38] De Cesare: *Fine*, ii, 164 ff.; he gives Riso's alleged confession in detail. Trevelyan, i, 156–61.   [39] That at Messina was the most vigorous. De Cesare: *Fine*, ii, 193–94.   [40] Mazzini: *Scritti*, xi, lx.   [41] Trevelyan, i, 159, says aptly: "Pilo was playing a game of bluff."   [42] "Piddu," Sicilian nickname for "Giuseppe" [Garibaldi].   [43] The Sicilian rustic guerillas.

tani, La Farina, Bixio, Sirtori and Medici, each from his special corner, but the Garibaldians generally in unison, worked to procure money and arms against the moment of action. Garibaldi, as head of the Million Muskets Fund, controlled both, and he promised, as we saw, to equip Rosalino Pilo: but the muskets, which were stored at Milan, were not shipped: for Finzi and Besana recognized their responsibility [44] to the Royal Government, and required to know how the arms were to be used, before consenting to release them from the depots. All the Radical conspirators plotted to compel Garibaldi to take the saddle: once there, they had no doubt but that he would gallop to victory. The wary Paladin, however, refused to mount, until he could feel sure that they were not starting him on a fool's errand. He could not easily get over his long-standing, wholesome distrust of Mazzini's schemes; [45] and he did not quite believe Mazzini's protestation that he would loyally support the Garibaldian program —"Italy and Victor Emanuel!"

The cession of Nice, announced on March 25, had a malign effect on Garibaldi, because it crystallized into undying and insensate hatred his antipathy for Cavour. Henceforth, he acted only too often on the assumption that Nice had been sacrificed not as a political necessity, but as a personal spite to himself. Had he possessed the reasoning power of a ten-year-old intelligent boy, he must have persuaded himself that Cavour had no motive for spiting him at the expense of depriving Italy of a province: but living by his instincts and his emotions, Garibaldi could not conceive that a statesman had any other guide than vulpine duplicity, or any other aim than the gratification of selfish ambition and private malice. Mischief-makers, hoping to open a breach between him and the Government, and thereby win him back body and soul to the Mazzinian camp, inflamed his rage. Even an outsider like Laurence Oliphant,[46] whose scatter-brains were soon to make him the victim of a terrible hypnotic servitude, had influence enough to egg Garibaldi on to interpellate the Government.

With that in view, he spoke for the first time in Parliament

[44] Mario: *Bertani*, II, 15; Medici to Bertani, March 10, 1860.
[45] Cf. Guerzoni, II, 24, who adds that Garibaldi accepted only up to a certain point Mazzini's maxim, "Martyrdom is a battle won."
[46] L. Oliphant: *Episodes in a Life of Adventure*, New York, 1887, pp. 137 *ff.*

on April 6.[47] The next day Crispi and Bixio, having news of the rising in Palermo, hurried to Turin, and implored him, "for the honor of the Revolution, for pity for the poor Island, and the salvation of the entire country," to go at once to Sicily. After long persuasion, he promised, but only on condition that the rebellion should be alive and vigorous when he arrived.[48] He sent Crispi to Milan, with a personal order to the Directors of the Fund to consign to him arms and money, while Bixio returned to Genoa to arrange secretly with Fauché the agent of the Rubattino Steamship Company for a steamer — the *Piemonte* or the *San Giorgio* — to transport Garibaldi "and some companions" to Sicily.[49] Then the General went straight to the King, revealed to him the entire plan, and asked permission to take the Reggio Brigade, commanded by his old comrade in arms Sacchi, and made up of a large number of former Garibaldians. It is significant to note that the canny Paladin, who publicly extolled the military virtues of the volunteers above those of the regulars, preferred the regulars when it came to so rough a task as he foresaw this would be. The King, always on edge at the thought of fighting Italy's enemies, listened sympathetically, but could say neither yes nor no offhand. Construing his sympathy as consent, Garibaldi summoned Sacchi, who was overjoyed. For a few days the Garibaldian officers in the Reggio Brigade lived on hope. Then the King told Garibaldi that, although he could not permit his regiments to go on this adventure, he wished them to make ready to face whatever consequences might spring from it.[50] The Mazzinians [51] attributed to wicked Cavour the King's apparent change; but they have never proved that he did change. Certainly, if Victor Emanuel dreamed of sending a brigade of the Piedmontese army to attack, without a declaration of war, the territory of a friendly Power, it would have been the duty of Cavour and the Ministers to lock him up as demented, and to appoint a regent. It is Guerzoni, one of Garibaldi's bravest officers and his best biographer, who has stated once for all the true relations between the Revolution and the Monarchy. "The Revolution,"

[47] *Ante*, p. 219. [48] Guerzoni: *Garibaldi*, II, 25.
[49] Ciàmpoli, 132; Garibaldi to Fauché, Turin, April 9, 1860.
[50] Guerzoni: *Garibaldi*, II, 26-27. [51] Mario: *Bertani*, II, 24.

he writes, "might stake everything on a single card; the Monarchy no. The alliance . . . could not be carried out or fruitful except on two conditions: that both should operate according to their natures, and that neither should usurp the part or embarrass the action of the other. A revolutionary party which had proposed to proceed with the regards, the caution, the scruples of a constituted government, would have worn itself out in sterility; a government which had chosen to follow the steps, to imitate the audacities and to affect the irresponsibility of a revolutionary party, would have dashed itself to pieces against the league of all the other constituted governments, and would have dragged down in its own ruin the very cause it wished to defend. It was permitted to Garibaldi and his men to dare the noble adventure, since at the worst they were risking many precious lives, indeed, but not the country as a whole: the Government of the new Kingdom of Italy, responsible not only for its existence, but for the future of the entire nation, could not, without renouncing its own special mission, run the same risk." [52] Well had it been for Italy if those whom Guerzoni's profound truth chiefly touched, had been guided by it.

Garibaldi was so enraged by his failure to compel Parliament to annul the cession of Nice, that, although he had just given his promise to launch the Sicilian Expedition, he suddenly resolved to rush to Nice and lead the Nizzards in a rebellion. Bertani, Medici, Bixio urged upon him the madness of this scheme; Sir James Hudson, whom he consulted, dissuaded him; and on the evening of April 12, he pledged himself again for Sicily. But going to Genoa next day, with Laurence Oliphant for traveling companion, he changed his mind, decided to invade Nice with two hundred men, and smash the ballot-boxes so as to prevent the plebiscite of April 15 from being taken. On arriving at Genoa, Garibaldi sent Oliphant to engage a diligence, while he attended a secret meeting of the conspirators. When Oliphant found him again, the weather-cock hero told him that he had abandoned that "little Nice affair" and would dedicate himself wholly to Sicily. Needless to say, in Oliphant's absence the Sicilian Committee had secured his undivided attention. [53]

[52] Guerzoni: *Garibaldi*, ii, 28.   [53] L. Oliphant: *op. cit.*, 137, 141–43. Oliphant wrote his recollections in 1887; but, in spite of some inaccuracies, they are in the main correct. La Rive confirms this story; 309.

For some time past Cavour had been considering whether it would be practicable to forestall the Party of Action by secretly supporting an expedition promoted by the National Society. Incidentally, he wished to encourage an insurrection in Sicily, in order to force the Neapolitan King to recall his troops from the Papal frontier.[54] He did not intend to stir until he had proof that the Sicilian revolt was irrepressible, but he wished to be prepared to act promptly if the need came. On April 4 La Farina was writing his confidant, Vergara, at Genoa, in regard to sending guns and munitions to Sicily. He was irritated at the activity of the Mazzinians, who, he feared, would spoil everything, and at the revival of the Muratists, whose plotting in the present situation he considered infamous. La Farina, criticizing from the stand-point of one who was striving to keep the movement out of the control of the Reds, was as severe towards them as they towards him.[55] On April 6, Fanti, Minister of War, wrote to General Ribotti, a Sicilian exile, serving in the Italian Army: "In case the revolution in Sicily comes off, would you go there, having, however, first resigned your commission? This is a question Cavour has asked me today."[56] Ribotti judged that he was hardly the man for the occasion. Shortly after, when La Masa, another Sicilian exile at Turin, interviewed Cavour and told him that whether he had help or not he intended to set out at once with as many as would accompany him, the Prime Minister replied: "This very day I will send [help] to you through La Farina."[57] La Masa went to Genoa to make ready, and on April 17 La Farina joined him there to complete the arrangements. They had difficulty over guaranteeing the owner of the steamer they engaged, in case it were lost: La Farina said that the National Society lacked means, nor did he approve of La Masa's securing some other guarantor;[58] but Cavour had ordered him to furnish all the arms in the Society's possession.[59]

Genoa by this time seethed with conspiracies. Garibaldi's headquarters were in Villa Spinola, which belonged to his old companion in arms, Candido Augusto Vecchi. "Good evening,"

[54] Carandini, 320.   [55] La Farina, II, 309; Turin, April 4, 1860.
[56] Carandini, 321, n. 1. Mazzini: *Scritti*, XI, lxxx.   [57] *Lettere*, IV, cxxii.
[58] La Farina's objection is not clear.
[59] Five chests of ammunition and 1500 guns. *Lettere*, IV. cxxiv.

he said to Vecchi, on arriving; "I come like Christ to seek my apostles, and this time I have chosen the richest. Will you have me?" "In God's name! General, with immense pleasure." From that time forth Villa Spinola, which overlooks the little cove of Quarto, a short three miles from the eastern outskirts of the city, was the rendezvous of the Garibaldians. Every day the Preparers, after laying out their plans by the bedside of Bertani, who was sick, would go to the villa to make them acceptable to Garibaldi; for the chameleon Hero still changed his purpose with each day's news or with each visitor. Being agreed that without him the expedition was doomed, the Preparers tried to keep him in a happy mood. La Masa's decision to start anyway, with or without La Farina's aid, seems to have been used to goad on Garibaldi, who went so far as to promise arms and money.[60] But why equip two rival expeditions? Garibaldi sent for La Farina, with whom he had been angry since the preceding autumn, suggested that the Garibaldians and La Farinians should unite, and protested that he and his nearest disciples — Medici, Bixio, Besana and Sirtori — were not under the thumb of the Mazzinians.[61] The bringing together of the indispensable Paladin and of Cavour's recognized agent meant that the former would not reject aid and that the Government would not withhold it. That La Farina acted in the hope of shutting out the Mazzinian, anti-Monarchist control over the ductile Hero, was undeniable.

This interview took place on April 20. Three days later Sirtori, who was at once an ardent Monarchist and Garibaldian, almost crushed by the realization that the expedition could succeed if backed by the Government, but must perish otherwise, felt it his duty to try to persuade Cavour, who happened to be passing through Genoa. The Prime Minister received him cordially. When Sirtori told him that the plan, following Mazzini's fixed idea, was to attack simultaneously the Pope's territory and Sicily, he said of the expedition against the Marches, "'no, absolutely no. The Government will oppose it in every

---

[60] Mazzini: *Scritti*, xi, lxxi, n. 1. [61] La Farina, ii, 313; La Farina to Cavour, Busseto, April 24, 1860. Mazzini, xi, lxxvi, Crispi's notes. Mario: *Bertani*, ii, 33–34. It is significant that Bertani, who with Crispi led the Mazzinian workers in Genoa, acted as peacemaker between the La Farinians and the Garibaldians. See his letter of April 19, to Garibaldi, and the reply.

way.' As to the Sicilian Expedition he uttered these precise words: 'This is well — to begin at the South in order to come up towards the North. When these undertakings are to the fore, no matter how audacious they may be, Count Cavour will be second to nobody.' . . . He said this," Sirtori added, "referring of course to all those ways by which the Government without compromising itself, could assist the expedition; he promised to assist it, provided the responsibility of the Government were wholly safeguarded, and this he did." [62]

Cavour was stemming a crisis, in which the Sicilian Expedition was not the only danger. He had just accompanied the King in his triumphal entry to Tuscany, and there had been a clash between them, the nature of which is still unreported.[63] He knew, however, that the King, in secret communication with Garibaldi, was inclined to show his sympathy more openly than prudence allowed, and actually had a confidant of the General, Count Trecchi, in his suite.[64] He knew that the opponents of the Government and his personal enemies were preparing a concerted attack when the debate on Nice should open. This might be another of Rattazzi's thrusts. "In truth," he wrote Farini, "the cup of power is full of gall, not of intoxicating liquid," and he even regarded the overthrow of the Ministry as so far possible that he was cogitating whether Ricasoli could not be persuaded to head its successor.[65] He returned to Turin, more anxious than ever lest the conspirators, regardless of any chance of success, should take their leap in the dark. If they did, then the Government must prevent the Mazzinians from dominating Garibaldi — a necessity which explains Cavour's offer to

[62] *Atti del Parlamento Nazionale.* Camera dei Deputati, June 19, 1863. Sirtori's statement was called out by Bertani's assertion that Cavour had said to Sirtori, " I do not know what to say," and then, rubbing his hands as was his habit when he was pleased, he concluded, " I believe they [the Bourbons] will capture them [the Garibaldians]." In his *Ire Politiche* (61), Bertani repeated his slander of that June 19. Was he impelled by malice to repeat the falsehood ? Or did he allow himself to be so blinded by his rancor towards Cavour (which became unbounded during the Sicilian Expedition) that he accepted as facts whatever calumniators invented against the statesman? Jessie Mario, Bertani's sympathetic biographer, discreetly omits Bertani's speech of June 19, 1863, from her collection of his speeches. It is to be noted that, at the utmost, Bertani could report only what he remembered Sirtori had told him Cavour had said.

[63] *Lettere,* iv, cxxxix. [64] Count Gaspare Trecchi; see Cavour's letter of April 22; *Ib.,* cxli. [65] *Lettere,* iii, 240; C. to Farini, Turin, April 24, 1860.

Sirtori; but Cavour still hoped that any expedition might be prevented. His enemies who, echoing Bertani, insinuated that he wished the conspirators to go because he felt sure that they would be captured by the Bourbons and quickly disposed of, imagined that his policy, like theirs, was determined by vindictiveness and personal spite. Had they reflected, they would have seen that from a selfish point of view Cavour must have dreaded such a calamity: for if Garibaldi and his men were captured and shot, as Pisacane's had been, a storm of wrath would break upon the Piedmontese Ministry for allowing them to rush to certain destruction. On the other hand, if they held out, all Italy would clamor for the Government to hurry troops to their rescue, while all Europe would call it to account for abetting an attack on a friendly kingdom. If, finally, the Garibaldians, without the connivance or against the express opposition of the Government, should go and conquer, they might sweep not only the Cabinet but the Monarchy itself away. Cavour's logical course, therefore, was to prevent the expedition if he could; if he could not prevent, to control it; if he could not control, to guide it. According as the situation changed, and its changes were swift, his acts and words aimed at one of these three ends. The last thing that he desired was Garibaldi's martyrdom.

With prevention in view, he sent Frapolli, an ex-Republican, to Quarto on April 24. Garibaldi listened willingly to his arguments and was much impressed at being reminded that in previous descents on Bourbon shores, Murat had been shot, the Bandiera party executed and Pisacane's legion destroyed. Frapolli returned to Turin that night, convinced that Garibaldi had given up his plan.[66] But the next day Raffaelle Motto, master of the bark which conveyed Pilo to Sicily, visited Villa Spinola. When Garibaldi, having read in the morning's paper that the Sicilian rising had been put down, spoke gloomily, Motto assured him, without any foundation, that all was going well, and that they needed only the General's name and arm. Garibaldi shook his head: "But France? but Cavour?" he asked, musing. Then, as if suddenly inspired, he roused himself and inquired, "How many can I count on?" "Three or four thousand," the bystanders replied. "No, no," Garibaldi retorted; "I don't

[66] Mazzini, XI, lxxvi; from Crispi's diary.

want useless flesh — few and good — a little more than a thousand will do for me." [67] He then conferred about transportation, arms, food and the Sicilian harbors. That very evening, Fauché, agent of the Rubattino Line, called, and, in reply to the General's questions, he promised to have two steamers, the *Piemonte* and the *Lombardo*, ready to sail at short notice. [68]

The 25th La Farina came to repeat his negative advice; consequently, Garibaldi blew cold again. The 26th unfavorable news drifted in. Garibaldi referred to the fate of the Bandiera brothers and 'of poor Pisacane.' Nevertheless, he assured Bandi, one of his volunteers, "We shall go! we shall go! but some things must be thoroughly thought over first." [69] Medici, whom Garibaldi greatly trusted, and Sirtori, poured out their dissuasion; Crispi and Bixio led the inflexibles who would not allow the General to abandon the enterprise, and they seemed to have won, for word was whispered throughout Genoa that he would sail during the night of the 27th. On the morning of the 27th, however, Crispi received a telegram from Fabrizi, dated, "Malta, 26 April, 1860," and reading: "Complete failure in the province and city of Palermo. Many fugitives, received by English ships, arrived in Malta. Do not stir." [70] "It would be madness to go!" said Garibaldi, wiping his eyes. "Patience! Our turn will come yet. Italy must be, and shall be." [71]

To the crowd of patriots waiting in the large hall, Crispi and La Masa brought the harrowing decision. Bixio remained for a while in the General's little chamber, to expostulate, beseech and upbraid. Garibaldi bore from him fury and oaths that he would bear from no one else: but they did not avail now. The Hero's fluid resolution seemed at last to have petrified. Bixio rushed out in wrath, shouting "To hell! to hell!" Most of the patriots hastened back to Genoa to spread the news. Rage and regret alternated in the hearts of those who were chafing to go, and of the far greater number who were in the secret. Angry Mazzinians began to whisper that Garibaldi was afraid: was this a spontaneous cry of theirs, or a premeditated taunt, to goad him to reconsider? In the evening a party of ten or twelve youths

[67] Mazzini, lxxiii *ff.*; Motto's narrative.
[68] *Gazzetta d'Italia*, letter of Fauché, June 13, 1882: quoted in *Lettere*, iv, cl.
[69] Bandi, 16.   [70] Crispi: *Mille*, 105.   [71] Guerzoni, ii, 34. *Lettere*, iv, cl.

2

came out to the Villa and asked to see the General. Bandi took their message, and when he hinted that they suspected him of cowardice, Garibaldi, flushing as red as a brazier, shouted in a terrible voice, "I am afraid, am I?" But he soon controlled himself, saw the young men, spoke to them with that wonderful voice of his which made every one love him, and soon he and they were sobbing with emotion.[72]

In this catastrophe one man, Crispi, was neither carried away by rage nor reduced to tears by regret. He believed that Garibaldi could still be won over. On April 27 he sent a cipher telegram to Fabrizi saying that having had no letter by the last mail from Sicily, the expedition was wavering and might not start: but he added that everything was ready, even the steamer. Late on the 29th Crispi was rewarded: at least he showed a batch of telegrams and letters announcing that the rebellion in Sicily was in full blast and awaited only Garibaldi's leadership.[73] That same morning, Garibaldi had decided to return to Caprera on May 2. Most of the volunteers had quitted for home. Bandi took his leave with a heavy heart. "For the present there is nothing to be done, but the time will come," said Garibaldi; "What a pity! what a fine expedition!"[74] At daybreak on the 30th, Crispi and Bixio, whose head was cool again, hurried to Quarto and told Garibaldi the astonishing news. The Sicilians were gaining ground in the principal cities — they had the upper hand at Marsala — Rosalino Pilo was commanding an army. Crispi produced a revised version of Fabrizi's despatch to this effect: "The insurrection put down in the city of Palermo holds fast in the provinces. News brought by refugees arrived in Malta on English ships."[75] Garibaldi was greatly impressed. A council of war followed. Bixio voted unconditionally to start. Motto and the other Mazzinians, clinging to their leader's program, urged a simultaneous attack on Umbria and the Marches. Sirtori opposed this resolutely, but said that, if Garibaldi went to Sicily, he would go too. After a little meditation, the General said, "Let us start, provided it be to-morrow."[76] They adjourned to the house of Bertani, who had been directing affairs

---

[72] Bandi, 21–23. [73] Crispi: *Mille*, 105 ff. [74] Bandi, 24–25.
[75] Mario: *Bertani*, II, 46. The text varies slightly in different books, but the purport is identical. See Crispi: *Mille*, 105–08, for details. But his editor evades stating how the decisive telegram originated. [76] Bandi, 29.

from his sickbed. The discussion turned now wholly on the necessary arrangements for sailing.[77] It was found that the ships and their passengers could not be ready on the following day, Wednesday, but all haste was made to sail by the end of the week. Despatches were sent to recall the home-faring volunteers, and to hurry the shipment of arms. The Preparers in Genoa worked without rest. Bixio directed the embarkation. Sick Bertani had still strength to scribble replies to innumerable correspondents.[78]

La Farina returned to Turin on May 1st, too early to know of Garibaldi's change of mind, and fully convinced that the expedition was shelved.[79] It appears also that La Masa and his Sicilians were not immediately informed, for on that day they resolved to set out without Garibaldi.[80] At Bologna that afternoon Cavour joined the King, who was continuing his royal progress through the newly annexed states. In the evening the rumor began to circulate that Garibaldi was on the point of sailing for Sicily. There occurred, probably the next day, an interview between Cavour and the King of which Count d'Haussonville has given a brief account, on the authority of the few witnesses. The Premier, he says, "wished to prevent everything. He purposed to have Garibaldi arrested. On this subject he was very animated. And when the objection was made that it would be impossible to find anyone who would undertake this mission, he said to the King: 'If nobody dares, I will go myself and take him by the collar.' A small number of witnesses, from whom I have this, alone know what singular scenes took place then be-

[77] Mario: *Bertani*, II, 46. She says the decision was reached there, and not at Villa Spinola. Crispi, on the other hand, claims for himself the sole credit of persuading Garibaldi, and gives May 2 as the date. Crispi: *Mille*, 109. But Guerzoni, loyal to his hero, declares that nobody had that honor, because Garibaldi always made up his own mind in solemn decisions. Like Socrates, he was guided by his daimon. Guerzoni, II, 35–36. The official despatches from Sicily, printed in the Genoese papers of April 29, and in the Turinese on April 30, read: " Insurgents, surrounded by powerful forces, have laid down their arms. Rigorous state of siege Catania, Messina, Palermo. A general disarming in progress." *Lettere*, IV, clix.   [78] Trevelyan, I, 194.   [79] La Farina, II, 314–15; letters of May 2, 1860.

[80] *Lettere*, IV, clv–clvi; telegrams from Orsini and Amari to La Farina, dated May 1. It seems improbable that the "secret" which, within a few hours, scores of persons knew, could have been kept for more than a day from the Sicilian group; or that La Farina, having the telegrams of May 1, could have written as he did. During the final week of this episode, it is impossible to make the hours, or even the days, stated by different witnesses, coincide.

tween the minister and the sovereign. The minister was not convinced, but he yielded, and, fulfilling to the utmost his constitutional duty, he never publicly admitted the dissent, but always
completely shielded, on this occasion as on every other, the person of the King." [81] When this story saw the light after Cavour's death, Garibaldi's partisans gloated over it as furnishing
proof, first, that Cavour did not desire the unification of Italy,
and, next, that he was impious enough to think of laying sacri-
legious hand on the sacred person of the Hero. His hopes for Italy
have been recorded on many pages of this history; his attitude
towards the Sicilian Expedition we have just described: as to his
reported willingness to brave even Garibaldi, we should regard
it as one of the supreme proofs of his statesmanship. For if the
incident ever happened, it means that Cavour found that even
the King was overawed into regarding it impossible to stop Garibaldi. Such a fear, Cavour saw, was tantamount to admitting
that Garibaldi was greater than the King, greater than the Government, greater than the Nation. No sovereign, no minister
responsible for the endurance of his country, can make such an
admission, and live. When Cavour said, therefore, that he dared
to collar Garibaldi, he made it clear that he at least did not recognize the right of any citizen to hold himself above the law, and
that, cost himself what it might, he would stand between the
Nation and dictatorship or anarchy. That he yielded, indicates,
as we have already seen, his belief that, although he would have
preferred to postpone the Southern Expedition, he could turn it
to Italy's advantage. Part of his heat at the interview was due to
his knowing that the King, for weeks past, had been secretly
communicating with Garibaldi: but he did not know just how
far the King had entangled the Government. If he had thought
it necessary for the country's welfare, he would have resigned,
as he did after Villafranca. Well had it been for Italy, and well
for the fame of Garibaldi, if in 1862 and 1867, King or Minister
had dared to lay his hand on the Hero's collar and save him and
his country from his madcap ventures.

Whatever were the 'scenes' between him and the King,
Cavour's peace of mind was not shaken, as it had been by the ter-

[81] O. d'Haussonville: "M. de Cavour et la Crise Italienne," *Revue des Deux
Mondes*, Sept. 15, 1862, p. 420.

rible interview at Villa Melchiorri. He visited the Bologna Gallery with zest, stood 'in ecstasy' before Raphael's "St. Cecilia," and discoursed to Artom on its beauty compared with that of the "Madonna of the Chair," which he had just seen in Florence. How quickly he adjusted himself to the certainty that the Expedition would start, is shown by his despatch that very day (May 3) to Rear-Admiral Persano at Leghorn, ordering him to sail as soon as possible with his three steam-frigates [82] and to cruise off Southern Sardinia between Cape Carbonaro and Cape Sperone, *but without using his engines*.[83] This part of the instructions has been much discussed. Cavour's enemies liked to suspect that it hid a plan to injure the Expedition; but until other information comes to light, we must regard it as more than favorable. For if Persano's frigates went under sail only, they could not be expected to overtake Garibaldi's steamers. This interpretation has at least the merit of harmonizing with the orders issued subsequently. In order to evade diplomatic pressure in the capital, Cavour lingered a day or two at Bologna.

At Genoa in those days all was bustle among the patriots; but they still lacked arms and money. In the middle of April, impatient at the delay, Crispi went to Milan to learn why the Directors of the Million Rifles Fund had not kept their promise. Finzi explained to him that when the guns were boxed for shipment they were sequestrated. Crispi appealed to Farini,[84] whom he found no longer the revolutionary Dictator of Modena, but a cautious Minister of the Interior, who informed him that this matter must be settled between Cavour and Garibaldi themselves.[85] The Mazzinians imputed the sequestration to Cavour's malice: the real offender, however, was the Governor of Milan — Massimo d'Azeglio. "As I have the reputation of an honest man to maintain," he wrote on May 15 to an intimate, "I follow at Milan my own policy. I refused the guns to Garibaldi, dismissed a syndic who published invitations to enroll for Sicily, and notified to the Italianissimi that, in my opinion, one might declare war at Naples, but not have a representative there and send guns to the Sicilians."[86] Massimo not only wished to keep his

---

[82] *Maria Adelaide, Vittorio Emanuele,* and *Carlo Alberto,* screw steam-frigates.
[83] Persano, 16. [84] On April 16. [85] *Lettere,* IV, cxxxi. Crispi: *Mille,* 98, 348.
[86] D'Azeglio: *Politique,* 162. *L' Opinione,* Sept. 6, 1869, contains an exhaustive explanation by Finzi; reprinted in *Lettere,* IV, cxxvii–cxxxi.

reputation unsullied, but to thwart, if he could, the cabal which, he thought, was using Garibaldi as a tool for undermining Cavour. "I have never been a blind approver of Cavour," he said . . . "but, in my view, he is the only man who has any chance of saving the ship. . . . The adventure of this true hero [Garibaldi] and not less great simpleton, is partly destined to place Cavour in an intolerable position. In short, we must either put ourselves outside the pale of the public law, or have against us Garibaldi and all those who use him as a marionette! That is the consequence of pushing eclecticism in the matter of parties too far."[87] D'Azeglio stuck to his decision, and would not give up the guns. Cavour might have overruled him: that he did not was probably due to the fact that their release could not have been kept secret.[88] It was imperative that whatever help he gave should appear unofficial, in order to estop European diplomacy from accusing the King's government of abetting the Expedition. Money, however, went in considerable sums from the Directors;[89] La Farina contributed 8000 lire in behalf of the National Society; and the King seems also to have begun his secret subvention which later ran into the millions. From all sources Bertani, the treasurer of the Expedition, received 321,870.06 lire up to May 6. Still lacking arms, Garibaldi sent for La Farina at Turin, who came and turned over 1019 guns and five chests of ammunition. The muskets were indeed no better than "old junk," as Garibaldi said; but they were the best the National Society had; and they could not, as was afterwards charged, have been picked out in the hope of ruining the Garibaldians in their first battle, because they were the very weapons which La Masa and his Sicilians expected to take with them ten days before.[90]

All day long on May 5, the preparations progressed openly,

[87] D'Azeglio: *Politique*, 162–63. Also Persano, 91, where d'Azeglio, in a letter dated July 16, 1860, assumes full responsibility for withholding the guns.

[88] Cf. Trevelyan, I, 198.   [89] Bertani stated that he received from them 140,000 lire, of which 50,000 were spent on equipment. Mario: *Bertani*, II, 51, n. 1.

[90] June 27, 1860, he wrote Commodore W. de Rohan: "I have already given three millions for Sicily; I will give two millions more." *Lettere*, IV, clxiii, n. 1. The relation of Finzi and the million muskets fund to the expedition is exhaustively analyzed by A. Luzio in *La Lettura*, April, 1910, pp. 289–301. H. N. Gay, *Deutsche Revue*, Dec. 1910, p. 313, shows that Cavour set aside a "special fund" to aid Agnetta.

feverishly. Every train brought carloads of volunteers. At every station crowds gathered to cheer the departing heroes. In more than one case, there was a struggle to board them and grief among the men left behind, the supply of cars being inadequate. The Vice-Governor of Genoa was the only person in the city who seemed to be unaware of what was taking place. At a sign from Cavour, he had become deaf to the noise and blind to the unusual throngs. To keep up appearances, Garibaldi had been cautioned that the sailing must not take place from the harbor itself, and guards were carefully posted along the Western wharves, as far as possible from his steamers. Throughout the evening, the eager patriots trudged down the shore to Quarto. Shortly before midnight, Nino Bixio and a small party of followers rowed a scow in which they had hidden to the *Piemonte* and *Lombardo*, which lay at a quay in the very centre of the water-front, crept aboard of them, roused and intimidated their willing crews, and began to get up steam. This act of piracy had been pre-arranged between the Preparers and Fauché, who, at his own risk, had agreed to furnish the steamers. Fauché took good care that his employers' company should be guaranteed against loss; but two months later, when the Expedition was dazzling the world by its triumphal march through Sicily, the Rubattino Company cashiered him, his fortunes were broken and he lived in great straits to be an old man. Rubattino, however, by one of those travesties which it is the duty of historians to expose, came to be honored as the patriot who had generously offered his ships without thought of profit to the Garibaldian heroes; and today his smug features in bronze greet strangers who land on the pier whence, had he caught Bixio playing the pirate on May 5, 1860, the *Piemonte* and *Lombardo* would never have sailed.[91]

Owing to bad engines and other delays, night was far advanced before the two ships moved from their berth, and headed down the coast: even then the *Lombardo* had to tow her consort. At Foce, they slowed up for a few boat-loads of volunteers. Opposite Quarto they stopped to take on more than a thousand youths and men who had been waiting impatiently [92] in little

---

[91] Cavour intended to recompense Fauché, but died too soon. Both Garibaldians and Monarchists allowed him to live neglected and die in poverty. Trevelyan, I, 200–01, and Appendix J.   [92] In Garibaldi's phrase "they pawed the sands like a high-spirited horse impatient for battle." *Mille*, 7.

boats or in the garden of Villa Spinola and upon the rocks, since long before midnight. As hour after hour passed, their impatience became almost unbearable; for they feared that the steamers had been seized by the government. When dawn was approaching, Garibaldi ordered his men to row his own skiff towards Genoa. In a little while, to his great relief the red, white and green signal lights flashed upon them, and a few minutes later the *Piemonte* and *Lombardo* drew up. Then there was a rush to embark; for the dawn was at hand, quenching the radiance of the full moon and diffusing instead its own light in which nothing could be hidden.[93] To and fro went the little boats for their cargoes of Argonauts, who soon crowded the steamers' decks. Then the sun came up and still many trips had to be made before the last passenger scrambled on board. The throngs from the shore waved good-byes to the throngs at sea. Bixio stood on the bridge of the *Lombardo;* Castiglia commanded the *Piemonte.* Garibaldi's sonorous "Forward!" rang above the hum of voices; the engines began to creak, the propellers to churn the indigo water and soon the watchers on land could distinguish only two black hulls, trailing long plumes of dark grey smoke, vanishing on the Southern horizon.[94] Not since the *Mayflower*, weighing anchor in English Plymouth's roadstead, set her course for the Northern Coasts of Virginia, had any ship borne seaward such a lading of destiny.

The Thousand who almost over-freighted the two wretched steamers,[95] numbered in reality about 1150 volunteers,[96] all but a few of whom were Garibaldian veterans. A handful had shared the Hero's exploits at Montevideo; more had fought beside him in the defense of Rome; the great majority had been Hunters of the Alps. They were drawn chiefly from the lower middle

---

[93] Crispi: *Mille*, 350, says they began to embark at 4 A. M., and started at 8.30 A. M.   [94] Guerzoni, II, 39.   [95] The dimensions of the steamers, as ascertained by Mr. Trevelyan, I, 209, n. 2, are: *Piemonte*, built in Glasgow in 1851; length, 50 metres, breadth, 7 m., draught, 3 m.; tonnage, 180 tons; horsepower, 160. *Lombardo*, built in Leghorn, 1841; length, 48 m., breadth, 7.40 m., draught 4.23 m.; tonnage, 238 tons; horse-power, 220.

[96] The official number of those who actually went to Sicily on the first expedition, given long afterward, varied from 1065 to 1095. 62 were detached at Talamone for Zambianchi's diversion. See *Elenco Alfabetico di tutti componenti la spedizione dei Mille di Marsala. Gazzetta Uff. del Regno d'Italia*, Nov. 12, 1878. Also *Illustrazione Italiana*, May 1, 1910.

classes — artisans, small shop-keepers, young lawyers and doctors, students, sailors.[97] Some loved adventure. Some had grown grey conspiring. Nearly all were stirred by genuine patriotism, although in the case of many, the form that their patriotism might take depended on their leader. Worship of Garibaldi was, indeed, the spell that bound that strange multitude together. Like Scottish clansmen, they would follow their chief blindly: but their devotion, instead of being hereditary, sprang from their own choice. Out of all the world they had chosen Garibaldi, as the lover chooses his mate, to idolize and adore. It is as impossible to conjure back to the printed page the sound of that deep, thrilling voice, as to paint the expression on his face which men called leonine and women called beautiful. Garibaldi was in fact neither commanding of stature, nor handsome according to the higher types of beauty. He was rather a glorified sea-captain or woodsman, whose features suggested an uncomplex nature, with a hint of shrewdness, perhaps of suspicion, in his nearset grey eyes, which he seldom opened wide. His auburn-brown hair, his deep-tawny beard and abundant moustache added dignity to the well-shaped head. But his contemporaries saw much more than this — they saw in him the embodiment of their ideals of heroism, of love of country, of chivalry, a Theseus in the flesh, a Roland or a Lancelot. He had that last gift of seeming to be one of themselves, and yet far above them. Historically, he was the final flower of that generous era whose seedtime was the French Revolution and whose harvest was the liberation of the peoples, and the redemption of Italy. Despite its excesses and its follies, its emotions too often merely hysterical and its enthusiasms too often ineffectual, that era, above all others, brought hope and a vision of perfectibility on earth to heart-sick humanity.

> " Bliss was it in that dawn to be alive.
> But to be young was very heaven." [98]

Garibaldi was the final flower of Romanticism, his Sicilian

[97] Some went in search of a country, says Guerzoni; the lover, of forgetfulness; the blasé, of an emotion; the wretched, of bread; the unhappy, of death. " A thousand heads, a thousand hearts, a thousand different lives, but their alloy purified by the holiness of the banner, animated by the unique will of that Captain, formed a formidable and almost invulnerable legion." Guerzoni: *Bixio,* 160.

[98] Wordsworth: *The Prelude,* Book xi.

Expedition its most fascinating embodiment in deeds. Unlike Jason and Columbus and the Pilgrims on the *Mayflower*, the Garibaldians had a glowing realization of their historic significance. "Sail on! sail on!" exclaims their leader, addressing the *Lombardo* and the *Piemonte* in his Ossianic dithyrambs. "You carry the Thousand whom the million will join on the day when these deceived masses shall understand that the priest is an impostor and monarchies a monstrous anachronism.[99] . . . O night of May 5 — lighted by the fire of a thousand luminaries, with which the Omnipotent — the Infinite! — adorned space. Beautiful, tranquil, solemn — with that solemnity which causes generous souls to throb, as they rush to the emancipation of slaves! Such were the Thousand — assembled and silent, on the shores of Eastern Liguria — gathered in groups, plunged in thought — penetrated by the great conception! Thou murmuredst in the heartstrings of those proud ones — with that indefinite sublime harmony, with which the elect are blest as they behold, in limitless space, the Infinite! I have felt that harmony on all the nights that resembled that night of Quarto — of Reggio, of Palermo, of the Volturno — And who doubts of victory when, borne by the wings of duty and conscience, thou art impelled to face dangers and death, as if they were the delicious kiss of thy beloved?"[100]

Such rhapsodical gushes, which are of the very essence of Garibaldi's nature, seem old-fashioned, sentimental rather than poetic, to the ears of a later age; but they explain him, and the spirit of his companions in glory. His was the simplicity of a Homeric hero, which did not preclude the development of other primitive passions in the highest degree. He was as self-conscious as a spoiled child, as vain as a coquette. His vanity led him to devise a costume for himself so odd that it became the symbol of his later career. On his head he wore a Spanish black felt hat, like a low cup inverted in a high-brimmed saucer, which gave him a boyish air. Round his neck he tied loosely a silk kerchief, gaudy-colored as the Italian peasants prefer. He buttoned his red flannel shirt into mouse-colored trousers, cut so broad at

[99] *Mille*, 4.

[100] Garibaldi: *Memorie*, 307–08. I translate as literally as possible, in order to preserve even the incoherent syntax of the original. An interesting parallel might be drawn between Garibaldi's best passages and Whitman's.

GARIBALDI IN 1860

the heel, sailor-fashion, that they almost covered his small feet. Over his shoulders he threw a little shawl, conspicuously checked, like a Scotch plaid. Finally, for outer garment, he wore the great grey mantle, or poncho, of the Argentine cowboys, with a triangular piece buttoned shield-like in front — the whole producing the impression, when he sat, of a child swathed in an enormous bib. In his belt, he stuck a revolver and knife. When he was walking, he sometimes carried his massive sabre, with heavy guard, over his shoulder; at others, he let it clank on the ground. A democrat of democrats, dear as an elder brother or father to every one in the Thousand, he was nevertheless careful to deck himself in this bizarre apparel so as to be as unique in appearance as in mission.[101] He did not intend to be mistaken for any one else. But on that radiant May morning had he stood before his men in the majestic glory of one of Tintoret's archangels, he could not have seemed to them more beautiful or more worthy of trust and admiration.

So was born the Sicilian Expedition, which the world saluted as the noblest offspring of modern chivalry. We who have watched the long gestation, with its uncertainties and pains, know that it was no sudden creation.[102] Had it depended on Garibaldi alone, the expedition would never have started; without Garibaldi, it could never have started. La Masa, Medici, Bixio, could not have drawn after them the host triumphant, nor the universal popular sympathy which even Diplomacy dared not ignore. Mazzini planned; Crispi prepared; Bertani organized; Bixio at the critical moment acted. Of the many other aiders in the preparations, Rosalino Pilo and Corrao, the Precursors who sped unsupported into Sicily, deserve unstinted praise: but for them, the preliminary revolt might have died out.

Equally necessary was the connivance of the Government. Garibaldi has denounced Cavour for not openly equipping the

---

[101] Whitman also, another protesting democrat, was most carefully careless in his dress.

[102] This episode, the most thorny in the history of the Risorgimento, is discussed by the biographers of all the leading participants, by historians, and by essayists. Recent reviews of the evidence have been made by A. Luzio, *Corriere della Sera*, May 5 and Aug. 23, 1907; by I. Raulich, *Rass. Contempo.*, July, 1909; and by R. Mirabelli, *Secolo*, Sept. 16, 17, 18, 1907, and *Rivista Popolare*, Jan. 15 and 31, 1910; by H. N. Gay, *Deutsche Revue*, Dec. 1910. For extreme Radical position see N. Colajanni's articles in *Rivista Popolare*, 1910.

Expedition: but this is an unfair charge, for it was Garibaldi himself who up to the last moment believed the adventure doomed to fail and refused to embark on it. If Garibaldi distrusted Mazzini, had not Cavour greater reason to distrust him? If Garibaldi, who had only his own reputation at stake, hesitated until he was assured that success was almost certain, how much more was it the duty of Cavour to hold back an exploit which, if fortunate, might bring down on free Italy the wrath of Europe, and, if Garibaldi perished, would arouse against the Monarchy the frenzy of millions of Italians! Actions speak louder than words. The freedom with which the conspirators were allowed to make their arrangements; the constant communications between their leaders and the Cavourians: their interviews with Cavour himself, with the King, with Farini; the public subscriptions voted by Cremona, Pavia, Brescia, and other cities, without hint of interference from Turin; the gathering of the volunteers unmolested at Genoa, not once but twice; the studied inattention of the Genoese officials to the final preparations; the gift to Garibaldi of the National Society's guns and ammunitions, without which he would not have sailed; the failure to order Persano to intercept the ships — these are facts which, singly and collectively, give the lie to the slander that Cavour and the King's Government refused to aid the enterprise. That slander sprang partly from envy, because Garibaldians and Mazzinians wished to take entire credit to themselves, and especially to have it appear that the Monarchists whom they hated could not share in any patriotic undertaking; and partly it sprang from Garibaldi's unreasoning hatred of Cavour. When that hatred was planted in his soul, and constantly nurtured by the evil suggestions of designing associates, Garibaldi interpreted by it every act of Cavour. Quite incapable of grasping the intricacy of Piedmont's international relations, on which her very existence depended, he accused Cavour of treachery and servility for heeding those relations; believing in a dictatorship with himself at its head as the panacea for social and political ills, he hated Cavour, who, as a constitutional minister, could not countenance would-be dictators. Garibaldi's hatred made him oblivious of speaking the truth. In a single page of his "Memoirs" he accuses Cavour of having abandoned a few months before, against the King's orders, the Hunters of the Alps to the Austrians [103] — a baseless falsehood.[104] He accuses Cavour of sequestrating the fifteen thousand muskets at Milan, — a baseless falsehood, as D'Azeglio's letter to Rendu, published in 1867, and his letter to Persano, published in 1869, prove. He accuses Cavour of getting a factitious popularity by buying up men and newspapers with the nation's money — a falsehood not only baseless but puerile. How should we judge Garibaldi, if we accepted as infallible Tennyson's maxim: " Every one imputes himself"? The test of zeal is not its intensity but its purpose: zeal forges alike the Anarchist and the Jesuit. Chivalry is picturesque, romantic exploits thrill: but no hero should feel himself absolved from obligation to speak the truth; and mankind has been better served in the long run by lovers of justice than by zealots.

It was well for Italy that Garibaldi's venomous charges against Cavour were not true. If none but approved Garibaldians had gone on the Expedition, though they had conquered Sicily and Naples, they would have postponed, perhaps for decades, the day of National Unity. Only by the participation, however indirect and unofficial, of the Monarchy in the preparations could the indispensable all-Italian quality be secured. This was Cavour's work. When he was convinced, says Guerzoni, "that the cry for Sicily was not the artifice of one man alone or of one party, but the clear deep echo of a sentiment of the whole nation, then he hesitated no longer, but conceded to the preparers all that the ruler of a constitutional State had a right to concede: power to make ready, to arm, and to set sail under the shadow of his Government and under the shield of his King." [105]

[103] *Memorie,* 384–85.
[104] See *Discorsi,* XI, 379.
[105] Guerzoni: *Garibaldi,* II, 30. The openness of the equipment speaks for itself. Daniel wrote Cass on May 12: " This is *undeclared war* of Sardinia against Naples." *Amer. Arch.*

CHAPTER XXX

FROM MARSALA TO PALERMO

WHILST his lieutenants on May 5 were making the final preparations, Garibaldi busied himself in writing letters to the King, to Bertani, and to others. Through most of them runs an undertone of melancholy. They read in parts like the last messages of one who suspects that he is setting out on a forlorn hope. In case the worst happens, he desires his countrymen and posterity to know his patriotic purpose. Garibaldi tells the King that he did not advise the Sicilian insurrection, but that, from the moment it cried for succor in the name of Italian Unity, he could not hold back. "If we succeed," he said, "I shall be proud to honor Your Majesty's crown with this new and most brilliant jewel; on condition, however, that Your Majesty will oppose any attempt of your counselors to cede this province to the foreigner as they have done with my native land. I did not impart my plan to Your Majesty; for I feared that, in spite of the reverence I feel for you, you could not succeed in persuading me to abandon it."[1] He addressed a manifesto to the Italian soldiers bidding them not to disband. He urged the Italians as a people to rise in multitudes, each arming himself as best he could, and to rush to the rescue of their down-trodden brethren in the Papal States and in Naples. "Italy and Victor Emanuel!" that battle-cry "shall reverberate in the fiery caverns of Mongibello," and cause the worm-eaten throne of tyranny to crumble.[2] He called upon the Romans and upon the Neapolitan army to come over to the cause championed by the volunteers who had approved themselves at Montevideo, at Rome in 1849, and at Varese.[3] He left Bertani with full power to act in his behalf. Italy, he said, could and should arm half a million soldiers at short notice. Let the Italians understand,

---

[1] Ciàmpoli, 136: Garibaldi to V. E., May 5, 1860. As to authenticity of letter see H. N. Gay: *Deutsche Revue*, Dec. 1910, p. 301, n. 1. For genuine letter see Trecchi, 417.　　　[2] Ciàmpoli, 137–38.　　　[3] *Ibid*, 139–40.

"that, if we are properly aided, Italy will be made in a short time at a small cost."[4] "It is better that you remain behind," he wrote Medici; "to send reinforcements not only to Sicily, but also to the Marches and to Umbria, where there will soon be an upheaval."[5] "The Sicilian insurrection carries in its womb the destiny of your nationality. I go to share its fate," he told a friend. "At last, I shall find myself in my element — action put at the service of a great idea."[6] In that phrase he showed that he knew his real strength. From these various messages we gather that he set out against his judgment, and with misgivings as to the outcome of the Expedition; that he believed that if the Italians rose to their duty, they could speedily make Italy; that he expected an immediate diversion in the Papal States and in Naples; that his watchword was "Italy and Victor Emanuel"; and that he nursed undying hatred for the ministers who had ceded Nice, and scorn for the government which, "through false diplomatic considerations,"[7] declined to give the Expedition its open support.

Before noon on May 6 everyone in Genoa knew that the Garibaldians had sailed. That morning Brown, the British Consul, telegraphed the news to Hudson at Turin. Hudson sent word to Cavour, who was, however, already informed. He had returned to the capital the night before, had received almost hourly messages, and was now on the alert in his office, awaiting the protests of European diplomacy and later tidings of Garibaldi. The protests soon began to pour in.[8] The most formidable was that of the French Ambassador, who reminded the Prime Minister that as long ago as April 28 he had warned him that an expedition was preparing, and that day by day he had imparted further details of the vast plot: but that the Prime Minister had apparently done nothing. Venetian, Roman and Neapolitan committees had been allowed to work openly. The Government was either powerless or unwilling. This fact needed no commentary in order to merit general reprobation.[9] Talleyrand uttered

[4] Ciàmpoli, 141.   [5] *Ibid*, 142.   [6] *Ibid*, 142.   [7] *Ibid*, 140. Yet on May 10, Daniel writes Cass that the Expedition was "gotten up under the patronage and with the assistance of the Sardinian Government." *Amer. Arch.*   [8] "For the last 24 hours," says the *Gazzetta di Torino* of May 9, " . . . protests against the Garibaldi expedition are raining down on the government."   [9] *Lettere*, IV, clxxi *ff.*; Talleyrand to Cavour, May, 1860. *Affaires Etrangères*, 1860, 138–40.

his official rebuke with proper severity. Diplomacy could not countenance the game of fast-and-loose which Piedmont had been playing, although Diplomacy knew perfectly well that this was the game which, under the circumstances, every statesman would have tried to play. In his private letter to Thouvenel, however, the French Ambassador admitted that his colleagues inclined "to think that it would have been a dangerous experiment for M. de Cavour to engage in a serious struggle at Genoa to prevent the embarkation of the volunteers." [10] The French newspapers called Garibaldi a filibuster, to whom no more mercy ought to be shown than to a pirate. Russia was profoundly indignant. Prussia regretted that she had no vessel in the Mediterranean to intercept the revolutionary buccaneers. Austria, while professing no intention of interfering, condemned the Expedition as a trick for aggrandizing Piedmont.[11] Official England looked askance. Queen Victoria thought that France — "who must needs disturb every quarter of the Globe and try to make mischief and set everyone by the ears" — was instigating Piedmont.[12] Even Lord John Russell had swung so far in his revulsion from Napoleon III that he was ready to believe that the Emperor designed to annex Genoa and Sardinia in return for allowing Piedmont to acquire the Two Sicilies.[13]

In expressing its horror, Diplomacy did only what was to be expected. The Law of Nations, as then codified, looked upon Garibaldian expeditions as crimes against international comity. The virtue or patriotism of the leader, and the nobleness of his purpose, no more affected Diplomacy's verdict, than the private character of an assassin can palliate in the eyes of the judge the crime of regicide. That Piedmont should connive with Garibaldi was a gross breach of etiquette,[14] nay, worse, a betrayal of caste: for the King's Government, ostensibly a constitutional mon-

---

[10] *Lettere,* iv, clxxiii.   [11] Martin, v, 96.   [12] *Q. V. L.,* iii, 399; Queen to Leopold, May 8, 1860.   [13] Martin, v, 96. In Ernest II : *Memoirs,* ii, 31, Napoleon himself tells of the various designs attributed to him. On May 17, Cavour telegraphed E. d'Azeglio to assure Palmerston that he would not cede an inch of Italian soil. Artom-Blanc, i, 111.   [14] Daniel believed that Hudson was actively helping the expedition. He asserts that Garibaldi sailed under the English flag; took out papers for English ports — Malta and Corfu; and received English passports from Hudson. Daniel to Cass, May 10. *Amer. Arch.* Although unproved, this gossip has value as an indication of diplomatists' opinions at Turin.

archy, thereby resorted to methods neither constitutional nor monarchical. The real cause for alarm, however, was not that Sicily might be freed from Bourbon despotism, but that this jar might dislodge the avalanche which had long been threatening feudalized Europe. The Treaties of 1815 were still the basis of international agreements. It was as if in an age of railways the laws of transportation of the days of the packhorse and the stagecoach were perpetuated. Every sane person knew that the States of Italy had reached the melting-point. What happened there might happen elsewhere; therefore, Diplomacy must use every effort to prevent a change. As usual in times of transition the Established System appealed to legality, which the innovators scouted, because legality meant to them merely a device by which the dominant party hoped to preserve its monopoly. Fate appointed Cavour to screen the innovators while they performed their task, and at the same time to hold them within the limits of the possible.

During thirty-six hours after the Expedition sailed he waited anxiously for news. Then the telegraph announced that the *Piemonte* and *Lombardo* had stopped at Talamone, a little port in the Maremma, not far from the Papal frontier. This news greatly increased Cavour's anxiety, for it seemed to indicate that Garibaldi, instead of making straight for Sicily, had decided to carry out his alternative plan of a diversion against Rome. The Piedmontese Prime Minister might feel equal to placate Diplomacy, already incensed at his collusion in an attack on the Bourbons, but he realized that a Garibaldian dash on Rome, which would involve the question of the Temporal Power and precipitate war with France, could not be explained away. To save appearances, Cavour had instructed Admiral Persano to arrest the volunteers in case they touched at any Sardinian port, but to let them proceed undisturbed if he met them on the open sea. The message from Talamone caused Cavour to telegraph the Admiral to prevent Garibaldi from landing on the Papal coast, and thereby to avert a calamity, the consequences of which nobody could foretell.[15]

[15] Persano, 18–21. "Cagliari" signified "arrest Garibaldi"; "Malta," "do not arrest." On May 11, Persano received this telegram from Cavour: "The Ministry has decided on *Cagliari*." Persano construed this to mean that Cavour did not agree with the Ministry. Accordingly he replied: "I understand," and re-

2

While the King's Government hung thus in suspense and Diplomacy was alarmed, the Expedition pursued its way as heedless of the world's care as a comet that speeds below the horizon. The ships were hardly beyond sight of Quarto, however, before a new danger arose — they failed to meet two luggers which were to await them opposite Bogliasco, laden with ammunition.[16] To put back would be suicidal; to land in Sicily without powder and ball for a single musket seemed crazy; but Garibaldi was undismayed. "No matter!" he said, "steer for the channel of Piombino!" The volunteers, unaware of what was going on, trusted implicitly to their leader; and he, as usual when in action, had perfect self-reliance. The rough waters on May 6 made many of them sea-sick, but nothing could check their patriotic enthusiasm. The next morning the *Piemonte*, miles in advance of the *Lombardo*, anchored at Talamone. Garibaldi put on his uniform of Piedmontese general, went ashore, appeared before the commandant of the old fort and made formal requisition for arms and ammunition. The Commandant handed over an antiquated culverin,[17] a four-pounder and two dismounted six-pounders: the real magazine, he said, lay at Orbetello. Accordingly, Garibaldi despatched thither his Magyar lieutenant, Türr, with a note ordering the chief officer — Lieutenant Colonel Giorgini — to furnish supplies for the Expedition, which had embarked with the approval of the King. Giorgini hesitated; but Türr was insistent and persuasive; Garibaldi had a name to conjure with; and after all, Victor Emanuel's well-known sympathy made it not improbable that he was secretly abetting the Expedition. Giorgini gave way, and sent several wagon-loads of military stores to the ships. At the same time, Garibaldi procured enough coal at Santo Stefano to enable him to steam to Sicily.[18]

solved not to molest Garibaldi. Cavour undoubtedly recognized the extreme danger of an invasion of the Papal States and intended to ward it off. See his letters: to Persano on May 14, *Lettere*, III, 248, and to Ricasoli on May 16, *ibid*, 250. His instructions to Persano seem to be inspired by this purpose; they were obviously and inexplicably inadequate, if he really meant to intercept Garibaldi's voyage to *Sicily*.

[16] The smugglers who owned these boats, after waiting a little while, absconded with their cargo. Abba hints that they were the same who had failed Pilo in 1857. Abba, 33. Garibaldi, writing to Bertani from Talamone on May 8, calls the head smuggler Profumo. Ciàmpoli, 144.   [17] Dated 1600; capable of throwing a 6-pound ball.   [18] Garibaldi: *Memorie*, 340.

He further improved these days — the 7th and 8th — by organizing his troops in eight companies, commanded respectively by Bixio, Orsini, Stocco, La Masa, Anfossi, Carini, Cairoli and Nullo. He appointed Sirtori chief-of-staff, Türr first aide-de-camp, and Ripari, head surgeon. Crispi and George Manin were also staff officers. Garibaldi declared the corps to be the Hunters of the Alps, belonging to the Italian Army, with the same war-cry — "Italy and Victor Emanuel!" — that resounded on the banks of the Ticino twelve months before.[19] When the Mazzinians heard this proclamation, they winced at being classed among the soldiers of the King, for they hoped that Garibaldi would conduct the campaign under Mazzini's neutral banner; nevertheless, all but three or four of them decided to go on; the majority being impelled no doubt by the pure desire of sharing in a glorious rescue, a few perhaps cherishing the expectation that if they clung to the Expedition they might succeed in republicanizing it. What would have happened if Mazzini had been on board, as he intended, we can only conjecture;[20] but we can be sure that his presence would not have made for harmony. The Paladin on the quarter-deck might have treated as mutinous the doctrines preached by the Apostle in the cabin.

From Talamone, Garibaldi despatched a troop to make a diversion against the Papal States. The plan was to hurry across country to Orvieto, alarming the Papalists, rousing and recruiting the patriots, and to invade Umbria. The inhabitants were expected to rise at the first signal. A general rebellion would ensue, and the Marches and Rome itself might swell the National crusade. The war would then be carried South over the Neapolitan border. For this undertaking, Garibaldi assigned 61 of the Thousand under Zambianchi and about 200 Livornese under Andrea Sgarallino, who had come down to join him.[21] They deplored being cut off from Sicily, but they obeyed. Zambianchi, it soon proved, had no fitness for such a task: being a

[19] Text in Menghini, 9–10.
[20] "At supper that night," Bandi says, "I well remember how Garibaldi, between one mouthful and the next, fell to discussing the hubbub at Talamone over the Savoy flag, and how he called down the wrath of God on Mazzini and his blind followers." Bandi, 67.   [21] That Talamone was the rendezvous of the Livornese, proves that Garibaldi had planned to stop there.

swaggerer, habitually drunk, without power to win either the respect of his men or their confidence. From the evening of May 7 to May 19, he led them along the outskirts of Tuscany. Crossing the Papal frontier, he reached Grotte di Castro, where, although the Papal gendarmes surprised him and his troops in a very unmilitary condition, they repulsed the Papalists, and made their way back into Tuscany. There they disbanded. Zambianchi was arrested and imprisoned, and died not long afterward on a voyage to America whither he had been banished. The Diversion [22] failed in its purpose of starting a revolution; but it served, during the few days which were indispensable to Garibaldi, to mystify the Italian, Papal and Bourbon governments as to his own destination. As long as even a handful of volunteers were wandering through Tuscany there might be danger. A match is a very small thing, but it may start a conflagration to destroy a city.

When Garibaldi reviewed the Thousand on the sands of Talamone, he beheld as miscellaneous a gathering of patriots as ever embarked on a crusade. In age they ranged from sixty-nine to eleven years; Tommaso Parodi, who had fought in the Napoleonic wars, was the oldest; Giuseppe Marchetti, a boy who accompanied his father, was the youngest. The larger number were under twenty-five. Of those above thirty, nearly all had served with Garibaldi at Rome. Probably four-fifths of the entire body had volunteered in 1859. In education and antecedents their diversity was equally striking. Many came from the universities, which were then in Italy, as they ought always to be in every land, the fountains from which students drank in the love of country and of duty, and awoke to ideals of self-sacrifice. One hundred and fifty were already, or became afterwards, lawyers, 100 were doctors, 50 engineers, 30 sea-captains, 10 painters or sculptors, and 20 druggists; there were several writers, several professors, three priests and a few seminarists. Rosalia Montmasson, Crispi's mate, was the only woman. Hundreds of business men and small merchants, hundreds of artisans, and many workmen completed the roll.[23] Among them all no peasant —

[22] The history of this fiasco is given in great detail by Gen. Giovanni Pittaluga in *La Diversione: Note Garibaldine sulla Campagna del 1860*. Rome, 1904.

[23] Abba, 73.

for the intelligence and the conscience of the peasantry were still brutalized by the priests. Nearly every district in Italy had sons in that great hazard, but the North sent nine out of ten. Lombardy led with 350 — of whom Bergamo claimed 160, Milan 72 and Brescia 59. Genoa's quota was 156, and Pavia's 58. Nearly 100 hailed from Naples and Sicily — all of them exiles, and seven of them released only a year before from Bomba's prisons, and bent now on consecrating their lives to opening prison-doors for the thousands still in bondage.[24] The roster showed also eighteen foreigners, including Kossuth's disciple, Colonel Türr.[25] Nor should we omit the 200 Tuscans, who, being assigned to Zambianchi's Diversion, could not share the first glories of Sicily.[26]

These men spoke many dialects. Their complexions were of every type seen in Italy from blonde to raven black. Their apparel, new or old, shabby or dandified, would have puzzled a theatrical costumer; it marked the class or occupation of each wearer, with an added tendency to eccentricity; so did their hair, worn in thick shocks or close-cropped, and their beards and whiskers and moustaches, either trimmed after the military fashion of the day or left in the unkempt exuberance affected by the professional revolutionists. Until they put on their Garibaldian red shirts, of which there were too few to go round, these crusaders had no common uniform. But a common spirit uplifted them. And whether they were hard-headed practical men, like Antonio Mosto, who commanded the Genoese Carabineers, or sentimentalists and dreamers, like scores upon scores, irrespective of age, class or condition, they united in adoration of Garibaldi. They were neither "fabulous heroes" nor "sublime madmen"; for, as one of the most sympathetic of them has written, there were thousands in Italy as eager as they, but to them fell the good fortune of being chosen.[27] "A mixture," says Guerzoni, "of all shadows and all splendors, of all wretchednesses and of all virtues."[28]

Having secured supplies, organized his forces and sent Zambianchi on his errand, Garibaldi weighed anchor at daybreak on

[24] The seven were Achille Argentino, Cesare Braico, Domenico Damis, Stanislao Lamensa, Raffaele Mauro, Rocco Morgante and Raffaele Piccoli. Abba, 74–75. [25] Garibaldi's son, Menotti, was registered as an American.
[26] Many of them reached Sicily later.
[27] Abba, 40. [28] Guerzoni: *Bixio*, 159.

the 9th and proceeded to Santo Stefano, where he took on
coal. That afternoon the Expedition started again, heading for
the Northwestern angle of Sicily. That night and the next day
passed tranquilly. The men learned to handle the old muskets,
which were scarcely better than blunderbusses, and under Orsini's
direction they moulded bullets and made cartridges. The officers
discussed drill and tactics. The schools of dolphins at play
around the prows delighted the landsmen. Garibaldi snatched
an hour's recreation for writing a song to be sung in the first
battle;[29] or, angry at some passing disturbance on deck, he
rushed out and gave warning that his voice alone was to be heard
on that ship, and that he would throw anyone overboard who
disobeyed.[30] Nino Bixio, more violent still, announced to his
men on the *Lombardo* that he came before everyone, even God
Almighty; that when they landed they might hang him to the
first tree, if they could, but that he was master on the *Lombardo.*
"Whoever called Bixio the Second of the Thousand did not lie,"
Bandi remarks, in narrating these incidents.[31] Bixio's furies and
Garibaldi's rages were hardly required to keep in order those
well-meaning but undisciplined crowds, who behaved decently,
although they were stived into quarters too small for half their
number, ill-fed, ill-clothed, and uncertain of what an hour might
bring forth. During the night of the 10th they narrowly missed
going to the bottom. The *Piemonte*, making two knots an hour
more than the *Lombardo*, stopped her engines and waited for the
latter to catch up. All lights were out on both ships to escape
Neapolitan cruisers. Suddenly Bixio on the *Lombardo* saw the
outline of a steamer loom up just ahead of him. Remembering
Garibaldi's order, to ram the enemy if they ever came to close
quarters, he called for all steam and himself rushed to the bow to
be the first to board after the shock. Suddenly Garibaldi's voice
rang out, "Oh Captain Bixio-o-o-o! Garibaldi!" There was just
time to prevent a collision. Without a quaver in his voice, Garibaldi called again, as if nothing had happened, "We will set our
course for Marsala."[32]

[29] Bandi, 77, who gives the stanza. Crispi's journal, written on board of the
Piemonte is one of the best contemporary documents. Crispi: *Mille*, 113–20.
[30] Bandi, 66.   [31] *Ibid*, 67.   [32] Guerzoni, II, 59–60; Abba, 90;
Bandi, 76; Garibaldi: *Memorie*, 342; Crispi: *Mille*, 117. Bandi and others state
that Garibaldi did not decide on the place of landing until the next day.

In his plan to outwit the Bourbon patrol, Garibaldi had steered beyond the usual steamer route westward, then southward to within thirty miles of Cape Bon, when he turned Eastward and came upon Marittimo, the outermost of the Aegades Archipelago. As soon as day broke on May 11, the Thousand looked eagerly upon the islands, and in a little while they saw the coast of Sicily rise in front of them out of the sea, from Monte S. Giuliano on the north to the lessening ridges beyond Marsala on the south. Two or three suspicious vessels, seen earlier, had disappeared. Garibaldi gave orders to make straight for Marsala. As the *Lombardo* and *Piemonte* approached the low-lying town, he discovered two men-of-war anchored near the roadstead. Every possible Garibaldian was sent below; the *Piemonte* slowed up and took on board the first fisherman they met, who reported that those ships were English, and that two Neapolitan cruisers had left hours before for Sciacco and Girgenti. Thus reassured, Garibaldi drove landward at full speed.

Marsala, the Lilybaeum of the ancients, the Haven of Ali[33] of the Saracens, occupies the western verge of a low and bare plain which stretches between the foothills and the sea. In 1860 its commune numbered some 25,000 inhabitants. A mole, curving along the waterside, formed a harbor of perhaps fifty acres' area, shallow but sufficient for the commerce of that time. The town itself, still enclosed by medieval walls, stood on a slightly rising ground less than 200 yards from the landing. Close to the sea were the establishments, protected by high walls, of the four great mercantile houses that made Marsala wine.[34]

It was past one o'clock when the *Piemonte* sailed round the lighthouse at the end of the mole and anchored among the shipping in the port. A little later the *Lombardo* came in, but, drawing four feet more water, she ran aground. As she passed the gig of one of the English men-of-war, Nino Bixio shouted triumphantly, "Tell them at Genoa that General Garibaldi disembarked at Marsala today, the 11th of May, at one in the afternoon."[35] The landing, however, was not to be untroubled; for already the

---

[33] *Marsa 'Ali.*   [34] Wood, Woodhouse, Florio and Ingham. The grape is said to have been brought from Madeira. The wine, which is fortified for export, first got its vogue during the Napoleonic wars, when it was supplied to the British fleet.   [35] Abba, 92; others state that he shouted this to an English merchantman, bound North.

smoke-pennons were seen of two Neapolitan cruisers hurrying up from the south. The British men-of-war, the *Intrepid* and the *Argus*, were anchored in the southwest, outside the harbor, a position which prevented the Neapolitans from firing until they had come up opposite to the mole itself. This delay, though only of a few minutes, enabled Garibaldi to disembark all his men from the *Piemonte*. By that time the steam sloop *Stromboli* was at close range, and if her captain, Acton, had had sense or resolution, he might have raked and sunk the *Lombardo*, which had stuck in the mud, and was forced to discharge her troops and munitions by means of small boats. But Acton hesitated. The presence of the English ships seems to have disconcerted him. He was not alone in inferring that the arrival of the *Intrepid* and the *Argus* that morning, quickly followed by Garibaldi, implied collusion.[36] The Bourbons had good reason to know that Palmerston's administration wished well to Italian patriots, and they did not believe that the English would refrain from helping them on the sly. In truth, however, those men-of-war had been sent round from Palermo to protect the British wine-merchants and British interests at Marsala, where disorder had prevailed for several weeks, and they gave Garibaldi absolutely no aid. But their presence made Captain Acton cautious, so that an hour or more elapsed before he interviewed the British officers, Marryat and Winnington-Ingram, and was told by them that they had not the slightest objection to his firing. The British consul, Collins, had already requested that they should aim so as not to harm the buildings flying the British flag. By this time the Neapolitan frigate *Partenope* and the steamer *Capri* had joined the *Stromboli*, and they opened fire.[37]

The vehement Bixio meanwhile literally tumbled his men ashore, but with such orderliness that there was no panic. So unwilling were the Marsalese boatmen to aid, that many had to be coerced. Bixio's men joined their comrades from the *Piemonte*, already lined up on the mole, and began to march, four by four, towards the town, whither Türr and a few others had preceded them and seized the telegraph office. The Neapolitan

[36] Garibaldi: *Memorie*, 343.
[37] See Lord J. Russell's denials in the House of Commons on May 21 that the British had protected Garibaldi's landing. Also Captain Marryat's report.

gunners sighted so badly that, instead of destroying the Thousand then and there, as good marksmen might have done, they wounded only one of them — and a non-combatant dog. Before five o'clock the Garibaldians with their scanty baggage, their arms, culverin and all, were safe within the town. The Genoese Carabineers waited for a time near the mole to prevent the Neapolitans from landing. Late in the evening Acton towed the *Piemonte* out of the harbor as a prize; but the *Lombardo*, grounded in slime and half-full of water, could not be moved.[38]

Garibaldi went up into the dome of the cathedral to inspect the country. Seeing no signs of Bourbon troops, he came down, and, in the presence of the town decurions, issued a proclamation urging every Sicilian to arm, and branding as a coward or traitor whoever held back. At the request of the decurions, Garibaldi, "considering that in time of war the civil and military powers must be concentrated in the same hands," decreed that he assumed the Dictatorship in Sicily in the name of Victor Emanuel, King of Italy.[39] At last, he held the supreme office which from his youth up he regarded as essential to a hero chief.[40]

Marsala, never a cheery town, was unusually gloomy that afternoon; for its inhabitants had just been terrorized by a Neapolitan column sent to punish them for recent political disturbances. At first, only a few boys and religious greeted the Liberators; then some of the townspeople crept out of their dark corners and began to fraternize; and before nightfall, the bakers and vintners were exchanging their wares for copper coins bearing the effigy of the much-mustachioed Victor Emanuel.[41] There was none of the delirious enthusiasm described, for obvious purposes, by the patriotic newspapers in Northern Italy a week or so later. The Marsalese were most curious to see Garibaldi, whose prodigies they had heard of, but they were

---

[38] Abba, 92–96. Guerzoni, II, 61–62. Guerzoni: *Bixio*, 167–69. Menghini, 19–29. Bandi, 79–98, gives a romantic account.   [39] Text in Ciàmpoli, 147; dated Salemi, May 14, 1860.   [40] "I accepted the [dictatorship] without demur," Garibaldi says, "because I have always regarded it as the plank of safety in case of emergency." *Memorie*, 344.

[41] "What is this Victor Emanuel?" a Sicilian was heard to ask; "male or female?" As a further example of the ignorance of the Sicilians, many Palermitans supposed that Garibaldi was descended from their patroness, Santa Rosalia, whose father's name was *Sinibaldi*. Trevelyan, I, 307, who had it from Prof. Pitré the folklorist.

somewhat disappointed to find him neither gigantic in stature nor godlike in face, and they did not respond to his appeal for volunteers. They wore rather the waiting air of neutrals, who, while they agreed that liberty would be a blessing, could not quite understand how it would fit into the routine of their daily lives; but they realized vividly the sufferings which beset Sicilians who unsuccessfully resisted the Bourbon Government. The elders had witnessed the quick smothering of too many up-flarings of patriotism to be sanguine now: and there within sight over the water rose as a warning to unwise enthusiasts Favignana, the island prison, where hundreds of political victims, including brave Nicotera and some of his Sapri companions, were languishing in misery which made death seem a boon. The unresponsiveness which Garibaldi met first at Marsala followed him so far on his way, that he had a right to feel that Pilo, Crispi and the rest had deceived him with their reports that the Sicilians were almost frantic for revolution; but for once he kept his counsel and showed no resentment.

That night he planned his campaign. He had been lucky in the incompetence of the Neapolitan cruisers, which failed either to intercept him on his voyage, or to destroy him at the landing. He had been lucky also in reaching Marsala a short time after the Neapolitan troops had marched off to Trapani. But having brought the Thousand to Sicilian soil, ill-provided with food, armed with rusty blunderbusses, ill-supplied with powder and shot, ununiformed and undrilled, what was he to do with them? The multitudes of well-equipped insurgents who were to have welcomed him, existed only in the imagination of Pilo. If all the country proved as unresponsive as Marsala, the game would soon be up; since he could not hope with so small a troop to stand long in the open against the massed forces of the Bourbons. At best, he might prolong a guerrilla warfare among the mountains; but that would not bring to Sicily the swift liberation which he desired. He must win an immediate success in order to draw fresh ship-loads of volunteers from Italy. Time was his chief concern. He had already lost two days by his detention at Talamone, and a third through the slowness of his steamers, and, as the Bourbon government was now on the alert, he could not expect to benefit by what might have been an invaluable ally — surprise.

With the instinct which rarely betrayed him in his military decisions, he resolved to march on Palermo by the shortest practicable route.

Before sunrise on May 12, the Thousand quitted Marsala. It was a beautiful, fresh morning; the dew glistened like hoar-frost on the low grass and flowers. Suddenly, a trumpet sounded, and Garibaldi came riding down the line. Some of his officers had also procured horses, and they now accompanied him with such modest splendor of motley uniforms as they could muster. The Thousand cheered, palpitating at this first glimpse of real war. The Chief led; the Thousand followed, to the tune of La Marmora's Sharpshooters' bugle-call. When the trumpeters paused for breath, the volunteers burst into song — patriotic airs, and choruses from the operas.[42] The column soon diverged from the highway to Sciacca and took the road that runs nearly due East to Salemi. They all knew then that they were bound for the capital. As the crow flies, it is 50 miles from Marsala to Palermo, but as the Garibaldians must go, winding through valleys and zig-zagging over mountains, there were nearly 80 miles. After leaving the narrow coastal plain, the country is rolling, and if it had sufficient water it would be unusually productive. But even in May the little streams run dry and a traveler from the North misses the verdure and vegetation which come with warm weather in his home. Cactus and aloe, and even the olive with its parsimony of shade, are but poor substitutes for elm and maple, beech and oak. The Garibaldians suffered much from thirst — so much that, when they reached a spring, Nino Bixio stood by with pistol cocked to prevent them from over-drinking. By eleven o'clock they were glad to halt, to munch their bread in a grove of olives, and to hanker for the waters of Lombardy.[43] In the afternoon, they resumed their march; footsore now, and dry-throated, but uncomplaining. No handsbreadth of shadow flecked the dusty road for them; and the country on either side seemed a desert, because between town and town in Sicily there were almost no farmhouses. At last, however, the weary Liberators came to a feudal castle — the manor of Rampagallo — where a company of three-score

[42] Abba, 101–03.
[43] Some of them sang Verdi's *Fonti eterne, purissimi laghi.* Abba, 104.

recruits, commanded by the brothers Sant' Anna and by Baron
Mocarta, greeted Garibaldi. There they stacked arms, ate their
bread, stretched their tired bodies on the grassy slope and went
gladly to sleep.

The next day a ten miles' tramp, short but uphill, brought
them to Salemi, a town perched on a crest. Forewarned by La
Masa, who had gone on ahead the night before, the natives were
expecting them in a body. Now at last enthusiasm burst forth
uncontrolled. The church-bells clanged, the throngs shouted and
sang popular tunes; and, as each dusty company panted up the
hill, into the piazza, they flocked round it and cheered. Soon
troops of horsemen came from all directions — but chiefly from
Monte San Giuliano, where they had eluded the Bourbons'
pursuit. They were genuine Sicilian countrymen, who, like the
Highland Scotch a century or so before them, easily transformed
themselves from farmers and country gentlemen into border-
raiders. Some had long-barreled flint-locks slung over the sad-
dle-bows; many carried rusty pikes or old swords. The poorer
were clad in leather breeches and in sheepskins, with the fleece
outside. The arrival of a band of a hundred, led by Fra Pantaleo, a Franciscan monk, gave Garibaldi great satisfaction, as
a sign that the clergy were not all Bourbons. He looked too for
wonders from these irregulars, to confirm his theory that mere
aggregations of patriots would always be more than a match
for the standing armies of despots. Good news now came in.
Rosalino Pilo had his bands ready near Palermo, and the insurrection, instead of being quenched, was kindling again through
the midland plateau as far south as Corleone. To effect a junc-
tion with Pilo and the other revolutionists, and to descend upon
the capital with what promised to be a formidable army, became Garibaldi's objective. He passed the 14th and the night
of the 15th at Salemi, taking the precaution to send scouts
forward. They reported that a Neapolitan force was approaching Calatafimi.

The announcement at Naples late on May 6 that an expedition, commanded by Garibaldi, had that morning sailed out of
Genoa, threw the Bourbon King and his advisers into consternation. Francis's first act was to pay his superstitious devoirs at
the shrine of St. Januarius; but the Saint's blood did not liquefy

to good purpose. Prince Castelcicala, a veteran of the Napoleonic wars, and for five years past general of the army in Sicily, sent nervous requests for reinforcements. On the 6th, the King despatched General Landi, a dawdler of seventy, with a column to keep order on the western coast. Landi drove in a carriage at the head of his troops, stopped to propitiate the saints at Sunday mass, and on May 13 rumbled into the town of Calatafimi. On learning there that a band of rebels had gathered at Salemi, he thought it prudent, before venturing farther, to wait for a fresh battalion which had been promised him. The next day, having verified that the rebels were in truth Garibaldians, he resolved, in an access of valor, to attack them: but sober second thought, which in the case of the Neapolitan generals was equivalent to what some may call extreme prudence and others cowardice, restrained him. He held so favorable a position at Calatafimi, that he decided not to move out of it.

Having rested his men, Garibaldi again proclaimed himself dictator, called for a general conscription, and gave the word to advance at daybreak on the 15th. He must either cut his way through Landi's opposing forces, or take to the mountains and creep towards Palermo by roundabout and precarious paths. Of course he chose the former. The first stage in the cool of the day brought him to the village of Vita, whence he went on, to the top of the Pietralunga, a rocky ridge. On an opposite hill, the Pianto dei Romani [44] (or Lament of the Romans),[45] he saw the Bourbon troops stationed. General Landi himself, enjoying what comfort he could in the wretched town of Calatafimi, sent forward Major Sforza, a younger and more vigorous officer, in command of a battalion of the Eighth Hunters. Sforza concluded that he would make an end of the crowd of tramps who occupied the slopes of Pietralunga and the valley between it and his own hill. Tramps, indeed, the Garibaldians looked, in their civilian clothes of all patterns, but mostly shabby. Even the minority in red shirts could not impress officers who judged soldierliness by parade dress. When the Bourbon bugle sounded forward, Garibaldi's bugle replied with the reveillée which had

[44] Pietralunga is 436 metres and Pianto dei Romani 422 metres above sea level (Abba, 116, n. 1). The descent into the valley between may be 400 feet.

[45] So called because it was incorrectly supposed that a Roman army had been wiped out there by the Carthaginians.

thrilled the Red Shirts at Como the year before. Sforza's men rushed down the hill, expecting to sweep the enemy before them, helpless as leaves before an October gust; but the Garibaldian outposts did not flinch. There was hot fighting, until Garibaldi ordered the signal for his little body of sharpshooters, who were outmatched, to halt and retire, but they paid no attention to it.[46] Then he called for a general charge. All his forces rushed at the double-quick into the hollow, and rolled the 8th Bourbon Hunters back, across the open valley to the foot of their hill, where Sforza gave them what support he could. The Pianto dei Romani was banked in seven terraces,[47] and the Bourbons now prepared to defend each terrace, which served as a narrow platform on which they could assemble, with a retaining wall as a breastwork in front of them. In numbers, in position, in arms, in ammunition the Neapolitans were far superior to the Garibaldians, and Major Sforza himself was no mean soldier. Nevertheless, after several hours of dogged combat, the Red Shirts planted the Italian tricolor banner on the top of the hill, and the Bourbons, in their dainty light blue uniforms, now sadly soiled, took to their heels, hurrying down into the valley which separated the Pianto from Calatafimi and up the opposite slope into the squalid town itself, where General Landi and his reserves received them. A squadron of cavalry, that had waited all day to cut the Garibaldians to pieces as soon as they should be routed, followed their terror-stricken comrades into Calatafimi. Landi regarded the retreat then made as "the best of victories."[48]

But the victor was Garibaldi and Italian Unity. His storming of Calatafimi, like Wolfe's capture of the Heights of Abraham, proved to be the turning-point not merely in a campaign but in the history of a nation. A hundred times during those fateful hours everything hung on the chance of his being killed: for he exposed himself recklessly, passing from point to point where the need of cheer or command was most urgent, and turning a deaf ear to the entreaties of his staff. Once, indeed, a flying stone struck him;[49] and once the odds seemed so overwhelming that Nino Bixio himself said, "I am afraid we shall have to retreat."

---

[46] Garibaldi: *Memorie*, 346.   [47] *Ibid*, 348.   [48] De Cesare: *Fine*, II, 210.
[49] As their ammunition gave out, the Bourbons rolled stones down the hill. Garibaldi: *Memorie*, 348.

"No, no!" Garibaldi replied solemnly, "here we make Italy one, or we die."[50] He knew that retreat meant ruin, and all the lion in him rose at the very thought of purchasing mere life by giving way. "Here we die!" he said again to Nino: "I had rather be a hundred yards underground, than have heard those words!"[51] When he saw the Bourbons at their last stand, some of them hurling stones for lack of ammunition, he shouted to his men: "Rest a few minutes, boys! then one more charge and we have won!"[52] For the seventh time the Neapolitans turned their backs and fled.[53] The Garibaldians lost in the battle about 180 men, of whom 30 were killed and 100 too badly wounded to proceed.[54] The thousand or more Sicilian Picciotti,[55] from whom much was expected, kept generally out of range on the surrounding hills, firing their guns in the air, and wondering what sort of warfare that could be in which soldiers stood up face to face and risked their lives against cold steel or bullets. They were not cowards; they were simply unused to fighting in the open. The Garibaldian losses, which probably fell a little short of those of the Bourbons, show that the Red Shirts fought stubbornly: they could hardly have won against better marksmen or braver troops.

While Garibaldi and his men bivouacked that night on the Pianto dei Romani, Landi wrote an astonishing account of the battle for his superior, Prince Castelcicala. "Help, and prompt help!" he began; and then described how his troops had been attacked by immense numbers of the enemy; how bravely they had fought; how they had killed the Grand Commander of the Italians and captured his banner.[56] After such a heroic introduction, it was certainly an anticlimax to announce that Landi's column had taken refuge in Calatafimi, and that his purpose

---

[50] Mario: *Garibaldi*, II, 220. [51] Guerzoni: *Bixio*, 176.
[52] Abba, 123. Guerzoni: *Bixio*, 176. [53] Guerzoni: *Garibaldi*, II, 79.
[54] The numbers are variously stated. Menghini quotes a correspondent of the *Unità Italiana*, May 30, 1860, who estimates "more than 30 dead and 60 wounded"; p. 28. The *Diritto*, June 3, 1860, says, "Our loss reaches 70"; *ibid*, 32. The Genoese led in losses, 5 dead, 54 wounded. Guerzoni: *Bixio*, 177. The *Movimento*, June 10, says, "we had 17 killed on the field and 120 wounded." Menghini, 37. Among the dead was the 13-year-old Luigi Biffi. Crispi: *Mille*, 139, 353.
[55] The *Picciotti* or Little Fellows, so called from their small size. One estimate gives their number as 1800. [56] The banner presented to Garibaldi by the Italians of Buenos Aires. Crispi: *Mille*, 353.

henceforth was to keep his line of retreat open, for use on the first occasion. What most "transfixed his heart," was the loss of a field-piece, which had fallen from the back of a mule.[57] Unnerved by defeat, and beset by dread lest his escape should be blocked, Landi was in such a state of hysteria that before midnight he had given the word to make for Palermo at full speed. While it was still dark the Bourbon fugitives reached Alcamo, and thence they hastened to Partinico, where the country-people, thinking the time for vengeance had come, fell upon them: but the soldiers, far outmatching them, put the town to fire and sword, and committed barbarities which date from the Stone Age. Then the Bourbons continued their flight. But woe to their wounded, and woe to their stragglers, who came after them by driblets, unprotected, into the smouldering town. The surviving Partinicans rushed back from their hiding-places and wreaked upon them bloodlust centuries old, whetted by that noon's horrors. They smote, they slew, they mutilated, they burnt the bodies of their victims, and fed the severed or charred members to their dogs. So inveterate in man are the traits of hyena and of rat! By day-break on May 17 Landi's main column, jaded and demoralized, slunk crestfallen into Palermo. In less than thirty hours it had covered thirty-five miles.[58]

Garibaldi spent the 16th at Calatafimi, making such provision as he could for the wounded. His men were much spent by fatigue, but victory is the best of tonics. The Paladin had now to face the future. His goal being Palermo, how should he reach it? He could no longer reckon on surprise, for Landi's battered troops bore witness to his presence. A sudden dash might be fatal. The capital had exterior fortifications, defended by a large army, and the commander-in-chief, as an extra precaution, had entrenched a large force four miles south of the city at Monreale, where he supposed the filibusters would first attack. Garibaldi judged rightly, therefore, that he must approach to within striking distance, establish communication with the insurgents and plan a united assault. He counted largely on a great revolution in the city as soon as he and his liberators drew near. On May 17 he resumed his march to Alcamo, where, at

[57] Text of Landi's report in Menghini, 34.
[58] Guerzoni: *Garibaldi*, II, 82–83. Abba, 139. Menghini, 38.

Fra Pantaleo's request, he went into the church and, with the cross laid on his shoulder, was blessed by that mystical friar as the soldier of God.[59] The news of the victory of Calatafimi having spread through the country, crowds of natives, rich and poor, rustic and urban, flocked for a sight of the marvelous Hero. Political trucklers who had yesterday cringed to the King's colors, cheered today the strange new conqueror. The recent volunteers marveled when they saw him asleep, wrapped in his cloak and pillowed on his saddle, like any common trooper. Partly his simplicity, and partly his success, lifted him in popular imagination to a superhuman level. The Bourbon soldiers whom he had driven from terrace to terrace up the Pianto dei Romani declared that he bore a charmed life; and his magic extended to his Thousand, from whose red shirts, the Bourbon soldiers reported, bullets rebounded, like hail from statues of bronze. The belief in magic, inculcated for centuries by sodden priestcraft, recoiled now upon its employers. On May 18 Garibaldi traversed the main street of Partinico, and after resting his men at a spot beyond the traces of Tuesday's barbarities, he pushed forward. That night, Bixio's battalion bivouacked at Borghetto, a crag-set village lying in the shadow of the mountains which hem in the Golden Shell on the southwest. "We shall soon be either in Palermo or in hell," the emphatic Nino announced to his men.[60] Garibaldi himself went on with the vanguard to the Pass of Renda and camped on a small plateau almost at the mouth of the defile, through which he looked down on Monreale and Palermo. There he waited three days, maturing his plans. Although it rained in torrents, the Volunteers, drenched and shelterless, kept up their spirits.

In great contrast to their confidence was the agitation of the Bourbon Government. Fully warned during April that a descent on the Kingdom was preparing, King Francis II and his advisers could fix on no definite policy. They were like a man who, when a robber is in the house, fumbles over half a dozen different weapons, unable to choose any one of them. They knew that after Pilo's arrival the insurrection in the mountains was scotched, not killed. As the Garibaldian expedition became imminent, they ordered fifteen ships to cruise round Sicily, and

[59] Abba, 138.   [60] Trevelyan, I, 268.

posted patrols at some of the loneliest points along the shore;[61] they also sent General Letizia with a punitive column to terrorize the western coast. But Letizia had quitted Marsala and the gunboats had just started for the south, when Garibaldi stole into port. Landi having already set forth by land, another force was shipped by sea, with the expectation of taking the Thousand front and rear; but Landi's usefulness vanished at Calatafimi, and the supporting troops, instead of stopping at Marsala, put back to Palermo, where nearly 20,000 Royal soldiers were already stationed. On May 13 Prince Castelcicala, whom the news of Garibaldi's embarkation had set quaking, begged to be relieved of his lieutenant-generalcy. After Filangieri and Ischitella declined the post, aged General Lanza, equally feeble and faint-hearted, was assigned to it. For his welcome at Palermo he had the rumor of Landi's mishap at Calatafimi, followed by the beaten soldiers themselves. Shutting himself up within easy reach of the gunboats in the harbor, Lanza entertained the King with frequent despatches in which, after describing the situation as desperate, he begged for reinforcements. The cutting of the telegraph wires made communications slow. With only 7000 troops in garrison at Naples, King Francis could spare no more for Palermo, but he sent supplies. Lanza walled up all the principal gates of the city, and massed his garrison at four points, thus leaving large sections unpatrolled and even unpoliced. After being at his post three days, during which he had not seen the enemy, he wrote to Naples that it would be most fortunate if the Royalists could retire to Messina.[62] Even as he wrote that despairing message, Garibaldi's men, peering from behind their rocky covert in the Pass of Renda, looked across to Palermo, less than nine miles off in a straight line. Had Lanza known that they were so near, he might, in his first access of senile fear, have taken ship and sailed away; for he belonged, like Landi, to that large class of warriors whose extreme prudence loses battles. His first thought was not to overtake and beat his adversary, but to provide a sure line of retreat for himself.

From his eagle's perch, Garibaldi's gaze swept the Conca d'Oro and its wonderful screen of mountains, which stretch from

[61] De' Sivo, II, 17.   [62] *Ibid*, II, 61–62.

Monte Pellegrino on the north to Monte Catalfano on the east. Palermo lies upon the sea, almost under the shadow of Pellegrino. At its walls begin the groves of oranges and citrons and lemons, whose yellow fruit, too abundant to be hidden by the dark green foliage, gives to the Golden Shell its name. The plantations creep up to the very feet of the mountains, which are for the most part without trees but clothed in colors so various and beautiful that you do not feel the lack of vegetation. From earliest dawn to nightfall and star-glimmer, each hour paints them with its peculiar charm. They suggest not overgrown rocky hills, but Alps or Andes in miniature, with the attributes which belong to true mountains. Abrupt and irregular, their tops are now pointed, and now they melt in undulations into the horizon. Their height runs from 2000 to 3000 or more feet, but occasionally a still higher peak looms up from behind. Paths wrinkle the lower slopes or zigzag among the gullies. More than one crag is crowned by the ruins of the castle which once defended the outlet to the pass below it. In their sickle curve, these mountains enfold one of the garden spots of the world, one of the spots where civilized men have longest faced the mysteries of life. It is the saturation of the human which hallows Nature everywhere. There are points in Greece that surpass Athens in natural beauty: Italy has many sites grander or lovelier than Rome: but the Athens and the Rome to which great-souled men and women will forever return, as to their home, mean far more than a patch of Attica or a few square miles of Latium. So whoever looks down on Palermo sees monuments of Saracen and Norman and of all who have come after them, and with the eye of memory he descries, as through a telescope, the first Phœnician ships rounding the cliffs of Monte Pellegrino and the Sicilians watching them from the shore.

We do not know what emotions stirred Garibaldi as he gazed over the Conca d'Oro on that 20th of May; he loved to rhapsodize and his slight grasp on history made it all the easier for him to shape the Past according to his fantasy of the moment. His attention that morning, however, was chiefly bent on studying the ground, a business at which he was as keen-eyed and practical as an Indian scout. The problem before him was how to break into Palermo. He followed with his eyes the roads which led towards the city; scrutinized the villages and clusters of buildings that dotted the plain up to the base of the mountains; weighed the possibilities of each approach, and decided that his best chance of success lay by way of Gibilrossa, one of the lower spurs of Monte Grifone on the east. To reach that point, however, he must make a long circuit. Immediately below him was Monreale, defended by a strong Bourbon force. Rosalino Pilo, with several hundred Picciotti, kept together by his zeal, was waiting at Sagana. Garibaldi planned that Pilo should occupy the heights overlooking Monreale on the west, where the vast monastery of S. Martino and the ruined castle, which the natives call Castellaccio, would afford shelter. Once in that position, he could render Monreale untenable for the Bourbons. To distract their attention, Garibaldi made a reconnaissance from Renda down the steep road to Pioppo. The Bourbon troops, however, happened to be commanded by two of the most energetic officers in their entire army, Colonel Von Mechel, a Swiss, and Major Bosco, and they, getting wind of Pilo's whereabouts, climbed with their columns to a height above the hollow where the Picciotti were encamped, took them unawares, and, after a skirmish, dispersed them in all directions. Pilo himself was shot while writing a letter — proof positive that he had been completely surprised. This happened on May 21.

Realizing that his own position at Renda was exposed to a similar attack, Garibaldi determined to carry out his movement on Gibilrossa, where La Masa had assembled large bands of natives. During the pitch-black night of May 21–22, amid a torrential downpour, over a wild mountain track, which led in one place through a morass, devoted mountaineers conducted him and his Thousand to the outskirts of Parco, another high village. When the bedraggled volunteers, during a respite in the storm, looked out and saw Renda still near them on the west and Palermo only eight miles away on the northeast, they felt that they had toiled much to gain little: but such is mountain manœuvring. Garibaldi's first thought was to defend Parco against Von Mechel's pursuing column, while La Masa attacked Palermo from Gibilrossa, and Corrao, who had a few hundred Picciotti within striking distance, made a dash for the city from the west. His great hope was that the Palermitans would rise whenever they learned that the Liberators were approaching from any quarter. With this in view, he spent May 22 and 23 entrenching himself in his position above Parco. Early on the 24th, however, he heard that Von Mechel had started to come in above and behind him, a plan which, if successful, would catch the Thousand in the same trap in which Pilo had been caught. Accordingly, he hurried his troops southward to Piana dei Greci, partly over the highroad and partly along mountain trails better suited to hunting than to military operations. They rested a few hours in the afternoon of May 24 at Piana dei Greci — so-called because of the Albanians who colonized it four centuries before: wild, rugged men, many of whose descendants had joined the insurgent bands. Towards evening, Garibaldi continued southward, sending his field-pieces and waggons ahead, under Orsini and a small escort. As the Thousand wound out of sight up the highway to Corleone, the hearts of the countryfolk sank: for they supposed that Garibaldi was beaten, and that, after he had been pushed farther and farther south, he would never return. Garibaldi himself, however, having followed Orsini for two miles, turned sharply to the east and scrambled over footpaths to the Chianettu woods. When day broke again, he went on to Marineo, a village near the top of a fertile valley. The Thousand passed most of the day there, torn and footsore and underfed, but cheerful, because they had eluded their pursuers and were almost near enough to deal their long-expected critical blow on Palermo.

On May 24 just as La Masa was leading his troops through the Mezzagno Pass into the Conca d'Oro, to carry out his part of the agreement, word reached him that Garibaldi was in full retreat southward. La Masa felt the ground give way under his feet: without Garibaldi, he knew that the game was up. He despatched a messenger to implore Garibaldi to come back at all hazards. In the interval it required all his eloquence and earnestness to keep the bands from vanishing altogether. Some of the Picciotti fled in dismay to the mountains. La Masa was greatly relieved on the following morning, May 26, to get word from the Paladin that he should be at Misilmeri on the 26th. Growing impatient, Garibaldi ordered his Thousand forward that same afternoon; at 11 o'clock that night they stacked arms and dropt asleep at Misilmeri. A few hours later, Garibaldi, La

Masa and their lieutenants held a council of war. La Masa
urged an immediate attack: for the Sicilians were losing confidence, and his own Picciotti had not refrained from attributing
Garibaldi's supposed retreat to treachery. Crispi and Türr supported La Masa; Sirtori, always brave but never hopeful, voted
for a retreat into the interior, where a desultory campaign could
be long kept alive; Bixio declared that there was not and could
not be any discussion.[63] The council decided to make the great
assault on the next day.

Meanwhile, Von Mechel and Bosco, with over 3000 of the best
Neapolitan troops, continued their pursuit to Corleone and
beyond, but Orsini and his ancient culverin and six-pounders
flitted tantalizingly ahead of them.[64] Saturn himself might have
smiled to behold the only energetic Bourbon officers in the Two
Sicilies fooled into such an empty scurry. No Sicilian betrayed
Garibaldi's secret; so that in perfect good faith the King's *Alter
Ego* (Lanza) at Palermo sent off a telegram to Naples announcing that the Royal troops had for a second time won a brilliant
victory over Garibaldi at Parco; that the rebel general was
fleeing in desperation towards Corleone, and that grave dissensions had broken out among the rebels.

If Garibaldi had any doubts, he did not reveal them. On that
last day before the ordeal, he went about as with a light heart.
And yet none understood better than he the odds to be overcome in order to take a walled city of about 180,000 [65] inhabitants, defended by an army of nearly 20,000 men, and by a fleet
which, from the harbor, could throw its bombs far into the suburbs. Between the foot of the ridge where he lay concealed and
the nearest gate, he must cross nearly four miles without cover,
most of the way over a highroad offering to the enemy frequent
opportunities for ambush and for temporary defenses. At any
moment his march might be interrupted by the return of Von
Mechel. He had no sure report from the patriots in the city, without whose coöperation the attempt might fail. He must strike
his blow swiftly, powerfully, once for all, because, if beaten off,
he would have no time to retire and try again, and he could

[63] Sirtori denied this later. Guerzoni: *Garibaldi*, ii, 93, n. 1.
[64] Menghini, 70–72, prints account of the retreat, by one of Orsini's men.
[65] The census of 1853 gave Palermo and suburbs 185,814 inhabitants.
Hachette: *Itinéraire de l'Italie.* Paris 1859. P. 736.

expect no reinforcements. The Thousand, on whom he placed chief reliance, were reduced to 750 men fit for service. The fortnight ashore had left them ragged in dress, but tougher in body. Their store of cartridges was so nearly exhausted, that they would have to rely on their bayonets if the contest were prolonged. The 3000 Sicilians recruited by La Masa, besides being ill-clad and ill-equipped — the more fortunate had old-fashioned fire-arms, the others pikes and scythes, — lacked not only the experience but even the sense of military discipline. A stranger would have mistaken many of them for bandits, — and indeed the line where the countryman ended and the bandit began was not clearly marked in Sicily, — but they were enthusiastic, and their numbers would be imposing, at least at the start, where the diminished Thousand would seem, if unaccompanied, too much like a forlorn hope.

At evening on the 26th Garibaldi led his men to the upland which forms the top of the pass of Gibilrossa. Thence in the twilight they looked across the Golden Shell to Palermo and the mountains beyond; near-by, on their right, stretched the sea. The moon came up, the matchless Sicilian moon. Before midnight the little army set out, the Picciotti first, but with a vanguard composed of picked men from the Thousand, commanded by Tüköry. The descent to the plain at Ciaculli was by a rocky path, fit for goats, down which they clattered at a snail's pace.[66] A runaway horse set the excitable Sicilians to firing off their guns, but the column was fortunately too far from the city to give the alarm there. A little later they lost their way, amid much confusion and some trepidation. Along different routes they now converged towards the city. Night was waning: they must hasten, if they hoped to fall upon the garrison unawares. At the Scaffa Crossroads, a mile from the Termini Gate, the divisions reunited. A furlong beyond, they scared up some pickets in the Scaffa Mills. "Probably to screw up their courage," says Guerzoni, the Picciotti raised such a clamor of yells and gunshots that the Bourbon vanguard, stationed at the Ponte del l'Ammiraglio, two hundred yards ahead, started from their sleep and seized their weapons. The Norman-Saracenic bridge which spans the Oreto — a shallow stream at all seasons, except in time

[66] Guerzoni: *Bixio*, 199.

of flood — made an excellent bulwark for the battalion that guarded it. Surprise, which Garibaldi had counted on, was no longer possible. Tüköry dashed at the bridge with a handful of Garibaldi's van, only to be checked by a volley of musketry. The Picciotti behind began to run. Seeing the peril, Garibaldi shouted "Forward! into the town!" to his own men, who rushed from their position at the rear of the Picciotti, and, captained by Bixio and Carini, charged the Bourbons, and charged again, and in a few moments sent them beaten towards the city.

The victory was Garibaldi's, but it was costly; for it warned the Bourbon garrison in Palermo that the rebels were at hand. From the bridge to the Termini Gate — a distance of less than three quarters of a mile — the highroad is lined with buildings which are almost continuous as you near the city wall. The gate itself had been closed and a barricade piled up in front of it. Day had now come. Rushing at the obstruction, the Thousand tore it down. But the space before it was swept by a double fire —from the garrison of Porta Sant' Antonino, and from a warship in the harbor. The Picciotti drew back, not daring to cross the supposed dead-line, until Francesco Carbone, a Genoese youth of 17, took a chair and seated himself there, in order to prove how wildly the Bourbon gunners aimed.[67] Then the Picciotti ran forward to the barricade, and on into the city through the Termini Gate,[68] which the Garibaldians had demolished. Garibaldi himself did not pause till he reached the Fiera Vecchia,[69] a small trapezoidal piazza a hundred rods nearer the heart of Palermo, once the Old Market Place, and the traditional haunt of sedition. Here flashed the signal for the Sicilian Vespers in 1282;[70] and here, on January 12, 1848, occurred the first tremor of that revolution from which all Europe quaked.[71] Garibaldi had some regard for the power of sentiment on his impressionable followers, who must count it as a good omen that their first charge brought them to that spot. It was about half past four: the sun was just rising. When the Thousand landed at Marsala on a Friday, some of the superstitious whispered of bad luck, — now, on the Sunday of Pentecost, the Liberators had stormed their way into Palermo. So much for omens.

[67] Forbes, 45.   [68] Now Porta Garibaldi.   [69] Now Piazza della Rivoluzione.
[70] This is disputed.   [71] *Dawn*, II, 77–78.

In 1860 Palermo within the walls was cut into four sections by two great streets — Via Toledo, which ran from the sea to the Royal Palace, and Via Macqueda, which met it at right angles in the little octagonal place of the Four Corners (Quattro Cantoni). These thoroughfares gave an air of symmetry to what was otherwise a city so irregular that you might imagine a fisherman had thrown his net down at random on the shore, and the tangle of its meshes had served as pattern for the ground plan. Winding streets, blind alleys, tunneled passages, crooked lanes, often so narrow that they were mere slits into which the sunlight never penetrated, with occasional small piazzas for breathing space, characterized the crowded districts. In these penetralia lay the hope of the revolution; for they could be easily barricaded, and they defied attack by any large force. In most of the passages two cavalrymen could not ride abreast; in many, even foot-soldiers must go single file. As soon as Garibaldi had established himself in the Fiera Vecchia, his men pushed forth into the tangled web of the city, sounding the tocsin from every belfry and shouting and banging to rouse the inhabitants, who, however, before showing their faces, cautiously waited to make sure that the Liberators had indeed come and were likely to hold their own.

The King's Alter Ego, the somewhat decrepit General Lanza, was wakened from his sleep at the Royal Palace shortly after sunrise that morning with news that Garibaldi had broken into the capital. Lanza, who had relied on his outposts at the Admiral's Bridge and on the blocked Termini Gate, was astonished. The Royal Palace, where he had his headquarters, faces a large square at the upper end of Via Toledo; from its roof the ships in the harbor a mile away could be easily signaled. On the western side of the square the Archbishop dwelt in another massive structure, separated only by a narrow street from the Cathedral, that stately Norman monument which men may gladly journey far to see. Having stationed his 18,000 men in the two fortresses and barracks, at the Palace, and at the two or three gates where he supposed the insurgents might try to enter, Lanza, seeing himself surprised, had but one resource — bombardment. And why not? In 1849, his former master, Ferdinand II, subdued the rebellious Sicilian cities by bombarding them. When Lanza realized that Palermo was in revolt, he unleashed his soldiers to plunder, burn and kill; he signaled the Bourbon frigates and the forts of Castellamare to shell the town from the north, while from the south his own guns raked the Toledo and adjacent streets with grape and canister. During three days, with occasional intermissions, the cannon battered down the most thickly inhabited districts, leaving a belt of demolition a thousand yards long and one hundred yards wide. The Bourbon soldiers were impartial in their barbarism — robbing churches and convents as eagerly as the houses of suspected Liberals; but it would have been better for the Royal cause if their energy had been more wisely directed; for when they came to close quarters with the emboldened insurgents, they faltered and gave way.[72]

In spite of the bombardment, the Garibaldians captured many important points on that first day. Sirtori stormed the Montalto Bastion, only a furlong from the Palace;[73] the Bergamasks captured Porta S. Agata; a brave troop of Picciotti seized Porta Felice, through which Via Toledo joins the quay;[74] Palermitan insurgents took Porta Macqueda, and pushed on into the Borgo or suburb in the northwest; Garibaldi himself drove the unmilitary Landi headlong from the small Piazza Bologni, occupied the Quattro Cantoni, and set up his headquarters a stone's throw distant, in the Pretorio Palace, or city hall.[75] Here he organized a Provisional Committee of Citizens[76] to act with his Secretary of State, Crispi, in governing Palermo, while he himself directed the fighting. When night came, the patriots had the interior of the city in their hands, except the Royal Palace and its neighboring wards, the Castellamare and the Mint. As if by a spell, a small body of ill-armed, undisciplined pirates, adventurers, or filibusters, as their enemies called them, had invaded the Sicilian capital in spite of its overwhelming garrison, and apparently they could not be dislodged.

Alter Ego Lanza concentrated as many troops as possible at the Palace — a mistake, though it added to his sense of personal

---

[72] Elliot, British Minister at Naples, wrote privately that the Papal Nuncio was almost beside himself with joy at the news of the bombardment of Palermo, and gesticulated in favor of shells and shrapnel, till his purple stockings got almost scarlet with excitement. Mundy, 164 *ff.* for bombardment.

[73] This seems to have been finally captured on the 29th.

[74] Abba, 189.   [75] Guerzoni: *Garibaldi*, II, 98-99.

[76] Ciàmpoli, 152, for Garibaldi's proclamation of May 27.

security. The rebels blocked the mile of streets between him and the harbor. On the 28th, the Garibaldians and the Bourbons fought desperately in the Upper Toledo, and round the Cathedral. On the northwest, from the Vicaria Prison, deserted by its guards, were unlocked 2000 prisoners, three quarters of whom were political, to swell the hordes of insurgents. The criminals among them doubtless improved the opportunity which the disorderly situation offered them: but there is a general agreement among the witnesses of those days, that Garibaldi did his utmost to put down lawlessness and that he succeeded. On that same Monday, the Royalists abandoned the Military Hospital, with 600 sick and wounded.[77] Aided by the townspeople, the Garibaldians not only extended their network of barricades, but strengthened those which they had hastily thrown up the day before. When Lanza saw that the insurrection, in spite of bombardment, of pillage, and of charges by his troops, was steadily growing, he bethought him of a trick by which to gain time, if not to commit the British in his behalf. He requested Admiral Mundy, of the gunboat *Hannibal*, to allow him to use the British flag to escort two officers from the Palace to the *Hannibal*, in order that they might confer with Captain Cossovich, who commanded the Neapolitan fleet, and with the commandant of the Castellamare. Too wary to fall into the trap, Mundy replied that he could not lend the flag, but that he would forward the request to Garibaldi. Without demur, the Liberator gave his consent for the officers to pass unmolested; but the Alter Ego scorned having any dealings with the Arch-Filibuster. Throughout that day and the 29th, therefore, the combat raged. The Bergamasks, who then earned by their valor the name of the Iron Company, took the Cathedral, rendered the Archiepiscopal Palace untenable, and actually occupied the buildings on the square opposite the Royal Palace. Thereupon the Bourbons, massed in great numbers, made a life-or-death onslaught, and drove their enemy back. When he heard of this, Garibaldi, who spent most of his time on the steps of the fountain in Piazza Pretorio, giving orders and flicking his whip, — as a charm to keep off bomb-shells, the superstitious Palermitans said, — went to the rescue. The Bourbons' advance was checked, and that

[77] Guerzoni: *Bixio*, 195.

night they were satisfied to be left in possession of the Cathedral. Before the next morning, two battalions of Bavarian mercenaries landed at Castellamare and made their way outside the town to the Palace, where they merely added to the number of mouths to be fed. Lanza's provisions were running low, and 800 of his men lay wounded, without proper care, in and near his headquarters.

On the morning of the 30th his pride, his scorn and his courage having melted like snow in April, he wrote a letter to "His Excellency General Garibaldi," humbly begging him to indicate at what hour two Neapolitan officers might meet him in conference on board the *Hannibal*, whose Admiral would act as mediator.[78] The haughty Alter Ego was now the humble suitor of the abominated filibuster. On first reading Lanza's petition, Garibaldi could scarcely credit it. His own straits were so desperate, that he was just considering how he could possibly hold out for another day. His ammunition was nearly exhausted; even the Thousand had only a few rounds left. He had sent secretly to Marquis d'Aste, who commanded the Piedmontese ship, *Governolo*, in the harbor, asking him for powder and cartridges; but the Marquis very properly replied that his duty as a neutral forbade him.[79] And now, at a stroke, Lanza's message reversed the situation! Having arranged for the immediate cessation of firing and for an armistice, to begin at noon, when the conference should assemble, Garibaldi put on his uniform as Piedmontese general, and, accompanied by Crispi, he went down to the Sanità quay, to be rowed to the *Hannibal*. While he was waiting, the Bourbon riflemen at Castellamare, though they knew of the truce, took several shots at him. Almost at the same time, Von Mechel, returning with his four battalions from his chase to Corleone, forced his way through Porta Termini and into the Fiera Vecchia. Falling on the Garibaldians by surprise, he would probably have penetrated to Piazza Pretorio, in spite of Sirtori's gallant rally, had not one of Lanza's messengers[80] appeared on the scene and compelled him to desist. Von Mechel himself saw no reason for respecting an armistice with bandits,

---

[78] English translation in Forbes, 54. *Correspondence*, 1861, viii, 2–4.
[79] Garibaldi : *Memorie*, 330.
[80] Nicoletti by name. Guerzoni : *Garibaldi*, ii, 109.

and only regretted that the Alter Ego was more squeamish. Had Von Mechel not been stopped there, or had he come a little earlier, he might have saved Palermo to the Bourbons and have destroyed Garibaldi's expedition. He had camped outside of Porta Termini the night before, but Lanza at the Palace was either unaware or heedless of this fact.

Much to the disgust of the Bourbon generals, Letizia and Chrétien, Admiral Mundy received Garibaldi on the *Hannibal* with the same honors as themselves. At quarter past two the conference began in the Admiral's cabin, with officers from French, English, American and Piedmontese ships as witnesses. Letizia, who pretended that Lanza wished Mundy to aid in framing proposals, which Garibaldi might accept or reject as he chose, was enraged at having to negotiate with the filibuster himself: but again, Bourbon hauteur suffered humiliation.[81] When it came to discussing terms, Garibaldi agreed that during the suspension of arms each party should keep its position, that the transport of the Neapolitan wounded from the Palace to the ships should be unmolested, and that the troops and their families should be allowed to procure food. But when Letizia proposed that the municipality of Palermo should "address a humble petition to his Majesty the King," "setting forth the real wishes of the town," Garibaldi jumped to his feet and roared that the time for humble petitions had passed, and that there was no municipality, for he himself was dictator, and would act accordingly.[82] He also announced Von Mechel's treachery. Letizia, who was prepared to concede everything, withdrew the objectionable Article 5, and signed the truce to last till noon the next day.

Late in the afternoon, from the balcony of Palazzo Pretorio, Garibaldi harangued the crowd which packed the little square below to hear what he had done. When he told them that, for humanity's sake, he had granted the enemy time to bury the dead and remove the wounded, there were loud cheers. When he added, "I rejected proposals that seemed to me ignominious to you, O People of Palermo," they broke into a shout: "War! War!" "We thank you, General! we thank you!"[83] "From the

[81] Guerzoni: *Garibaldi*, II, 110 ff. Mundy, chap. 13.   [82] *Ibid*, 111–13. Zini, I, ii, 614.   [83] Guerzoni: *Garibaldi*, II, 114–15.

bottom of the piazza," said one of the Thousand, "I too waved
a kiss to him. I believe that Garibaldi never seemed so resplen-
dent as in that moment from that balcony; the soul of that people
seemed to be wholly transfused into him."[84]

During the truce, whilst the Bourbons were removing their
wounded, Garibaldi provided himself with ammunition as best
he could, buying a small store of powder from a Greek ship and
keeping the Palermitans busy making cartridges. But even
now he believed that the chances were so great against him that
he debated with himself whether it would not be better to retreat
to the mountains. Fortunately, a more acute self-distrust prevailed at the Palace, so that when Lanza's officers reported that
the rebels seemed to be impregnably barricaded in the city, he
decided to ask for a prolongation of the truce. Garibaldi, who,
whatever his inner doubts were, always presented a victorious
front,[85] magnanimously agreed on a three days' extension.[86]
Some of his men censured him for granting the Bourbons so long
a respite: but he was wiser than they. Whilst his display of generosity added to his popularity, his feint of being the grantor and
not the suitor imposed mightily on friends and foes alike. He
employed the three days in strengthening his military position,
in organizing a provisional ministry, and in sending northwards
joyful messages, with a call for reinforcements and supplies.
The Sicilian treasury,[87] which was now handed over to him, contained five million ducats.[88]

The Alter Ego meanwhile despatched Letizia and Buonopane
to Naples for instructions. King, Court and Council were distracted, for at last they had to deal with brute facts and not
lying telegrams. On a single day Bombino telegraphed five times
to Rome for Pius's pontifical blessing, which was duly sent — the
last three times by Antonelli, without bothering His Holiness.[89]
It was proposed to promise a constitution as a blind, but to
concentrate the troops on the plain of Sant' Erasmo, so that the
bombardment of Palermo might be resumed. Filangieri objected that the insurrection had passed beyond the stage where
cannon could quell it, and that Liberal Europe would rise up

[84] Abba: *Noterelle*, 154.   [85] For instance, his manifesto after returning
from the conference. Guerzoni: *Garibaldi*, II, 114.   [86] Terms in Ciàmpoli,
155.   [87] Or Regio Banco.   [88] De' Sivo, II, 74.   [89] Walpole:
Russell, II, 327; June 7, 1860.

against further barbarities. The Generals returned with orders for the garrison to retire to the suburbs of the Quattro Venti.[90] But Letizia found the situation already so changed, that Lanza, at a loss to know what to do at the expiration of the truce, begged for three days more. Again Garibaldi acquiesced, now certain that capitulation was near. On June 6, Garibaldi on one side and the Alter Ego on the other signed a convention[91] calling for the immediate evacuation by the Royal troops of all parts of Palermo except the Castellamare, which was to be delivered over after the evacuation was effected. Having the option to withdraw his troops and trains by land or by sea, Lanza chose the latter; and until June 19 transports plied day and night between Palermo and Naples.

The 19th century saw few spectacles stranger than the marching out from that walled city, with its forts and fortresses and forty cannon, of more than 20,000 soldiers, well-armed, uniformed, with frogs, epaulettes and buttons according to the manual, with its pompous cavalrymen and prancing horses now crestfallen, and its batteries now silenced. As regiment after regiment tramped from the Palace down to the Quattro Venti to await its turn for embarking, it would pass, at the intersections of the streets, little knots of unshaven, gaunt men, in threadbare clothes and red shirts, armed with poor muskets or pistols, or with swords of any pattern. Yet that Bourbon host, despite its numbers, and its leaven of foreign mercenaries, who had at least courage, was quitting Palermo and Sicily, because of those handfuls of Garibaldians, because of them and of the Picciotti and townspeople hidden behind the network of barricades; because of them, and, above all, because of the fear which Garibaldi inspired. Bixio declared that on June 7, as they watched Lanza's brigades file past,[92] only 390 of the Thousand had guns! So amazing was the Bourbons' collapse that their official historian could account for it only by treachery. From the Landing of Garibaldi's Thousand at Marsala to the sailing of Lanza's 22,000 at Palermo, every Bourbon commander, according to De' Sivo,

[90] De Cesare: *Fine*, II, 242–43.   [91] Text in Guerzoni: *Garibaldi*, II, 118–19.

[92] Guerzoni: *Bixio*, 206. "The rest," says Bixio, "have been sold or stolen! This is the discipline of the soldiers before whom at least 18,000 men are withdrawing from Palermo." What are we to think of *patriots* who sell their weapons or allow them to be stolen?

either sold out or ran away.[93] Although such accusations throw a flood of light on the standard of honor which critics, who ought to be qualified, believed to obtain in the Neapolitan army, they were exaggerated if not malicious; still, the fact that only four officers were killed and only 33 wounded [94] during the three days' combat, shows that self-preservation had indeed become the first law among the military chiefs whom Bomba bequeathed to his son. "In Sicily," Garibaldi remarked sarcastically, "I fought an army without generals." [95]

But the transcendent figure is Garibaldi himself. Never was a leader more adequate to cope with every vicissitude that fortune sprang upon him. No fatigue tired him; hunger could not irritate, nor rains depress. He played with danger. For everyone he had the fittest mood — affection for the wounded, grief for the dead, encouragement for the faltering. He made even the unstable Picciotti realize that in sharing in this holy ordeal they were privileged beyond ordinary mortals. His unassumed buoyancy — now singing snatches of popular operatic airs, now declaiming bits of patriotic poetry — was beyond price, because his men thought it indicated that he felt no anxiety. His perfect democracy captivated that legion of outlandish democrats. If the poorest volunteers went thirsty, so did he; if they were drenched, so was he; and he exposed them to no peril which he had not dared. It was as natural to him to say to the adoring peasants who crushed round him: "No, no! Not my hand! Kiss my face!" as to peel an orange and offer slices of it, skewered on his poniard, to the starched Neapolitan generals who came to negotiate the truce. But neither his simple ways nor his familiarity lessened the awe in which everybody held him. "I could never imagine a man more terrible than Garibaldi enraged," writes his infatuated disciple, Bandi.[96] His rage was truly terrible because his victims perceived that it was just. Even Bixio, who seldom attempted to control his own furious

---

[93] See De' Sivo passim. He states (II, 60) that Landi retired from Calatafimi because Garibaldi bribed him with a check which, when presented at the bank, was declared a forgery. Poetic justice could demand no more. For De Cesare's criticism of this tale see *Fine*, II, 211.

[94] De' Sivo, II, 76. He gives the total Bourbon losses: 4 officers and 205 soldiers killed; 33 officers and 529 soldiers wounded. This seems to omit the losses of the third day.   [95] De Cesare: *Fine*, II, 237.   [96] Bandi, 192.

outbursts, quailed before the Chief's reproof. "How are you going to command ten thousand men, you who cannot command
yourself?" Garibaldi asked him, after one explosion; and Nino
had no reply.[97]

On the military side during the brief campaign, Garibaldi
could not have been excelled. He judged rightly that to take to
the hills and keep up a guerilla contest would never do. To win
the enthusiasm of the Sicilians, he must be swift, brilliant and
decisive. His evasion of Von Mechel's pursuing column and his
success in reaching undiscovered the point from which he could
best attack Palermo, were strategic feats which Europe had not
seen the like of since Suwarow eluded Macdonald. In directing
the defenses of the city throughout the three days' struggle, he
made no tactical mistake. His bluff in his dealings with Alter
Ego Lanza was incomparable. The imaginative Sicilians, in
whose minds flourishes a composite superstition, — Punic, Greek
and Roman, Norman, Arab and Catholic, — regarded Garibaldi
as a magician. No one dealt in magic, though of a kind they
dreamed not of, more truly than he.

[97] Guerzoni: *Bixio,* 206.

CHAPTER XXXI

FROM PALERMO TO THE FARO

AT Turin late in the evening of May 13, a little man went merrily down Via Carlo Alberto, rubbing his hands and whistling "*Di quella pira,*" with the vigor of a schoolboy.[1] On his way home from the Ministry of Foreign Affairs, where news had just come of Garibaldi's safe landing at Marsala, Cavour gave vent to his joy in this fashion, although, as he used often to assert, he scarcely knew one tune from another. He felt immense satisfaction that Garibaldi — the symbol and banner-bearer of that Italianism to which he had himself since youth devoted his life — had reached Sicily unscathed; and immense relief, that the threatened attack on the Papal States had been given up. The next morning, he telegraphed Persano to concentrate his fleet in the Gulf of Cagliari, so as to be ready to move at a moment's notice.[2] Among the possibilities which he foresaw was a declaration of war from Naples. Instead of that, however, the Bourbon government launched only a protest against the "act of savage piracy permitted by a friendly State."[3]

Cavour now formulated the policy which, for better, for worse, he adhered to thenceforth to the end. He would support every movement towards Italian Unity, openly if he could, secretly or indirectly if he must; but always by, through and for the Monarchy. He would countenance no action that threatened either to jeopard what had already been won or to prejudice the future of the Monarchy. In all capital matters the King's government alone should decide. This program evidently gave an excuse for hostile critics who charged Cavour with caring more for the dynasty of Savoy than for Italy, or with wishing to Piedmontize Italy, or with intending to impose the Monarchical principle against the desires of a nation which, they alleged, was Republican

---

[1] G. A. Cesana: *Anedotti sulla Vita del Conte di Cavour.* Quoted in *Lettere,* IV, clxxviii.   [2] Persano, 20.   [3] Circular despatch of Carafa, Neapolitan Foreign Minister, dated May 12, 1860; *Lettere,* IV, clxxx.

at heart. To everyone of these charges, if interpreted in the sense he attached to them, he would have pleaded guilty; and he would have added that Italy could not have been made without the Monarchy. His critics and enemies have still to prove that had a republic been set up at Turin in June, 1860, the liberation and unification of Italy could have been accomplished. We smile to-day at the mere suggestion of substituting Brofferio and Guerrazzi and Mazzini for Victor Emanuel, Ricasoli and Cavour, either to carry on the routine administration of the Kingdom or to lead its international negotiations to a successful issue. It was Crispi himself who proclaimed in 1862: "The Monarchy unites us and the Republic would divide us." It was Carducci, an ingrained Republican, who declared in 1895 that Italy was still too undeveloped by fifty years for a republic.

Those, therefore, who censured Cavour for insisting on the Monarchy as the ark of Italy's salvation, did not in 1860 see facts as they were. To be logical, they ought to have revered him for taking the one sure road towards Unity — the goal which they professed to hold dearer than life itself: but men are seldom continuously reasonable as individuals; in masses, almost never. To the Party of Action it seemed preposterous that Victor Emanuel's Government, which had tried to dissuade their going, and had, as they supposed, given them no assistance, should presume to direct their course after they had begun to conquer, and should appropriate their conquest. Some of their Party were undeniably impelled by that love of dominion which is common alike to men of really great power, and to the untrained and undisciplined: but others sincerely believed Mazzini's warning that Unity could never be genuine or holy or permanent unless it were achieved by Republicans. "Praise be to God and to Italy," he wrote on May 31, "that the Sicilian insurrection cancels the initiative of Plombières and hands it over to the People." [4]

The "materialistic idolater,"[5] as Mazzini dubbed Cavour, had an immense advantage over the embittered Apostle in knowing how to handle men in their political relations. Mazzini could preach; but it is one thing to exhort a congregation from the pulpit on Sunday, and quite another thing to lead it to practise virtue every day and night through the week. Cavour was a doer,

[4] Mazzini: *Scritti*, XI, 43.   [5] *Ibid*, 189.

not a preacher. And having outlined the policy he regarded as necessary, he set about applying it with his usual vigor. The first blast of diplomatic scolding had done Piedmont no harm. It served chiefly to show that, however sternly foreign sovereigns might disapprove, none of them was prepared to interfere. When the news of Garibaldi's landing in Sicily brought a second squall of censure, Cavour formally announced in the *Official Gazette* that the King's Government, disapproving of the General's expedition, had sought to hold it back, so far as prudence and lawful means permitted; that the Royal fleet had been ordered to follow the two ships and stop disembarkation, but had been no more successful than the Neapolitan; and that, although the Government did not hide its solicitude for the common country, it was resolved to respect the law of nations.[6] Informally, or through the Piedmontese diplomats abroad, Cavour magnified the danger that threatened if the Sicilian crusade were antagonized. When foreign governments frowned on Piedmont, he bade them consider the alternatives: they must choose between the existing Liberal Cabinet, which would do all in its power to guide the Expedition, and an upheaval, which might destroy the Monarchy and plunge not Italy merely but Europe into war. His reasoning, which seemed Machiavellian, was honest. If the King's government had attempted to arrest the Expedition, especially during the great unrest over the cession of Nice and Savoy, it might have brought the Kingdom to the verge of civil strife. That such a combat would have swept away the House of Savoy is uncertain; but that it would have shattered the hopes of Italian Unity, by kindling irreconcilable passions and by calling back foreign domination, can hardly be doubted.

Cavour made no thorough effort, therefore, to interfere with the patriotic preparations. He allowed subscriptions for the Sicilian Expedition to be opened in almost every town. Arms, rations and clothing were collected, and might be sent with impunity. Everybody knew that several ships, with volunteers who came forward by thousands, would sail in a few days, but not from Genoa; because, "to save appearances," Cavour forbade that. The Garibaldian furor grew and grew, and thrilled all classes. Aged Marquis Robert d'Azeglio, on the brink of the

[6] *Gazzetta Officiale*, May 18, 1860.

grave, regretted that he had no longer either arms or legs to give
to that "scandal," Garibaldi's "noble temerity," which he could
not sufficiently deplore nor sufficiently admire.[7] "What will happen now?" Cavour wrote Ricasoli on May 16. "It is impossible
to foresee. Will England aid him? Possibly. Will France oppose
him? I do not think so. And we? We cannot openly support
him; neither can we repress individual efforts in his behalf." [8]
This letter crossed one much more incisive from the Iron Baron,
who urged that the King's Government must not allow the country to suspect that it was less Italian than the "true Italians."
He insisted that enthusiasm must unite with wisdom, abnegation and opportuneness, and that the national task called for
concerted action by both People and Government. While allowing no attack on the Papal States, the Royal policy, he said,
should be to tolerate, and even to aid, the Sicilian insurrection
just so far as this could be done without compromising the Government. The Italians' right to help those of their compatriots
who were still subjected to bad rulers, could not be sufficiently
proclaimed before Europe. If the French aided the Americans
to throw off the English yoke, much more ought Italians to assist
each other towards independence and union under a common
sceptre.[9] On May 18, Ricasoli repeated this advice. The participation of the Government was necessary not only to further
the National Cause, but to increase its own authority and popularity among the people, to direct the popular movements and to
claim its proper share in the glories and results of the campaign.
"I recommend supporting prudently with the Royal ships the
vessels that transport the new volunteers to Sicily. I recommend to the foresight, which has no equal, of Count Cavour, to
profit by the English inclination to favor the Sicilian revolution.
If all this is done with prudence, France will stand mutely by.
The Emperor of the French will be forced to conclude that he
can have no better ally than Victor Emanuel, King of Italy." [10]

Ricasoli's counsels, which he repeated at short intervals, confirmed Cavour, who was already acting according to their spirit.
As responsible Prime Minister he had the delicate task of ap-

[7] C. d'Azeglio, 636.
[8] *Lettere*, III, 250; C. to Ricasoli, May 16, 1860; in full in Ricasoli, v, 62–65.
[9] Ricasoli, v, 58–9; Ricasoli to C., Florence, May 15, 1860.
[10] *Ibid*, 70–72; Ricasoli to C., Florence, May 18, 1860.

plying maxims which were innocuous until applied. The news of Garibaldi's prosperous landing in Sicily, with the likelihood of further success, precipitated another shower of protests. Gortchakoff remarked solemnly that, if Piedmont were too feeble to prevent the Revolution from unhorsing her, the Powers ought to adopt a common policy towards her, and he only regretted that geographical remoteness kept the Czar from defending the Bourbons.[11] The Papal Nuncio at Naples called Europe to witness that Piedmont had committed an act more villainous than the medieval invasion of the Saracens.[12] These fangless hisses, however, did not disturb Cavour, whose eyes were fixed on Paris and London, the two points where Italy's fate might be decided. He instructed Nigra to persuade Napoleon that it would be better for France that Southern Italy should belong to her ally, than to a brutal and antipathetic government. Cavour hoped that England would do in the South what France had done in the North — a suggestion to pique the Emperor's pride.[13] Expecting at the utmost to restrain the Imperial Government from hostile interference for the present, Cavour exerted himself chiefly to secure England's active coöperation. The long-standing sympathy of the English Liberals for the Italian cause had not lessened, but their trust in Victor Emanuel's Government, and especially in Cavour's sincerity, had been shaken by the cession of Nice and Savoy. They had reason to feel that, as the Queen expressed it, they had been made regular dupes. But three months had elapsed since Cavour apparently prevaricated in stating that he had not agreed to cede, sell or barter Italian territory; and the English recognized that political avowals, whether at Turin or at London, were seldom absolutely true. Lucky if, as in Cavour's case, they were technically true at the time of utterance. The practical men at the head of the Liberal Ministry had not the habit of crying over spilled milk. They argued that, since Cavour ceded Nice and Savoy unwillingly, Piedmont being unable to defend herself against French coercion, the person for them to blame was Napoleon III, and not Cavour. By showing their friendship for the Italians, therefore, they ac-

---

[11] *Stor. Doc.*, VIII, 291–92; despatches of Regina, Neapolitan Ambassador at St. Petersburg.   [12] *Ibid;* despatch of May 18, 1860.
[13] Artom, 110; C. to Nigra, May 18, 1860.

complished the double purpose of helping the Italian cause and of punishing the Emperor. In May, 1860, that schemer awoke to the fact that the English Alliance, on which he had lavished his blandishing arts and his energy for six years, had crumbled away. The English People, roused to one of their periodic scares at foreign invasion, volunteered as riflemen, and Prince Albert, who, more than any other individual, had labored to spread the epidemic of Gallophobia, proudly wrote Uncle Leopold on May 15 that 124,000 men were already enrolled.[14] The Prince Consort and the Queen did not stop here, but sounded Austria and Prussia as to entering into a secret triple agreement by which each should make known to the others whatever overtures any of the three might receive from France tending to a territorial change in Europe; and that the Government so approached should give no answer to Napoleon until it had consulted its allies.[15] Thus by a compact which, without wearing the menace of a formal coalition, aimed at isolating Imperial France, they unintentionally served Italy.

When the Italian Ambassador presented Cavour's explanation to Palmerston and Russell, he met with a kind hearing. Through Hudson, who was scarcely less Cavourian than Cavour, they had long since understood the truth about the cession; from him also, they had been apprised, day by day, of Garibaldi's preparations and of the Government's ambiguous complicity therein. They had no ulterior designs on Sicily. They readily believed Cavour's protest that he had worked to remove every pretext for France to traverse Italy's national policy. Probably these worldly-wise statesmen smiled, when they heard Cavour's malign questions: If the entire Neapolitan fleet could not prevent Garibaldi's landing, why should our two ships be blamed? And if Austria openly permits Austrian, Irish, French and Belgian volunteers to embark at Triest, in order to enlist in the Papal Army, how could Victor Emanuel's Government, even if aware of it, prevent Sicilian exiles from rushing to aid their brothers?[16] The British Ministers knew that Cavour was sincere when he declared: "I am Italian above all, and it was to enable my country to enjoy, at home and abroad, self-government, that I undertook the

---

[14] Martin, v, 107.   [15] *Ibid*, 121; Queen to Palmerston, June 3, 1860.
[16] Artom, 110–11; May 18. *Stor. Doc.*, VIII, 292–93; May 30, 1860.

difficult task of driving Austria out of Italy, without substituting therefor the domination of any other Power."[17] They saw that national interest was a sufficient guarantee of Cavour's veracity; and when Naples begged England to help her against the revolution in Sicily, Lord John Russell replied bluntly that the Government would take good care to do nothing of the kind.[18] Lord John gave the Queen his opinion that there would be no moral wrong for Piedmont to assist in overthrowing the Neapolitan Government. "The best writers on International Law," he said, "consider it a merit to overthrow a tyrannical government, and there have been few governments so tyrannical as that of Naples. Of course the King of Sardinia has no right to assist the people of the Two Sicilies unless he was asked by them to do so, as the Prince of Orange was asked by the best men in England to overthrow the tyranny of James II — an attempt which has received the applause of all our great public writers, and is the origin of our present form of government." [19] The Queen held the pen while Prince Albert replied that the cases of Victor Emanuel and of William III were not parallel, because William III had no thought of annexing Great Britain to Holland, whereas Victor Emanuel was presumably seeking to aggrandize Piedmont.[20] The Royal Couple were greatly relieved when they could deny as calumnious the report that British ships had protected Garibaldi's landing at Marsala.[21] Nevertheless, they began to treat the Italian patriots less coldly; not so much because they sympathized with the struggle for Italian Unity, as because they wished, by blocking Napoleon III, to prevent the further dismemberment of Austria and to preserve peace, which was, in truth, their dearest aim.

The Neapolitan Government spent the fortnight between Garibaldi's landing at Marsala and his entry into Palermo in forging lying despatches for the delectation of Europe. They made the mistake, however, of reporting too often that the Arch-

[17] Artom, 111.   [18] *Lettere*, vi, 563; E. d'Azeglio to C.

[19] *Q. V. L.*, iii, 397–98; Russell to Queen, April 30, 1860.

[20] *Ibid*, 398; Queen to Russell, April 30, 1869.

[21] *Ibid*, 400; Queen to Leopold, Osborne, May 22, 1860. "Affairs are in a most bewildered state. Lord Palmerston is *very stout and right* about our neighbour [Napoleon III]. I am glad to be able to *refute most positively* the report of our *ships* having *prevented* the Neapolitans from firing; the *case* is *quite* clear, and the French and Neapolitan Governments themselves have spread this falsehood."

QUEEN VICTORIA AND PRINCE ALBERT

1860

Filibuster had been utterly routed or captured. As if to give these bulletins the stamp of infallibility, Cardinal Antonelli manifolded them to Papal Delegates,[22] and Pius himself waited impatiently for news of the extermination of the Garibaldian pirates. But while the Bourbons were enjoying congratulations over spurious victories, Garibaldi kept on winning real ones: and on May 30, King Francis II, at the solemn conference with his family and advisers, had to face the truth. The Ambassadors at his Court, whom his Foreign Minister, Carafa, had besought to save the dynasty in Sicily, declined to commit their governments, although the Papal and Spanish agents characteristically hoped that a conflagration which threatened to devour Europe would be quenched in the blood of the filibusters and rebels.[23] A really brave man, much more a monarch with one drop of kingly honor in his heart, would have gone straight to Palermo, taken command of the 20,000 soldiers there, and perished, if he could not conquer: but Francis, like his father and grandfather and great-grandfather, had no conception that being a king should imply readiness to risk death. Honor was a quality of whose existence his family had known nothing for at least seventy years. Francis gladly approved the suggestion, therefore, that they should appeal to Napoleon III to mediate.

The Emperor graciously consented to receive De Martino, as special envoy, and Antonini, the Neapolitan Ambassador in Paris. He had no desire that the Kingdom of the Two Sicilies should be annexed to the Kingdom of Italy, but he could see at the moment no safe way for meddling. His interview with the Neapolitan suppliants took place at Fontainebleau on June 10. As they passed into the audience chamber, Thouvenel followed, saying, "Let us go and hear what lies they will tell the Emperor";[24] and on this occasion, the French Foreign Secretary did not use language to disguise truth. Napoleon listened while the envoys assured him that Francis II, with the best intentions in the world, had not had time to carry them out; then he replied that it was too late — that he was bound by obligations to his allies. "The Italians are indeed cunning," he continued;

---

[22] *Stor. Doc.*, VIII, 670; Antonelli's despatches of May 19, 20, and 28.
[23] *Ibid*, 295; Villamarina to C., Naples, May 31, 1860.
[24] *Stor. Doc.*, VIII, 297; Antonini to Carafa, Paris, June 20, 1860.

"they understand marvelously that, having given the blood of
my soldiers for their country's independence, I shall never fire
my cannon against it."[25] Cavour's remark to Benedetti, "Now
we are accomplices,"[26] had sunk in. Napoleon warned the envoys
that, as Piedmont alone could save Naples, they must go to
Turin without delay, and see Cavour. At this, they naturally
shuddered. But Napoleon did not mince matters. Cavour, he
said, was a man of sense, who had good reason to prevent the
triumph of the Revolution. King Francis must form an alliance
with Piedmont, grant very liberal concessions in Naples, consent
to the autonomy of Sicily — under a Bourbon prince, if possible
— and show himself unreservedly favorable to the National
sentiment.[27] Had a sheep, whose ewe lamb had just been de-
voured by a wolf, consulted a fox and been advised by him to
make friends with the devourer, she could not have felt more
repugnance and trepidation than De Martino and Antonini felt
then. Having pointed out the difficulties, they tried to touch the
Emperor's heart to go to the rescue of their King, but Napoleon
had no alternative to suggest; and if he had hesitated, there was
Thouvenel, who detested the Neapolitan régime, and spoke out
bluntly. Napoleon's advice, though it seemed bitter, was the
best that he could have given to the Bourbon envoys, and it had
the further advantage of serving his own purpose — which was,
to convince Europe that he was a man of peace, innocent of any
scheme for extending the French domain. In urging Francis II
to save himself by joining Piedmont, he both disavowed the long-
standing Muratist designs, and slily put a stumbling-block in Cavour's path. But neither by his apparent disinterestedness towards
Naples, nor by his protestations to the German princes at Baden
(June 15) could he rid himself of the suspicions which, since the
Savoy-Nice affair, had clung to him like the shirt of Nessus.

Before the Bourbon embassy came to Turin, however, a crisis
was at hand. On sailing for Marsala, Garibaldi left Bertani with
full powers to represent him, and with instructions not only to
send reinforcements to Sicily but to organize or support insur-
rections in Umbria, in the Marches, and in the Sabine and Neapolitan provinces.[28] The Revolution, of which Garibaldi was the

[25] *Stor. Doc.*, VIII, 298.   [26] *Ante*, p 214.   [27] *Stor. Doc.*, VIII, 298.
[28] Mario: *Bertani*, II, 53–54; Garibaldi to Bertani, Genoa, May 5, 1860.

standard-bearer, aimed at nothing less than freeing the entire Peninsula, including the city of Rome and Venetia. The descent on Sicily was only one movement in this enterprise. By Zambianchi's Diversion, Garibaldi set an example which he expected his lieutenants to follow. Instead of the policy of the Artichoke, the Revolutionists were for adopting boldly the policy of All-or-Nothing. No man of greater energy than Agostino Bertani, no man more persistent or more thorough than he, could have been deputed to manage Garibaldi's interests: but in becoming the Alter Ego of the Paladin Dictator, he lost that clearness of vision and that sobriety which during the years of conspiracy distinguished him above his associates in the Party of Action. We shall meet no more the Bertani who in January, 1860, declared that to bring Cavour and Garibaldi together would be of the greatest benefit to Italy; in his place we shall find a sleepless fanatic, implacable and deaf to argument, who devoted his unusual gift of vituperation to whetting Garibaldi's already excessive hatred of Cavour, and who did not scruple, after Cavour was dead, to utter in speech and in writing calumnies which he had ample means of knowing were unfounded and falsehoods which he knew had been exposed.

We must not attribute Bertani's apparently sudden change to a low cause. Degeneration is too easy an explanation. We must seek rather in the psychology of fanaticism. The fanatic nature may seem open and elastic; but when it closes on its object, like the steel trap which has been sprung, it never yields. The cession of Nice and Savoy set off Bertani. He regarded it as unnecessary, then as unpatriotic, and finally as criminal. Although neither he nor its other opponents could show how it might have been avoided, he held Cavour wilfully guilty of an unavoidable act. He lost his sense of proportion and talked in Parliament as if Nice were more important than all the rest of Italy. He indulged in sentimental gush on the sacrilege of betraying to a foreign despot the birthplace of Garibaldi and the plot of ground where Garibaldi's mother was buried. In thus mistaking a part for the whole, he took his stand definitely among the irreconcilables. He not only distrusted Cavour, but came to believe with Mazzini that the Republic alone could unite Italy. To prevent further cessions, to have done with delays, to abolish the threadbare hypocrisies of monarchy and aristocracy, he held to be the task of the Revolution. Cavour's evasiveness during the preparations for the sailing of the Thousand confirmed his suspicion that Cavour was an enemy, if not a traitor. La Farina's bustling officiousness filled him with indignation. He resented the attempt to claim credit for equipping the expedition; and after Garibaldi was safe in Sicily and advancing from glory to glory, Bertani grew wroth that anyone except himself — Garibaldi's Alter Ego — should direct the National Movement. Some of his critics, friends as well as foes, thought that the sudden access of power made him arrogant; others believed that his head was actually turned, and that for several months disease and the strain of responsibility upset his normal mental poise. Disease must certainly have troubled his judgment: because nobody could, for weeks together, direct a revolution from a sickbed, without seeing events, like his own sensations, magnified by his sufferings. The arrival of Mazzini in Genoa in the middle of May, and his constant injection of revolutionary virus, did not soothe the sick man's nerves, much less check his Radicalism. Still, the truth seems to be that Bertani, on being put to the test, fell back, as all men do, on his ultimate convictions and powers. These were Republican and Revolutionary. His common sense had kept him out of the earlier fatuous attempts; but now he saw the Revolution at the helm, progressing daily, with every likelihood, he thought, if properly steered, of redeeming Italy. If the Two Sicilies, the Roman State and Venetia should owe their emancipation to the Revolution, the Revolution might well expect to dictate the form of government of United Italy. Garibaldi, the hero of this crusade, chose for his motto "Italy and Victor Emanuel"; but Garibaldi at heart was a Republican; Garibaldi always seemed pliable to those who wished to mould him; Garibaldi hated the Moderates, and suspected them of betrayal; and if the Revolution went on conquering, Garibaldi might declare that it and not the Monarchy should possess Italy.

Bertani reached these conclusions soon, but not all at once. Immediately after the sailing of the Thousand he set about equipping the expeditions against the Papal States and Naples which Garibaldi had urged and Mazzini proclaimed to be indispensable. In this, he came into conflict with many Garibaldians, who would not agree to cut loose from government coöperation. The smouldering feud with La Farina burst into flame. La Farina, on behalf of Cavour and of the National Society, insisted that all parties should concentrate to help the revolution in Sicily. Bertani, however, was so loyal to his instructions, that those who differed from him complained that he used Garibaldi's appointment as a patent of autocracy. He would neither compromise nor listen to argument. La Farina was not alone in calling him the evil genius of the undertaking.[29] Regardless of appearances, Bertani was said to telegraph unciphered messages, from which, when published, the public and Diplomacy might guess that the Government was openly conniving at an attack on the Papal States and on Naples. He was also accused — but this was not proved — of coaxing soldiers in the Piedmontese Army to desert. It did not make him less irascible to know that Medici, to whom Garibaldi assigned the command of the Second Expedition, having been captured by Cavour, would not listen to going elsewhere than to Sicily. Now Medici was easily the most competent military commander, not excepting Bixio, among all the followers of Garibaldi; his refusal to be bound by the pro-dictator, therefore, was significant; and when Finzi, the head of the Million Muskets Fund, and Malenchini and Amari and Cosenz, took the same side, a man less inflexible than Bertani might have faltered; but he simply redoubled his efforts, having Mazzini and the Marios, Maurizio Quadrio and a few other intransigents to support him. He and they acted on the assumption that the Party of Revolution enjoyed a monopoly of further plans for Sicily and the Mainland.

The news of Garibaldi's victory at Palermo thrust the political problem to the front. It was no longer a question whether the Thousand could escape destruction at the hands of the Bourbons, but whether the Island should be controlled by the Revolution. Garibaldi was pledged to act in behalf of Victor Emanuel: who could guarantee that the exercise of dictatorial powers, the influence of Republican and Extremist agitators and his aversion for the King's Ministers might not cause him to change his mind, or at least to postpone the settlement? Cavour's guiding principle

[29] La Farina: *Epist.*, ii, 319; May 12.

— to prevent the National Cause from being swamped by the
Revolution — now led him logically to desire the annexation of
Sicily to the Kingdom of Italy at the earliest moment possible.
With this in view, he despatched La Farina to Palermo, and bade
Admiral Persano to proceed thither with his fleet. La Farina, a
Sicilian, a leader of the Sicilian exiles in Piedmont, and the man-
ager of the National Society, was to persuade his fellow-islanders
of the necessity of immediate union with their brothers in the
North. He was also to win over to this view the victorious Garibaldians — a crucial task. Looked at theoretically, La Farina's
mission seems flawless: the King's interests required a champion
and the Sicilians needed to be instructed in Italianism: who could
better be trusted than the Sicilian exile whose acquaintance
among his countrymen was widest, a leader whose energy and
alertness had stood every test, who had been behind the preparations of the Thousand, and who, above all, enjoyed the confidence
of the Prime Minister?

Many historians have agreed with the Garibaldians that
Cavour made a mistake in insisting upon immediate annexation.
If Sicily, they say, had been annexed at the end of June, the Italian Government could not have permitted Garibaldi to go on and
conquer the Neapolitan mainland. Diplomacy would have interfered, and blocked the Straits. Cavour would have been as powerless at Turin as Garibaldi penned up in the Island. But unless
Naples were invaded that summer, the chance to oust the Bourbons might slip away for many years. Garibaldi was logical,
therefore, in refusing to surrender his dictatorship before completing his work. To this argument it might be replied that
Cavour could have connived at Garibaldi's passage to the mainland, as easily as he had connived at the sailing from Quarto.
As to Diplomacy, so long as he could play England against
France, he would be reasonably safe. Still, experience proved
that the Neapolitans themselves would not rise unless either Garibaldi or Victor Emanuel came with an army of liberation. For
Victor Emanuel the risk was too great in June: therefore, Garibaldi must move then, or perhaps never. The two policies, the
Cavourian and the Garibaldian, could not indeed be reconciled:
but it is indisputable that Cavour would have been less anxious to
annex Sicily immediately, if Garibaldi's radical advisers had not

declared very emphatically that they should dispose of Sicily and conduct further operations regardless of instructions from Turin. It was their attitude quite as much as Diplomacy's growls, which impressed on Cavour the need of annexation without delay.

Having been the guest of Persano on the flag-ship *Maria Adelaide*,[30] La Farina went ashore at Palermo on June 6, and after spending three days in sounding public opinion, he wrote Cavour a report at once vivid, terse and comprehensive, which showed that he saw exactly what he had come to see: Garibaldi's new-born government already sinking through incompetence and corruption; Mazzinian hot-heads in league with uncaged jail-birds; Bourbon turn-coats slily fraternizing with too gullible patriots; avalanches of laws and ordinances concerning every detail of the city and the Island; and Garibaldi, too humane and too easily duped, a hero out of his element, bored, irritated, wearied by it all to an incredible degree. In this state of things, La Farina writes naïvely, "all eyes are turned on me." From the upper-crust aristocracy "to the heads of the masses, all come to me to ask counsel and direction. If I pass through the streets, they give me a festive welcome; whereas nobody salutes the governing officials. . . . My house is always as full of people as a ministry. They want the immediate convocation of the Assembly to vote annexation and to order universal suffrage. The Government knows that it could not live a day if the Assembly were convened, and it opposes on the pretext that the hurried annexation would render the Naples undertaking impossible."[31]

Cavour discounted the apparent conceit; what weighed with him was La Farina's description of the alarming condition of the Dictatorship — a condition which other observers soon confirmed, only to make Cavour feel that the consummation of his plan became hourly more imperative. Throughout the month of June he labored in every way to hasten the union of Sicily to Piedmont. To this end he instructed Persano that, besides aiding the passage of new cargoes of volunteers, and of safeguarding the Royal interests, so far as he could do this from his quarter-deck, he should persuade the officers of the Bourbon ships to come over to the

[30] Persano, 32–33.
[31] La Farina; *Epist.*, II, 327; La Farina to C., Palermo, June 10, 1860.

2

Italian cause. Persano was allowed to use funds and to offer promotion in the Italian Navy as inducements to desertion: but although Captain Vacca and some of his colleagues were quite willing to be induced, they shrank from taking the decisive step. That treachery called for a little courage: but they were sodden in cowardice or indifference. Only Count Anguissola, captain of the corvette *Veloce*, handed his ship over.

When La Farina flattered himself that Garibaldi esteemed him personally and only repelled him because he was Cavour's agent, he misread the Paladin and his followers. The Radicals hated him because, having once been one of them, he had seceded to the Monarchy; they hated him because they believed that he had withheld the means to equip the Thousand; they hated him because, without risking a hair himself, he now came to teach them, who had dared everything and won, what to do with their victory; they hated him because he represented Cavour, the vendor of Savoy and Nice; above all, they hated him because he was La Farina. Whether anyone else, dedicated to the work which he had undertaken, could have succeeded in it may be doubted: there are labors in which tact itself does not avail — and the Garibaldians accused La Farina of wholly lacking tact.

The truth about Palermo under Garibaldi's dictatorship still puzzles historians. Eulogists paint it as a Golden Age, in which the shackles were struck from the feet of political prisoners, orphans were cared for, feudal titles and servile hand-kissing were abolished, patriots' widows were pensioned, Jesuits suppressed. Garibaldi dispensed blessings with Saturnian largesse. All who supported him were paragons of virtue;[32] neutrals and opponents were all minions of tyranny. The laws he found, being Bourbon, must be bad; many of the laws he substituted bore the stamp of haste, arbitrariness or ignorance; but his flatterers assured him that all were perfect. In truth, however, Garibaldi in most cases simply signed what his advisers laid before him. The brains of his administration was Crispi — a born political boss, unscrupulous, able, domineering, persistent in action, tenacious in hatred. His legislation, if read between the lines, aimed at planting the Revolution in Sicily. He did not intend that the

[32] Jessie Mario admits, however, that *one* Garibaldian was sentenced to the galleys for embezzlement. *Garibaldi*, I, 236.

Party of Action, which had engineered Garibaldi's Expedition, should supinely efface itself before the Monarchists, whose principles he detested and whose patriotism he did not trust. How far he consorted, as his enemies charged, with the scum, cannot be proved now. That offices went by favor; that sometimes four or five persons drew salaries for the same office; that contracts were bestowed on the highest bidders; that public moneys were allowed to flow wastefully, or were openly embezzled; that life and purse ran great risks from robbers; that many harmless Sicilians were despoiled or persecuted on the pretext of being Bourbons; that rascals were fêted who strutted as patriots — is the bill of indictment that its critics have brought against the Garibaldian régime. Liberals had always ridiculed the reactionary King of Piedmont who, at his restoration in 1815, called for the Court Almanach of 1798 and reappointed the survivors to their old places; were the Garibaldians less ridiculous, who in 1860 quite consistently called back the Sicilian placemen of 1849?

That incompetence and corruption, that injustice and disorder, should characterize Garibaldi's dictatorship ought not to astonish us. Garibaldi himself was the most lawless of men: he lived by his heart and his instincts, and despised as slaves or hypocrites those who lived by laws. With no more training for government, that most intricate of human trades, than for running an astronomical observatory, he had to work with material which required not months or years but a generation before it could begin to practice a civilized political system. For centuries Church and State had deliberately brutalized the Sicilians, until they thought of government as of a vampire that bled, burdened and killed those subjects who could not secure immunity by bribes or violence. In the country, the Sicilian always carried a gun for self-defense; and he banded with his fellows in the Mafia, a secret society with far-reaching vengeance, which protected its members from Bourbon justice, and slew landlords and bailiffs who showed no mercy to starving tenants. To the Sicilian, government meant also the domination of Naples, which he detested more virulently than the Irish detested the domination of England. Though Garibaldi had been a Trajan, an Alfred or a Washington, he must have failed. Circe transformed the companions of Ulysses into swine; but mythology conceived no enchantress with a spell sufficiently potent to turn swine into perfect citizens. Whoever recalls the story of revolutions, will not be so much surprised that Garibaldi's régime in Sicily displayed most of the usual symptoms of anarchy, as that it had some traces of order amid the general chaos. The truth seems to be that after the first weeks order was fairly well enforced in Palermo itself, but that in the other cities and provinces lawlessness reigned.[33]

Personal feuds vied with party passions in fierceness: as was natural among men who, having clung to their opinions through years of exile, suddenly found themselves free to speak and to act. Most rasping was Crispi. His colleagues in the Ministry, men without a tenth of his ability, could not tolerate his domineering ways; and he resigned, rather than cause a scandal.[34] But Garibaldi retained him as Secretary to the Dictatorship, a post of undefined authority, in which his influence lost none of its reach (June 27). La Farina and his friends kept urging immediate annexation to the Kingdom of Italy, a proposal against which Crispi and the Mazzinians fought ferociously. They roused the Sicilians' inherited desire for autonomy; they sowed suspicions of the Monarchists' patriotism; they preached Unity, but with the implication that Unity could be achieved through the Republic only. They did not scruple to circulate printed sheets with the announcement that Cavour intended to cede Sardinia and Genoa to the French Emperor as an offset to the acquisition of Sicily.[35] Garibaldi himself told the Civic Council of Palermo that his program was "Italy under Victor Emanuel"; but that annexation must not be spoken of for the present because it would put Sicily in the hands of Diplomacy, and prevent him from completing his undertaking. "When all Italy shall be free," he said, "Diplomacy cannot prevent the unity of the mother country."[36] Nevertheless, three days later Garibaldi, in response to a shower of addresses, published an electoral law, and promised that the Sicilians should soon be asked to vote on the question of annexation.[37]

Although the Dictator changed his mind from day to day, and

[33] Cf. Amari, *passim* : one of the soberest eye-witnesses of these events.
[34] Three Ministers, Torrearsa, Pisani and Guarneri, resigned first; upon which there was a riot, followed by Crispi's resignation. Persano, 63. La Farina: *Epist.*, II, 337.   [35] Amari, II, 121–22, for one of the many allusions to this lie.
[36] La Farina: *Epis.*, II, 336–37.   [37] *Ibid*, 338.

reversed his decisions with a suddenness fatal to law and discipline, he never wavered in his hatred of La Farina. In their final interview he berated La Farina for voting for the cession of Nice and Savoy, and for having hustled him out of Central Italy the autumn before.[38] Such hostility, in which Garibaldi indirectly avenged himself on Cavour, could have but one end. On July 7, one of Garibaldi's officers and two policemen delivered La Farina on board the royal flagship, *Maria Adelaide*, and demanded of the astonished Admiral Persano "a receipt" for the same, as if the outraged statesman were a case of lemons. Garibaldi not only expelled La Farina in this fashion, but permitted the *Official Gazette* to couple his name with those of two spies, expelled at the same time, whose criminal records were familiar to the police of many cities.[39] "The Government," said the *Gazette*, "could no longer tolerate among us the presence of these three individuals come hither with guilty intentions." Like earlier paragons of chivalry, Garibaldi was not above taking a savage delight in venting barbaric spite on an enemy.[40] So the Cid not only broke his promise to the Moors of Valencia, but, when they surrendered in good faith, he threw them alive to feed his dogs.[41] Any ruler would have been justified in expelling La Farina on the ground that his propaganda tended towards sedition; but expulsion after that manner was unworthy of Garibaldi.

Wrath, however, ran too high for common humanity. When they argued, the men at Palermo had their hands on their daggers' hilts. All felt that the cause of a thousand years was being decided then and there, according to their action; and besides the zeal of patriotism, the fires of party or of sect kindled them. In such a crisis, the ruthless Crispi, assured of the Dictator's backing, outmatched La Farina, who, while wanting in neither vigor nor courage, was personally and politically unacceptable. Garibaldi kept on good terms with Persano, who not only represented Victor Emanuel, but gave valuable aid in convoying the ships

[38] La Farina: *Epis.*, II, 342; interview of June 25.

[39] Persano, 72, 73, 76, 82. At Persano's urgence, Garibaldi promised that the *Gazette* should retract; but he did not keep his promise. See also Guerzoni: *Garibaldi*, II, 128–32.   [40] The article itself was probably by Crispi, for Garibaldi was scarcely capable of such sharp-edged, poison-dipped writing.   [41] *Chronicle of the Cid* (Lockhart's translation), bk. VI, chap. 27, bk. VII, chap. 5.

that brought new cargoes of volunteers and supplies. The Dictator, heartily sick of wrangles, longed to take the field again: still he had his compensations in the idolatry in which he was held. Always a favorite with women, he became irresistible when he issued a manifesto asking "the fair and gentle sex of Palermo, to offer their breasts to the infants at the Orphan Asylum, nine out of ten of whom were dying of starvation for lack of wet nurses." [42]

While Garibaldi, master at Palermo, was awaiting reinforcements in order to take possession of the entire Island, the Bourbon Government at Naples sank from terror to terror, madly clutching at any stay, like the climber, who, having missed his footing, rolls helplessly to the brink of the precipice. When De Martino brought Napoleon's advice,[43] the King and Ministers could scarcely credit it. The Obscurantists even insinuated that the envoys exaggerated, in order to force the King's hand. But in a family council at Portici on June 21, it being no longer possible to blink the truth, eleven voted for and three against offering a constitution. The three incorrigibles were Troya, Scorza and Carrascosa — the last prophesying that the Constitution would be "the tomb of the Monarchy." [44] Francis II sent secretly to consult Pius IX, who, much flustered, said that the King had better make concessions, but that they must in nowise endanger the "sacrosanct" rights of the Church. Against his own inclination, Francis signed the Sovereign Act which declared that he conceded a constitution in harmony with the National Italian principles; that he granted an amnesty for political offenders; that he intended to arrange with the King of Piedmont an agreement for the mutual interests of their crowns; that the Neapolitan flag should combine the tricolor with the Bourbon arms; and that Sicily should have a suitable government, with a Royal Prince as Viceroy. This was dated Portici, June 25, 1860.[45] The Neapolitan Bourbons had two remedies for the insurrection which their abominable rule engendered, bombardment and perfidy. Bombardment had failed; Francis II, in falling back on the promise of a constitution, perhaps hoped that it would be

[42] Guerzoni; *Garibaldi*, ii, 122, n. 1, prints this curiosity.
[43] A summary had been already telegraphed. *Stor. Doc.*, viii (Canofari, June 12), 663; (Antonini, June 16), 664.
[44] De Cesare: *Fine*, ii, 251–52.   [45] *Ibid*, 253–54, for text.

as easy for him to forswear, as it was for his father in 1849 and for Ferdinand I in 1821.

On June 26 De Martino, the new Minister of Foreign Affairs at Naples, broached to Villamarina the question of an alliance with Piedmont. Villamarina was polite, but inconclusive. The same day the French Ambassador, who had already informed Cavour of the Emperor's earnest wishes,[46] pressed them again. Seldom has a Prime Minister been more embarrassed. Not only could there be no sincere alliance between Piedmont and Naples, but the mere pretense of a compact would let loose howls of anger and derision from every patriot in Italy. But to rebuff the Emperor, would expose Piedmont to the joint attack of Austria, of the Pope's army of 25,000 men under Lamoricière, and of the Neapolitans, who still had 80,000 troops on the mainland. In order to keep France friendly, Cavour dissembled. "We must hold ourselves in a great reserve," he wrote Villamarina, "declaring that we shall refrain from any act which might thwart the Liberal course which the Government of Naples intends to follow; and that we are disposed to second it if it adopts a policy truly National, having for end to attain the absolute independence of the Peninsula."[47] Cavour did not disguise from the Neapolitans, however, that he believed they had suffered their change of heart too late. He never dreamed that the arrangement could succeed, nor, as it soon appeared, did he mean that it should succeed. At the outset, he imposed conditions which he knew the Bourbons, however loudly they might promise, could never fulfil. He instructed Villamarina to demand that Naples must give up every intimacy and cut every tie with Austria; must bring the Pope to adopt the National cause, by extending the vicarial system; and must abandon every effort to reduce Sicily by force under Bourbon domination. As if these terms were not sufficiently harsh, Cavour hinted that Piedmont could not countenance a policy which included civil war.[48] This was equivalent to requiring that Naples should come to an immediate understanding with Garibaldi. As a token of good faith, King Francis must put from him the Queen Mother, with the Camarilla that had fastened their evil system on the Two Sicilies. Cavour confessed

---

[46] On June 9, 1860.
[47] *Lettere*, III, 273; C. to Villamarina, June 27, 1860.   [48] *Ibid*, Artom, 118.

privately that he took up the alliance in the hope, and almost in the certainty, of being betrayed.[49] He argued that if the constitutional experiment were honestly carried out for a few months, the Neapolitans would vote for annexation to Upper Italy.[50] "Let the Italian flag fly but once at Tarento," he wrote Ricasoli, "and Italy is made, the Temporal Power dead, the presence of the Austrians at Venice impossible." [51] If, on the contrary, the Bourbons, either through unwillingness or inability to reform, should prove false, there would obviously be no further excuse for tolerating them.

During the following weeks, Cavour pursued a double policy: he formally announced that Piedmont was ready to listen to the King of Naples, if he would accept, as a preliminary to negotiations, the terms which Victor Emanuel's government drew up. While waiting, Cavour spared no means that might strengthen the National spirit in Naples and lead the Neapolitans themselves to expel the Bourbons. Without Sicily, he thought that Francis II could not surmount his troubles at home. Without Sicily, the Neapolitan Liberals would all become Unitarians, and make their choice between Annexation and the Revolution. He planned to let Francis II fall, while saving appearances. Public opinion was his compass.[52] "We must go neither too fast nor too slow," he wrote Villamarina, "and above all, we must not be caught by their birdlime" [53] — a warning which has a comic sound when we reflect that the relative ability of Cavour and the moribund Bourbons was as that of a hawk and a bantam. When the Neapolitan envoy insisted that Piedmont should check Garibaldi, Victor Emanuel returned an unqualified no, and stipulated that Francis must not employ force to subjugate the Sicilians. "This condition," said Canofari, the Neapolitan minister at Turin, "denatures our demand for a simple temporary truce." [54] When the panic-stricken Neapolitan minister in London sounded the Queen's Government on this astonishing requirement, Lord John Russell not only approved it but added: "Three months ago the King of the Two Sicilies might have saved

---

[49] Artom, 117; the words are Artom's but they express C.'s thought.
[50] *Ibid*, 116.   [51] *Lettere*, III, 274; C. to Ricasoli, June 27, 1860.
[52] *Lettere*, III, ccxcv *ff*., letter of July 4, 1860. *Ibid*, III, 281; C. to Villamarina, July 7, 1860.   [53] *Ibid*.   [54] *Stor. Doc.*, VIII, 666; Canofari to De Martino, July 5, 1860; also despatch of July 7.

Sicily; three months hence he may not be able to keep Naples":
therefore Lord John advised him to come at once to terms with
Piedmont.[55] Berlin and St. Petersburg gave barren sympathy;
Paris promised nothing, although the Emperor's desire that
a separate Kingdom should be preserved in the South was well
known. Thus Cavour succeeded in staving off foreign intervention, which would have both paralyzed Garibaldi's project and
hurried Italy into a war in which her recently annexed provinces
might have been wrenched away.

But Cavour's greatest anxiety was Garibaldi himself, not
Naples. The capitulation of Palermo left the Paladin master of
Sicily. His actual military strength increased rapidly; his prestige, which alone was worth an army corps, was fabulously magnified. While he adhered to his war cry, "Italy and Victor
Emanuel," he ruled that he alone should interpret its meaning. Just what secret understanding he had with the King will
probably never be divulged: but he acted on the assumption
that he might do many things in the King's interest, which the
King himself could not only not do but must perfunctorily disavow. The King had to pay respect to Diplomacy — Garibaldi
flouted Diplomacy. The King must listen to his Ministers —
Garibaldi despised those Ministers, hating one of them with
a mortal hatred, and instinctively opposing any course which
Cavour upheld. He believed that as the Monarchy, attempting
to redeem Italy along regular lines, had come to an impasse, the
Revolution, seizing the initiative, would carry the work through
along irregular lines. Whoever denounced it for being irregular,
simply defined and glorified it. But while Garibaldi exultantly
captained the Revolution, he honestly intended that it should
conquer in the name of Italy under Victor Emanuel. He soon
gave warning, however, that he construed his mission most liberally — very differently, indeed, from the King's advisers. To
him, Sicily was only the first stage in his campaign of Liberation;
the next was Naples, then Rome, and finally Venice. From the
beginning of June, every vessel brought a flock of strangers to
Palermo — homefaring exiles, volunteers, adventurers, sensa-
tion-hunters — among whom the partisans of the Revolution
predominated. With Crispi for mentor, Garibaldi was not likely

[55] *Lettere*, IV, ccxcvii.

to lack dynamic Republican suggestion, although Crispi, like Mazzini and Bertani, who directed operations in Genoa, protested that he thought only of Unity and not of the Republic. That Garibaldi was at heart Republican, he never denied. The question which not even he could answer was, how long his personal loyalty to Victor Emanuel would hold out against the incessant persuasion of his intimates, and the conviction that if the need arose, everything, including the dynasty of Savoy, must be sacrificed for Italy. Evidently, the first duty of Victor Emanuel's Prime Minister was to forestall this peril by getting control of the movement; this he could accomplish most effectively by securing the immediate annexation of Sicily. It is equally evident that Garibaldi was perfectly logical in opposing annexation, which threatened to cut him off from the main part of his task — the liberation of the Continent.

But if Garibaldi was acting in the name of Victor Emanuel, the King might well claim a right to be consulted, because, at the settling of accounts, the world would hold him responsible. The two had their quasi-secret communications — but a more official bond was needed. The King suggested Depretis or Lorenzo Valerio as pro-dictator. Garibaldi chose Depretis, in whose judgment, principles and executive ability Cavour placed no reliance, not only because he had been a Mazzinian, but because he "could not face unpopularity"[56] — a trait which the Prime Minister, who had dared to be unpopular ever since he was Charles Albert's page at the Military Academy, despised. But Garibaldi sent word that he knew better than the King the sort of man Sicily needed, and that, so far as concerned annexation, he, as Dictator, could decree it without recourse to popular vote whenever he deemed it necessary. In regard to the expedition to Calabria, he first promised not to start without the King's permission; then, simply to let the King know that he had decided to undertake it; and finally, to come to an agreement with the King. He ignored the Ministers, as completely as if Victor Emanuel were an absolute monarch. This was on July 9 or 10.[57]

[56] Persano, 79–80; C. to Persano, July 7, 1860. "[Depretis] would be a very good executor under a decisive chief," C. adds. "He will turn out a very mediocre director of a great political movement."

[57] Artom, 112; memorandum of instructions to Count Emerico Amari, sent directly by Victor Emanuel to Garibaldi, and Garibaldi's reply.

During these weeks, when the vital questions to be adjusted were diplomatic and political; when personal animosities raged; when party and sectarian feuds ran riot; when that inveterate dualism of the Italian nature, which anciently embodied itself in Guelf and Ghibelline, menaced the dawning unity of Italy, the world thought only of the heroic achievement of Garibaldi and his red-shirted companions. The effect of their amazing story can hardly be described. It seemed to millions of men and women as if all they had ever heard or dreamed of valor, chivalry, self-sacrifice, had come true — as if the heavens had opened and revealed to them that the ideals, which baffled mankind had grown to regard as myths, were the only reality. No other hero's glory had been so instantaneous. The legends of Arthur's Knights and of Charlemagne's Peers, of Godfrey and Tancred and Richard the Lion-hearted, spread slowly by word of mouth, after troubadour and poet had embellished them. But the electric telegraph flashed day by day to an astonished world tidings of Garibaldi's exploits; and so widely latent was the conviction in the hearts of that generation that Liberty, like Faith, could move mountains, and that Liberty would not only prevail but justify herself, that they saw in Garibaldi the Messiah of Liberty, and in his marvelous victories the confirmation of their belief. The almost universal worship which he inspired was an important though intangible factor in international deliberations. His enemies hoped to bury him under an avalanche of opprobrious names — "pirate, filibuster, bandit, adventurer and Anti-Christ"; but in a few weeks two continents greeted him as "Italy's heroic son, as the Italic Genius, the Redeemer, the Archangel Gabriel." [58] The world outside heard very little of disagreements, and then only tardily; it saw only results, achieved against apparently immense odds; and it assumed that whatever Garibaldi desired, he ought to have, and that whatever he planned must be right. How shall the historian, who listens dispassionately to masses of testimony, — most of which no contemporary knew, and all of which was beyond the access of any single contemporary, — how shall he at once chronicle events as we now understand their sequence, and still keep that glamour and that glory, sometimes unwarranted and sometimes

[58] De' Sivo, II, 54.

mistaken, no doubt, which the actors and spectators themselves beheld in them? The Risorgimento, we cannot too often repeat, was a drama surcharged with Emotion, and no account of it can approach life-likeness which seeks to interpret it unemotionally — least of all its Garibaldian climax, in which Emotion threatened more than once to degenerate into hysteria.

Although Garibaldi, like other soldiers, prided himself on his superiority as a civil administrator and law-maker, the weeks of bickering at Palermo sickened him. He turned eagerly to military preparations for relief. His calls for conscripts, which he expected would provide him with 90,000 recruits, passed unheeded among the Sicilians. The bands of Picciotti, in whom he had set high hopes, before experience at Calatafimi and at the assault on Palermo had disappointed him, he weeded out, dismissing all but the best. Troops that wasted their ammunition by firing volleys into the air whenever they became excited, were not the proper stuff for the task he had before him. But Medici's arrival on June 22, with the Second Expedition of 3500 men, gave him great joy. Cosenz followed on July 7 with 1500 more.[59] "Excursionists" as they called themselves, who were really volunteers, many of them old Hunters of the Alps, reached Palermo in small unorganized parties almost every day. These forces which, with his Thousand and their accessions, numbered about 8000 fairly reliable men, Garibaldi divided into four brigades. One he kept with himself at Palermo; the second, Medici's, he sent along the northern coast to Messina; the third, commanded by Türr, marching southeast to Caltanisetta, he ordered to come out at Catania; the fourth, under the fiery Bixio, striking southward through Corleone to Girgenti, and then following the coast, was to join Türr.[60] Towards the end of June they set out and advanced by easy stages, almost unopposed, towards their different goals.

The Bourbons had now evacuated most of the Island except the fortresses of Milazzo, Messina, Agosta and one or two other places. About twenty miles west of Messina the promontory of Milazzo juts northward towards the Lipari Isles — a rocky ridge, commanded on its landward end by a citadel, protected

[59] See Luzio: "Le Spedizioni Medici-Cosenz," *Lettura*, June, 1910, pp. 481-91.
[60] Guerzoni: *Garibaldi*, ii, 126-127.

by two lines of walls which would have been impregnable before
the days of heavy guns. The shabby town sprawls over the low
isthmus and scrambles up the slope under the shadow of the
outer circumvallation. The low land along the main coast to
the west is marshy in the wet season, cut by watercourses and
a meshwork of irrigating ditches and covered by a growth of tall
reeds. To avoid this flat with its reedy jungle, the highroad
bends inland from Barcellona, skirting the foothills, and coming
out at Gli Archi, two miles to the east of Milazzo. On July 5
Medici reached Barcellona and took up his quarters there, to
await reinforcements. He could not safely proceed to Messina
because that would enable the garrison of Milazzo to cut off his
communications with Palermo. Clary, who commanded the
Bourbon forces [61] at Messina, decided that the Garibaldian advance could best be blocked at Milazzo; and accordingly, on
July 14, he despatched on this errand Bosco, the fighting general,
who still smarted at having been tricked by Garibaldi at Piana
dei Greci. On the 17th Bosco encountered Medici's outposts at
Gli Archi and drove them back. Medici saw that he must deliver
a battle. Garibaldi was warned, and, leaving Sirtori in charge at
Palermo, he hurried, partly by ship and partly by carriage, to the
front. On the 19th he explored the ground between Barcellona
and the enemy, ordered up the columns of the Englishman,
Dunne,[62] and Cosenz, and placed his little army of 4000 men so
as to prevent the Bourbons from breaking through and intercept-
ing his retreat. Bosco had in every respect the superior position.
With his left at Gli Archi and his right at Santa Marina, his
shorter line could, if imperiled, fall back on the town of Milazzo, behind which towered the fortress. Garibaldi's line, being
the outer, was longer, and although he had fortified the most critical spot, Meri, with his few cannon, he lacked a strong base.

At seven o'clock on the morning of the 20th the fight began
by Malenchini's attempt to drive in the Bourbon right. He was
forced back; so were Dunne's men, sent to assist him. Bosco's
Hussars dispersed them among the reeds, and were riding away,
when Garibaldi himself, with the Genoese Carabineers, took them

[61] 20,000 strong according to De' Sivo, ii, 120.
[62] Garibaldi brought Dunne's 400 with him on the *Aberdeen* from Palermo to
Patti, on the 18th. Guerzoni: *Garibaldi*, ii, 138. Persano, 89.

in the flank; and after a fierce hand-to-hand mêlée, in which the
Paladin barely escaped being cut down by a cavalryman's sabre-
stroke, they were so worsted that but few of them succeeded in
returning to Milazzo. Finding his operations hampered by the
tall reeds, which prevented his seeing the enemy, Garibaldi rowed
out to the gunboat *Tüköry*, anchored a mile off-shore, climbed
a mast and surveyed the field. After bringing the *Tüköry* so far
inshore that a broadside from her took a Bourbon column by
surprise and shattered it, he landed and concentrated his attack
on the town. The afternoon was wearing away. Bosco's lieutenants had lost heart, while Garibaldi's brigades, having reformed, felt a fresh appetite for victory. They assailed the chief
gate of the town, and chased the defenders, very willing to go,
up the straggling street into the citadel. At five o'clock Garibaldi was the victor. His losses bespoke the tenacity of his men:
out of 4000 engaged, 750 were killed or wounded; of 82 Genoese
Carabineers, only 32 were left.[63] The Neapolitans, who fought
much under cover, alleged that they lost only 40 dead, 83
wounded and 21 prisoners. They also claimed that Bosco had
brought only 1500 men into action.[64] These numbers are obviously too small to account for either the various engagements
or the result. Garibaldi estimated the Bourbons at 3000.

The next morning he summoned Bosco to withdraw: Bosco
refused unless he were allowed to take everything with him. His
telegraph wire being cut, he had to use the semaphore, and while
he was begging Clary to be allowed to surrender, the Garibaldians were deciphering his message.[65] In due season four men-of-
war entered the harbor, but, instead of attacking the Garibaldians, they embarked Bosco's troops and the garrison of Milazzo,
who, by the terms of capitulation, went out with their arms
and baggage and with the honors of war, leaving to Garibaldi
the fortress with its guns, ample munitions, horses and mules
(July 24). He was glad to be rid of the Bourbons so cheaply:
because to reduce Milazzo by siege would have been a difficult
job, requiring long delay, and, in case the place were reinforced,
involving possible reverses. Time being one of his chief allies,
he could not afford even to seem to be checked. At Milazzo he
delivered a telling stroke in the welding of Italian unity.

[63] Forbes, 100.   [64] De' Sivo, ii, 124–25.   [65] Forbes, 104.

On July 27 General Clary, commanding 20,000 Bourbon troops at Messina, wrote the King's Secretary: "Now Mr. Garibaldi wishes to amuse himself with me. Let him come. He will find me more than ready. I assure you that he will dance well!"[66] The next day Garibaldi's vanguard drove Clary's outposts from the environs of Messina into the citadel. On the 26th the main body of Garibaldians, under Medici, entered the city. On the 28th Clary signed a convention agreeing to withdraw his army from Sicily, but stipulating that until this could be carried out, his garrison should remain in the citadel, under bonds to keep the peace. This was Clary's war dance.

In Bosco's attempt at Milazzo the Bourbon Government hoped to recover prestige to weigh in their negotiations with Piedmont. After his interview with Cavour, De Martino reported those terms, which were very hard for Francis II to hear. The Neapolitans renewed their entreaties with the Emperor, who would gladly have given direct aid, if he could have induced England to join him. Failing in that, he tried to intimidate Cavour. Ambassador Talleyrand regaled the Prime Minister with more than one Tiresian warning: diplomatic rupture with the Northern Powers — possible destruction of Italian independence — a European war and an Italian revolution — the French diplomat conjured up one of these monsters after another. Then Cavour, who "had listened with emotion," replied: "If we were to do what is demanded, [the people of Piedmont] would throw us out of the window. The popularity of the King himself could not save him. Nobody in Italy would counsel me to accede, because nobody believes in the King of Naples. He will do what his father and grandfather did. The situations are identical, and we have experience to tell us what will happen. . . . This is not one of the most difficult positions I have been in, it is the most difficult."[67] Nevertheless, he consented to give another audience to the Neapolitan envoys, and on July 17 and 18, when Winspeare and Manna conferred with him, he received them courteously. They repeated the proposals made by De Martino ten days earlier, were even more profuse in good intentions, and they left no persuasion untried to induce Pied-

[66] De' Sivo, ii, 128.   [67] *Aff. Etrang.*, 1860, 153; Talleyrand to Thouvenel, July 16. Also, *Lettere*, iv, ccciv, *ff*.

mont to insist on an armistice and to guarantee the Bourbon dynasty in Sicily.[68] Before Cavour could hand his written response to the envoys, on July 22, news of Bosco's defeat at Milazzo reached Turin, and the envoys informed him orally that their Government had given up the Island.[69] Cavour announced to them that, although General Garibaldi was at the head of a separate government, the Piedmontese Ministers, in the hope of putting an end to civil war in Italy, had recommended to Victor Emanuel to advise the Dictator that he should suspend hostilities and refrain from crossing to the Mainland.[70] Cavour made it clear not only that the King could exert only a moral influence, but that His Majesty held himself unpledged in case the King of Naples should fail to recognize the Sicilians' right to choose their own lot. That Cavour expected any result except a gain of time is unlikely: but to him, as to Garibaldi, time was invaluable. "I have had the entire diplomatic corps, except Hudson, on top of me," he wrote Emanuel d'Azeglio that same day. "But I let them talk, and I shall stop only before fleets and armies."[71] The Neapolitan envoys lingered on in Turin, although they saw the prospect of the alliance fade away.

On July 27,[72] Count Giulio Litta Modignani delivered to Garibaldi the letter in which, after disavowing absolutely any connexion with the expedition, Victor Emanuel said that, if Francis II should evacuate Sicily and carry out his promises, "it would be more reasonable for us to give up every ulterior movement against the Kingdom of Naples. If you are of a different opinion, I expressly reserve for myself entire liberty of action, and I refrain from giving you any suggestion in regard to your plans."[73] This was the document intended for publication. Privately, Count Litta conveyed a message with a different ring. "Now, having written as King, Victor Emanuel suggests to you to reply to him nearly in this sense, which I know to be his. To say that the General is full of devotion and reverence for the King, that

---

[68] Neapolitan memorial of July 20, 1860; *Lettere*, IV, cccvii, *ff*.

[69] *Ibid*, cccviii.   [70] Bianchi: *Politique*, 375; July 23, 1860.   [71] *Ibid*.

[72] Guerrini, 13–15, for Litta's account of meeting Garibaldi at Messina.

[73] Text in *Lettere*, IV, cccxi, *ff.*; dated Turin, July 22, 1860. Bandi, p. 252, quotes this version of the letter. Mario: *Garibaldi*, I, 252–53, prints a variant version. Guerrini, 38–40, shows almost conclusively that both these are apochryphal. On p. 7 he gives Litta's abstract of the King's genuine letter.

he would like to follow his advice, but that his duties towards
Italy do not permit him to pledge himself not to succor the
Neapolitans if they appeal to his arm to free them from a Gov-
ernment in which loyal men and good Italians cannot have trust.
To be unable therefore to follow the King's wishes, desiring to
reserve fully his own liberty of action."[74]

Cavour wrote at the same time to Persano: "I hold that the
fate of the Bourbon dynasty has been sealed by Providence,
whether Garibaldi accepts the advice offered, or refuses to follow it. I request you therefore not to attempt to influence his
decision. . . . You have done and will do well to keep on the
best terms with the General Dictator. I advise you, however,
not to trust unreservedly in him. Remember that he has lived
many years in America, and more still in solitude. So he has
contracted habits of excessive reserve and general diffidence. He
is sincere in his affection for the King, but he loves him in his
own way. He wishes to unify Italy, and that is well; but I fear he
intends to employ very dangerous means. Nevertheless, so long
as he is in the least reasonable, the King's Government must
go along with him. I shall try my utmost to bring this about.
I would not hesitate a moment to retire, in order to facilitate
the establishing of perfect harmony between Garibaldi and the
Ministry: always provided that he would not act madly." [75]

Garibaldi replied at once in a famous note which merely
embellished the laconic sentences the King sent him to copy.
"Your Majesty knows," he wrote, "with how much affection
and reverence I am filled for your person and how much I long
to obey you. However, Your Majesty ought to understand in
what embarrassment a passive attitude to-day would place me
in the eyes of the people of the Neapolitan Continent, whom I
have been compelled to rein in so long a time, and to whom I have
promised my immediate support. Italy would call me to account
for my passivity, and would suffer immense injury from it. At
the conclusion of my mission I will lay at the feet of Your Majesty the authority which circumstances have conferred upon me,
and I shall be most fortunate in obeying for the rest of my life."[76]

[74] Guerrini, 43; facsimile on p. 33.   [75] Persano, 99; C. to Persano, July
23, 1860.   [76] Stor. Doc., VIII, 318; Garibaldi to V. E., Milazzo, July 27,
1860. For confusion of dates, see Guerrini, 43. L. Rava: "Documento Capi-
tale," Corriere della Sera, Jan. 30, 1911.

Both letters, which were merely blinds, looked well in print. The King's was so skilfully worded that Diplomacy could not pick a flaw in it. The fanatical anti-Cavourians, however, cited it as a further proof of Cavour's hatred of Unity. Being in Garibaldi's confidence, and knowing the real purpose of the letter, their imputation against Cavour was unusually shameless.[77] The unprejudiced saw that it might just as well be construed as an encouragement to Garibaldi to go ahead; and no one who knew him doubted that he would do so.

Cavour had already changed his mind as to the invasion of the mainland. On July 25, with the news from Milazzo still fresh, he wrote Persano to present Garibaldi his sincerest congratulations: "After so splendid a victory, I do not see how he could be prevented from crossing to the Continent. It would have been better if the Neapolitans had completed, or at least begun, the work of regeneration; but since they will not, or cannot, move, — room for Garibaldi! The undertaking cannot remain half-finished. The national flag raised in Sicily must travel up the Kingdom, and push on along the coasts of the Adriatic until it floats over the Queen of the Sea. Prepare therefore to plant it with your own hands, my dear Admiral, on the bastions of Malamocco and on the towers of St. Mark's."[78] Nothing could better illustrate Cavour's open-minded statesmanship than this apparent change of front. At each stage of this drama, we shall understand his action if we remember that he was guided by two cardinal motives: first, to prevent the Revolution from swamping the Monarchy; and next, to make sure that whatever was won should benefit Italy. Hence, he had not checked the sailing of the Thousand, because to have done so might have stirred up civil feuds more injurious than the Expedition could possibly be. And when Garibaldi, by taking Palermo, held Sicily in his grasp, Cavour urged immediate annexation, in order to secure Sicily to the Kingdom of Italy beyond the risk of loss in an unsuccessful battle, besides lightening the pressure of Diplomacy and stemming the torrent of

[77] Victor Emanuel's *open* letter was originally misprinted with the date *June* 23, instead of *July* 23. Tivaroni, Mario, Bandi and other Republican writers build upon this wrong date a characteristic series of motives for Cavour. In general, their respect for dates and accuracy is slight.

[78] Persano, 101–02; C. to Persano, July 25, 1860.

Revolution. So long as this seemed the utmost attainable, Cavour labored for annexation, and would not have shrunk from blocking the Straits of Messina to Garibaldi. But La Farina proved an irritant instead of a peacemaker; the better class of Sicilians were agreed on annexation, but did nothing; Garibaldi, controlled more and more by the Republicans, went forward, openly professing that not Sicily but Rome was his goal. The victory of Milazzo added so much to his prestige that the danger from thwarting him had increased tenfold. The point had been reached where the Revolution might overflow, if Cavour attempted then and there to dam it up. He was too wary to commit that fatal blunder. Had he forced the issue just after Milazzo, the Garibaldians would probably have declared Sicily independent, and Victor Emanuel's Government could neither have sent an army to subdue them, nor have decently joined the Bourbon King, if he had proposed to reconquer the Island. At the same time, every patriot in North and Central Italy, were he Monarchist or Republican, would have denounced the Ministers for their anti-National policy. Riots were certain to follow: perhaps civil war. And there was Austria impatiently watching for such a chance, in order to win back Lombardy for herself and to restore the Pope and the fugitive Dukes in Emilia and Tuscany. While a doctrinaire would have clung fast to the formula "no crossing before annexation," Cavour recognized that this formula had failed, and that the new combination of events called for a new handling. To persist in his failure, would strengthen the Revolution, and lessen the chances of unifying Italy under Victor Emanuel.

He determined, therefore, to postpone to the last moment the life-or-death grapple with the Revolution, seeking meanwhile so to control the new conditions that there need be no war to the knife. The attitude of England gave him immense support in this decision. Lord John and Palmerston were slowly recovering from the distrust which his apparent insincerity had aroused in them. Hudson saw him at all hours, knew his staggering difficulties, discussed possible remedies, and never doubted that Cavour's statements were true. Hudson's beliefs and observations, communicated to his chiefs in London, carried great weight. Although the British Ministers saw in them not merely

2

a reason for encouraging the Italians but also a confirmation of their deep-rooted suspicion of Napoleon III, they chose to act in concert with the Emperor, so long as he stood by their policy of non-intervention. After the capture of Palermo, they would have been satisfied to have Sicily declared autonomous under a Bourbon prince; not because they desired the perpetuation of the Neapolitan dynasty for its own sake, but because they feared that if the Revolution spread to Naples, the unification of Italy would necessarily come next; then the united Italians would attack the Austrians in Venetia, and be forced to appeal to Napoleon III for succor. In that case, there must either ensue a general war, or Italy, shorn of more territory, would be completely subservient to France. To destroy this series of possibilities at their beginning, Lord Russell favored Napoleon's suggestion that English and French fleets should intercept Garibaldi if he attempted to cross the Straits. The Emperor had his special reasons for not wishing the Garibaldian Expedition to invade Terra Firma: he feared the destruction of the Bourbon throne, and, above all, he feared that any jar might precipitate the Roman Question upon him. Great was his surprise when on July 25 he learned that Russell had informed Persigny that England declined to oppose Garibaldi's passage, lest such interference might cause a counter-revolution. Russell intimated that the army and navy of Naples, if loyal, ought in any event, to be able to protect Francis II from invasion; and that, even if the Revolution should triumph there, Garibaldi would certainly not attack Rome while the French garrison occupied it, and the Piedmontese would not be so foolhardy as to attack the Austrians in Venetia unless Napoleon III abetted them.[79] The Emperor was upset by this news. Who had turned Lord John Russell from his purpose? Cavour was the culprit; he worked so privately, that his method was not published for many years.

Having decided that Garibaldi must not be stopped at the Straits, he lost no time in disposing Diplomacy to that end. It was essential to get England's concurrence; but England, he knew, was half pledged to France to interfere. He could not approach the British Foreign Office directly, because that would be

[79] *Correspondence;* Russell to Cowley, July 26, 1860; Russell saw Persigny the day before.

tantamount to admitting, what he had consistently denied, that
Piedmont had an official connection with the Garibaldian Expedition. Then he bethought him of Giacomo Lacaita, a trust-
worthy Neapolitan gentleman, who had lived in exile in London
and was on intimate personal relations with Lord John and Lady
Russell. To him Cavour telegraphed the need. On July 25[80]
Lacaita drove without delay to the Foreign Secretary's. When
the flunkey told him that his Lordship was engaged, Lacaita
replied, "Then I must see Lady Russell." "But her Ladyship
cannot be seen; she is in bed, ill." "Never mind, take up my
card." The astonished flunkey obeyed, and two minutes later
Lacaita was explaining to her Ladyship that to block Garibaldi might ruin Italy and kindle a European war. Lady Russell
took in the peril, and summoned Lord John, who was conferring
downstairs with Neapolitan agents. Lord John was somewhat
surprised to see the grave Lacaita, wrapped in the black mantle
which Italian bandits wore in opera, standing at the foot of his
wife's bed. On learning the cause of the visit, Lord John shook
his head. He had half given his promise to Persigny, he said,
and besides, Garibaldi must be stopped, or the Revolution would
break beyond control. Lacaita urged, argued, entreated. Lady
Russell seconded him. She recalled how her father, Lord Minto,
had suffered remorse during his last years because he failed, at
a critical moment, to support the Italians. She bade Lord John
to avert a similar sorrow; but he still shook his head, declared
that he could not change his policy, and left the room. On his
way downstairs, however, turning the matter over, he perceived,
as by a flash of inspiration, that his wife and Lacaita and Cavour
were right. When Persigny called to draw up a formal agreement, Lord John told him that Her Majesty's Government had
concluded not to forbid Garibaldi's passage.[81] If France, he
added, decides singly to interpose, 'we shall limit ourselves to
disapproving of her conduct and to protesting against it.'[82]
But France was too discreet to take this risk.

[80] The date was either July 24 or 25.   [81] P. Villari in *Albo Commemo-*
rativo del Gran Re Vittorio Emanuele II (2d edit., Bologna, 1884), pp. 77–83.
I have heard the story, with additional details, from Senator Villari himself;
who had it from Hudson, and he from Cavour and Lacaita. The first printed
account of the episode is in Fagan's *Panizzi*, ii, 207; where will be found a
notice of Lacaita. See also *Lady John Russell*, London, 1911.

[82] *Correspondence;* Russell to Cowley, July 26, 1860. Also *Lettere*, iv, cccxx.

On July 30, the London *Morning Post* published the translation of a letter, dated "St. Cloud, 25th July," from the Emperor to Persigny. Napoleon assumed to perfection the rôle of a virtuous man whose neighbors persisted in calumniating him. They thought him warlike, but he desired peace; he was above all, and had always been, eager for England's friendship. He grieved that his motives in taking Savoy and Nice had been misunderstood. No thought of territorial aggrandizement seduced him: he had flung away ambition. Great conquests he had still to make — but they were in France, where he must organize his Empire morally and socially, and develop its languishing internal resources. He chafed at the conspiracy of distrust which misconstrued all his acts, and maligned all his motives. "To sum up," he said, "this is my innermost thought. I am anxious that Italy should obtain peace, no matter how, so that I can withdraw from Rome, and that foreign intervention may be averted." [83] This letter went ricochetting over Europe, startling everybody, and no one more unexpectedly than the French Foreign Minister, M. Thouvenel, who had had no inkling that the Emperor intended to write it. Talleyrand, laboring at Turin in behalf of Naples, was dumbfounded; the Neapolitan envoys themselves, though floored, divined that it meant that Napoleon intended to throw Francis II over. [84] Cavour rejoiced, for he saw in it the Emperor's approval "of the program of Unity." [85] As the time approached for Garibaldi to cross the Straits, three essential points had been gained: non-intervention; a passage unhindered by either France or England; and the official sympathy of the British Ministers for Italy. For three months Cavour had stood between the Garibaldians and Europe.

Difficult as this task was, that of dealing with the Revolution itself exceeded it. Bertani and his helpers at Genoa adopted an independent attitude. The initiative, as Mazzini kept preaching, had passed to them. They were cunning enough to act on the assumption that the Government, already involved in the Expedition of the Thousand, would not dare to interfere with the great popular movement, and that Napoleon III, snared as an accomplice by the cession of Nice and Savoy, could not attack

---

[83] London *Morning Post*, July 30, 1860; reprinted in Martin, v, 154–56.
[84] *Lettere*, iv, cccxxi.   [85] *Lettere*, iii, 322; Aug. 9, 1860.

Italy. From his sickbed Bertani directed operations with amazing vigor.[86] A surgeon himself, he knew that fourteen or sixteen hours a day of racking labor, compounded of mental fatigue, physical weakness and worry, were no medicine for the gastric catarrh which gnawed him: but he could not be persuaded to desist. If he died then, he was giving his life for his cause as surely as if a bullet found him in battle. His devotion and activity deserve admiration; not so the venomous spirit in which he worked. The virtual dictatorship which Garibaldi conferred upon him brought out his latent fanaticism. His old comrades found his arrogance hard to bear. Even Mazzini, who was constantly pouring the virus of intransigence into his mind, could not conceal his chagrin that the Disciple presumed to dictate to the Master.[87] He treated Bertani with almost abject deference, as if he had reason to foresee that in a fit of irritation Bertani might send him to the devil. Once Mazzini, after making suggestions, remarks that he hopes that he may still venture to consider himself a partner in the enterprise. So was the mighty fallen! And yet Bertani was risking everything to carry out Mazzini's pet project of attacking the Papal States and Naples. When we remember how much those men had suffered from hope deferred; how bad a school exile was for teaching them breadth of view, tolerance and generosity; how painfully the charge rankled that they, who were conscious of dedicating all they had and were to patriotism, aimed at destroying Italy; how the thought galled them that the Monarchy, which they insisted had not only not helped but had done its utmost to hinder, would step in and claim the kingdom which they had redeemed — we cannot wonder that they were as implacable as hornets, as merciless as steel. Had they been otherwise, they would have belonged with Washington and Lincoln for generosity, and not with Cassius and with Cato.

Bertani recruited volunteers, collected funds, arms, and uniforms, secured with the aid of Cowen, Ashurst and other Eng-

[86] Saffi (Mazzini: *Scritti*, XI, xc) sums up what was done in three months, chiefly under Bertani's direction.

[87] "If I *venture* to give you advice," Mazzini writes (*Scritti*, XI, cxxi). Again: "Here is my advice for you — *which will not be followed* — but which from duty I give you." (*Ibid*, cxiv.) Again: "I too am so far involved in this affair . . . that I have the right to say something." Mario: *Bertani*, II, 157.

lish Friends of Italy [88] several vessels, and perfected his plan
of campaign. Two thousand were to cross from the Romagna
and as many more from Tuscany into the Marches and Umbria,
while 8000, embarking at Genoa, were to land on the Papal
Coast.[89] When Mazzini predicted that the Pope's subjects would
rise almost to a man to welcome the troops of Liberation,
Bertani seems to have shared this vision. Despising as riffraff
the polyglot Papal Army which Lamoricière had recently organized, they both assumed that the emancipation of the Pope's
dominion would render Naples, beset on the north by them and
on the south by Garibaldi, an easy achievement. Throughout
June and July, Bertani pushed these preparations with the air of
a dictator who wished to show that, on principle, he should pay
no heed to the Government at Turin. The Revolution was in the
saddle: the Monarchy, if docile, would be allowed to ride behind;
if it attempted to thwart or to control, it would be pitched off.
On the theory that the Monarchy rejected Italian Unity and, by
ceding Nice and Savoy, disclosed a fatal lack of both patriotism
and initiative, Bertani's procedure was logical; but fanaticism
blinded him to the truth. Even his friends called him rigid, narrow, exclusive: but he seemed to himself more than generous
towards the Monarchists, for he offered them harmony — if they
would allow him to carry out his projects undisturbed.

When Cavour made it plain that the King's Government, so long
as it existed, must be master, which was, indeed, the condition
indispensable for creating Italy, the Bertanians sent up a howl
against him as a fomenter of discord. Still we must not forget
that the sectaries regarded themselves as models of self-abnegation and conciliation, although at the very time when they professed concord to be their aim, they were as unyielding as flint.
The conflict was, indisputably, irreconcilable. Yet the loving
Saffi expatiates on Mazzini's self-effacement as not merely extraordinary but unique: had he not held in abeyance his Republican creed, and allowed Piedmont to prosecute the campaign in
1859? Had he not stayed his hand that autumn when by a signal
he could have roused the Papal States and Naples, and have
distracted the inchoate Kingdom of Upper Italy by civil war?

[88] Through W. Ashurst they sent 100,000 lire. Mazzini: *Scritti*, xi, cxxi, n. 1.
[89] Pianciani gives the most detailed account of the preparations.

So great was his self-abnegation that he had even suffered the monstrous betrayal of Nice and Savoy to be consummated, and permitted his followers to serve with Garibaldi, in spite of the Paladin's watchword, "Italy and Victor Emanuel." Having sacrificed his dearest principles so many, many times for the sake of Patriotism, as Saffi says, what wonder that he and his disciples believed that he was the embodiment of conciliation? When, however, history asks dispassionately what would have happened if Mazzini had taken the opposite course in each of these cases, the answer is, Nothing different. Mazzini could no more prevent Piedmont and France from fighting Austria than the fly in the fable would make the wheels of the chariot run backward. At the beginning of 1859, when his influence was sinking beyond recovery, he was sufficiently adroit to graft himself on to the National movement. His disciples, Crispi and Pilo, fanned the flame in Sicily; but one and all admitted that without Garibaldi nothing could be done: and when the time for action came, Crispi and Bertani, the ablest of the Mazzinians, threw in their lot, as became the keen, practical men they were, with Garibaldi. A blunt Cavourian might have silenced the lauders of Mazzini's supposed fanatical allegiance to principles, by asking for a single instance when Cavour, from boyhood up, ever sacrificed a principle which he professed to hold as fundamental. Zeal for zeal, which was more loyal—the Statesman who, having declared that Italy could be redeemed only through the Monarchy, never wavered in working by the Monarchy; or the Agitator who, having preached that Italy could be united only by a republic, let his republican principles lie dormant, at the prompting of expediency? The key to Mazzini's conduct in 1860 is found in his secret avowal in 1859, that the Mazzinians must capture and use Garibaldi.

So at Genoa during the early summer, Bertani pushed forward his project for invading the Papal States, according to Garibaldi's written directions. Mazzini, chafing at playing second fiddle to Bertani, conspired for a raid into Umbria, to be led by Nicotera, Pisacane's brave lieutenant, recently released from the dungeon of Favignana. Bertani took no pains to keep up appearances: he seemed rather to wish to appear absolutely indifferent to what the Government at Turin proposed; but when the test came, he learned that he was not above the law. Cavour retaliated on the expulsion of La Farina from Palermo, which the Mazzinians had instigated, by refusing to have further dealings with Bertani.[90] Next, he forbade the sailing of other expeditions from Genoa. Those already under way, with reinforcements destined for Garibaldi, were allowed to proceed. The Bertanians, supposing Cavour afraid, laughed at his prohibition. They had difficulty in finding a commander for their forces. Medici, a real soldier, on whom they counted, refused, preferring to join Garibaldi in Sicily: and as a punishment, Bertani to the end of his life vilified Medici, who, be it said, was more than able to ward off abuse. Cosenz too, another trained soldier, led his legion to Palermo. Bertani at last persuaded Charras, a French incendiary, to take command; and when he failed to appear, Pianciani, a violent Red, accepted the task. On August 1, Farini, by Cavour's orders, had an interview with Bertani, telling him decisively that the Ministry would not allow an expedition against the Papal States to sail from Genoa. Bertani hurled recriminations; accused the Ministry of lack of patriotism, and tauntingly declared that force alone could stop the revolutionary movement. "Do you want to resort to it?" he asked. Farini replied that the King must decide that, but that Cavour would resign sooner than consent to the sailing of the expedition. As a way out, he suggested that the Bertanians, having assembled at some point in Sardinia, should proceed thence to Sicily. From Sicily, over which the King's Government exercised no jurisdiction, they could go wherever they chose.[91]

"A terrible day was that first of August to me!" Bertani acknowledged later. He might play the dictator to the top of his bent so long as Cavour did not interpose: but when Cavour spoke, he knew how hollow his own bravado was. His sole hope now was to persuade the King, who had constant secret relations with the other leaders of the Revolution besides Garibaldi, and was more friendly than Cavour to their projects, — partly because he disliked Cavour, partly because he did not yet realize fully the risk of giving a free hand to the Revolution, and partly

---

[90] *Lettere*, vi, 568; C. to Magenta, Vice-Governor of Genoa, July 10, 1860: "You will furnish no more to the agents of Garibaldi, without a precise order from the Ministry."   [91] Mario: *Bertani*, ii, 150.

because he envied anybody who was actually fighting for Italy. Still, the King shrank, however unwillingly, from deserting the Prime Minister on a vital question. He sent word to Bertani to hold back the movement in the Romagna, because France would not stand passively at Rome while Italians were overturning the Papal régime. The Roman States would be redeemed, he hinted, by freeing Naples: but he would permit no expedition to set out, except for Sicily. Bertani, nearly frantic, was compelled to yield. Thus Cavour, at whose right to safeguard the Kingdom of Upper Italy he had arrogantly sneered, saved the Peninsula from imminent intervention by the French Emperor. Bertani's volunteers, to the number of over 5000, embarked quietly at Genoa and Leghorn for Terranova, on the Gulf degli Aranci, on the northeastern shoulder of Sardinia. Some 2000 more, who had been recruited in Tuscany, waited under Nicotera near the Umbrian frontier.[92] On August 8, Bertani himself, perplexed and full of wrath, slipped away from Genoa to confer with Garibaldi.

On the back of a telegram dated August 5, Count Trecchi jotted down in pencil the following memoranda, "dictated by V[ictor] E[manuel] to be reported to General Garibaldi." "Garibaldi in Naples. According to opportunity he will regulate himself, either to have Umbria and the Marches occupied with his troops, or by letting the volunteer corps go. As soon as Garibaldi is in Naples he will proclaim Union with the rest of Italy as in Sicily. He will keep the Neapolitan army intact, because Austria will shortly declare war. Allow the King of Naples to flee, or, in case he were taken by the people, defend him and let him flee." [93] We have no report of the date when Trecchi communicated this to Garibaldi: but such a message, together with that brought by Litta, simply adds to the amazement with which posterity reads the reiterated falsehoods of Garibaldi and his associates that the King's Government did all in their power to prevent the passage to Terra Firma. There is no doubt that Cavour knew of the Litta letters, and he probably knew of this message.

The sure way to Rome lay through Naples. For weeks, Cavour had been hoping that a revolution there would anticipate

<hr/>

[92] Mario: *Gar. Supp.*, 314, letters of Sanfront and Bensa, July 30, 31. Pianciani, 155 *ff*. Pianciani estimates the entire force at 8940 men.

[93] Trecchi, 426. This memorandum is dated " Bagni di Valdieri, 1860."

the possible invasion by Garibaldi from Sicily or by the new legions collecting at Genoa. The Neapolitans, however, hung fire.
Their Committee of Order,[94] of which Silvio Spaventa, Pier
Silvestro Leopardi and Mariano d'Ayala were the dominant
spirits, worked as openly as they dared to unite Naples to Upper
Italy. They plotted in the city itself; they fomented revolts in
the provinces. In rivalry with them, the Committee of Action —
Agresti, Albini, Libertini, Mignona — old Mazzinians nearly all
of them — were busy in behalf of the Revolution. Both bodies
agreed in endeavoring to rouse the country before Garibaldi's
arrival, and they had their reward in intermittent but inconclusive explosions. Cavour planned on a far larger scale. He hoped
to entice the Bourbon army, navy and government to achieve a
bloodless revolution, — an end to which Villamarina, the Piedmontese Minister, had long been intriguing. As the Bourbon
cause became desperate in Sicily, he redoubled his efforts to persuade Neapolitans in authority that the time had come when
patriotism as well as self-interest demanded that they should
join the National movement. Besides these appeals, Villamarina
had at his disposal money for bribing, and promises to the officers
of the army and navy that they should be cared for. For awhile,
these manœuvres seemed likely to succeed. Liborio Romano, the
reform Minister of the Interior; General Nunziante, a soldier of
great reputation under Bomba; and even the King's uncle, the
Count of Syracuse, were enlisted, more or less sincerely, in the
plot. Piedmontese agents reached Naples by almost every
steamer. Muskets and ammunition were sent down. On August
3, by Cavour's order, Admiral Persano anchored his flagship in
the harbor of Naples, under the shadow of the Castel dell' Ovo,
ostensibly to protect the Countess of Syracuse, sister of the
Prince of Carignano, in case of an outbreak; really, to act as
Cavour's executive agent.[95] To serve him in case of need he had
a detachment of Piedmontese bersaglieri stowed away in his
ships.

The aim of these intrigues was "to cause the National principle to triumph in Naples without the intervention of Gari-

[94] Reorganized on July 9.

[95] "When you wish to conclude," C. wrote De Vincenzi, one of his emissaries,
"go to Persano; when you do not wish to conclude, go to Villamarina." De
Cesare ["Memor"]: *Fine* (Edit. of 1895), p. 409.

baldi."[96] "Do not assist Garibaldi's passage to the Continent,"
Cavour wrote Persano on August 1; "but instead, try to delay
it by indirect means as long as possible."[97] "It is greatly to be
desired," he wrote Villamarina, "that the liberation of Naples
shall not come about through Garibaldi's work; because, if that
happens, the Revolutionary system will take the place held by
the constitutional monarchical party. If the Dictator reaches the
capital in triumph, the Revolution, anarchy, will take root, and
that will create a most unfavorable feeling in Europe. Add also
his crazy design of going to Rome, in spite of and against France.
That would be the complete ruin of the Italian cause. Hence a
National movement must occur in Naples before Garibaldi
arrives there. The attempt is hazardous; but it is necessary that
the Revolution shall not burst bounds in Naples."[98] Politically,
Cavour's reasoning was irrefutable: morally, his plot to overthrow the Bourbon government can no more be justified than
can the party of William of Orange in conniving at the overthrow of James II, or the American Patriots in plotting against
George III, or the European Legitimists in resorting to every
device for crushing Napoleon I. If we admit that every government, no matter how bad it may be, ought to be upheld, then
we must condemn any attempt, from inside or out, to destroy it.
If we believe, on the contrary, in the claims of patriotism, we
shall exonerate the motives of the Piedmontese and the Neapolitan Liberals; but without blinding ourselves to their methods,
which, like ambuscades and surprises in warfare, have no moral
sanction. "I should have much preferred," said Massimo
d'Azeglio, "an open conduct, rather than the use of so many
artifices, by which, after all, nobody has been duped."[99]

On Cavour's fiftieth birthday, the crisis seemed at hand.
While he was waiting impatiently at Turin for a telegram announcing the success of the great plot at Naples, Garibaldi in
the upper room of the Faro at Messina was deliberating where to
cross the Straits, Bertani was hurrying to confer with him, and
Mazzini, from his hiding-place in Florence, was cursing the
hand which held back the raid into Umbria.

[96] *Lettere*, III, 301; C. to Persano, July 30, 1860.   [97] *Ibid*, 305.   [98] *Ibid*, 300.
[99] Persano, 91; M. d'Azeglio to Persano, July 16, 1860.

CHAPTER XXXII

COLLAPSE OF THE BOURBON KINGDOM

EARLY in August the great drama was nearing a crisis. At Turin, Cavour, having abandoned his impracticable idea of checking Garibaldi's passage to the Mainland, was intriguing to superinduce a revolution at Naples, and while he labored to screen Garibaldi from foreign interference, he meditated a new plan for preventing the Revolution from overwhelming Italy. The last Bertanians had sailed from Genoa, but not for the Papal Coast, in spite of Bertani's high and mighty purpose to ignore the Government. At Naples the Bourbon King was beginning to perceive that the advent of a so-called Liberal Ministry had not exorcised the Demon of Revolution. Napoleon was trying to formulate a North by South policy which should please England over the Channel without sacrificing French prestige across the Alps.

Day after day from his outlook in the light-house tower, Garibaldi scanned the Straits of Messina with his field-glass. At its narrowest point the channel is scarcely two miles wide. Just opposite the Faro, the ancient Charybdis, the small town of Scilla rests upon a shelf-like ledge. Above it, the Calabrian coast slopes away in purpled outline to the northeast; below it, the shore trends southeast; and as the Sicilian coast recedes towards the southwest, the Straits grow rapidly broader. It is as if Vulcan had riven the Island from the Mainland by a wedge, the narrow end of which cut the outlet between Scylla and Charybdis. The imposing range of Aspromonte, whose highest peak falls just short of 7000 feet, forms the toe of the Boot: a wild and for the most part uninhabited region, furrowed by purple ravines, and meeting the water in steep slopes or sheer cliffs. There are few havens, and no large harbors. The towns are few; the villages cling like barnacles to the rocks, or fringe the sandy beaches.

Garibaldi studied every wrinkle in the Calabrian Coast, which

to him and his men was the Promised Land. He watched the
ebb and flow of the currents in the Straits, those perilous currents into which the Sirens lured unwary mariners in Homeric
days. Unlike Ulysses, he did not stop his ears to their enchant-
ing song, with its burden "Come over! come over!" But a score
of Neapolitan vessels patrolled the eastern shore, troops occupied the forts and barracks, and watchmen were stationed along
the desolate stretches. At length, on the night of August 8
he despatched 200 picked men under Musolino and Missori to
surprise the fort of Altafiumana, opposite the Faro. They crossed
silently, evaded the patrol and landed safely. But a false alarm
caused some one to fire his gun, which put the Neapolitans on
their guard, and obliged the Garibaldians to take to the mountains. There they easily maintained themselves, too nimble to
be caught by the Bourbon regulars, and they began to draw
bodies of Calabrians to their camp. Three nights later, Castiglia
attempted a second crossing with four hundred men: but the
Neapolitan cruisers discovered him, and he was forced to put
back. Nevertheless, the first step had been gained.[1]

To Garibaldi, just risen on the morning of August 12, Bertani
appeared unexpectedly. "You are Providence!" exclaimed the
Paladin to his Alter Ego full of gall. Then he listened to Bertani's report, approved of everything, and doubtless in his
explosive fashion discharged a volley of oaths at Cavour. Having performed his task with extraordinary energy, Bertani felt
that his Chief must now decide. There is a strong presumption
that he hoped to persuade Garibaldi to postpone attacking the
Bourbons in Calabria in order to lead the Bertanian legions
against the Papal States. Bertani, Mazzini and their Extremist
cronies would have had Garibaldi quit Sicily a month earlier,
after the Bourbons evacuated Palermo, and hurry forward the
invasion of Umbria and Latium, so obsessed were they by this
project. But he knew better than they that, until the Island was
secured, his departure might bring the Bourbons back. Now,
however, having possession of every important place except the
Citadel of Messina, he was ready to listen to Bertani. That very
forenoon he and Bertani sailed away on the *Washington*, leaving

[1] Guerzoni: *Garibaldi*, II, 153–54. Garibaldi: *Memorie*, 373. Forbes, 129. Bordone, 290–95.

no whisper as to their destination. The army, bivouacking along the strand from Messina to the Faro, was mystified, and in a day or two, when the telegraph had spread the news, Europe watched to see where this latest melodramatic stroke of the Paladin would hit.

On the voyage, the two had eager discussions. According to Bertani, Garibaldi agreed to captain the expedition. The Ministerial requirement, that the troops must touch some point in Sicily before proceeding, gave him no trouble: his only question being whether to fall like a thunderbolt on the Roman coast, or on the Neapolitan. "I say nothing," Bertani writes; "I cannot see any difference. I study the map of Italy and see her unity completed wherever Garibaldi may land."[2] Garibaldi himself, however, leads us to infer that he deliberately played a trick on the Bertanians. His fortnight's watch at the Faro had taught him the desirability of securing a larger force before he invaded Calabria: and when Bertani told him of seven or eight thousand well-equipped men chafing for action, he quickly resolved to appropriate them to his own use. He had no intention that another expedition, sufficiently large to be formidable, should operate in the Papal States, or elsewhere, except under his control. Much as he professed to trust Bertani, he still regarded him as Mazzini's man at heart: many of the volunteers were avowed Republicans; if they succeeded in freeing the Pope's dominion and the adjacent Neapolitan provinces, they and their leader, Mazzini, would justly claim equal glory with the Garibaldians in Sicily, and would demand an equal voice in determining the form of government when the day of reconstruction should come. "Mazzini, Bertani, Nicotera, etc.," Garibaldi writes in his Autobiography, "without disapproving our expeditions in Southern Italy, thought that diversions ought to be made in the States of the Church, or against Naples! or perhaps they felt repugnance to submitting themselves to obey the Dictatorship. In order not to run counter entirely to the strategic idea of those gentlemen, the thought came into my head of taking myself those 5000 men, and with them attempting a sudden stroke against Naples."[3] With his usual disregard of truth, the Paladin ignores the fact that on July 30 he had written Bertani: "Concerning

[2] Mario: *Bertani*, ii, 168.   [3] Garibaldi: *Memorie*, pt. iii, chap. 11.

N'ayant pas eu le plaisir de vous trouver
a Londres, et doutant fort que vous reveniez
dans cette ville avant que je la quitte,
je voudrais bien pouvoir vous rencontrer
quelque part pendant le tour que
je vais entreprendre dans le nord de
l'Angleterre et dans l'Écosse vraiment
je ne saurais me consoler si je devais
quitter l'Angleterre sans avoir eu le
plaisir de vous serrer la main

C'est pourquoi je vous prie de me faire savoir où je pourrai aller vous chercher dans les premiers jours d'août. Je n'ai pas préparé d'itinéraire de mon voyage en Suisse, ainsi je puis le combiner de façon à vous rencontrer d'ailleurs vous m'aurez fixé un rendez-vous.

Croyez, mon cher Monsieur, à mon sincère dévouement

C. Cavour

Londres 1. Regent Street
19 juillet 1852

the operations in the Papal and Neapolitan States, push them to the very utmost."[4] He conveniently forgets that before embarking for Marsala, he had impressed upon his lieutenants that those operations were an integral part of his plan,[5] and that by starting Zambianchi on his wild-goose chase, he had himself pointed to the goal he expected his followers to reach. His extraordinary triumph in the intervening three months changed his outlook. In mid-August he was prepared to welcome all the help that "those gentlemen," the Mazzinians, would give him; but he insisted that they should act under his command. There should not be a divided allegiance, or conflicting counsels, or two Paladins. In other words, Garibaldi adopted towards Mazzini and the Republican Extremists the very policy which Cavour pursued towards him and the Revolution.

Early on August 14,[6] the *Washington* steamed into the Gulf degli Aranci to find there four vessels with 4000 volunteers. Bertani and Garibaldi learned with rage that the *Torino* and *Amazon*, with the remaining 2000, had been ordered to Palermo by the commander of the Piedmontese gunboat *Gulnara*.[7] Garibaldi used this as an excuse for giving up the proposed descent on the Roman or Neapolitan littoral. *Four* thousand men would be too few — although he had expected to command only *five* thousand — and too much time had been lost — although when he sailed from the Faro he must have known how long it would require for him to go to Terranova and thence to the Mainland. Obviously, he was not prepared to disobey the Government's condition, that the Bertanian expedition must touch first at some Sicilian port; he must also have realized that the eager Bertanians would on all accounts be safer under his own command. So he reviewed them, roused their enthusiasm by one of

[4] Ciàmpoli, 168. This letter did not reach Genoa till Aug. 15. The delay has not been explained. Doubt has been cast on the genuineness of the letter, but another, written by Garibaldi to Ricasoli on the same day, did not reach Florence till Aug. 19. Ricasoli, v, 171, n. 2. Pianciani, 147 *ff.* On p. 152, he says that he read this letter himself.   [5] Garibaldi to Bertani, May 5, 1860; Ciàmpoli, 141; to Medici, *ibid;* to Finzi and Besana, *ibid*, 143.

[6] On Aug. 14, C. telegraphed Persano that the Bertanians, having promised to go to Sicily, were in the Gulf degli Aranci, with the probable intention of landing on the Papal coast — "which would ruin everything." As a precaution, C. ordered the *Monzambano* "to those waters." Persano, 139.

[7] Pianciani, p. 310, states that the force intended for Terranova numbered 8940 men.

his stirring harangues, and, having bidden them to obey Bertani, he sailed off for a few hours' distraction at Caprera. Returning, he put in at Cagliari, where the Bertanians had arrived. He gave instructions for them to follow, and proceeded to Palermo, and on without delay to the Faro, only to learn that Nino Bixio intended that very night to attempt a passage from the beach of Giardini, below Taormina. Having ordered Sirtori to make an ostentatious feint from the Faro and Messina, the Paladin jumped into a carriage and with joy in his heart drove at top speed the thirty miles to Bixio's camp.[8]

Bertani's legions were incensed at seeing their expedition thus diverted from the objective for which they had volunteered. Of all Garibaldi's acts, this was the one they were least disposed to forgive him.[9] Their resentment was natural: because now, instead of enjoying the prestige of an independent corps, with whatever glory they might win, they were simply another division of the Garibaldian army. To their questions, Bertani replied laconically: "We shall go where, when and how Garibaldi shall command." Though trembling with anger, they kept silent; for they knew that, whatever their preference, their fortunes depended on Garibaldi. When they disembarked in Sicily, they heard no more of an invasion of the Papal coast or of surprising Naples, but they were summoned by Garibaldi to join in his attack on Calabria. At this order, Pianciani, their military head, resigned in dudgeon.[10] Almost simultaneously the attack on Umbria by the Mazzinian troops under Nicotera was prevented by Ricasoli, whom they accused of breach of faith.[11] With further exasperation, the Party of Revolution read the warning issued on August 13 by the Minister of the Interior, who announced that the Government would tolerate no more the private recruiting of volunteers or launching of expeditions against friendly states, and he declared, with too evident harsh-

---

[8] For the Bertanian side, see Mario: *Bertani*, chaps. 16 and 17, and Pianciani. In general: Garibaldi: *Memorie*, pt. iii, chap. 11. Mario: *Garibaldi*, ii, 246–49. Bordone, 297–310. Guerzoni: *Garibaldi*, ii, 154-60. Bandi, 260–62. Forbes, 123–24, 134–38. [9] Guerzoni: *Garibaldi*, ii, 157. [10] In accepting Pianciani's resignation, Garibaldi assured him that he had not given up his plan against the Papal States; but often, he said, one can accomplish more with 2000 men than with 10,000. Meanwhile he discreetly appropriated the 6000 Bertanians for his own use. Mario: *Bertani*, ii, 170. [11] Mario: *Nicotera*, 34–47. Mario: *Bertani*, ii, chap. 13. Pianciani, *passim*. Ricasoli, v, *passim*.

ness, that "Italy must belong to the Italians, and not to the sects." [12] Thus as the Revolution was preparing to invade the Mainland, the Italian Government took pains to disavow connexion with it.

On the strand of Giardini, Garibaldi found Nino Bixio, who, having traversed the Island and suppressed as best he could some atrocious anarchical outbreaks among the Sicilians along the way, had been waiting for days in a frenzy of impatience for orders to embark. He had with him the *Torino*, a screw steamer of 700 tons, and the *Franklin*, a paddle boat of 200 tons, which together might safely accommodate two thousand passengers. Nearly four thousand [13] Garibaldians, however, stowed themselves like sardines into these vessels. Late in the "dark and fitful evening," well suited to their adventure, the *Franklin* and the *Torino*, having weighed anchor, laid their course to the east. Just before daybreak they prepared to run inshore near Melito, the very tip of Calabria. But here, as at Marsala, Bixio's ship grounded, and although when Garibaldi came up with the *Franklin*, he did his utmost to tug the *Torino* free, she still stuck fast. Without thought of his own peril, the Dictator quickly put his helm about and steered straight for Messina in search of tow-boats. He had not gone far before two Neapolitan cruisers, the *Aquila* and the *Fulminante*, bore down upon him. He hoisted the American flag, which caused them to refrain from firing, while he steered landwards and disembarked his forces. The cruisers, discovering the *Torino*, bombarded her at short range, and then set fire to her: but Bixio had already sent all his men ashore, seized the telegraph office and started northward. Garibaldi followed, having cut off his retreat by ordering the *Franklin* back to Messina.

But retreat was no more in Garibaldi's thoughts than in those of a hound on the scent of a hare. His amazing success in Sicily inspired him with a belief, which his followers shared, that he was invincible. The public of two hemispheres regarded him as a sort of demi-god, while the Neapolitan soldiers, and even more their officers, felt a superstitious dread of him. And yet his descent on Calabria, though less foolhardy than his Marsala

[12] Text in Bordone, 308–10.
[13] Forbes, 148, says that the *Torino* took 3000 and the *Franklin* 1200.

2

landing, was highly audacious. True, he had nearly 4000 men, and 12,000 more were encamped on the Sicilian shore, waiting for their chance to cross: but the Bourbon troops in Southern Calabria numbered at the lowest estimate 20,000, they held several fortified places and the lines of communication, and they were supported by some twenty ships, large and small, which could easily be concentrated at any point along the coast. To these odds Garibaldi paid as little heed as to the spasms which Diplomacy might suffer at his daring. Happy as a Scottish chief to be once more in the saddle, he led his men a long day's march over difficult paths to attack Reggio. A strong citadel defended the town, and reinforcements under Melendez and Brigante were hurrying to aid its garrison. At daybreak on the 21st Garibaldi and Bixio, with Musolino's column, now commanded by Missori, tried to take the Bourbons by surprise; but they were on the alert, and held out till midday. Having captured Reggio, Garibaldi hardly gave his men time to breathe before pressing on to meet Brigante. During the night of May 21-22, Cosenz crossed with part of his division to Scilla. A few hours later Brigante and Melendez, finding themselves hemmed in and unable to make their men fight, surrendered. Europe was again amazed to hear that Bourbon regulars, equipped with arms, artillery and the outward trappings of soldiers, gladly submitted to "shirtless" adventurers. "From that day," writes Guerzoni, "the melting away continued with the terrible swiftness of putrefaction." [14] Each night saw Garibaldi a stage nearer Naples —his march being not so much an invasion as a triumphal progress. As the passage of the Straits was now no longer barred, the troops he had left in Sicily crossed over and hastened to catch up with him; volunteers from the North flocked to his standard; and a few recruits came from the Neapolitan provinces, where revolts instigated by Cavourians and Revolutionists alike had broken out in many places. But the Bourbon soldiers, who threw away their arms and ran, could not be persuaded to enlist under him. He had expected that they would welcome the first opportunity to exchange the service of Tyranny for that of Liberty: but there was no patriotism in them; nor even manliness. They dispersed over the country in robber

[14] Guerzoni: *Garibaldi*, II, 163.

bands, — terrorizing, stealing, outraging, slaying, — true exponents of Bourbon ideals. But the Liberator swept on towards the capital, with the victorious rush of a torrent in springtime.[15]

At Turin, meanwhile, Cavour was beaten against by conflicting gusts of opinion. Ricasoli kept urging him to assert the primacy of the King by extreme measures. Victor Emanuel's prestige, he said, would be halved if he accepted Sicily from Garibaldi, and everyone would declare that Garibaldi ought to be king himself.[16] "I will never suffer," he wrote, "that any other principle shall rise up in Italy save that which embodies itself in the King."[17] "Better war than anarchy!" was his motto. He could not tolerate the idea that anybody should have permission to be bold, except the Representatives of the Nation, the constituted Authority itself.[18] Victor Emanuel ought to be the real Garibaldi. "If Garibaldi lands at Salerno, the [Bourbon] King will probably flee; in which case, one of [Victor Emanuel's] Generals, . . . followed by troops of the Italian Kingdom, must quickly seize, provisionally and dictatorially, the government of the city and kingdom of Naples. At the proper moment, a civil government can be set up composed of native Neapolitans. . . . We need a *coup d'état* after Napoleon's pattern. . . . This is not the time for scruples; this is the time for saving Italy."[19] Three days later, Ricasoli returned to the charge and begged Cavour to have done with Diplomacy. "You possess very great genius," he said, "and must see that the time for fighting by means of genius alone is passed." The King's Government must regain its authority at home and abroad, and escape from the toils of Diplomacy. "They are already prophesying the downfall of Count Cavour," he added.[20] The next day he bids Cavour to face Diplomacy's menaces, "and to expose all to a war with one power or with three, but save us from the Garibaldian anarchy."[21] When such a sober man as the Iron Baron emulated Danton in urging audacity! audacity! evermore audacity! we can infer that the Revolutionists did not enjoy, as they supposed,

[15] Guerzoni: *Garibaldi*, II, 159–65. Garibaldi: *Memorie*, 375–80. Bandi, 262–69. Bordone, 317–22. Mario: *Garibaldi*, I, 256. Forbes, 148–57.

[16] Ricasoli, v, 161–62; Ricasoli to C., July 15, 1850.

[17] *Ibid*, 162; July 16, 1860.   [18] *Ibid*, 172; July 31, 1860.   [19] *Ibid*, 173.

[20] *Ibid*, 177; Aug. 2, 1860.   [21] *Ibid*, 180; Aug. 3, 1860.

a monopoly of zeal. Cavour listened gladly to his urging, although he saw that the real problem was how to be bold successfully. "Garibaldi's doings have produced in him the greatest exaltation," he wrote of Ricasoli to Gualterio; "he would like to have the Government surpass in audacity the Dictator of Sicily, initiate uprisings, organize revolutions — in a word put down (*soverchiasse*) both Pope and King of Naples by proclaiming the unity of Italy. He writes and writes again, and telegraphs day and night to goad us on with counsels, notices, reproofs, I would almost say with threats. I hope that he will calm down; otherwise I don't know how we can get on, because we are resolved to be bold, even audacious, but not foolhardy or crazy. The Italian movement follows a determined course; in desiring to hurry it one runs the risk of ruining it completely."[22] Reading between the lines, we suspect that Cavour, while professing to be embarrassed by Ricasoli's importunities, really took this means of informing Gualterio — and through Gualterio many others — that the Cavourian policy, which the conservatives were censuring as too bold, was condemned by Ricasoli as too timid.

Lanza also, a man of deliberate decisions, found fault with Cavour for lack of courage and frankness. The Prime Minister, he said, ought to have prevented Garibaldi from becoming so powerful as to menace the existence of the Monarchy; and he ought to have declared war openly on the King of Naples. Lanza did not state how either of these suggestions could be sagely carried out; he simply asserted that the danger from increased diplomatic tension would have been less than from the formation of a Revolutionary army in the South.[23] Massimo d'Azeglio, always a dilettante in politics, threw up his position as Governor of Milan, although at that crisis any defection from the Liberal party must do harm, especially the defection of a veteran like Father Massimo, whose early reputation as a patriot followed him as luminously as its tail follows a comet. But he refused to serve a government guilty of duplicity towards the King of Naples and guilty of allowing Mazzinian volunteers, under the transparent mask of Garibaldians, to enlist in Lombardy.[24]

[22] *Lettere*, iii, 317; C. to Gualterio, Aug. 8, 1860.
[23] Tavallini, i, 245, 246, 247, 249.
[24] M. d'Azeglio: *Politique*, 168; D'Azeglio to Rendu, Sept. 22, 1860.

Massimo seems to have supposed that Cavour was simultaneously the witless dupe of the Revolution and the Bourbons, of Napoleon III and the Pope.

While others were criticizing, Cavour was working like a Titan to set off the military revolution at Naples. Necessary as it was to forestall Garibaldi, it was not less certain that, unless the Neapolitans showed a determination to embrace the National Movement, they would not profit by the expulsion of the Bourbons. "Who would be free, *themselves* must strike the blow." [25] He acted on the assumption that, provided a large proportion of the better element in Naples desired to be Italians, he needed only to place a ladder at their prison window, and they would come out of their own accord. Even a revolution in which the natives were steered from outside would serve. The obvious instrument was the Bourbon army: let that issue a pronunciamento and raise the Italian flag, and the Kingdom would support it. So Cavour's agents were busy persuading, and tempting. But before an army goes over to the enemy, it must know what it has to expect. Cavour therefore authorized his agents to promise to the officers similar rank in the Italian service and to incorporate the privates in the Italian army. Money was offered and accepted. To those who hesitated, the alternative to desertion was emphasized: since the Bourbon Kingdom was doomed and United Italy was sure to be established, those Neapolitans who had not seized their opportunity could look for no employment under the new Kingdom. In short, patriotism coincided with self-interest to impel them to secede. The annals of political ratting — whether it results in the restoration of a Charles II or the coming of a William III — are never savoury. In this case, Cavour had no qualms at hastening by underhand means the revolution which he regarded as inevitable; he saw only the patriotic need of having Naples emancipate herself and vote for union with the Kingdom of Italy, before the Garibaldians, borne along with their torrent of revolutionary discord, should flood the capital.

On July 30 Cavour telegraphed Admiral Persano to proceed to Naples,[26] where, with Villamarina, he was to carry through the proposed seduction. "We are at the end of the drama," the

<hr>

[25] Byron: *Childe Harold*, II, 76.   [26] Persano, 105.

Prime Minister wrote. "The moment is critical." Persano replied that he had "a hard bone to gnaw," but that he would do his best.[27] Arrived at Naples, he seems to have spared no effort. Cavour sent down bersaglieri, money, arms and various emissaries. General Nunziante, formerly the merciless instrument of Bourbon tyranny, now accepted the inducements offered him to become Italian, and went secretly to Naples to win over his former troops.[28] Liborio Romano, the new Minister of the Interior, a gentleman of easy virtue, while still serving Francis II, saw no difficulty in promoting the plot. The King's own uncle, Count of Syracuse, made no secret of his collusion. The Committee of Order, which avowedly existed to spread Unitarian doctrines, became bolder, whilst its rival, the Committee of Action, pushed its mines for a Republican upheaval. Among the officers and crews of the Bourbon navy, and among the civilians of the administration, the Cavourians plied their powers of persuasion. In the night of August 11, Piola, commanding Garibaldi's ship, the *Tüköry*, made an unsuccessful attempt, in collusion with Persano, to surprise a Bourbon ship, the *Monarca*, at Castellamare, and to precipitate a stampede of desertion.[29] On August 15 General Nunziante reached Naples incognito. Two Italian generals, Ribotti and Mezzacapo, in whom Cavour had confidence, arrived there. Emilio Visconti-Venosta, one of the ablest of Cavour's younger aides, who had begun his career as a Mazzinian, suddenly appeared, to energize the project, bringing with him Finzi, Director of the Million Muskets Fund; "eminent patriots, both of them," Persano thought, "and of serious and valid operosity." Nisco, an unpolluted Neapolitan Liberal, worked with them. Still the yearned-for military revolt hung fire. Persano's marines on shore leave provoked a street brawl, but nothing came of it. On the 19th news of an outbreak at Potenza, and of the Basilicata in a ferment, brought cheer. The Count of Syracuse read Persano the draught of a letter he was sending the King, urging him to retire. Still the pronunciamento lagged, although bundles of proclamations had been printed. The next day the report from the provinces showed that the insurrection was spreading. Liborio Romano, the reform minister, grew bold and

[27] Persano, 106. [28] *Lettere*, vi, 578. De Cesare: *Fine*, ii, 329.
[29] Persano, 137–38.

wrote in plain terms to Francis II, assuring him that the situation
had become untenable, the State being honeycombed by plots
and discontent on the inside, and menaced from without by the
National movement. Romano advised the King to absent himself for some time from the Kingdom, to appoint a ministry to act
as his regent, and to announce to his subjects that he wished to
save them from the horrors of civil war.[30] On the 21st the telegraph bore the death warrant to the Bourbon dynasty: "Garibaldi has landed at Melito with 4,500 men."[31] To the Cavourians, that message acted as a final spur. Visconti-Venosta advised
sending arms to the insurgents to enable them to harass the
Neapolitan armies in the rear, while Garibaldi assailed them in
front: the arms were sent. A last desperate effort to provoke the
revolution in the capital failed.

But the Neapolitans, while refusing to join the Italian Party,
had no thought of supporting Francis II. Such a disgrace of
desertions as he witnessed during the last week in August and the
first week in September has rarely been recorded. It was rather a
slinking away, than an overt change of sides. Upon the miserable
King were visited the sins of his fathers. Their long régime of
corruption, in which their chief ally had been the Church, had so
debased the Neapolitans that there was no manliness, no sense of
honor, nor even the recognition of the ordinary family and social
ties in them. The kings had sown deceit, injustice, cruelty,
fraud; the priests had sown bigotry and superstition hardly less
crass than the fetish-worship of the Papuan. Kings and priests
alike had gloried in the 90,000 lazzaroni who polluted Naples,
because they could be held in check by the sleight of liquefying the
blood of St. Januarius ; they not merely winked at the Camorra,
they had filiations with it. And now, at the day of reckoning, the
people, who had been thus deliberately depraved by their temporal and spiritual guides, proved themselves the degenerates they
were bred to be. The courtiers melted away. Some of the more
conspicuous officials resigned. One — the martial General Bosco
— had a timely attack of sciatica. Every steamer bound north
took a crowd of despicable fugitives. When the Ministry resigned, the King could get no one to replace them. Falconi,
Ulloa, Gigli resolutely said no: the hour of dissolution had come,

[30] Text of Romano's letter in Persano, 152-56.   [31] Persano, 157.

and neither they nor any other notables would compromise themselves by serving as official pall-bearers to the dynasty.[32] The King's kinsmen — his half-brother, Count of Trani, and his uncle, Count of Trapani — threw up their commissions; while the Count of Syracuse, dallying with the seductions of the Italian Party, in which he saw hope of aggrandizement for himself, addressed to Francis the above-mentioned letter in which, having declared that the doom of the dynasty could not be averted, he implored his royal nephew to make "a sublime sacrifice" and retire from the Kingdom. Europe and his subjects would bless, God would reward him![33] Another uncle, the Count of Aquila, having plotted with the reactionary Camarilla to compel the King to abdicate and to appoint himself regent, had already taken to flight.[34]

Every hour the telegraph brought news of Garibaldi's triumphal advance, and told how the Bourbon troops vanished before him, without firing a shot. Francis knew that the regiments garrisoning his own capital, the sentries at his door, the very guards who escorted him, were faithless. "If Europe does not want him," said De Sauget, one of his officers, "why should we let ourselves be killed for him?"[35] Francis listened to one adviser after another, but did nothing. He seems to have been cognizant of the plot of the Clergy to organize a second Saint Bartholomew, in which the Liberals should be massacred,[36] but whether he approved or not we do not know: for, although his ears listened, his mind was dazed and his will numb. When aged Carrascosa, with laudable bravado, said to him, "Mount your horse, and we will all follow Your Majesty; we will either fall like brave men, or pitch Garibaldi into the sea!" the King did not rouse. From long dealing with phantoms, he was incredulous of any reality. He had only too much reason to suspect that the Minister, who spoke so valiantly, would bow himself out of the room with protestations of devotion, and return no more. The Bourbons from sire to son for generations had exploited the evil in mankind; now their miserable descendant was punished by a monomania of suspicion and distrust, which left him powerless to discern the good.

[32] De Cesare: *Fine*, II, 357.   [33] Text of letter, dated Aug. 24, 1860, in Persano, 164–65; English translation in Whitehouse, 382–84.   [34] The details of Aquila's conspiracy are still veiled. De Cesare: *Fine*, II, 358. Whitehouse, 274–77.   [35] De Cesare: *Fine*, II, 350.   [36] Whitehouse, 277.

He gave no sign of motion except to vacillate. The Bourbon dynasty in dissolution cumbered the shore of the beautiful Bay of Naples, like the carcass of some sea-monster, putrefying in the sun.

But in spite of this rottenness, which had become a stench in the nostrils of Europe, the National Revolution failed to materialize at Naples. Miscalculating the depth of degradation to which the Neapolitans had sunk, Cavour supposed that they were really so disgusted with the Bourbon régime, that, as their leaders assured him, they needed only a push from the outside to rise up and destroy it; in truth, however, the number of high-minded Neapolitans ready to run any risk, much more to sacrifice themselves for any cause, was pitifully small. Poerio, Settembrini and their patriot band of 1848–49 did not represent their countrymen; neither did Spaventa and his handful of zealots in 1860. The great mass of the people of the capital were inaccessible to ideals, Patriotism meant nothing to them. They had the Camorrist's instinct for dishonest gain, the lazzarone's content with the sensual moment. The ignorance of the upper classes was incredible. Intelligence among the bourgeoisie commonly took the form of cunning. Even those who would have preferred a decent government had suffered too cruel a disillusion in 1848 to care to venture their safety in another attempt. They would wait warily, evade taking a stand that might commit them, and be prepared to hurrah for the winner. The officers of the fleet and army who found Cavour's inducements agreeable, felt no immediate hurry to carry out their part of the contract; for possibly Diplomacy might step in and save the Bourbon King: then where would be their profit? On the other hand, further delay might bring them another crop of inducements. Cavour wronged them, by imputing to them that residual sense of honor which is supposed to exist among thieves. Like Garibaldi and Mazzini, he had enormously overestimated the influence among them of the saving remnant who, intelligently desiring to be freed from Bourbon tyranny, were willing to risk a drop of blood for the sake of patriotism. It has been said that revolutions cannot be made to order; it would be more correct to say that they require proper material and leaders. The Neapolitans had neither. The Party of Action probably contained most of the violent conspirators, but they were working to welcome Garibaldi, rather than to cause an upheaval in advance of his coming; and their propaganda conflicted with that of the Cavourians.

Cavour at Turin must have wished himself at Naples, where, as he believed, a resolute man could have accomplished the task. On August 12 he telegraphed Persano to prevent the Party of Action from seizing Francis II;[37] he would have no orgy of bloodshed after the French fashion. On the 16th he announced the crisis as at hand.[38] Three days later he urged the Admiral to "go ahead."[39] On the 20th he hoped that the insurrection in the Neapolitan provinces would ignite the explosion in the capital.[40] In response the Admiral's despatches described superhuman difficulties, amid which he, like Hercules, was toiling undismayed.[41] On August 23 he telegraphed: "Great softness here. If anything is done, it is because I tug them by the hair."[42] His bulletin of the 24th had a different sound: "I act with calm and poise to such a degree that I hold in whoever would go too fast."[43] That same day Cavour instructed him to protect the passage of the remainder of Garibaldi's troops — which protection Garibaldi had asked for — but to save appearances. He added: "This Government begins to be tired of the hesitations and backslidings of the Neapolitans, in whose behalf it is compromising itself."[44] Persano inclined to criticize Villamarina for losing himself in parleying.[45] The moments sped fast; still the revolution balked. There was talk, in case the King should leave Naples, of making Persano dictator, but he rightly foresaw that, though this might free them from the Mazzinian danger, it would embroil them with Diplomacy. He advised, therefore, using the Count of Syracuse as the "symbol."[46] Cavour replied affirmatively; but suggested that, at a pinch, Finzi or Visconti-Venosta might serve.[47] In case of revolution, he bade Persano to take possession of the Neapolitan fleet and fortresses, in order to control the movement.[48] If this "does not happen before Garibaldi's arrival," wrote Cavour, "we shall be in a very grave fix. But we shall not be at all troubled on that account."

[37] *Lettere*, III, 326; C. to Persano, Aug. 12. [38] *Ib.*, 331, to Ricasoli; and 332, to Cassinis, Aug. 12. [39] *Ib.*, 339; to Persano, Aug. 19. [40] *Ib.*, 340; to Persano, Aug. 20. [41] *Ib.*, 342; Persano to C., Aug. 21. [42] *Ib.*, 343; Persano to C., Aug. 23, 2.30 P. M. [43] *Ib.*, 344; Persano to C., Aug. 24, A. M. [44] *Ib.*, 344; C. to Persano, Aug. 24, noon. [45] *Ib.*, 345; Persano to C., Aug. 25, 1 P. M. [46] *Ib.*, 346; Persano to C., Aug. 26, 1.30 P. M. [47] *Ib.*, 346; C. to Persano, Aug. 26, 5.50 P. M. [48] *Ib.*, 346, 347, 394; C.'s despatches of Aug. 26 and 27.

He gave minute directions as to swearing in the Neapolitan Marine, issuing commissions, and taking steps to prevent anarchy from breaking out at the capital. Whilst this message was going to Naples, Persano was sending to Turin one in which he regretted to report that their party had become inert, while the Garibaldians had the upper hand, and that he therefore recommended that the Cavourians should attempt to direct the Garibaldians instead of pursuing their own listless policy.[49]

At last Cavour realized that his efforts at Naples were hopeless. Nothing now except accident could prevent Garibaldi from entering the capital, and with him the deluge of Revolution would pour in. Still Cavour was not dismayed, for he held in reserve one plan in which he trusted. He had, indeed, considered the advisability of adopting a very different means, as this letter to Nigra shows: "To call the Chambers together and deliver a great parliamentary battle would be mightily to my taste. But I am persuaded that even though I should succeed in saving my prestige I should ruin Italy. Now, my dear friend, I tell you without emphasis that I prefer to lose my reputation, but to see Italy made. To make Italy at this juncture, we must not set Victor Emanuel and Garibaldi in opposition. Garibaldi has great moral influence; he enjoys an immense prestige not only in Italy but above all in Europe. You are wrong, in my opinion, in saying that we are placed between Garibaldi and Europe. If I engaged in a struggle with Garibaldi tomorrow, it is probable that I should have the majority of the old diplomats for me, but European public opinion would be against me. And public opinion would be right, because Garibaldi has rendered to Italy the greatest services that man could render to her. He has given the Italians confidence in themselves: he has proved to Europe that the Italians know how to fight and die on the field of battle to reconquer their mother country. . . . We must not enter the lists against Garibaldi except in two cases: (1) if he wished to involve us in a war with France; (2) if he disowned his program, by proclaiming a different political system from the Monarchy under Victor Emanuel. So long as he is loyal to his flag we must act in accord with him."[50]

[49] *Lettere*, III, 348; Persano to C., Aug. 27.
[50] *Ibid*, 321–22; C. to Nigra, Aug. 9, 1910. Chiala heads this letter: "To an Intimate Friend," but there is little doubt that the friend was Nigra.

Three things appear from this letter: Cavour's perfect appreciation of Garibaldi's unique services; his own generosity; and his
patriotic self-abnegation. As a master parliamentarian, he might
well hanker after a forensic duel on ground where he felt sure of
victory: but his success might mean Italy's ruin, and he dismissed the plan — dismissed it, only to adopt another which, for
audacity, is quite as amazing as Garibaldi's expedition to Marsala. He would send an Italian army, commanded by the King,
to invade Umbria and the Marches, thence to push on into the
Kingdom of Naples, to beat the Bourbons, if they still had troops
in the field, and to come up with Garibaldi. Two compelling
reasons justified this policy. If the Monarchy, without lifting a
finger, should accept either Sicily or the Two Sicilies from the
hands of a free-lance and his comrades, it must suffer an irreparable loss of prestige. On the other hand, if Garibaldi should go
over to the Revolution, abandon the Monarchy, and declare that
the Southern Italians would establish a republic and govern
themselves, the presence of Victor Emanuel and his army would
check such secession at the start. The dangers were formidable.
Royal interference might exasperate the Garibaldians. The withdrawal of Italian troops from Emilia might cause the Austrians
to cross the Po. The presence of the French garrison at Rome
must complicate any violation of the Papal States. Napoleon
III, already displeased by the aggrandizement of the Italian
Kingdom, might forbid further expansion. But by far the most
delicate matter was the proposal to attack the Pope's dominion
at all: Europe, Christendom claimed an interest in that. Cavour
scrutinized the difficulties, one by one, as deliberately as a surgeon weighs the chances for and against a capital operation. Even
the possibility of a war with Austria failed to terrify him. "We
will all fight," he wrote to an intimate friend. "If I possessed the
military art as I possess the political, I would answer to you for
the result. After all, when a way has been proved the only one to
follow, we must not calculate the dangers it involves, we must
study the means for surmounting them."[51]

At what moment he conceived this, the master-stroke of all his
statesmanship, does not appear.[52] He communicated it to Nigra

---

[51] *Lettere*, III, 322.

[52] Many projects were broached during that summer. Towards the end of

at Paris and to Emanuel d'Azeglio at London on August 1 in an "ultra-confidential letter," which he bade them destroy in case they should absent themselves from their embassies.[53] On that very day, when Farini told Bertani that the Government would not countenance the volunteers' expedition against the Papal States, he hinted that the Ministers had decided on the King's intervention.[54] This was more than a month before Cavour decided to act. His plan was kept with such secrecy, however, that, when he sent Farini and Cialdini to bear the King's official greeting to Napoleon III, who had come to Chambéry for a few days, the public suspected nothing. The object and result of their mission Cavour himself described in a letter to Nigra on the 29th. "Farini and Cialdini returned this morning from Chambéry. The Emperor was perfect. Following Conneau's advice, Farini explained to him the plan we have adopted. Here it is in a few words. It is too late to prevent Garibaldi from reaching Naples and being proclaimed Dictator there. We must no longer fight on this ground; consequently, I have written Persano to content himself with seizing the forts and collecting the Neapolitan fleet and above all to act in harmony with Garibaldi. Being unable to forestall Garibaldi at Naples, we must stop him elsewhere. That will be in Umbria and the Marches. An insurrectionary movement is about to break out there; immediately, in the name of the principles of order and humanity, Cialdini enters the Marches, Fanti Umbria; they throw Lamoricière into the sea and take Ancona, while declaring Rome inviolable. The Emperor approved everything. . . . He said that Diplomacy would utter shrieks, but would let us go ahead; that he himself should be placed in a difficult position, but that he would put forward the idea of a congress. . . . It is essential that the result of Farini's interview be unknown; I shall say here that the Emperor washes his hands of the affairs of Italy, but nevertheless wishes us good luck."[55]

June, the Prince of Carignano suggested to Cavour that it would be well to profit by the trouble at Naples by sending a strong expedition. ,Vayra, 56. Prince Napoleon gave similar advice, and Cavour was quick to give the Prince the credit for it. *Ibid.* [53] Cavour: *Politique*, 379; C. to E. d'Azeglio, Aug. 1, 1860. [54] Mazzini: *Scritti*, XI, cxxx, n. 1; this is the statement of Saffi, who attended the interview with Farini. [55] *Lettere*, III, 353–54. French official statement, Oct. 18, 1860, in *Aff. Etrang.*, 162–63.

According to tradition, Napoleon dismissed Cavour's envoys with the words, "Do it, but do it quickly!"[56] French historians have endeavored to discredit Farini's report of the interview. They insinuate that the Italians, misinterpreting the Emperor, chose to assume, as usual, that his silence implied consent.[57] In all likelihood, however, Napoleon recognized that this plan was the fatal sequel to Cavour's "Now we are accomplices." He saw himself caught beyond escape in the toils of a dilemma. If Garibaldi came northward unchecked, the Revolution might overthrow the Italian Monarchy and spread to France, kindling a European War; if the Cavourian project succeeded, the vanity of the French would be wounded at the erection of a kingdom of 22,000,000 Italians on their southeastern frontier, while the desecration of the Pope's dominion would enrage Clericals all over Europe, but especially in France. Napoleon took the lesser evil. We need not be surprised that he railed against being forced to take it: men curse Nemesis, even in the act of submitting. Posing as the protector of the Pope, who stood for medieval authority and despotism, and of regenerate Italians, struggling for modern Liberty, Napoleon III was in an impossible position. Again, as so often in the course of this history, we see him trying to wriggle himself free from the consequences of a policy of lies. Having told Farini to "do it — but do it quickly," he gave vent to his annoyance by berating the Piedmontese. "I am broken-hearted," he wrote Arese, "at the conduct of your government towards Naples, for one is always very sensitive to the faults of one's friends; but, really, no honest man can approve a policy which has all the characteristics of weakness, that is to say, of ruse and duplicity. And then, whither will it lead? to another Novara?"[58]

Cavour telegraphed Arese to see the Emperor, and to describe the situation of Italy since Villafranca, as follows: "Continuous underhand war by Austrian enrolments at Rome and Naples. Alliance almost formed among the Pope, Austria and the Bour-

[56] *Faites, mais faites vite.* Balan, II, 221, says Napoleon's words were: "We understand each other; do not touch Rome; and above all make haste." Cantù's version (III, 479) is, "Destroy this rabble for me, and be quick about it."

[57] Cf. La Gorce, III, 405–09, Ollivier, 473–76.

[58] Arese, 267; Napoleon to Arese, St. Cloud, Aug. 20, 1860; Bonfadini gives the wrong date, Aug. 30. Cf. Dina, I, 329, n. 3.

bons. Very keen sentiment in all Italy of the danger of this league. After the cession of Nice impossible to hold Garibaldi back. Admit that the Government has tolerated and even supported him. But it has energetically prevented and repressed Mazzinian expeditions. Impossible to allow itself to be distanced by demagogy at Naples. As soon as the annexation is accomplished, we shall try not to attack either Rome or Austria. The Emperor will save Italy by preventing attack before spring. If need be, single-handed, we will fight Austria. We are sure that the Emperor will not destroy by a coalition the only ally of France. Explain that it is not at Turin but at Paris that we are blamed."[59] It would be hard to pack more into so short a despatch. Cavour drove deep into Napoleon's mind the fundamental facts, and then added suggestions which should tinge his interpretation of them.

The Emperor is believed to have given Arese benevolent assurances;[60] but even had he scolded, Cavour would not have drawn back. French historians, supposing that the object of Farini's mission was to ask the Emperor's consent, declare boldly that "a single word would have stopped the Italians: a 'no' very clear, very brief, very French. This 'no' was not said"; and they argue therefrom that, while "complicity" would sound too harsh, "weakness" would be too mild a term to describe the Emperor's conduct.[61] Cavour's purpose, however, was not to sue for permission, but to inform Napoleon of the Italian policy. Unquestionably, he desired Napoleon's goodwill; but he saw the situation so much more clearly than the Emperor did, that he was resolved to act at whatever cost. Without a friend in Europe, except Piedmont, Napoleon could not destroy the ally whom he had just supported in a great war. If he openly intervened against the cause of Liberty as symbolized by Garibaldi, he would have to reckon with the Revolutionists of France. England's sympathies were for the Italians; and English antipathy for the French Emperor had become a bond that now gathered Liberals and Tories, Victoria, Albert and Palmerston into one fold. The Germans, led by Prussia, would

[59] *Lettere*, III, 360–61; Aug. 31, 1860. Also, Arese, 267–68. Note that Bonfadini mixes the dates, putting Arese's interview *before* Farini's.
[60] Arese, 268.   [61] La Gorce, III, 408.

not shun a challenge to meet France on the Rhine. Even the Pope, to protect whom Napoleon was slowly undermining his own throne, despised him. Thus the consequences of his acts left the Imperial arbiter powerless to oppose by force the Italians' plan.

As a pretext to excuse trespass on Papal soil, Cavour encouraged uprisings among the Pope's subjects. The first splutterings occurred on August 28, after which the National Committees, in connivance with the Prime Minister, prepared for a general insurrection during the second week of September. Persano received instructions to take his fleet to Ancona;[62] two army corps were put in marching trim, and Cavour ordered Villamarina to inform Garibaldi at the earliest occasion of the King's project. The King himself, in whose veins the blood of twenty generations of fighting ancestors tingled, rejoiced at the prospect of smelling powder: not only his warrior instinct, but his pride rejoiced; for he realized keenly that in proportion as Garibaldi's prestige waxed, his own waned. He had not forgotten the taunts of a Republican, who said to him point-blank: "What have *you* done for Italy? Napoleon gave you Lombardy; Garibaldi is on the point of giving you Sicily; all the rest, they say, Cavour's ability has won for you. So you see I have reason to speak to you in this fashion."[63]

Whilst these plans were maturing in the North, Garibaldi, more scornful than ever of Diplomacy, pursued his triumphant way towards Naples. On August 30 at Soveria, General Ghio, without striking a blow, surrendered more than 10,000 troops to him. Melendez had already surrendered his forces near Palmi; Brigante's brigade, after its general had been slain by mutineers, melted away; Caldarelli's made common cause with the Garibaldians, and then disbanded, deserting his flag as quickly as it had deserted their King's; Vial capitulated at Pizzo.[64] Thenceforward, the Bourbons made no pretense of resistance; but their craven conduct does not lessen Garibaldi's merits. He was

[62] Persano, 194–96; C. to Persano, Aug. 31.

[63] Guerrini, 31. Victor Emanuel related this to Litta on Aug. 4, adding: " I replied, 'Perhaps it is as you say, but now there is one thing left for me to do and that is to have all you gentlemen shot.' " The Republican made his insult more pointed by addressing the King " you," instead of " Your Majesty."

[64] Rüstow, 286 *ff*. De Cesare: *Fine*, II, 351 *ff*. Revel: *Ancona*, 18.

swift and alert, and ready for any emergency. He could not be sure, when the enemy vanished before him, that they were not resorting to Parthian tactics, and that he must not face them in a great battle before he reached the capital. That plan, indeed, so attracted the bewildered Bourbon staff that they decided to assemble their still available forces, numbering at a fair estimate, 40,000 men, on the broad plain between Eboli and Salerno, and there to block Garibaldi's passage. But as the Liberator's vanguard drew near, their courage evaporated. One column of Garibaldians followed the coast, gaining time by using transports where they could; the main army, under Garibaldi, moved along the consular road; the right wing kept more to the east.

The consternation that reigned in the Royal Palace at Naples may well be exaggerated: because it is evident that Francis II, and the few who intended to stand by him, gave up all thought of defending the city of Naples from the moment they had news of Garibaldi's coming. The rumor that the King sent an agent to Garibaldi offering him the command of the Bourbon army and pledging his word to allow it to attack the Papal States and Venetia, although unfounded, illustrates the opinion of his subjects as to the Bourbon King's extremity and as to his loyalty. Learning by telegram on September 4 that 15,000[65] Garibaldians had landed at Sapri, Francis II held a council. Thereupon his cabinet resigned, and when he desired them to continue until he could secure their successors, they replied that there would be no successors. And so it proved. Five generals had been sounded, but not one would serve as Minister of War. General Ulloa, the King's last hope, also refused, to the great relief of all parties, because they understood that Ulloa would rather be besieged in the capital than retreat without contesting Garibaldi's advance. That same day orders were telegraphed to the generals at Eboli to abandon the battle which had been talked of, and to withdraw their troops to La Cava. On September 5, at a final Cabinet meeting, the King announced his purpose to retire to Gaeta, collect there his fleet, mass his troops at Capua and along the Volturno, and defeat the Garibaldians on a field of his own choosing. Meanwhile, he would protest to

[65] Fear magnified their number at least five times. Rüstow, 287. See Trevelyan, II, appendices, for discussion of numbers.

2

the universe against the outrage committed against his legitimate rule. "If Your Majesty sets foot outside of Naples," said
the aged Carrascosa, "there will be no return."[66] Having
screwed his will up to the point of making a resolution, the King
seemed to be light-hearted. He bade the heads of the National
Guards good-bye half jokingly, telling them that he left the city
"because your Don Peppino[67] — and *ours* — is at the gates."
He and his attractive young queen, Sofia Maria, — who had the
beauty, spirit and courage of her Bavarian kin, — drove in an
open carriage through the streets; smiling, bowing, in apparent unconcern at their calamity. Once, when their carriage was
stopped by a ladder, at the top of which stone-cutters were
chiseling out the Bourbon lilies from the sign of the Court Apoth-
ecary, the royal pair may have reflected on the fickleness of their
servants' devotion; but they laughed and passed on. At four that
afternoon the Ministers went to the Palace to take leave of their
sovereign. Francis was far from downcast. "Don Liborio," he
said in banter to Romano, "if I come back, look out for your
neck." The Minister replied that he certainly should.

That night and throughout the next day there was bustle in
the Palace as workmen and porters dismantled it of many valuable objects, some of which were loaded into waggons and
started for Capua, whilst others were sent aboard the *Delfino*
and the *Messaggero*, which were to convey the King to Gaeta.
Although he professed to expect to return soon, he prudently
carried off much booty; the Queen, less thrifty, left even her
wardrobe behind her. There came a dismal parody of the ceremony of kissing hands, at which hardly a score of persons attended. A few charwomen wept. About half past five that
afternoon, the King and Queen quitted the Palace by the winding staircase, crossed the quay, and in a few minutes were safe
on the *Messaggero*. Their departure was not exactly a flight, as
of fugitives in dread of assassination, or of thieves fearing arrest;
but it resembled both, rather than the departure of sovereigns.
This had been the favorite way of absconding with the Bourbons
ever since Louis XVI fled from the Tuileries. Francis II had
ordered the Neapolitan fleet to accompany him, but only the

---

[66] De Cesare: *Fine*, II, 367.   [67] *Ibid*, 368. "Don Peppino," a nickname
for Garibaldi. "Peppino" is the Italian equivalent of "Joe."

Partenope obeyed. Two Spanish men-of-war acted as his escort. The *Delfino*, with baggage and booty, was already out of sight, when, at six o'clock, the *Messaggero* steamed out of the Naval Harbor into the Bay. Before night fell, the last pitiful king of the dynasty which had reigned for 126 years, saw Naples for the last time. All things have an end — even governments which are a negation of God.[68]

The Bourbon beneficiaries allowed their King to depart as heartlessly as the Papal entourage of Gregory XVI left him to die alone while they scrambled to loot the Quirinal. The Neapolitans of all classes were too eager to see Garibaldi, to heed the fading out of Francis. The officials displayed wonderful promptitude in turning to the new régime. In a brief conflict between the two Committees, the Men of Action easily prevailed. Villamarina's hope of landing the Piedmontese bersaglieri, and, under the pretext of keeping order, of controlling the revolution for Victor Emanuel, collapsed noiselessly. High and low, the Bourbon placemen knew that Garibaldi was master: high and low, they played their cards to propitiate him. The Ministers despatched two officers that evening to greet the Dictator at Salerno. The next morning, Prince d'Alessandria, Syndic of Naples, and General de Sauget, Commander of the National Guard, followed thither to arrange for his entry. Garibaldi had already telegraphed to Don Liborio, who replied in a message "to the Most Invincible General Garibaldi": "With the greatest impatience, Naples awaits your arrival to salute you the Redeemer of Italy, and to resign into your hands the power of the State and its own destiny. In this expectation, I shall stand firm in preserving public order and tranquillity."[69]

The Prince and De Sauget gave so alarming a report of the condition of Naples that Garibaldi decided to go there at once. His intimates tried to dissuade him: for many regiments of Bourbon troops remained in the capital, and still occupied the town of Nocera, through which he must pass. But he feared a Cavourian plot at Naples more than all the Bourbons, and,

[68] De Cesare: *Fine*, II, 368–85. See p. 369, n. 1, for a list of articles "missing" from the Royal Palace. See also Clara Tschudi: *Maria Sophia, Queen of Naples* (translated by E. H. Hearn. London: Swan Sonnenschein & Co., 1905), chaps. 17–19, for a sympathetic description of the plucky Queen.

[69] De Cesare: *Fine*, II, 348.

accompanied only by his staff and the two envoys, he drove to
La Cava, then the terminus of the railway. Before his train
started the women and girls insisted on kissing him, an act of
adoration to which he was never averse. His journey was a triumph. The crowds at every station almost went mad with enthusiasm. National Guards perched on the tops of the railway
carriages, waving tricolor flags and evergreens. The tracks so
swarmed with human beings that the locomotive could proceed
at only a snail's pace.[70] At Portici the train stopped with a jerk,
and a breathless naval captain announced that, as the Bourbon
cannon were trained upon the Naples station, Garibaldi must
not go on. "Cannon, indeed!" the Dictator replied; "when the
people give such a welcome as this, there are no cannon. Forward!" And the train crept on into the city.

There a reception that baffled description awaited the Hero.
The open spaces and the avenues round the station, and every
street, lane and alley leading to it, were packed with people.
Ladies rubbed elbows with lazzaroni; Bourbons, Republicans,
Nationalists, policemen and Camorrists, National Guards,
Clericals, mere sightseers, and that great rabble which, like the
muddy scum on a freshet, is always present at Naples, lifted their
voices to cheer Garibaldi. A solemn deputation, with Romano
as its spokesman, formally received him on the platform.
Horses had been prepared for him and his staff to make a soldierly entry; but the crowd pressed so close that he found it
better to occupy an open barouche. Three of his comrades drove
with him, others followed on horseback or in carriages; and so he
made his way through the city, now standing, now sitting,
acknowledging salutes and cheers, or greeting by word or gesture
acquaintances whom he recognized, apparently unheeding the
stray detachments of Bourbon troops, and blind to the cannon on
the Castel Nuovo, whose muzzles glowered upon him as he came
up the Strada del Piliero to the Royal Palace. But the cannon
slept, and the Bourbon gunners, as eager as the rest of Naples
to catch sight of the Hero, peered over the battlements of the fort.
Instead of taking up his quarters under the roof which Francis II
had just quitted, he paused at the Foresteria, the residence of the
Queen Dowager. Later in the afternoon, he pursued his way

[70] Forbes, 232.

up the Toledo, the noisiest street in Christendom, now noisier than ever, and gay with banners and hangings at every balcony and window of its many-storied buildings. After visiting the Cathedral, where some say he witnessed the liquefaction of the blood of St. Januarius, he established himself in the Angri Palace.

In the great hall of the Foresteria, D'Ayala, surrounded by the notables of Naples, greeted the Hero in a speech as florid as a plot of petunias, but no doubt not less sincere than those gaudy flowers. He begged to be allowed to imprint a kiss on that forehead; and "this kiss," he said, "is the kiss of 500,000 inhabitants."[71] The Dictator's first official act was to transfer to Persano, in the name of Victor Emanuel, the navy, mercantile fleet, arsenals and naval munitions of the Two Sicilies. He appointed a provisional ministry headed by Liborio Romano (Interior), Cosenz (War), Pisanelli (Justice), De Cesare (Finance), Giacchi (Interior, under Romano), and Sauget (War, under Cosenz).[72] D'Ayala commanded the National Guard, which numbered only 7000 ill-equipped volunteers.[73] These appointments indicated an attempt to mix the oil of one faction with the vinegar of another, but the Monarchists preponderated. During the next two days Naples gave itself up to an orgy. Crowds gay or surly poured through the streets. Bands of ruffians masqueraded as patriots. Prostitutes of every class drove to and fro and challenged the politics of any one they met, and unless he shouted "Italy One," or held up the forefinger, the symbol of the Unitarians, they might strike at him with their daggers, which they carried openly.[74] Aristocratic ladies harangued the populace. The regiments of Bourbons marched unhindered out of the city, shouting "Long live Victor Emanuel! Long live Garibaldi!" as lustily as if they were Garibaldians. September 8 being the Festival of the Madonna of Piedigrotta, Garibaldi drove in a street-cab to the grotto and by his presence kindled the multitudes to the pitch of delirium. To the Neapolitans, with their surface passions and their infantile response to the stimulus of the moment, it was all one whether they cheered St. Januarius, whose blood they believed possessed magic virtue, or Garibaldi, who told them roundly that the blood and its liquefaction were the imposture of besotted priests.

[71] Ayala, 323.   [72] Persano, 224.   [73] Ayala, 332.   [74] Forbes, 237.

While Garibaldi's welcome by the populace would have honored an archangel, every hour impressed upon him the fact that he had plunged into a whirlpool. Two vital issues had to be dealt with: the immediate needs of Naples and the policy of the Revolution towards Italy. The provisional ministers, except Cosenz, having played their parts in Naples during the summer, were already found out. They represented, so far as weathercocks can be said to represent anything fixed, the Monarchical party. Liborio Romano alone among them was endued with unusual ability. An eel could not surpass him in gliding among rocks or in burrowing in mud; a compass does not follow a magnet more obsequiously than he followed his self-interest. He had that gift of protective coloration which enables politicians to survive a revolution, Among moderns, Talleyrand is the master of this species — Talleyrand who, in taking his last oath of allegiance, remarked sardonically, "This is the thirteenth." Don Liborio fell far below the Bishop of Autun in natural talents, in complete cynicism, and in opportunity; and he even preserved just enough self-deception to suppose that he acted from pure motives. He desired the good of the Kingdom. If that could have been attained under the Bourbon despotism, with him as chief minister, he would have stood by Francis II; when the upheaval began, and it seemed probable that Victor Emanuel would attract the votes of the Neapolitans, he turned to Turin for inspiration; when, however, Garibaldi outstripped the King, he idolized Garibaldi. The tale is ancient and always unedifying, — we expect so much more of patriots than of ourselves, — but this must be said to Don Liborio's credit, that throughout that distracting summer, when the Bourbon authority was paralyzed, he, as Prefect of Police, preserved order in the city. Thanks to his device of entrusting the policing of the capital to the Camorra itself,[75] neither riots, nor pillage, nor more than normal Neapolitan violent crimes, occurred.

But now Liborio Romano's eel-like proficiency would not serve. The Republicans who surrounded Garibaldi did their work without hesitation or circumlocution. These men, whom Bertani, General Secretary of the Dictatorship, led, had not conspired in Northern Italy, campaigned in Sicily, and conquered in Calabria,

[75] New York city imitates this practice when it puts Tammany in power.

to be put off by shifty politicians. They insisted that the Dictatorship should dictate. Within three days they harassed the Ministry so mercilessly that it offered to resign. Garibaldi refused to let them go, but he soon saw them reduced to insignificance. Don Liborio hoped by a phantom of constitutionalism to bridge the interval until the Kingdom of Naples should be annexed to Upper Italy. Garibaldi's advisers, on the contrary, desired for the present neither constitutionalism nor annexation. As a result of this conflict, anarchy flourished in Naples. Garibaldi himself, more and more occupied with preparations for destroying the Bourbon army encamped round Capua, gave little time to civil affairs, which always bored him. The administration fell quite naturally, therefore, into the control of Bertani and the Implacables; and under them, Naples became a cauldron of political rage, and Garibaldi's attitude towards Italy was determined. Confident in his own heart of his loyalty to Victor Emanuel, he maintained with equal stubbornness that it was for him and not for the Government at Turin to decide when he should resign his dictatorship into the hands of the King. Having assumed for months that he could do what the King wished to have done but was checked by Diplomacy from doing, he held, logically, that he knew better than the King himself what needed to be done. Accordingly, in his first interviews with Villamarina and Persano, he made no secret of the intention which he had been publishing for weeks of liberating the entire Peninsula before he hung up his sword. Having promulgated the Piedmontese Statute in Sicily and at Naples,[76] having turned over the Bourbon navy to Persano, having on all occasions declared himself the soldier of Victor Emanuel, he scouted the idea that the Republicans might lead him astray, or that the bond between his provinces and the Kingdom of Italy ought to be legalized forthwith.

On September 10 Mr. Elliot, the British Minister, met Garibaldi on board the *Hannibal*, and, after congratulating him on his marvelous exploits, told him that Lord John Russell hoped that no attack would be made upon Venetia. Garibaldi replied, with perfect frankness, that he intended "to push on at once to Rome, and when that city shall be in his hands, to offer the crown

[76] For Naples, in the decree of Sept. 14.

of an united Italy to King Victor Emanuel, upon whom will then devolve the task of the liberation of Venetia, and in which he would himself be but the Lieutenant of His Majesty. If this liberation could be accomplished by purchase or negotiation, so much the better; but if Austria would not voluntarily abandon the Kingdom, it must be wrenched from her by the sword; and he was confident, in the present humour of the Italian people, that the King could not decline the undertaking without the sacrifice of his whole position and popularity." Elliot pointed out the danger of such a course, and warned him that the English, who almost to a man applauded the Garibaldian achievements in the South, would turn against him if he threatened to involve Europe in war. Garibaldi dismissed the suggestion that an attack on Venetia would have any such result. "The Empire of Austria," he said, "was rotten at the core, and ready to crumble to pieces." Elliot then asked him whether he had considered the consequences of attacking Rome "and a collision with the French garrison, which must at once bring about the intervention of France in the affairs of Italy." But Garibaldi made as light of France as of Austria, "saying with vehemence that Rome was an Italian city, and that neither the Emperor nor anyone else had a right to keep him out of it." Whatever the risks, "he had no alternative but to go to Rome," an enterprise which he did not regard as very difficult. He spoke bitterly of Cavour, "who," he said, "by the cession of Savoy and Nice, had dragged Sardinia through the mud at the feet of France, of whom he was afraid." "For my part," added the General, "I am not afraid of her, and never would have consented to such a humiliation." [77]

The victorious Hero, whose recent exploits seemed to justify him in believing himself equal to every undertaking, would evidently not be dissuaded from the dizzy plan he unfolded to Mr. Elliot. When Villamarina confided to him Cavour's projected invasion of Umbria, Garibaldi showed at first real joy; but in a few moments, having reflected long enough for his suspicions to be aroused, he said: "If this expedition is aimed at drawing a cordon of defence round the Pope, it will produce the worst effect on the mind of the Italians." [78] Garibaldi's suspicion, like a drop

[77] *Correspondence*, 1861, vol. 67, pt. vii, 68–70; Elliot to Russell, Naples, Sept. 10; received, Sept. 17, 1860.　　[78] *Stor. Doc.*, VIII, 338.

of vitriol, soon corroded his heart; and near him were advisers, who, if he showed signs of wavering, knew how to play upon him. Bertani's ascendency was pre-eminent: Bertani, who had now hardened into a rigid fanatic, as logical, as immovable, as autocratic as Robespierre, with a talent for organization, and a gift of incisive thought and of decision which made him, by contrast, invaluable to Garibaldi. Unlike Robespierre, he preferred not to rely on the guillotine: but he never shrank from killing reputations by calumny or from sowing discords. He belongs in his later phase among the terrible Incorruptibles, who, because they lack broadness of vision and magnanimity, leave blight in their path. Zeal may act either as medicine or as poison. We cannot fail, therefore, to detect Bertani's influence in the note which, on September 11, Garibaldi sent by Trecchi to the King. "Sire," he said, "dismiss Cavour and Farini; give me Pallavicino Trivulzio for pro-dictator. Give me the command of one of your brigades, and I answer for everything."[79] To a correspondent, who apparently had urged him to harmony, he wrote: "You assure me that Cavour asserts that he is in accord with me and my friend. I can assure you that disposed, as I have always been, to sacrifice on the altar of the country every personal resentment, I cannot ever reconcile myself with men who have humiliated the national dignity and sold an Italian province."[80] Anger and vanity had branded the cession of Nice as indelibly on Garibaldi's heart, as remorse burned the damned spot into Lady Macbeth's distraught mind.

Garibaldi's perplexity was indeed maddening. He desired the liberation and unity of Italy; he accepted Victor Emanuel as his titular chief, the Monarchy of the House of Savoy as the government of the nation; but he would brook no control from Turin, and the Revolution, which was his weapon, desired either a republic or such a complete change of direction in the Royal administration that the Revolutionists themselves should dominate. In a word, Garibaldi's attempt to face both ways was as evident as that of Napoleon III whom he loathed, and the contradictions into which it betrayed him were unedifying. His appeal to Victor Emanuel to send Pallavicino as pro-dictator indi-

[79] Mario: *Bertani*, II, 208. Trecchi, 412, does not confirm that he bore the letter.
[80] Ciàmpoli, 181; Garibaldi to Brusco, Sept. 15, 1860.

cates that a crisis was at hand in his political arrangements. On coming to the Mainland three weeks before, he had left Depretis to shoulder the Sicilian burdens alone. That politician had, indeed, the velvet glove, but the times called for the iron hand. His course as pro-dictator typified that Transformism, or painless gliding from one party to another, which became the boast of his prime. He went to Sicily in July as the King's representative. Yet he spent the night before sailing from Genoa with Bertani, and the forenoon of his arrival at Palermo he spent with Crispi. His task was to appear to promote immediate annexation, in order to satisfy the Ministry at Turin, while keeping on the friendliest terms with Garibaldi, who would not hear of annexation. He found the Island in a shocking state. Garibaldi counseled him to limit his activity to unpolitical reforms; Cavour kept prodding him to hasten annexation. Garibaldi hinted that, when he himself deemed it necessary, he would decree annexation; Cavour insisted that the union must result from a plebiscite. Petitions for a plebiscite reached Depretis from all parts of Sicily: but wherever he moved, the shadow of Crispi fell across his path. Crispi ridiculed the apparent sentiment for annexation : the petitions, according to his partisans, were either paid for or forged. The Cavourians, on the other hand, charged Crispi with debauching the administration; they cited his intimacy with many well-known Bourbon renegades, and the propaganda of Republicanism and of Autonomism which he promoted. The historian has still too scanty testimony to pronounce a final verdict; but he can safely assume that Depretis and Crispi worked each after his kind, and that, as Crispi was far the abler, he was the more likely to outstrip his adversary. Depretis, at best, was a promising fox, while Crispi was a seasoned wolf. Neither had scruples; but Crispi, besides his superior natural talents, had a relentless singleness of purpose which made him more than a match for the time-serving Depretis. In the conflict between them, Depretis leaned with increasing weight on Cavourian support, until he came to work zealously for annexation. At Fortino, on September 4, he was so persuasive that Garibaldi said: "Annex whenever you will." Then Bertani, who was present, thrust in: "General, you are abdicating." Whereupon Garibaldi changed his mind.[81]

[81] Bertani: *Ire,* 73–77.

When Garibaldi crossed the Strait, Depretis's antagonism with Crispi, unchecked and undisguised, broke into open rupture. Crispi accused him of treachery; he hurled the charge back. Crispi resigned from the Ministry and started for Naples to lay his grievance before Garibaldi. Depretis went by the same steamer. The Dictator took Crispi's side and wished him to return to Palermo: but the Sicilian, either from anger or because he realized that he could pursue his policy best by staying at Garibaldi's elbow, would not go. The Dictator himself, by one of his unexpected moves, appeared in Palermo on September 17, installed Mordini the Tuscan Radical as pro-dictator, and set up a Revolutionary cabinet. Then he harangued the populace — denouncing Depretis and his corruptors, and declaring that at Rome he would proclaim Victor Emanuel King of Italy. "At Palermo," he said, "my enemies cried for annexation to prevent my crossing the Straits; now that I am at Naples, they cry for annexation to prevent my passing the Volturno." Having straightened out, as he hoped, the Sicilian feud, he hurried back to Naples.[82]

There he found Mazzini and Cattaneo — one eager to seize the helm, the other to decant into the ears of any listener who could not escape him, his obsolete Federalist dogmas. Cattaneo had lost touch with reality since 1848; but he now added his voice to those who decried annexation. The city was a volcano on the eve of an eruption. Garibaldi waited angrily for a reply to his note demanding Cavour's dismissal, but the King did not flatter him by hurrying. Bertani had made their position so intolerable that Liborio Romano and his colleagues, who had been scarcely more than half-alive, insisted on resigning. Bertani complained that, without consulting him, they sent decrees for Garibaldi to sign, and even conducted business without consulting Garibaldi; the Ministers complained that Bertani ignored their existence.[83] The combination was, in fact, impossible: a ministry, assumed to be bound by constitutional checks, being yoked to a dictatorship which recognized no checks. The Extremist inner ring, which encircled Garibaldi, was strengthened

[82] Mario: *Bertani*, II, 209–11, 222–23. Rosi: *Mordini*, 201–03. Ciàmpoli, 138, does not print Garibaldi's speech entire. Garibaldi: *Memorie*, 350. Stillman: *Crispi*, 92–97; Stillman himself is never to be relied upon, but as Crispi inspired this book, it represents presumably what Crispi wished posterity to believe. Crispi: *Mille*, 298–304.   [83] Mario: *Bertani*, II, 215.

by the appointment of Crispi as Secretary of State for the Mainland.

At this juncture, George Pallavicino, privately summoned by the Dictator, arrived (September 20). His friendship for Victor Emanuel was as sincere as for Garibaldi; and during the past year he had held himself aloof, in a position from which he criticized independently whoever seemed to him harmful to the true cause of Italy. Weeks earlier he had warned Garibaldi to beware equally of Mazzini and of Diplomacy, to consult alone his own great heart, and to remember that he was not a man, but a principle — the incarnation of the Revolution.[84] Pallavicino now set before himself the patriotic task of mediator. He saw that Garibaldi was very angry, especially at Farini and Fanti, who had 'made a fool of him' the previous autumn, and was on the point of breaking with the government at Turin. He was persuaded, however, — the latest comer usually persuaded him, — to allow Pallavicino to go unofficially to the King and to see how they could be reconciled. On September 23, when Pallavicino reached Turin, the King was so irritated that he at first declined to receive any Garibaldian emissary. That evening, however, he changed his mind, and at 10 o'clock, Victor Emanuel and the Survivor of the Spielberg sat facing each other on two stools at the Palace. The King burst into a philippic against Garibaldi, who arrogated to himself the chief place in Italy, and had the effrontery to dictate to Victor Emanuel to dismiss his ministers. The King scoffed at the Garibaldian proposal to crown him at the Quirinal. He had no fear of the "impertinent fellow"; on the contrary, he would march down to Naples, unless things changed there, and restore order. If the Mazzinians broke loose, so much the better, because then he would have an excuse for chastising them. Pallavicino tried to pacify the monarch, whose royal blood was thoroughly roused: but the only reply he could get was: "Tell him to annex at once, or to retire."

Not wishing to return to Naples with this message, Pallavicino had two interviews with Cavour, who listened with perfect courtesy, appreciating the peace-maker's noble intentions, but stood immovable. In August he and his colleagues would

[84] Pallavicino, III, 589; Pallavicino to Garibaldi, June 19, 1860. *Ibid*, 599-600; Aug, 5, 1860.

have resigned, for the sake of harmony, had the King requested them; but now, when the demand came from Garibaldi, their resignation would be equivalent to admitting that a private citizen, though he were the Dictator of the Two Sicilies, was above the King and the Constitution. "If Garibaldi wants war," Cavour said solemnly, "I accept it. I feel myself strong enough to combat him." Pallavicino urged that, if Garibaldi retired, Mazzini and then anarchy would reign at Naples. "So much the better," Cavour rejoined; "we will then make an end of Mazzinianism." "But that would be a fratricidal war!" Pallavicino remonstrated. "The responsibility for this war," said Cavour, "will recoil on those who instigated it."

Pallavicino hastened to report to the Paladin. With true tact, he stated frankly the attitude of the King and Cavour, but omitted the phrases that might rankle. He made it clear that, while everybody at Turin had faith in Garibaldi, they distrusted his intimates, Bertani, Mario, De Boni, and especially Mazzini. They were willing to discuss whether annexation should be carried out now or later, and to arrange for the incorporation of the Garibaldian volunteers in the regular army: but on the question of the Cabinet's resigning, or of permitting the Republican agitators, who worked under cover of Garibaldi's prestige, to jeopard the safety of Italy, they were adamant. Doubtless, Pallavicino intimated that the King and Cavour felt strong enough, both in public opinion and in troops, to beard Garibaldi himself and the Revolution in arms, at Naples, and that, rather than accept dictation which would mean suicide to constitutional monarchy, they would not shrink from a contest. Perceiving that during his brief absence Bertani had been discrediting him, Pallavicino told Garibaldi that he did not hanker for the prodictatorship, but that, before he accepted it, Bertani and Mazzini must go. Garibaldi protested that Mazzini was harmless, that the King's people trumped up accusations against him, and that, after all, it would be ungenerous and unjust to deny a refuge on Italian soil to men like him who had deserved much of Italy. He consented, however, that Bertani should return to Turin. He did not reveal that Bertani had actually resigned three days before; neither did he admit that he was trying to persuade Cattaneo to be pro-dictator.[85]

[85] Mario: *Bertani*, II, 220, 223.

In spite of his headstrong moods, which expressed themselves in threats and in denunciations of Cavour, Garibaldi's instinct warned him when to yield: and now, hearing that Cavour would risk war rather than sacrifice the Monarchy, he took care not to force the rupture. In his heart, he had little liking for his Mazzinian entourage; but they abetted his pet scheme of deferring annexation until the war was over, and so he tolerated them. But he knew that they sowed hatred, and that Bertani, with his fanaticism and his implacable nature, his dictatorial manner and his venomous tongue, was almost as much detested by the Garibaldians as by the Piedmontese. Bertani quitted Naples on September 30, the victim, as he declared, of ignoble intrigues and calumnies. Garibaldi did not formally accept his resignation,[86] but he appointed Crispi Secretary of State in his place. This appointment, Pallavicino wrote, "is a great mistake," for Crispi "is an entire programme, and this programme is not *ours*." [87] "The General's evil genius," said Bonghi, "was called Bertani and is now called Crispi." [88] Like Napoleon III, Garibaldi blew hot or cold with bewildering abruptness. By letting Bertani go, he signified his realization that it would not be safe to exasperate Victor Emanuel into war: by appointing Crispi, he wished the Revolution to infer that he was still Dictator, intent on freeing the Peninsula, and resolved to postpone annexation. Probably he did not reason this out in set terms, for he seldom reasoned. The real secret of their power over him was that both Bertani and Crispi, men of remarkable ability in fields where he was helpless, dominated him by their personality. They had the art of doing their will with him while making him think that they were simply doing his. Mazzini, endowed with genius before which the talents of Bertani and Crispi pale, could never sufficiently dissemble his imperiousness to succeed with Garibaldi.

Partisans will always clash in their opinions of these men. Their friends extolled their patriotism, their unflinching zeal, their refusal to compromise, their trenchant and often ruthless conduct of affairs: and they deserve praise for all these things. When their enemies, on the other hand, accused them of narrowness, of rancor, of an unbridled passion for domineering,

[86] Mario: *Bertani*, II, 222.   [87] Pallavicino, III, 611–12.   [88] Mario: *Bertani*, II, 224–25.

which they carried to the rule-or-ruin extreme, and vindictive-ness, they too had justification. These qualities, whether they be approved or condemned, got their special edge from the very nature of the men themselves. Others, pursuing the same policy, might conceivably have equalled Bertani's and Crispi's achieve-ment, without kindling the terrible fires of sectarian hatred, and without leaving behind them a trail of recriminations and irre-concilable feuds. If it be urged that they had much provocation — that the Cavourians distrusted and maligned them — the re-ply must be that this might explain but not excuse. Patriots of a higher type, like Washington or Lincoln, would have blushed to have it recorded that in lies, malice and injustice, they merely copied or outrivaled their opponents.

Italy's indictment against Crispi and Bertani in 1860 rests on deeper grounds. They failed to understand the conditions neces-sary to the very end they had in view. Having chosen Italian Unity for their watchword, they proceeded to exclude the large monarchical element without which the process of unification could never have been completed. Once launched in their cru-sade, they determined to carry it through in spite of or against the Monarchy. They set having their own way above concord: yet what would United Italy be worth, if its components were virulent factionaries? It would have been better to defer the Expe-dition than to win it at the expense of creating undying discords. If the Extremists imagined that Victor Emanuel's Government could be dispensed with in their undertaking, they showed an un-statesmanlike blindness. If they schemed to use Royal help until they themselves waxed sufficiently strong to throw the Monar-chy over and set up a republic which they should rule, they were base. In attacking Victor Emanuel's Government, they played into the hands of the enemies of Italy. When they spread broad-cast the slander that Cavour abhorred the idea of unity, and was merely the tool of Napoleon III, they lied as palpably as Abolitionists lied when they attributed Lincoln's acts to a secret sympathy with the slaveholders. When they printed and show-ered broadcast circulars announcing that Cavour had ceded Genoa and Sardinia to France, they allowed partisan fury to degrade them to the level of their Austrian antagonists, who cir-culated similar falsehoods from Vienna. When they warned the

Sicilians and Neapolitans that Victor Emanuel wished to Piedmontize their provinces instead of Italianizing the entire Peninsula, they employed a diabolic means for rekindling and perpetuating those fires of sectional wrath which had kept the Italians divided, despised and enslaved for fourteen hundred years.

The truth is, they took it for granted that the King's Government stood behind them, as a headstrong son assumes that his father, though incensed, will not disown him: but when the Government finally gave notice that *it* must decide, they instinctively shrank from the irrevocable plunge, for they realized that, while civil war might leave them temporarily masters of the South, it would blast the work of unification. If they had seen any prospect of final victory, they would have persisted; their instinct, rather than reason or conscience, warned them that they had better stop. When they acted on the assumption that Cavour's only springs of action were envy, jealousy, and selfish ambition, they reflected their own natures. It is possible to conceive of leaders who should have prepared and equipped the Garibaldian expeditions with as much energy as Bertani and Crispi displayed, but who, accepting the collusion with the Government in a proper spirit, would have loyally coöperated with it, not regarding the Monarchy as either a competitor or as an enemy. Garibaldi's military triumphs would have been promoted by such harmony, and his peace of mind would not have been harassed. He would have been saved from temptation to meddle in political and civil matters, for which he was unfitted. His heart would not have been poisoned against Cavour — a calamity which changed the course of history. If, therefore, the work of liberation could have been accomplished without the accompaniment of hatred which Bertani, Crispi, Mazzini and the little knot of irreconcilable Mazzinians created, Italy and posterity will not absolve them. The plea that they acted from patriotic zeal will not absolve them: zeal untempered by reason, justice and charity is common to savages and to madmen.

Even Garibaldi, by accepting their resignations at the critical moment, dimly realized this. Yet he would allow no one to deny their devotion, although he himself sometimes chafed at their coercion, and knew that they exasperated his best friends with as little consideration as the Cavourians. During the last half of

September, when he was vexed by these feuds, his real business lay in the field: for the Bourbon King had decided to give battle. Thirty thousand Bourbon troops were drawn up at Capua along the Volturno. Thither Garibaldi concentrated his own army. Having accepted Bertani's resignation, installed Crispi, with Mazzini and the Extremists round him, and chosen, somewhat reluctantly, Pallavicino as Pro-dictator,[89] he went to the front. As Garibaldi departed to fight the Bourbons in the field, Bertani went to Turin to fight Cavour in Parliament. In quitting Naples, the indefatigable surgeon could take satisfaction in the transformation he had wrought. Bertani worked swiftly, how swiftly can be measured with precision. On September 7 Garibaldi appointed a pro-Monarchist ministry favorable to union with Upper Italy, handed over the navy to Persano and professed friendliness to the King's invasion of the Papal States. Within a fortnight, Bertani had rendered their position so uncomfortable that the Ministers would not stay. He had persuaded Garibaldi to replace Depretis by Mordini, the Republican, as Pro-dictator in Sicily, and to appoint Saffi, an extreme Mazzinian, as Minister in Sicily, and Cattaneo, a doctrinaire Republican, as Pro-dictator at Naples.[90] He had secured the banishment of Silvio Spaventa, the most honored and influential of the Neapolitan Liberals. He had approved, if he did not instigate, Garibaldi's letter demanding Cavour's dismissal. Finally, he had received Garibaldi's assurance that there should be no annexation until the war was over.[91] And even though Bertani himself had to step down, he knew that Crispi, who stood in his place, would carry on his work with equal vigor.

[89] His commission was dated Oct. 4, 1860. declined.   [90] Saffi and Cattaneo   [91] Mario: *Bertani*, II, 209.

2

CHAPTER XXXIII

ITALY ABSORBS THE REVOLUTION

WHILST Garibaldi was tossed to and fro in the conflict between his instinct and the advice of his intimates, Cavour pursued his course with the steadfastness of a pilot who knows his port and trusts his compass. From Napoleon he feared no armed interference. Plon-Plon, who probably spoke with the Emperor's cognizance, wrote that Piedmont might, if she chose, take the risk, but that she must not count upon French aid in case Austria attacked her.[1] This peril was very real, for Austria hardly needed an excuse to attempt to win back Lombardy, and to restore the ousted reactionist princes in Emilia and Tuscany. If Beust is to be believed, Napoleon III secretly informed Francis Joseph that France would not interfere if Austria made war.[2] Bach, the Austrian Minister of the Interior, had already intimated that, in case Austria went to war, she would not reclaim Lombardy.[3] But for Cavour, the cardinal factor was the neutrality of France. Assured of that, he dared the rest.

During the first fortnight of September, the Piedmontese army was divided into two parts; one, to guard the frontiers,[4] the other, to invade the Papal States. On September 7 Cavour sent Cardinal Antonelli a note, in which he set forth the excesses committed by the foreign mercenaries who constituted the Papal Army, and threatened that, unless they were immediately disbanded, the King's troops would cross the border and, in the name of humanity, suppress them. No civilized government, he said, had the right to turn over the lives and property of its subjects to the brutality of soldiers of fortune.[5] Cavour's pretext was specious, unless the doctrine were admitted that a State, whose tranquillity was disturbed by the internal disorders of a neighboring State, was justified in protecting itself

[1] *Stor. Doc.*, VIII, 339.   [2] Beust, I, 202–03.
[3] Thouvenel: *Secret*, I, 184–85; Gramont to Thouvenel, Rome, Aug. 18, 1860.
[4] *Lettere*, IV, 4–6; C. to La Marmora, Sept. 13, 1860.
[5] Text in De Cesare: *Roma*, II, 62–63.

by putting them down. But this infringed on that very principle of non-intervention on which Piedmont had long relied for her very existence. Antonelli replied with Papal hauteur denying the charges: there was no brutality; the Pope had a perfect right to hire soldiers; the disorders, after all, were fomented by Cavour himself; the Pope would protest against any encroachment on his Temporal authority.[6] For a government which had depended since 1814 on foreign garrisons to prop it up, the Cardinal's denunciation of Piedmont's proposed interference might seem specious too. Cavour's contention that the Papal Army, made up of foreigners, recruited largely by Austria's agency, was really an instrument of foreign intervention, was quite as plausible as most of the other quibbles. But pretexts lay on the surface only: the reason beneath them was that the obsolete Papacy blocked the path of Italian Unity. Against the new principle of Nationality, the medieval Pontiff protested as impotently as the Danish King against the North Sea's in-rushing tide. If moribund institutions had the grace to die quietly and disappear, the progress of mankind would be simple: but they grow tenacious of life in proportion as they become senile, and they not only refuse to be set aside, but they advance claims in their decrepitude which would have been preposterous in their prime.

The conflict between Cardinal and Premier was irreconcilable. If the Cardinal appealed to the letter of international law, the Premier could appeal to its spirit and to its practice. If the Cardinal insisted, " Thus was it in the Past," the Premier replied, "The rights of subjects to be properly governed, the rights of peoples to unite as a nation, are of the Present." The world cannot live under a perpetual mortmain to ideals of Innocent III. The Piedmontese invasion of Umbria can no more be justified according to the letter of the law prevailing in 1860, than the abolition of slavery against the will of the slaveholders in 1863 could be technically justified. But living human aspirations will not forever be bound by dead laws.

Before Antonelli condescended to answer, Cavour instructed General Fanti to warn General Lamoricière, who commanded the Papal Army, that, if the Papal mercenaries should attempt to put down any National movement, the King's troops would

[6] De Cesare: *Roma,* ii, 63–64.

occupy Umbria and the Marches.[7] This message was shorn of
diplomatic or other ambiguity. Somewhat taken by surprise,
Lamoricière telegraphed to Rome for instructions. There De
Mérode, Pius's fanatical war minister, and Antonelli replied that
the French Embassy had received word that the Emperor had
written Victor Emanuel that, if he attacked the Pope's domain,
the Emperor would oppose him *with force*.[8] De Mérode sent
similar telegrams into the provinces, whereby the spirits of the
provincial monsignori were temporarily kept up. The ghosts of
Gramont, Antonelli and Mérode are still disputing as to who
launched this falsehood. Probably Gramont, in his hatred of
Piedmont, gave the impression that his own truculent views were
inspired by his Emperor. Only too soon, however, the truth
came out that the Pian Ministers had added the words "*with
force*," and that Mérode's message to the Apostolic Delegate at
Spoleto to the effect that "a great French division would be in
Rome between the 15th and 17th to stem the current," was likewise mendacious, in that it created the belief that this army was
coming to defend the Pope against the Piedmontese.[9] Napoleon,
as usual, was floundering in an ambiguous situation. He wished
at the same time to save his prestige as the friend of Italian
independence, and to keep the French Clericals docile by protecting Pius. Thouvenel implored him to forbid the Piedmontese to cross the frontier; but Napoleon preferred the course
which faced both ways. In strengthening the garrison at Rome
as a personal safeguard for the Pope, he intimated to Garibaldi, not less than to the King, that he should allow no attack
on the Holy City itself.

Victor Emanuel appointed Fanti provisional commander-in-
chief of the army of invasion, which numbered 45,000 men.[10]
Lamoricière had some 25,000 men,[11] of whom less than half were

[7] De Cesare: *Roma*, II, 67. Fanti wrote from Arezzo on Sept. 9; Antonelli's
reply to C. is dated Sept. 11.   [8] *Ibid*, 68. *Stor. Doc.*, VIII, 673–83, gives telegrams sent from Sept. 5 to Sept. 15. Antonelli's of Sept. 10 (p. 679) is typical.
For text of Napoleon's despatch, see Thouvenel: *Secret*, I, 197. Balan, II, 226–31.
[9] Zini, II, ii, 668–69; Gramont to Antonelli, Oct. 25, 1860. De Cesare: *Roma*, II,
68.   [10] Rüstow, 397; this means effective troops; on paper there were 54,000.
Mariani, IV, 376, and Carandini, 330, give 35,000 as the effective. See also Fanti's
official *Relazione sulla Campagna di Guerra nell' Umbria e nelle Marche, Settembre, 1860*. Turin, n. d.   [11] Mariani, IV, 374. Rüstow, 394, gives Lamoricière
only 9000 men. Carandini, 328, says that only 20,000 Papalists could take the
field. Tivaroni's estimate is 14,000; II, 308. Fanti says about 25,000; p. 5.

the foreign mercenaries recently drawn into the Pope's service. The latter came from Belgium, France, Switzerland, Ireland, Germany, and Austria; some out of blind devotion to the head of their Church, some for pay, others for titles, or for excitement, or to win a passport to Paradise. They represented many social layers, from the younger sons of Old Régime aristocrats [12] to Polish peasants and Irish bog-trotters. Nearly all the French, including Lamoricière, hated Napoleon III, and many of them, like the fire-eating Vendean, Athanase Charette, said openly that they hoped for the Bourbon restoration in France.[13] Most of the nobles, survivors of medieval fanaticism, inspired by intense zeal, regarded themselves as Crusaders and potential martyrs. Before hostilities began, the Pope sent plenary absolution to any one who might be at the point of death; but his soldiers would have fought better, it was hinted, if he had also sent them rations for their empty stomachs.[14] On the eve of the battle, their pious leaders comforted them by the assurance that, though they were probably doomed to be beaten on earth, they could count on eternal bliss.[15] At dawn before the fight at Castelfidardo, Lamoricière, Pimodan and others, prostrated themselves on the floor of the shrine of Loreto, their foreheads on the pavement, during the mass.[16] In a word, nothing was left undone to fortify the Papalists with those supports which dated from the golden age of superstition.

Lamoricière was taken by surprise by Fanti's ultimatum. He had been distributing part of his troops to the southward, as if to go to the aid of the Neapolitan King — indeed, the Pope and the Bourbon were become like Siamese twins in their insepara- bleness — and he assumed, just as Antonelli and Mérode as- sumed, that, in case of need, the French Emperor would prevent the Piedmontese invasion. Perhaps their wish was father to their thought; perhaps they mistook Gramont's denunciations of Piedmont and Italian Unity for pledges of French assistance. From that day to this Papal partisans have not ceased to declare that Napoleon III betrayed Pius IX.[17]

[12] De Cesare: *Roma*, ii, 52.   [13] *Ibid*, ii, 72–73. Colleville, 153.   [14] Colleville, 157.   [15] De Cesare: *Roma*, ii, 72–73. Colleville, 153.   [16] Colleville, 163. [17] For instance, Balan, ii, 227: "We fought because we trusted in powerful aid, we fought because we believed we should not be alone, we fought because others had encouraged us." Colleville throughout arraigns Napoleon III. Cf. La Gorce, iii, 411–22. Lamoricière said of Gramont: "He decoyed me." Revel, 49.

From his headquarters at Spoleto, Lamoricière had sent several small detachments to put down popular demonstrations which Papal Liberals, in concert with Cavour's agents, provoked at Orvieto and other towns. Now he planned to concentrate the bulk of his army at Ancona. Fanti despatched the Fifth Army Corps under Della Rocca into Umbria, and the Fourth, under Cialdini, into the Marches, to follow the coast to Ancona. Both crossed the frontiers on September 11. In short order Orvieto,[18] Perugia, Urbino, Pesaro, Foligno surrendered; but not without occasional displays of pluck against overwhelming forces. When the Royal troops prepared to bombard Perugia, Cardinal Gioacchino Pecci bestirred himself to secure a truce. It was remembered that when the Papal soldiery massacred the Perugians the year before, the Cardinal not only did nothing to stop the atrocities, but conducted the service to thank God for the happy results of the massacre.[19] At Spoleto, the garrison of 800 foreigners under Major O'Reilly bravely delayed Della Rocca during a day, until the heavy artillery knocked at the gates.[20] But Cialdini's rapid march on Ancona disconcerted Lamoricière, who realized the necessity of holding that fortress, the key both to the approaches to Naples and to the great central route to Rome. Ancona was also the nearest port for landing Austrian troops, in case Francis Joseph should decide to intervene in behalf of the Pope. Lamoricière hastened thither, only to find his way intercepted by Cialdini, who occupied the ridges of Osimo and Castelfidardo, a dozen miles south of Ancona. There on September 18 the Papalini were easily defeated.[21] The Piedmontese army greatly out-totaled the Papal, but the troops engaged were of nearly equal numbers, about 3,000 on each side.[22] Except for its results, Castelfidardo scarcely deserves to rank as a battle; for the Piedmontese lost only two score in killed and about 140 in wounded.[23] The Papal losses from bullets were not much greater, but panic fear dissolved most of the Pope's troops in a trice.[24] Whilst his army was running away in all directions, Lamoricière and a handful of horsemen managed to scamper off to Ancona.

[18] Orvieto was freed by the Hunters of the Tiber, under Masi.
[19] Revel, 38. Rüstow, 421–22.   [20] Revel, 39. Balan, II, 233–34.
[21] Military details in Rüstow, 410–21; Mariani, IV, 395–401; Carandini, 352–58. Papal story in Balan, II, 236–43.   [22] Carandini, 358. Fanti says Italians numbered only 2525; p. 13.   [23] Carandini, 358.   [24] Colleville, 168.

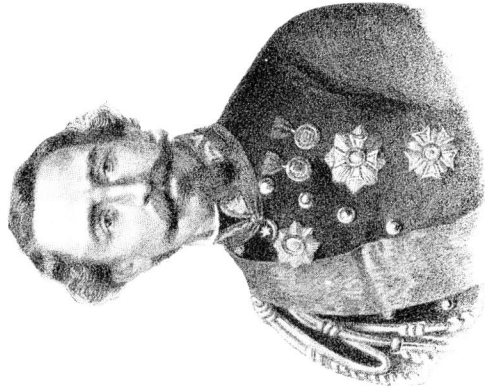

ALFONSO LA MARMORA

MANFREDO FANTI

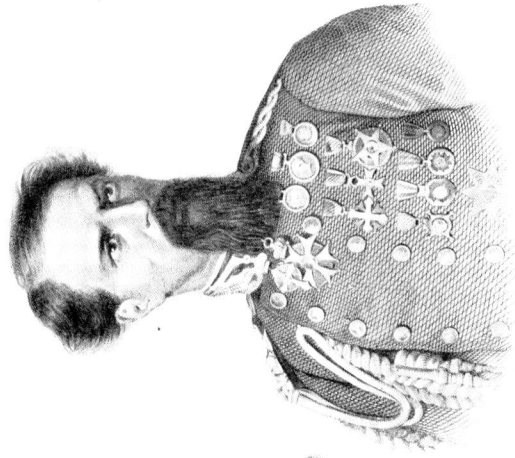

ENRICO CIALDINI

THREE PIEDMONTESE GENERALS

The Papal chronicler[25] asserts that Lamoricière had only 3000 troops against Cialdini's more than 20,000; by what miracle was it that 8000 Papal fugitives or more were captured that day and the next? Four thousand of the fugitives took refuge in Loreto, which looks down on Castelfidardo: but when neither the Holy House nor the special relics wrought a miracle in their behalf, they surrendered the next day. Nearly four thousand more, disguising themselves in peasant clothes, dispersed through the land, but the Piedmontese arrested most of them.[26] Fanti summoned both his corps to invest Ancona. Persano lay just outside with the Piedmontese fleet. Attacked by sea and land, Lamoricière, although he had a garrison of at least 5000, saw no hope of rescue. He held out until September 29, when, being convinced that neither Austria[27] nor France would interpose, he raised the white flag.[28] In eighteen days the Pope's army was annihilated, and 18,000 Papalini were prisoners. Again had mere zeal, though upheld by ecclesiastical incantations, proved wanting in warfare against disciplined and well-equipped troops; as it has always proved, no matter what the cause or what the religion.

Piedmontese military historians have tried to magnify this campaign into a mighty feat of war. It was not that. The official Papal chroniclers describe it as "brief but terrible,"[29] and they compare the feats of Lamoricière and his fugitives to those of Leonidas at Thermopylæ![30] Brief it was, but not terrible in any other sense than that it blasted forever the pretense of the Pope as a temporal sovereign. He had chosen to enlist a nondescript horde of foreign Catholics to defend him in his rôle of worldly prince — a rôle in which religion was no more implicated than in that of the Neapolitan Bourbon. Having staked his fortune on the decision of battle, and been beaten, he passed ignominiously

[25] Balan, II, 243. [26] Carandini, 358. Larousse, *Castelfidardo*. Fanti, 13.
[27] For incidents of siege, see Revel, chap. 5; Rüstow, 423–31; Balan, II, 244–52.
[28] At the beginning of the campaign, Lamoricière wrote Francis Joseph begging him to send cannon to fortify Ancona, and to prevent the invasion of the Papal States. Otherwise, he said, "if the Pope, abandoned by all the Catholic sovereigns, is forced to quit Rome, we will take from the sanctuary of Loreto the standard given by Pius V to Don John of Austria, the hero of Lepanto; we will conduct the Pope to Ancona, and then we shall know whether Christian Europe will behold unmoved Pius IX besieged and bombarded by the —— of the 19th century." Balan, II, 244. Balan discreetly suppresses the General's characterization of the Pope's enemies. [29] Balan, II, 229. [30] Carandini, 354.

into the limbo of pretenders to lost crowns. With perfect logic, he thenceforth protested that temporal and religious were so inseparably joined in him that both were harmed if either was touched.

Upon Lamoricière fell the blame of a disaster he could not avert: but posterity feels little sympathy for him. He was too arrogant a swaggerer. He learned soldiering in the worst school — fighting Arabs in Algiers — which made him contemptuous of the enemy, conceited, and often cruel. He had no fixed political principles. In 1849 he denounced his French Government for sending an army to subdue the emancipated Romans; in 1860 he accepted from the Pope the command of an army to rivet Papal despotism more securely on those re-enslaved Romans. His one abiding passion was hatred for Napoleon III; yet perhaps that might have been soothed if the Emperor had flattered him. His braggart order of the day,[31] in which he likened the Revolution to Islamism, remains as one of the humors of the crisis.[32] The modern "Islamites" against whom he banned his crusade, treated him and his army after their surrender better than he had a right to expect; for they were foreigners, hired by an Italian despot to crush his Italian subjects. Cavour wished, however, to leave as little rancor as possible in the hearts of the population which had inevitably suffered by the military campaign; and his orders were not to exact from the Papalists, whether native or foreign, a conqueror's terms. He took steps for the temporary administration of Umbria and the Marches, and for a plebiscite.

Whilst the Piedmontese army swept Umbria and the Marches clear of the Pian crusaders, Cavour was battling at Turin to hold Diplomacy at bay. The French press arraigned the unjustifiable aggression. The French Government increased its garrison at Rome. Napoleon, though whispering privately to Cavour's messenger, "Go ahead,"[33] publicly withdrew the French Ambassador from Turin, as a sign of his disapproval (September 14). France is showing her teeth to Piedmont, a witty Parisian remarked, "but I don't know whether they are artificial teeth."[34] From England, however, Cavour received strong encouragement. Hudson,

[31] Text in De Cesare: Roma, ii, 50.   [32] When Lamoricière died in 1865, Pius IX sent his widow, for *consolation*, a skeleton from the Catacombs, to which he gave Lamoricière's name, "Christopher." Larousse.   [33] Arese's letters, printed in *Lettere*, vi, 590, 595.   [34] Doudan, quoted in *Lettere*, vi, 598.

a Dualist in the spring, had become, since Garibaldi took Palermo, a consistent Unitarian; and as soon as Cavour confided to him the project of invading the Papal States, he persuaded Lord John Russell of its excellence. By acquiring Umbria and the Marches, the Kingdom of Upper Italy would stretch continuously to the Kingdom of Naples: the territorial gap between North and South would be bridged. An enlarged Italy, instead of conflicting with British interests, would promote them, not only through the ordinary ways of trade, but, politically, by shutting out French schemes for establishing Murat at Naples, and by curtailing French influence throughout the Peninsula. Lord John and Palmerston, who had long ago given up the Papal Government as incorrigible, could only applaud the prospect of its abolition over a large portion of the Pope's domain. Although they had hoped for such an overturn in the Two Sicilies as would ensure an enlightened régime, they had not been willing to abet any suggestion which might lead to a general war. They sympathized heartily with Garibaldi, but not with the Revolution, which they foresaw might capture him and overrun Italy. Cavour's bold plan offered a solution which they approved all the more because it flouted the French Emperor.

Garibaldi's dictatorial message to Victor Emanuel to dismiss Cavour and Farini, and his apparent surrender to Bertani and the Extremists, seemed to Cavour to indicate that he had at last thrown off the mask. If this suspicion were confirmed, it behooved the King's Government to act resolutely and at once. Garibaldi's undisguised hatred of Cavour showed that not only the Paladin but the faction that was using him regarded the Prime Minister as the chief impediment in their way. The King replied "calmly but categorically" to Garibaldi's insulting demand.[35] Whatever Cavour felt as to personal affront, he kept to himself, for he would not put Italy in jeopardy in order to avenge his private grievance; he therefore bade Villamarina to keep on good terms with Garibaldi, without compromising the King.[36] He debated sending Persano to Palermo, to expedite the vote of annexation, and Cialdini with a corps of observation to the Neapolitan frontier.[37] The victory of Castelfidardo cleared the horizon;

[35] *Lettere*, IV, 7; C. to [Nigra] Sept. 15, 1860. *Lettere*, VI, 600; C. to Fanti, Sept. 17, 1860. [36] *Lettere*, IV, 8; C. to Villamarina, Sept. 17, 1860. [37] *Lettere*, VI, 600.

it would, Cavour believed, either bring Garibaldi to his senses or "give us a sufficient force to prevent him from ruining us." With the instinct of a statesman who knew where his strength lay, he convened Parliament to meet on October 2.

He regarded the withdrawal of Talleyrand as a cheap price to pay for the campaign in the Papal States. On September 22 he wrote Nigra, who was to take a leave of absence from Paris, to speak very frankly to the Emperor. Admit, he said, that, in the eye of Diplomacy, our conduct is blamable; but make the Emperor understand that it is essential in order to save Italy. "Garibaldi," he continued, "is a visionary [*illuminé*], intoxicated by unhoped-for successes. He believes that he has received a providential mission and is authorized to employ whatever means he chooses in order to accomplish it. At present, he imagines that he ought to go with the men of the Revolution. Hence it follows that he sows disorder and anarchy along his route. If we fail to remedy this situation, Italy will perish without Austria's taking part. We are resolved not to permit this. Tell the Emperor very plainly that if Garibaldi persists in the fatal way he has entered, we shall go in a fortnight to restore order at Naples and at Palermo, though it were necessary to throw all the Garibaldians into the sea. The immense majority of the nation is with us — the debates in Parliament will prove it. Gianduja is furious with Garibaldi. The National Guard of Turin would march against him in case of need. Fanti's and Cialdini's soldiers ask nothing better than to rid the country of the Red Shirts. Tell the Emperor to have no uneasiness on this score. We have waited, we have been conciliatory, even feeble in appearance — so as to have the right to smite, and to smite hard, at the proper moment. It was necessary to wait till these gentlemen threw aside the monarchical mask they were wearing. Now the mask is off, and we shall go ahead. The King has decided to have done with it. Moreover, I would not tolerate vacillation." [38]

To construe this letter aright we must remember that Cavour wrote it to be read to Napoleon III, upon whom he wished to impress four facts: that Garibaldi was under the control of the

[38] *Lettere*, IV, 12–13; C. to Nigra, Sept. 22, 1860. When Chiala first printed this letter in 1885, he omitted some phrases which might then have given offence. *La Rivista di Roma*, Jan. 25, 1906, printed it in full. See also De Cesare: *Roma*, II, 59–60.

men of the Revolution; that the Revolution must be stopped unless the Italian cause were to be ruined; that Victor Emanuel's Government had resolved to intervene at all hazards; and that both the army and the great majority of the country would heartily support this decision. Napoleon expressed great regret at Nigra's going, and hoped to see him soon again. He admitted to Panizzi a few days later that the King's expedition was necessary, in spite of being rather too sudden and too regardless of conventions. As to Naples, he thought that, if a parliament could be called there, it would proclaim the decadence of Francis II and would elect Victor Emanuel, thus stamping with legality an affair which might otherwise seem revolutionary.[39] Castelfidardo confirmed Cavour's belief that the King must go to Naples with an army corps.[40] When this was communicated to Palmerston, he heartily approved.[41] The capitulation of the Papal garrison at Ancona opened the way to the new move. "Every regard for Garibaldi," Cavour wrote the King and Farini; "no compromise with the system."[42]

At that moment Garibaldi's power seemed more formidable than ever, owing to his victory over the Bourbons in a great battle. Since his flight from Naples on September 6 the Bourbon King had brought his troops into such condition that they could take the field. Indeed, on September 21 they had driven the Garibaldians out of Cajazzo, a strong post on the Volturno above Capua, which Türr had imprudently occupied during Garibaldi's absence. Bourbon partisans, among whom was the Bishop of Ariano, had already started a backfire of insurrection in Eastern Campania. The Bourbon headquarters were at Capua, round which the river winds on its meandering course towards the sea. Above Capua it makes an ample curve, and bounds a cluster of foothills which jut from the Apennines into the plain. Skirting these hills, on the edge of the level country, runs the railway from Capua to Naples, which passes first Santa Maria di Capua (three miles), then Caserta (four miles farther) and then Maddaloni (another four miles). From Maddaloni to Naples by rail

---

[39] *Lettere*, VI, 605–08; Panizzi to C., Oct. 1, 1860.   [40] *Ibid*, 602–03; C. to Fanti, Sept. 21, 1860. At least a fortnight earlier Cialdini had been agreed upon to command the corps.   [41] *Ibid*, 610; C. to Farini, Oct. 2, 1860.   [42] *Ibid*, 611; the King had started for Ancona, where he arrived on Oct. 3.

was only sixteen miles; by the highway, a little less. In 1860 two broad roads and half a dozen narrower routes led to the capital. Irrigating canals, whose general direction was from east to west, intercepted these. Besides the towns, villages and large farms dotted the luxuriant Campanian Plain. Gorges and valleys, cutting the mountains, set free several streams. The Volturno, too deep and swift for fords, was crossed at many points by flying bridges, which the Bourbons, who numbered nearly 30,000 men, controlled. The King planned to celebrate his fête, October 1, in Naples. The success of Victor Emanuel over the Papalists spurred him to action; because, if he could defeat Garibaldi and enter Naples in triumph, he would dispose of the pretense that the Piedmontese were called to Naples to put down anarchy.

On the afternoon of September 30, Garibaldi, perceiving that battle was at hand, distributed his men along an irregular line, 13 or 14 miles in length, at six points where the enemy might break through. Bixio, with 5600 men, occupied the extreme right at Maddaloni; the reserves, 4500 strong, waited at Caserta under Türr; near Sant' Angelo Medici, with the centre numbering over 4000, fronted Capua and had Monte Tifata behind him; while Milbitz, with 4000 more, supported Medici's left at Santa Maria; on the extreme left, near Aversa, Corte had 1500. Bronzetti with 200 bersaglieri held the isolated Castel Morrone; and Sacchi, with 1500, at S. Leucio, was to prevent the Bourbons from burrowing through the valley behind Monte Tifata to Caserta. These various commands were as well entrenched as circumstances permitted; but for a successful defensive their line was far too long, and the space between one division and the next was often so wide that communications could not be kept up.

General Ritucci, the Bourbon commander, planned a simple battle. His centre, comprising 17,000 men, issued from Capua in two columns under Afan de Rivera and Tabacchi, and proceeded to attack the Garibaldian centre under Medici and Milbitz. Von Mechel, with 8000 men, led the Bourbon left through the eastern roads towards Maddaloni. Five thousand more, under Ruiz, supported the right of the Bourbon centre; while Perrone, with 1200, was to pass Castel Morrone and strike Caserta in the rear. On the map, the field resembles a half-drawn bow. Capua is the left and Maddaloni the right tip, and the string is the almost straight line of railway connecting the two. The curving Volturno corresponds roughly to the arc of the bow, and the space between is occupied by the foothills and a strip of plain. Ritucci's object was to force a passage either across the level country, or through the valleys which debouched at Maddaloni and Caserta.

At dawn, Tabacchi attacked Milbitz, and for five hours it was to and fro between them, but the Garibaldians held their own. Afan de Rivera, however, hurled his 10,000 against Medici's 4000 with such vigor that Medici's division was ground down to half that number, and, after a brave resistance, he had to fall back to the heights behind Sant' Angelo. By noon, both sides were so exhausted that they paused to rest. The Bourbons renewed their attack at 2 o'clock, and but for Garibaldi's summoning up fresh reserves from Caserta, Medici's remnant might have been driven from the field. Meanwhile, round Maddaloni, Bixio was fighting all that morning against Von Mechel, who proved a stubborn foe. At the first onset one of Bixio's brigades (Eberhard's) retreated in utter disorder; then Bixio himself, being pushed back and back, took up his station on the slopes. He was ably seconded by his lieutenant, Dezza, who grimly held Monte Caro, the key to the valley. As the afternoon wore on the Bourbons lost energy, for Ruiz, Von Mechel's second, had failed to come up with the 5000 men under his command, having been delayed half the day by Bronzetti's 280 heroes on the crag of Castel Morrone. Bixio, whose force outnumbered Von Mechel's, recaptured his earlier positions, and narrowly missed cutting off Von Mechel's retreat. At this same hour, the arrival of the reserves at Santa Maria turned the tide on the left. Tenacious Milbitz was relieved; indomitable Medici at Sant' Angelo was saved. Covered by their cavalry, the Bourbon troops sought refuge in Capua. At five o'clock Garibaldi telegraphed to Naples: "Victory all along the line."

After the fighting was over, two companies of Piedmontese bersaglieri and two companies of infantry, sent by rail from Naples, came upon the scene. They fought next day in the recapture of Caserta, but they were too few — some 400 men in all — to justify the claim, put forth by superserviceable Piedmontese reporters, and repeated subsequently, that they saved the Garibaldians on the Volturno.[43] A few British sailors from the *Hannibal*, spending their holiday in witnessing the engagement, helped the Garibaldians to remount two captured Bourbon guns, and to drag them into Santa Maria. Throughout the day Garibaldi displayed his military talents on a larger scale than ever before. His plan of defense, although he knew its weakness, was the only practicable one. His vigilance and swiftness showed him to be as alert to see where the danger threatened as he was quick to parry it. He exposed himself recklessly, not merely to bullets, but to risk of capture, and at least twice just missed being made prisoner. From his lookout on Monte Sant' Angelo, he scanned the battle far and near, and when he saw the need, like one of the Homeric gods watching the conflict between Greeks and Trojans, he swooped down from his eyrie and suddenly appeared in the midst of the combat. Great praise belongs to his lieutenants, to Medici and to Bixio, to Milbitz and Dezza, but for whose valorous endurance Garibaldi's magical presence would have been of no avail. Beyond all in heroism on that day were Bronzetti and his 280 bersaglieri, who held their isolated post for hours against overwhelming odds, and only laid down their arms when they had no ammunition left, and every one who survived had been wounded. The chief criticism of the Bourbons touches their mistaken plan of battle. Instead of attempting to break through at six different places, over so wide an area, they should have massed half their army against a single point, while the other half engaged the Garibaldians at the other points. The Bourbon troops fought well; their commanders were not incompetent; in drill, morale and tenacity there was nothing to recall the ignominy of Calatafimi and Calabria. But the result of the battle was that nearly 30,000 Bourbons had been checked and driven back by 19,000 Garibaldians. Garibaldi's loss amounted to about 3200, of whom over 300 were killed, 1328 wounded, and 389 missing. The Bourbon losses in killed and wounded are uncertain, though not less than 1000; and 2000 prisoners were taken on October 2, when the Garibaldians had an aftermath of victory near Caserta. The Bourbons also left seven cannon on the field.[44]

[43] Forbes, 304; Mariani, IV, 347. On the other side, Revel, 55.
[44] For the battle of the Volturno Rüstow's is still the best of the detailed con-

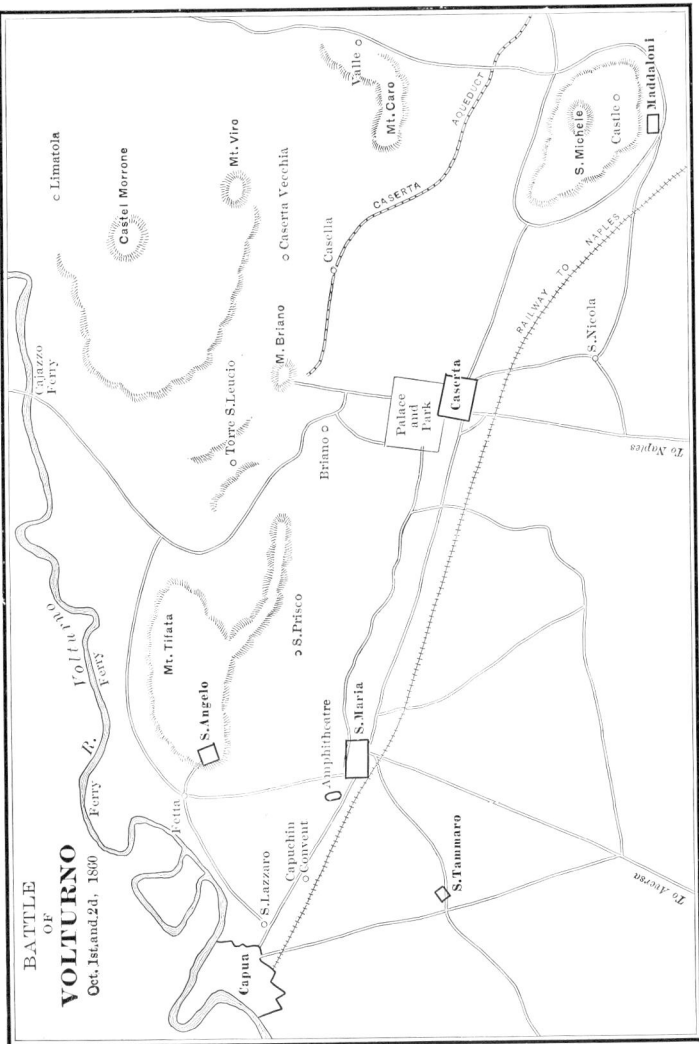

BATTLE
OF
VOLTURNO
Oct. 1st and 2d, 1860

Capua

S. Lazzaro
Capuchin
Convent

Retta

R. Volturno

Cajazzo
Ferry

c Limatola

Castel Morrone

Mt. Vira

o Caserta Vecchia

o Casella

Valle

Mt. Caro

AQUEDUCT

CASERTA

S. Michele
Castle o

Maddaloni

M. Briano

o Torre S. Leucio

Mt. Tifata

S. Angelo

o S. Prisco

Briano o

Palace
and
Park

Caserta

S. Nicola o

RAILWAY TO NAPLES

To Naples

S. Maria

Amphitheatre

S. Tammaro

To Aversa

When the smoke cleared away, it appeared that Garibaldi's victory on the Volturno, like that of the Allies at Solferino, concluded nothing. It would have been fatal to him if he had lost; having won, he was simply master of the territory he had possessed before the battle. The Bourbons shut themselves up in Capua, protected by fortifications too strong to be taken without a siege. Even if Garibaldi had succeeded in crossing the river above the city, he would have been insane to march north while Capua not only menaced his rear, but also offered cover for a Bourbon attack on Naples itself. Mazzini and other fanatics, blind as usual to remorseless fact, urged him to hurry forward to Rome;[45] but Garibaldi's military sense prevailed over their madcap visions. The soldier in him forbade the idea of leaving unconquered behind him a hostile army of 40,000 men, who had Capua and Gaeta for their defenses. His own troops would barely have sufficed, in the opinion of Guerzoni, to save Naples from a sudden assault,[46] if the Bourbons had ventured to make it: and yet a few months later, in one of those moments of magnifying retrospect to which he was subject, Garibaldi declared that he could have taken Capua in a couple of days, but that, as he received a private letter from Victor Emanuel begging him not to attempt it,[47] he had to content himself with standing on the defensive.[48] While the Piedmontese army advanced as rapidly as it could by wretched roads through the Abruzzi and Molise on Naples, the Bourbons, overcome by inertia, left him unmolested. But he would gladly have exchanged the disgusts and ferocities of political quarrels, which now beset him, for active campaigning, whatever its hardships, risks or perils.

To anyone whose heart has beaten faster at the tale of heroic achievements, the bare record of the Garibaldian anticlimax in that month of October must bring sorrow. The scene shifts from Campania to Turin, where the constitutional govern-

temporary accounts. See also Mariani; Garibaldi, *Memorie* and *Mille*; J. W. Mario, *Garibaldi*; Guerzoni, *Garibaldi* and *N. Bixio*; Zini; De' Sivo; Forbes; M. Du Camp. Trevelyan, ii, chap. 12, for best modern description. His discussion in Appendix J of the forces engaged is exhaustive.

[45] A. Mario: *Garibaldi*, 53.   [46] Guerzoni: *Garibaldi*, ii, 206.

[47] J. W. Mario: *Gar. Supp.*, 285–86.   [48] Forbes, 279, writing *before* the battle of the Volturno, thought that Garibaldi could take Capua.

ment must organize the newly liberated provinces, welding North and Centre and South together into one nation. But first Parliament must settle the great contention between Garibaldi and Cavour. Garibaldi has demanded that Cavour be dismissed, and that Ministers approved by himself be substituted. Garibaldi has further intimated that he intends to retain his dictatorship, until he has freed the Papal States and Venetia. Cavour's reply is to convene the Chamber, to which it belongs to make and unmake ministers, and to extend or to limit the dictator's term.

The session opened on October 2. Cavour read an address in which he reminded the deputies that the 11 million Italians of six months before had become 22 millions; that the means by which this had come to pass was the necessary consequence of Charles Albert's policy; that Venice alone was in bondage, but that it would be imprudent then to go to war in her behalf; and that the City of Rome must likewise be untouched for the present. The Two Sicilies, having signified their desire by a plebiscite, must be relieved as soon as possible from their provisional status. They shall vote in the same form as Tuscany and Emilia voted; and their preference shall be respected: but Cavour said frankly that he and his colleagues believed in neither Federalism nor Centralization, but in a compact union, in which all sections of the country should abide equally under the authority of Parliament and of the Nation. Although some patriots hoped to postpone it until Venice and Rome were free, he declared that the plebiscite must not be delayed; for to prolong a situation in which the Revolution and the constitutional government existed side by side, would inevitably cause friction from which the common enemy alone would benefit. He eulogized Garibaldi, the "generous patriot," but prophesied that, if the provisional state were allowed to continue, authority in the South would pass from the hands of him whose practical formula was "Italy and Victor Emanuel," into those of persons who used the dark and mystical symbol of the sectaries, "God and the People." The Two Sicilies had been liberated by Garibaldi in the name of the King: how could the King suffer them to be governed as if they were conquered provinces, forbidden to express their will? Cavour concluded that the Ministry, in order to do its duty

amid the new difficulties, must be assured of the confidence of
Parliament — all the more since "a voice justly dear to the
multitudes" had requested the King to dismiss them. "It is the
absolute duty of the Ministers of a constitutional King," he
said, "not to yield to claims which are scarcely legitimate, even
when they are backed by a splendid popular aureole and by a
victorious sword." [49]

The address was a fine example of Cavour's reliance upon
reason to recommend his words. In phrase most propitiatory, he
was in substance irremovable. He placed the King and Constitution above debate. He paid the highest tribute to Garibaldi,
but assumed that the Paladin was sincere in protesting his loyalty to the King. And he left no doubt as to the Ministers' resolve to postpone the liberation of Rome and Venice, and to
resist the sects. Whoever reads this speech without knowing the
situation when Cavour delivered it, would not imagine that he
spoke from the very vortex of a crisis, when foreign invasion
seemed imminent, and when faction ran so high that many good
Italians believed that civil war, if not the splitting of Italy into
two hostile states, could not be prevented. Cavour spoke with
as much assurance as bronze Colleoni sits invincible on his
bronze war-horse; and amid the eddies of conflicting proposals,
he defined a clear, sane, fearless policy.

He would not listen to those who urged him to let Parliament
declare the immediate annexation of the new provinces, but insisted that there must first be a plebiscite; for to rob the Umbrians and Neapolitans of their right to express themselves
would be as unjustifiable as to set up, as many begged him to do,
a royal dictatorship to govern the new Italians by martial law.
When Salvagnoli, the Florentine lawyer, pressed this upon him,
he replied: "Your advice would result in realizing Garibaldi's
idea, which aims precisely at securing a vast revolutionary dictatorship to be exercised in the name of the King, uncontrolled
by a free press or by individual or parliamentary safeguards.
I think, on the contrary, that it will be not the least title to glory
for Italy to have been able to establish herself as a nation without sacrificing liberty to independence, without passing through
the dictatorial hands of a Cromwell; but to have unshackled her-

[49] *Discorsi*, xi, 237–47. Artom-Blanc, ii, 504–25.

2

self from monarchical absolutism without falling into revolutionary despotism. Now there is no other way to attain this end except by drawing from the concurrence of Parliament the sole moral force capable of conquering the sects and of preserving for us the sympathies of Liberal Europe. To go back to the committees of public safety, or, what amounts to the same thing, to the revolutionary dictatorship of one or more, would be to kill at birth that legal liberty which we desire as the inseparable companion of national independence." [50]

At this crisis, which more than any other in his career seemed to justify a temporary resort to Absolutist methods, Cavour did not even feel that as a temptation, so fundamental was his reverence for liberty. His trust in constitutional methods was quickly rewarded by the goodwill the Chamber of Deputies showed him. Of the orators of the Extreme Left, only Ferrari spoke vehemently, and rather as the advocate of Federalism than as a denouncer of the Ministry. [51] The Moderate Chiaves, on the other hand, indulged in scathing condemnation of the Mazzinians. [52] Bertani, who was listened to with the keenest curiosity, surprised his audience by his gentleness. Instead of the enraged hawk they expected, he came as the dove with the olive branch. He appealed for peace and concord among all the sons of Italy, and begged Cavour to go to Naples and seek to grasp Garibaldi's hand in reconciliation. He could not tell whether Garibaldi's hand would be offered in return, but in that act Bertani and posterity would behold the agreement of the Revolution with the Monarchy, and would applaud more than ever the Count's efforts for Italian liberty. Bertani failed to state why Cavour, who had neither started the feud nor allowed it to influence his attitude towards Garibaldi, should be the suppliant. [53] If sincere, this appeal was a noble outburst of patriotism; but judged by what went before and came after, there is some ground for believing that Bertani made it in order to be able to say that he and his party were the first to plead for harmony, and had been rebuffed. Minghetti in commenting on Bertani's proposal argued that it was impracticable, if not specious. On October 11 Cavour closed the debate for the Government in a speech

[50] *Lettere*, IV, 24; C. to Salvagnoli, Oct. 2, 1860.   [51] Mario: *Bertani*, II, 240. Zini, II, ii, 763–64.   [52] Cavour called this "one of the most brilliant and spirited speeches ever delivered in the Chamber." *Lettere*, III, 36.   [53] Mario: *Bertani*, II, 239–41.

in which, after stating with great frankness the Ministerial policy, he declared that United Italy would never rest until Rome was its capital. Amid wild cheers of approval the deputies proceeded to vote. Two hundred and ninety-six supported the Ministers' program, only six — among whom were Ferrari and Bertani — opposed it. In the Senate the ayes numbered 84, the noes 12; the irreconcilable Clericals naturally could not approve the spoliation of the Pope's Kingdom.

Annihilated! was the verdict of Parliament on the pretensions of the Revolution. The Extremists tried to console themselves by explaining that Parliament was made up of members obsequious to Cavour's will who did not represent the country; or, if not quite that, that it was packed by Monarchists pledged not to listen to arguments in favor of either a federation or a republic. In truth, that verdict expressed the sober second thought of all but a small minority of enlightened Italians in every part of the Peninsula; and had it not been that that Mazzinian remnant exploited Garibaldi's unique popularity, as a cover for their own designs, their influence, after the vote of October 11, would have been negligible.

Before that vote was taken, Cavour, having discerned that he had public opinion overwhelmingly with him, proceeded to fulfil the policy of which the invasion of the Papal States was merely the prologue. Since July, he had planned to send an army to Naples in case either Garibaldi should cross to the Mainland or a revolution should break out in the capital. The surrender of Ancona left Fanti's corps free to march south; the Garibaldian victory on the Volturno made haste imperative. Victor Emanuel joined the troops at Ancona on October 3. Three days later Cavour handed to Winspeare, the Neapolitan envoy at Turin, a note announcing the King's intention of going to Naples in response to innumerable petitions of the inhabitants of the Two Sicilies. Francis II, he said, had virtually abdicated by abandoning his capital, and leaving his Kingdom in a state of civil war. Anarchy, to be followed by an attempt to set up a Republican Utopia, must be suppressed. Victor Emanuel undertook the task in the interest not merely of the Neapolitans but of the entire Peninsula.[54] Winspeare protested. Francis II likewise

[54] Text of draft, dated Oct. 6, 1860, in Artom, 152–53.

protested, and besought the Great Powers to defend him against this monstrous breach of international comity.[55] Recalling his Minister (Stackelberg) from Turin, the Czar warned the King's Government that while pretending to wish to check the Revolution they had abetted it in order to enjoy its fruits.[56] Prussia recalled her Minister (Brassier de Saint Simon) and lectured Piedmont on the wickedness of allowing the claims of nationality to override long-established rights. Schleinitz added, pertinently, that Victor Emanuel, who had most ardently supported the doctrine of non-intervention by the Great Powers, was now intervening himself in flagrant fashion. Whereupon Cavour, who saw further into the future than Schleinitz, remarked that Prussia would some day be grateful for the example they were setting in Italy.[57] Spain also recalled her Minister (Coello), protesting that Europe would never accept universal suffrage as the basis for a new state. Most serious of all, Napoleon III, whose envoy had been recalled three weeks before, was in one of his uncertain moods, trying to propitiate the French Clericals by seeming to support the Pope; loth to abandon his long-cherished dream of installing a Murat at Naples ; frowning on the Garibaldian victories; resolved to win back English goodwill; bent on currying favor with Prussia, Austria and Russia, whose sovereigns were to confer at Warsaw late in October; and yet secretly persuaded that both his honor and his interest required him to save from wreck the Italy which he had helped to create. In part, the contradictory policy was due to the fact that Napoleon was pursuing one path and Thouvenel another.

Cavour realized, however, that the final risk must be taken. He feared Napoleon less than Austria, whose armies, massed on the frontiers, were eager to cross.[58] But he had in England, in Palmerston and Russell, the support which reassured him. Palmerston said emphatically, "Go to Naples!" and he took pains to point out how England, by her influence, had been as useful to Italy as the French armies had been.[59] Napoleon confided to Panizzi that he had no objections to seeing Victor Emanuel in Naples, but that he advised the Piedmontese not to hurry and to

[55] *Stor. Doc.*, VIII, 354–55.   [56] *Ibid*, Gortchakoff Note of Oct. 10, 1860.

[57] *Ibid*, 256–57. Schleinitz Note of Oct. 13, 1860; C.'s reply of Oct. 29, 1860.

[58] *Lettere*, IV, 31; C. to V. E., Oct. 5, 1860.   [59] *Lettere*, VI, 608; Panizzi to C., London, Oct. 1, 1860. *Ibid*, 610; C. to Farini, Oct. 2.

observe legal forms. He even went so far as to declare that, if the Pope should quit Rome — as then seemed probable — Victor Emanuel would naturally occupy and govern the city, and the French would withdraw from it at once.[60] The Emperor's underlying motive — in case his own designs were thwarted — was to check Garibaldi, whose purpose of freeing Rome and Venetia threatened a general war and the aggrandizement of the Revolution.

Cavour outlined the following programme which he forwarded to the King and to Farini, who attended the King, at Ancona: Send Cialdini directly to Naples with a corps; reëstablish order in Naples first, and then subdue Francis II ("Woe if this procedure were reversed!"); let Victor Emanuel push on to the nearest Neapolitan city, Aquila, for instance, summon Garibaldi, and "magnetize him." The Paladin, Cavour wrote, "will be overjoyed to lay his dictatorship at the feet of Your Majesty, and to give up the command of all his troops to Cialdini." On no account must the siege of Gaeta precede Victor Emanuel's entry into the capital. Cavour was most solicitous that nothing should occur to offend the Great Condottiere. There must be, he said, "no compromise with the Mazzinians, no weakness with the Garibaldians, but infinite consideration for their General. Garibaldi has become my fiercest enemy, and yet I earnestly desire for the good of Italy and of Your Majesty that he shall retire fully satisfied. That is why I look with displeasure on General Fanti's going to Naples, which is calculated to irritate Garibaldi to the highest pitch. If you can come to an agreement with him before Fanti passes the frontier, you will have done a noble thing." [61]

Again and again Cavour insisted on this line of conduct. "We must show ourselves generous towards all those who have fought," he wrote Farini. "If Garibaldi's army acclaims the King, it must be well treated. Here you have to struggle against military exactions and pedantries. Do not yield; a supreme State reason demands it. Woe to us if we show ourselves unresponsive and ungrateful towards those who have shed their blood for Italy. Europe would condemn us. At home a tremendous reaction in favor of the Garibaldians would set in. On this point, I have

---

[60] *Lettere*, vi, 606.   [61] *Ibid*, iv, 30–31; C. to V. E., Oct. 5, 1860. *Ibid*, 32; C. to Farini, Oct. 5, 1860.

had a very sharp discussion with Fanti. He spoke of the army's exigencies. I replied that we were not in Spain, that among us the army obeys.

"I do not mean by this that all the ranks conferred by Garibaldi or his deputies must be preserved. Heaven forbid that such an absurdity should lodge in my brain! but no more ought we, as Fanti desires, to send all the Garibaldians home with a simple bounty. In my opinion we should appoint a commission composed of Cialdini, president; of two generals of our army — Sonnaz and Villamarina, for instance — and of two Garibaldian generals, Medici and Cosenz. This commission would divide the Garibaldian officers into three classes. The first composed of the very few, who would enter the Army. The second would constitute one or two special divisions, called after the Hunters of the Alps, detached from the Army with its own rules of seniority. The third, certainly the most numerous, would be sent home with one year's stipend. The above commission would distribute a certain quantity of medals and of Savoy crosses, and of pensions for the wounded.

"Talk about this to Cialdini, who is, in this respect, more reasonable than Fanti. Make him perceive that a cry of reprobation would be raised if the grades were kept for the Bourbon officers who ran away shamefully and if the Garibaldians who whipped them were sent home. On this point I will not compromise. Rather than assume responsibility for an act of black ingratitude, I will go and bury myself at Leri. I despise ingrates to such a degree that I do not feel angry at them, and I pardon their offenses. But by God! I could not bear the merited blot of having failed to recognize services like that of the conquest of a kingdom of nine millions of inhabitants." [62]

Such was the policy, just, generous and far-seeing, of the statesman to whom Garibaldi and the Mazzinians then and thereafter imputed the basest motives — envy and personal spite, class hatred and sectional jealousy.

The Italian army moved south without delay. Cialdini's corps started on October 7; Della Rocca's followed two days later. Victor Emanuel accompanied this, having addressed to the people of Southern Italy a manifesto in which he announced

[62] *Lettere*, IV, 34–35; C. to Farini, Oct. 8, 1860.

that, at their call, he was hastening to restore order among them, to afford them free opportunity to express their wishes by a plebiscite, and to close, in Italy, "the era of revolutions." This last phrase incensed the Radicals,[63] who were in so irascible a state that eider-down would have rasped them. Cialdini and Della Rocca advanced as rapidly as the bad roads permitted. As they passed out of reach, Cavour took steps with La Marmora to defend the North against the much-feared Austrian invasion. He also sent several regiments by sea to Naples to ward off an attack from the Bourbons, who might, if their commanders had been either able or daring, have endangered the capital.

During the weeks of waiting, the war of factions at Naples raged to a conclusion. Garibaldi himself foresaw in September that when the King resolved to invade the Papal States he would not stop until the Italian banner flew on the Castle of St. Elmo. At the King's coming the Garibaldian dictatorship must either cease, or there would be civil war. Not for a moment does Garibaldi himself appear to have dreamed of forcibly resisting the King, in whose name he had dazzled the world by his mission of liberation; but his loyalty did not preclude him from harboring contradictory desires. He resented the interruption to his work in the Bourbon Kingdom. He had the love of power natural to a self-confident and enormously successful man. Nor would he give up his hope of freeing Rome and Venetia before he had crowned Victor Emanuel King of United Italy at the Quirinal. It had become impossible for him not to regard himself as a person above the law, who might obey the law if he chose, but was not to be criticized if, for reasons which satisfied him, he decided to act contrary to law. Devoted though he was to the cause of Unity under Victor Emanuel, he felt that he, and not the King, knew best what to do. The King must be saved from his advisers. Therefore, the truest service he could perform was to carry out the work of unification, sure that in the end the King and Italy would applaud him. In his belief that destiny conferred upon him more than human powers, thereby enduing his plans, simply because they were his, with a sacredness which only the profane

[63] Farini wrote the Manifesto. Cavour objected to the phrases, " *accozzaglia di gente* " (as applied to the beaten Papalists) and " *nido di sètte* " (which does not appear in those words, but is implied). *Lettere*, VI, 616.

would question, he strangely resembled Pius IX, the popular demigod of 1847 and 1848. Unfortunately, the resemblance held further: for Garibaldi, like Pius, was ruled by men stronger than he. So while his speeches, which were his own, breathed union and harmony, his acts, which were his advisers', inevitably bred discord. Only by keeping in mind the fact that his contradictions sprang from these sources, shall we judge him fairly.

On September 27 he issued an order of the day telling his troops that Cialdini had beaten Lamoricière, freed the Papal provinces, and crossed the Neapolitan frontier. "Very soon," he added, "we shall have the happiness of grasping those victorious right hands."[64] On October 4 he announced to Victor Emanuel the glorious days of the Volturno and Capua. Then he suggested that the King send troops into the Abruzzi to put down Bourbon supporters and he thanked him for the proposed despatch of four regiments to Naples, where they would be useful. After advising Victor Emanuel, as father of all his people, to welcome all the "honest," whatever their previous party colors, he urged the King to come to Naples, preferably by land, at the head of a division. "I will join my right to that division, and will go in person to do you homage and receive orders for further operations. Promulgate, Sire, a decree recognizing the rank of my officers. I will undertake to weed out those who ought to be weeded out."[65] The next week, he announced to the citizens of Naples, that the King would soon be among them. "Let us receive worthily the envoy of Providence," he said, "and let us strew on his path, in token of our redemption and of our affection, the flowers of concord, so pleasing to him and so necessary to Italy. No more political colors! no more parties! no more feuds! Let Italy One, as the people of this metropolis and King Galantuomo dreamed her, be the perennial symbol of our regeneration, of the grandeur and prosperity of our mother country."[66]

Fine words, soft words, and doubtless sincere words, at the moment when Garibaldi wrote them. But like intermittent gleams of sunlight through cloud-rifts on a stormy day, they did not represent the prevailing conditions.

At the end of September, as we have seen, Garibaldi reluctantly accepted Bertani's resignation, replaced him by Crispi, and

[64] Ciàmpoli, 185.   [65] Ibid, 186–87.   [66] Ibid, 188–89; Oct. 12.

offered the pro-dictatorship to Pallavicino, a man who, although he had broken with the National Society and voted against the cession of Nice and Savoy, was supposed to be esteemed by the King. Small of stature, pompous, and frankly conceited, Pallavicino allowed no bushel to hide the halo which, as the "martyr of the Spielberg," he was privileged to wear. But, not content to live on his past, he labored with great zeal and much success for the national cause. Egotism has not prevented many men from laying down their lives for their country, as Pallavicino would have done now, had the call come. At sixty-four he found himself, though inexperienced in administration, set over Naples, at all seasons one of the most degraded and barbarous of cities, and at that time seething with party passions, in addition to its usual ferment of crime and graft and vice. It was as if the wild beasts in a menagerie had broken out of their cages and flown at each others' throats, and Pallavicino were sent to play the part of lion-tamer. The little man, unterrified by their ferocity, confident in his own powers and upheld by his sense of duty, strode boldly in among them. His policy he summed up for Garibaldi in a single sentence: "Neither *Cavourian* nor *Mazzinian!* Like you, my great friend, I desire Italy one — and *indivisible* — under the constitutional sceptre of the House of Savoy."[67]

Pallavicino's first act, performed before he had received his commission as Pro-dictator, was to address a letter to Mazzini, urging him, as a patriot, to go away from Naples for the good of his country. "*Even not wishing it*," he said, "*you divide us.*" Though Mazzini might honestly declare that he had sunk his personal preferences for the sake of unity, still his life-long record as an invincible Republican aroused the distrust of the King and Ministers. "Your presence in these parts creates embarrassments for the Government and perils for the nation. . . . I do not doubt that the facts correspond to your words. But not everyone believes you; and there are many who abuse your name with the parricidal purpose of raising in Italy another banner. Honor enjoins you to put an end to the suspicions of the former, and to the intrigues of the others. Show yourself great by departing, and all decent persons will praise you for it."[68]

[67] Pallavicino, III, 613; Pallavicino to Garibaldi, Oct. 5, 1860.
[68] *Ibid*, III, 611; Pallavicino to Mazzini, Oct. 3, 1860.

This blunt request disturbed Mazzini, who did not know whether Garibaldi approved of it, or whether Pallavicino, in case the Apostle refused to go, intended to banish him, as Garibaldi had just banished Spaventa.[69] Mazzini's disciples vibrated between rage and alarm. Garibaldi himself, angry at what might be construed as the committing of his government to an anti-Mazzinian policy, sent for the aggrieved Apostle, who went to Caserta late on October 4. Crispi, who was present, described the interview thus more than twenty years later:

"Garibaldi was in bed, and the two, as soon as they were near, shook hands cordially, like friends who meet for the first time after a long and irksome separation. Garibaldi was the first to speak. — 'I hope you will not quit Naples according to the advice given you. Pallavicino's letter is an aberration: and you must know well that I can neither distrust you, nor suppose that your presence in Naples can be a hindrance to the triumph of the National Cause, for which we have both worked.' — 'General, I was sure of your mind; but the letter, because written by your Pro-dictator, has made a deep impression on the country.' — 'Pallavicino has been Pro-dictator only a few hours, and what he has written is on his own responsibility, and cannot be an act of the government. However that may be, I ask you not to stir, and I assure you that nobody will dare to molest you.'" [70]

Fortified by the knowledge that he had not lost his ascendency over Garibaldi, Mazzini wrote a beautiful reply to Pallavicino. To go, he said, would be to admit the charges of his calumniators; to go would be to convince Europe that Italy was governed by a tyrant — that an Italian had not the right to live in his native land; it would imply that he acknowledged an obligation to the Ministers at Turin, those politicians whom he deemed fatal to national unity. He had already, he added, made the greatest sacrifice possible, in accepting, for the sake of concord, at the popular will, the Monarchy. He had himself taught his very accusers to lisp the word Unity. That men were ungrateful was

[69] B. Croce: *Silvio Spaventa dal 1848 al 1861.* (Naples, 1898.) De Cesare: *Una Famiglia di Patriotti,* ccxii-ccxiii.

[70] Crispi: *Scritti,* 642; reprinted from *Nuova Antologia,* June 15, 1886. Historians may well distrust reports of interviews written many years later; but Crispi's statement here contains nothing unexpected, and he had no special reason for distorting.

no reason why he should voluntarily submit to their injustice, and thereby sanction it.[71]

Undeterred by Garibaldi's apparent rebuff, and unmelted by Mazzini's rehearsal of grievances and merits, Pallavicino forced the issue. In the Council of Ministers held on October 7, Crispi proposed that they should imitate Sicily and hold general elections for an assembly. Pallavicino, Conforti and others stood out for a plebiscite, and the next day Pallavicino proclaimed that on October 21 a plebiscite would be held, to accept or reject, by a simple "yes" or "no," the following formula: "The People wishes Italy one and indivisible, with Victor Emanuel, constitutional King, and his legitimate descendants."[72] Pallavicino declared that Garibaldi had approved of this act; Garibaldi contradicted him; perhaps the Martyr misunderstood; perhaps the Hero, as frequently happened, changed his mind. Whatever may be the truth, the proclamation threw the Mazzinians into a frenzy.

Many reasons urged them to put off to the latest day the union of Naples with the Kingdom of Italy. The most evident, if not the most influential, was that with union their occupation would be gone. They resented seeing the Kingdom, which the Revolution had acquired, pass into the hands of the Monarchy they hated. They claimed that the nine million South Italians ought not to be merged in the Northern Kingdom, but that a constituent assembly should be convened of representatives of all the free provinces of Italy to determine the form of government for the new nation. They pointed out that neither the Neapolitans nor the Sicilians had had the slightest part in framing the Statute of Piedmont, which they were now asked to adopt, without being given an opportunity to modify it according to their preferences or special needs. A statute suited to the Piedmontese might not be the best for the Neapolitans; a statute passed hurriedly in the inexperience of 1848 might not be the best even for Piedmont in 1860. The Mazzinian contention that so vital a matter should not be settled in haste, seemed plausible; but, as Abraham Lincoln remarked in a similar crisis, the deliberation which proceeds in the front of a house when the back is on fire

[71] Pallavicino, III, 615–17; Mazzini to Pallavicino, Oct. 6, 1860. Also in Mazzini: *Scritti*, XI, cxlv–cxlvii.   [72] Pallavicino, III, 621.

cannot be sane. The Mazzinians taunted the Italians with inconsistency in having waited nearly a year before annexing the Tuscans, who had kept begging to be annexed, whereas they now proposed to rush through in a month the absorption of the Neapolitans who did not wish to be absorbed.[73] This plea, which wholly ignored the fundamental difference between one case and the other, was so specious that it betrayed the insincerity of those who uttered it. Upon Garibaldi they employed arguments well-calculated to kindle his wrath and his ambition. Nice had been ceded after a spurious plebiscite — would he doom the Neapolitans to a similar sacrifice? The Revolution Triumphant was pledged to march forward to free Rome and Venetia; would he stop half-way, and surrender the leadership into the hands of the Monarchy, the timid and selfish Monarchy — the Monarchy which slavishly did the bidding of the French Emperor — the Monarchy which was always more ready to dance attendance on Diplomacy than to heed the appeal of Italian patriots? At their first sally, the Mazzinians seemed sure of capturing the Paladin. To complicate the situation, Mordini, Pro-dictator of Sicily, had refused passports to the committee bound for Turin to implore immediate annexation,[74] and he had ordered a general election for a constituent assembly to be held on November 1. Garibaldi not only approved this device for staving off Piedmontese intervention[75] but also stated that he wished the elections on the Mainland to be held in precisely the same manner as in Sicily. Pallavicino rendered uniformity impossible, unless either his or Mordini's move were revoked. Parisi, Mordini's Minister of the Interior, went to Naples to defend their side, and with Mazzini, Crispi, Cattaneo and the Marios he besieged Garibaldi.

For four or five days there was hurrying to and from Caserta, the Dictator's headquarters. He had the knack of allowing the latest comer to infer that *he* was the favored one. In truth, Garibaldi was tormented by indecision like that which had plagued him during the fortnight before the sailing of the Thousand. His heart went with those who urged him not to stop till liberation was completed; his intuition told him that he must submit to the King, whose champion he had proclaimed himself. His moral struggle grew intense, and took shape in contradictory acts. To

---

[73] Mario: *Garibaldi*, II, 6. [74] Rosi, 215. [75] *Ibid*, 216.

calm the tumult in the city, Pallavicino ordered the political clubs to disband. Thereupon the National Unitarian Association, made up of the most vehement Mazzinians, appealed to Garibaldi, who stated that this association was under his special guarantee, and annulled the Pro-dictator's ordinance. But the question of the Plebiscite overshadowed all others. On the evening of October 11 Garibaldi summoned a conference at which Pallavicino insisted that, if the Dictator were bent on holding the election to the assembly, that body ought simply to ratify the result of the plebiscite, and adjourn forever. A prolonged session, at which constitutional details were discussed, would inflame the already overwrought country and might easily lead to civil war. Garibaldi, much moved, retorted that he would never permit a civil war. Cattaneo, the venerable doctrinaire, put forward the quibble that Victor Emanuel was legally only King of *Piedmont*, not of *Italy*, and implied that the people of the Two Sicilies had no cause to wish to be annexed to Piedmont. Crispi defended the proposed assembly. Pallavicino, whose temper was never tightly corked, burst forth in an arraignment of Crispi, as the man who caused all the dissensions. "Without him," hissed the Pro-dictator, "Italy would be made already; with him, she will never be." Crispi, who did not let passion show in his speech, repelled the charge. Garibaldi, with accustomed chivalry, defended his mentor as his best friend — a man devoid of selfish aims, who had shared all dangers and had surpassed everyone in usefulness. "I ought not, I cannot, I will not sacrifice my friends to the ill humor or to the caprices of anyone," Garibaldi replied. "Stay or go, Marquis, as you choose. If you stay, I shall be content; but if you want to go, I shall certainly not hold you back." Pallavicino, repeating that, since the Dictator preferred Crispi it was not worth while to have summoned him from Turin, took his hat and left abruptly.[76]

As soon as the news of this break reached Naples, there was widespread dissatisfaction. On the following morning the city was strewn, as by a snowstorm, with white slips bearing the single word "*Yes*," to indicate that the Neapolitans favored annexation. The National Guard and a group of citizens signed

[76] Rüstow, 458–59. Pallavicino, III, 626–27. Mario: *Bertani*, II, 247–48. Crispi: *Mille*, 327–30, quoting letter to Mazzini of March 18, 1865; 331–32.

petitions in which they declared themselves amazed to hear that Pallavicino had resigned.[77] When Garibaldi came to the capital on the 13th, he found crowds surging through the streets and mingling their cheers for him, Victor Emanuel and Pallavicino with cries of "Death to Crispi! Death to Mazzini! Down with the Assembly!" "I hear that some one has shouted *death!*" he said indignantly, addressing the multitude from the balcony of the Foresteria Palace. "Italians ought to live, in order to make Italy. Let us have concord. A few days hence our King, Victor Emanuel, will come. Let us show ourselves worthy of the high destiny which Providence has reserved for Italy." Another conference followed. The leaders clung to their former sides. Garibaldi continued to lean towards the Assembly, when General Türr, who commanded the city of Naples, entered and presented the address of the National Guard. Garibaldi, deeply stirred, said that the popular will should be satisfied. "No one is readier than I to bow my head to so solemn an authority," he assured them. He bade Pallavicino to withdraw his resignation and continue his labors. A few hours later, Crispi — who like Bertani knew when his game was lost — resigned.[78]

Almost simultaneously, the telegraph announced that the Subalpine Parliament by an all but unanimous vote had upheld Cavour, declared for immediate annexation, and, by implication, repudiated Garibaldi's evil counselors. On the 15th Garibaldi, officially, as Dictator of the Two Sicilies, decreed that they made "an integral part of Italy, one and indivisible," under Victor Emanuel.[79] This served the double purpose of proving that he was true to his watchword, and of enabling any casuist who chose to assert that Victor Emanuel owed his new kingdom not to popular vote but to the fiat of the Dictator. Mordini at Palermo adjusted himself to the new orders, by proclaiming that the Sicilian plebiscite would be held on October 21, to vote for or against annexation. Thus failed on both sides of the Straits the struggle for an assembly.

There was nothing now but to await the coming of the King —

[77] Texts in Pallavicino, III, 630–32. Crispi: *Mille,* 333, n. 1.

[78] Pallavicino, III, 632–33, who quotes Caranti: *Il Plebiscito delle Provincie Napoletane,* p. 42. Caranti was Pallavicino's secretary. For Crispi's account of the crisis see *Mille,* 330–34. For his resignation, 337.

[79] On Oct. 12, decree for Sicily. Crispi: *Mille,* 336.

a painful interval, which Garibaldi and his men spent trying to learn how to retire with some show of grace. After the battle of the Volturno, the army lost its enthusiasm. Troops like the Garibaldians need the constant stimulus of going forward. The Bourbons at Capua checked its advance. The best of his legions were tired. Bivouacs amid the chills and rains of autumn caused many desertions. At least half of the army was composed of men much inferior in every respect to the veterans of Marsala and Palermo. The proportion of riff-raff had increased as soon as he triumphantly established himself on the Mainland. Adventurers, eleventh-hour patriots, spoils-seekers, and lovers of notoriety pressed in. The General created an appalling number of officers. At the first whisper that the Italian army was coming down to Naples, anxiety as to their own future filled the Garibaldians. Many demanded that they should be maintained in the service on equal terms with the regulars: all clamored for adequate recognition in pay and honors. Although they could not be expected in their hearts to welcome the National regiments, which were to close their campaign, they nevertheless loved Italy and were disposed to treat the regulars as fellow-countrymen. Garibaldi himself, having submitted to the plebiscite, uttered in public no unfriendly word. He meant to live up to the instructions he telegraphed on September 24 to Colonel Tripoti: "If the Piedmontese enter our territory, receive them as brothers."[80]

The elections passed off with but slight disturbances. Suggestion there was, and pressure, and in some cases intimidation. When the ballots were placed in two baskets, under the eyes of inspectors and of the crowd, it required resolution for the voter to select his slip from the basket of "Noes."[81] But the results were so nearly unanimous, that not even much coercion could account for them. In the Kingdom 1,302,064 voted yes and 10,312 no; in Sicily 432,053 yes and 667 no.[82]

On the 21st, while the plebiscite was being held throughout the Two Sicilies, Cialdini routed the Bourbons near Isernia, who

[80] Mario: *Bertani*, II. 267. The Turin newspapers of Oct. 2 stated that Bertani's own message was — "Receive them with musket volleys." *Ibid*. 266. See also, Bertani: *Ire*, 67.   [81] Tivaroni, III, 343. Mariani, IV, 360.

[82] A fortnight later the Marches voted, 133,072 ayes, 1212 noes; Umbria voted 99,628 ayes, 380 noes.

then withdrew their troops, except the garrison at Capua, behind the Garigliano. In announcing the victory in cordial terms to his men, Garibaldi told them that the valiant soldiers of the Army of the North would very soon grasp the hands of the courageous soldiers of Calatafimi and of the Volturno.[83] The road being now open, he went to meet the Royal Army, taking three brigades and the English Legion — that battalion which, unable to resist the wine which flowed in plenty, was drunk most of the time and gave him the greatest annoyance. At the cross-roads near Teano, very early in the morning of October 26, Garibaldi's outposts heard military bands playing, and presently the Piedmontese regiments approached down the highway. Garibaldi dismounted to await the King. Under his felt hat he had tied a silk muffler, which covered his ears and the back of his head, to keep off the dampness. Many of the troops passed without saluting, because they did not recognize him; but when Della Rocca, the courtier-soldier who commanded the vanguard, came up, the two shook hands, and talked for a while in friendly fashion. Then the Royal March was heard; the Royal Body-Guard, tall men and fine, and glistening with burnished trappings, hove in sight; and the King himself, riding an Arab horse and wearing a general's uniform, was heralded by cheers. Garibaldi lifted his hat, disclosing the silk kerchief, and went forward with the greeting, "Health to the King of Italy!" Victor Emanuel, who was already burly in figure, took off his fatigue cap and replied, "Health to my best friend!" They shook hands heartily and rode on ahead at a walk, conversing, while the staffs followed a little behind them. What they said has been variously reported, but there seems to be no doubt that the King was cordial in his hail-fellow-well-met way. Next to a pretty woman, he loved a soldier, and in Garibaldi he had the most amazing soldier alive. "How is your army?" one historian makes him ask the Paladin. "Tired," Garibaldi replied. "I believe it," said Victor Emanuel; "now it's the turn of mine to fight. Hold yourself in reserve with yours."[84] Having passed in review the Garibaldian detachment, the King informed Garibaldi that he had sent Della Rocca forward to invest Capua immediately, while a part of the

[83] Ciàmpoli, 189; Oct. 21, 1860.
[84] Mariani, IV, 483-84. Nisco: *Francesco II*, 179.

army proceeded to Sessa in order to cut the Bourbons' communications between Capua and Gaeta. A little later, the King and the Dictator parted, after another exchange of salutations and every appearance of friendliness. The waters of the Revolution and the river of Constitutionalism had met.[85]

The meeting had been correct in its formal informality: but the King had let slip a golden opportunity. It would have puzzled a stranger to understand the somewhat perfunctory courtesies. Were the two armies enemies, whose chiefs had come together to parley? or were they rivals, jealous of each others' prowess? The blame did not lie wholly with the Italians, because until a few days before they had misgivings as to how the Garibaldians would act towards them. The telegram, imputed to Bertani, and saying that the Piedmontese were to be received with musket volleys, had been generally accepted as genuine. It certainly harmonized with the known hostility of the Mazzinians, who seemed to control Garibaldi. If the Dictator's purposes were distrusted, he had only himself to blame, because up to the last moment he had persistently announced that he would not stop until he reached Rome, and he had delayed granting permission for the plebiscite, till Cialdini's army was well on its way to Naples. Only ten days before they met, Victor Emanuel himself had regarded a conflict with Garibaldi as not unlikely.[86] But since Garibaldi had yielded and the King had assumed that their relations were to be friendly, it was a stupid blunder to allow the first meeting to pass without more enthusiasm. For months the Garibaldians had been greeted everywhere with unstinted applause: the world had acclaimed them as heroes; they fully appreciated their own achievements; and they now were consenting, reluctantly but peaceably, to be superseded. If Paris was well worth a mass to Henry IV, the goodwill of the Garibaldians would have been bought cheap at the cost of even simulated gratitude and fervor. Instead of an effusive welcome, however, they had only stiff politeness: and there, at the King's right hand, was Fanti, the soldier whom Garibaldi hated most of all, and who Cavour had urged should not on any account accompany the King; and

[85] For this meeting see also Forbes, 332. Della Rocca, II, 76. Carandini, 397. J. W. Mario: *Garibaldi*, II, 19-21. Dicey: *Vic. Em.*, 258. A. Mario: *Garibaldi*, 78. Mario: *Supp.*, 298-99.   [86] Massari: *Vitt. Em.*, 357.

2

among the Royal suite was also Farini, who might well have kept in the background until negotiations had been concluded. Where was common tact, or even common sense, to prevent such a blunder?

The hypersensitive Garibaldians construed every oversight as studied insult. To Alberto Mario, the implacable Cassius on Garibaldi's staff, the well-fed, well-uniformed Royalists seemed hardly able to conceal their contempt for the humble Red Shirts, gaunt and shabby and bedraggled. He read on their faces that they thought themselves the liberators and Garibaldi the liberated. He gloated over the unwillingness of the country people to cheer Victor Emanuel, whilst they rent the very heavens with their shouts for Garibaldi.[87] Mario's temper boded ill for concord; the aggrieved patriot cannot be appeased. Equally ominous, on the other side, was the temper of the regular troops, as embodied in Fanti. Armies are at all times hotbeds of bickerings, jealousies, and envy between officer and officer, regiment and regiment: but when question arises between regulars and volunteers, the spirit of caste unites the regulars to defend their prestige against outsiders. The professional instinctively resents the success of the amateur. If raw volunteers can equal disciplined veterans, what becomes of the pretense that war is a business to be mastered only by much drill and study, and to be proved, if possible, by experience in the field? What becomes of marshals' batons, and of generals' bosoms plastered with medals and crosses? What becomes of titles and of social precedence in peace, and of pensions in old age and of bounties to widows and children? And yet, there were the Garibaldian Volunteers, with their record that dazzled mankind. Fanti and the majority of the army looked upon them as a College of Surgeons might look upon a layman who, in an emergency, had performed with his penknife a most difficult operation: they might be amazed; they would certainly point out that he had not followed the manual; but they would never think of electing him to be president over them. Something of this professional hauteur marked that first meeting of the two armies: it should have been neutralized by a deliberate effort, on the part of the Italians, to appear admiring and grateful. After all, Garibaldi was bestowing a kingdom on

[87] Mario: *Garibaldi*, II, 19–21.

the King. In excuse for this oversight, it might be said that the time and place of meeting were not prearranged; that the Royal troops were in the enemies' country and hastening to give battle — indeed, that same afternoon they fought an engagement; that the proper occasion for glorification would come later.

Garibaldi did not openly berate Victor Emanuel, but his chagrin took definite shape, as he realized that the bitterness of abnegation had come. The next day, Jessie Mario, hearing a cannonade on the Garigliano, asked him for instructions for her ambulance corps. "My wounded," he replied dolorously, referring to his army whose work of glory was cut short, "lie on the *other* bank of the Volturno." In a little while he added, very sadly: "Jessie, they have sent us to the rear."[88] Part of the King's troops, under Della Rocca, besieged Capua, which surrendered, after a feeble resistance, on November 2;[89] the main body proceeded to invest Gaeta, where the Bourbons were preparing for their last stand. Garibaldi passed the first days of November in making ready to depart. He hoped against hope that Victor Emanuel would still decide to keep him at the front till the end of the campaign. His most feverish concern was the fate of his Volunteers, whom he wished to have accepted as a separate corps in the regular army. To his Hungarian Legion he presented a flag,[90] worked by the ladies of Naples, and to the survivors of the Thousand a medal, decreed to them by the City of Palermo.[91] He sent the King a letter, written by Crispi, in which he praised the Neapolitans as a people not less docile than intelligent — a Delphic saying, true, if interpreted as it might be; praised the Garibaldian régime in Sicily, which had bestowed upon that island unexampled tranquillity; assured the King that the country was well started on the path of national unification; but, above all, he begged that his Majesty would take the Southern Army under his own protection.[92] Despite the surface shimmer of egotism, the letter was admirable in spirit, as in fact were all Garibaldi's published utterances — whoever dictated them — in these trying days.

On November 6 he assembled his legionaries at Caserta, to be

[88] Mario: *Garibaldi*, II, 21.   [89] Rüstow says that scarcely half-a-dozen projectiles caused any damage. P. 479.   [90] Oct. 31.   [91] Nov. 4. [92] Ciàmpoli, 198–99, who misdates the letter, Nov. 9; it should be Oct. 29. Crispi: *Mille*, 338, facsimile.

reviewed by Victor Emanuel: but the King failed not only to keep his promise but to send word that he could not be present — an unpardonable breach of tact, which cut the Garibaldians to the quick, and seemed to typify the growing arrogance of the Army cabal towards the Volunteers.[93] The next day came the official entry of the King into Naples. He and Garibaldi sat side by side in an open carriage, with the Pro-dictators Pallavicino and Mordini facing them. Rain fell in torrents, and Garibaldi and Mordini spread the flaps of their cloaks over the King's knees. They drove first to the Cathedral. Cardinal Riario Sforza, the Archbishop of Naples, had joined Bombino at Gaeta; but the clergy welcomed the new King with the impartial fervor of the proverbial inn-keeper. When he had been solemnly blessed, he went and knelt at the shrine of St. Januarius, and was given the cruse containing the thaumaturgic blood, which he kissed. There had been discussion between Victor Emanuel and his intimates as to whether he should countenance this humbug or not. "I should wish by all means to inaugurate the new era by respecting religion and the Church," said Della Rocca, "but by abolishing superstitions." The King inclined to agree, until Farini and some of the others pointed out that, as the miracle had been worked for Garibaldi a few weeks before, the Neapolitan clergy and populace would be incensed if Victor Emanuel slighted their patron.[94] So the King kissed the vessel, and some chroniclers report that the blood obligingly liquefied, while others are sceptical. But as the crowds believed that St. Januarius had accepted the new ruler, the end was attained.

The King escaped with difficulty from the crush. Little Pallavicino, nearly suffocated, kept shouting, "Make way for me! I am the Pro-dictator!" but nobody heeded him. Hundreds pressed round Garibaldi to kiss his hands and garments. Priests had their cassocks burned by the candles or torn off. Pandemonium reigned. On regaining their carriage, the triumphant quartet proceeded down Via Toledo, which, in spite of the deluge, was packed with enthusiastic throngs. From the windows, women showered flowers; on the sidewalks, from under their umbrellas or dripping hats, the men shouted indiscriminately for Garibaldi

[93] No excuse for this tactless oversight has been given.
[94] Della Rocca, ii, 94–95, 103–104. Rosi, 423–27.

and the King. The triumphal arches, made of cardboard, as if to symbolize the durability of Neapolitan enthusiasm, went to pieces in the wind and the rain. Thirty cardboard Victories, portly female figures, representing the chief cities of the Kingdom, each holding up the forefinger of her right hand, drooped or collapsed. Nothing, however, could dampen the ardor of the people, and the King, despite his soaking, kept in good humor. On reaching the Royal Palace, he received the authorities.

Garibaldi, on the contrary, appeared preoccupied and discontented, and with reason: for he was brooding over the work he was not allowed to finish, and he felt keenly what he regarded as the supercilious attitude of the Royal retinue. To suspect that Fanti or Farini was dogging him at every turn, stirred his bile. That evening, being irritated by some pin-prick of etiquette, — a chamberlain had requested him to take his hat off at the Royal reception, — he declined to attend the San Carlo Theatre with the King. The next day, he said in disgust to Persano that men were treated like oranges, — to be thrown into the corner as soon as the last drop of juice is sucked out. He refused the Collar of the Order of the Annunziata as a tainted honor, since Fanti and Farini had received it; but when it was conferred upon Pallavicino, and not upon Mordini, he was angry. At a formal audience, the Pro-dictators presented the plebiscites; Conforti, Minister of the Interior, addressed Victor Emanuel as King of the Neapolitan People; the act of union was read and signed; as at a wedding, everyone seemed overjoyed, although those experienced men knew only too well that marriage does not always bring concord. After the ceremony, Garibaldi had a private interview with the King, who wished to force honors upon him. The title of General, equivalent to a marshalship — a royal palace for his residence — a steamship — ample provision for his sons — a dowry for his daughter — a generous donation — even a dukedom — by these offers Victor Emanuel strove to express his gratitude. But Garibaldi shook his head at them all. He would accept nothing, he said, except the lieutenant-generalship of the new Kingdom, with full powers for a year. It is variously stated that he demanded this, and that he offered his services in the hope that by his popularity he might make the Herculean task of reconstruction easier. The King, however, could not grant his

request. Then Garibaldi urged again the claims of his Southern
Army, and the King seems to have promised very liberally.

The next morning, November 9, before the town was awake,
Garibaldi rowed from the landing to the *Hannibal*, where he bade
good-bye to Admiral Mundy and for half an hour poured out his
grievances into that officer's sympathetic ears.[95] Then he proceeded to the *Washington* near by, and embarked for Caprera.
Three or four of his bosom friends and his son Menotti accompanied him. He carried with him a bag of seeds, another of vegetables, and a roll of salt codfish. Although the treasury of the
Two Sicilies had been at his disposal for more than five months,
he had taken nothing for himself. At his departure, having only
a few pennies in his purse, he was forced to borrow 1500 lire from
Adriano Lemmi, the unfailing benefactor of the Revolution. As
the *Washington* steamed past the Italian fleet, Persano's impulse was to salute the Dictator, but etiquette forbade firing
salutes for anybody save the King, when he was in the city.
Garibaldi left behind a farewell manifesto to his crusaders in
arms, telling them that they must consider the campaign just
ended as the penultimate stage to their national resurrection;
that Providence had favored them by allowing them to fulfil
the stupendous conception which the elect of twenty generations
had cherished; that they would go on conquering. He exhorted
the women of Italy to cast cowards out of their sight. He had his
fling at Diplomacy and at Napoleon III. The Italian People, he
said, would not go crawling and begging its liberty, nor be towed
by men with hearts of mud. Victor Emanuel was its chief. He
besought every able-bodied Italian to arm himself. "If March,
1861, does not find a million Italians in arms — poor liberty, poor
Italian vitality!" "To-day," he added, "I have to withdraw,
but for a few days only. The hour of conflict will find me again
with you, alongside of the soldiers of Italian liberty."[96]

The spectacular informality of his going impressed the imagination much more than if he had embarked, as he might well
have done, with full honors, escorted to the waterside by the
King's regiments and his own veterans, acclaimed by myriads
of Neapolitans, and by all the ships in the harbor beflagged in his
honor. But the studied simplicity which he preferred, served to

[95] Mundy, 280–87. Also in *Correspondence*. [96] Text in Ciàmpoli, 197–98.

advertise him as a new Cincinnatus, as a patriot purged of personal ambition, and so modest that he shrank from even being thanked. It served also to give color to the suspicion that the King had not been duly grateful to his stupendous benefactor. The Collar of the Annunziata dangling at his neck and a dozen stars blazoning his coat, would not have made Garibaldi's farewell so conspicuous as did the bag of seed-corn and the bundle of salted cod. The world, ignorant of the gifts he had refused, contrasted the glory of his achievements with the penury of his rewards: and it was right in honoring his apparent self-effacement. The King-makers of earlier days, the Monks and the Warwicks, were not like him. Had the *Washington* gone down on that voyage to Caprera, Garibaldi would have been transfigured for all time at the noblest moment of his life. Remembering only the shining qualities by which he wrought his transcendent exploits, posterity would have come to regard him as indeed a modern demigod. But Fortune, having permitted him to lift his laureled head among the immortals, brought him back to earth and doomed him to twenty years of anticlimax.

CHAPTER XXXIV

THE SEAMY SIDE OF PATRIOTISM

WHILE Victor Emanuel was marching southward and Garibaldi with his Radical inspirers was regretting the King's approach, Cavour at Turin had to bear the brunt of Diplomacy's displeasure. More serious than chiding despatches was the menace of an attack by Austria. During the second and third weeks in October, when every day's advance towards Naples put the King's army farther and farther beyond call, the danger seemed pressing.[1] But Austria, having failed to go to the rescue of the Pope, now hesitated to declare war. She distrusted Napoleon; her treasury and army had not recovered from the drain of 1859; and she hoped to persuade Prussia and Russia to join her in a common crusade against Revolution triumphant in Italy. When the sovereigns of the three despotic Powers met at Warsaw on October 22, it appeared that none of them cared to hazard a policy that might lead to a European war.[2] Russia openly favored France; which meant that unless Napoleon III moved against the Italians nobody else would. "Accustom Europe to see you persevering in the direction you have once chosen," was Gortchakoff's advice to the French, given in a private letter to his intimate, De Morny. "Spare her the unexpected. She needs repose."[3]

Before the result of the Warsaw meeting was generally known, Lord John Russell sent Hudson a despatch which, when published, caused the Italians unspeakable joy. In it he said squarely that the Italians themselves were the best judges of their own interests: that the Papalists and Neapolitans had revolted because

---

[1] On Oct. 22, C. wrote Prince Napoleon that the nomination of Benedek to command the Austrian army in Italy, made an attack certain. C.'s intent was, of course, to rouse Napoleon III. *Lettere*, iv, 61. See also C. to Fanti, Oct. 27; *Ibid*, 71.   [2] For C.'s prediction as to Congress, see his letter to V. E., Oct. 23 ; *Lettere*, iv, 62–63.   [3] La Gorce, iii, 438; quoting Gortchakoff's letter of Oct. 22, 1860, from Morny's *Une Ambassade en Russie*, p. 231. See also, *Lettere*, iv, 85–86; C. to V. E., Nov. 2, 1860.

the Pope and the Bourbon King governed abominably, and that since 1849 Italians had come to recognize that their only remedy lay in a United Italy. With his English devotion to precedent he shrewdly quoted Vattel, who justified the revolution of 1688, on the ground that "when a people from good reasons take up arms against an oppressor, it is but an act of justice and generosity to assist brave men in the defense of their liberties." So Russell argued that if it was right for William of Orange to aid Englishmen to overthrow the tyranny of James II, it must be equally right for Italian patriots to aid their brothers groaning under Bourbon and Papal misrule. At any rate, he insisted that they were the best judges, and he did not shrink from asserting that the British Government believed that the Southern Italians had good reasons for throwing off their allegiance to Francis II, and that Victor Emanuel could not be blamed for assisting them. He declared that the Italian Revolution had been conducted with singular temper and forebearance; that Austria, France, Prussia, and Russia, had no sufficient grounds for their severe censure of Victor Emanuel's acts; and that the Queen's Government rejoiced at "the gratifying prospect of a people building up the edifice of their liberties, and consolidating the work of their independence amid the sympathies and good wishes of Europe."[4]

Lord John's bolt floored the conventional statesmen of the Continent — it was so shockingly irregular! "That is not diplomacy," said the Muscovite Brunnow; "that is sheer blackguardism." Vitzthum, the Saxon man-of-the-world, denounced it as being "unique in the annals of diplomacy."[5] Others found the reference to Vattel pedantic. It was all as irregular as if, in a community of cannibals, a chief should suddenly propose that they stop killing and eating their captives. For the Italians, however, Lord John's despatch was as precious as a page of Holy Writ. "You are blessed night and morning by twenty millions," his nephew Odo wrote him from Rome. "I could not read it myself without deep emotion. Thousands of people copied it from each other to carry it to their homes and weep over it for joy and gratitude in the bosom of their families, away from brutal mercenaries and greasy priests."[6] When Hudson read this

[4] *Correspondence*, 1861, pt. vii, 125–27; Russell to Hudson, Oct. 27, 1860. Walpole: *Russell*, II, 325–37.   [5] Walpole: *Russell*, II, 327.   [6] *Ibid*, 328; Odo Russell to Lord John, Dec. 1, 1860.

despatch to Cavour, "he shouted, rubbed his hands, jumped up, sat down again, then he began to think, and when he looked up, tears were standing in his eyes. Behind your despatch" (Hudson wrote Lord John) "he saw the Italy of his dreams, the Italy of his hopes, the Italy of his policy." At Naples, Villamarina told Elliot that the despatch was worth more than a hundred thousand men, and Victor Emanuel spoke almost as strongly to Admiral Mundy. Thenceforward, Cavour could concentrate his energy on making the Italians one people: for England blocked the way to Austrian or other intervention.

His chief enemies were the Italians themselves in Naples, Bourbon Reactionists and Muratists; in Sicily, Reactionists and Autonomists; in the States of the Church, Papalists; and everywhere, the Party of the Revolution, which made Garibaldi its screen. The hero or paladin of old was born to slay dragons and to rescue lovely ladies in distress, not to engage in conflicts which call not merely for courage and the sword, but for wisdom, foresight, decision and justice. Unhappily, since Garibaldi took Palermo, he had had thrust upon him tasks for which he was wholly unfit. Pegasus harnessed to the plow was not more out of place than Garibaldi amid the political factions at Naples. The condition of that city under his régime has been fiercely discussed. If we believe a dear fanatic like Jessie Mario, that Hell's kitchen became, in the twinkling of an eye, at the coming of the Liberator, pure, law-abiding and noble. This is as improbable as if it were asserted that the day after a great musician visited a deaf-and-dumb asylum its inmates performed perfectly one of Beethoven's symphonies. Much nearer the truth is Elliot's private verdict, sent to Lord John on the day when Garibaldi left for Caprera: "The corruption which has prevailed in every branch of the administration during his dictatorship has far surpassed anything that was known even in the corrupt times which preceded it." [7] The British Minister, an ardent supporter of Italian unity, having had much experience at Naples and having mixed with all sets, can hardly be gainsaid. And yet Naples may not have been so anarchical as the anti-Mazzinians described it. The National Guard kept crimes of violence within normal limits. Vice, which never took the trouble to wear a mask there, was

[7] *Correspondence*, 1861, vii, 141; Elliot to Russell, Nov. 9, 1860.

SIR JAMES HUDSON
British Minister at Turin

not more flagrant than it had been under Liborio Romano and his Camorrist allies. But there was inevitably a welter of political agitation. Cavourians and Mazzinians worked openly and the Bourbon reactionists and Muratist intriguers by stealth. If the crowds shouted "Annexation" and "Death to Crispi," the Mazzinians denounced the corrupting power of Piedmontese gold: if they hurrahed for the Assembly, the Mazzinians took it as proof of the high political culture and undying patriotism of the Neapolitans. As always happens in such an overturn, the criminal classes were quick to disguise themselves under a political cloak. The legion of the lawless naturally wished the period of disorder to continue. Most of the higher nobility, although they were too debased to risk anything for any cause, would have welcomed Bombino's return. Property-holders, tradesmen, merchants and professional men — unless they had selfish reasons for desiring the Bourbon — looked forward to Victor Emanuel's coming to put an end to the perturbed conditions which caused hard times. There was also an army of Bourbon placemen, with their families, friends and hangers-on, to be disposed of. If retained, they would perpetuate the methods in which they had been bred; if dismissed, they swelled the multitude of malcontents. Garibaldi was justly criticized for making many unfit appointments; he might have pleaded in extenuation that he had no body of trained men to pick from: but as he went on the assumption that all Garibaldians were saints, he did not trouble to notice his critics, unless it were to brand them as calumniators. His real mentors were Bertani and Crispi, who very logically put in office the agents with whom they had conspired. Garibaldi's ability to pick administrators was typified by his appointing as minister of art and education Alexander Dumas the Elder, who turned up at Naples with one of his mistresses dressed as a boy, and was given a royal villa. The Prince of Romancers never invented a situation more improbable than that of his being taken seriously by the Modern Paladin!

When the military operations of the Garibaldians drew to a close, after the Battle of the Volturno, the war of words rose to a tempest. Personal abuse, which had been hardly checked during the summer and early autumn, overflowed on all sides as when a drain breaks loose. That dualism planted in the hearts of the

Italians by the ancient conflict between Church and State, a dualism embodied in medieval times by Guelfs and Ghibellines, threatened under new leaders and changed forms to cleave Italy asunder at the moment when her unity seemed assured. The Party of the Revolution was as reluctant to abdicate, as it had been ready to seize and resolute to wield power. It had come permanently to adopt a policy of grievance. It attributed every act of the King's government to jealousy or spite. Piece by piece, it had built up a legend in which only the basest ingratitude — not to mention political imbecility — could account for the conduct at Turin. It regarded Cavour as little better than a traitor who, in order to keep his own ascendency and to save the House of Savoy, had truckled to the French Emperor, coquetted with the King of Naples, and sold two provinces to France. So diabolical was his heart that he was described as gloating over the likelihood that Garibaldi's expedition would founder at sea on its way to Marsala. Pianciani gravely reports that some one had seen in Cavour's study a map on which, marked in blue pencil, were Genoa, Sardinia and other places that the wicked Minister had agreed to throw to the French Cerberus. Day in and day out, Mazzini kept preaching that the King did not intend to unite Italy, but to Piedmontize it. Bertani, whose keen mind, whetted by a sense of personal wrongs, had given edge to many vindictive shafts during the summer, had no compunction against writing from Turin on October 6 that Cavour was thinking of proclaiming Garibaldi an outlaw and a felon![8] Crispi was neither more scrupulous nor less scathing than Bertani. To cite Maurizio Quadrio or the Marios or others of the inner circle, would illustrate again how sectarian zeal absolves its victims not merely from the claims of truth-telling and ordinary charity, but even from the obligations of common sense.[9] Outside of these was a larger ring, composed of adventurers, if not of rogues, who found patriotism a convenient refuge and a source of profit and promotion. Accepting everybody who volunteered under him as a brother hero, Garibaldi flattered the Neapolitans by

[8] Rosi, 419; Crispi to Mordini, Turin, Oct. 6, 1860.

[9] Among the documents of the Risorgimento with which I am familiar, none is more depressing than Maurizio Quadrio's *Il Libro dei Mille*, which shows how, because of hope deferred, a worthy spirit became shriveled and sour.

lauding them as a noble people, although only a few inhabitants of their city joined his army.

On the other side there was a similar flood of misrepresentation, calumny and hatred, in swelling which the Clericals vied with the Liberals. They persisted in arraigning Mazzini as an upholder of regicide, an instigator of social and political revolution, a brand of perpetual discord, an autocrat: and unfortunately they could produce ample evidence, in his writings and career, for thus arraigning him. When he protested that he had sacrificed his Republicanism on the altar of Unity, they had reason to put no faith in the conspirator who only a little while before had attempted to capture Genoa, heedless of kindling a civil war which must have ruined Piedmont as the leader of the Italian cause. Prudence dictated to the Government to have no transaction with this man or his irreconcilable disciples. If the Garibaldians had been left to themselves, it seems most probable that the Mazzinian minority, which supplied will-power to them all, would have attempted to set up a republic. There is no doubt that Garibaldi was honest in declaring that he would stand by the Monarchy: but in the hands of Bertani or Crispi he was as putty. When, therefore, the conservatives accused him of playing a double game, they wronged him in his present intention, although his future change of mind might justify them.

The savagest attacks centred on Bertani. He was charged with appropriating a fortune by peculation, by dishonest railway concessions and by other forms of graft. None of these charges was ever proved; indeed, Bertani was the unlikeliest of men to enrich himself by such means. He lived poor; he died poor. The luxury of his hatreds from 1860 onwards procured him a satisfaction which he would not have exchanged for millions of francs. He was accused of sending the atrocious order to Colonel Tripoti to receive the Piedmontese with bullets. That a telegram so worded and signed by him exists has never been shown: that it was sent, could never be proved. Bertani alleged that his message dated September 23 read: "If the Piedmontese should wish to cross the frontier, tell them that before allowing it you must ask instructions of the Dictator." He alleged further that on the 24th Garibaldi himself telegraphed: "If the Piedmontese cross our territory, receive them as brothers." Later, when the Italian newspapers castigated Bertani for the "volleys of musketry" order, he appealed to Bixio; but Bixio replied that, as he had never seen the despatch, he could affirm or deny nothing. Medici, likewise appealed to, gave a similar answer, as any man careful to have his testimony correspond to his knowledge, must have done. Their respect for truth seemed little better than betrayal to Bertani and his intimates. The devoted Jessie Mario, whose idea of judicial evidence had not advanced beyond the primitive stage of compurgation, berated Bixio and Medici for not declaring openly that Bertani was too noble a patriot to be capable of writing such an unpatriotic telegram. There the matter stands.[10]

The difficulty in clearing Bertani lies in the fact that there was nothing in his reported views and conduct during the summer and autumn of 1860 to make the despatch seem improbable. To the last he had fought the idea that the King's Government should be allowed to interfere with his own expedition against the Papal States; he had consistently maintained that Garibaldi and not the King was the sole judge of what needed to be done for Italian Unity; he vilified Cavour; he exacted from Garibaldi the promise to defer annexation; he warned continually, with the inherited venom of a Lombard, against the selfish purposes of the Piedmontese. That Medici, Bixio and others had heard him utter sentiments in comparison with which the telegram to Tripoti was mild, can hardly be questioned. His subsequent writings give no sign that he was softened. In his "Account Rendered" of the receipts and expenses of the campaign, he unblushingly attributed to himself and his friends the collecting of all the money and material. There came from him no acknowledgment of the assistance of the National Society; no word as to the subvention from the Million Muskets Fund; no recognition of the secret aid which the Government, with Cavour's connivance, rendered in fitting out those who followed the Thousand; no hint of the King's personal contributions. And in his "Political Rages Beyond the Tomb," although he wrote nine years after the event, when his fury might have cooled sufficiently to give scope for fair-play, if not for magnanimity, he laid bare a heart corroded by malice and hate. La Farina's "Correspond-

[10] Mario: *Bertani*, ii, chap. 109; but especially 266-71. Also, Bertani: *Ire.*

ence," which called forth his rages, contained mistaken statements, snap judgments and hostile imputations: but they were
written to intimates in the heat of a volcanic conflict, without
expectation that they would be published. The delight which
Bertani takes in mauling the dead La Farina is literally ghoul-
ish: for ghouls and not generous men feed upon carcasses; and to
rebut calumnies by other calumnies is the practice of either
rogues or fanatics. Until the spring of 1860, Bertani was the
sanest of the Radicals; thenceforth, he was the most intractable.
Lease of power, as Garibaldi's second, made him dictatorial;
opposition embittered and thwarting infuriated him. Conscious
of his own rectitude, he came to regard those who questioned the
wisdom of his acts, as enemies of rectitude itself. Being by nature
an intense partisan, he never saw the whole. From leader of a
party, he shrank to be leader of a faction, and so, by an inevitable process of contraction, he became a fanatic without a following. It was not from mere pique that Medici and Bixio,
Cosenz and Türr, Sirtori, Guerzoni and Malenchini, and even
Crispi, dropped away from him during 1860 or soon afterward.
But Italy, remembering that his devotion helped towards unity,
may well forget his venom which, thanks to wiser patriots than
he, failed to poison the life-blood of the new nation.

Close upon Garibaldi's departure from Naples, another pro-
tagonist in the Drama of Italian Independence made his exit.
Still under the ban and disguised for a time in a Garibaldian red
shirt, Mazzini glided out of reach of Victor Emanuel's police.
In these pages, we shall encounter no more that spare figure,
seemingly frail, yet capable of unlimited fatigues; we shall see no
more that face, grave with sorrowing for an unworthy world, nor
those eyes, which, whether glowing with benediction or flashing
with scorn, no one ever forgot; we shall not hear again that voice
which had once been the voice of conscience for thousands of
Italians, and uttered doctrines so seductive that his enemies
almost feared to listen to him. If Europe in the nineteenth century bore any prophet of the celestial lineage, Joseph Mazzini
was he.

But immense injustice has been done to Mazzini the Prophet
by confounding him with Mazzini the Politician. Nothing could
be more preposterous than the claim that, having been the

forerunner, he must therefore be the best pilot to Italian Unity. If Piedmont had taken his advice after 1850, there would have been neither independence nor unity; if his own Party of Action had followed him, Italy would never have been freed or united. Beginning with his tragical fiasco at Milan in February, 1853, he proved by the mad enterprises which he instigated and by the wild propaganda which he poured forth, that he misunderstood the time, the men, the means. He not only lost all sense of proportion, but deceived himself by supposing that his formulas would work automatically, irrespective alike of the intelligence and special aptitude of the Italians or of their previous training. If he had had his way there would have been no Crimean Expedition, no spokesman for Italy at the Congress of Paris, no agreement at Plombières, no War of 1859 which resulted in the liberation of Lombardy and the union of the Centre. Instead, there might have been civil war in Genoa and a succession of tragically inept conspiracies.

But far worse than his abortive opposition, — which, after all, merely proved that he never

> "Knew the seasons when to take
> Occasion by the hand," —

was Mazzini's ten-year-long sowing of discord. Thanks to his genius for invective, seldom equaled and never surpassed, he planted in the hearts of many Italians distrust or hatred of the monarchical majority without which Unity could not have been achieved. He imputed selfish motives to the King, he vilified Cavour, he set circulating the poisonous insinuation that the Peninsula was to be Piedmontized, he scornfully reproved Manin and other Republicans who recognized that the time had come to unite under the King's leadership, and when the National Society drew nine-tenths of his party away from him, he reviled that. Then, the seeds of his sowing having borne fruit after their kind in factions and feuds, he protested that he was the champion of Unity, a peace-maker, a conciliator. That he believed this, who can question? Mazzini would always be reconciled to any opponent who submitted to him. But there is no appeal from Pallavicino's indictment: "Your presence divides us." None of his avowed enemies have equaled Crispi, his ablest disciple, in blasting Mazzini's pretensions to practical statesmanship.

Crispi's arraignment, delivered in 1865, could not be explained away, because it was substantially true.[11]

Gradually, however, as Mazzini's career ceases to be distorted by being falsely appealed to by partisans of the issues of our day, his failure as a politician will seem less important, while his glory as prophet will be magnified. His genius was to quicken deadened consciences, to reveal patriotism as a duty and a religion to Italians who had forgotten the very meaning of country. An authentic spokesman of the ideal, he was pathetically ineffectual before the concrete facts of life. Fate seems never more sardonic towards great men than when, having raised them up by giving opportunity to their extraordinary talents, it discredits them by transferring them to a position which exposes their defects. So was it when Mazzini the Prophet and Garibaldi the Soldier of Liberty went astray in the realm of statesmanship.

Among the cardinal errors of both was their belief that the common people and peasantry of Italy would respond to the call of freedom. The Party of Action, which made so proud a boast of being the true representative of the nation, probably never numbered more than a few hundred thousand adherents, and of these only a fraction enlisted. When Garibaldi retired, his army mustered 51,000 men, but fully 16,000 of these were soldiers only on paper, and several thousand more would have been rejected by any recruiting officer who knew his business. This maximum, drawn from 17,000,000 or 18,000,000 of the lower classes, disposed of the Mazzinian claim, which Garibaldi once echoed and later denounced, that the vast majority of Italians were on tiptoe to rebel. The remnant of three or four millions, drawn from the aristocracy, the tradespeople and the professional men, really achieved the Risorgimento. Among them, four out of five preferred a constitutional monarchy to a republic; and even among the avowed Republicans, the more prudent admitted that the monarchical form ought to be preserved until national unity had become indissoluble. Crispi, who was destined to surpass all his brother Mazzinians in that "tact for the possible" which Cavour defined as the hall-mark of a statesman, was quick to declare, "The Monarchy unites us and the Republic would divide us." In becoming a Monarchist, in 1862, Crispi tacitly confessed

[11] Crispi, 307–60; Lettera a Giuseppe Mazzini, March 18, 1865.

2

that Cavour's policy of 1860, which saved the Monarchy, that policy against which Crispi himself had fought most savagely, was, indeed, the salvation of Italian Unity.

By grace of the plebiscites, Victor Emanuel was at last King of Italy; but the labor of unification was increased by the antagonism, which never flagged, although it was not always open, of the Mazzinians and Garibaldians. They professed to acquiesce in the triumph of the Monarchy, but they could refrain neither from showing their disappointment and disgust nor from venting recriminations. As when husband and wife quarrel, everything which one does exasperates the other, so it was with them. Quite inexcusably, the King and his suite omitted to pay court to the touchy liberators. The *Official Gazette* contained no notice of Garibaldi's departure. The King referred too grudgingly to the Paladin's unexampled services. The Royal offers of honor and wealth being little advertised, the public talked of ingratitude, and idolized the simplicity and self-effacement of the Hero, who had retired to Caprera with his bag of seeds, bundle of codfish and few pounds of borrowed money. Conscious that he was heroic and self-sacrificing, Garibaldi could not understand how anybody could overlook this fact. His followers were like him; only, where he mulled over his grievance, they screamed it to the universe. The King went ahead in unemotional fashion to introduce a new administration; whereas the Garibaldians would have had him keep thanking them for a month or so: but Victor was never cut out to play Romeo, and the Revolution was not the Juliet of his choice.

Appointed Lieutenant-General for Naples, Farini, that alert administrator who had shown his mettle at Modena the year before, was overwhelmed by his task. Even if the Neapolitans had sincerely desired an honest government, months would have been required to plant it and years to make it flourish: but to them, all government was a hateful restraint, to be circumvented by brute violence or by bribes. Everyone now scrambled for the spoils. The Liberals naturally expected, and they received, most of the plums; this enraged the Garibaldians, who asked pertinently why they, who had won the Kingdom, should be set aside for their feckless rivals. Reactionaries — priests, nobles and lazzaroni — hoped by stirring up the turmoil to improve their

LUIGI CARLO FARINI

GIUSEPPE LA FARINA

own chances. Any criminal needed only to put on a red shirt in order to pass himself off as a patriot. Although ex-Bourbons who loyally accepted the new régime had of course the right to be treated as Italians, the Garibaldians denounced such equalization as a concession to reaction. That Ghio, who led the troops against Pisacane's band in 1857, should now be allowed to command the Castle of St. Elmo, seemed dastardly to Jessie Mario. Poor Farini had hardly measured his task, when the sudden death of his son-in-law seemed to crush him. He fell into a melancholia, the first symptom of the mental break-down which eclipsed his later career. Losing control of his power of action, he had to be recalled. Among his most efficient colleagues was Silvio Spaventa, the Minister of the Interior, who toiled indefatigably to reduce the capital to order; but we are not told that even Hercules cleansed the Augean stables in a day.

More ominous than the lawlessness of Naples, was the brigandage which infested many parts of the Kingdom. To be brigands had been as natural a trade for enterprising provincials under the misrule of the Bourbons, as to be Camorrists was for the dwellers in the great city itself. A brigand might almost be regarded as a self-respecting person, who protested against the extortions and iniquities of Bomba's system. Now, however, from his refuge at Gaeta Francis II organized brigandage on a large scale. The bands of highwaymen, armed with his leave, committed atrocities, sparing neither women nor children, robbed, burned and intimidated; and the Bourbons had the effrontery to claim that in so doing they were honest patriots, defending their homes against the Piedmontese invaders. They rendered the introduction of orderly government impossible. They cut off communications, by guarding the country roads. The fastness of Civitella del Tronto served them as a refuge; and if they were hard pressed they found safety by merely crossing into the Pope's country. Had not Francis II been seconded by the Papal leaders, brigandage might have collapsed with his downfall; but its real arsenal was Rome, where the Papal advisers did not scruple to give instructions to the priests and friars of the Neapolitan provinces to foment an insurrection. The superstitious mountaineers of the Abruzzi, only too glad to have an ecclesiastical sanction for their banditry, pocketed eagerly the spurious coins, bearing Bombino's head, which were sent from Rome[12] to be distributed to them from the monasteries and curates' houses. It was characteristic of the Bourbon-Papal decadents, that they should pay even their hired assassins in false money.

Only by a remorseless hunting down, could brigandage in its openly violent form be exterminated. The work required years; called eventually for the employment of 70,000 or more troops; cost tens of millions of lire in direct losses, and an incalculable sum in the check to agriculture, industry and habits of civilization; destroyed hundreds of soldiers' lives in actual combat and many more by disease; and retarded by several decades the Italianization of the Two Sicilies. In the 23 months from May, 1861, through March, 1863, no fewer than 7151 brigands were rendered innocuous. Of these 2413 were killed in conflict and 1038, captured in arms, were shot.[13] That Pius IX and Francis II should abet brigandage, in order to blight the provinces which, through misrule which the world had long condemned, they could not retain, marks the last stage of decomposing despotism. Apologists of both tried to make it appear that the brigandage they organized was a holy war, and the Abruzzi were another Vendée, but the world was not deceived. Pope and Bourbon hoped, by promoting anarchy in the Centre and South, that they could persuade Europe not only that the Union of Italy was a sham, but that a large part of the country would not submit to a union forced upon it by Piedmontese ambition aided by French arms. Posterity has simply reaffirmed the verdict of a contemporary English historian, who said: "There can be no greater crime against society than that of organizing, paying, and directing the rogues of a nation for the purpose of destroying it. For though it may not be a crime to destroy a nation, it is always the greatest of crimes to corrupt, befoul, disorganize society. Brigandage strikes deeper than nationality."[14]

In Sicily, other difficulties confronted the new government. The inveterate feuds cropped out. Autonomists, Reactionaries, Mazzinians, plied their conflicting propaganda. That section of the population which was always against the government,

---

[12] M. Monnier: *Notizie Storiche Documentate sul Brigantaggio*. Florence, 1863, p. 41. [13] David Hilton: *Brigandage in South Italy*. London, 1864. 2 vols. II, 268. [14] De Witt, 392. Hilton, II, 13.

because government either fleeced it or tried to curb its criminal acts, swelled rapidly. To provide new tools for the new task, Cavour sent Marquis Montezemolo, a Piedmontese Liberal, to replace Mordini, who had not yet sufficiently purged himself of his Republicanism. La Farina and Cordova accompanied Montezemolo,—a questionable move, in view of the wrath they had stirred up in the summer; but Cavour required agents there whom he could trust, and he wished to atone for La Farina's expulsion. When the King visited Palermo, he was welcomed with frantic demonstrations. The populace unhitched his horses, dragged his court coach up Via Toledo to the Cathedral, and then they surged with him into the building. Royally incensed at this indignity, Victor Emanuel told the Mayor to inform them that he was neither an opera tenor nor a ballet-dancer, and that he wished men to behave like men and not like beasts. The Garibaldians carefully noted that he made no acknowledgment in public of their Chief.[15] He avoided further ovations, by not appearing in the streets on foot. But as La Farina wrote Cavour: "Our Southerners need to know the person *materially* and to see it, in order to love it. . . . Four or five promenades . . . would arouse greater sympathy for the King, than four or five acts of civic virtue or of military valor. . . . *Garibaldi showed himself lavishly.*"[16] The King, however, lacked both the will and the art to curry favor with anybody, least of all with the populace, and after a brief stay, he left for Naples. The Sicilian situation grew worse. La Farina found three or four times as many office-holders as the work called for; pensions assigned to wives, daughters and even lemans of self-styled patriots; and patriots themselves drawing each four or five salaries.[17] He endeavored to reform these abuses. As a result, he and Cordova had to flee from Palermo in peril of their lives. La Farina's enemies charged him with want of tact: in truth, however, political spoilsmen have never discovered tact in the reformer who deprived them of their spoils. Although Montezemolo labored conscientiously, more than goodwill on his part was needed to redeem Sicily. Farini's collapse enabled Cavour to suggest the appointment, January 9, 1861, of the King's cousin, Prince Eugene of Carig-

[15] Tivaroni, iii, 355.   [16] La Farina, ii, 453; La Farina to C., Dec. 1, 1860.
[17] *Ibid*, ii, 466; Jan. 12, 1861.

nano, who went to Naples with Costantino Nigra, the ablest of Cavour's young pupils, as his secretary.

Looked at thus minutely, the new Kingdom of Italy seemed at the beginning of 1861 to be in a perilous state. There were many reasons why it might never be knit together. Internal troubles, due to chronic causes, rarely appeal to the imagination. War may be decided by a single battle, whereas reconstruction demands years: after the brief flash of glory, the long tedium of character-building. The Italians had not only to face the common obstacles to reconstruction, but a host of special evils. No doubt there were high-minded citizens everywhere who earnestly desired national unity, but did not realize, until they made the experiment, how roughly their habits conflicted with their desires. The Past of every town, province and state rose up like an unbidden spectre, in denial of unity. Concessions must be made, but who should begin? Compromise and mutual forbearance are the essentials of friendly relations, whether public or private: but if they did not emerge spontaneously, who should compel them? And so much could be settled only by experience, that discussion seemed imperative.

In such a crisis, the statesman is he who never loses sight of fundamentals. Italy needed first a uniform government. One law must prevail before the people could feel united, or would respect any law. To extend the Piedmontese Constitution, already acknowledged by half the Peninsula, was simple common sense; later, if necessary, it might be amended. So too Piedmontese — that is, national — methods of administration must be introduced everywhere in order to carry that law out uniformly. That the men who had proved themselves ablest in such administrative work should be chosen to establish it in the new states was again as indispensable as that they should reap unpopularity and odium for their reward. The Two Sicilies could not be governed as a conquered state — that would have been easy — but must be treated as equals to Piedmont, with her thirteen years of constitutional experience, and to Tuscany, with her long inheritance of culture. But in Sicily only ten persons out of every hundred could read and write, and the Church held one third of the island in fee. The Regno was quite as bad in both respects. Heart-rending and widespread poverty, superstitions that reduced their victims to the level of savages, and ignorance, — these were the returns the Church made for the exemptions she had enjoyed during a thousand years. Small wonder that the factions found it mere child's play to inflame this vast brutalized mob against the "foreigners" from the North. Nevertheless, on constitutional government would follow the curtailing of Clerical greed, and, it was hoped, the introduction of popular education and of means to economic improvement.

These were the ends Cavour sought in the first distracting months of liberation. He knew well the defects of the men he sent to Naples and Palermo but they were the best he had to send. He discounted the cries against Piedmontizing, in which Clericals, Bourbons and Republicans joined. Convinced from youth that structural changes in a people come best gradually, he perceived the irony of heaping upon him blame for the chaos which he had struggled to prevent. Without faltering, he turned the stream of National Government into every section: for it was the symbol of unity, however the people might chafe at it. Although circumstances were extraordinary and menacing, he would not consent to employ unconstitutional methods for subduing them. "The salvation of Italy," he wrote La Farina, "resides in Parliament. If it has a majority honest, liberal and hostile to the sects, I fear nothing. But if the majority is sectarian or merely weak, I cannot foresee the calamities that might threaten us." [18] His devotion to constitutional principles made it quite impossible for him to think of entrusting the reconstruction of the Two Sicilies to Garibaldi, who, when the King told him that his proposed dictatorship with full powers would be unconstitutional, replied that "when one wished, one could do anything." [19] So an American political boss remarked at a similar objection, "What does the Constitution matter between friends?" The truth was, as we have often observed, that, in his perfectly sincere admiration of Democracy, Garibaldi always assumed that it could at pleasure be tempered by a dictatorship controlled by himself. Cavour, on the contrary, revering constitutional government as the true safeguard of modern liberty, never felt so secure as when he had Parliament behind him.

[18] La Farina, ii, 455; C. to La Farina, Dec., 1860.   [19] Solaroli, 345.

CHAPTER XXXV

ITALY UNITED — ROME FOR CAPITAL

EXAMINED element by element, the new Italy disclosed these grave hindrances, not merely to a healthy union but to the attainment of a civilized state; to the world, however, she seemed a miracle. On January 1, 1859, only Piedmont was free; on January 1, 1861, only Venetia and the Patrimony of St. Peter were not free. Such a transformation in so short a time amazed Europe. Compared to the enemies already overcome, the difficulties of reconstruction seemed almost negligible, so that generous spirits predicted that the Italians would make a strong nation. From the outside, everything looked rosy. While war lasts men pray for peace as the sure dispeller of all evils; but peace often merely dispels war, and then unloads a cargo of evils of her own, besides those which war has bred.

Elections for the first Parliament of United Italy were held in January, 1861. The Bourbon King, besieged in Gaeta since November, must have surrendered earlier by blockade and bombardment, if the French Emperor had not instructed Vice-Admiral Tinan [1] to interpose his squadron between the Italian fleet and the forts. Napoleon's action, devious as usual, Lord John Russell rightly characterized as unintelligible. [2] Having permitted the dismemberment of the Papal States and the liberation of the Two Sicilies, why did he connive at the prolongation of a hopeless struggle? Unless Francis II were saved by foreign intervention, his doom was sealed. Yet he was being aided by the very monarch who frowned on intervention. Did Napoleon himself, through whose mind strange thoughts flitted, cherish the idea of restoring the Bourbon? or had he still hopes that some unforeseen chance might enable him to set up Murat at Naples? So long as he kept the Italians out of Gaeta, he exposed them to dangers which might

[1] For his instructions see *Affaires Etrangères*, 1860, pp. 163–64. Thouvenel, i, 269–71; Thouvenel to Tinan, Oct. 30, 1860.

[2] *Correspondence*, 1860, pt. vii, 187; Russell to Cowley, Dec. 24, 1860.

turn out to his advantage. Meanwhile, he held a rod over them,
because every week's delay postponed the work of reconstruction. The Reactionists took heart; brigandage multiplied;
the Bourbon King could proclaim that his subjects still longed
for him and that the new government was far worse than his own.
At first Napoleon gave out that he simply wished to save Bombino's dignity, so that he might depart without seeming to run
away.[3] After the plebiscite, he pretended that he kept advising
Bombino that, having saved his honor, he had better quit Gaeta:
but his true purpose appeared in the continuance of the French
men-of-war in the harbor. In lieu of better evidence, however,
we may believe that Napoleon took this means of disavowing
sympathy with the Revolution, as embodied in Garibaldi, and
of reassuring the Papalists in France and at Rome that he had
not abandoned the Pope. Empress Eugénie, Thouvenel and
Gramont supported this policy, which in the end brought only
ignominy on the Empire; but they would have gone further
and actively interfered. Gramont protested that it was cruel to
dangle a cord, intentionally cut too short, just out of reach of a
drowning man.[4] Cavour himself tried in vain by friendly remonstrance to cause Napoleon to withdraw; help came at last from
England. Lord John addressed despatches to Paris which grew
in pungency until the Emperor thought it unwise to ignore them.[5]
Tinan steamed away from Gaeta on January 10. Francis II,
encouraged by his gallant Queen, held out until February 14;
then he capitulated. The siege, which had cost both sides heavily
in money and had reduced the garrison by a third, enabled the
Bourbon troops to show a last gleam of valor before they ceased
to fight under the Bourbon flag forever.

Having a momentous project on his hands, Cavour allowed no
irritation over Gaeta, which he treated as a side issue, to creep
into his communications with Paris. Napoleon, however, hinted
that he was displeased with him. "It matters little to me," Cavour wrote Farini, "that the Emperor finds fault with me. I
serve my country not for the pleasure of princes; therefore the
Emperor's displeasure does not trouble me. The day when I can

[3] *Affaires Etrangères*, 1860, 164. *Correspondence*, 1860, pt. vii, 132.
[4] Thouvenel, II, 276; Gramont to Thouvenel, Nov. 3, 1860.
[5] *Correspondence*, 1860, pt. vii, 185, 186, 187.

honorably retire, I shall lay down power with greater gusto than
he will have at seeing me go."[6] Before that day should come,
however, the little man intended to complete the Unity of
Italy. To that completion, one thing was absolutely essential —
Rome. When North, Centre and South were welded together,
Rome alone could satisfy the conflicting requirements of a capital. To Neapolitans and Sicilians, Turin seemed a foreign city.
Lombards insisted that Milan should be preferred to it. Tuscans clung to Florence. On the other hand, the Piedmontese
pleaded with justifiable devotion that Turin, the cradle of national independence, the asylum of Italian patriots, the residence
of the King, the home of the Subalpine Parliament, should continue to be the capital. Without Rome, geography pointed to
Florence, as being nearest to the Centre: but considerations
of geography cannot smooth away prejudices or even compen-
sate for civic emotions and patriotic desires. Cavour wished that
there might be two capitals — his beloved Turin for business,
and Rome for state and pleasure: but he knew that personal preference ought not to weigh against the supreme national considerations. Rome was neutral — Milanese or Florentines, Turinese
or Neapolitans could not set up their local city before her.
Rome was universal, the symbol of unity for Italians, the centre
to which, from the remotest corners of the world, all roads led.
Ricasoli not less than Garibaldi acknowledged the spell of
Rome. Mazzini had long prophesied the Third Rome, which
should be to modern life what Imperial Rome was to antiquity
and Papal Rome to the Middle Age.

Sentiment, political expediency, history, the claims of structural symmetry and of geographical convenience, called for Rome
as the capital of Italy. But Rome was the seat of the Roman
Catholic Pope, who happened also to be a petty Italian despot.

The Papacy, the temporal institution, stricken with senility,
infected with the vices of old age when it is corrupt, had for sixty
years required foreign support to save it from its own subjects.
Now, however, Austria, the pledged protectress of despotism in
Italy, had been expelled; a large part of the Papal territory had
already been united to the new Kingdom; and if the French garrison were withdrawn, the narrow Patrimony of St. Peter would

[6] *Lettere*, IV, 111; C. to Farini, Dec. 3, 1860.

throw over Papal government in a day. The time seemed propitious, therefore, for persuading the Pope to come to terms with modern conditions. He could hope nothing more from Austria; the Catholic Powers had not lifted a finger to prevent the spoliation of the Legations; the French Emperor was known to be tired of propping up the ungrateful and incompetent Papal régime; Pius could be satisfied that he had loyally striven to preserve intact the impossible political legacy handed down from one pope to another since the Renaissance.

Cavour's splendid project, however, did not stop short at securing the predestined capital for United Italy; it went on to embrace the vision of a renewed Church, whose influence would be immeasurably enhanced as soon as it was freed from its worldly consort. Impressed by the part which religion should play in the life of a people, he recognized, as many of the devoutest Catholics of that century recognized, that one of the chief causes of moral decadence and spiritual torpor was the confusing of religion and politics. So he aimed at a solution in which, by the divorce of Church and State, the service of God should no longer be neglected for the service of Mammon. As a proof that this was his desire, he based his first appeal to the Pontiff on the benefits which religion would derive from the proposed compact. Free from hatred and malice, he approached the question with the detachment of a mathematician, who endeavors to discover a solution which shall be approved long after the original parties to the transaction have vanished. This habit of his of subordinating his personal feelings for the sake of the cause — as he had done in his relations with Garibaldi — was so unusual, that his critics failed to recognize it, or if they faintly surmised it, they imputed it to hypocrisy.

In order to make Rome the capital of United Italy, he must either persuade the Pope to consent to give up his temporal power, or, if that failed, arrange with Napoleon to withdraw the French garrison, upon which the Eternal City would speedily welcome the Italians. He proposed to exhaust his efforts with Rome direct, before trying the roundabout and less satisfactory dealings with Paris. After the occupation of Umbria and the Marches, Cavour asked Diomede Pantaleoni, a physician at Rome, who was a friend both of Cavour and of several of the cardinals, to sound very discreetly whether there were any possibility of opening the way to a reconciliation. In the course of a fortnight, Pantaleoni sent a favorable reply; and he made such progress that by the middle of December he presented a memorial to one of the most influential cardinals. This was Santucci, known as the opponent of that Antonellian policy by which the Papacy had been wrecked and the Church was being forced back into medieval intransigence. Pantaleoni's rough draft of proposals began with Cavour's formula, "A Free Church in a Free State," and specified that the Pope should relinquish temporal power, in return for which he should be acknowledged as nominal sovereign, inviolable in his person, absolutely free to exercise his ecclesiastical functions according to canonical forms, to communicate with the clergy in Italy and abroad, and to convoke synods. He should retain the Vatican and certain other palaces, besides receiving a munificent annual subsidy. To the clergy should be assigned revenues sufficient to support every priest who had the cure of souls entrusted to him. Liberty of teaching and of preaching, of founding theological schools and ecclesiastical corporations, was stipulated, subject only to the civil laws which applied to all persons in the Kingdom.[7]

Before these bare proposals were made, however, Cavour wished to prepare the minds of the Papalists by showing the benefits which the compact would bring to the Church. The Italian people, he said, was profoundly Catholic. Schism had never taken deep roots among them. All the more desirable, therefore, was it that the antagonism between them and the directors of their religion should cease. Much of that antagonism was traceable to the fact that in his character of Italian prince the Pope had seemed a political rival to his fellow Italian princes, who had consequently imposed many restrictions upon his ecclesiastical functions. Hence the Tannuccian Laws in Naples, the Leopoldine laws in Tuscany, the Josephine Laws in the Austrian provinces; hence concordats, bargains and reciprocal favors with the Catholic Powers outside the Peninsula. "To vindicate the complete independence of the Church from the State in spiritual affairs," he urged, "is doubtless the noblest and loftiest mission that Pope Pius IX could undertake." He pointed out that the

[7] Text of proposals, with C. comments, *Stor. Doc.*, VIII, 415-19; Nov. 28, 1860.

failure of the recent concordat with Austria showed that the method chosen to secure it was not the best adapted to either the spirit of the times or the actual aspirations of Christian peoples. Italy, he said, was the only Catholic country which could aid Pius to fulfil his glorious mission, and Victor Emanuel the only sovereign who could set the example of renouncing franchises, to guard which had been till then one of the hinges of European politics. By these and other considerations, Cavour hoped that the Pope and his advisers would realize that the great boon of a Free Church must far more than offset the loss of Temporal Power. That Temporal Power itself had been hewn down to a precarious minimum, which would vanish in turn whenever the French evacuated Rome. As the Church had always been strongest when the Papacy was weakest, so the culmination of the Papacy, when in its luxury, splendor and worldliness it surpassed the other unbridled princedoms of the Renaissance, saw the falling away from Catholicism of half of Christendom, followed by the degeneration of Italy, Spain and Portugal and the spread of scepticism in France. Providence seemed to have set before the Pope the opportunity of making the Church once more a mighty religious and moral influence, untrammeled by the political, mundane and corrupting interests of the Papacy.

Cavour hoped that, though his appeal to the spiritual side should fail, the practical benefits which he offered would win over the Pope and his counsellors. He believed that, when the bishops and lower clergy understood what the change would mean to them, they would welcome it. To the objection that he was conceding too much — that the Church, freed from the Papacy, would acquire a real influence over the country — he replied: "I do not fear liberty in any of its applications."[8] He did not allow the fact that the Curia was the most reactionary body in the Roman Catholic world to discourage him.

Although the details of the negotiations have never been officially revealed, we can trace with some definiteness the course taken by Cavour's agents. Pantaleoni was joined by Father Passaglia, a Jesuit, who had commended himself to the Pope by writing a strong polemic in behalf of the dogma of the Immaculate Conception, and who now, being convinced of the immense

---

[8] *Lettere,* VI, 101; C. to Pantaleoni, Nov. 28, 1860.

harm which the moribund Temporal Power was causing the Church, bravely advocated its abolition. Passaglia and Pantaleoni found sympathetic hearers in Cardinals Santucci and D'Andrea, and probably some others, whose names were held back. Their reports cheered Cavour, who regarded any rift in the Cardinals' College as a hopeful sign. He wrote Passaglia on February 21, 1861: "I trust that, before this coming Easter, you will send me an olive branch, symbol of eternal peace between the Church and the State, between the Papacy and the Italians. If that comes to pass, the joy of the Catholic world will be greater than that which, nearly nineteen centuries ago, the entry of our Lord into Jerusalem produced." [9] On January 13, Cavour received a despatch announcing that when Cardinal Santucci spoke out, the Pope appeared to resign himself to the suggested surrender of the Temporal Power; then Antonelli was called, and he too, after a brief opposition, seemed to acquiesce. Both he and Santucci begged the Pope to release them from their oath, in order that they might be canonically free to treat this question. Cavour secretly informed Napoleon III of the transaction and received word that the Emperor hoped he would proceed, although he predicted that there was slight chance of success. Before authorizing even an officious overture, Cavour still waited. Passaglia had an interview with Pius and Antonelli, from which he made favorable deductions, [10] and went to Turin to confer with the Prime Minister, who had taken Minghetti and Artom into the secret. When the Jesuit Father returned to Rome, he bore with him the systematized proposals. During the next two or three weeks, he and Pantaleoni felt their way towards a favorable moment; but the Jesuits already had wind of the intrigue, and they drew so close a ring round Pius that Cardinal d'Andrea advised that Cavour should instruct his agents to go direct to the Pope and tell him that the Government would be glad to negotiate. Cavour consented. [11] His credentials scarcely reached Rome, however, before Pantaleoni was commanded to quit the city within twenty-four hours. [12] What had happened? We can only

---

[9] *Stor. Doc.*, VIII, 422.   [10] *Ibid*, 421; Teccio's despatch of Feb. 5, 1861.

[11] *Ibid*, 440; C.'s telegram to Pantaleoni, March 9, 1861.

[12] Pius wished to expel Pantaleoni's family also, but on learning that his wife was English and that Palmerston would make trouble, he exclaimed, "Ah! that cursed Lord Palmerston." Pantaleoni, 91.

conjecture as to what induced Antonelli's sudden revulsion —
for he it was who gave the drastic order.

While Passaglia and Pantaleoni had been attempting to work
upon the Pope through the more Liberal Cardinals, other Cavourian agents — Omero Bozino, Salvator Aguglia, one of Antonelli's intimates, and Antonio Isaia, secretary of the Dataria
— approached Antonelli himself. As it was certain that Pius
would take no final action without the approval of his political
mentor, common sense dictated the expediency of propitiating
that personage. Bozino, therefore, drew up general overtures
similar in most respects to Pantaleoni's. In addition he proposed
that the Italian Government should approve all the contracts
made by the Antonelli family with the Papal Government, besides bestowing on Cardinal Antonelli himself three million lire,
and conferring special honors upon his brothers.[13] The price
would have been cheap, most Italians would have declared, to
pay for amputating the Papal cancer from Italy and the Catholic world. Antonelli, whose piety could be reached only through
his purse, is described as being ready to close the bargain; for
after Castelfidardo he looked upon the Temporal Power as lost
and was watching for the best way in which to provide for his own
future. According to Isaia and Aguglia the negotiation had gone
so far that nothing more was needed except Antonelli's signature
to the compact, before he presented it to the consistory.[14] Then
without warning, the transaction blew up. Pantaleoni fled from
Rome on March 21, and was soon followed by Isaia and Passaglia. What made Antonelli change his mind? The leaking out of
the secret, says Isaia: but the Cardinal needed only to disavow
any knowledge of the affair, in order to remain diplomatically
correct. More probably he found in the Curia so strong a body
of opponents to the scheme, that he deemed it safer to cast it
aside, at least for the present. The coming to Rome of the Bourbon King and Queen after the fall of Gaeta must also be taken
into account. In collusion with the Pope's Government they were
organizing brigandage on a vast scale and labeling it a holy war.
The condition of the Kingdom of Italy was so disturbed that
Francis and his fellow-pretenders might dream that either civil

[13] Text of proposals in *Stor. Doc.*, VIII, 433–34; C. to Bozino, Feb. 14, 1861.
[14] Aguglia; cited by De Cesare: *Roma*, II, 106–07.

war or foreign intervention would give them a chance to recover their thrones. So long as that chance existed, the wary Antonelli might very well reason that it would be foolish to throw away the Temporal Power. Pius also, from being resigned, became suddenly immovable. Had his Jesuit entourage intimidated him? Did he remember that Clement XIV, the last pope who had dared to resist the Company of Jesus, sickened mysteriously and died, of poison their enemies believed? On March 18, he uttered an encyclical breathing anathema upon the government at Turin, and that same day, he flew into one of his periodic rages and so berated Santucci that the poor Cardinal lost his mind and died insane a few months later.[15]

Thus ended, not inappropriately in a burst of pontifical fury, Cavour's attempt to harmonize Church and State in Italy. Cynics smiled at seeing him outwitted, as they thought, by Antonelli. The friendly rather pitied him as the victim of a Utopian aberration. Those who knew the circuitous methods of the Curia said that he had not taken time enough. But the underlying obstacle was the astuteness with which the Curia, composed almost wholly of Italians, used the doctrine of the Temporal Power to serve their own ends and to perpetuate the preponderance of the Italians in the hierarchy.

The claim that the Temporal Power was indispensable to the Pope's spiritual functions was, like the claim of the divine right of kings, a comparatively modern invention. In the New Testament there is not a hint that a religious leader must also possess political authority. Herod, not Jesus, was King of Judea. The disciples of Jesus and their successors acquired no pomp as satrap or proconsul. It was only in the Renaissance that the King usurped the first place over the Pope in the Pope-King partnership. Popes not only used the Papacy to build up the fortunes of their families; they even disposed of Papal territory for their private benefits. The cynical remark attributed to the sybarite, Leo the Tenth, that "we Medici have profited mightily by the legend of Jesus Christ," though apocryphal, set forth an evident fact. And as the pontiffs' incapacity to govern what remained of the Kingdom of the Church became notorious, they protested all the more vehemently that their temporal rule was necessary

[15] De Cesare: *Roma*, II, 14. Cf. Cesaresco: *Cavour*.

to the Church. Such stubbornness is common to men and institutions far gone in senility. Yet no Papalist would admit that during the exile of Pius VI and VII, when the Papal State ceased to exist for fifteen years, or during the Republican interregnum of 1848–49, the decrees of the Church were diminished by a hair's breadth in authority. The historic evolution of the Papacy was clear to anyone allowed to consult history; but when the politicians of the Curia saw Temporal Power slipping away, they insisted more desperately on its preservation, and some of them would have embodied it in a dogma. The reasons chiefly urged by them were that without the Temporal Power the Pope might be hindered in his communications with the Catholic world, or he might fall under the influence of the Italian Government. To this Liberal Italians replied that as the Pope had depended since 1815 upon the armed protection of either France or Austria, or of both, he could not be regarded as free, while the fact that the sovereigns of Austria, France, Spain and Portugal could and did exercise a veto at the election of a pope, was proof direct of secular interference.[16] Many declared that the true reason for pressing the claim to Temporal Power could not be avowed: it was to prevent the monopoly of the Catholic hierarchy from passing out of the hands of Italians. The offices, the sinecures, above all the power, should not be shared with foreign Catholics; four sevenths of the College of Cardinals and nine tenths of the Papal bureaucracy should remain Italian. Foreign Catholics, at least among the higher ecclesiastics, accepted this condition, because it gave them a special authority at home. The foreign cardinal or bishop owed his place not to his local sovereign but to the Pope; and if there were conflict of interest, he sided with the Pope. In many cases these ecclesiastics connived with pretenders, in the hope of getting larger favors for themselves. Conversely, a Legitimist pretender, in France, for instance, would have no hesitation in making lavish promises to Clerical supporters. Thus while the hierarchy was being exploited for the benefit of the crafty Italian minority, foreign ecclesiastics acquiesced because the arrangement gave them certain privileges in return for their birthright. They were, moreover, scattered in many countries, so that a union

[16] In the Conclave of 1903, which elected Pius X, Cardinal Rampolla was excluded through the indirect intervention of the German Emperor — a *Protestant*.

2

among them against the central authority would be difficult, if not impossible. As a result, if any local movement gathered volume enough to send delegates to Rome, those delegates were quickly ground to powder by the great machine, which was always orthodox and always Roman.

Now Cavour appealed from the Pope as a petty temporal sovereign, to the Pope as the head of a world religion — from mundane ambition to conscience. He had in view not merely the immediate benefits that would come to 25 million Italians, if, through securing Rome as their national capital, the long irreligious struggle of the Papalists for temporal power should cease; he looked forward to the time when the Church, purged of worldly lusts and freed from political competition, should fulfil its mission, the mission of Christ, to sanctify and solace the souls of men. He offered it liberty, the condition through which it might thrive as never before. To Americans, accustomed for generations to the absolute separation of Church and State, and to unrestricted freedom among the churches, Cavour's proposal needs no defense. Europe, however, received it now with cynicism and now with scepticism; for Europe was too sophisticated to suppose that any body of ecclesiastics would voluntarily give up claims to power they had once possessed. Europe was too jaded by immemorial disappointments to believe that ecclesiasticism could be got rid of any more than militarism, or poverty, or the other burdens which oppressed mankind and were regarded as incurable. Some of Cavour's admirers even regretted that he should risk being ridiculed as simple, for seeming to expect that an appeal to holy motives might stir the Roman Curia. They little knew him, whom fear of derision or of failure never deterred. The vision of the incalculable good that would come to a free Church in a free State, justified every risk. When he discussed it, Artom says, his speech became exalted to the level of poetry, and one marveled to hear him, the master economist and rational statesman, express himself with such fervor over the possible and even near accord of Catholicism and liberty.[17]

The rebuff neither surprised nor disheartened him. "Time," he said, "is the powerful ally of him who is on the side of reason and progress." [18] He knew that, in spite of the unmeasured con-

[17] Artom-Blanc, I, 195.   [18] *Lettere*, IV, 110; C. to Matteucci, Dec. 2, 1860.

servatism inherent in human nature, dead institutions must sooner or later go to the graveyard. "Do you think the Temporal Power still exists?" he asked Artom. "The proof that it is really dead is that the occupation of Rome by the French troops fails to arouse jealousy in the other Catholic Powers. . . . It is our duty to end the long struggle between the Church and civilization, between liberty and authority. . . . Perhaps I shall be able to sign, on the summit of the Capitol, another religious peace, a treaty which will have for the future of human societies consequences far greater than those of the Peace of Westphalia. . . . It is an insult to assert that Catholicism is incompatible with liberty. I am convinced . . . that as soon as the Church has tasted liberty, she will feel herself rejuvenated by this healthful and strengthening regimen." [19]

The immediate answer to his noble effort at conciliation came in the Pope's allocution of March 18, when he denounced progress and liberalism, and upheld the inviolability of the Temporal Power, to which he imputed a religious sanctity.[20] His speech was the official declaration that the Roman Papacy and modern liberty were incompatible — a conclusion which the Syllabus of 1864 reaffirmed. Officially, indeed, consent would never be given to this readjustment, for the Curia never relinquishes a claim; but against facts, Rome herself can only protest: and to her protests the course of things pays no more attention, in the long run, than the comet paid to her bull. Institutions, political, social or religious, are subject to that law of growth and decay which controls not only man and every plant and animal on earth, but the life of the earth itself and the solar system, and star, and star-dust. In the presence of this universal fact, what becomes of the pretension of any church that it has not changed? Cavour no doubt instructed his agents to persuade the hierarchs that "the Papacy, which pretends to be immovable, has changed and gradually transformed itself along with Christian society. Without going back to apostolic times, one may recall that the councils offered to the nascent civilization of Europe the first model of parliamentary government. Feudal in the Middle Age, the Papacy became little by little an absolute monarchy, and thereby simply followed the general law which established the royal

[19] Artom-Blanc, ii, 570–71.   [20] Text in Balan, ii, 338–44.

power as the centre of development in modern states." [21]   When the time came for democratizing monarchy, however, the Papacy could not adapt itself to the new ideals — the ossification of old age had set in. By making the great refusal at the behest of his advisers, Pius IX simply certified that the Temporal Power was dead. A few weeks after the Pope read his allocution in Rome, the supporters of another institution,[22] before whose hoary age the millennial lifetime of the Temporal Power was but a span, began in America a civil war to make slavery perpetual.[23]

During the winter and early spring of 1861, Turin, in aspect and by tradition a somewhat sober city, acquired the bustle of a metropolis. Crowds flocked to it from all parts of the Peninsula. Foreigners, who usually passed it by in their haste to reach the shrines of art, now paused long enough to see what sort of a place and people those were that had just created a nation. The general elections, held on January 27, brought an overwhelming Cavourian majority to the capital. Even Naples and Sicily, the Radicals' strongholds, stood by the Government. Several of the leaders of the Left — Bertani, Cattaneo, Mordini, Guerrazzi and Ferrari — failed on the first ballot, but were returned on the second. Parliament convened on February 18, and greeted Victor Emanuel with outbursts of genuine enthusiasm, when he delivered a brief but tactful speech from the throne. He touched on the help given by France, England and Garibaldi in creating Italy; he went out of his way to compliment William I, the new King of Prussia; he invited the Chambers to devise laws which should ensure political unity for peoples accustomed to different methods; he praised the army and navy. "Devoted to Italy," he said, "I have never hesitated to hazard my own life and crown, but no one had the right to hazard the life and destiny of a nation." The joy of all classes that day was mingled with

---

[21] Artom-Blanc, II, 567; the words are Artom's, but the substance is Cavour's.

[22] Beauregard took Fort Sumter, April 14, 1861.

[23] The documents in this transaction are necessarily Italian, for the Curia has allowed none of the Papal to be printed. *Stor. Doc.*, VIII, 405–63. Pantaleoni, 43–97 and documents. Passaglia: *La Question de l'Indépendance et de l'Unité de l'Italie vis-à-vis du Clergé* (Paris, 1862) is valuable as giving Passaglia's criticism of the Temporal Power. *Lettere*, IV and VI. Bianchi: *Carlo Matteucci e l'Italia del suo Tempo* (Turin, 1874), chap. ix. The official Papal annalist, Balan, usually follows Bianchi, but implies that nobody need believe the story. Cantù: *Cronistoria*, III. 718, thinks that Cavour was duped by Antonelli.

SUBALPINE SENATE CHAMBER
Palazzo Madama

X Cavour's seat

wonder approaching incredulity that at last the dream of every patriot since Dante was realized. On March 17 Parliament confirmed by a unanimous vote the decree proclaiming Victor Emanuel King of Italy. Some persons favored the title "King of the Italians," but Cavour insisted that "King of Italy" was alone appropriate, because it expressed the great fact — *Italy*. The King himself preferred to be counted Victor Emanuel *Second* instead of *First*, in order to keep his sequence in the line of Savoy.

Three days later (March 20) Cavour announced that the Ministry, wishing to leave his Majesty untrammeled to choose a Cabinet which should represent every section of the New Kingdom, had resigned.[24] Victor Emanuel accepted the resignation with what seemed to many unbecoming satisfaction. He was too much the King to suffer gladly the primacy of his chief minister; and since the Rosina affair and the outburst at Villa Melchiorri, he had nursed a strong personal dislike for Cavour: but, true to his constitutional oath, he had loyally accepted the leader whom Parliament had designated. Now, however, he was free to choose a man more to his fancy, and to give to his choice a semblance of political wisdom. Cavour was hateful to one of the great parties, and he was accused of being too Piedmontese: by throwing him over, therefore, and taking a non-Piedmontese, the King hoped to avoid many difficulties. Accordingly, he urged Ricasoli to accept the post of premier, both to show Europe "that we have other men besides Cavour," and to unite all factions.[25] Ricasoli resisted the King's blandishments, however, declaring that Cavour could not be dispensed with, and the King reluctantly bade his antipathetic Prime Minister to remain. Changes were made in the Cabinet to lend it a national complexion: Pietro Bastogi of Leghorn became Minister of Finance; Ubaldino Peruzzi of Florence took the portfolio of Public Works; Francesco de Sanctis, of Naples, that of Public Instruction; and Giuseppe Natoli, of Messina, was Minister of Agriculture and Commerce. Minghetti, of Bologna, was already Minister of the Interior,[26] and Fanti and Cassinis were continued in the departments of War and of Justice.[27] What might not Italy have been spared if

[24] *Discorsi*, XI, 306. Bianchi, March 21, 1861.   [25] Gotti, 272–73. Ricasoli, v, 403–04; Ricasoli to C. [26] He succeeded Farini in November, 1860, when the latter went to Naples.   [27] *Discorsi*, XI, 308–10.

Ricasoli, by accepting the premiership, had fronted the storms of the next three months and saved Cavour's life!˙

Cavour himself would have been the last to shift the burden to other shoulders. Secure in his leadership, he proceeded to carry forward without delay the work of reconstruction. And first he turned to the transcendent question of Rome. His secret overtures having been rebuffed, he deemed it expedient to state publicly the purposes and desires of the nation, and to explain their reasonableness. In three great speeches, which, taken together, form a single oration, he treated the question from every point of view, facing the objections candidly, defining the reservations that must be made, and picturing in eloquent but solid phrase the incalculable benefits which conciliation would bring. He emphasized the need of persuading the Catholic world that the change would in nowise affect the Pope's religious and spiritual relations. He set forth two things as necessary, the Pope's consent and the acquiescence of France. He proclaimed anew the doctrine of a Free Church in a Free State. Many French Clericals, he said, now wished that the Liberal principles advocated by Lamennais, and by his disciples Lacordaire and Montalembert, had been adopted in France. Belgium he pointed to as a nation where the Church enjoyed liberty without troubling the State. He drew historic parallels and inferences. At times he was solemn, as when he said: "Assuredly, they cannot be the followers of the religion of Him who sacrificed his life to save humanity, who would sacrifice an entire people, and condemn it to perpetual martyrdom, in order to maintain the temporal dominion of his representative on this earth." [28]   Again, he relieved the tension by a half-playful touch, as when he predicted that, under the régime of liberty, the Catholic Party would be in the ascendant, "and from now on," he added, "I am resigned to finish my career on the Opposition benches." [29]

When Ferrari accused him of being a conspirator, Cavour replied: "I thank him for it, and I seize this occasion to declare to the Chamber that for twelve years I was a conspirator. For twelve years I have conspired with all my strength; I have conspired to procure independence for my country. But I have conspired in a singular fashion; I have conspired by proclaiming in

[28] *Discorsi*, XI, 327.   [29] *Ibid.*

the newspapers, by proclaiming in the face of Parliament, by proclaiming in the Councils of Europe the aim of my conspiracy. I conspired too by seeking out adepts and affiliates, and I had for comrades all or nearly all the Subalpine Parliament; moreover, I have had adepts in all the provinces of Italy; in past years I had for adepts nearly the entire National Society, and today I conspire with 26 millions of Italians." [30]

In construction, his speeches were supple and flowing, as far removed as possible from that oratory which aims at overpowering its hearers by an onset of serried demonstrations or from dazzling it by flashes of wit: but when examined closely, they reveal the art of a master of persuasion. That the Temporal Power had failed to give the Pope independence, and that its abandonment under the conditions of a Free Church in a Free State, would bestow upon him independence, influence and universal respect unknown to his predecessors — these were Cavour's main themes, which he illustrated in many ways. He never confused the secular and religious natures of the Pope — as Ultramontanes, for too obvious reasons, do. He neither criticized doctrine nor hinted at the personal defects of the Curia. He was as sympathetically straightforward as a physician, who tells how a disease of many years' standing, which has brought the patient to the verge of death, can be cured. And emotion was so woven into his historic instances and statements of fact that it thrilled the Chambers. When he concluded with this appeal, which, he said, he hoped would ere long be addressed to the Quirinal from Catholics the world over, his hearers were electrified. "Holy Father, accept the terms which emancipated Italy offers you! accept the terms which must assure the liberty of the Church, enhance the lustre of the see where Providence has placed you, augment the influence of the Church and at the same time carry to completion the great edifice of the regeneration of Italy, assure the peace of that nation which after all, in the midst of so many misfortunes, of so many vicissitudes, has remained most faithful and most attached to the true spirit of Catholicism." [31] Boncompagni's resolution, embodying Cavour's policy that Rome be declared the capital, and be united to Italy, was passed almost unanimously.

[30] *Discorsi*, XI, 335-36.   [31] *Ibid*, 361-62.

Although Cavour, aware of the power of suggestion, habitually
implied that the policy which he deemed right could be realized
soon, he did not deceive himself as to the tenacity of Papal ambition. He could foresee that the politicians who connived at the
fanatical Mérode's "crusaders," would not scruple, if the occasion
came, to invent and maintain the subterfuge that the Pope was
a prisoner in the Vatican, if by so doing they could stimulate the
blind zeal of gullible Irish, ignorant French peasants and bigoted
Austrians, and exasperate Catholic governments against the new
Kingdom of Italy. But Cavour had the centuries in view, and
the centuries transform the Roman Church with the races on
which, like all other institutions, it depends for its existence. He
was as unmoved by the denunciations of Montalembert, whom
Rendu aptly characterized the "eloquent zouave," as by Massimo d'Azeglio, who, with an eye to the present only, advised
making Florence the capital and letting Rome, the "medieval
fantasticality," alone. Cavour saw that the Temporal Power
was doomed. He held that the separation of Church and State
which had been the guiding principle of Catholics like Dante and
Sarpi in the past, and of many recent devout Catholics, could
work no possible injury to the Spiritual Church. He knew that
an institution which secures conformity by silencing, and if
it cannot silence, by outlawing, those of its members who are
most sensitive to conscience and most accessible to ideas, is far
on its way towards petrifaction. Not merely did Cavour recognize great Catholics of his own generation, like Döllinger and
Rosmini and Lacordaire, as forerunners, but he perceived that
their gospel of liberty and of purifying the Church by freeing it
from worldliness, was stirring the hearts of many of the younger
men. It was one of these, Lord Acton, the most learned Catholic
of his time and one of the most learned men of all time, who
spoke later of Ultramontanism as a compounding with murder.[32]
It was another of these, Cardinal Hohenlohe, one of Pius's fav-
orites, who wrote boldly in 1889 to Leo XIII: "God has so or-
dained that the Church can never again get back her temporal
power. The salvation of souls requires that we resign ourselves

[32] Lord Acton's *Letters to Mary Gladstone*, London, 1904, pp. 298–99. In the
same passage he chides Rosmini and Lacordaire for being too Papalist. "The
most awful imputation in the catalogue of crimes rests, according to the measure
of their knowledge and their zeal, upon those whom we call Ultramontanes."

TURIN. ROYAL PALACE

Monument of the Milanese on right

TURIN. PIAZZA CASTELLO

Palazzo Madama on the left ; Hotel Europa facing at left hand corner of street

to this fact." [33] It was a third of these, the lovable Franz Xavier Kraus, who predicted that, as soon as *"religious* Catholicism" should supersede *"political* Catholicism," it would in a few decades conquer a world and build a new home for Christianity. [34] These men had and have troops of disciples and fellow-believers. Their existence points to the day when Cavour's vision of a Free Church in a Free State may be realized. "Who knows?" he once said, with a laugh, to an intimate; "perhaps in the end the Church will canonize *me.*"

The strategic importance of his public announcement that Rome must be the capital of Italy was evident. By it, he warned the Party of Action — which hoped to follow Garibaldi to the war-cry of "Rome or Death!" — that the Government had the solution of the Roman Question in hand, but that it would not suffer premature ventures. He also warned foreign Catholics that, by virtue of the fact that the Temporal Power made the Pope an Italian prince, the question was Italian, to be settled by Italians.

[33] W. R. Thayer: *Italica.* Boston, 1908. P. 291.
[34] F. X. Kraus: *Cavour.* Mainz, 1902. P. 94.

CHAPTER XXXVI

CAVOUR'S LAST VICTORY AND DEATH

BY far the most pressing duty, before setting out to redeem Venetia and Rome, was to weld together in peace and brotherhood the Kingdom which already acknowledged Victor Emanuel as sovereign. Although the national cause had triumphed, each of the new states contained minorities which still cherished the old régime and would oppose more or less openly the effort to nationalize them. In the former Papal States and Naples brigandage, financed and directed from Rome, had by April swollen into a wide-spread insurrection. The relations between the King's government and the country had to be defined. Should the old territorial divisions be kept, or should Italy be reapportioned? If reapportioned, should the French system of departments be copied, or the ancient Roman system of regions be revived? Minghetti drew up a scheme for regional administration. Others preferred provinces. The ingrained individualism of the Italians, expressed for centuries in their political particularism, needed to be overcome, if there were to be real national unity; on the other hand, it must be treated with such deference that the citizens of the former States should not feel that, in becoming Italians, they had lost their identity. Among French or Germans, the Tuscan wished, indeed, to be recognized as an Italian; but among Piedmontese or Sicilians or Romagnoles, he was a Tuscan. Such deep-rooted instincts could not be suddenly outgrown; least of all, could they be removed by statute. To discover the happy mean between centralization and local autonomy, was, therefore, the task.

Similar problems confronted every department. The finances must be reorganized. The army, the judiciary, the diplomatic service must be enlarged, or remodeled. Public works — railways, telegraphs, steamship lines, post offices — required planning on a national scale. New taxes were called for. Many of the recently emancipated Italians supposed, in their ignorance, that

Unity would mean Utopia — a happy state in which there would be no more work, or imposts, or police, or restraint on their personal desires. After a few months of Unity, they began to perceive that free government not only cost more than despotic, but laid upon them civic obligations which they did not understand and could not discharge. They felt deceived and were inclined to throw the blame of this deception on their liberators instead of on themselves.

No other statesman in the 19th century had to face such a complication of internal difficulties as challenged Cavour in the spring of 1861. Reconstruction with old materials is tenfold harder than construction with new. To William de La Rive, who invited him to go to Pressinge and refresh himself in that air, moral and physical, which always restored him, he replied, regretfully: "I greatly fear that, unless the Parliament which is about to meet overthrows me, it will be impossible for me to cross the Alps. My task is more laborious and thorny than in the past. To constitute Italy, to fuse together the divers elements of which she is composed, to put North and South in harmony, offers as many difficulties as a war with Austria and the struggle with Rome." [1] Even while he was writing, the tempest which had long been gathering was about to burst.

Garibaldi had passed the winter at Caprera not wholly in bucolic peace of mind. Having turned his war-horse and donkeys — one of which he irreverently named Pio Nono — out to pasture and having planted his seed-beans, he had much leisure to ruminate over his grievances. The more he thought upon them, the more his heart grew wroth. His own patriotism loomed before him, like a vast and shining cloud dwarfing and dimming everyone else. He was obsessed by the loss of Nice, as Achilles by the abduction of Briseis. His magnanimity made the ingratitude of the Government seem inexplicable. Had he liberated a kingdom, merely to see it pass into the clutches of Cavourian placemen? Had he told the world that in March he should return to lead half a million Italians against Rome and Venetia, only to learn that the Government would neither permit the enrolling of volunteers in time of peace, nor hand over to self-constituted autocrats the direction of international relations,

---

[1] *Lettere*, IV, 201; end of March, 1861.

which the Constitution imposed upon the Ministers, subject to parliament? Whenever these grievances ceased to gnaw him for a moment, resentment at the slight put upon his Southern Army nettled him. And throughout the winter, every boat brought to Caprera visitors bursting with complaints and letters breathing indignation and revenge. Garibaldi honestly believed that he had sacrificed his personal wrongs and was moved solely by those of his companions in arms. His conduct is intelligible only when we remember that he had just achieved the most glorious feat of chivalry in modern times; that the whole world was showering him with praises and laurel; that he was fully conscious of the magnitude of his achievement; that he believed that, just as he had known better than the Government how the Two Sicilies could be freed, so he and not it should be followed in regard to Venetia and Rome. He was almost agonized at the thought that the supreme opportunity of completing his mission of liberation was being wasted. Majestically ignoring that Cavour, by warding off diplomatic intervention, had enabled him to win in the South, he defamed the Prime Minister as a truckler to Diplomacy, a timorous intriguer, if not a traitor, who danced attendance on the most loathsome monster living — Napoleon III. Garibaldi's contempt for the regular army, and especially for the War Department, equalled his scorn of Diplomacy. Had he not proved that volunteers were more than a match for disciplined troops? Field marshals and corps commanders had gone down before his own superior military genius, and their army before his nondescript legions: ergo, the art of war must be revolutionized. The more he thought it over, the more outrageous it seemed to him that the Ministers, instead of accepting his merest suggestion as a command, actually paid no heed to him. Never doubting that he himself was infallible, he regarded this as a proof of their lack of intelligence not less than of their dishonesty.

He had had, in truth, to suffer treatment to try the temper of Socrates. Before he quitted Naples, Farini and even the King had slighted him, apparently with intention. What purpose serves a royal retinue, who hold etiquette in greater reverence than the Decalogue, if they fail not in tact only, but in common courtesy towards the popular hero whom, above everyone else, they should keep in good humor? Not even slaves are callous to disdain; much less was the hypersensitive Garibaldi, who discovered it in every act. When some of the Liberal press both criticized his volunteers and went so far as to insinuate that he owed the victory of the Volturno to Piedmontese succor, his indignation knew no bounds. The publication by the French Government of a reference to the Chambéry interview, in which Farini was reported, and no doubt correctly, as urging upon Napoleon III that Piedmont was going to interfere in Umbria in order to check "the Revolution embodied in Garibaldi," [2] further enraged the Paladin: for, although the definition was literally accurate, he liked to imagine himself as the incarnation of all Italians, except the hated Cavourians and the Papalists.

The disbanding of his Southern Army inevitably fed his wrath. Victor Emanuel, who often promised more than his Ministers could perform, had assured Garibaldi in their last talks at Naples, that his Garibaldian army should be preserved on an equal footing with the regulars. The Cabinet, however, declared this impossible, and Victor Emanuel, being a constitutional king, bowed to their decision. The Minister of War, Fanti — next to Cavour the man most detested by Garibaldi — was an admirable organizer, a soldier of conscience, but rigid and uncompromising. He was certainly right in protesting that the regular service would be seriously impaired, if thousands of red-shirted guerillas, unused to discipline and restive under it, were distributed among the regiments. To perpetuate an independent corps of volunteers would destroy that uniformity in the personnel and training which are indispensable to an army. Nevertheless, this arrangement, intended to be provisional, was accepted by the Ministry in order to appease Garibaldian clamors, but its possible harmfulness was guarded against. A joint commission examined the records of the volunteers. When Garibaldi retired in November there were 51,000 names on his rolls. Of these, some 16,000 were of men who had seen little service or none. Barely 25,000 of the remainder composed the real army with which, in Sicily and on Terra Firma, he had conquered the Bourbons. He had issued commissions so recklessly that 7002 officials were on the rolls, of whom 3736 remained in the reorganized army —

[2] *Aff. Etrang.*, 1861, p. 163.

an indication that the weeding out was not cruelly thorough. A special Corps of Italian Volunteers was created, and the Garibaldian soldiers might choose between enlisting in that or being mustered out with six months' stipend (162 francs) and sent home free of expense. Within two months all except 238 subalterns and common soldiers had disbanded. A few officers of proved ability — like Medici, Bixio and Cosenz — received generals' commissions in the regular army.

The disbanding of the Bourbon Army, with provision for the reënlistment of the rank and file as well as for the immediate reception into active service of certain men of high rank, went on at the same time. The Garibaldian sympathizers denounced Fanti for treating the Bourbon troops as if they were entitled to similar consideration with the Southern Army. If the Neapolitans were henceforth to be regarded as Italians, however, justice demanded that their oath of allegiance to Victor Emanuel should be recognized as giving them equal standing with the natives of Lombardy or Piedmont. That mistakes were made in this reorganization can no more be doubted, than that Fanti was strict, and sometimes harsh; for among both Garibaldians and Bourbons, impostors, scamps, and deserters swarmed. His general plan, which aimed at nationalizing the army in its personnel and of bringing it under a uniform system of education and discipline, does not need to be defended. His sternness in dealing with rascals was warranted. But the genuine Garibaldians had unique claims to national gratitude. Like their Chief, they were not deterred by patriotism or modesty from pressing those claims, and they preferred to see ten fraudulent claimants rewarded rather than one honest Garibaldian slighted. The lugubrious Sirtori, Garibaldi's agent in the transaction, repeatedly acknowledged the justice of the Royal Commissioners' charges, but he censured the commissioners for being influenced by them. "They treated us like enemies," he declared in Parliament; and Medici made a similar complaint. Later, when the issue had cooled, they were both less inclined to condemn unreservedly.[3]

[3] Carandini, 429–42. Della Rocca, chap. 18. Revel: *Ancona*, chaps. 8 and 9. Revel said that the Commissioners' task was to distinguish Garibaldi's real volunteers, who numbered not more than 20,000, from the 40,000 who rushed for the spoils, and had nothing Garibaldian about them except the red shirt. P. 167.

As news of this business came to Garibaldi, his resentment grew hot. It was bad enough for the Liberals to refuse to hand over the Government to him and his, and deprive them of finishing their patriotic task: it was worse to rob them of their glory, and infamous to withhold those honors and rewards which they had earned with their blood. Most tantalizing to his patriotism was the conviction that, if he were listened to, Italy could be made in a few weeks. He had reached that familiar stage of obsession, when he no longer attempted to reason, but attributed all his injuries to Cavour. He could not be persuaded that Cavour had not instigated the royal chamberlain's snubs, the uneffusive greeting of the King's entourage or Fanti's inflexibility. Like other victims of the persecution mania, he found a simple explanation for his persecutor's conduct: Cavour was jealous of his fame and influence. Unable to hold in longer, Garibaldi decided to go to Turin. "Let not thine hand draw the sword," said bright-eyed Athene to his Homeric prototype, Achilles, "yet with words indeed revile him." [4] Garibaldi's counselors urged his going, because they too for a year past had kept pouring into his head hatred of Cavour: some honestly, being as unreasoning as himself; others, the larger number, for personal or partisan reasons.

During the last week in March a delegation of workmen visited Caprera, bearing an address which reeked with pessimism over the condition of Italy. Garibaldi replied that perhaps the situation was not so gloomy as they painted it, for they still had Victor Emanuel for a pivot; but, he added, no nation ought to depend on one man. And the King, he went on, "is surrounded by people without heart, without patriotism, by men who have created a dualism between the regular army and the volunteers. . . . These wretches have sown discord and hate, have checked the work of fusion and of unification so well initiated by us. . . . But, I repeat, the King is deceived; he desires Venice to be free, and we desire to crown him in Rome." [5] Garibaldi assured his hearers that he relied on the horny right hand of men of his own station in life, and not on the fallacious promises of the political intriguers. Having refused to be a candidate for Parliament, he suddenly changed his mind, and on March 31 he telegraphed to

[4] *Iliad*, I, 210–11.   [5] J. W. Mario: *Garibaldi*, II, 26.

Naples that he would stand for the first college of that city. On April 1 he crossed to Genoa, where he was irritated to hear that the police had visited the rooms of a patriotic committee, and where his friends inflamed him further by their tale of wrongs.[6] The next day he went on to Turin, by invitation, one newspaper reported, of Count Cavour, a statement which Garibaldi promptly denied.[7] Yet so natural was it to suspect his sudden movements, that the French journals insisted that he and Cavour were in collusion, and even the Emperor seems for a moment to have credited this error.

Fearing an explosion, the King sent for Garibaldi, whom he found angrier than ever with Cavour, for ceding Nice and Savoy. The King repeated that if he himself could submit to the loss of the cradle of his race, Garibaldi might do as much: but the Paladin, in no mood to sacrifice his darling feud on the altar of concord, told Victor Emanuel that that cession was the wickedest of all Cavour's acts. Among his friends, during the next few days, he let his tongue play without restraint, stinging nearly everyone except his trusted few. He forgot, however, that, being no longer dictator at Naples, beyond reach of criticism, his irresponsible arraignments could not pass unchallenged in the capital. One citizen there was, the fittest of all, to call him to account in Parliament, the place where every Italian was amenable to the law.

That challenger was Bettino Ricasoli, the man of iron will, of self-control, of downright speech. On April 10 he rose in the Chamber of Deputies, a Puritan patrician, austere in dress, gloved, soberly serene in demeanor, with the poise of a man who can never be thrown off his feet, but who shuns rather than seeks to express his opinion. As Ricasoli had saved Tuscany and Emilia the year before, a positive achievement, second only to that of Garibaldi in the South, no one could question his service. Only the half-educated imagine that victories on the battlefield are nobler or more difficult or more important than victories which statesmen may sometimes win. Ricasoli spoke without rhetoric and without recrimination. He said that the conscience of every deputy had been wounded by words attributed to General Garibaldi — words which offended alike the majesty of Par-

⁶ Guerzoni: *Garibaldi*, II, 256.   ⁷ *Ibid*, II, 255, n. 2.

liament and the inviolability of the King. But he refused to believe that Garibaldi could have uttered them. In the summer of 1859 he and Garibaldi pledged each other to fulfil their duty to the country. 'He has done his duty, I have done mine.' It cannot be, Ricasoli continued, that Garibaldi would insult either the King or Parliament. The King being the Liberator of Italy, there was under him no first citizen and no last. If two or three or half a dozen had been privileged to perform their duty on a wider sphere of action, they ought not therefore to arrogate to themselves special glory, or to set themselves above the law, but humbly to thank God for granting them the larger opportunity, and for permitting them to declare: "To me belongs the example of abnegation and of modesty; the example of showing others how everyone ought to obey the law." It was impossible, therefore, Ricasoli concluded, to believe that Garibaldi had used the words imputed to him.[8]

Seldom was sarcasm used more properly, never with better effect than on that day. Ricasoli's unadorned sentences seemed as irrefutable as a self-evident axiom in geometry. They captured his audience not by their sarcasm, but by their truth. The nation drew a long breath of relief, because it felt that one of its great citizens dared to announce that no citizen, not even Garibaldi, stood above the law, above Parliament, above the King. When the session broke up, Cavour grasped Ricasoli's hand and said: "Were I to die to-morrow, my successor is marked out." Massimo d'Azeglio, the free-lance patriot, who had grown pessimistic during the last twelve-month, wrote: "Bravo, Betto! May God bless you! There was one post — the best and most useful in my opinion — to fill in Parliament: that of vindicator of the law, of the moral law, as well as the political and every other. This post is now no longer vacant. You occupy it, and you deserve to occupy it. Now I begin to hope. Had I not known for a good while that great deeds are done by great and noble characters rather than by talents, I should have learned it now."[9] Massimo spoke the truth: character, not talents, makes men and nations great. It was Ricasoli's righteousness that served Italy on that day. Others had courage equal to his, but only he could perform that singular service.

[8] Text of speech in Ricasoli, v, 439–43.   [9] Gotti, 275–79. Ricasoli, v, 417.

2

Suffering from rheumatism, Garibaldi delayed appearing in the Chamber. But he improved every hour by conferring with his Radical friends. They hoped to use him to overthrow Cavour, and he was more than eager to aid them. As usual, they shrewdly allowed him to suppose that he, and not they, led. Their programme was to accept the Monarchy, as the symbol of unity, but to insist that they should shape the foreign policy of the government, and decide when to attack Rome, or to liberate Venetia, or to attack France in order to win back Nice. With Cavour out of the way, they might even capture the control of the Kingdom itself. Their pretension seems arrogant now, but in 1861 they regarded their moderation as most magnanimous; for they held that the Revolution, which had freed the Two Sicilies, had a supreme claim to Italy's gratitude and obedience. In their secret conferences Rattazzi, Depretis, Brofferio and others joined, whose primary interest was not to set up a Mazzinian republic, but to get rid of Cavour, in order that their own ambition might secure the right of way.[10]

While waiting until he felt disposed to attend, Garibaldi, quite after the fashion of a sovereign communicating with his parliament, sent to the deputies a letter which Rattazzi, their president, laid before them. In this, after thanking the Prime Minister for postponing the debate on the Southern Army until he could be present, Garibaldi stated that he should protest against the disbanding of his old comrades, and that he was displeased to learn that his private remarks about the King and Parliament had been discussed by Ricasoli. He concluded by reaffirming, in a tone which many found patronizing, that his trust in the person of Victor Emanuel was known of all.[11] This haughty letter failed either to relieve his mind or to satisfy the large majority of deputies whom his virulent speeches had roused. Accordingly, he wrote again to Rattazzi, to inform the Chamber that he still approved of the King; that his conscience forbade him to condescend to justify himself either towards the King or the Parliament; that he was moved to indignation at the condition of the South and the abandoning of his comrades in arms; but that, in

[10] Rattazzi, Depretis, Pepoli and a few others tried to organize a third party to hold the balance of power.

[11] Ciàmpoli, 215–16; Garibaldi to Rattazzi, April 11, 1861.

the presence of the holy National Cause, he should trample under foot any personal contest whatsoever.[12] He enclosed suggestions concerning the Southern Army, the foremost being that he should be appointed royal commissioner in the South for an indefinite period.

On April 18, the day set for the debate, Garibaldi limped into the Chamber, accompanied by Macchi and Zuppetta, two Mazzinian friends. The deputies met at half past one, but he put off his coming till nearly two, as if to make sure of a spectacular reception. The Liberator of a kingdom, however, had no need to stoop to set traps for applause. Long before he reached the Chamber, his progress was registered by the cheers of the crowds in the streets. Instead of taking the main entrance into the hall, he chose to slip in by a small side door, which connected with the topmost row of seats of the Left, and in this most conspicuous position, all eyes were at once turned upon him. Whilst the members of the Left and the Garibaldians in the tribunes cheered him for five minutes, the rest of the House waited expectantly. He was dressed in his legendary bizarre costume, — red shirt, gray Scotch plaid poncho, and little Spanish hat. Although his face was flushed, he bore no signs of illness, but he appeared older to those who had not seen him since he sailed from Quarto. One spectator found that the lion aspect "was sobered by a profusion of gray about the long mane"; but the "usual benignant, calm, supremely dignified look,"[13] which magnetized high and low, shone in his face. That air of self-confidence and relish of the fight which he always wore in battle, could be discerned as he glanced right and left. Order being restored, he took the oath of deputy and sat down between his friends.

The debate on Fanti's army bill, interrupted by Garibaldi's theatrical entrance, was resumed. Ricasoli spoke. He exhorted the Chamber to concord, and again insisted that the remarks recently attributed to Garibaldi must be calumnious. In questioning Fanti, he referred to the Volunteers in phrases which irritated the Garibaldians;[14] but his criticism irritated equally the War Minister, who read a long businesslike reply, in which he showed the undesirability of maintaining in time of peace a corps

[12] Ciàmpoli, 217.   [13] London *Times*, April 23, 1861.
[14] Text in Ricasoli, v, 443–46.

of volunteers side by side with the regular army. He gave his reasons for each step frankly, so frankly that when he described many of the promotions in Garibaldi's army as "fabulous," the Left, and especially Garibaldi himself, grew restive. If Fanti's general scheme had been referred to unprejudiced experts like Generals von Moltke and von Roon in the Prussian Army, they would have upheld it without a question. No military expert, indeed, could approve of the creation of a corps of volunteers in a country where military service was compulsory. But for Garibaldi and his friends, sentiment and wounded vanity, mingled with a quivering sense of patriotic wonders wrought and of threatened injustice, shut out a dispassionate consideration of the best military system.

Before Fanti had finished, Garibaldi, in spite of his outward calm, was inwardly chafing to reply. Crispi and Bixio suggested that Fanti's report be printed for public distribution, but to this both the War Minister and Ricasoli objected. Then Garibaldi rose. Deputies and spectators in the galleries, and the Ministers at the green table just below the President's chair, knew that the storm, which had been visibly gathering, was about to break. Good-natured Peruzzi sat on the ministerial bench between Cavour, who listened intently but calmly, and Fanti, who seemed ready to repel an attack. From his shrewdly-chosen seat Garibaldi could be seen clearly by all the deputies; for the Chamber was not large. In one hand he held several sheets of paper on which was written — by Rattazzi, many believed — the speech he intended to deliver. To read it he put on his glasses. He began pacifically, but everyone suspected that he was barely holding himself in. His rich and beautiful voice filled the hall; he spoke slowly, as an orator does who intends that his words shall express neither more nor less than his exact idea. After the first few sentences, however, he hesitated for his words, tried to read them from his manuscript, failed to catch the whispered promptings of Macchi and Zuppetta, and then plunged into an extemporaneous invective. Having thanked Ricasoli for bringing the question before Parliament, he repelled the charge that he was responsible for the dualism which existed. He said he had heard proposals of reconciliation, but only in words, acts were always unconciliatory. "I am a man of deeds," he continued. "Whenever this dualism might have harmed the great cause of my country, I have yielded, and I shall always yield. And yet, considering me not as Garibaldi but as anybody you please, I appeal to the conscience of these representatives of Italy to say whether I can offer my hand to him who has made me a foreigner in Italy." Cheers of approval from the Garibaldians in the galleries caused the President to give warning that he should order the tribunes cleared, if there were further disturbance.

Having now thrown discretion to the winds and scattered his written speech on the desk in front of him, Garibaldi continued, angrily: "Italy is not split in two; it is whole: because Garibaldi and his friends will always be with those who battle for it." Then he addressed himself to Fanti, whom he charged with asserting that he (Fanti) went to Central Italy the year before to put down anarchy. After a brief dispute over Fanti's exact phrase, Garibaldi swept on to take up the real subject of his speech — the Southern Army. "I ought above all," he said, "to narrate very glorious feats. The prodigies wrought by it were overshadowed only when the cold and hostile hand of this Ministry caused its maleficent effects to be felt. When, for love of concord, the horror of a fratricidal war, provoked by this very Ministry — "

At these words, a cyclone of passion swept through the Chamber. The deputies jumped to their feet and beset the President with calls to order, and he, having rung his bell without avail, attempted to speak. "I beg the honorable General Garibaldi — " his voice was drowned by the hubbub. Cavour, who had listened with growing indignation to Garibaldi's tirade, sprang up as if stung at the words "fratricidal war," pounded on the ministerial table and shouted so that many heard him in spite of the din: "No one has the right to insult us in this manner! We protest! We have never had such intentions. Mr. President — cause the Government and the Nation's representatives to be respected." At the first partial lull, Garibaldi, with unsophisticated egotism, said that he thought he had earned, by thirty years' service to the country, the right to tell the truth to the Chamber. Rattazzi requested him to express his opinions so as not to offend any deputy or minister present. In a flash Cavour protested: "He said that we provoked a fratricidal war. This is very different from the expression of an opinion." More outcries! more rushing to and fro! more waving of arms and shaking of fists! Garibaldi, the effigy of stolid rage, wholly unabashed, bellowed unrepentantly, "Yes, a fratricidal war!" From the Right came cries of "Order! Order! he has insulted the nation!" while voices from the Left replied, "No! no! let free speech be respected!" The uproar broke out afresh, not to be controlled. After frantically ringing his bell to no purpose, Rattazzi put on his hat, the sign that the sitting was suspended.

Then, as is the Italian fashion, the deputies poured down the aisles into the small semicircle below the President's dais, to press as close as they could to the Ministers. One Garibaldian supporter, beside himself with excitement, aimed a blow at Cavour, but was intercepted and carried out of the Chamber to cool off. Groups hemmed the Prime Minister in, approving, expostulating, advising, or merely yelling. "The mêlée in the centre of the hall, round the Ministers' table, was truly appalling," says a looker on. "In the midst of it all, Crispi was seen bawling, gesticulating like a maniac."[15] Friends surrounded Garibaldi on his upper platform, some to applaud, and some to pacify. The sanest deputies of every faction perceived that an outrage on parliamentary dignity had been committed: worse still, if the scene were renewed, irreparable harm might be done. The Red Shirts in the galleries had reached that pitch of resentment where, if they could not get what they demanded for themselves, they could gloat over the injury Garibaldi was inflicting on the Monarchy.

But the patriots of the Left joined with their least agitated colleagues of the Right to urge peace, and at four o'clock, after a quarter of an hour of pandemonium, Rattazzi, who with characteristic slyness had pretended to be faint and retired to his private room, called the Chamber to order. Garibaldi still had the floor. Rattazzi neither reproved him nor requested him, in the name of the Chamber, to retract his unparliamentary words. Garibaldi himself, perfectly unconcerned, had enjoyed the luxury of speaking his mind regardless of consequences — a performance in which the victim of obsession feels a strange sense of discharging a public duty. Having once broken through the inhibitions of self-restraint, the danger that he would let himself go again was

[15] London *Times*, April 23, 1861.

increased tenfold. And he had still much venom to rid himself of. He stood there defiant, with almost a peasant's insensibility to the havoc he was creating. To some his manner seemed leonine, to others theatrical. Oblivious to the larger issues, he was not to be diverted from the two objects he held to be paramount — the venting of his pent-up grievances against Cavour, and the defense of the Volunteers. He attacked again Fanti's law to disband the Southern Army. Those volunteers, he said tauntingly, won two kingdoms for you: why accept the kingdoms and reject the army that bestowed them? Garibaldi went still further, and demanded that the Government should arm the nation, creating perhaps half a million volunteers, who would outnumber the regular army three or four to one, and form an invincible weapon for the Paladin himself to use against Rome or Venetia. He urged that without such a bulwark Italy lay at the mercy of France and Austria.

Fanti replied that he could not agree with General Garibaldi's views. The air grew thunderous again. Then Bixio, the fiery and impetuous Nino, the Second of the Thousand, rose "in behalf of concord and of Italy," and made a very noble appeal to sink party and personal quarrels for the sake of national union. He said that, although the regular army must be respected, even in its prejudices, the element of strength offered by the Garibaldians ought also to be cherished. He deplored as a calamity that a multitude of mischief-makers had sown discord between Garibaldi and Cavour. "I would give my family and my own person," he concluded in a burst of patriotic emotion, "if I could see these men, and those who, like Signor Rattazzi, have directed the Italian movement, grasp each other's hands."[16]

Bixio did not appeal in vain. Cavour rose instantly to speak. His face still showed the effect of the terrible agitation through which he had just passed. Never had a prime minister resisted a greater temptation than he that afternoon. Attacked in his personal honor, accused of being a traitor, charged with fomenting a fratricidal war, — all this but the culmination of nearly two years of calumny and malice aforethought, — his first impulse was to hurl back his assailants, cost what it might. But to do this, though the great majority of Italians would justify him and

[16] Guerzoni: *Bixio*, 267–68.

Europe approve, might lead to civil war. The unification of Italy, to which he had devoted thirty years of his manhood, would be shattered. To avert that, by a Titanic exertion of will he held his passion as in a vise. "If emotion could have killed," he said afterward, "I should have died during that hour." Mingled with his patriotism was a noble pity for Garibaldi, the man so heroic of stature in one field, so dwarflike in others.

On rising, Cavour paid due tribute to Bixio's generous words. Then he confessed that he had been profoundly moved by the accusations leveled at him, especially because his accuser was Garibaldi. But who, he asked, created the Volunteers whom he was charged with wronging? Was it Garibaldi? No, it was Cavour himself, who more than two years before had summoned Garibaldi from Caprera to organize that very corps. It was he who, despite the opposition of the War Department, despite also grave political difficulties, had seen the Volunteers equipped in time for the War of 1859. Garibaldi listened attentively but made no attempt to deny this. Cavour acknowledged the great service rendered during that campaign by the Hunters of the Alps, because he said they showed Europe that Italians from all sections knew how to fight and die for the cause of Liberty. Having created and upheld this corps on his own responsibility, he felt the more keenly the injustice of certain accusations. "In spite of that," he said, and he spoke with great feeling, "I will be the first to accept the appeal made me by General Bixio. For me, the first part of this sitting is as if it had never happened." Prolonged cheers greeted this magnanimous avowal. Four fifths of the deputies breathed easier, hoping that the worst had passed. Garibaldi, however, sat immovable through it all, nor could he "be got to say one generous word."[17]

Cavour went on to unfold the plan of military reorganization. He showed how impossible it was to continue the Southern Army in active service as a volunteer corps. The Garibaldians had

[17] Mme. de Bunsen: *In Three Legations*, 138. The London *Times* correspondent says that Garibaldi's impulse, on hearing Cavour's words, was to go down and shake hands with him, but that Zuppetta "forcibly prevented him." *Times*, April 25, 1861. Amari wrote Cartwright that the "only generous movement of our popular hero during this sitting, from which he came out very much smaller than when he went in," was an instinctive rush of tears to his eyes, when Bixio spoke. "Cavour, on the contrary," Amari adds, "was admirable in dignity, tact, and even in eloquence." I, 153.

enlisted for no specified term: at Garibaldi's call they rushed to battle; the fighting over, they as quickly dispersed; they neither were qualified for routine service nor did they desire it: their strength lay in their very mobility. The Government proposed that the Volunteer Corps should consist of skeleton regiments, each of which should have a permanent staff in order to summon the volunteers in time of war. Another reason forbade adopting Garibaldi's scheme. To continue the Garibaldians under arms, would be almost equivalent to a declaration of war; and that, he stated emphatically, the Government would not countenance.

Garibaldi followed Cavour, but without a hint of retractation or apology or of meeting half-way the Premier's conciliatory speech. Confronted by arguments which he would not accept and could not refute, he fell back on that store of grievances which were his obsession. He accused the War Department in 1859 of having kept the able-bodied volunteers for the regular army, leaving him only the hump-backed and the halt. Cavour might have retorted by asking how it happened that at all times except when he was attacking the Ministry Garibaldi boasted that these alleged cripples — to wit, the Hunters of the Alps — were the finest soldiers in the world.[18] But Cavour refrained from sarcasm, merely stating that during the weeks of enrolment in 1859 Garibaldi had frequently expressed himself to Cialdini as well satisfied.[19] So Cavour explained that the sending of Garibaldi and the Hunters of the Alps into the Valtellina was made against his express advice, and that, to avoid a similar blunder, he himself ordered the Hunters of the Alps to the Mincio, where they might take part in the battle against the Austrians. The Paladin had cherished this grievance as one of the early proofs that Cavour was jealous of him and wished to shelve him; he now professed to be satisfied with the statement, but he continued to reiterate the falsehood to the end of his days.[20]

Cavour prefaced his explanations with the words: "I do not

[18] Even Jessie Mario thinks that Garibaldi exaggerated. *Garibaldi*, II, 32.
[19] La Marmora at once telegraphed a denial of Garibaldi's accusation.
[20] In his *Memorie*, 284, he says. "Besides the five regiments — Hunters of the Alps — at last had come the regiment, Hunters of the Apennines, which *Cavour, in spite of the King's orders, [which he] received at the beginning of the campaign, would not send us, under different pretexts, and which he sent us when the war was over.*"

indeed flatter myself that I can bring about that concord to which the honorable deputy Bixio invited us. I know that there exists a fact which creates between General Garibaldi and me — perhaps — an abyss.[21] I believed that I performed a painful duty, the most painful of my life, in advising the King and proposing to Parliament to approve the cession of Nice and Savoy to France. By the pain I felt, I can understand what General Garibaldi must have felt, and if he does not forgive me for this fact, I shall not bear him a grudge."[22]

To Garibaldi, however, the idea of forgiving Cavour for the crime of ceding Nice never occurred as a possibility. In his reply, he remarked that he had not doubted that Cavour also loved Italy; and that the disputes between them could be quickly removed if the Prime Minister would accept Garibaldi's project for arming the nation, and would send the Southern Army back to active service in the Two Sicilies. " That," he said, quite as a sovereign might, "is my desire." In other words, Garibaldi, yielding nothing, and feeling no thrill of magnanimity, had no glimmer of realization of the jeopardy into which his violence was forcing Italy. At the end of the debate, as at the beginning, he clung with bull-dog stubbornness to the demand that justice as he defined it should be done to his Volunteers and that his will must prevail, cost what it might.

After adjournment, Cavour remarked to a companion, as he was walking home: "And yet if war came, I would take Garibaldi's arm in mine, and say to him, 'Let us go and see what they are doing at Verona.'" So habitual was it for him to subordinate personal passion for the good of Italy. The next day and the next the discussion was continued. Orators of the Left attacked Fanti's plan from many angles; Ministerialists defended it. Garibaldi introduced another resolution to the effect that the Ministry should recognize the commissions issued by him as dictator, and should call out the Volunteers as early as it deemed best.[23] On both sides there was much latent heat, with occasional explosions, and the purpose, evident though tacit, to avoid an open rupture. Cavour spoke twice on the 20th, answering objections

[21] Here Garibaldi interrupted and requested Cavour to turn towards him, so that he could hear. Cavour complied, repeating this sentence.

[22] *Discorsi*, XI, 378.   [23] Text in *Discorsi*, XI, 386, n. 1.

and restating with great clearness the intentions of the Cabinet, in order that, under the momentary glamour of assumed conciliation, there should be no misunderstanding. The next day the Chamber passed Ricasoli's resolution[24] by 190 votes to 79. Thus was Garibaldi's policy overwhelmingly repudiated by the representatives of the nation to whom he had appealed.[25] "Who Garibaldi is," Ricasoli wrote to an intimate friend, "is shown in these last debates; but what whoever was absent could not see is the *expectation* of all honorable hearts, after Cavour's generous and chivalric words, that Garibaldi would withdraw his resolution, and quitting his seat would go and grasp Cavour's hand."[26]

That afternoon General Cialdini sent to the newspapers an open letter to the Hero. Garibaldi despised parliament men; Cialdini was a soldier. Garibaldi was the sworn enemy of Cavour and Fanti; Cialdini had been his friend, his loyal admirer. Garibaldi regarded the Piedmontese as banded in a conspiracy against him; Cialdini, though he had long served in Victor Emanuel's army, was a Modenese. And now Cialdini wrote:

"Your reply to the address of the Milanese workmen, your words in the Chamber, caused me a disillusion very painful but complete. You are not the man that I thought, you are not the Garibaldi I loved. With the disappearance of the spell, the affection that bound me to you has disappeared. . . .

"You dare to put yourself on a level with the King, speaking of him with the affected familiarity of a comrade. You mean to place yourself above usage, presenting yourself to the Chamber in a very outlandish costume; above the Government, branding its ministers as traitors because they are not devoted to you; above Parliament, heaping with vituperation the deputies who do not think as you do; above the country, desiring to drive it whither and how pleases you best. Very well, General! There are men disposed not to tolerate all that, and I am with them. The foe of every tyranny, whether it be clothed in black or in red, I will combat even yours to the end.

"I know the orders given by you, or by yours, to Colonel Tripoti to receive us in the Abruzzi with musket volleys; I know

[24] Text *ivi*.   [25] For this famous session see Parliamentary reports; *Discorsi;* letters of Cavour, Ricasoli and other participants; descriptions of eye-witnesses — Mme. de Bunsen, D'Ideville, *Times* and other correspondents.   [26] Ricasoli, v, 418; Ricasoli to C. Bianchi, April 21, 1861

the words uttered by General Sirtori in Parliament; I know those spoken by you; and by these successive tracks, I travel surely, and I penetrate the intimate thought of your party. It wishes to get control of the country and of the army, threatening us, otherwise, with a civil war. I am not in a position to know what the country thinks of this, but I can assure you that the army does not fear your threats — it fears only your government.

" General, you achieved a great and marvelous undertaking with your volunteers. You have reason to be proud of it, but you are wrong in exaggerating its true results. You were on the Volturno in the very worst conditions when we arrived. Capua, Gaeta, Messina, and Civitella did not fall by your work, and 56,000 Bourbons were beaten, dispersed and made prisoners by us, not by you. Therefore, to say that the Kingdom of the Two Sicilies was wholly liberated by your arms is inexact. . . .

"I will end by telling you that I have neither the pretension nor the mandate to address you in the name of the army. But I think that I know it well enough to count on its sharing the feeling of disgust and of pain which your own intemperance and that of your party have roused in me." [27]

This letter came as a godsend to multitudes throughout the land, who were, indeed, either disgusted with Garibaldi's vanity, or alarmed at the prospect of civil war. The inner circle of his intimates read it with justifiable rage. The deputies of the Left even talked of resigning in a body: but the saner heads among them saw that they had already gone too far, and Garibaldi himself began to suspect that his Radical friends had misused him. There were neither resignations, therefore, nor retractions. But Garibaldi addressed to the doughty Cialdini this reply, which seems to have been composed by a more experienced rhetorician than the rhapsodical Paladin:

"I too was your friend and the admirer of your deeds. Today I will be what you choose; not being willing certainly to condescend to justify myself so far as regards what you point out in your letter as indecorous on my part towards the King and towards the Army: strong in all that, in my conscience as soldier and as citizen. As to the style of my dress, I shall wear it until I am informed that I am no longer in a free country where every

[27] Mario: *Garibaldi*, ii, 33–35.

CHÂTEAU CAVOUR AT SANTENA

Cavour's Room is the last on the right in the top story

one wears what he pleases. The message to Colonel Tripoti I hear for the first time.[28] I know no other orders than that given by me — to receive the Italian soldiers of the Army of the North as brothers; although we knew that that army was coming to combat the revolution personified in Garibaldi (words of Farini to Napoleon III). As deputy, I think I have exposed to the Chamber the very smallest part of the wrongs received by the Southern Army from the Ministry. The Italian army will have one soldier more when there is question of fighting the enemies of Italy — and that will not come as a novelty to you. We were on the Volturno — on the eve of our most splendid victory won in Southern Italy, before you arrived; and quite otherwise than very badly off. So far as I know, the army has applauded the free and moderate words of a deputy soldier for whom Italian honor has been a religion during his whole life. If, however, any one takes offense at my manner of procedure, I, speaking in my own name only, and alone responsible for my words, await calmly a demand for satisfaction on account of them." [29]

It would be unjust to many soldiers to call this a soldier's letter. Put in a nutshell, it announced that Garibaldi refused to acknowledge that anyone had the right to criticize his words, acts or dress; that whoever insinuated that the Garibaldian army was in a bad condition when Victor Emanuel's corps reached the Volturno, lied; that the Dictator would prove these things by fighting a duel with the first person who challenged him. The public, which regarded Garibaldi's letter as weak, waited anxiously for the next move. Early on the 25th, the Dictator himself, restive at being in an unpopular position, sent his future son-in-law, Canzio, to inform Cialdini that they must fight. Meanwhile, friends of both worked to prevent a meeting. The King had had news of Garibaldi's intention, through Trecchi, who intimated, however, that the Paladin would not be loath, if appearances could be saved, to have a double reconciliation. At noon the King saw Cavour and told him that that same evening Garibaldi would meet him in the Royal Palace. Cavour replied that, as a public man could not decline to see anyone, he consented

[28] This is a plain untruth, because the alleged Tripoti telegram, apparently put forth by some liar from the Piedmontese army, had been a current topic for seven months. Bertani: *Ire*, 87.   For Napoleon's remark: *Aff. Etrang.*, 1861, p. 163.   [29] Mario: *Garibaldi*, II, 35–36.

to the interview. At seven o'clock they met in one of the ground-floor rooms of the Palace. Garibaldi was polite, if not affable. Cavour treated him with much courtesy, and once more outlined the general policy of the Government towards Rome, Venice and military reorganization. Garibaldi reiterated his demands for the Southern Army and for national armament. They parted in peace. Knowing that Garibaldi had sworn that rather than take Cavour's hand he would chop off his own, Cavour made no advances. He did not wish to expose Garibaldi to the obligation of carrying out so foolish a vow.[30] A few hours later at Pallavicino's palace Garibaldi and Cialdini made up with an effusiveness that appeared to be genuine.[31]

Garibaldi's onslaught had failed. Some one described him as having the heart of a child and the head of a buffalo —that creature which, seeing a red object in the distance, charges it with indiscriminate fury, and gores and tramples it, though it be his red-cloaked master, the farmer, or the farmer's little daughter picking flowers. Equally insensate was Garibaldi's fury in the final duel with Cavour and in his conduct for nearly two years previous. He might plead that he honestly believed that Cavour was persistently trying to destroy him; yet serious judges will scarcely acquit a public personage, wielding a mighty influence, who does not feel the obligation of verifying a single accusation, and even dispenses with reason. Statesmen and soldiers may engage in life-or-death antagonisms over vital principles; but when they are impelled by personal pique, or vanity or ambition, or when they mistake their blind prejudices for patriotism, we may indeed pity them, but we can neither admire nor respect.

Garibaldi's ostensible purpose in attacking Cavour on April 18, was to secure what he regarded as justice for his volunteers. Grant that they had cause for grievance, grant that he had not received the full measure of official recognition which he hungered for, was it patriotic to precipitate a conflict which might shatter his country? Is Achilles, who sulks in his tent, or hurls taunts at his opponent, or threatens to blast the national cause

[30] "I never saw his hands at all," Cavour told Ricasoli; "he held them under his Prophet's mantle all the time."   [31] Memorandum written by Ricasoli from statements by Cavour and others, April 25, 1861. Ricasoli, v, 422–25.

unless he is satisfied — is this barbarian product of the youth of Greece, the best model of patriotism for civilized men? Garibaldi's Red Shirts risked life and fortune on their splendid enterprise: was it becoming that, even before they had finished their task, they should begin to clamor for rewards? Was it edifying to see them through Garibaldi's agency attempt to seize the State by the throat and bid it yield or perish? Why is it that the very men who, in an ecstasy of devotion, sacrifice everything in order to save or to create a nation, will not sacrifice their selfish claims when they have weathered the crisis? Better, a thousand times better, like Leonidas and his Three Hundred, to sleep in glory on the field of a lost battle, enshrined forever in the gratitude of mankind, than to go forth under the spell of patriotism at the call of duty, and, having performed deeds of undying lustre, to come back and pose as heroes, demanding pensions and honors and offices, and by vanity and greed to make patriotism odious!

But the indictment against Garibaldi goes deeper than his hatred of Cavour; it concerns Italy herself. National unification was achievable only through the coöperation of the two elements — the Monarchy and the Revolution. By promoting the National Society, and by enlisting Garibaldi on the side of the Monarchy, Cavour secured this indispensable coöperation. Garibaldi undertook to lead the Revolution in the name of the Monarchy, but though loyal at heart to the King, he rebelled against the policy of the King's government. Dictatorial by nature, he neither understood nor respected the prosaic working of a constitutional régime. Relying on his emotions, with hardly the reasoning power of a child, he despised or resolved to ignore facts which, like his bug-bear, Diplomacy, he found inconvenient.

Tested by the touchstone of patriotism, his mad outbreak in Parliament must be unqualifiedly condemned: for he made the interest of his few thousand volunteers paramount to the welfare of Italy: to sacrifice all to a clique is not patriotism. If they had been unjustly treated, they might have waited to have their wrongs redressed. But Garibaldi, in order to get commissions for his officers and pay and a billet for his soldiers, was ready — although he did not realize it — to wreck his country. What Italy needed above all was harmony: his speeches to his friends, his harangues to visiting delegations, every sentence that he uttered in the Chamber, was a warning that there should be no harmony until the Garibaldian demands were appeased. With Sicily and Naples in a state of insurrection, and the possibility of a reaction still in sight; with all the new provinces eyeing each other and Piedmont with misgivings; with the reinforced Austrian army mobilized along the Venetian frontier; with the Pope intriguing among the Catholic Powers to recover his lost territory; and with the intentions of the French Emperor uncertain, — Garibaldi decided that the most patriotic thing he could do was to go into the Parliament of his just-created nation and threaten ruin if the minor object on which he had set his heart were denied. He held further that, instead of welding together the 22 million of Italians, — peoples as mutually unrelated as Scotch Highlanders and Cornishmen in the days of the Stuarts, — instead of even ascertaining whether they could be welded together, — this new, tentative Italy must be put in jeopardy in order to rush to the liberation of three million Venetians and of 400,000 Romans. The annals of patriotism have no counterpart to this Garibaldian outbreak, for the simple reason that it was not patriotism: as must appear if we ask, How would Hampden or Washington, Lincoln or Pisani, have acted?

The best excuse we can find for Garibaldi is that, like the small boy who does a great injury, he did not realize what he was doing. His obsession of hatred for Cavour, his innate megalomania, his inability to reason, from which came his lack of historical perspective, his accessibility to flatterers, his unwavering devotion to whatever plan he adopted, and his certitude that whatever he planned was the final evangel of patriotism, predestined him to threaten the very existence of Italy in April, 1861. If it be argued that he served Italy by goading the reluctant forward and by enabling Cavour to hasten unification by scaring Diplomacy with the spectre of the Revolution, the reply is yes: but Garibaldi might have done this service without adopting the policy of hatred which so greatly impaired his achievement. Much more was involved than the explosion of his personal wrath. The Party of Action made him their tool. They hoped, under cover of his immense prestige, to shape the foreign policy of the new Kingdom; as they might have done, had their move for the enrolment of a half-million volunteers, to be led by him, been successful.

In resisting him and them, at the risk of his own popularity and, as it proved, of his life, Cavour performed the best service that a patriot could perform at that crisis. As in the previous October, so now he carried the contest into Parliament, an arena which Garibaldi could not decline, although he was placed at as great a disadvantage there as his statesmen adversaries would have been in the saddle. Cavour showed by this that under a constitutional régime no man, not even the monarch, is above the law: that was the stern lesson which the Italians, and Garibaldi above all, most needed to learn.

Garibaldi assured his friends after the explosion that, far from conceding anything, he intended to prosecute his war on the Ministers until he secured justice for the Southern Army and a general arming of the Nation. "In case those gentlemen continue to croak," he added, "then we will take up our interrupted task." [32] Happily, however, he returned to Caprera (May 1), where the absence of virulent instigators gave him time to calm down. He wrote Cavour in behalf of certain of his friends who sought offices. Cavour stated his position as sympathetically as possible, and then, as a hint that, although the time was not ripe for another expedition, he did not mean to be idle, he referred to a proposed understanding with the Magyars and Croats, of which Garibaldi should be kept informed.[33] The Paladin answered this note on May 18 in a tone that seems to indicate that he had suddenly awakened to some sense of Cavour's position in the work of National resurrection. Having spoken of the appointments in question, and praised the Prime Minister's "parsimony in conferring high rank in the Army and Navy," he went on to offer some suggestions. "The sacrifices with which you were obliged to pay for the magnanimous alliance," he said, "will have opened your eyes as to what may be expected from it; your superior intelligence will surely have enabled you to understand fully the actual situation. I am wholly with you in welcoming the French alliance, but, Count, *you* ought to be the arbiter of Europe and treat at least as an equal with whoever

[32] Guerzoni: *Garibaldi*, II, 270; Garibaldi to Guerzoni, April 29. Also, Amari.
[33] *Lettere*, VI, 707–08; C. to Garibaldi, May 10, 1861.

2

wishes to pose as Master. Italy represents today the aspirations of the World's Nationalities, and you rule Italy. But to rule Italy well, one must not descend to weaknesses appropriate to the intrinsic present condition. Kossuth, Manin, Guerrazzi, Mazzini, more than by the strength of their enemies were overthrown by the defect inherent in their intrinsic condition. They were Dictators, but they were not Soldiers. A single example, in order not to weary you. Mazzini, Dictator in fact, but having neither the indispensable qualities, nor the courage to assume the title, bends under miserable individual susceptibilities, keeps at a distance those capable of commanding the Army, and raises from the lower ranks of the Militia that poor old soul, Roselli, to be general-in-chief, excellent perhaps at the head of his regiment, but inadequate to the difficult circumstances in which the Republic was involved. . . .

"Let Victor Emanuel be the arm and you, Count, the brain, and thus form that powerful Whole which alone is lacking to-day to the Peninsula. I will be the first to utter in Parliament the word Dictatorship, indispensable in great emergencies. Give Victor Emanuel the Army-Nation, and call to his side the men capable of quickly realizing it. Italy will give with enthusiasm whatever is needed.

"These are the guarantees which will cause us to throw ourselves blindly into the arms of the Dictatorship. With this there will not be in the State a single opposing voice. You will sleep tranquilly, confident that the very last of the Italians will do his duty. To others will be left the miserable subterfuges of deceit, in order to govern, and the Dynasty of King Galantuomo will rest perennially on Italy like an emanation of Providence. If human progress is not a lie, the Army-Nation will supersede the standing army, and you will have advanced Italy an immense distance on the right road. Then too, I beg you to believe me, Count, Italy and her ruler ought to have friends everywhere and to fear nobody! In '49, I quitted Rome with 4000 men, and I was obliged to hide in the forests only. In '60 you have seen what we did with 1000. Tomorrow we will achieve in geometrical progression with the people which gave the Romans to the Universe. Trusting in your superior ability and firm will to accomplish the welfare of the father-land, I shall await the happy word which summons me once more to the fields of battle." [34]

Whether this letter, which epitomizes so much of Garibaldi,— his ancient grudge against Mazzini, his belief in a dictatorship, his grandiose dreams of the Nation Armed, — ever reached Cavour, does not appear. But the fact that he wrote it at all, that he voluntarily admitted that Cavour had done well and that he himself was ready to serve under him, might have brought, but for an unforeseen and terrible calamity, internal peace to Italy. Later, indeed, Garibaldi never acknowledged these admissions, nor was the existence of his letter generally known for nearly half-a-century. Instead of that impulse to reconciliation, which passed almost in a day, he perpetuated in his Memoirs the malice with which whispering tongues had corroded his heart against Cavour. His written word remains, to the sore distress of Italy and to the soiling of his own reputation.

The truest admirers of Garibaldi are those who admire him for his noble qualities, not those who idolize his failures, his blunders, his defects. He belonged by nature to the simple, Homeric brood, but Fate placed him in the complex nineteenth century, amid rotting tyrannies and an effete ecclesiasticism. He loved liberty, he loved the ideal of country, with a consuming passion. Not understanding the intricacy of the modern problem, he plunged ahead and expected that the system which had sufficed for patriarchal or tribal life would suffice still. So he lacked that tact for the possible, which is the first mark of a statesman, and saves those who are privileged to achieve inestimable benefits, from doing irreparable harm to their countrymen. But he let the world see that the youth of Italy could fight for an ideal. He bequeathed to the story of his country's redemption the aureole of a legendary exploit. The contradictions in his character and deeds may well be the despair of historians, who must so often pass in a single breath from admiration to censure. He personified the patriotic Emotion of his time, and Emotion will always be its own justification. His contemporaries did not scrutinize him minutely — they submitted joyfully to his fascination. He stood for the few simple primal

[34] P. Vayra: "Garibaldi e Cavour," *Riv. Stor. Ital.*, III, 461–63. *Centenario*, 30–32, where Garibaldi's letter is given in facsimile.

things, which mankind forever comes back to as essential — for freedom, whether it be freedom from priestcraft or from civil despotism; for love of country; and for human fellowship. In a world that had become stratified into social layers, he was the comrade of any man, high or low, who shared his code of honor and his enthusiasms. Forgetting his defects, his rancors and his political blunders alike, Posterity will probably remember him as the modern Paladin, who set forth against great odds to free a kingdom, and, having accomplished his task, and refused honors and rewards, retired to his island crag. In the childhood of the world, when myths and poems sprang up, gods and demigods and heroes wrought in this imperial simplicity. But for us, who live near enough to know the truth, it is better to see Garibaldi as he was, human to the core, a paradox of pettiness and of glory.

This forensic duel with Garibaldi was, however, only an episode in Cavour's overburdened life.

Besides attending to the routine tasks of two ministries, he was required, as President of the Council, to discuss the multitude of questions submitted to it by all of his colleagues. He seems to have neglected nothing. At the Ministry of Foreign Affairs, he toiled not merely to ward off the harsh criticisms of the Great Powers, but to secure their recognition of the New Kingdom, being most solicitous to persuade Napoleon III, who would secretly have been glad to acknowledge Italy and see the Pope quit Rome, as it was commonly supposed he would do, and take refuge in Austria. Perhaps the Emperor did not suspect that it was his Ambassador, Gramont, who, according to his own statement, dissuaded the Curia from letting Pius depart. Throughout the winter and spring, scarcely a week passed without fresh rumors that the Pope could bear his humiliation no longer and would go. The humor of it was that Pius, far from being grateful to Napoleon for preserving Rome, upbraided him for allowing the wicked Italians to seize Umbria and the Marches. After the Bourbons collapsed at Gaeta, Napoleon could cherish no further hope of getting a foothold in the South. To continue to garrison Rome for Papalists who hated him, became, therefore, repugnant to him; especially since he thereby made himself unpopular among the Italians, whose benefactor he wished to appear, and distrusted by the English and the Germans, whose goodwill he craved. When Cavour now secretly urged that the French troops should be withdrawn, the Emperor listened. That withdrawal was about to be carried out a year before, but the sailing of the Thousand upset Napoleon's calculations. Now he listened; at first inscrutably, according to his habit, then more and more favorably. Cavour had Plon-Plon for an ally. The terms finally agreed upon were: the King's Government promised, after the departure of the French army, neither to invade nor permit anyone else to invade the Patrimony of St. Peter; the Emperor agreed that no other foreign power, or international army, should occupy Rome. The intent was obvious. If the Papalists, after being thrown on their own resources, were unable to preserve order, and if the Roman Liberals appealed to Victor Emanuel for protection, it would be less difficult for the Italians to come to an agreement with the Pope. When a sufficient interval elapsed, Napoleon could no longer feel bound to send back an army, and the Roman Question, so far as it was political, would soon be generally regarded as an Italian Question, to be settled by the Italians and not by Europe. By the end of May, Vimercati, who was conducting the negotiations at Paris, wrote the glorious news that Napoleon had consented, that the compact would be signed before the middle of June, and that the recognition of the new Kingdom would then be proclaimed without delay. Cardinal Antonelli having barred the direct way to Rome, Cavour thus found the key to a side entrance.

He told a friend that he hoped Rome would be Italian within a year. At the same time he was conferring with Kossuth and Türr as to a Magyar revolution, during which the Venetians might throw off their Austrian yoke. The creation of a navy adequate to the protection of the new Kingdom took much of his thought. The possibility of the reopening of the Garibaldian dispute still hung over him. The condition of the Neapolitans and Sicilians gave him no sleep. His intimates remarked that, since the fatal 18th of April, his face had been now flushed, now livid or ashen; his manner was often unwontedly brusque, and sometimes even in the Chamber he showed an excitability which surprised everyone. Martin Tosco, the trusty body-servant of many years, who slept in a room just below the Count's chamber, reported that his master spent many nights pacing up and down, apparently talking to himself or rehearsing speeches. The interviews at dawn were still kept up. But although these things were noted at the time, they aroused no real alarm. Cavour had come to be regarded as a Titan, whom no burden could crush.

On May 26 his friend Salmour had an early morning appointment with him. Business over, they fell to discussing the situation. Cavour explained that, having twice been reconciled with Rattazzi, for the sake of harmony, and having found him faithless, he should trust him no more. The two old friends talked about their youth, and Cavour lingered tenderly on this memory and on that. Salmour was shocked at Cavour's face, and at the evidences of exhaustion. "I do not feel well," Cavour said; "ever since that unfortunate sitting when I was so unjustly attacked by Garibaldi, I have never felt well." Salmour urged him to dismiss that ordeal from his thoughts, assuring him that it had discredited Garibaldi and immensely increased Cavour's popularity. Cavour replied that he had argued with himself, but that there are certain sensations we cannot control — one spot where we are vulnerable — and that his effort to stifle his indignation had struck him in that spot. The friends parted with a spontaneous fervor of affection: but Salmour was haunted by Cavour's lustreless eyes — "their whites very yellow" — and by his hue like that of a disinterred corpse.[35]

On May 27, Cavour spoke in the Chamber on the project of modifying the customs tariff. On the 28th and 29th he took part in the debate over the status of the disbanded troops. On the 29th he said, in discussing a resolution in the interest of the Mazzinians of 1849, that all who had fought for national independence should be held worthy by the country: "It has been said that we must fuse all parties, at least on the foreign question; when the foreign question is finished we will discuss among ourselves; we will even fight each other:[36] but first let us finish the foreign question. Now, to reach this end no difference must be made between those who fought at Venice or at Rome; between those who fought at Rome or at Bologna; between those

---

[35] F. Crispolti: "Cavour alla Vigilia della Morte." *Corriere della Sera*, Jan. 6, 1911. [36] Here the stenographer adds: "Hilarity and cries of 'No! no!'"

who fought at Bologna or at Palermo. This is the thought of concord which Deputy Bixio's resolution expresses — that is to say, that all who fought, though even under a Republican banner, previous to 1859 — because since then there has been no more fighting under this flag — have indeed deserved well of Italy. We support this declaration; and therefore I think that we perform the greatest act of conciliation that is possible under existing conditions." [37]

Cavour went home tired. Tosco begged him to take a holiday. "I am fagged," Cavour replied; "but I must work in spite of it; the country needs me. Perhaps I can go to Switzerland this summer." He dined as usual with his brother and nephew; chatted freely on many subjects; and urged Gustavo to put Santena in order. "I mean to repose there some day," he said, "beside my own people." After dinner, he smoked a cigar on the balcony, but feeling a chill, he returned indoors and took his customary nap. On waking an hour later, he had bad sensations, then vomitings, and went to bed. He would not allow Tosco to stay with him; but about midnight the devoted servant heard him walking to and fro. Presently, Cavour rang his bell violently, and on Tosco's rushing up to him, he said, "I have one of my usual attacks and fear apoplexy. Go for a doctor." Very early in the morning of Thursday, May 30, Dr. Rossi, for twenty years the family physician of the Cavours, came; but being unable to stop the vomiting, he ordered bleeding. A surgeon, hastily summoned, bled Cavour and a temporary calm followed. Again at eight o'clock, and again at five that afternoon, the patient was bled. On Friday, Cavour seemed so much better, that, against Dr. Rossi's advice, he held a two-hours' cabinet meeting at his bedside, and spent the rest of the forenoon working with Nigra and Blanc. When his niece, Countess Josephine Alfieri, saw him later, he congratulated himself that the bleedings had prevented an illness which might have kept him in bed a fortnight. He could not waste his time in that way; for "Parliament and Italy need me," he said earnestly. Before daybreak Saturday, however, there was another access of chills. Dr. Rossi ordered quinine, which his stomach rejected. During the day, he was bled twice, and the natural quiet of extreme weakness supervened.

[37] *Discorsi*, XI, 456.

Sunday, the 2d of June, Turin celebrated the National Festival of the Statuto — when, for the first time, all Italy rejoiced. While merry-making went on in the streets and gardens, with the city in gala costume, and while the churches resounded with *Te Deums*, the sick man grew no better, but he inquired eagerly for reports of the festivities.

That day Countess Alfieri discovered, to her horror, that his left hand and arm were cold as marble. The servants began to whisper to each other, "The Count will not get well." Cavour, nevertheless, kept in good spirits, and if he had doubts, he did not reveal them. On trying to read a book — the latest volume of Thiers's "History of the Consulate and Empire" — he found his head troubled. "This is extraordinary," he said to Tosco; "I cannot read." Then, at a sudden movement, one of his wounds opened, and he lost much blood before the surgeon could arrive. By evening, a raging fever set in, his breathing became short, his mind wandered. On Monday morning Dr. Rossi requested to call a colleague, Dr. Maffoni, in consultation.[38] Before he came, however, Cavour insisted that his head was so confused that nothing could save him except another bleeding. When the cut was made, no blood issued, until the surgeon by dint of much pressure, succeeded in squeezing out two or three ounces of black, coagulated blood. At Dr. Maffoni's entrance with Rossi, Cavour said, "Gentlemen, cure me promptly, I have Italy on my hands, and the time is precious. Saturday, I must be at Bardonnèche to inspect the Mt. Cenis tunnel." Maffoni prescribed more quinine, to which Cavour had a mortal repugnance, but when his niece implored him, he drank it, "for I do not wish to refuse you anything." In the evening, the Prince of Carignano saw him for a few moments. Countess Rorà, Cavour's cousin, watched with his niece. Faithful Castelli and Farini came and went, until their growing alarm kept them permanently in the anteroom.

On the 4th the doctors ordered mustard plasters for the cold limbs and bladders filled with ice for the burning head. Being

[38] The doctors never satisfactorily diagnosed Cavour's disease. According to different opinions it was a "mild form of typhus," "congestion of the brain," "inflammation of the intestines," threatened apoplexy, malignant malaria, *perniziosa*, etc. Whatever it was, modern authorities agree that the excessive bleeding made recovery impossible.

left alone with Tosco, he said suddenly: "Martin, we must part. When the time comes, send for Fra Giacomo, the curate of Madonna degli Angeli, who has promised to be with me at the end. Now send for M. Castelli and M. Farini." To the trusty Castelli, he could not utter the confidences he intended. To Farini he said, "You cured me of an illness like this a few years ago; I put myself under your charge now." Farini ordered more ice and mustard, but to no avail. Over and over again that day he asked whether word had come from Vimercati — the message he hungered for, that Napoleon had signed the agreement. He talked much on administrative and other matters, but those who watched him remarked that through all his delirium he never revealed a secret, nor uttered a word of hate or rancor.[39] By this time, Turin knew the danger he was in, and crowds gathered in the streets near his house, in the courtyard and even on the staircase. Wednesday morning early, his case was so desperate that the physicians advised that the friar be sent for. When this news spread among the crowds, remembering how the Church had persecuted Santa Rosa in his death agony, they resolved that their dear "Papa Camillo" should not suffer likewise. An upper-class person asked for Castelli, who was watching in the antechamber. "I come to warn you," said the stranger, "that if the priests refuse, there will be a grave scandal. Be prepared." Soon after, a workman, with trembling voice and red eyes, exclaimed, "If the priests refuse, one word is enough and we will end it." And the warnings and threats were not vain, Castelli adds. But Fra Giacomo kept his promise.[40]

Meanwhile, it fell to Countess Alfieri — who like a beautiful presence hallows the sickroom during all these days and nights — to warn the patient. "Uncle," she said, "Fra Giacomo has called to get news of you; will you see him for a moment?" "He looked at me fixedly," she reports, "understood me, pressed my hand, and replied, 'Have him come in.'" For a little while the curate remained alone with the dying man. Later, Cavour said to Farini: "My niece has had Fra Giacomo summoned; I must prepare for the great passage to eternity. I have confessed and received absolution: later, I shall take communion. I desire the good people of Turin to know that I die like a good Christian. I

[39] Castelli: *Carteggio*, I, 362.   [40] Castelli: *Cavour*, 99-100.

am at peace; I have never done injury to anyone." At five that afternoon, Fra Giacomo returned to administer extreme unction. The populace escorted him from the church a block away, silently, reverently, as many as could bearing lighted candles.

From this time on Cavour's mind wandered frequently. At nine in the evening, when the King entered unannounced, — by a private staircase, in order to escape the multitude which now thronged the palace, — Cavour recognized him, tried to lift himself to a sitting posture, and at once launched into a feverish review of Italy's needs. He spoke earnestly of "the poor Neapolitans," corrupted, not through their own fault, but by "that rascal Ferdinand." "The bad must be cleansed; yes, yes, Sire, let them be cleansed, cleansed." The King, much moved, grasped his great Servant's hand, and on going out, begged Dr. Riberi, a specialist of the highest reputation, who had been called in, to try cupping the jugular vein. When Cavour saw Riberi, he said, with his characteristic raillery: "I have sent for you a little late, because till now I was not sick enough to be worthy of you." But no remedies could affect him any more.

Throughout that night, the beloved niece sat by the bedside. Cavour poured out directions, opinions, questions. He had Naples continually in mind. "Let there be no state of siege," he said; "none of those means used by absolute governments. Everybody can govern with the state of siege. I will govern them with liberty and I will show what ten years of liberty can do for those fine lands." He spoke of Prussia; of the civil war just broken out in the United States. Gradually, his voice, which had been strong till then, failed. The servants, alarmed, remarked: "When the Count stops speaking, he will stop living." He drank with relish a cup of beef-tea and a glass of Bordeaux. "Were they good?" his niece asked. "Too good," he replied smiling: "Riberi will scold us both to-morrow. Tell the cook his beef-tea was too succulent for a sick man like me." His legs grew cold; a cold sweat gathered on his forehead, and he complained of pain in his left arm. A mustard-plaster was applied, but he soon asked Countess Josephine to remove it, and he assisted her with his right hand. He spoke now with great difficulty. Reaching up to his niece, he drew her head down to his mouth, kissed her twice and said, "Good-by, dear little one." Then he bade his

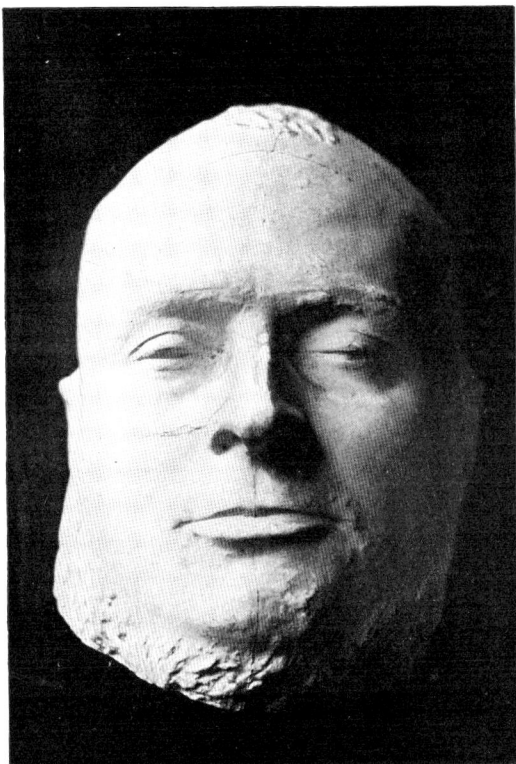

From a replica belonging to Princeton University

CAVOUR'S DEATH MASK

brother good-bye very tenderly. His pulse failed fast. Fra Giacomo, hastily summoned, brought the holy oil, at half past five. Cavour recognized him, grasped his hand, and murmured, "Friar, friar, a Free Church in a Free State!" For an hour longer, during which his niece moistened his lips, he showed signs of life. His last intelligible words were: "Italy is made — all is safe." [41] Then, after coughing very faintly twice, he died at a quarter to seven in the morning. It was Thursday, June 6, 1861.[42]

[41] Castelli: *Cavour*, I, 361; Castelli to M. d'Azeglio, June 7, 1861.

[42] For Cavour's last illness the chief document is Countess Alfieri's narrative, La Rive, 319–32; Italian version in Artom-Blanc, II, 617–39. Next in importance is Castelli: *Cavour*, 93–110. See also Castelli: *Ricordi*, 135–48; Ideville, 189–201; Massari: *Cavour*, 433–34; Artom, 211–14; *Moniteur*, June 5, 6, 7; London *Times*, June 4, 5, 6, 7.

CHAPTER XXXVII

CONCLUSION

HAVING hardly realized that Cavour was desperately ill before they heard that he was dead, the Turinese would not believe that their "Papa Camillo," the incarnation of life, lay that morning a mere corpse, beyond reach of their grief, their gratitude, their dire need. The Cabinet met at nine o'clock and voted, as a safeguard from alarm, not to resign until the King should secure a new prime minister. At half past one, Rattazzi called the Chamber of Deputies to order with a few conventional phrases. But the general emotion was indescribable: members of every party wept; Minghetti broke into sobs when he announced the action of the Cabinet. In the Senate, the grave patrician Sclopis declared that the history of Italy commemorates no statesman who conceived so vast a design as Count Cavour — none who employed such a wealth of means to achieve it. The imprint of Cavour's policy on Italy, he said, "will never be blotted out, either through lapse of time or through the vicissitudes of fortune." National mourning for a period of twenty days was decreed,[1] but the shopkeepers of the city had already, of their own accord, put up their shutters, and they transacted no business until after the funeral. "Whoever has not seen Turin in that day of lamentation," says Massari, "cannot understand what the sincere grief of an entire people is." The news of the disaster of Novara, the impending invasion of the Austrians in May, 1859, the untimely check to national hopes at Villafranca — none of these ordeals caused such consternation as Cavour's death.[2] The throngs discussed it with bated breath, and the rumor ran among them that a secret agent of the French Emperor had poisoned the Count.[3] Nothing less than that seemed credible to their distraught minds.

[1] Proceedings of Parliament, *Discorsi*, xi, 457–63.   [2] Massari: *Cavour*, 435.

[3] This suspicion was followed up by the secret police, who found nothing to justify it. Sensation-mongers still repeat it. See, for example, Cappa's *Memoirs*, or *Cavour Avvelenato*.

On Friday Cavour's body lay in state at his home, and was viewed by thousands of grief-stricken mourners. That afternoon, amid a drenching rain, it was taken to Fra Giacomo's church for the funeral mass. The King, who, whatever his personal dislike of the masterful Prime Minister may have been, always sank his private preference for the good of the State, now desired that Cavour, in recognition of his unique services to Piedmont and to Italy, should be buried at Superga with the princes of the House of Savoy. Florence also craved the honor of placing him among the mighty dead in Santa Croce. But in his last weeks Cavour had remarked more than once that he wished to lie beside his own people at Santena, and there, in the simple mortuary chapel of the family, his coffin was laid on June 9. Neither epitaph nor monument distinguishes his tomb from those of his parents, of Marina and the aunts and uncles, of the beloved nephew killed at Goito, and of his brother. A slab of unadorned marble bears for each an inscription giving the name and the dates of birth and death.[4] The family circle knew no greater and no lesser. During his life he whom Europe had come to recognize as a transcendent statesman allowed no barrier of fame or genius to shut him out from the perfect equality of family affection: in his death, he slept among his own.

At Cavour's vanishing, friends and foes joined in acknowledging what he had done for Italy. Even Don Margotti's *Armonia* freely commended his character and the honesty of his purposes. Only the Mazzinian *Italia del Popolo*, steeped in sectarian gall, rejoiced at the striking down of the statesman whom it branded as a sceptic, a despiser of principles, a man who devoted himself wholly to working evil, by all the instruments of evil.[5] But wherever there was an Italian accessible to generous impulses, there was a mourner. "Poor Cavour!" wrote Massimo d'Azeglio, amid his tears, "I realize how much I loved him. I might well enough have died, who am no longer of any use. These two days past I seem to be dreaming, and I pray God to aid Italy; and one idea has at last given me a little calm. If Providence wishes to save Italy — and I believe it does — it will save her even without Cavour."[6]

[4] The list is given in G. Bosio: *Santena*, 6-7.

[5] Tivaroni, II, 400.   [6] Castelli: *Carteggio*, I, 363.

Beyond the Alps, there was a general regret: for the very leaders of European conservatism, who had opposed Cavour living,
deplored his death, which they feared would let loose the flood
of revolution. Napoleon III immediately showed his sympathy
by officially recognizing the Kingdom of Italy. "The driver has
fallen from the box," he said, on receiving the first telegram;
"now we must see whether the horses will bolt, or will go back
to the stable."[7] In the British Parliament, Lord Palmerston paid
a noble tribute to the statesman whose "memory will live em-
balmed in the grateful recollection of his countrymen and in the
admiration of mankind so long as history records his deeds."
Sir Robert Peel declared that Cavour's death had "darkened the
prospects and the peace of Europe."[8] Lord John Russell and
Monckton Milnes joined in praise: the latter deplored "the disappearance of this foremost man in Europe," whose "best panegyric is to be found in the sympathy of the whole civilized
world."[9] With perfect appropriateness it was an Irish member,
The O'Donoghue, whose intimate knowledge of the Divine Will
had not previously been suspected, who announced that God had
removed Cavour as a punishment for seizing Papal territory.[10]
In the House of Lords, Clanricarde, Brougham and Malmesbury
spoke in high eulogy. The Marquess of Bath, however, is saved
from the oblivion which otherwise enwraps him, for having protested that Cavour "violated every law, human and divine."[11]

At Rome, Pius IX exclaimed, "Let us pray for Cavour —
God's mercy is infinite." And later: "He was a great patriot!"
Gregorovius, who had good means for hearing gossip from all
sets in Rome, says that Pius's comment on Cavour was: "He
was not among the worst: the worst enemies of the Church come
after him"; and that Pius even said a funeral mass for him.[12]
Antonelli dreaded that the new pilots of Italian diplomacy would
be less candid than the dead Prime Minister, who had never
concealed his policy.[13] Nevertheless Fra Giacomo was summoned to Rome and disciplined for administering the viaticum

[7] *Q. V. L.*, III, 441, n. 2.   [8] Hansard, CLXIII, 778.   [9] *Ibid*, 776.
[10] *Ibid*, 775. "I am not afraid, even in this House of Commons, to say that I
see the finger of God's justice in the death of Count Cavour." The Irishman's
further remarks were drowned in cries of "Oh! Oh!"
[11] *Ibid*. The sitting of the Lords was on June 6; that of the Commons on June
7, 1861.   [12] Gregorovius, 163.   [13] Ollivier, 566.

to a person under the ban, and the Liberal papers asserted, and it has always been believed, that the monk was forced to reveal what Cavour had confessed to him: this the Papal organs deny as a matter of course.[14]

Ricasoli succeeded Cavour as Prime Minister, and if an inflexible will, directed solely to patriotic ends, could have availed, the new nation must have prospered. Erelong, however, it saw that mere rigidity would not suffice: that an iron bar was no substitute for a Toledo blade. Then followed the incorrigible politician Rattazzi, wanting in deep principles, equipped with the talents of the successful lawyer, unhampered alike by consistency and by ideals. He thought that by copying Cavour's tactics in the Garibaldian Expedition, he could win an easy solution of the Roman Question — and Aspromonte was the result. Unchastened by that stupendous blunder, he connived again, and inflicted another calamity — Mentana — on Italy.

When Cavour died, only the Patrimony of St. Peter and the province of Venetia lay outside the fold. The lucky alliance of Victor Emanuel with Prussia against Austria in 1866 served, in spite of the defeat of the Italians at Custozza and at Lissa, to redeem the Venetians. The French garrison having been withdrawn to give Napoleon III what help it might in his death agony, the Italians entered Rome on September 20, 1870. As had been asserted for over twenty years, the Pope could not, without foreign aid, maintain his detested government against his subjects. Italy was made. The tale which Palmerston characterized as the most extraordinary and romantic recorded in the annals of the world was written.

But during those years of suspense, not a week passed when there was not the consciousness of a great void. The new kingdom went on, as a steamer, whose engines have stopped, drifts first with its own momentum, then with the tide. The initiative was gone. Men remembered only too vividly the days when little Piedmont, captained by Cavour, dared to break with Austria, sent her troops to the Crimea, spoke up boldly at Paris, forced France to join her in war, prepared the liberation of the Centre, abetted the emancipation of the South. Although she had relied upon France, yet Piedmont never gave up her independence: for,

[14] Balan, 357–58; he cites also *Civiltà Cattolica*, ser. IV, 11, 613–14.

thanks to Cavour, the Emperor did Piedmont's bidding, while seeming to dictate. Though Napoleon chafed, Cavour, when the time was ripe, accepted Tuscany into the union; though Napoleon threatened, he covertly supported the Garibaldian Expedition and boldly invaded Umbria and the Marches.

Between 1861 and 1870, however, Italy was openly subservient to France. Mazzini fulminated, but his fulminations now had only the quality of stale gunpowder smoke. Garibaldi pushed his ineffectual enterprises, which involved much peril to the country, and in return kept alive a somewhat vociferous patriotism. Ricasoli, Minghetti and their colleagues tried loyally to continue Cavour's victorious foreign policy. Rattazzi played the fox. In vain: Europe perceived, and, what was worse, the Italians themselves realized, that Italy lacked the clear vision and the downright will. Happily, the foundations laid by Cavour were too staunch to give way, and Fate spared the King to be the national moderator and the symbol of unity, until unity was well consolidated. To-day, after fifty years, Italy stands upright, stronger than ever before.

It used to be contended that Cavour died opportunely for his fame. How he would have met the prosaic decades of financial and economic difficulties, how he would have warded off the undue pressure of France and opened the gates of Rome to the Italians, how he would have dealt with organized brigandage in the South or overcome the incessant feuds of the Party of Action, no one can say. But surely our best guide in such speculations is the statesman's record. To argue that Pericles, or Lincoln, or Cavour, who up to the moment of death commanded their situations, would have been unequal to cope with the confusion and panic caused by their death, is to employ a false logic.

Anyone can brandish the magician's wand; only the magician himself can conjure with it. Slowly the world has come to see that Cavour's achievement was not due to a succession of dazzling dexterities, but to the genius of the man — genius in which we must reckon temperament and natural aptitude, character, training, and an almost infallible eye for opportunity. He was a lifelong pupil of experience. He knew his time and his people through and through. Having accepted certain principles, he never betrayed them. He devoted himself to Liberty, as a divine guide against which, until mankind shall cease to advance, the blasts of tyrannies and of hierarchies cannot prevail. He understood that progress is a growth and not a manufacture; that the harvest shall be according to the seed sown; that evolution, which is a mechanical process in the brute creation, can be assisted and even hastened by man's forethought for his kind.

He wore his extraordinary faculties with a naturalness that made him the most accessible of men. Garibaldi was born of the people, a sailor's son. Mazzini sprang from the lower bourgeoisie. Cavour came of a long ancestry of aristocrats; yet no one, whether high or low, ever felt that a sense of class distinctions affected his contacts. It was fortunate for Italy, if not indispensable, that her cause should be championed before the aristocratic cabinets of Europe by one to the manner born, whom they regarded as belonging to their caste. A bourgeois or a plebeian might never have reached a common ground for negotiation.

Again and again, it is this naturalness — the simplicity of real greatness — that impresses us. In imagination we join him on his daily walk under the porticoes of Via di Po; we hear his rapid comments; we see him rub his hands together in sign of satisfaction, or to mark a witty sally; we catch his friendly greetings, by word or nod, to half the passers-by: and we ask ourselves whether this little man is indeed the statesman who has turned European Diplomacy from its channels in London, Paris and Vienna, to wait at Turin upon his word. His play of irony, his frolic spirits, — which rarely failed, except in the last overburdened months, to enliven even his hours of business, — bridged the gulf between him as prime minister and the humblest who had dealings with him. To strangers, his smile seemed baffling, but his intimates learned to foretell by the quivering of his lips what reply to expect. He had a very rich capacity for friendship. Perhaps generosity was his dominant moral trait — the generosity which impelled him to ask forgiveness of Farini for a petulant word, and saved him from becoming embittered by misunderstandings among his family and by false accusations from political opponents.

In his public conduct, this generosity expressed itself by his

2

solicitude to be more than fair and more than kind to his adversaries. "If you want to get anything from Cavour," Castelli said, "you have only to treat him outrageously." Out of reverence for justice, he returned good for evil, and he shunned the appearance of vindictiveness. "Bear in mind," he said, "that I never do ill to anyone, not even to my enemies." "I am accustomed to forget insults, perhaps even too much; but services done me are never erased from my memory or from my heart." "In politics I have always practiced broadly the penultimate precept of the Lord's Prayer." These items of self-evaluation, set down hastily in his correspondence, sprang from profound self-knowledge. The trait of generosity to which they bear witness did not in the least preclude him from surface outbursts of anger. "My temperament," he wrote, "is subject to fury." Meekness was as foreign to him as vanity. He despised the mock modesty which assumes that a great man should alone be unaware of his powers. The proof of character in him came when, although knowing his importance to his cause, he was always ready to sacrifice himself.

Except Lincoln, no other master statesman of that century was equally disinterested. It was so much a matter of course for him to ignore his personal ends, that he looked for a similar self-denying spirit in his colleagues; who, for the most part, justified his trust, although occasionally one of them found him ruthless or imperious when he called for a resignation. He could say without pose, "Perish my name, perish my fame, if only Italy may be!" And he signed without faltering the treaty of cession which, he foresaw, must draw down upon him the wrath of the Garibaldians, if it did not lead to actual impeachment and disgrace.

His intellect was scientific, of a very high order. Hence his unquenchable thirst for facts and his recognition that truth could be relied upon, if stated clearly, to persuade and conquer. So complete was his confidence, that he never hesitated, in his parliamentary expositions, to lay bare the defects as well as the advantages in the measures he proposed. Had he been permanently shut out from public life, he might, by devoting himself to science, have won renown as an investigator. Mathematics, the favorite study of his youth, had indeed 'formed his head and taught him how to think.' He tolerated everything except empty theorizing. Fact had for him the allure which fantasy exerts over minds less positive or less robust. He used to regret that he lacked literary imagination, saying that it was easier for him to make Italy, than to make a sonnet. But in an Italy thousands of whose languid sons had for three centuries reeled off millions of sonnets, and regarded that as the supreme purpose of existence, it was well that Providence took care to deprive Cavour of the sonneteer's fribbling facility. His letters, although they often ignore syntax, and are sometimes mere batches of memoranda, jotted down in haste, are models of clear statement, if by clearness we mean the quality of conveying just the idea, no more, no less, than we intend. In addition, they are saturated with his personality. The briefest of them, no matter on what subject, rarely lacks the Cavourian phrase or touch, and never the Cavourian point of view. His play of irony lights up the dullest page. He invariably addresses the correspondent to whom he is writing, stating the fact precisely and then interpreting it as he wishes it to be viewed in London or Paris, in Florence or Naples, according to its destination. Critics who do not discover this habit of his are often puzzled, and attribute to him inconsistency or even deceit. They judge as absolute, opinions which he intended for a single person at a particular time and place. Thereby they wrong him grossly.

To the end he kept his simplicity of nature, being equally at home in the salons of Paris, the library of learned Genevans, the offices of Turin or his own farmhouse at Leri. Such elasticity, such adaptability, coupled with immense strength, is the rarest of social gifts. It is one of the springs of charm: it assures poise. His poise, indeed, cannot always be distinguished from courage. Thus in 1850 when Deputy Avigdor imputed venal motives to the editors of the *Risorgimento*, Deputy Cavour challenged him to a duel. The seconds fixed the meeting for four o'clock on that very afternoon. Cavour, quite unperturbed, spoke with his usual vigor in the Chamber until half-past three, when a signal from Castelli warned him that it was time to go. In the duel which followed, Avigdor fired first without hitting. Then Cavour's bullet whistled past his ear. "I did not aim to miss," Cavour said bluntly, and walked away. Dueling was stupid enough, but if he engaged in it, he went in to win.

Although Cavour despised "rancid aristocracy," and laughed at the legendary long-descent of the Bensi, he never lost the ideals of his caste. He insisted that nobility implies obligation. However democratic he might be in his informality, he neither undervalued breeding nor held manners cheap. When a Parisian hotel-keeper presented a bill for twelve hundred francs for a three days' stay, Cavour bade his valet pay it without a protest. The grand seigneur in him would not stoop to haggle with a vulgar extortionist: but in his business affairs or in official accounts he would battle for the last shilling due.

As Piedmont reckoned fortunes then, Cavour through his talents as farmer, manufacturer and banker became a rich man — rich, but unmercenary: for he gave large sums in charity, and died 300,000 francs poorer than when he became premier. It was getting to be the fashion among public men everywhere to make money out of their offices — Cardinal Antonelli, conveniently placed "there where Christ is bought and sold every day," [15] annually pocketed a million or more: but Cavour drew generously on his private purse to pay his ministerial expenses; and if the King ever hinted to him of a dukedom or a donation, a point on which we have no testimony, Cavour certainly declined.

At Turin, he lived in his quarters in the Cavour Palace, joining his brother and niece and nephew at meals, where Gustavo, being the elder and the marquis, sat at the head of the table. Camillo never married. No other woman except Nina Giustiniani, the love of his youth, seems to have touched the depths of his passion. Once indeed, when he was already famous throughout Europe, it was rumored that he offered himself to an English marchioness, but that she, whose patent of nobility was of recent date, feared to marry beneath her station: so insular and local, and withal so amusing, are the exigencies of pedigree! But Cavour fascinated many women, as various in kind as Madame de Circourt and Princess Belgiojoso, and reference to his gallantries sometimes enlivened even parliamentary debates.

That in his statecraft he employed the accepted methods of diplomacy, many pages of this history have frankly shown. He could no more dispense with them, than a general who hoped to win could abandon modern artillery and revert to arquebuses.

[15] Dante: *Paradiso*, xvii, 51.

THE OLD TOWER, SANTENA

No one recognized more clearly than he the conflict between private and public morals. "If we were to do for ourselves what we are doing for Italy," he remarked of the intrigues in the Two Sicilies in 1860, "we should be great rogues." [16] He would be the first to welcome a happier era in which diplomacy as well as business and social life had the habit of perfect straightforwardness and crystalline candor.

But neither Cavour's scientific detachment, nor his readiness to sacrifice everyone, including himself, for his ideal, would have enabled him to make Italy, if he had not also possessed a vivid appreciation of the concrete. For him, persons were not abstractions, though in respect to the great design they must consent to be used or discarded as the need of the hour required. He saw his fellow-men as individuals, — compounded of flesh and blood, of passions, foibles and prejudices, — and he knew how to employ each, as the painter chooses and mixes the colors on his palette, for the special work in hand. And they, in turn, never thought of Cavour as an embodied formula or mere doctrinaire, but as the most real of human beings, energized in every nerve, who could toil like a Titan yet pause to play like a boy, who never did things by halves, yet could do many things simultaneously and do them supremely well. Objective as the chemist in his scrutiny of laws and elements, Cavour was as subjective as a woman in his human relations. It is that marriage in him of two natures commonly regarded as incompatible, that distinguishes him from the few other statesmen who are his peers.

He was a master Opportunist: but Opportunism is as futile as the veerings of a weathercock unless it be rooted in principles. How deep, how immutable, his principles were and how compelling, we have seen at every turn. They quickened his conscience; they clarified his vision; they guided his will. Whether to them or to temperament he owed his poise and his resilience who can say? Although he had no anxiety lest Truth should die with him, yet he labored as unceasingly as if on him its existence did verily hang. He believed so intensely the truths which his reason approved as final, they were to him at once so definite and so demonstrable, that he felt no need of a faith based on the supernatural. Never confounding religion with theology or

[16] Persano, 463.

ecclesiasticism, he knew its importance, and he desired that the Church in Italy, by stripping off the political and the formal and by purging herself of the worldly, might become once more religious. It was the appeal to the spiritual that stirred him in the addresses of Abbé Cœur and in the impassioned writings of Lamennais. But he himself remained a rationalist, and after he reached his prime, he seldom refers to religion in his letters or reported conversations. To Castelli, who was discussing the nature of God, the plurality of worlds and the destiny of man, he replied with Montaigne's poignant query, "What do I know?" Accepting as unknowable the ultimate mysteries, he seized with all the more ardor on the life that must be lived and can be moulded by the intelligence of men. Having become a Cabinet Minister, on whom lay the duty of freeing the State from ecclesiastical usurpation, he took the strictest care to have it understood that the validity of Catholic dogma was not even remotely involved. Privately, indeed, he said that he could no more believe in the infallibility of the Pope than that twice two make six. He arranged with Fra Giacomo to receive the last rites and to die as a Catholic, in order that after his death his enemies might have no ground for imputing his anti-Papal statesmanship to infidelity. In that acquiescence he respected, too, the belief of the devout among his kindred and in the community which he loved. Burial by the Roman ritual made neither him nor Montaigne a Romanist; as little did the funeral service over Darwin in Westminster Abbey prove him an Anglican; and Socrates deferred to the religious custom of his people by ordering that a cock be sacrificed to Aesculapius in his name.

To Italians, Cavour will stand for all time as the builder of their state. Many quarried: he took the blocks, of every size and shape and quality, and made United Italy out of them. He used the material at hand, as the true architect does, uncomplaining, in default of better: and though he died before the edifice was completed, yet the walls were up, the roof was on and the general plan finished. Like Michael Angelo, he left to others to add the façade and details. If only later Italians do not spoil Cavour's Doric design or hide it beneath a Baroque exterior!

But to the world, Cavour has a still larger significance. He was one of the few statesmen whose mission it is to mediate between an era that is passing away and a new era that has not yet taken definite form. This task is of far deeper import than that of founding a dynasty or of aggrandizing a state. The rise of Prussia under Frederick the Great, for instance, simply meant that a man of very uncommon powers carved a kingdom for himself out of existing conditions: but his success marked no turning-point in civilization nor advanced civilization; it merely measured the vitality of the Old Régime, when its waning strength was wielded by a Frederick on a people as sturdy, as rigid, and politically as backward as eighteenth-century Prussians. Cavour, on the other hand, was confronted by innovations. The French Revolution destroyed; the generation that followed patched together the débris; the men who came on the scene about 1840 saw that the make-shifts and compromises could not endure. Thenceforth, their business was to construct. Democracy, a new force, which the partisans of the Old feared and hated but could not annihilate, must be grappled with. Democracy had arisen to make an end of Feudalism, which, however transformed and wearing many names and strange disguises, was still, after a thousand years, the accepted principle of official Europe. Democracy was no longer a theory, but the ideal of multitudes whose numbers swelled every day.

In such a conflict between two mutually destructive systems, the consummate statesman is he who, averting the brute shock of a bloody revolution, — which often settles nothing, — leads out of the Old into the New by steps so gradual that the clash of readjustment may be minimized. This was Cavour's method. He did not destroy the Old, merely because it was old; nor did he rush fanatically to the New, merely because it was new. But perceiving that Liberty, the ideal which underlies Democracy, is a universal principle, by properly obeying which society may be organized on a higher level than the opposing principle of Authority can ever attain, he dedicated his genius to promoting Liberty in all fields. No one knew better than he how much Liberty presupposes, and how little hitherto mankind in the mass has possessed the qualifications required for working Democracy on a high plane; but he held that it is better to fall short or to fail in striving for the highest, than to be content with the corroding prosperity of a system admittedly inferior. "Better the worst of Chambers," he said, "than the best of antechambers": and he set up reverence for Liberty as the test of man's moral nature.

Cavour did not pretend to foresee — how can anyone foresee? — what will be the outcome of Democracy: but he recognized that it was, in its modern form, a new force, bound, like electricity or steam, to revolutionize human affairs. To understand it, to control it, to apply it for the amelioration of the race, became his life-work: and in so far as he could he infused it into institutions which were perishing. Thus by democratizing Monarchy, he secured the symbol without which Italy could not then have been united, or, after unification, have been held together. Where he could, he waited, relying upon time; careful not to sow too early or before the soil was plowed; treating Liberty not as a nostrum, any dose of which is warranted to cure any disease, but as the elixir of life, provided it be administered with due regard to the need of each individual. This is what it means to mediate between the Old and the New in epochs of transition.

In such a crisis the alternative is to fall back on the Past, as Bismarck did, when he constituted the German Empire on the basis of Authority. It is plausible that a system of stratification into classes, with the resultant privileges for those above and burdens for those below, since it is the product of many centuries, must contain a deposit of human nature which a statesman is justified in assuming to be permanent. Conservatism, tradition, inherited interests which have become idealized until they inspire loyalty, class greeds which are sanctified into rights — these, and the immense inertia and the instinct for imitation which are deep-rooted in the mass of mankind can always be enlisted by the partisans of Authority. History tells of so many forlorn hopes, so many failures and mistaken enthusiasms, such splendid ideals crushed and trampled by the brute Course of Things, that cynicism towards all reforming zeal seems wisdom. So Bismarck scoffed at Liberty and predicted that Democracy would be played out within fifty years: but, since even he was not powerful enough to be rid of it at once, he proceeded to denature it, so far as he could, by curtailing freedom in speech and print, and in every other avenue to political activity.

Whereas Cavour made parliament the great school of education in patriotism and in government, listening patiently to opposition, however specious, and only content when he had won over a majority by reasonable persuasion, Bismarck, on the contrary, treated the nation's representatives as a pack of intruders and impertinents, upon whom he used not argument but the compulsion of his autocratic will. Those whom he could not bludgeon into silence — Bunsen and Lasker, Virchow and Mommsen (no less!) were among his victims — he condemned to persecution and imprisonment. Authority has had in modern times no other champion of his calibre: and it may be that Authority as he conceived it has still a long life ahead among the Germans, who responded so readily to his will, and whose very virtues predispose them to submission. But "anyone can govern by martial law," said Cavour, on his deathbed. Bismarck's ideal was a country where martial law should be universal and perpetual, strong enough to stifle political discussion and to enforce the least behest of the central autocracy.

We draw here no Plutarchian parallel between the personal genius of Bismarck and Cavour,[17] or between the states they builded. Cavour should have lived until 1880, when he could have legislated for his united nation, as Bismarck was permitted to do, in order that we might judge him as a law-maker in time of peace. As it is, he wrought during a ten years' crisis, so that many of his measures were war measures and his first duty had to be the securing of independence and of union. But since all his acts are vitalized by the same spirit and point in the same direction, we cannot believe that a day could ever have dawned, no matter how long his life, when he would have denied the dreams of his youth, the ideals of his prime. "I am the son of Liberty; to her I owe all that I am."

Amid the tangle and confusion and tragic futilities which have made up so much of history, one fact is clear: Reason has steadily come to play a greater part in the lives of men and of nations. Were this not true, the experience of the past would be as the bubbles on last year's stream: and the human race, looking nei-

---

[17] In the *Atlantic Monthly* for March, 1909, and in the *Fortnightly Review* for March and April, 1909, in a paper entitled "Cavour and Bismarck," I elaborated this theme.

ther before nor after, but locked up in bodies subject only to instincts and physiological interactions, would remain as stationary as any species of the animal kingdom.

No one disputes now the primacy of Reason in the machinery of our daily existence. Our railways and telegraphs, our steamships and factories cannot be run by whim or repaired by miracle. Equally true is it that Reason extends its sway over our human relations, whether they affect the individual or the community. The nineteenth century revealed the interdependence of state and state, of nation and nation, and close upon that recognition follows the sense of international solidarity. To rationalize life, not merely in its material and political interests but in its highest social concerns and in its morals, is therefore the task set for man to prove that in his destiny he differs from the beasts of the field. To rationalize life does not mean to make it mechanical, or to extirpate the passions to which it owes its variety and glow, its dignity, its charm. Electricity is not less wonderful when, under man's control, it serves millions of human beings, than when it loses itself in flashes of lightning.

Now Cavour was probably the earliest statesman of the first rank who, having foreseen the scope of Reason in government, attempted to apply it consistently and with a trust so unshaken, that he would not resort to prejudice in order to win a fleeting success. "Reason is omnipotent when it has love for an ally," he wrote as a young man, and this creed he embodied in his life, but never more nobly than in that final scene with Garibaldi, when he met the Paladin's frantic obsession with Reason allied with Love. So to those who like to believe that men may be in some measure masters of their fate, that Reason does indeed transcend Caprice, and that Love, woven of sympathy and justice, is loftier than instinct, Cavour stands out as a victorious exemplar. And in the future, as the rationalizing of life goes on, the number of those who comprehend and value him will increase.

Youth comes to men only once; but to some peoples and nations Fate grants divine periods of renewal, or of transformation and expansion which betoken the replenishing of life at its sources. Those are the great moments in the history of the race when, as in youth, there is breathed into the souls of men a mighty ideal, before which the adamant of custom melts away as if it were mist, and the ugliness and cruelty of the Old cannot abide in the radiance of the New. Then duty burns with the incandescence of desire. Then life is nothing if it be not dedicated to the ideal, and death for the ideal is sweeter than any life. Once more, as in the morning of the world, men seem to themselves to be endued with godlike powers, and they behold, unastonished, gods working among them. Life, the creative force, which is all we know and all we are, reasserts itself imperially. The darkened windows of Time's chamber wherein we dwell are opened, to let in the light and deathlessness of Eternity. Truth, ceasing to be a revelation echoed out of the Past, becomes the supreme certitude of the Present. Such periods of revitalization are the floodtide of religion, of patriotism, of liberty, and of all other noble expressions of collective zeal.

It is because Cavour, by the rare blending of Reason and disciplined Emotion, guided to victory the most marvelous and difficult struggle for freedom recorded in modern times, that his name will be cherished by generations yet unborn and by races yet uncivilized. Whoever fights for liberty anywhere, fights for the uplifting of mankind everywhere. All creeds agree in making absolute freedom an attribute of the Almighty: and finite man has in no way shown his kinship with the Infinite more clearly than by his incessant craving to be free. Without Liberty, the best loses for him its savor, and even religion becomes an anodyne instead of an inspiration. Among the champions of Liberty, since the beginning, none had a nobler vision of her beauty, none confided in her more loyally, none served her more wisely than Camillo di Cavour.

GENEALOGICAL TABLES

I. Cavour – De Sellon

1. Jean de Sellon, Huguenot; burgher of Geneva in 1699
2. Jean François de Sellon
3. Jean de Sellon (b. 1736) = Anne Marie Suzanne Victoire Montz

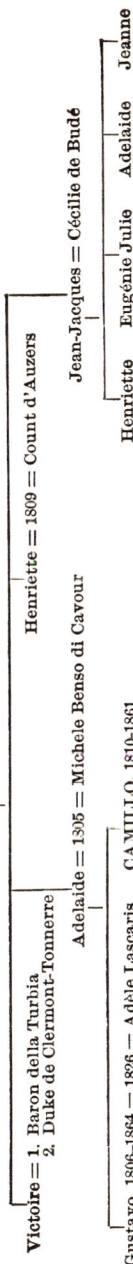

Henriette = 1809 = Count d'Auzers

Jean-Jacques = Cécilie de Budé

Henriette Eugénie Julie Adelaide Jeanne

Adelaide = 1805 = Michele Benso di Cavour

Victoire = 1. Baron della Turbia
2. Duke de Clermont-Tonnerre

Gustavo, 1806-1864 = 1826 = Adèle Lascaris   CAMILLO, 1810-1861   Aynard, 1833-1875

Augusto, 1828-1848   Giuseppina = 1851 = Carlo Alfieri

Louise = Emilio Visconti Venosta   Adèle

II. De Sales – Cavour

Paul François de Sales, d. 1795 = Françoise de Regard de Disonche de Ballon

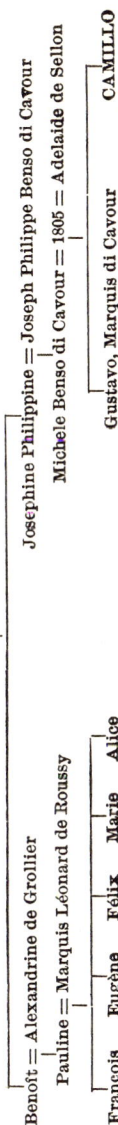

Josephine Philippine = Joseph Philippe Benso di Cavour

Michele Benso di Cavour = 1805 = Adelaide de Sellon

Gustavo, Marquis di Cavour   CAMILLO

Benoît = Alexandrine de Grollier

Pauline = Marquis Léonard de Roussy

François Eugène Félix Marie Alice

ABBREVIATED TITLES OF WORKS FRE-
QUENTLY REFERRED TO

C. = Cavour.   V. E. = Victor Emanuel.

Abba = G. C. Abba: *La Storia dei Mille.* Florence: Bemporad, 1884.
Aff. Etrang. = *Documents Diplomatiques.* 1860. Paris, Imprimerie Impériale, 1861.
Amari = A. D'Ancona: *Carteggio di Michele Amari.* Turin: Roux, Frassati and Co. 3 vols. 1896-1907.
Amer. Arch. = Despatches from American diplomatic and consular officials to the U. S. Department of State. The originals were examined by me at the American Embassy, Rome, in 1906.
Arese = R. Bonfadini: *Vita di Francesco Arese.* Turin: Roux, 1894.
Arrivabene = Charles Arrivabene: *Italy Under Victor Emanuel.* London, 2 vols. 1862.
Artom = E. Artom: *L' Opera Politica del Senatore I. Artom nel Risorgimento Italiano.* Parte Iª. Zanichelli: Bologna, 1906.
Artom-Blanc = *Opera Parlamentaria del Conte di Cavour.* (Compiled by his secretaries, I. Artom and A. Blanc.) Leghorn: E. Razzanti, 2 vols. 1863.
Ashley = Evelyn Ashley: *The Life and Correspondence of Henry John Temple, Lord Palmerston.* London: Bentley, 2 vols. 1879.
Ayala = *Memorie di Mariano d'Ayala e del Suo Tempo.* Scritte del Figlio Michelangelo. Rome: Bocca, 1886.
Bandi = Giuseppe Bandi: *I Mille.* Da Genova a Capua. Florence: A. Salani, 1903.
Bazancourt = Baron de Bazancourt: *La Campagne d'Italie de 1859.* Paris: Amyot, 2 vols. 1859.
Benedek = *Benedeks Nachgelassene Papiere.* Herausgegeben von Heinrich Friedjung. Leipzig: Grübel & Sommerlatte, 1901.
Bersezio = V. Bersezio: *Il Regno di Vittorio Emanuele II.* Trent'Anni di Vita Italiana. Turin: Roux e Favale, 8 vols. 1878 *ff.*
Bert = *C. Cavour: Nouvelles Lettres Inédites recueillées par* Amédée Bert. Turin: Roux, 1889.
Bertani: *Ire* = Agostino Bertani: *L'Epistolario di Giuseppe La Farina: Ire Politiche d'Oltre Tomba.* Florence: Polizzi, 1869.
Berti, I = D. Berti: *Il Conte di Cavour avanti il 1848.* Rome: Voghera, 1886.
Berti, II = D. Berti: *Diario Inedito con Note Autobiografiche del Conte di Cavour.* Rome: Voghera, 1888.
Beust = *Memoirs of Friedrich Ferdinand Count von Beust, Written by Himself.* With an Introduction by Baron Henry de Worms. London: Remington, 2 vols. 1887.
Bianchi: *Cavour* = N. Bianchi: *Il Conte di Cavour.* Reprinted from *Rivista Contemporanea.* Turin, 1863. (3d edit.)
Bilotti = P. E. Bilotti: *La Spedizione di Sapri.* Da Genova a Sanza. Salerno: Fratelli Jovane, 1907.

Bonfadini=R. Bonfadini: *Un Mezzo Secolo di Patriottismo Italiano.* Milan, 1882.

Brofferio=Angelo Brofferio: *Storia del Parlamento Subalpino.* Milan: Battezzeti, 6 vols. 1866-70.

Cantù=Cesare Cantù: *Cronistoria della Indipendenza Italiana.* Naples, 3 vols. 1872-77.

Carandini=Federico Carandini: *Manfredo Fanti, Sua Vita.* Verona: G. Civelli, 1872.

Carpi=Leone Carpi: *Il Risorgimento Italiano.* Biografie Storico-politiche d'Illustri Italiani Contemporanei. Milan: Vallardi, 4 vols. 1884-88.

Castelli: *Cavour=Il Conte di Cavour.* Ricordi di Michelangelo Castelli. Editi per cura di Luigi Chiala. Turin, 1886.

Castelli: *Ricordi=Ricordi di Michelangelo Castelli,* 1847-75. Editi per Luigi Chiala. Turin, 1888.

Centenario=Nel Primo Centenario della Nascita di Camillo Cavour. Turin: Bona, 1911.

Cesaresco=E. Martinengo Cesaresco: *Cavour.* Foreign Statesmen Series. London: Macmillan, 1898.

Chambrier=James de Chambrier: *La Cour et la Société du Second Empire.* Paris: Delachaux et Nestlé, 1902.

Chantrel=J. Chantrel: *Annales Ecclésiastiques de 1846 à 1860.* Paris: Gaume Frères, 1861.

Chiala: *Une Page=*L. Chiala: *Une Page d'Histoire du Gouvernement Représentatif en Piémont.* Turin: Botta, 1858.

Ciàmpoli=Domenico Ciàmpoli: *Scritti Politici e Militari, Ricordi e Pensieri Inediti di Giuseppe Garibaldi.* Rome: Voghera, 1907.

Colleville=Comte de Colleville: *Un Crime du Second Empire. Le Guet-Apens de Castelfidardo.* Paris: Juven, 1910.

*Correspondence=*English Foreign Office Blue Books, under their respective dates.

Crispi=Francesco Crispi: *Scritti e Discorsi Politici.* Rome: Unione Cooperativa Editrice, 1890.

Crispi: *Mille=*F. Crispi: *I Mille.* Milan: Treves, 1911.

*Dawn=*W. R. Thayer: *The Dawn of Italian Independence.* 1814-1849. Boston, 2 vols. 1893. (1st edit.)

D'Azeglio: *Lettere=*N. Bianchi: *Lettere di M. d'Azeglio al Marchese E. d'Azeglio.* Turin: Roux e Favale, 1883.

D'Azeglio: *Politique=Correspondance Politique de Massimo d'Azeglio,* 1847-1865. Paris: Didier, 1867.

C. d'Azeglio=Constance d'Azeglio: *Souvenirs Historiques.* Turin, 1894.

De Cesare: *Fine=*R. De Cesare: *La Fine di Un Regno.* Città di Castello: Lapi. 2 vols. 1900. (1st edit.)

De Cesare: *Roma=*R. De Cesare: *Roma e lo Stato del Papa dal Ritorno di Pio IX al XX Settembre.* Rome: Forzani and Co. 2 vols. 1907.

De' Sivo=Giacinto De' Sivo: *Storia delle Due Sicilie* dal 1847 al 1861. Trieste, 2 vols. 1868.

Della Rocca=Enrico Della Rocca: *Autobiografia di un Veterano.* Bologna, 2 vols. 1898. (References for vol. 1 are to 1st edition; for vol. 2 to 2d edition.)

Dicey: *Vic. Em.=*Edward Dicey: *Victor Emanuel.* New York, 1882.

Du Camp=Maxime Du Camp: *Expédition des Deux-Siciles.* Souvenirs Personnels. Paris: Calmann Lévy, 1881. Originally printed in *Revue des Deux Mondes,* March 15, April 1 and 15, and May 1, 1861.

Duquet=A. Duquet: *La Guerre d'Italie,* 1859. Paris, 1882.

Ernest II: *Memoirs*=Memoirs of Ernest II, Duke of Saxe-Coburg-Gotha. English Translation, London: Remington, 4 vols. 1890.

Fagan=L. Fagan: *Life and Correspondence of Sir Anthony Panizzi.* Boston: Houghton Mifflin & Co. 2 vols. 1881.

Friedjung=H. Friedjung: *Der Kampf um die Vorherrschaft in Deutschland.* Stuttgart, 2 vols. 1901.

Gallenga=Antonio Gallenga: *History of Piedmont.* London: Chapman and Hall, 3 vols. 1855.

Garibaldi: *Memorie*=G. Garibaldi: *Memorie.* Edizione Diplomatico dall' Autografo Definitivo a Cura di Ernesto Nathan. Turin: Società Tipografico-Editrice Nazionale, 1907.

Garibaldi: *Mille*=Garibaldi: *I Mille.* Bologna: Zanichelli, 1874, 2d. edit.

Gioli=Matilde Gioli: *Il Rivolgimento Toscano e l'Azione Popolare.* 1847–60. Florence: Barbèra, 1905.

Gotti=Aurelio Gotti: *Vita del Barone Bettino Ricasoli.* Florence: Le Monnier, 1895.

Greville=C. C. F. Greville: *A Journal of the Reign of Queen Victoria, from 1852 to 1860.* Edited by Henry Reeve. New York: Appleton, 3 vols. 1887.

Guerrini=D. Guerrini: *La Missione del Conte G. Litta Modignani,* in *Risorg. Ital.,* vol. II, i, pp. 1–48.

Guerzoni: *Bixio*=Giuseppe Guerzoni: *La Vita di Nino Bixio.* Florence: Barbèra, 1875.

Guerzoni: *Garibaldi*=Di Gius. Guerzoni. Florence: Barbèra, 1889, 2 vols. 3d ed.

Hansard=T. C. Hansard: *Parliamentary Reports,* under date cited.

Hohenlohe-Ingelfingen=*Lectures on Strategy.* By Prince Hohenlohe-Ingelfingen. London, 2 vols. 1898.

Hübner=Comte de Hübner: *Neuf Ans de Souvenirs d'Un Ambassadeur d'Autriche à Paris,* 1851–59. Paris: Plon, 2 vols. 1904.

Ideville: *Journal*=Henry d'Ideville: *Journal d'un Diplomate en Italie.* Turin, 1859–1862. Paris: Hachette, 1872. (2d edit.)

La Farina: *Epist.*=A. Franchi: *Epistolario di G. La Farina.* Milan, 2 vols. 1869.

La Rive=W. de La Rive: *Le Comte de Cavour.* Recits et Souvenirs. Paris, 1863.

La Rive: *Ital. Ver.*=W. de La Rive: *Il Conte di Cavour. Racconti e Memorie.* Turin: Bocca, 1911.

Larousse=Pierre Larousse: *Grand Dictionnaire Universel du XIXᵉ Siècle.* Paris: Larousse et Boyer, 17 vols. 1866 *ff.*

Lettere=*Lettere Edite ed Inedite di Camillo Cavour.* Raccolte ed Illustrate da Luigi Chiala. Turin, 6 vols. 1882–87.

Loliée: *Morny*=Fréderic Loliée: *Le Duc de Morny et la Société du Second Empire.* Paris: Emile-Paul, 1909. (9th edit.)

Mariani=Carlo Mariani: *Le Guerre dell'Indipendenza Italiana dal 1848 al 1870.* Turin, Roux and Favale, 4 vols. 1884.

Mario: *Bertani*=Jessie White Mario: *Agostino Bertani e i Suoi Tempi.* Florence: Barbèra, 2 vols. 1888.

Mario: *Garibaldi*=Jessie White Mario: *Vita di Giuseppe Garibaldi.* Milan: Treves, 2 vols. 1893.

Mario: *Gar. Supp.*=*Autobiography of G. Garibaldi.* Authorized Translation by A. Waerner. With a Supplement by Jessie White Mario. London: Walter Smith and Innes, 3 vols. 1889.

Mario: *Mazzini*=J W. Mario: *Vita di G. Mazzini.* Milan, 1886.

Mario: *Nicotera*=J. W. Mario: *In Memoria di Giovanni Nicotera*. Florence: Barbèra, 1894.

Martin=Theodore Martin: *The Life of His Royal Highness the Prince Consort.* London, Smith, Elder & Co., 5 vols. 1880.

Massari: *Cavour*=*Il Conte di Cavour, Ricordi Biografici*. Per Giuseppe Massari. Turin, 1873. (2d edit.)

Massari: *La Marmora*=Giuseppe Massari: *Il Generale La Marmora*. Ricordi Biografici. Florence: Barbèra, 1880.

Massari: *Vitt. Em.*=Giuseppe Massari: *La Vita ed il Regno di Vittorio Emanuele II di Savoia*. Milan. 1880.

Mazade=Charles de Mazade: *Le Comte de Cavour*. Paris: Plon, 1877.

Mazzini: *Scritti*=*Scritti Editi e Inediti di Giuseppe Mazzini*. [Aurelio Saffi, editor.] Rome, 1875 *ff.*

Menghini=Mario Menghini: *La Spedizione Garibaldina di Sicilia e di Napoli*. Turin: Soc. Tipogr.-Edit. Nazionale, 1907.

Mérimée=P. Mérimée: *Lettres à M. Panizzi*, 1850–70. Paris: Calmann Lévy, 2 vols. 1881.

Minghetti=M. Minghetti: *Miei Ricordi*. Turin: Roux, 3 vols. 1889–90. (With 4th edit. of vol. I; 2d edit. of vol. III.)

Moltke=*La Campagne d'Italie en 1859*. Rédigée par la Division Historique de l'État-Major de Prusse. Traduit de l'Allemand. Paris: Dumaine, 1862. This is practically the work of General H. von Moltke.

Morley: *Cobden*= John Morley: *The Life of Richard Cobden*. London: Chapman & Hall, 2 vols. 1881.

Morley: *Gladstone*=John Morley: *The Life of William Ewart Gladstone*. London, 3 vols. 1903.

Mundy=Sir Rodney Mundy: *H. M. S. "Hannibal" at Palermo and Naples*. 1859–61. London, 1863.

Nielsen=F. Nielsen: *A History of the Papacy in the 19th Century*. English Translation. New York: Dutton, 2 vols. 1906.

Nigra=*Le Comte de Cavour et la Comtesse de Circourt*. Lettres inédites publiées par C. Nigra. Turin: Roux, 1894.

Nisco= Nicola Nisco: *Gli Ultimi 36 Anni del Reame Di Napoli*. Naples, 3 vols. 1889. Vol. II. Ferdinando II. Vol. III. Francesco II.

Oddo=Giacomo Oddo: *I Mille di Marsala*. Milan, 1863.

Ollivier=Émile Ollivier: *L'Empire Libéral*. Vol. IV. Napoléon III et Cavour. Paris, 1899.

Pagani =Carlo Pagani: *Milano e la Lombardia nel 1859*. Milan: Cogliati, 1909.

Pallavicino=*Memorie di Giorgio Pallavicino, Pubblicate per Cura della Figlia*. Turin: Roux, Frassati & Co. 3 vols. 1895.

Panizzi=*Lettere ad Antonio Panizzi* (1823–70.) Edite da L. Fagan. Florence: Barbèra, 1882.

Pantaleoni=D. Pantaleoni: *L'Idea Italiana nella Soppressione del Potere Temporale dei Papi*. Turin, 1884.

Paoli: *Azeglio*=*Lettres di M. d'Azeglio a G. Torelli*. Pubblicate per Cura di Cesare Paoli. Milan: P. Carrara, 1870.

Pasolini=P. D. Pasolini: *Giuseppe Pasolini, 1815–1876. Memorie*. Turin: Bocca, 1887. 3d edit.

Persano=C. di Persano: *Diario Privato-Politico-Militare*. Turin, 1880. (4th edit.)

Pianciani=Luigi Pianciani: *Dell'Andamento delle Cose in Italia*. Rivelazioni, Memorie e Riflessioni. Milan: Editori del *Politecnico*, 1860.

2

Poggi=Enrico Poggi: *Memorie Storiche del Governo della Toscana nel 1859–60.* Pisa, 3 vols. 1867.

Précis=*Précis de la Campagne en Italie.* Brussels, 1887.

Predari=F. Predari: *I Primi Vagiti della Libertà Italiana in Piemonte.* Milan. 1861.

Q. V. L.=*The Letters of Queen Victoria,* 1837–61. Edited by A. C. Benson and Viscount Esher. London, 3 vols. 1908.

Raulich=Italo Raulich: *Il Conte di Cavour e la Preparazione dei Mille. Rassegna Contemporanea,* July, 1909; II, pp. 87–117.

Reuchlin=*Geschichte Italiens von der Gründung der regiereden Dynastien bis zur Gegenwart.* Von Dr. Hermann Reuchlin. [Geschichte der neuesten Zeit, Band 18.] Leipzig, 4 vols. 1873.

Revel: *Ancona*=Genova di Revel: *Da Ancona a Napoli.* Miei Ricordi. Milan: Dumolard, 1892.

Ricasoli=*Lettere e Documenti del Barone Bettino Ricasoli.* Pubblicati per Cura di M. Tabarrini e A. Gotti. Florence: Le Monnier, 5 vols. 1888.

Risorg. Ital.=*Il Risorgimento Italiano.* Rivista Storica. Turin: Bocca, 1908 *ff.*

Rosi: *Mordini*=Michele Rosi: *Il Risorgimento Italiano e l'Azione d'un Patriota, Cospiratore e Soldato.* Rome: Roux e Viarengo, 1906.

Rubieri=E. Rubieri: *Storia Intima della Toscana dal 1 gennaio 1859 al 30 Aprile, 1860.* Prato, 1860.

Rüstow: 1860=W. Rüstow: *La Guerre Italienne en 1860.* Traduit de l'Allemand par J. Vivien. Geneva, 1862.

Sanders: *Palmerston*=Lloyd C. Sanders: *Life of Viscount Palmerston.* Philadelphia: Lippincott, 1888.

Scritti=*Gli Scritti del Conte di Cavour.* Editi da Domenico Zanichelli. Bologna: Zanichelli, 2 vols. 1892.

Senior: *Conversations*=Nassau Senior: *Conversations with Thiers, Guizot, etc.* Edited by M. C. M. Simpson. London, 2 vols. 1878.

Stillman: *Crispi*=*Francesco Crispi, Insurgent, Exile, Revolutionist, and Statesman.* By W. J. Stillman. London: Grant Richards, 1899.

Stor. Doc.=Nicomede Bianchi: *Storia Documentata della Diplomazia Europea in Italia.* 1814–18. Turin, 8 vols. 1865–72.

Sybel=*The Founding of the German Empire by William I.* By Heinrich von Sybel. Translated by M. L. Perrin and Gamaliel Bradford, Jr. New York, 4 vols. 1891.

Tavallini=Enrico Tavallini: *La Vita e i Tempi di Giovanni Lanza.* Turin: Roux, 1887.

Thouvenel: *Secret*=M. Thouvenel: *Le Secret de l'Empereur.* Paris: Calmann Lévy, 2 vols. 1889. (2d edit.)

Tivaroni=Carlo Tivaroni: *L'Italia degli Italiani.* Turin: Roux, Frassati and Co. 3 vols. 1896.

Torelli=*Ricordi Politici di Giuseppe Torelli.* Edited by C. Paoli. Milan, 1873.

Trecchi=Giuseppe Manacorda: *Vittorio Emanuele e Garibaldi nel 1860 secondo le Conte Trecchi. Nuova Antologia,* June 1, 1910, pp. 407–36.

Treitschke=H. von Treitschke: *Il Conte di Cavour.* Tradotto da A. Guerrieri Gonzaga. Florence: Barbèra, 1873.

Trevelyan, I=G. M. Trevelyan: *Garibaldi and the Thousand.* London: Longmans, 1909.

Trevelyan, II=G. M. Trevelyan: *Garibaldi and the Making of Italy.* London, 1911.

Vayra=Pietro Vayra: *Il Principe Napoleone e l'Italia.* Turin: Casanova, 1891.

Veuillot: *Mélanges*=Louis Veuillot: *Mélanges Religieux, Historiques, Politiques, et Littéraires.* 2ᵉ Série. Paris: Gaume, 1861.

Vitzthum = *St. Petersburg and London in the Years 1852–1864.* Reminiscences of Count Charles F. Vitzthum von Eckstadt. Edited by Henry Reeve. Translated by Edward F. Taylor. London. Longmans, 2 vols. 1887.

Walpole: *History*=Sir Spencer Walpole: *The History of Twenty-five Years.* London, 4 vols. 1904–08.

Walpole: *Russell*=Spencer Walpole: *The Life of Lord John Russell.* London, 2 vols. 1889.

Whitehouse=H. Remsen Whitehouse: *The Collapse of the Kingdom of Naples.* New York, 1889.

INDEX

bears the brunt of Diplomacy's displeasure during V. E.'s southward march, 424; Russell's despatch to Hudson leaves him free to concentrate his energy on forwarding Unity, 426; his chief enemies, 426; regarded as a traitor by the Party of Revolution, 428; its foolish charges against, 428; Mazzini's vilification of, 432; sends La Farina and Cordova to Sicily with Montezemolo, 437; suggests Eugene of Carignano as Lieut.-Gen. of Naples, 437, 438; ends sought by, during early months of liberation of Naples, 438, 439; urges withdrawal of French men-of-war from Gaeta, 441; bent upon the completion of Unity, to which Rome was essential, as capital, 442; his vision of a renewed Church, 443; basis of his first appeal to Pius IX, 443; applies to Pantaleoni to open the way to a reconciliation, 443, 444; his exposition of the benefits to accrue to the Church by abolition of the Temporal Power, 444; the course pursued by his agents, 445, 446; their cheering reports, 446; is advised to send his agents direct to Pius, 446; sudden rupture of the negotiations, 446–448; his aim therein, 450; neither surprised nor disheartened by the rebuff, 450, 451 and n.; on assembling of first Parl't of United Italy, resigns with his cabinet, 453; V. E. reluctantly bids him remain, 453; remodels his cabinet, 453; proceeds with work of reconstruction, 454; his three great speeches on the Roman Question, 454, 455; proclaims anew the doctrine of a Free Church in a Free State, 454; "a conspirator," 454, 455; his closing appeal to the Pope, 455; has the future in view, 456; strategic importance of his announcement that Rome must be the capital of Italy, 457; the complication of internal difficulties which faced him in 1861, 459; G.'s hatred of, further inflamed by his visitors at Caprera, 460, 461; G. attributes all his injuries to, 463, 464; G.'s radical friends hope to use him to overthrow C., 466; G.'s speech in Parl't, accusing the ministry of provoking "a fratricidal war," calls forth an indignant protest from, 469; is again attacked by G., 471; Bixio appeals for reconciliation between G. and, 471; his speech in reply, 471–473; his noble pity for G., 472; his plan of military reorganization, 472, 473; further debate with G., 473, 474; refers to the cession of Nice as creating an abyss between them, 474; other speeches by, 474, 475; interview with G., 477, 478; folly of G.'s rage against, 478, 479, 480; in resisting G. and his advisers, he performed the best services a patriot could perform, 481; G.'s pacific and complimentary letter to, 481–483; did he ever receive it? 483; G.'s subsequent acts and his written Memoirs inconsistent with the letter, 483; his multifarious duties, 484 ff.; urges withdrawal of French troops from Rome, 485; is informed by Vimercati of N.'s consent, 485; evidences of failing health, 485, 486; his talk with Salmour (May 26), 486; takes part in debates on the following days, 486; in his last speech (May 29), urges fusion of all parties on the foreign question, 486, 487; beginnings of his fatal illness, 487; its progress, 487, 488; his disease never satisfactorily diagnosed, 488 n.; receives the last sacraments from Fra Giacomo, 489, 491; last interview with V. E., 490; preoccupied by the question of Naples during his last night, 490; the end (June 6, 1861), 491; uni-

versal grief in Turin and in Parl't at news of his death, 492; rumor of poison at N.'s instigation, 492 and n.; buried at Santena, 493; tributes of friends and foes to his services to Italy, 493, 494; the only jarring notes, 494 and n.; Fra Giacomo disciplined for administering sacraments to, 494, 495; the great void left by his death, 495, 496; he did not die opportunely for his fame, 496; his career reviewed, 502 ff.; his method of proceeding from the Old to the New, 503; dedicated his genius to promoting Liberty in all fields, 503, 504; sought to infuse Democracy into moribund institutions, 504; his method contrasted with Bismarck's, 504, 505 and n.; the first statesman who attempted to apply Reason consistently and with unshaken trust, 506; his creed nobly exemplified in his final struggle with G., 506; his place among the champions of Liberty, 507.

VII. *In Private Life: Personal Characteristics.* — Anecdotes of his childhood, **1**, 3, 4; his temperament, 4; his boyish characistics as revealed in extracts from his letters, 6, 7; eulogizes Franklin and Santa Rosa, 7; leads his class at Turin Military Academy, 8; his studies outside the regular course, 8; his views on gambling and on Turinese society, 8, 9; his interest in mathematics and the exact sciences, 9; his early opinions become convictions, 9; his character shaped and hardened by the Absolutist régime under Charles Felix, 15; the precocious ripeness of his mind 15, 24, 31; his youthful ordeal described in letters to his brother, 16–18; his friendship with Cassio, 16, 17; social relations at Genoa, 19; his passion for Nina Giustiniani, 19, 35, 36, 37, 38 ff.; his status of family black sheep galling to him, 24; self-training of his five years in the army, 24; the bitter lot of a second son, 25; improved relations with his family, 26; his diary (1833–38), 26 ff., 33, 34, 38, 39, 45, 46, 61, 62; suffers from lack of sympathy, 26; doubts Cassio's affection, 26; effect of self-repression on, 26; his despair of the future, 26, 27; importance of his self-revelations, 27; not moved by personal ambition, 27; his spirit goes seeking Liberty, 28; further self-revelation in letters to Marchioness Barolo, 28, and to Cécile and J. J. de Sellon, 28, 29; his genius for the positive side of life, 31, 34; Liberty and Growth his guiding principles as soon as he could reason, 32; his reading in political economy and philosophy, 32; maxims from his commonplace books, 32; his religious belief, 32; from a Catholic becomes a sceptic, 32, 33; his emotions and enthusiasms, 34; his admiration for Rousseau, 34, 35; Rousseau's influence on, 35; his period of storm and stress closed by Countess Giustiniani's death, 41; his longing for Geneva described in letter to Madame de Sellon, 44; in Geneva (1833), 44–46; visits to Ferney, etc., 45, 46; again at Geneva (1834), *en route* to Paris, 47; in Paris (1835), 47 ff.; first meeting with Madame de Circourt, 48; his sterling qualities as revealed in letter to Madame de Waldor, 51; on the tomb of Juliet, 56; his visit to Paris (1842–43) and extensive contacts with Parisian life, 61, 62; his great talents already recognized, 61; his activity, 61, 62; attends lectures, 61; deeply impressed by Abbé Cœur, 61; in Parisian society, 62; his first essays at authorship, 62 and n.; writes

English Court INDEX **533**

Diplomacy, European, and the Sicilian Exped'n, **2**, 271 *ff.*; displeased at overturn in Naples, 424 *ff.*, and Lord J. Russell's despatch of Oct. 27, 1860, 425.

Diritto, Il, **1**, 394.

Disarmament, question of, in spring of 1859, **1**, 589 *ff.*

Disraeli, Benjamin, Chancellor of the Exchequer, on Queen Victoria, **1**, 504; 506, **2**, 207.

Dolfi, Giuseppe, **2**, 56, 59, 134, 155.

Döllinger, Johann J. I. von, **1**, 456.

Donation of Constantine, the, **1**, 342.

Donnet, Cardinal, **2**, 146.

Dora Baltea, river, **1**, 555, **2**, 55.

Drouyn de Lhuys, Edouard, **1**, 168 n., 223, 298, 322, 334.

Duchies, the, C.'s plans concerning, **1**, 378; movement toward independence in, **2**, 67, 68; all united to Piedmont before Solferino, 68. And *see* Modena, Parma, Piacenza.

Dumas, Alexandre, père, appointed Minister of Art and Education by G., **2**, 427.

Dunne (English Garibaldian), **2**, 331.

Dupanloup, Monsignor, Bishop of Orleans, **2**, 146, 171.

Durando, Gen. Giacomo, **1**, 80 n., 83, 328, 329, 350, 354, 356, 358, **2**, 3, 22, 42.

Durando, Gen. Giovanni, **1**, 178.

Eastern Question, in the Congress of Paris, **1**, 391 and n.

Ecclesiastical corporations, proposed legislation concerning, **1**, 120, 124.

Ecclesiastical courts and immunities, abolition of, proposed by D'Azeglio ministry, **1**, 120, 122; evils of, 120; abolished by Parl't, 124.

Ecclesiastics, under Piedm. Constitution, on same footing with other persons, **1**, 115; dispute between Church and State thereon, 115, 116; exemption of, from trial in civil courts, 286.

Edinburgh, C.'s impressions of, **1**, 149.

Education, state of, in Rome, **1**, 474 and n., 477 n.

Electoral Law (Piedmont), first election under (1848), **1**, 91, 92.

Elliot, Sir H., British Minister to Naples, interview of, with G., **2**, 375, 376; on condition of Naples under G.'s dictatorship, 426.

Emilia, remains autonomous under governorgeneralship of Boncompagni, **2**, 153; Farini dictator of, 157; N. stipulates for plebiscite in, on annexation to Piedmont, **2**, 193, 194; result of plebiscite in, 202 and n.; celebration in, 204.

Emilians, deputation of, to V. E., **2**, 139.

Engineer Corps, C. joins, **1**, 8.

England, in 1835, **1**, 51, 52; C.'s enthusiasm for, as the abode of Liberty, 51; C.'s first visits to, 52, 53, 62; and the Italian situation in 1848, 87, 88; Alfieri Cabinet seeks mediation of, 98; attitude of, towards Piedmont, in 1849, 109; and Protestantism, 119, 120; C. negotiates commercial treaty with, 130; her economic policy praised by C., 131; House of Commons, his model, 140; C.'s visit to, in 1852, 144, 147; the Reaction in, 151; flurry over Chartism in, 151; public opinion in, touching Piedmont and Austria, 209; refuses to abandon right of asylum, 248; reëstablishment of Roman hierarchy in, 304; and the origin of the Crimean War, 317; sends fleet to Besika Bay, 317; joins with France to preserve Turkey, 317; her reasons for keeping Russia out of Constantinople, 318; conscience of, condemns

the war, 318; declares war on Russia (Mch. 1854), 319; and France, seeking allies against Russia, 321 *ff.*; their treaty with Austria, 324, 325; incompetence of her troops in the Crimea, 362 and n.; and the continuance of the war, 366; at the Congress of Paris, 376 and n.; and Turkey, 377; lesson of Congress to, 391; would not abet Piedmont in war with Austria, 393; opinion in, adverse to Treaty of Paris, 403; inclined to renew friendship with Austria, 403, 404; advises Austria to adopt milder methods in Lombardy-Venetia, 417, 487; Austria urges her to force apology from Piedmont, 418, 419; C. resists pressure of, 419, 420; reason for her change of front, 421; encouraged by C. to oppose election of Murat at Naples, 430; agrees with France to urge reforms on Ferdinand II, 431, 432 and n.; estopped from moral reproof, 432; her minister presents an ultimatum and leaves Naples, 433; Don Margotti's denunciation of, 472; Walewski's note of remonstrance to, 501; policy of, concerning political refugees, 502; French abuse of, 502 and n.; reactionary movement in, 503; N.'s real purpose toward, 504; lack of cordiality between Piedmont and, 522; alarmed at prospect of war, 548, 549' 556; her pledges to Austria, 549; and the redemption of Italy, 552; her wish to avoid war leads her to Austria, 558; disaffected toward C., 561, 562; her position in Feb. 1859, 563; her attitude, 565, 566; propositions submitted to Austria by, 567; and the proposed European Congress, 573, 574; her urging disregarded, 589; offers to mediate between France and Austria, 601; adopts policy of strict neutrality, **2**, 53; fall of Tory ministry in, 83, 84; great strength of new ministry, 85 and n.; distrust of N. in, 86, 209, 367; and Prussia's action in June, 1859, 89, 90; her new policy does not include furtherance of N.'s ambition, 91; comes to Italy's rescue, 123 *ff.*; change of opinion in, 128; moral support of, and the Italian cause, 147; conditions on which she will enter proposed congress, 164; vetoes Pius's claim to precedence there, 164; insists on Piedmont's admission, 164; supplants France as promoter of Italian independence, 165; N. anxious to regain her friendship, 181; commercial treaty with France, 182, 190; Lord John's proposal to N. concerning Italy, 190, 191; and the cession of Savoy and Nice, 192, 205, 206, 207; urges immediate annexation of Tuscany, etc., 198; and the possibility of war with France, 221; tries to get Upper Savoy for Switzerland, 224; and the Sicilian Exped'n, 272; feeling in, toward V. E. and C., 310; goodwill of Liberals to the Italian cause, 310, 311; agreement of, with Austria and Prussia, 311; her attitude in summer of 1860, helpful to C., 337, 338; declines to oppose G.'s crossing the Strait, 338; change in her attitude due to C., 338 *ff.*; encourages C. in invasion of Papal States, 392, 393. And *see* Clarendon, Malmesbury, Palmerston, Russell (J.), and Victoria.

English, the, admired by C. as the vanguard of civilization, **1**, 62; not made to understand other races, 557 and n., 558; their contempt for foreigners, 557; their assumption of superior virtue resented by other nations, 557, 558; great majority of, sympathize with Italians, **2**, 147.

English Court, always pro-Austrian, **1**, 209, 221, 403, 503, 504.

pivot of the Congress," 380; consents that Italian Question be brought before Congress, 381; C.'s interview with, 390, 391; apparent effect of Congress on his position, 391, 392; C. tries to make him champion of the Italian cause, 401; gives Piedmont his moral support, 415, 416; dreams of making France paramount in Italy, 428; suggested remodeling of the map of Italy,— Plon-Plon and Murat, 428; imposes no restraint on Murat, 429; C. anxious not to antagonize, 430; his backing of Murat keeps C. from open opposition, 439; Orsini's attempt to murder, 494 ff.; Orsini's letters to, 496, 497; was he terrorized? 497; inclined to spare O.'s life, but deterred by his advisers, 498; his early self-control, 498, 499; address to the Chambers, 499; his promises neutralized by the terror of his accomplices, 499, 500; falls back on military despotism, 499, 500; various opinions on his change of front, 500, 501; congratulations of army colonels to, 502 and n.; tries to ride two horses, 503, 514; his policy towards England, 503; lurches towards reaction, 503; and Della Rocca, 508, 509; V. E.'s letter to, and its effect, 509, 510; promises to assist Piedmont in case of war with Austria, 510; and the publication of Orsini's letters, 516, 517; invites C. to meet him at Plombières, 526; details of their conference, 528 ff.; they seek and find a pretext for breach between Austria and Piedmont, 529; reorganization of Italy discussed, 530; hopes for neutrality of great powers, 530, 531; proposes match between Plon-Plon and Princess Clotilde, 531, 532; Plombières agreement a personal one on his side, 536; his perplexing character discussed, 536, 537; his two ideals, 537; various motives of his action, 537; effect of Orsini's attempt, 537, 538; shy of G., 545; C.'s chief task to keep him to the mark, 546, 547; his vacillation, 546; difficulties of his enterprise, 547, 548; his own interests and those of France not identical, 547; negotiates with Russia and Prussia, 547; begins to "drop hints," 548; interviews with Clarendon, Palmerston and Cowley, 548, 549; Victoria tries to turn him from war, 549, 550; deals in mystification, 550; contradictory statements, 550, 551; his New Year's (1859) speech to diplomatic corps, 553; his significant remark to Hübner, and its effect, 553, 554, 558, 585, 591; Malmesbury tries to dissuade him from war, 558, 559; desires war but uncertain as to time and manner thereof, 556; his Sphinx-like qualities in evidence in early 1859, 563; uncertainty of ministers as to his real intentions, 563; his political philosophy and views set forth in La Gueronnière's pamphlet, 563, 564; Victoria's letter to, 565; his speech at opening of the Chambers (Feb.), 565, 566; and Cowley's mission to Vienna, 568; professes eagerness for peace, 569; V. E. and C. had it in their power to expose him, 571; instigates Russia to propose a congress, 572; interviews with C. with, 575, 577; C.'s threat of disclosures, 575, 578, 579 and n.; C.'s letter to, 577, 578; makes no promises, 578; G.'s distrust of, 584; Mazzini's abuse of, 586; accepts plan of general disarmament, 592, 593; his shiftiness wears out C.'s patience, 595; C. holds him to his engagements, 602, 604.

And the official reports of the war, 2, 1; delays his preparations, 2; his purpose, 2; decides to lead the army, 2; orders troops to

Savoy, 7, 8; goes to the front, 12; warm reception at Genoa, 12, 13; his manifesto and its effect, 13, 14; takes command of allies at Alessandria, 14; his military proficiency, 14; his dispositions, 15; his plan of campaign, 17, 18 and n.; his repugnance to G. and his corps, 21; inactive after Montebello, 22; puzzled by Gyulai's indecision, 25; orders troops into Lombardy, 26; at Magenta, 27 ff.; his bearing during the period of suspense, 30, 31; retires to San Martino, 34; conduct of the battle discussed, 34 and n., 35 and n.; his horror of bloodshed, 35, 50, 88; enters Milan, 36 and n.; dispositions for battle, 42; tardy arrival on the field, 42; opposed to V. E.'s becoming dictator of Tuscany, 62, 71; V. E. suspects his purpose to create an Italian kingdom for a Bonaparte, 63, 64; interview of C. with, 64, 65; denies rumors about Central Italy, 65; first signs of schism between C. and, 65; difficulties of his situation in Italy, 65, 66; his obligation to the Clericals, 70; effect of his proclamation after Magenta, 74; his reception at Milan, 74; complains of ineffective coöperation of Italians, 75, 76; works secretly to keep Naples neutral, 78; sends Fleury to Francis Joseph to propose an armistice, 80, 81; reasons for his decision, 81 ff.; his growing aversion to C., 82; and the Whig ministry in England, 86; his military successes alarm British public, 86; has no militant ally save Piedmont, 86; his generals torn by jealousy; the direct military problem, 87, 88; physical condition, 88; Plon-Plon's pessimistic reports to, 88, 89; final decision due to Prussia's action, 90; reads Eugénie's letter to V. E. on eve of Solferino, 90; after the battle, asks England to mediate, 90, 91; decides to appeal to Francis Joseph directly, 92 and n.; interview with V. E., 93; various interpretations of his conduct, 94; requests personal interview with Francis Joseph, 94; their conference at Villafranca, 95–98; his three historic interviews, 98 and n.; discusses terms of treaty with V. E., 98, 99; sends Plon-Plon to Francis Joseph, to conclude, 99; his joy over the treaty, 101; stormy interview with V. E., 101, 102; his slurs at C., 104; regarded by Europe as V. E.'s master, 105; draws away from C., 105; and Kossuth, 106, 107; refuses to meet C., 108 and n.; seeks to make C. his scapegoat, 108, 109; altered demeanor of Italians towards, after the treaty, 112, 113; interview of C. with, at Turin, 112; his betrayal of Italy, 115; justified in stopping the war, not in his hypocrisy, 115, 116; his lack of principle, 117; why Italians should be grateful to, 117; his address at the Tuileries, 118; and the Confederation idea, 119, 120; opposed to Italian unity, 120; distrusted by Palmerston and Russell, 128; attitude of the Clericals, 128, and of Eugénie, 128; suggests a European congress, 129; beset by Italian delegations, 129; disturbed mainly by England, 129; and Arese, 130; refuses to change his plans for Italy, 130, 131; again irresolute over Tuscany and Piedmont, 138; publishes statement of his position, 138, 139 and n.; favors restoring the despots, 139; and the Central Italian movement toward Piedmont, 144, 146; attacked by French Clericals, 146; declares his purpose to withdraw Roman garrison, 146; and the suggestion of C. as regent of Central Italy, 146; desires annexation of Savoy, 146; an-

THE   END

The Riverside Press
CAMBRIDGE . MASSACHUSETTS
U . S . A